ARTHURIAN MYTHS AND ALCHEMY

A modern photograph from Minnesota of the astrological phenomenon known as a parhelia that inspired Edward, Earl of March. (Geoffrey Wheeler)

To save my bretheren I have so great delight. – And for I dread the venemous serpent my tender youth I must now win.

The Vision of George Ripley (1470)

ARTHURIAN MYTHS AND ALCHEMY

The Kingship of EDWARD IV

JONATHAN HUGHES

SUTTON PUBLISHING

First published in the United Kingdom in 2002 by
Sutton Publishing Limited · Phoenix Mill
Thrupp · Stroud · Gloucestershire · GL5 2BU

British Library Cataloguing in Publication Data
A catalogue record for this book is available from the British Library.

ISBN 0-7509-1994-9

Typeset in 11/12pt Ehrhardt MT.
Typesetting and origination by
Sutton Publishing Limited.
Printed and bound in England by
J.H. Haynes & Co. Ltd, Sparkford.

Contents

According to this mythology [the grail] there is no fixed law, no established knowledge of God, set up by prophet or by priest, that can stand against the revelation of a life lived with integrity in the spirit of its own brave truth.

Joseph Campbell, *Creative Mythology: The Masks of God*

The prophets gathered around the Throne of Reason foretell the coming of Edward IV. In the sky are depictions of parhelia and a comet heralding Edward's arrival. (British Library MS Harl. 7353)

Foreword

Just over twenty-five years ago Charles Ross brought out his Eyre Methuen biography of Edward IV. I can remember the excitement of the event. As a young undergraduate at Bristol University I had been inspired by his teaching of the Wars of the Roses. It was wonderful to see the book in print, and I felt a real sense of pride in its obvious quality. Time has passed. Looking back now, I see the biography as Charles' finest piece of work. A groundbreaking study, it surpassed Cora Scofield's earlier narrative of Edward IV's reign in its analytical clarity and cogency of argument.

Now our understanding of this fascinating monarch moves on again with Jonathan Hughes's hugely challenging book. Hughes offers us a dramatic backdrop for an engagement with fifteenth-century personalities and politics, presenting a potent mix of contemporary belief systems: the powerful model of Roman antiquity, the abiding hold of prophecy and its infusion with the Arthurian mythology of Britain. At their centre is a major re-evaluation of the significance of late medieval alchemy. This is a sustained exploration of remarkable quality. It yields a host of insights on the expectations of participants in the Wars of the Roses. It is also a bold attempt to penetrate the mental world of the man at the very eye of the storm, King Edward IV.

A number of attributes make this book important. It is the first study to look at the whole personality of the king, and here its endeavour in grappling with Edward's complex and contradictory emotional life gives the work much of its fascination and ensures it will be highly controversial. In his pursuit of the images and myths that appealed to the house of York, and particularly Edward himself, the lavishly illustrated pedigrees and genealogies, the intriguing if frustrating profusion of prophecies, the author is to some extent rehearsing ideas already explored. What makes his approach fresh and stimulating is the fusion of this material into a coherent personal vision of kingship, and the placement of alchemy at the very heart of that vision. We are offered an extraordinary map of the psyche, anchored in concepts familiar and relevant to a late medieval audience, that seeks to reconcile positive aspects of Edward's character with more disturbing traits. One is reminded of the startling treatment of the idealism and excesses of a more recent charismatic leader, Jack Kennedy. This will be a journey to the dark side of Camelot.

Embarking on this, Hughes establishes a larger construct, exploring expectations of kingship associated with Edward IV's predecessors, the Lancastrian kings Henry V and Henry VI. His treatment of Henry V is original and worthwhile, and puts a different emphasis on the legacy of this great warrior, that his early death created 'a climate of restless dissatisfaction', a longing for a successor able to carry on his work. The author gauges the contemporary intellectual climate, and the ideals found in classical mythology and history, to identify the inspiration drawn on by the king and his circle. This leads Hughes to argue that Henry's achievement transcended political success, at home and abroad, in re-establishing a sense of historical destiny for his nation. It is a refreshing stance, reminding us of a quality academic studies sometimes lose sight of, the visionary power of kingship. What was understood by Old Testament leaders and prophets remains true for medieval kings: where there is no vision the people perish.

This theme underlies Hughes's work and merits expansion. On his deathbed Henry V expressed a heartfelt wish to go on crusade and reconquer Jerusalem. This remark has received scant attention from historians, being seen as either a throwaway line or a belated statement of contrition. As a result, we have underestimated Henry's intent. Close to the end of his reign the king sent an experienced soldier, Gilbert de Lannoy, on a spying mission to the Holy Land. Henry died before his return and never saw Lannoy's report, but others did, and were moved by its contents. It was not some vague, romantic discourse but a highly practical survey, referring to techniques of war practised and understood by the king, and set out as an intended course of action. Its wealth of military detail was shaped by acute observation: the firmness of soil, and its suitability for mining operations; the thickness of walls, and their capability of resisting artillery bombardment. It culminated with an assessment of the defences of Jerusalem itself. When we discover that Henry had also borrowed a book containing the chronicles of Jerusalem, and the story of Godfrey of Bouillon (who took the holy city by assault in 1099) it is hard not to take his crusading interest seriously.[1] It certainly fired the imagination of his contemporaries. It is we who have become distanced from it. The aspirations of kingship, the vision, what was read, what was dreamed or imagined possible, remain as important as the practical affairs of government.

Hughes counterpoints the achievement of Henry V with the disturbing lethargy of his son, who became increasingly distant from his subjects. This became so marked that by the 1450s Henry VI's ill-health was likened to a sickness afflicting the entire country. Henry's aversion to the hands-on reality of running a kingdom has led some historians to speculate that he was a simpleton, incapable from birth. In fact the king showed considerable early promise, making the subsequent crises all the more painful. Given the later frustration of so many of his countrymen, it is perhaps surprising to find the chancellor John Kempe, in a private letter of March 1428, moved to extol his mental and physical accomplishments. He gives us an intimate personal description of the six-year-old child. The infant Henry had already 'perfectly' learned matins, litanies, the hours of the Blessed Virgin, the seven penitential psalms and was beginning the psalter. Never before in England, Kempe enthused, had there been seen in any person of such tender years such ability, such 'amazing understanding', not only in his studies but everything else. Kempe's skein of optimism ran through to Henry VI's coronation in December 1431, when he noted with obvious pride that the young king was now able to sign letters of state in his own hand.[2] These hopes were later cruelly dashed. The adult Henry retreated behind a severe religious practice, the *devotio moderna*, that removed him from meaningful interaction with most of his subjects. His lack of interest in everyday government, and increasing ill-health, created a frightening void out of which, Hughes argues, physicians and alchemists led the quest for a youthful replacement, whose energy and vigour would restore the vitality of the realm.

The stage is set for the dramatic entrance of Edward IV. There is an almost audible sigh of relief from the populace at his youthful grace and courage. The king literally towered above his contemporaries, at a height of six feet four inches, and was stunningly attractive. His 'beauty of personage', praised in the first parliament of the reign, led the shrewd observer Philippe de Commynes to note 'he was more handsome than any man alive'. The contrast with the hapless Henry VI could not have been greater. Hughes analyses the complex web of prophecy and genealogy spun around the change of dynasty, seeing beyond the workings of partisan propaganda a serious search for the renewal of the monarchy. This informs his presentation of Edward as a 'redeemer' of his people, a view held by a broader political community, in which alchemists played an important part, and also the way this charismatic ruler began to see himself.

At the heart of Jonathan Hughes's portrayal is a belief that the extraordinary circumstances by which Edward came to the throne helped shape a personal sense of destiny. Faced with the death of his father and brother in battle, Edward responded to this devastating blow in a courageous, inspired way. To examine his possible motivation, Hughes explores sources closely linked to the young monarch, a number of visually striking genealogies. In one of these, we find Old Testament episodes paired up with events from Edward's own life. This deserves explanation. In a society which felt comfortable in drawing parallels between figures of contemporary importance and biblical characters, a change of dynasty would almost inevitably be accompanied by signs and portents. Someone representing this change might find such signs in his own life, or more consciously might set about ensuring such signs were present, so that they could then be publicly displayed as a form of approbation. Here there is an overlap between responding to the expectations of others and imagining oneself as the chosen one. To argue for Edward's having a messianic sense of himself requires evidence of his personal input in such representations. A messianic figure must have a good pedigree, and this could be communicated visually – the late medieval equivalent of the company video – presenting the images which put the message across the best. In this we see the interweaving of the Zeitgeist and the personal and intimate, creating a constellation of Edward's youth, attractiveness and victory in battle and the response of those around him. This would then sweep him forward on a wave of self-belief.

Handling such evidence is notoriously difficult, yet Hughes marshals a substantial body of material that is at the very least highly suggestive. In the biblical sequence, the infant Moses floats down the Nile in a woven basket foreshadowing Edward's escape across the Channel to Calais, when he was suddenly separated from his father and brothers. This could be a personal contribution, for, as I have argued elsewhere, Edward came to see this separation as the provident working of his own destiny.[3] Hughes rightly emphasizes the symbolic importance of Mortimer's Cross, where Edward's victory was presaged by the appearance in the sky of three suns, a meteorological phenomenon known as a parhelion. There is little doubt that he saw this as a divine portent, a sign that he had been chosen to lead after the earlier deaths of his father and brother.

A telling example is found in another rich genealogy closely associated with the young king, now known as the Philadelphia Roll. In one part of the manuscript, Edward's links with a glorious past are signalled by the banner of St George, patron saint of the Order of the Garter, followed by the arms of Brutus, the legendary founder of Britain. Hughes amply demonstrates the centrality of both figures to the emerging Yorkist dynasty. But opposite St George is a far more obscure choice, the Saxon king Sebbi. There is no obvious reason to account for his presence, unless it be a personal choice of Edward himself. For according to Bede, shortly before he died Sebbi saw a vision of three men in bright clothing, who foretold the time and manner of his passing. Sebbi thus shared with Edward IV, who saw three suns at Mortimer's Cross, a powerful experience that could be interpreted as a vision of the Trinity. There is a pleasing additional touch. When Sebbi died, the sepulchre brought for him was found to be too short, but then miraculously stretched to fit. Sebbi, like Edward, was unusually tall.

The reign opened with the vital optimism of a man believing himself divinely chosen to govern his people. Following the defeat of the Lancastrians in the north, Edward expressed bright confidence in a seemingly pre-ordained path in a little-known letter to King Pedro of Portugal, with the uplifting sentiment: 'we welcome the victories and successes in war granted by God in what seems to us a just quarrel'.[4] Hughes traces its flowering to the elaborate joustings and displays celebrated in Edward's court, likened by contemporaries to another Camelot. Hughes argues that it was through his passionate interest in genealogy that Edward was able 'to inflate his sense of power . . . through myth, alchemy and prophecy'. Yet there was a darker aspect. What goes up must come down, and the king's wildly fluctuating energy levels, his increasing resort to the pleasures of women, banquets and the hunt, masked a worrying lack of purpose, seen in his breach with the Nevilles, his brief exile abroad and finally the débâcle of the French expedition of 1475, persuasively characterized by Hughes as an act of 'self-destructive betrayal'. Commynes captured this well in his description of Edward as 'a very handsome prince, but not an outstanding man'. There is here a king unable to fully grow up, too much in love with his early promise to fulfil the expectations of his subjects.

Perhaps the most novel element of Hughes's survey is his consideration of Edward IV's enthusiasm for alchemy. By showing the strength of the king's association with a coterie of alchemists, who worked under his patronage and dedicated treatises to him, Hughes illuminates an increasingly controversial dimension of his kingship. Edward's predilection seems to have doubly damaged him. Those who had been inspired by the seeming potential of his youthful vision for the realm, and hoped for a great transforming focus – the crusading ideal that had so deeply impressed Henry V's contemporaries – grew disillusioned with a man more interested in amassing wealth for his hedonistic lifestyle. Others were alienated by Edward's dabbling in increasingly arcane magical practices. Hughes depicts with verve the growing fear of witchcraft and sorcery that eddied round the Yorkist court, culminating in the insinuation surrounding the death of the king's brother, Clarence.

Faced with the harm caused by this strange and damaging obsession, one is left wondering why, after such an auspicious beginning, Edward took such a personally destructive path. It is my own belief that allegations of the king's bastardy, made on a number of occasions during the reign, deserve much fuller consideration. The sad decline of this once imposing figure, and the growing affliction of his ill-health, a worrying blight on the last period of the reign, disaffected many around him and helped fragment the political community, setting the scene for the terrible violence that followed the king's death.[5] This is a tragic story, told by Jonathan Hughes with sensitivity and insight, in what will become a valuable and intriguing addition to our understanding of the Yorkist age and the fifteenth century as a whole.

Michael K. Jones

NOTES

1. J. Webb, 'A survey of Egypt and Syria, undertaken in the year 1422, by Sir Gilbert Lannoy', *Archaeologia* XXI (1827), pp. 281–444.
2. British Library, Cleopatra CIV, ff. 169v, 175–6.
3. M.K. Jones, 'Edward IV, the earl of Warwick and the Yorkist claim to the throne', *Historical Research*, LXX (1997), pp. 342–52.
4. J. Calmette, 'Une lettre d'Edouard IV à D. Pedro de Portugal', *Annales du Midi*, XXXI (1919), pp. 193–6.
5. Evidence for Edward IV's ill-health becoming a serious issue soon after the abortive French expedition is set out in M.K. Jones, '1477 – the expedition that never was: chivalric expectation in late Yorkist England', *The Ricardian*, XII (2001), pp. 275–92. The issue of Edward's bastardy is explored in my forthcoming book for Tempus, *Bosworth 1485 – Psychology of a Battle*.

Preface and Acknowledgements

This book was conceived around a vision or epiphany experienced by a charmed eighteen-year-old youth, Edward earl of March, on St Blaise's day 3 February 1461 at a crossroads on the River Lugg on the morning of the Battle of Mortimer's Cross. The young man had just learned of the defeat of his family at the Battle of Wakefield and of the deaths of his father, Richard duke of York and his younger brother, Edmund earl of Rutland. Around 10 that morning three suns (or parhelia) reflected from the frozen ice particles in the frosty morning air were interpreted as a sign of Divine approval of Edward's mission to become king of Britain. It was a moment of intense realization of self, when he became convinced that God had chosen him. He exhorted his troops to take heart, leading them to a victory culminating in a seizure of the throne that was accompanied by an extraordinary manifestation of optimism and hero-worship on the part of his people.

Contemplation of this event led me on a four-year-long quest to write a book on the cultural forces that had contributed to Edward's emergence as a heroic redeemer of a nation languishing under years of military defeat, civil war and inept kingship. It has answered some questions posed since my youth by artistic and historical examples of moments of realization of heroic destiny. One concerned a painting by the Swiss artist active in the 1930s and 1940s, Peter Birkhauser, of a dream about a marvellous youth with four arms, representing the integrated wholeness of the four elements, before whom hovers a magical flower. Behind this rider of a white horse resembling a boar is a round object like the sun. The boy was interpreted by Maria von Franz in her essay 'The Process of Individuation' as a manifestation of the self, a symbol of the renewal of life and a new spiritual orientation by means of which everything becomes full of energy and enterprise. Another relates to William Wordsworth's reflection in book twelve of *The Prelude* of the feelings he experienced at the age of thirteen after the death of his father, and how an awareness of the birth of his self and sense of destiny as a poet with a special relationship with the divine parent that is nature was to be forever linked to those moments when he used to wait on a craggy eminence for his father at a crossroads:

> . . . the wind and the sleety rain
> And all the business of the elements,
> The single sheep, and the one blasted tree,
> And the bleak music of that old stone wall,
> The noise of wood and water, and the mist
> Which on the line of each of those two Roads
> Answered in such indisputable shapes,
> All these were spectacles and sounds which
> I often would repair and thence would drink,
> As at a fountain.

A historical parallel to Edward IV's moment of insight is provided by the decision of the twenty-four-year-old Alexander the Great, four years after the murder of his father, Philip of Macedonia, to deviate from his strategic route to make a pilgrimage to the oracle of the ram-god, Ammon, in the Libyan oasis of Siwah. Here a priest told Alexander that he was the son of Zeus; and it was therefore as a Homeric hero that he rejoined his troops and proceeded to conquer the world.

It was Shakespeare, with his understanding of the way that Henry V's mythology dominated the fifteenth century, who demonstrated in his trilogy of plays, *Henry IV Parts I and II* and *Henry V*, the importance of self-definition and how, especially for an heir apparent, the father could stand in the way of the realization of a sense of destiny. He showed how the Prince of Wales had to struggle with his actual father, Henry IV, and his surrogate father, Falstaff, before breaking ruthlessly with his past to undertake his messianic task. I have attempted to trace the emergence of another king with a powerful mythology, one who consciously attempted to emulate and surpass his predecessor from the rival house of Lancaster. One key to Edward IV's sense of self and destiny is alchemy which, with its preoccupation with the creation in the alchemist's womb like vessel of the artificial man, the homunculus, was especially well adapted to inspire a sense of an emerging self independent of those traditional sources of identity, the family and society. This is a theme explored in such modernist novels as Fyodor Dostoyevski's *The Idiot* and Thomas Mann's *The Magic Mountain* which follow the gestation in a 'hermetic retort' of their heroes, Prince Myshkin and Hans Colthorp, in the isolation of sanatoria. My attempt to understand the key protagonists of the Wars of the Roses, Henry VI and Edward IV, in the context of the heroic myths and Arthurian legends that contributed to a growth of self in the royal student of the alchemical arts will inevitably arouse controversy; and it is therefore with special gratitude that I wish to acknowledge the support and help of a number of friends, scholars and specialists as I entered these fields.

I owe a special debt to Carole Rawcliffe who generously gave her time and expertise to guide me through the field of medical history. She carefully and incisively commented on an early draft and is responsible for suggesting many of the additions which I am sure have improved the book while testing the good humoured patience of Christopher Feeney of Sutton Publishing, the editor who has watched this work expand far beyond its original perimeters. Michael K. Jones has been an enthusiastic supporter of this project since its inception. He has shared his ideas on Edward IV and the period and provided insightful comments on the typescript. Others who have read and helpfully commented on the text in its different forms include: Jeremy Catto who, as ever, has offered me friendship and encouragement; Geoffrey Wheeler who has advised me on matters of heraldry and allowed me to select images from his picture collection; Sarah Cook, Michelle Tilling and Anne Bennett who have patiently and enthusiastically handled the many corrections and additions to the text.

Many others have helped at different stages. Anthony Gross communicated his forthright views on late medieval alchemy and shared his particular expertise on Friar Bungay/Robert Barker; and with James Campbell I have had many interesting discussions on 'the matter of Britain'. Others who were willing to share their ideas and in many cases their unpublished works include: Laura Blanchard, Cecil Clough, Mark Haeffner, Catherine Duncan Jones, George Keiser, Margaret Kekewich, P.M. Jones, Ursuzula Szulokowska, and Linda Voigts.

The narrative that follows (based heavily on manuscript evidence) would not have been possible without the patient co-operation of the library staff of various archives. In particular I would like to thank the Philadelphia Free Library for allowing me to publish images from Philadelphia Free MS E 201 without charge and the staff of the British Library and Trinity College, Cambridge. I would also and in particular like to thank the staff of Duke Humfrey's in the Bodleian Library for their help, always delivered with patience and humour. Much of the initial research for this book was undertaken with the help of two study grants awarded by the British Academy in 1998 and 1999. The final stages of research and the writing over the last two years have been facilitated by a Research Fellowship at the School of History in the University of East Anglia awarded by the Wellcome Trust. The support and encouragement of my colleagues at this university has been greatly appreciated.

When I first contemplated emigrating to England from New Zealand to undertake academic research I was encouraged to do so by Lynne Cargill, who has read this book in its different stages and offered unfailing encouragement and support. And back in 'Middle Earth' I am grateful for the back-up always provided by my parents R.O. and B. Hughes and my sister Deborah Hohneck. This book is dedicated to my children Venetia and Timothy who make 'a July's day short as December' and cure those 'Thoughts that would thick my blood'.

For Venetia and Timothy Hughes

CHAPTER 1

Introduction: The Image of Edward IV

> The most knowing scholar hath found a period which his curious search could not move.
>
> William Habington, *The Historie of Edward IV (1640)*

The fifteenth century was an age when kingship meant more than effective government and the management of the ruling class. The monarch was the focus of myths, and projections in which there was a close identification between the energy and health of the monarch and the well-being of his people. For many of these monarchs Shakespeare has perpetuated the myths that surrounded them during their lifetimes: Henry V the warrior; Henry VI the reluctant saintly king; and Richard III the demonic manipulator of men. The mythic status of these men, aided by repeated performances of Shakespeare's plays, has grown in the succeeding centuries. Edward IV, however, has not enjoyed such status in spite of his being the most charismatic and complex of the late medieval kings. He ruled England for twenty-three years, the only king ever to have lost and regained his throne. Undefeated in battle, he had a considerable reputation as a military leader, and his court was renowned throughout Europe for its wealth and glamour. He was the first English king to found a royal library, the dedicatee of English works on alchemy, chivalry, history, Roman philosophy and Arthurian romance. It was during his reign that Caxton established the printing press. Despite his reign being a cultural watershed, at least as significant as the reigns of those better known cultural icons, Richard II and Elizabeth I, the cultural achievements in the period between 1460 and 1483, and the personality of the king who inspired many of these activities, have not been closely studied.

One of the reasons for the comparative neglect of Edward IV is that he had a personality of baffling contradictions. He burst on to the political stage as a charismatic eighteen-year-old and seized the kingdom after leading his armies to victory at Mortimer's Cross and Towton. However, he threw away the advantages of his early popularity and the support of his former mentor the earl of Warwick in a clandestine marriage to a widow of mere gentry origins from a Lancastrian family. His energy levels fluctuated wildly, to the extent that he lost his throne to Warwick and Clarence without a struggle, only to emerge after six months' exile in Burgundy to recapture the kingdom in an astonishing military campaign where he once again displayed inspired leadership and courage. He was as erratic in the second reign: after marshalling the largest invasion force ever seen to invade France, he returned to England with a large pension without having fought a battle. He had a reputation for great beauty and charm, yet he suffered bouts of inertia and over-eating: at his death he was a corpulent travesty of his former self. He was frequently easy-going and forgiving to the point of folly, especially in his relationships with such committed Lancastrians as Henry Beaufort, the duke of Somerset (and chief favourite of Henry VI), and with his unstable younger brother George. He was also capable of displays of petulance, capricious cruelty and impulsive violence. At the Battle of Tewkesbury, for example, Edward reversed his order to spare the commons after the battle, and even ordered the killing of men seeking sanctuary in the abbey. Most contemporary sources say the young Prince Edward of Lancaster died during the Battle of Tewkesbury, but one source reported that the king himself slapped the captured prince across the face before Gloucester executed him; in similar vein he finally authorized the murder of his brother George duke of Clarence. He was lavish and ostentatious in his dress and a generous host, yet he had a reputation for avarice, especially in his second reign. He enjoyed an easy familiarity with his subjects and yet he was regarded as a tyrant, especially after the death of Clarence.

Such contradictions and Edward's often noted similarities to his grandson Henry VIII have perhaps not encouraged dramatic representation. Contemporaries certainly saw Edward as a heroic, inspirational figure: he was described as a God in poems celebrating his accession, and chroniclers such as Philippe de Commines (the Burgundian servant of Charles the Bold and Louis XI), the Italian friar Dominic Mancini, and the author of the second continuation of the *Croyland Chronicle* all alluded to his heroic and inspirational qualities – his striking good looks, his ability to inspire men, his charm, energy and intelligence – but they did not evade his contradictions and his darker side – his periodic bouts of indolence, his compulsive sexual activities and gluttony, his avarice and in later years his melancholy. Such contradictions are the stuff of flawed heroes and around this complex personality there accrued, as we shall see, alchemical and Arthurian myths that played an important part in the political and cultural history of the late Middle Ages. Little of this, however, seems to have survived the anti-climax of his premature death, and the figure that emerges in the subsequent writings of the historians, poets and dramatists is a bland shadow of the compelling presence that dominated the period of the Wars of the Roses.

The most vivid portraits of Edward IV came from the Tudor historians Polydore Vergil and Sir Thomas More, who both had access to people who knew the king. Polydore Vergil captures the sense of Yorkist destiny and the unatoned sins of the house of Lancaster that certainly motivated Edward and his supporters and which were used in the histories and genealogies commissioned by him. He depicted Edward as a tall, handsome, charming, courageous man, familiar with courtiers and poorer subjects, bountiful towards friends, and terrible towards enemies, one who had the charisma to inspire the people and at least sporadically to achieve great things:

> Edwarde was much desired of the Londoners, in favor with the common people, in the mouth and speeche of every man, of highest and lowest he had the good willes. He was, for his liberalite, clemencie, integritee and fortitude, praysed generally of all men above the skyes; wherefore there was no concouerse to him of all ages and degrees of men, with wonderfull affection, insomuch that some gave in their names to goe to the felde with him; others, in the behalfe of the cities, promised him good willes, and all that they might doo, and swore to be his true subjectes: by which occasions this Edwarde, brought in hope of victory, prepared as great forces as he could possible.[1]

He was an instrument of fortune, blessed with amazing luck, which allowed him to triumph over all his enemies because God had chosen him as an instrument to avenge the original perjury of Henry IV (who professed when he invaded England that he was intending only to claim the Duchy of Lancaster) and the subsequent deposition and murder of Richard II.[2] This much Edward would have readily accepted, but Vergil went on to point out that Edward had also perjured himself 'heinously' in 1471 in exactly the same circumstances when he promised the citizens of York that he wanted only to regain his earldom. Vergil maintained that at the same time as Edward was perjuring himself, the saintly prophet Henry VI had met Henry Tudor earl of Richmond in London and prophesied that he would be the future king. Edward consequently was supposed to have spent the rest of his reign in secure prosperity but unlike Henry VI, who showed Job-like patience in good and bad fortune alike, he succumbed, when secure and prosperous, to various compulsions and fears concerning Richmond.[3] The most compelling aspect of Vergil's account of Edward IV is his suggestion that Edward was impressive in adversity and that he had great potential to be a 'liberal, bountiful prince, profitable to the common weal but for his falling into such a sudden and horrible temptation as putting Clarence to death'.[4] Vergil's portrayal of a reign dominated by the working out of providential destiny and of a gifted, talented man succumbing to his inner demons comes closest, as we shall see, to the sense that Edward and his people had of the powerful forces of light and darkness that were seen to motivate political life in this period. Vergil's concentration on the irrational dimension to the king's character allows him to make sense of the contradictions that enabled Edward to be both an amiable if over-familiar prince, who won the affection of his people to the extent that his passing was mourned, and at the same time an avaricious and increasingly tyrannical and feared ruler.[5]

Sir Thomas More's evocation of Edward is equally powerful but mainly by virtue of the dramatic contrast with Richard III, the man who dominates and mesmerizes the narrative. Although Edward was no Abel to Richard's Cain, More ignored Edward's irrational darker side and seems to have projected it on to his brother, who becomes almost literally his dark shadow. This allows More to present a sanitized, one-dimensional Edward, the exact opposite of his demonic brother, an Augustus embodying the Roman qualities of good sense, decency and good rule in contrast to the tyrannical Tiberius.[6] Whereas Richard is shown to be deluded and isolated, Edward is depicted as a humane figure, a husband and father in touch with his family – a family about to be shattered by Gloucester. Edward's relationship with his mistress Elizabeth (Jane) Shore was used to demonstrate his humanity, sanity and compassion. These qualities, so notably absent or warped in his younger brother, would have been readily recognized by contemporary chroniclers and observers.

Something of the complexity and diversity of Edward's character was preserved in the first purely literary testament to his reign, the 75th sonnet of the *Astrophel to Stella* sequence. The author, Sir Philip Sidney, had reason to be sympathetic towards a king who had granted the earldom of Pembroke to the ancestors of his in-laws, and in this sonnet he chose to present Edward as a complex and talented person of many roles, rather like the narrator of the sonnets, but one who, as the embodiment of chivalry and courtly love, was prepared to sacrifice everything for love, including his friendship with Warwick and his crown, when he chose to marry Elizabeth Grey.

Shakespeare's depiction of Edward as earl of March and king in *Henry VI Parts II and III* could not have been further from Sidney's courtly lover. Shakespeare's Edward is a sexually rampant figure, a shallow, compulsive womanizer who is something of a figure of fun to his brothers Clarence and Gloucester. He is prepared, in the pursuit of a woman, to sacrifice his friendship with Warwick and his relationship with his brothers, and Shakespeare does not depict this as heroic but as an irresponsible compulsion and a perverse assertion of will. The playwright may well have been constrained by the awareness that many saw in Henry VIII significant resemblances to his grandfather, but he does nevertheless capture the sense that Edward was a man of unfulfilled heroic potential. This potential is captured in the scene before the Battle of Mortimer's Cross when the earl of March sees three suns in the sky and decides to bear them on his targe. However, from this point on Shakespeare (perhaps influenced by More) chooses to portray Edward as an insignificant figure, at times a buffoon, manipulated by his more intelligent and charismatic younger brother: under the dark power of the duke of Gloucester Edward becomes increasingly morbid and superstitious as his vital energies are sapped. In *Richard III*, however, Shakespeare, like More, emphasizes Edward's role as a devoted family man when he is depicted as an invalid making provisions for his relatives. This is a recurring theme in literature on Edward: in fact he was the first king since Edward III (before his senile infatuation with Alice Perrers) to present such an image.

Between them these sixteenth-century writers at least captured some aspects of Edward's personality, his charm, intelligence, and easy-going familiarity, vitiated at times by displays of cruelty and irrational fears. Little was made of the culture and sophistication of his court or of the way he occasionally acted as if he were sustained by powerful myths. Shakespeare, perhaps wisely, did not choose to invest his genius in an attempt to reconcile Edward's many contradictions and focused instead on kings whose lives could be more consistently defined with reference to a single simple myth: Henry V therefore was immortalized as a warrior, Henry VI as a saint and Richard III as an evil tyrant. When a lesser talent such as Thomas Heywood devoted a play to Edward IV at the beginning of the seventeenth century entitled *The First and Second Part of King Edward IV's Histories*, the contradictions in the king are ignored and the result is a burlesque farce.[7] Shakespeare's *Henry VI Part III* ends with the word 'joy', perhaps a reference to Edward IV's motto 'comfort and joy', and Heywood took this as his cue to depict Edward's reign as a merry hiatus before the irruptions of evil tyrannies and superstitions associated with the emergence of the duke of Gloucester. Edward in this play is an innocent, easy-going, jovial and charming, if shallow, Englishman: the mayor of London remarks: 'Have you ever seen a prince more affable than Edward is? What merry talk he had upon his way'. Edward uses his charm to prey off his people and to secure benevolences, but his shallowness and that of his court is contrasted to the dignified burgher values represented by the mayor's cousin, John Shore, and his wife Jane. Edward, while preparing to invade France, is more intent on the siege of Jane Shore's chastity and he goes to her in disguise, prompting the mayor to remark:

> I wonder in this serious busy time
> of this great gathered benevolence
> For his regaining of his right in France
> The day and nightly turmoil of his lords,
> yea of his whole estate in general,
> He can be spared from these great affairs,
> And wander here disguised in this sort.[8]

Edward's invasion of France is depicted as a jolly jape and the kings of England and France, both plain-dealing men, arrange an honourable peace when they become aware of the double-dealing and perfidy of Charles the Bold, duke of Burgundy, and Louis of Luxembourg, count of St Pol. Edward returns to England preoccupied with the impending showdown with his wife and mistress, both stronger personalities who have become friends, and anxiously exclaims to the queen: 'Bess, I greatly was afraid I should not find ye in so good a tune.' This almost clownish figure is totally eclipsed towards the end of the play by the couple he ruins, Jane and John Shore, who devote the rest of their lives to good deeds and compassionate intercession as the shadow of Gloucester's evil falls over London.

This eclipsing of Edward by Richard III continues to be a feature of literary creations in the twentieth century, to the extent that while there are a number of romantic novels devoted to the last Yorkist king, Heywood's play remains the last work of literature exclusively devoted to the founder of the Yorkist dynasty. These novels continue to perpetuate the tradition that Edward's personality could be simply explained by his addiction to sensual pleasure. For Rosemary Hawley Jarman in her 1971 novel *We Speak No Treason*, Edward, in contrast to his serious and chivalric younger brother, was the embodiment of sensuality – 'I have seen King Edward's smile often. A merry smile, or a kindly glance, or a mischievous smile full of white bodies or soft beds' – and his end was the fitting climax to an overindulged life – 'the huge gross body bloated like a wine bag. We heard the fat choking the organs.' The same contrast was maintained in a 1989 film adaptation of Shakespeare's play starring Ian McKellen and set in England in the 1930s; Gloucester is the embodiment of cold, disciplined fascism, and the weak, besotted playboy Edward and his upstart domineering queen are meant to represent the contemporary royal couple, Edward VIII, the misguided Nazi sympathizer, and his American wife, Mrs Simpson. The spirit of Heywood's sensual and charming king can be seen in Julian Rathbone's 2000 novel on the outset of the Wars of the Roses, *Kings of Albion*. A bisexually rampant and virile earl of March, after stabling his black stallion, comes on to the deck of the ship bearing him from Calais to England and thrusting himself against the buttocks of a figure draped over the rails, looks towards the white cliffs of Dover, and when he discovers the sexual identity of his prey breathes in her ear, 'Albion, my new-found land . . . one day I shall be King.'

The consistent theme in all these fictional creations is that Edward, despite his vices and weaknesses, was, in contrast to his saintly predecessor and evil successor, a good king and a reasonably well-adjusted human being who enjoyed the trust and affection of his fellow men. One feature of Edward noted by all those who knew him and wrote about him was his charm: he was the favoured son, and lucky. His charm seems to have beguiled subsequent historians as well as contemporaries, and he is consequently a much-diminished figure from the king who inspired a generation of artists, poets, scholars and philosophers to weave around his personality, acts and aspirations some of Britain's most enduring myths – myths that have also been ignored by historians from the seventeenth century onwards in their attempts to steer attention away from Edward's private life to focus on his political achievements.

The first political account of Edward's reign, published in 1640, comes closest to understanding the king in the terms of his own time. The antiquary Thomas Habington (1560–1647) wrote part of *The Historie of Edward IV of England* and it was completed and published by his son, William Habington, at the request of King Charles I.[9] When William Habington dedicated his *Historie* to Charles I, he was well aware of the parallels between his own time, when the threat of civil war loomed, and the period of the Wars of the Roses. He asks his king to look back to Edward's age and congratulate himself that they were living in a time of peace, and prays that if war does come the king's enemies will submit to his sword and taste his mercy. Habington's Edward lacked such clemency. The *Historie of Edward IV* is full of examples of his vengefulness and cruelty. However, Habington's portrait has the virtue that it sees the king as a complex, contradictory and charismatic figure. He emphasizes his beauty, charm and ability to inspire an almost idolatrous following: 'His presence was easie to any mans love or curiositie, his aspect cleere and smiling, his language free and familiar. And to the ladies who have also their share in the motion of states, he applyed a generall courtship: which used by a Prince and of so amiable a personage, made them, usually the Idolls of others, Idolaters of him.' Habington appreciated his public relations skills, his sitting in the Court of the King's Bench for three days to 'court the opinion of wisdom', and acknowledged that the basis of his popularity was in Wales and London. He understood that Edward was a theatrical man who was most impressive in times of danger: 'Never liv'd Prince whom adventure did more to harden to action; and prosperitie more soften to voluptuousnesse.' He was also alert to the strange periods of inertia and indecision that afflicted Edward at times, and reported that Warwick's rebellion prompted a 'strange diffidence in the king himself'. Like many people of great charm who are subject to idolatrous worship, Edward had a degree of insubstantial shallowness and fragile sense of self: 'The king was of waxen nature, apt to receive any impression best pleased his present humour.' The real strength of the Habingtons' portrayal of this period comes from the empathy that the proximity of civil war gave them. They understood the Wars of the Roses in broader terms than those of a feudal conflict between affinities and saw them in a more alchemical, holistic sense as a national disorder, 'a universal disease of the kingdome'. Thomas Habington also translated the *Liber querulus de excidio Britanniae* of the Romano-British historian Gildas (516?–570?) and he was consequently more in touch than later historians with the issues of British identity that surrounded Edward's accession. As Habington and his son saw it, Edward's tragedy (and his country's tragedy) was that he employed all his military and leadership skills and courage as head of the body politic in the shedding of his own *nation's* blood and never applied his gifts to a foreign adversary. Habington wrote at a time when court alchemists diagnosed political ills as they had done 180 years earlier, and therefore deployed some of the methodology and terminology which will be used in this study.

The philosopher/historian David Hume, in his *History of Great Britain* (1762), noted some of the cultural achievements of Edward IV's reign, such as the use of printing, and saw this as especially incongruous in such a dark age of war and unnatural violence. His Edward IV was a product of the times: 'His hardness of heart and serenity of character rendered him impregnable to all the moments of compassion which might undo his vigour in the prosecution of the most bloody revenges against his enemies.' His reign was seen as a reign of tyranny where the scaffold in the field streamed with the noblest blood of England. The antithesis of the enlightenment values of Hume's time, Edward was at least a man of destructive power, dark sexual energies and intermittent inspiration; a man who lacked the prudence and foresight to prevent ills, yet was capable of rising above his natural sloth to remedy those ills that did occur with activity and great vengeance. The paradox of his popularity is explained by Hume as a consequence of his easy-going familiarity and life of pleasure. In 1768 Horace Walpole similarly projected the rationalist values of enlightenment on to his brief account of Edward IV in his *Historic Doubts on the Reign of Richard III*. He criticized the Croyland chronicler for showing a monkish partiality for the king 'whose cruelty and vices he hardly noticed'. For Walpole the king was above all else a rational, political opportunist, and this rather than superstition lay behind accusations of sorcery. He was described as a brave man who pursued his hereditary right 'with all the arts of a politician and the cruelty of a emperor'.

Bishop Stubbs, applying the high Victorian morality of his times, similarly rescued Edward IV from the bland, innocuous reputation he had in the seventeenth century to suggest that he was very much the equal in evil of his younger brother Richard of Gloucester. While giving qualified approval for Edward's activities in foreign policy and his success in keeping the court at peace by means of his popularity and the force of his will, Stubbs nevertheless described his reign as one of exactions and executions, and the king himself as more vicious than anyone since King John, more bloodthirsty and cruel than any king England had known, far outshining his ancestors in bloodshed. The death of Clarence

Views of historians

was the crowning act of an unparalleled list of judicial and extra-judicial cruelties, which those of the next reign would supplement but not surpass.[10]

Stubbs was the last of the Victorian moralists to write about the Yorkists, and the publication of James Gairdner's biography of Richard III in 1878 sees the start of an attempt to present an objective, historical appraisal of Edward IV. Historians writing in the last decades of the nineteenth century were preoccupied with the growth of nationalism and the formation of modern nation states in Italy and Germany. They naturally reflected on the example of the modern nation state that England provided for these emerging nations, and they therefore tended to evaluate Edward's reign in terms of the evolution of the English state from a feudal society divided by feuding barons to a centralized absolute monarchy. Gairdner therefore considered Edward's political achievements in the realms of law and order, foreign policy and finance and concluded that he was a reckless gambler who threw away all the advantages secured by hard fighting; a man no more capable of holding the kingdom together than the rival he supplanted, and one who left a legacy of a bitterly divided court. In contrast, Gairdner's contemporary J.R. Green saw behind Edward's indolence and gaiety a profound political ability which enabled him to lead England out of the Middle Ages. While he was jesting with aldermen, dallying with his mistresses or idling over the new pages from the printing press at Westminster, Edward was silently laying the foundations of an absolute rule which Henry VII did little more than develop or consolidate.[11]

It is a measure of the neglect Edward has suffered in comparison to his younger brother that the first study devoted exclusively to his reign did not appear until 1932. Cora Scofield's detailed two-volume biography, however, is more a study of the period and there is little evaluation of the king himself.[12] The 1950s and 1960s saw the emergence of professional historians who scrutinized the contention of their predecessors that Edward contributed to the emergence of the state under a strong monarchy. Both J.R. Lander and Bertram Wolffe gave favourable assessments of Edward's work in areas of law and order and finance and suggested that he was an able forerunner of Henry VII.[13] This view was qualified from the 1970s by Charles Ross, Keith Dockray and Sandy Grant. Regarding Edward's sexual adventures as an irrelevancy, they focused on Edward's mistakes: his mismanagement of his over-mighty subjects, in particular Warwick; his disastrous marriage; and his failure to prevent the development of a Woodville clique at court which facilitated the Readeption of Henry VI in 1470–1 and the occurrence of destructive feuds which destroyed the Yorkist dynasty after his death. They therefore concluded that Henry VII's reign was the real turning-point in English history.[14] These recent studies have been enlightened by close attention to original fifteenth-century documents and can be seen as a product of the expansion of the universities in Britain from the 1960s. They do, however, like preceding works, bear the hallmarks of their own time. Edward is seen as a hard-working, hard-drinking and womanizing monarch, a professional who never allowed his private life to interfere with his close attention to the details of administration. He seems to have stepped out of the common room of a provincial university or the pages of Kingsley Amis's *Lucky Jim*. Colin Richmond seems to associate Edward's second reign with the greed of the British during the Thatcher regime of the 1980s when he sees Edward sharing the ruthless, materialistic and professional interests of those pragmatic, managerial lawyers, the Pastons.[15] It is my contention that the real Edward can only be found if we focus on the projections of his contemporaries rather than those of eighteenth-century rationalists, nineteenth-century nationalists or twentieth-century professional academics. The key to seeing Edward as contemporaries saw him, to understanding his own self-image, the many contradictions in his character and his wildly fluctuating energies, is to be found in the beliefs and myths that motivated people in the fifteenth century.

The story of Edward's life is well known. His reign can only be understood in the context of the fifteenth century as a whole. His destiny was marked in September 1399 with the usurpation of Richard II's throne by Henry duke of Hereford, of the house of Lancaster, who was proclaimed Henry IV by Parliament. The controversial and autocratic yet anointed and divinely ordained king he replaced was subsequently murdered. Hereford's task had been made easier by the fact that Richard II was childless, but nevertheless the legitimate claims of the Mortimer family through Philippa, the daughter of Edward III's second son, Lionel of Antwerp, duke of Clarence, had been ignored. Fortunately for Henry, the earl of March died in 1398 and his son, the eight-year-old Edmund earl of March, never pressed his legitimate claim when he grew up. However, Henry IV's reign was as troubled and unpopular as Macbeth's: he faced plots from Ricardian courtiers (rumours that Richard II was still alive abounded) and had difficulty securing English lordship in Wales, Ireland, Calais and Gascony. Moreover, the 1396 treaty with France, cemented by Richard II's marriage with Charles VI's seven-year-old daughter Isabel, was invalidated by the usurpation. War with Wales and Scotland followed, and Henry also had to contend with growing opposition to his policies from his own son Harry Monmouth, the prince of Wales, from the Percies in Northumberland, and from the archbishop of York, Richard Scrope. Somehow the king survived all these crises, but he was a sick and disfigured man (widely, but wrongly, rumoured to be suffering from leprosy)[16] when he handed his shaky crown on to the son with whom he was reconciled near the end of his life.

The new monarch, Henry V, had to survive one abortive plot against his life in 1415 by supporters of Edmund earl of March; these men included Edward IV's paternal grandfather Richard earl of Cambridge. Mortimer, uninterested in the crown, himself informed the king about the plot. From this point Henry V set about establishing the legitimacy of the Lancastrian dynasty by fair, firm and judicious rule at home, and a brilliant campaign of conquest in Normandy. By the time of his early death in 1422 at the height of his powers he had established himself as a king of mythical proportions. His military campaigns had brought him the title of Dauphin, heir to the realm of King Charles VI of France (or at least to those parts of Northern France that he had conquered). He had revived the prestige of the English monarchy to a position it had not enjoyed since the earlier years of Edward III.

He was succeeded by his eleven-month-old son, and for the next fifteen or so years a conciliar government, led by the deceased king's two talented brothers, John duke of Bedford and Humphrey duke of Gloucester, continued the work of conquest and consolidation of an English empire in France. As the child king entered his majority his inability to follow in the footsteps of his formidable father became apparent. Henry VI was temperamentally unsuited to rule and suffered a form of mental illness, the precise nature of which it is now impossible to define, but which he no doubt inherited from his insane grandfather Charles VI, king of France. Even in his lucid moments Henry VI showed little enthusiasm for defending his father's territories, and as the English were inexorably pushed out of France royal authority dwindled in the realm of England itself. A power struggle developed between William de la Pole earl of Suffolk and Edmund Beaufort duke of Somerset, the two men who dominated the king's council and court, and Richard duke of York, the father of Edward IV, who in 1425, after the death of Edmund Mortimer, the last direct male heir of the Mortimer line, inherited through the female line the Mortimer claim to the throne. After a series of crises – the sudden death in royal captivity of Humphrey duke of Gloucester in 1441; the popular Kentish uprising of the spring of 1450, known as Cade's rebellion; and the murder of Suffolk in May of the same year – the king fell into a completely debilitating bout of mental illness lasting eighteen months. Richard duke of York emerged as a leading figure in the hopes for a restoration of credible authority. However, the king recovered and the struggle continued between the house of York and the court, dominated by the Beaufort affinity; the struggle came to a head at the first Battle of St Albans in May 1455. The king lost his senses after this battle, in which his favourite, the duke of Somerset, was killed, and he probably never fully recovered. His queen, Margaret of Anjou, emerged as the real leader of the Lancastrian cause, which was now realistically focused on her son Edward, the prince of Wales. An attempt in 1459 to impose on the king a settlement in which York (like Henry V) was named as the heir to the sick king was inevitably followed by armed conflict between York and his supporters, drawn from the Neville family, and those supporting Margaret of Anjou and her son. Civil war followed at the beginning of 1460, and after the death of the duke of York at the Battle of Wakefield in January 1461 Edward earl of March emerged to seize the throne three months later after a series of bold military manoeuvres.

This charismatic young king, identified by his badge of the sun in splendour, started his reign with great promise, but those who helped him to the throne, his Neville kinsmen, were eventually responsible for deposing him and attempting to rule England by releasing Henry VI from captivity. Edward, after a six-month exile in Burgundy in 1470–1, again proved his qualities of leadership and his military skills and recaptured his throne. This time he ruled for thirteen years without any serious challenge to his authority, until his premature death in 1483 at the age of forty-two left his two young sons at the mercy of his inscrutable younger brother Richard duke of Gloucester. He seized the throne, imprisoning the boys, who were never seen again. The last survivor of the house of Lancaster, Henry Tudor, earl of Richmond, capitalized on Richard III's lack of political credibility following rumours that he was responsible for the murder of Edward's children, and seized the throne after the Battle of Bosworth in 1485, uniting at last the two warring factions of York and Lancaster by marrying Edward's daughter Elizabeth, and establishing the Tudor dynasty.

This is a familiar tale, and it was Shakespeare in his history plays who established it as a myth about the emergence of a nation from over eighty years of dynastic conflict and bloodshed in atonement for the original crime of regicide in 1400. Historians, however, have approached the fifteenth century from a rational, twentieth-century perspective, studying the complex, political interplay of factions within the court and the households of the magnates. I propose to retell this story from a very different, controversial, but late medieval perspective.

Most historians of medieval statecraft have failed sufficiently to appreciate the relationship between medicine, alchemy and such related practices as magic and astrology in government. This presumes that the educated and governing classes of the fifteenth century had a more holistic attitude towards their society and their natural environment. It was common knowledge that a close relationship existed between the celestial spheres and the individual. At the most rudimentary level it was universally understood that the Earth was composed of the four elements air, earth, fire and water, each influenced by four of the seven planets, Venus, Saturn, Mars and the moon, all ruled by the sun. These planets were composed of metals that specifically influenced the behaviour of the elements. Venus was the planet of copper and connected to the air; Saturn was lead and linked especially to earth; Mars was the planet of iron and affected fire; and the Moon was the silver planet influencing the element of water. All these planets were governed by the sun, the planet of gold, which in the hierarchy of metals was king. These elements gave rise to the different humours in the human body. Air formed blood; earth the black bile; fire led to choler; and from water came phlegm, the last of the elements to be created. In a mid-fifteenth-century treatise ascribed to Bacon on the four humours, water and phlegm are particularly associated with the old age of the earth and man himself; the humours of youthful spring, choler and blood, give way to those of phlegm and bile. The stock medical theory transmitted through the copious writing of the Greek physician Galen (AD 129–216) was that illness, physical or mental, was the result of an excessive and dangerous imbalance of one or more of these humours. Excess choler gave rise to fever, excess phlegm to colds. Treatment involved attempts to redress the balance by applying the opposite elements and later by the application of the metals associated with these opposing elements. Hence, fevers, caused by an excess of choler, would be treated by a sophisticated attempt to rectify the imbalance of moisture in the body through the application of water and perhaps the use of silver amulets; colds, derived from an imbalance of phlegm, required the application of fire and such warm metals as iron or even gold. The other standard treatment involved phlebotomy, the release of the excess humour through blood-letting.

A knowledge of the working of the humours in the body could also explain personality differences and behaviour. A preponderance of choler produced a 'choleric' personality, which was aggressive, extroverted and warlike (Henry V's horoscope established that his ruling planet was Mars). Black bile dictated the development of a saturnine, melancholic character. Saturn tended to be the ruling planet of scholars and introverts prone to moods and depression. Hamlet was the classic literary representative of this type. Phlegm was the characteristic humour of the phlegmatic man who was sluggish, indifferent, lazy and lifeless. In extreme cases he was prematurely aged. Blood produced the most fortunate of the four personality types, the sanguine personality, warm, creative, sensual and optimistic. Such humoral theories could be used in turn to explain the complex interplay of cooperation and conflict that characterized human societies formed from the mixture of different personalities dominated by different humours. This was best expressed by Geoffrey Chaucer towards the end of the fourteenth century in his prologue to *The Canterbury Tales*, in which he describes a society of pilgrims sharing fellowship, conviviality and story-telling, and yet also competing and quarrelling among themselves. The company contained a whole range of characters: choleric extroverts such as the abrasive Miller; the romantic and elegant Prioress who must have been born under Venus; the generous, sanguine and hospitable Franklin; the phlegmatic Pardoner with his thin yellow hair, his asexuality and lack of vital life force, symbolized in his trading in dead bones; and the sinister, saturnine Reeve who rides at the back of the company and lives by himself in a house shaded by a wood. The subtlety and complexity of humoral and astrological explanations of personality is revealed in Chaucer's portrait of the Wife of Bath, born under the competing influences of Mars, which gives her an argumentative nature and a red face, and Venus, which contributes to her wistful, creative side. The warring influences of both planets at her birth (which she is aware of) probably determined the predatory twist given to her sexuality. This society is held together by the host, the innkeeper Henry Bailly, who organizes the tale-telling competition. He is a born leader, warm, affable and confident:

> a large man he was with eyen stepe
> And of manhood hym lakkede right naught,
> Eek thereto he was a right myrie man.[17]

He is therefore naturally identified with the sun. The pilgrims set out for Canterbury in late springtime in April, his time:

> Up roos oure Hoost, and was oure aller cok
> And gadrede us togidre alle in a flok.[18]

The two main protagonists in this story, Edward IV and Henry VI, and the wars that were fought between their respective supporters, would have been understood by contemporaries with reference to planetary and humoral forces. Edward was born at 2.44a.m. on 28 April,[19] a child of the young and vigorous spring sun, and close enough to the house of Aries to come under the influence of this constellation; in contrast Henry VI was born in mid-winter, on 6 December 1421, when the sun was at its weakest and the moon relatively stronger. Two treatises on the four humours have considerable bearing on this dramatic polarization of the two most important contending personalities of the fifteenth century. One is the *Treatise on the Four Humours* which occurs in a mid-fifteenth-century manuscript containing Guy De Chauliac's treatise on surgery.[20] The other, written in 1486, is the *Book of the York Barber Surgeons' Guild*, containing information on the four humours and their regulation, useful for men whose tasks included phlebotomy (blood-letting).[21] In the *Barber Surgeons' Book* it is advised that spring is the prime time of the year, the time of the first of the four elements, air, and a time of abundant moistness and a good time to bleed,[22] whereas winter is a time of the fourth element, the phlegm, when people should avoid bleeding, eat salt meat and dry foods and counter phlegm with strong wines.[23]

This division of the year into two opposites had political as well as medical significance. The *Treatise on the Four Humours*, prefigured by a diagram showing the astrological influences on the human body, provides information on the different star signs. Aries is described as the sign of attraction. Men born under this sign are sanguine, full of face, of great heat and moistness, and inclined to grow fat. But a man born under Aries will also be full of deeds and have abundant grace.[24] Few of Edward's contemporaries would fail to observe how he corresponded to this description. Interestingly, those born under Scorpio (Richard III's sign according to John Rous, although strictly speaking Richard was born on 2 October, on the cusp of Scorpio), have much tribulation and anger. In the *Book of the York Barber Surgeons* it is demonstrated that when the moon is in the lusty sign of Aries it is a good time to speak with great lords and kings, 'to fight battles against foes' and to deal in gold. This is the time of year of blood, of the sanguine man, of the first element of air and the highest of the metals, gold.[25] Edward took the throne at the beginning of March and much was made (as we shall see) of his associations with gold, the spring, and the vigorous and new rekindling sun in the poetry, genealogies and proclamations that accompanied his accession. The *Treatise on the Four Humours* identifies Aries and the month of March with the creation of a new world, for it was during this sign that God made the earth. Similarly in an alchemical treatise entitled *On the withdrawing of the Accidents of Old Age*, copied in the mid-fifteenth century, Spring is described as the most noble time of the year.[26] The most powerful demonstration of the medical and astrological dimension to this struggle between York and Lancaster is in the account in the *Book of the York Barber Surgeons* of the respective qualities of the child born under the sun and the child born under the moon. As if to stress the important implications of what he is saying the author instructs his readers: 'I counsel every man to take good kepe there to.'[27] The child born under the sun is described as benign, much favoured in speech, fair mannered, and of high sovereign wit. He gets much good and spends it with a good cheer and good will (in other words he is full of largesse). Such a man is full lusty and willing, with a clear, shining face and inclined to love women over much.[28] This accords with all contemporary observations about Edward's charm, good looks, generosity and sensuality. The child born under the moon, however, is more variable and unstable, unsure in his speech and susceptible to colds, lethargy and melancholy. He makes light causes into heavy and forgives too easily the wrongs done to him. He is also unstable in his wits, heart and thoughts, always staring around him like a wild man. The sign of the moon in his body is a pale, even white face, and a small mouth. He has a liking

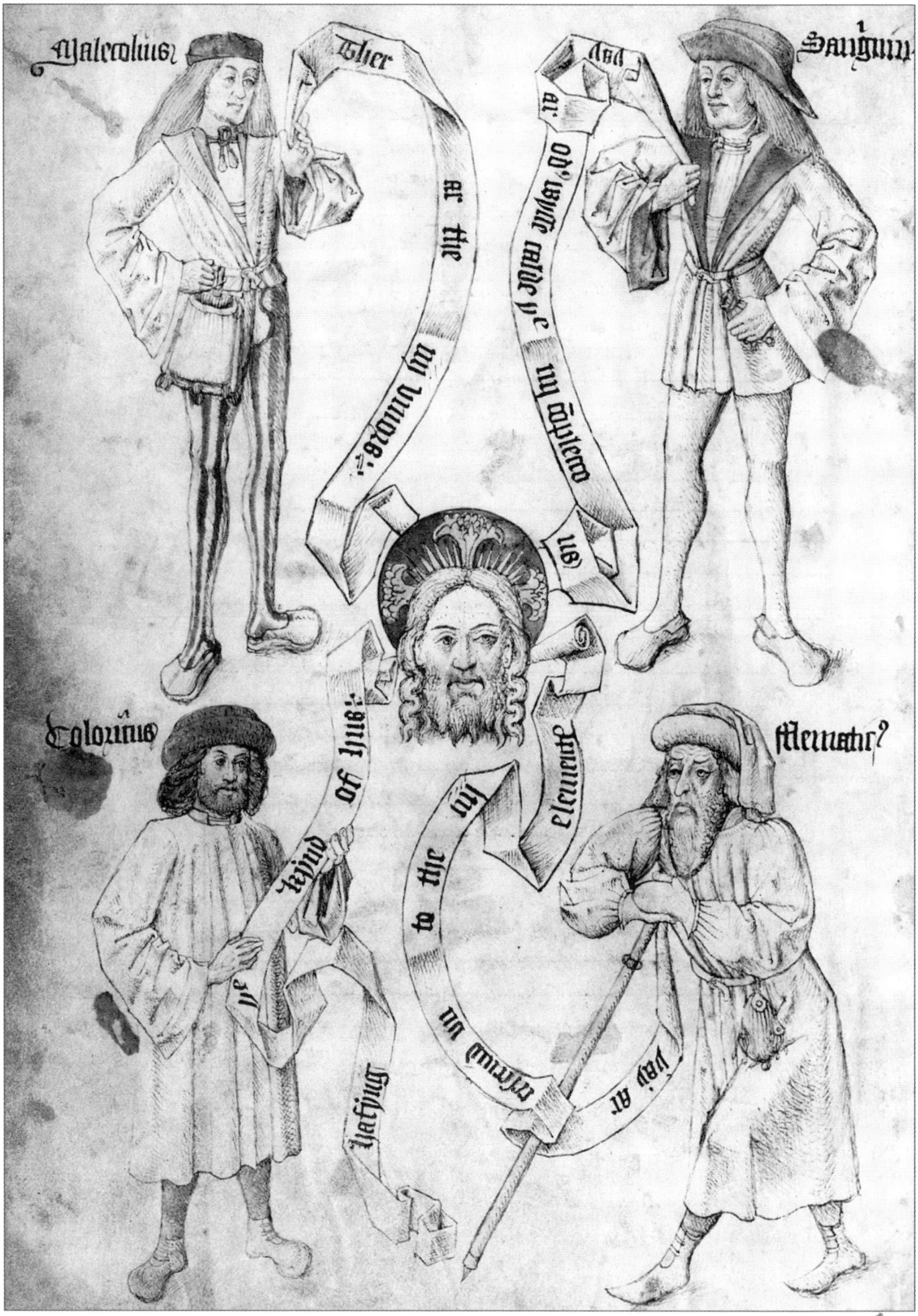

The four humours personified surround Christ, representing the quintessence, the perfect state of equilibrium. Behind Christ shines the sun in splendour and before him Phlegm (the predominant humour of Henry VI) is depicted as an old man. (British Library Egerton 2572, fo. 54v)

for silver.[29] This too accords with the physical and mental characteristics of Henry VI, who was officially diagnosed as suffering from an excess of phlegm by his physicians. The difference between the two kings was summed up in the diagram of the four humours around Christ, who is shown with the sun shining behind his ruddy face, while the phlegmatic man, prematurely senile, leans on his stick.[30] The author also accorded different countries with different ruling planets. The sun rules in Greece and the moon in England.[31] It must have seemed in the 1450s that England was entering a barren and cold wintry old age under its phlegmatic king. And then in the spring of 1461 the earl of March burst on to the political stage, taking control like the host of the Canterbury pilgrims Henry Bailly, like the young ascendant sun he bore on his shield, adopting the cognomen Sol (Gold) to dispense the chilly mists of England's winter king.

This stark contrast between the respective heads of the houses of Lancaster and York gives a profound medical/astrological dimension to the Wars of the Roses. There was a close identification between the health of the king, the head of the body politic, and his land. This is not a construct of late nineteenth-century anthropologists popularized in Jessie Weston's study of vegetative religion, *From Ritual to Romance* and T.S. Eliot's *The Wasteland*, but a truism of late medieval life. In a fifteenth-century poem in praise of Edward there is the recurring refrain:

> long ever preserve under thy myghty hand
> The king, the queen and thy land.[32]

St Augustine of Hippo (d. 430) first elaborated the image of Christ as physician (*Christus Medicus*) and surgeon,[33] and surgeons provided secular rulers with metaphors on the usefulness of control and sometimes amputation. The court poet John Lydgate, concluding his *Troy Book* in 1420 and celebrating Henry V's marriage to Katherine, the French princess, expresses the belief that once Henry is crowned king of France and the two realms are united there will be a golden age:

> the tyme fortunat,
> Of the olde worlde called aureat,

in which there will be no suffering and:

> With full ceessyng of deth and pestilence.[34]

Shakespeare perpetuated the myth of Henry V as a physician to his troops, depicting him visiting them on the night before the Battle of Agincourt, like a compassionate physician, bringing his men 'a little touch of Harry in the night'. The healing touch of kings was specifically applied to scrofula, a tubercular infection of the lymph nodes, which was known as the king's evil. The earliest recorded instance of a king healing through touch was in the reign of Edward the Confessor, and Edward III touched about five hundred people annually. Henry VII, to legitimize his position, made much of the ceremonial of the king's touch.[35] The *Somnium Vigilantis*, a Lancastrian document produced in defence of the proscriptions of 1459, compared the Yorkist lords to a rotten tooth; Richard duke of York countered this by likening his opponents to a wasting fever or pernicious cancer, and he invited his audience to reflect upon the inadequacies of a royal *medicus* who had so conspicuously failed to heal either himself or the ills of his kingdom. He enlisted the support of the commons in the Parliament of October 1460 as a physician calling on his apothecaries:

> I, beyng the partye greved, and complaynaunt, can not minister to my self the medicine that should helpe me (as experte leches and chyrurgians may) except you be to me both faithful ayders, and also trew counsaylors. Nor yet this noble realme, and our naturall countrey shall never be unbukeled from her quotidian fever, except I (as the principall physician) and you (as trew and trusty appotecaries) consult together, in makyng of the pocion, and trye out the clene and pure stuffe, from the old, corrupt and putrified dregges. For undoubtedly, the route and botome of this long festered cankar is not yet extripat–.[36]

One writer even identified Jack Cade, the leader of the Kentish rebellion in support of the duke of York, with the Surrey physician John Aylmer.[37] Giles of Rome (d. 1316), an Austin friar and scholastic theologian at the University of Paris, explained the ruler's task in *De Regimine Principum* as primarily keeping the body politic in a state of balance:

> We must understand that just as the essence of medicine, by the diet and potions and by syrups and other things which concern it, relates principally to the management of the humours and to make the human body healthy, so the science of governing cities and realms relates principally to ruling human affairs by law.[38]

War was seen by Giles in medical terms as a form of phlebotomy, of blood-letting to redress humoral imbalances in the body politic:

> It remains to be explained why war is waged – Just wars are meant to make peace and quiet for the people, and are waged for the sake of the common good. Wars should have the same effect on society as potions and blood-letting have on the human body: – the superfluity of bad humours which disturbs its health should be removed – when kings and princes are intent on the common good and the peace of their people they themselves will earn that eternal peace in which there is perfect rest.[39]

Lydgate in his *Troy Book* described how Achilles and Hector, the main warriors in the Greek and Trojan armies, were motivated by a predominant humour when they fought and killed. The Wars of the Roses especially came to be regarded in this medical dimension.

The political community (the body politic) was itself conceived in organic terms and shown to be susceptible to illnesses which were used as political metaphors. Leprosy and sexual diseases were attributed by the house of York to the founders of the house of Lancaster. Thomas Gascoigne maintained that John of Gaunt suffered from the pox, which contributed to his death.[40] John Capgrave, the Austin friar, recorded in his *Chronicle of England* the rumours that Gaunt's son, Henry IV, met with divine retribution after the execution of Archbishop Richard Scrope: 'As the comoune opinion went, fro that tyme onto his death he was a lepir and evyr fowlere and ffowlere. For in his deth, as thei recorded that swey of him, he was so contracte, that his body was scarse a cubite of length.'[41]

John Hardynge too claimed that Henry IV's face was 'so foule that leprous doth apere'.[42] In reality Henry IV suffered after Scrope's execution in 1405 from a combination of stress-related disorders, a skin condition (probably psoriasis) and circulatory disorders manifesting in leg ulcers in 1406, a seizure in 1408 and a fatal heart attack in 1413.[43] What is significant is that this enabled opponents to conceive both the Lancastrians and destructive infections such as *lupus*, which consumed the flesh, as ravening wolves devouring the body politic. The health of this body depended ultimately on the health of its head, the king. As Carole Rawcliffe's work has shown, the medieval physician plumbed the recesses of the soul rather than the body, often being more familiar with his patients' spiritual health and psychological anxieties than with their physical infirmities. This was a holistic approach to medicine, and when the balance of the king's mind was disturbed this affected all the members of society. The Wars of the Roses will be appraised in a novel way by studying attempts made either to redress the imbalance of Henry VI's humours or to bring in the new spring son of March to warm the land and bring it physic. One of the keys to the physician's political influence in the fifteenth century, as this book seeks to establish, lay in his involvement in alchemy.

Some misconceptions concerning the medieval alchemist need to be laid to rest. One of the problems facing historians is that alchemy is seen as a literary conceit, a product of the imagination. The image of the crazed lunatic in his cell, deranged by his futile quest and the noxious fumes he has inhaled, still dominates. This is in part because of the popular supposition that alchemy involved the pursuit of various chimeras, either the elixir of life (the source of eternal youth), or the transmission of base metals into gold and silver, all of which has been trivialized to little more than the search for the philosopher's stone, now the subject of children's books.[44] Literary treatments of alchemy have tended to emphasize the element of deception involved in the pursuit of wealth. Dante and Petrarch described it as a fraud; Langland, in the tenth book of his *Vision of Piers Plowman*, regarded alchemy as a science permeated with occultism aiming only to deceive.[45] Chaucer, in the *Canon Yeoman's Tale*, satirized the gullibility of those fooled by an alchemist who inserted silver into coals and into a hollow stick with which he stirred his crucible. Ben Jonson in his 1603 play *The Alchemist* focused on the humour of the alchemist Subtle's farrago of pseudo-learning and crude tricks with which he duped the greedy and the credulous.

However, in the concluding lines to the *Canon Yeoman's Tale*, Chaucer alluded to a very different alchemical tradition, one of obscure symbolism of such emblems as the dragon, Sol and Luna. Far from satirizing the verbal miasma of this tradition, as Jonson was to do, Chaucer writes:

> 'Lat no man bisye him this art for to seche,
> But if that he th'entencioun and speche
> Of philosophres understonde kan;
> For this science and this konning,' quod he,
> 'Is of the secree of secrees, pardee.'[46]

In this book I shall be attempting to unravel some of the mysteries of the alchemical emblems and allegories to show that they had a very down-to-earth application to political and social issues in the fifteenth century. Chaucer's skill with words and metaphors was matched by his scientific knowledge (the 'secret of secrets' was the term for the hidden and profound learning of the alchemist), and his reputation as an alchemical authority was such in the fifteenth century that he was cited by Thomas Norton, an alchemist at Edward IV's court.[47] Chaucer gave ample demonstration in his prologue to *The Canterbury Tales* of his ability to see the relationship between scientific and medical learning and the way society operated. The key to this more realistic and influential dimension to alchemy was medicine.

The alchemist was an important reality of fifteenth-century life. In a manuscript of the *Ordinal of Alchemy*, dedicated to Edward IV by Thomas Norton, there is a contemporary fifteenth-century illustration of an alchemist's cell with a stillatory, six furnaces for the making of potash glass, with two servants tending them, stacked alembics including one standing in hot water to maintain a constant temperature, and a distillation tower.[48] Alchemical distillation was a growing industry in this period. Most monastic infirmaries had distillation equipment and at Sandal Castle, owned by Richard duke of York, thirty-two alchemical vessels have been found. Over 225 Middle English texts refer to distillation.[49] There were two types of distillation, the refining of gold and the distillation of alcohol from wines and (in Scotland) whisky, and both had a medical purpose. Gold was widely used in medicines, as Chaucer slyly hinted in the *Physician's Tale*:

> He kept what he wan in pestilence
> For gold in physic is a cordial,
> Therefore he lovede gold in special.[50]

It was especially important in the treatment of leprosy. The court alchemist Sir George Ripley, in a letter to the chancellor and archbishop of York George Neville, wrote of the 'quintessence of gold as a 'precious portable liquor that helpeth lepers',[51] and in his *Marrow of Alchemy*, dedicated to Neville in 1476, he wrote about the true elixir of gold that cleansed the body's alchemy bringing it from whiteness to the glow of gold.[52] Distilled alcohol in various forms of concentration was a panacea for many ailments, especially melancholia. The Catalonian monk John of Rupescissa, one of the main authorities on distillation, proposed in his *De Consideratione quintae essentiae* (*On Consideration of the Fifth Essence*) in 1351–2, that alchemy could produce new kinds of drugs, such as compounds from chemical rather than organic sources. In this respect it represented a breakthrough in pharmacology. All those involved in the production and administering of medicines – apothecaries, physicians and surgeons – needed to have some knowledge of alchemical procedures. Bernard of Gordon (b. 1258), a learned physician who practised at Montpellier for over thirty years, showed in his popular *Lilium medicinae* (1303) a knowledge of alchemical procedures including the distillation associated with the production of medicines (he recommended the distillation of sea-water as an eye bath), and such ingredients of alchemy as sol ammonia and vitriol.

But any physician claiming to be learned needed to know the basic principles of alchemy beyond distillation procedures. This involved the maintenance of the balance of the humours. The English surgeon John Arderne (b. 1307) begins his *Treatise on Surgery* with a diagram of the four elements.[53] The surgeon of King Philip the Fair of France, Henri de Mondeville (d. 1320), in his *Book of Surgery* (1306) saw the surgeon as a craftsman working with fire to maintain the even temperatures of the body's humours. Like a blacksmith or an alchemist he burned with cauteries certain parts of the body. Like a jeweller he wielded with white-hot pincers his cauterizing tools, used to evacuate or keep away evil humours. Surgeons, like metal workers, had to make instruments. Mondeville thought that the using of cauteries of gold and silver was so complicated that the surgeon might seek a jeweller's assistance, and he used the same techniques as an alchemist in preparing oils and soldering the limbeck. These humours were produced in the body by a process of cooking, the source of the heat being the liver. The body was therefore seen as an alchemical furnace with the stomach as its cauldron inside an oven which was the trunk. The body over which the surgeon laboured was something like the athenar of the alchemist, the seat of incessant boiling, combustion and calcination, on which the lungs blew like a blacksmith's bellows. The surgeon and the physician presided over this cooking process to ensure a gentle heat was maintained, to prevent the boiling or freezing of the humours. Too much cooking produced an excess of choler and fever, and too little heat produced unnatural amounts of phlegm. This frequently involved a long fight to maintain the gentle, natural heat of the human furnace with bleeding and the application of cauteries.[54] The link between alchemy and phlebotomy is illustrated by John Aldeward, rector of Stoke Bruerne and an Exeter College fellow, who gave to Oxford University a manuscript containing tracts on the philosopher's stone,[55], on the quintessence[56] and on phlebotomy.[57] The luted vessel of the alchemist was likened to a womb in which the cooking process took place, imitating the gestation of a human offspring. A manuscript containing Rupescissa's treatise on the quintessence completed 'on the last day of March 1461' is accompanied by accurate drawings of distillation equipment that are made to resemble such organs of the body as the stomach, the small intestines, and the heart. Illnesses were seen in alchemical terms. Mondeville described how when a sick body lost its equilibrium corrupted humours took on metallic tints: bile goes rusty, blood turns to tin, gangrene invading a limb gives it the appearance of lead – all in sharp contrast to the golden glow of healthy flesh.[58] An English version made in 1446 of a Latin surgical treatise originally written by John Bradmore (d. 1412) described in alchemical language 'herpes' (a form of sexual disease or pox) and leprosy attacking the privy members and limbs of the body, putrefying and rotting them, alluding to the base states of matter that the alchemist attempted to transmute.[59] The quintessence, or the philosopher's stone, the perfect fifth essence from which all the other humours derived, was not an illusion. Symbolically it represented the state of perfect health which came from the peaceful equilibrium between the contending humours. For the alchemist Robert Barker, writing in the mid-fifteenth century, the production of gold from the four elements was a medical process, the creation of a medicine from the harmony between the elements:

> put gold unto thy spirit and it shall be amended more than a man may believe. And also then it may not be corrupt of no other thing. – in hym are all the four elements evenlike joined when softness and hardness be so evenlike then man of his qualities hete cold drye nor moist is overdrown of other-part thou the stone by the four elements, for everyone of them hath his operacion and his kynd in purpose like other. And put together that stone they hath no division ne no parting.[60]

This is the image of Bosch's peaceful Christ, surrounded by the four humours represented by his four tormentors (National Gallery, London). When the king's mind was at peace so too were the potentially contending humoral factions of his body politic.

Alchemists, and physicians with some alchemical knowledge and interests, played a vital role in maintaining the humoral balance of the king. The secret of secrets (the term for the most important hidden secrets of alchemy) was also used as the title of one of the most popular advice manuals of the Middle Ages. This was a handbook for princes, but with a much wider readership; though widely accepted as the instructions of Aristotle to Alexander the Great, it was actually a compilation put together from several Arab versions in the early Middle Ages. One copy, celebrating the marriage of medicine and astrology under the auspices of a great king, was presented to Edward III and contains an illustration showing doctors attending the king, one of whom holds a laxative herb to be prescribed when the moon is right.[61] The text of the *Secreta secretorum* was devoted in equal portions to statecraft, personal health, natural magic and astrology, and, in a version adapted by Roger Bacon, the English Franciscan thirteenth-century scientist, and owned by Edward IV, to alchemy. All physicians practised prognostication, consulting astrological charts before treating patients, using volvelles (astrolabes that tracked the path of the sun and moon through the heavens), and inevitably were drawn into making political prophecies, or at least into advising royal and aristocratic patients on the advisability of conducting certain enterprises at a particular time. One of the key texts used by Edward IV in his campaign to take the throne, and in his efforts to consolidate his position, contained prophecies of his coming and a genealogical history of his family to back up his claim to the crown. However, these were combined with medical texts that included a table of planetary influences and days, and a diagram showing the astrological influences on the human body.[62]

A sixteenth-century list of Great British alchemists in *A Lookeing Glasse for Illiterate Alchymists* is dominated by fifteenth-century practitioners, some of whom will play a prominent role in this study. What is striking about this list is that it is not confined to monks but includes prominent laymen such as Humphrey duke of Gloucester, brother of Henry V, who nominated him as regent of England in his will; Thomas Norton, a Bristol customs official and clerk of the household of Edward IV; and Sir George Ripley, an Augustinian canon who acted as counsellor to Edward IV. To this list can be added other prominent figures in English political life, such as George Neville, chancellor of England and archbishop of York; Gilbert Kymer, physician to Humphrey duke of Gloucester; and John Kirkby, Henry VI's chaplain. Just as the academic pursuit of medicine was increasingly becoming an interest among the laity, so too alchemy had ceased to be the preserve of a narrow clerical elite. Recent research demonstrates how alchemy became absorbed into the mainstream of intellectual life in fourteenth-century England. Faye Getz has studied the impact of Roger Bacon's alchemical manuscripts; Michela Pereira has examined the texts ascribed to Raymund Lull; and Linne Mooney, Peter Jones and Linda Voigts have described and catalogued other medieval alchemical manuscripts. Building on these studies, this book focuses on the intellectual and social underpinnings of medieval therapeutics by establishing the importance of the medical philosophy and mindscape of alchemy in the fifteenth century. It will explore the hitherto neglected and uncatalogued writings of George Ripley (*c.* 1470–90), physician and counsellor both to Edward IV and to George Neville, chancellor of England. Political historians have failed fully to appreciate the enormous differences between medieval and modern medical practitioners and have neglected to set the former in a meaningful context. These differences in perception go far beyond the obvious disparities in medical technology and the understanding of human psychology that separate the fifteenth century from the twentieth. I shall re-evaluate the power and status of the late medieval court physician. The question needs to be addressed as to why these practitioners exercised so much authority and grew so affluent. One of the keys to the physician's influence in the fifteenth century lay in his involvement in alchemy, as I shall seek to establish. Alchemists saw political life, history and myth in terms of conflicting personalities whose antagonisms sprang from the incompatibility of individual humours. A proper balance of choler, phlegm, blood and bile would resolve these conflicts. By learning from the alchemist the royal patient would be equipped to perform the multifaceted practical and heroic duties required of a late medieval head of state. The physical and spiritual health of the king was therefore bound up with the welfare of the realm.

George Ripley made the most influential application of alchemical ideas to these fundamentals of kingship, achieving prominence at the royal court by adapting Catalan alchemical texts posthumously attributed to Raymund Lull. Ripley is a significant and neglected figure. He features as one of Subtle's authorities in Jonson's play, *The Alchemist*:

> Ananias: 'A faithful brother, if please you.'
> Subtle: 'What's that?
> A Lullianist? A Ripley. Filius Artes?
> Can you sublime and dulcify?'[63]

John Dee, the Elizabethan alchemist, had in his library fifteenth-century manuscripts of Ripley's writings and according to his diary he consulted him in February 1588.[64] Ripley's works survive in nearly two hundred manuscripts, some from the fifteenth century but most from the sixteenth. They are full of compelling material: remedies for royal and baronial patients, medical theories, writing on natural philosophy, political prophecy, and advice on morality and statecraft. These iconographically rich manuscripts also contain mysterious, disturbing emblems. Jung appropriated some of these archival sources in an ahistorical way, applying what he saw as an illustration of the workings of the unconscious mind, thereby giving alchemy and Ripley an occult new age association that has deprived them of academic credibility.[65] But Ripley was at the hub of political and intellectual life. Alchemy played an important part in Edward's claim to the throne and with Ripley it is possible to understand a more subtle aspect of late medieval alchemy, a concern with maintaining the balance of the mind, especially the mind of the king: his will, courage and self-belief. Specifically I will show how Ripley's writings and visual images taught the royal patient to meditate on the physical processes of alchemy as a way to understanding his humoral disposition, personality and political potential. Most historians of medieval statecraft have failed sufficiently to appreciate the interface between medicine, alchemy and government in an age when the court physician was also a political animal. Ripley and his fellow alchemists advised Edward IV not only on matters of the physical body but also on issues of diplomacy, military strategy and religious policy. Had Jung looked differently at Ripley's writings he might have discovered a key to the understanding of the fifteenth-century body politic; conceptually they are comparable to the twentieth-century unravelling of DNA.

Another new aspect of this study will be the important place assigned to myths that alchemists, genealogists and poets believed held the key to the nation's recovery of its health, sense of purpose and destiny. The myth of the sick Fisher King and his wasted kingdom is not just a twentieth-century literary conceit of Jessie Weston (*From Ritual to Romance*) and T.S. Eliot (*The Wasteland*); it has a firm political foundation in the fifteenth century and especially in the reign of Henry VI. This mythological interpretation of the Lancastrian king may seem radical to modern historians, but it is how Henry's courtiers and physicians saw him. The legends of the Fisher King were being circulated at the Lancastrian court; the Great Vulgate cycle of Arthurian myths was owned by the Lancastrian courtier Sir Richard Roos, and by Edward IV's queen, before it was further popularized in Sir Thomas Malory's great epic, *Le Morte d'Arthur*.

A key to Edward's success was his willingness to allow himself to be the focus of an alchemical and allegorical exploration of the reinvigoration of an ineffectual monarchy in which he was seen as the embodiment of Sol, the rising sun of alchemy. Alchemists at Edward's court succeeded in fusing medicine with politics to project a cult of renewed kingship replete with myths and symbols. This celebrated the emergence of a united nation from the alembic of war. Alchemy was concerned with more than the physical health of the king; it involved a search through the past to the myths that could inspire a king and a nation. The founding father of British alchemy, according to the sixteenth-century list of Great British alchemists, was Merlin, King Arthur's guide and the prophet who predicted the coming of a British king who would reunite his nation. This king was widely interpreted at the Yorkist court as Edward IV. Merlin was an important figure in the political imagination, and it is likely that some influential alchemists, like Ripley, consciously identified with him. Edward made full use of the British myths by emphasizing his ancestry through the Mortimer line to the Welsh kings of Britain. This involved his identification with Arthur himself, and his claim that he was the 'once and future king of Britain'. This was something which would enable Edward to more than measure up to the formidable Henry V.

The concept of Britain as a holy land ruled by Arthur and his knights is no more of a literary conceit than alchemy. In the fifteenth century it became a political reality.

Winchester may have inspired the nineteenth-century romantic poet John Keats' beguiling and haunting evocations of a chivalric medieval world,[66] but in the fifteenth century it was believed that Winchester was the site of Camelot. The Round Table was there (*La Belle Dame Sans Merci* was even written in this period by Sir Richard Roos)[67] and Edward so convincingly attempted for a time to recreate his kingship in Arthur's image that Malory was inspired to set the legends of the British king and his grail knights into the coherent narrative that was to have such influence on the nineteenth-century fascination with the Middle Ages. What we shall witness at Edward's court, with the flowering of Arthurian romance and a Yorkist genealogical history stressing Edward's links with a lost period of British greatness from Brutus to King Arthur, is an assertion in the wake of the defeats in the French wars of a national identity based on a largely mythic history, Britain's isolation as an island from Europe, and its Celtic roots. Alfred Lord Tennyson adapted Malory's *Morte d'Arthur* to his vision of high Victorian British imperialism in his tediously moral *The Idylls of the King*, but here too we can see the fifteenth-century political reality that precedes subsequent literary and romantic projections. For it is at Edward's court that a sense of the imperial mission of Great Britain is first expressed.

Henry VI and Edward IV were also at opposite ends of a spectrum of religious sensibility. Henry was a lay practitioner of the contemplative life, a follower of the school of Richard Rolle and his disciples who placed the life of contemplation, of rejection of the world, above the active life. But Edward's court was a centre of religious change, of an increasingly secular outlook in which the eremitic life, the ascetic's rejection of human society and the natural needs of his own body, had little place.[68] Edward's chancellor, George Neville, illustrates these developments. On the one hand Neville was a member of a Yorkshire family that in the fourteenth century had been patrons of Richard Rolle and John Thweng (St John of Bridlington). He was also a pastoral bishop, one who consciously attempted to continue the work of his great predecessor as archbishop of York, John Thoresby. In 1466 Neville issued constitutions for the diocese dealing with the education of clergy and laity in the tradition of Thoresby.[69] But Neville was also a friend of George Ripley and a practising alchemist. Alchemy, with its investigations into the nature of matter, into all aspects of the natural world and into human history, can be seen as part of an increasingly empirical, scientific curiosity about nature and human society, as demonstrated by the antiquary William Worcester and by men at Edward's court such as William Caxton, the mercer and printer, and Anthony Woodville earl Rivers, the writer and translator and the king's brother-in-law. This court witnessed an increasing interest in the literature, history and philosophy of ancient Rome and the provision of this literature to a wider audience in vernacular translations and printed editions. The Yorkist court was the centre of a Renaissance that had little to do with the elitist view of Italian clerics' appreciation of Latin style which was mediated to England through such scholars as Erasmus, but everything to do with the growth of an educated ruling class dedicated to the ideals of public service and to the creation of a strong, rational and secular state.

The reign of Edward IV is a cultural watershed not just because it offers us fascinating insights into the imaginative world of fifteenth-century chivalry, myth, alchemy and medicine. The arid political labels of Lancaster need, whenever possible, to be laid aside, for this is the story of a family splitting apart as various myths and ghosts resurfaced. A conscious attempt was made to find a holistic solution to these conflicts, to discover the soul of the nation and to lay the foundations for England's future development. Behind it all lay the personal initiative and inspiration of an intelligent, charismatic, fascinating but deeply flawed man.

Ed.

NOTES

1. *Three Books of Polydore Vergil's English History*, ed. H. Ellis (London, 1844), p. 116.
2. Ibid, p. 154
3. Ibid, p. 159.
4. Ibid, pp. 159–68.
5. Ibid, p. 172.
6. *The Complete Works of Sir Thomas More*, ed. R.S. Sylvester, vol. ii, *The History of King Richard III* (Yale, 1963), pp. 4ff.
7. Thomas Heywood, *The First and Second Part of King Edward IV's Histories* (London, 1842). It is just possible that this play was written by the epigrammatist John Heywood (1497–1580), who wrote dialogue plays. During the reign of Edward VI John Heywood, thanks to the intercession of a gentleman of the king's chamber, escaped hanging. In this play Edward IV, in disguise, is befriended by one Hobbes. Edward, once he resumes his role as king, returns this favour by pardoning Hobbes's son, who is sentenced to be hanged.
8. Heywood, *Edward IV*, Act 1 Sc. 4.
9. William Habington, *The Historie of Edward IV* (London, 1640).
10. W. Stubbs, *The Constitutional History of England* (Oxford, 1878), vol. 3, pp. 225–6.
11. J.R. Green, *A Short History of the English People* (London, 1874).
12. C.L. Scofield, *The Life and Reign of Edward IV*, 2 vols (London, 1923).
13. B.P. Wolffe, 'Yorkist and Early Tudor Government 1461–1509', Historical Association Pamphlet, 1966; *The Crown Lands 1461–1536* (London, 1971); J.R. Lander, *Government and Community, England 1450–1509* (London, 1980).
14. K. Dockray, 'Edward IV: Playboy or Politician?', *The Ricardian*, x, 131 (December 1995), 306–24; C. Ross, *Edward IV* (London, 1974); A. Grant, *Henry VII* (London, 1985).
15. C. Richmond, '1485 and All That, or what was going on at the battle of Bosworth', in P.W. Hammond (ed.), *Richard III: Loyalty, Lordship and Law* (London, 1986).
16. P. McNiven, 'The Problem of Henry IV's Health, 1405–13', *English Historical Review*, 396 (1985), 747–72.
17. Chaucer, *The Canterbury Tales*, ed. L.D. Benson, The Riverside Chaucer 3rd edition (Oxford, 1988), ll. 753–8.
18. Ibid, ll. 822–3.
19. BL MS Harl. 543, fo. 130; BL MS Cotton Domitian A IX, fo. 83b; Scofield, *Edward IV*, vol. i, p. 1.
20. BL MS Sloane 965, fos 106vff.
21. BL MS Egerton 2572, fos 50–68.
22. Ibid, fo. 54v.
23. Ibid, fos 55–55v.
24. BL MS Sloane 965 fo. 147v.
25. For Richard III and Scorpio see A.J. Pollard, *The Princes in the Tower*, pp. 24–7; BL MS Egerton 2572, fos 58–58v.
26. Trinity College Cambridge, MS R.14.52 fo. 61; BL MS Sloane 965, fo. 147v.
27. BL MS Egerton 2572, fo. 54v.
28. Ibid, fos 62–62v.
29. Ibid, fos 62v–63.
30. Ibid, fo. 51v.
31. Ibid, fo. 52.
32. Trinity College, Cambridge, MS R.3.21, fos 242ff.
33. Carole Rawcliffe, *Medicine for the Soul. The Life, Death and Resurrection of an English Medieval Hospital* (Stroud, 1999), p. 104.
34. *Lydgate's Troy Book*, ed. H. Bergen (EETS, London, 1906), ll. 3400 and 3438.
35. P.T. Stone, 'A Brief History of the King's Evil', *The Ricardian* (1982 vol. VI, no. 76); R.H.P. Crawford, *The King's Evil* (Oxford, 1911).
36. Edward Hall, *Hall's Chronicle Containing the History of England During the Reign of Henry IV and the Succeeding Monarchs* (London, 1809), p. 245; C. Rawcliffe, *Medicine and Society*, p. 45; Rawcliffe, 'Status of the Royal Court Physician', 86.
37. R.A. Griffiths, *The Reign of Henry VI* (London, 1981), p. 617; Kingsford, *English Historical Literature*, p. 365
38. Rawcliffe, 'The Status of the Late Medieval Court Physician', 86; J. Watts, *Henry VI*, pp. 20–1; J.L.G. Pritchert, *La metaphore pathalogique et therapeutique a la fin du moyen age* (Tubigen, 1994), p. 20.
39. Giles of Rome, *De regimine principum Librii III* (Rome, 1567, repr. Facsimile, Frankfurt, 1968), bk 3, pt 3,

ch. 1. Quoted in A. Sutton and L. Visser-Fuchs, '"Chevalrie – in som partie is worthi for to be comendid, and in some part to ben amended": Chivalry and the Yorkist Kings', in *St George's Chapel, Windsor, in the Late Middle Ages*, ed. C. Richmond and E. Scarfe (Windsor, 2001), p. 115; A. Sutton and L. Visser-Fuchs, 'Richard III's Books: V Aegidius Romanus' De regimine principum', *The Ricardian*, 1985–7, pp. 541–52.

40. Thomas Gascoigne, *Loci e Libro Veritatum*, ed. J.H. Thorold-Rogers (Oxford, 1881), p. 228.
41. John Capgrave, *Chronicle of England*, ed. F.C. Hingeston, Rolls Series I (London, 1855), p. 291.
42. John Hardynge, *Chronicle*, ed. H. Ellis (London, 1812), p. 320.
43. McNiven, 'The Problem of Henry IV's Health', 747–72. The king's remains were examined in 1832 and there was no evidence of leprosy.
44. J.K. Rowling, *Harry Potter and the Philosopher's Stone* (Bloomsbury, 1997).
45. W.H.C. Ogrinc, 'Western Society and Alchemy from 1200–1500', *Journal of Medieval History*, 6 (1980), 103–32.
46. Chaucer, *The Canon Yeoman's Tale*, ed. M. Hussey (Cambridge, 1965), ll. 889–94; George Keiser, 'The Conclusion of the Canon Yeoman's Tale: Readings and (Mis)readings', *Chaucer Review*, vol. 35, no. 1 (2000), 1–19; E.H. Duncan, 'The Literature of Alchemy and Chaucer's Canon Yeoman's Tale: Framework, theme and characters', *Speculum*, 43 (1968), 633–56.
47. Thomas Norton, *The Ordinal of Alchemy*, ed. J. Reidy (EETS 272, London, 1965), ll. 1163–5.
48. BL MS Add. 10302, fo. 1v; J.E. Murdoch, *Albumen of Science and Antiquity in the Middle Ages* (New York, 1984).
49. Voigts, 'The Master of the King's Stillatories', paper delivered at the 18th Harlaxton Symposium on The Lancastrian Court, July 2001.
50. Chaucer, *General Prologue*, ll. 442–4.
51. BL MS Sloane 3580 B, fo. 178.
52. Bodley MS Ashmole 1479, fo. 9v.
53. BL MS Sloane 56, fo. 1.
54. M.C. Pouchelle, *The Body and Surgery in the Middle Ages* (New Brunswick, 1990); Jacquart Danielle, *La Medicine medievale dans le cadre Parisien xiv–xv siecle* (Fayard, 1999); *Chirurgie de Maître Henri de Mandeville*, ed. E. Nicaise; J.L. Pagel, *Die Chirurgie des Heinrich von Mondeville* (Berlin, 1892).
55. St John's College, Oxford, MS 172, fo. 316.
56. Ibid, fo. 212b.
57. Ibid, fo. 264b.
58. BL MS Sloane 338, fo. 56v for date. Distillation drawings to 30. See also BL MS Sloane 1118, fos 8–8v.
59. BL MS Harl. 1736, fos 94v–96.
60. From the alchemical treatise of Robert Barker or Frimitor (Friar Bungay), BL MS Stowe 1070, fos 26–32.
61. BL MS Add. 47680, fo. 54v.
62. BL MS Cotton Vesp. E VII, fo. 164; cf. BL MS Sloane 965, fo. 14.
63. Ben Jonson, *The Alchemist*, ed. F.H. More, Act II sc. V, ll. 6–11.
64. *Diary of John Dee*, ed. J.D. Halliwell (Camden Society, 1842), p. 21.
65. Carl Jung, *Psychology and Alchemy*, pp. 412ff; Carl Jung, *Mysterium Coniunctionis*, transl. R.F.C. Hull (Princeton, 1963).
66. See his *Eve of St Agnes*, *La Belle Dame Sans Merci* and *Eve of St Mark*.
67. BL MS Harl. 372; E. Seaton, *Sir Richard Roos, Lancastrian Poet* (London, 1961).
68. Jonathan Hughes, *Pastors and Visionaries: Religion and Secular Life in Late Medieval Yorkshire* (Woodbridge, 1988).
69. Wilkins, *Concilia*, vol. iii, pp. 599–665; Borthwick Institute Historical Research Register, Neville, vol. i, fo. 62.

CHAPTER 2

The Legacy of Henry V: Myths of Antiquity and the House of York

Shallow: 'That thou hadst seen that that this knight and I had seen.
Ha, Sir John, said I well?'
Falstaff: 'We have heard the chimes at midnight, Master Shallow.'
William Shakespeare, *Henry IV Part II*, *Act III sc. 2, ll. 228–32*

Henry V in his short but momentous life bequeathed more than a stable kingdom and an empire in Normandy to his successor. He raised himself to mythic dimensions in the eyes of his subjects, who ranked him with such heroes of antiquity as Hector of Troy, Alexander the Great of Macedonia, Julius Caesar of Rome and King Arthur of Britain. He therefore created in his subjects expectations of greatness, of a strong secular state led by a great imperial king, and of an overseas empire, all based on the inspiration of ancient Rome. Despite his early death these ideals persisted and, coupled with nostalgic recollections of the achievements of his reign, they created a climate of restless dissatisfaction, of an eager expectation of the arrival of a successor who would continue his work. As the failings of his son in all these areas became obvious, these hopes were entertained by courtiers associated with the house of York, and ultimately they were to be rest on the young earl of March.

Ironically the source of the Roman inspiration was Henry V's conquered lands in northern France and in particular Paris. It was during the second phase of the Hundred Years War between England and France, from 1415 to 1435, that the ideals and myths of Roman antiquity reached the forefront of the ruling classes in both countries. At the Valois court of Charles V and Charles VI French translations were made of classical myths and Roman history. The most important sources of classical mythology, the story of Troy and the *Metamorphoses* of Ovid, were translated into French around this period. Between 1342 and 1350 a moralized Christian allegorical version of *Metamorphoses* was written by Pierre Bersuire and a second version in prose was made in 1466–7. Boccaccio's *De casibus vivorum illustrium*, which drew on myths for moral exempla, was translated by Laurent de Premierfait in 1407 and dedicated to Jean duke of Berry. Another source of classical myth, the *Epitre d'Othea* of Christine de Pisan, employed a similarly allegorical treatment of classical myths for Charles V. It was also at this court that French translations were made of Roman history. Pierre Bersuire translated Livy's *Ab urbe condita* and Nicholas Gonese compiled for John de Berry between 1400 and 1401 Valerius Maximus' *Facta et dicta memorabilia* (*Memorable Deeds and Sayings*), a large body of anecdotes taken from Roman history up to the time of Tiberius, illustrating Roman practices and the workings of Roman institutions with examples of virtue and prudent actions. In the French royal library of Charles V there were six copies of the *Faits des Romans*; four in combination with the *Histoire Ancienne*; two of a French translation of Livy; three of prose works on the life of Caesar, possibly a translation of Lucan's *Pharsalia*, a popular classical epic; three of the Latin *Pharsalia*; one of books I–IV of Simon de Hesdin's translation of the *Memorabilia* of Valerius Maximus and another of the French version of Sallust. Such works, along with the writings of Cicero and Seneca, formed the nucleus of the royal library of the Louvre. Christine de Pisan grew up in the court of Charles V and in this library. She wrote a biography describing Charles as the wise king of France who was 'sovereignly governed by cunning and loued singularly philosophres', and a rhetorician who measured up to the ideals of the Romans: 'It was a grete pleasaunce to her his goodly and eloquent language whether in counceil or anuy other matter – it was a mervellous thyng to her him speke.'[1] Christine became the most influential fifteenth-century adaptor of Roman classics. She greatly admired Charles V as a philosopher king in the tradition of great Roman rulers, and it was in her adaptations and translations at his court that admiration for Roman civilization and empire was openly expressed for the first time and the possibility of emulating Rome was being considered. An introduction to a fourteenth-century translation of Livy began: 'considering that the Roman people among all others, by the virtues of constancy and prudence and by their chivalrous deeds – knew how to achieve so much that by their wisdom and labour they conquered the whole world, we may see that every ruler may take examples from their wonderful deeds'.[2] It was a French translation of Vegetius's *De re militari*, the Roman military textbook first written in the fourth century AD in an attempt to stem barbarian invasions by a revival of Roman military discipline, that provided practical advice on how to emulate their military feats: 'Men should read it because they know the Romans conquered the world and wanted to know how they did it.'[3] In the vernacular adaptations of Roman history and in the original writings of Christine de Pisan, Froissart and Bouvet an attempt was made to address the issue of the French defeats at the hands of the English in the fourteenth century. It was argued that the wheel of fortune could only be stopped by an assertion of the Roman military virtues of courage[4] and prudence.

Ironically this French literature was appropriated by their English conquerors. The most successful emulator of the Romans (and a reader of Vegetius) was Henry V, the scourge of the Valois dynasty. One of the most far-reaching cultural consequences for fifteenth-century England of the war with France between 1415 and 1430 was the spreading of the influence of these French adaptations of Roman military and political theory among the English court and aristocracy. The earliest English translation of Vegetius's *De re militari* was made in 1409 for one of Henry V's commanders, Thomas Lord Berkeley, who was serving in the prince of Wales's first imperial venture, fighting against Owain Glyndwr.[5] According to the privy seal clerk and poet Thomas Hoccleve, Henry V consulted Vegetius.[6] The characteristic phrase Henry V used to gain approval for his campaigns was 'one wages war to make peace', an echo of Vegetius's remark 'he who desires peace prepares for war'. Another influential model for Henry was Julius Caesar's *Gallic Wars*. There is little doubt that Henry V identified with Caesar. The main campaigns of the Gallic wars, such as the crossing of the Loire, influenced the conduct of Henry V's military actions. The campaigns of both Caesar and Henry V were marked by an emphasis on siege warfare; protracted winter campaigns requiring bureaucratic organization of food supplies; siege tactics; and discipline in armies of permanent occupation. Henry V and his brother John duke of Bedford adopted the policy of expelling natives of Normandy who refused to be loyal to their conquerors, a policy that was reminiscent of the discipline imposed by Caesar on his legions occupying Gaul. One of Henry's captains, Sir John Fastolf, owned histories of the civil war between Caesar and Pompey and the war between Rome and Carthage. But his most important acquisition was Caesar's *Gallic Wars* which he obtained in Paris in 1428. The qualities that were to guide Fastolf's subsequent career as a military commander in Normandy were determined by his reading of this work. Caesar ordered the forests of Normandy to be cut down and the crops destroyed to prevent the enemy foraging. Caesar considered prudence to be the hallmark of a great general and placed the welfare of his troops ahead of other considerations; he was therefore prepared to make strategic retreats and reprimanded his generals for being too ruthless and headstrong. Fastolf similarly ordered a strategic withdrawal at the Battle of Patay and defended it in terms of Roman prudence at the court of chivalry. He also advocated the destruction of the enemies' hinterland in Normandy. All this bore the hallmark of a serious campaign of conquest very different from the more haphazard summer chevauchées involving the collections of prisoners, booty and honour recounted by Sir Walter Manny in his descriptions of the campaigns of Edward III and the Black Prince in the fourteenth century.

The degree to which Henry V identified himself with a conquering Roman general can be seen in the victory processions organized in London after the victory at Agincourt and in the valedictory sermon preceding the king's final journey to France, following the footsteps of Caesar's conquest of Gaul. This sermon took the form of a prayer sent for the preservation of the king so that he can say 'alle the lands aboute me I am sovereign lord'. The preacher employed an analogy from Vegetius's *De re militari* of a ship trapped in the narrow harbour at Syracuse by a blockade of ships until Sextus Julius, using his wits, put all his soldiers in the front of the ship and broke out through the chain. Henry V is identified with the great Roman general similarly driving the ship of state out of the harbour and through the French, Normans and Scots.[7]

By this stage Henry V was achieving mythic status, and the Benedictine monk John Lydgate, who had access to a considerable collection of classical literature in the library at the monastery of Bury,[8] became the bard who developed the myth of Henry V which was to have such an influence on the policies and image of Edward IV. The epic story of the siege of Troy was known in the Middle Ages in Benoit de Saint Maure's *Roman de Troie*, composed in about 1160 from forged eyewitness accounts of the fifth to seventh centuries.[9] This was adapted by Guido in 1278 and turned into English by Lydgate at Henry V's request between 1413 and 1421 because Henry:

> hath joye and gret deynte
> To rede in bokys of antiquite,
> To fyn (fynde) only, vertu for to swe
> Be example of hem, and also for to eschewe
> The cursyd vice of slouthe and ydelnesse.[10]

The prince, according to Lydgate, busies himself to exercise his body in martial exercise 'after the doctrine of Vygecius'. Henry is depicted therefore as self-consciously following in the footsteps of the Romans. Moreover he is shown to be aware of the common ancestry he shared with the Romans and the Trojans who fled their city under Brutus to found New Troy or London. Lydgate's description of the ancient city shows he conceived it as a classical city with theatres and amphitheatres where poets glorified the deeds of emperors, a city of circular buildings enshrining the principles of reason, an imperial city containing people from many provinces. The prince who will succeed to 'gouerne Brutys Albyoun'[11] therefore bade Lydgate to translate 'the drery pitus fate of hem of Troye'[12] because he wished

the noble story openly wer knowe
In oure tonge, aboute euery age
And y-writen as wel in oure language
As in Latyn and in frensche.[13]

Henry therefore secured for his own ambitions an epic that through Lydgate's services would help define the nation and serve his own grandiose pretensions. Lydgate may have complained of the inadequacies of the English language in dealing with an epic previously treated by Ovid and Virgil, and admitted that Chaucer was no longer alive to do it justice,[14] but he nevertheless set about creating the epic story of Britain's origins which as much as Malory's *Morte d'Arthur* defined the self-image and aspirations of the fifteenth century's two most charismatic kings, Henry V and Edward IV.

For Lydgate the trauma of Troy's defeat represented the birth pangs of the Roman and British civilizations. Aeneas, an exile from Troy, conquered Italy and his descendant was Augustus Caesar,

that was whilom so noble a conquerour,
That his renoun to this day doth schyne.[15]

Referring his readers to Virgil if they wished to know more about this emperor, Lydgate set out to demonstrate that Henry V, another descendant of the Trojans, was a great conqueror. Lydgate was aware that as a writer he had the opportunity to draw on powerful myths and to evoke the inspirational example of heroes of the past. He saw his *Troy Book* as a work of history, for without such books knowledge of the past would disappear, and with it the glory of old heroes would vanish. Writing, he claimed, stopped the earth from dimming the brightness of a hero's fame, and without knowledge of the past our ancestors (the Trojans) would die. The Trojan war in particular was seen as a mirror of the current enterprise in France, which similarly locked two chivalrous nations together in mortal combat. Through his writing the heroes of this war are

refresched newe,
of oure auncetrys left to us by-hynde;
To make a merour only to oure mynde,
to seen eche thing trewly as it was.[16]

Contemplation of the Trojan war would therefore enable Henry and his troops to understand what they shared with their Trojan ancestors in terms of chivalry and courage, and to see where the Trojans went wrong. Hector, Henry's ancestor, was depicted as the embodiment of chivalry, but he and his people were held back by their chivalry. They lacked ruthlessness. Hector allowed the Greeks time to bury their dead, a three-month reprieve when he could have defeated them. He also proudly displayed his arms, allowing himself to be identified by the vengeful Achilles. The message for Henry V and his troops was clear: they were presented with an opportunity to reverse this ancestral tragedy and to fulfill their ancient potential by adopting the tactics of the Greeks. The British were now the invaders, not the besieged. Lydgate emphasizes this by describing the Greeks in terms reminiscent of Henry V's invading army: they debate the invasion of Troy in parliament and advance in fifteenth-century armour and with scaling ladders. The subliminal theme of Lydgate's narrative is that Henry V and his captains had to pursue the same logical, disciplined, ruthless pursuit of military advantage, with no half-measures, as Achilles and the rest of the Greeks had done.

Henry V's cynical diplomatic manoeuvres before the invasion were reminiscent of the way the Greeks boxed in the Trojans with unacceptable peace terms. Henry V's public gesture in executing a soldier accused of stealing a pyx from a church was perhaps a deliberate allusion to the way Hector was fatally struck by Achilles' spear when he was distracted by taking gold from a dead knight. Henry would not make the same mistakes as his great forebear.

The importance and originality of Lydgate's *Troy Book* reside in his secular view of history which allowed full scope for the impact of a personality such as Henry V's, and explored the working of fate through history. In denying the intervention of the pagan gods of Ovid and Virgil, Lydgate paradoxically created a more secular world dominated by fortune's wheel. The unpredictable fluctuations of this wheel were set in motion when great men like Jason and Priam followed their passions and went to war. For Lydgate war was frightening and horrific rather than chivalrous. He is full of dread at the suffering caused by war, describing the fear of the Trojan women when their husbands ride out to battle, the horror of Achilles slaughtering fathers before their sons' eyes and the destruction of a beautiful city. It is seen in the terms of alchemical medicine as an aberration caused by humoral imbalances of the great who have to let blood. Hector is 'Brennynge ful malencolye' and Achilles goes on the rampage because

> – it dide him good
> with his swerde Troyan blood to schede,
> and on the soil to sen hem lyn and blede,
> Routheles in his malencolye.[17]

Nevertheless Lydgate does not impose a Christian morality about the falling of the proud. His sense of awe at the forces of history unleashed in war encourages him to express an admiration for the great personalities behind wars. His interest in the forces of history leads to his approval of Jason's intransigence (which prefigures Henry V's stubbornness), and although the subsequent fall of Troy is a tragedy, from it emerges the forces that shaped the Roman Empire. Reflecting on the fate of Troy and all empires subject to the vagaries of fortune and war, Lydgate admits to his own lacklustre skill in describing this and his fear of the wrath of Prince Henry who commissioned this work. He subtly identifies his patron with the protagonists of this historic drama:

> My penne quake and tremble in my hond,
> list that my lord, dredde on see and lond,
> whos worthiness thorogh the world doth spred,
> My makyng rude schal beholde and rede.[18]

This magnificent and ambiguous reaction to war, anticipating Tolstoy's, was to mark the subsequent generations who grew up with stories of the campaigns of Henry V, Bedford and Talbot, and was to influence the formulation of policies under Edward IV.

Henry's premature death in 1422 created a profound sense of loss among members of the governing class and the intelligentsia, including Lydgate. They were deprived of a leader who had given them a sense of participating in an epic that would have placed their civilization on the same level as that of the Romans. However, Henry did bequeath a lasting legacy that was to have reverberations throughout the fifteenth century: a secular, pragmatic view of the state. Despite his much-vaunted piety, Henry made religion serve the needs of the state; he organized public processions after his victories, harnessing the cults of saints and the services of religious houses to his dynasty, making religion a public ceremony, a politically binding force, just as the Romans had done, and in a way that Machiavelli was to recommend. This was something Lydgate understood and reflected on in the work that stands as a meditation on the implications of the king's death, *The Fall of Princes*. This translation and adaptation of Laurent of Premierfait's *Des cas des Nobles Hommes et Femmes* (a French prose version of Boccaccio's *De casibus vivorum illustrium*, written in the years 1355 to 1360, made for the Duke of Berry between 1405 and 1409) was undertaken by Lydgate from April 1430 to January 1432 at the instigation of Humphrey Duke of Gloucester. In this compendium of the legends of antiquity Lydgate contemplates the mutability of great men and their empires at the hands of nature or fortune. He regards with pathos the fate of ancient Rome, which in the two centuries after the birth of Christ subjected almost the whole inhabited world to its rule.[19] He praises the achievements of antiquity, enumerating its contributions to the founding of the various sciences including medicine, astronomy, warfare and the science of weights and measures,[20] and in particular notes the qualities of the writers of ancient Rome:

First in Rome, be souereyn excellence,
Off rethorick Tullius fond the flours.[21]

He follows this with an envoy on Rome, an appreciation of the achievements of its empire and the emperors Julius Caesar and Caesar Augustus (Octavius), and its writers, Publius Vergilius Maro (Virgil), the greatest poet of Augustan Rome and author of the epic story of Rome's origins, *The Aeneid*; Marcus Tullius Cicero (Tully), the statesman of the Roman republic, orator and moral philosopher; and Anneus Seneca the younger, the essayist and stoic philosopher of the Rome of Tiberius. This encomium is not in the original source and Lydgate asks:

Where is now Cesar, that took possessioun
first off thempire, the tryumph usurpyng?
Or wher is Lucan, that maketh mencioun
Off al his conquest be cerious wrytyng?
Octavioun most solepneli regnyng?
Wher is become ther lordeshep or ther lyne?
Processe of yeris hath brought it to ruayne.
Wher is the palace or royall mancion
With a statue clere of golde shining
By Romulus wrought and set on that dongeon?
Where is thy temple of christal bright shewing,
Made half of gold most richelly moustryng.[22]

He also laments the disappearance of the writers who were beginning to have such influence in Lydgate's courtly circles:

where is Tullius cheef lanterne off thi toun,
in rethorik all other surmountyng?
Moral Seneek or prudent sad Catoun?[23]
Thi comoun proffit alwei preferryng?
Or rihtful Traion,[24], most just in his demyng.[25]

and he concludes: 'long processe hath brought al to ruyne'. Such writers are bracketed with Boccaccio and Chaucer as bringing renown to their nations. Finally he asks what has become of Rome's great empire:

Wher is become thi dominacioun?
The grete tributis (enrichyng) thi tresours?
The world al hool in thi subieccioun,
The swerd off vengaunce, all peeplis manacyng.[26]

Fortune, or nature, is fickle and this is emphasized when Lydgate meditates on the fate of Troy, the civilization that was the harbinger of Rome and the England of Henry V. The fall of this city shows that there is little order or justice in the world:

to us declaryng the mutabilite
off false Fortune, whos fauour last no while,
Shewing ay trewest when she will begile. –
Hir wheel untrusti and frowardli meuyng.[27]

This is the context for the death of Henry V. When Lydgate writes about Priam, the legendary king of Troy, and the siege of his city, he comments that he has already written about this at the request of Henry V, whom he describes as:

Henry the Fiffte, most myhti off puissaunce,
. . . for knyhtli suffisaunce,
Worthi for manhod, rekynd kynges all,
With nyne worthi for to haue a stall,[28]

a great man whose purpose was to bring peace between England and France, but who, alas, died too soon; a legendary figure who ranked with the heroes of antiquity and who dwarfed his fellows:

But, o allas, ageyn deth is no boone!
This lond may seyn he deied al to soone
For a-mong kynges he was oon the best,
So alle his deedis conueid were with grace.
I pray to God, so yiue his soule good reste,
With hooli seyntis in heuene a duellyng-place.
For heere with us to litil was the space
That he abod; off whom the remembraunce
Shal neuer deie in Ingland nor in Fraunce.[29]

Lydgate therefore sees Henry V as a man whose colossal ambition introduced him into the pantheon of such heroes of antiquity as Julius Caesar and Octavius, who have long-since entered mythology. Lydgate does pay lip-service to the doctrine of Christian humility by claiming that the Romans overreached themselves:

In thi most hiest exaltacioun,
Thi proude tirantis provyncis conqueryng,
To God cntraire be long rebellioun,
Goddis, foddessis falsli obeieng,
Aboue the sterris bi surquedous clymbyng,
Till olde vengaunce thi noblesse dede ontoyne
With newe complyntis to shewe thi ruyne[30]

and he exclaims:

> ley doun thi pride and thi presumcioun,
> Thi popmpus boost, thi lordeshepis encresyng,
> Alle false goddis pleynli diffieng!
> Lifft up thyn herte onto that heuenli kyng.[31]

Lydgate objects to the gods of the Greco-Romans because they were ruled by their passions, and his counsel to Christian humility is really an exhortation to the sort of stoic obedience to the unfathomable laws of nature counselled by the Roman writers he admired:

> O thou Pouert, meek, humble and debonaire,
> which that kepeth the lawes off nature.[32]

The stoic writers of ancient Rome, such as Cicero and Seneca, taught that happiness came from an acceptance of nature and all that happens, which was in no way dependent on the fulfilment of desires or of things outside one's control. Such an outlook could lead to peace of mind, health and freedom from the dictates of the emotions. Lydgate frequently quotes Seneca on the contentment that comes from finding joy in adversity. In the *Troy Book* and the *Fall of Princes* he advises his readers to be rational and detached and to obey the vagaries of fortune. Fortune's capriciousness can be mitigated by human virtue, reason and prudence, and obedience to the laws of nature can release one from the tyranny of fortune. It was also incumbent on great rulers, according to Lydgate, to show this sort of stoical detachment and obedience in which they never succumbed to excess emotion or humour. He interprets the riddle of the sphinx in the *Fall of Princes* as an allegory on the need for prudent moderation:

> Agayn nature is no proteccioun;
> Worldli estatis echon thei be mortall, –
> who clymbeth hiest, his fal is lowest doun;
> a mene estat is best, who koude it knowe
> Tween hih presumyng and bowyng doun to lowe.[33]

If the great princes are reasonable and learned in stoic literature then there is a chance that the world will be reasonable and the turning of fortune's wheel can be slowed:

> Vertu on Fortune maketh a diffiaunce,
> That Fortune hath no domynacioun
> wher noble pryncis be gouerned be resoun[34] –
> offte reedyng on bookis fructuous
> The hertis sholde off prudent prynces perse,
> Synke in ther mynde and make hem vertuous.[35]

The hero is the one who can turn fortune's wheel. Lydgate saw obedience as the source of political stability on which the foundations of the state, the manifestation of God's natural order, were built. This is a secular outlook that places little emphasis on an interventionist God or on an easily moralized view of history. Instead the emphasis is on stoic obedience and conformity to the laws of nature and the great which is seen as the guarantor of personal and political stability. This is an attitude that anticipates Protestantism in its emphasis on obedience and conduct at the expense of the numinous and magical.[36] The Bible, instead of being used as a source of multi-layered meanings, was becoming a source of moral exemplars and exhortations to obedience. The city of Abel (the shepherd martyred at the hands of his more practical and earthy brother Cain), the heavenly Jerusalem in Augustine's exegesis of the destinies of the two cities of Jerusalem and Rome that dominated the outlook of educated men for a thousand years, was being replaced by a new sympathy for Cain's earthly Rome, the model for the ideal state.[37]

What was becoming palpably clear to Lydgate when writing the *Fall of Princes* was that there was no immediate successor to Henry V to provide this stability, and as Henry VI came of age the reverse started to happen. His disturbing brand of religiosity, his dependence on the mystical outlook of fourteenth-century devotional writers following the traditions established by Richard Rolle (the influential Yorkshire hermit who counselled his followers to reject the responsibilities, ties and temptations of the active life in society),[38] meant that religion was far from being the means to creating a strong state and instead was becoming a potentially disruptive force and one that could encourage self-indulgence. The king who emerges from the pages of the biography by his chaplain, John Blacman, is a practitioner of the contemplative life who turned away from the world, a man of passive temperament. He was an Abel whose eyes are set on the heavenly Jerusalem and who implicitly rejected the imperialistic, secular values of Rome, the city of Cain. Henry V would not have approved. For him religion was always subservient to the interests of the state and his strong stand against heresy shows how alert he was to the potentially divisive threat posed by religious enthusiasm. He saw the teachings of antiquity as the antidote to such extremism. In 1415 Thomas Hoccleve, always ready to offer opinions on topical issues in his poetry, reproved Sir John Oldcastle (the leader of the first Lollard revolt in 1414) for his heretical opinions, and urged him to

> rede the storie of Lancelot de Lake
> Or Vegece [Vegetius]. Of the art of chivalrie,
> The siege of Troie of Thebes. The applie
> To thyng that may to Th'ordre of knyght longe
> rather than delve into holy scripture.[39]

The preacher whose valedictory sermon of 1419 compared Henry to a Roman general commanding a ship reflected that this ship of state, once honoured throughout Christendom, had been nearly wrecked in the previous thirty years by Lollardy but had been saved by the present king.[40] The governing classes were therefore searching for a successor to Henry V who embodied the secular, expansionist values of ancient Rome. With the inadequacies of his son, politically never advanced beyond infancy, so apparent, they looked to various forms of government that owed their inspiration to Roman models, from conciliar rule along senatorial lines to a more imperial form of authority; and they naturally looked for guidance to Henry's two brothers, John duke of Bedford and Humphrey duke of Gloucester.[41] Through these two men the intellectual traditions started by Henry V descended to Richard duke of York, Bedford's widow, Jacquetta of Luxembourg, her son Anthony Woodville, and ultimately to Jacquetta's son-in-law, Edward IV.

Humphrey duke of Gloucester, an avid collector of classical literature, was the obvious successor to uphold Henry V's Roman imperial ambitions. Humphrey owned a French version of Vegetius's *De re militari* and Suetonius's *History of the Twelve Caesars*. In a letter of thanks from Oxford University for his donation of books, many of which were Roman classics, Humphrey is compared to Julius Caesar, who founded a library in Rome and who, like Gloucester, embodied the attributes of a great soldier and scholar. Pietro del Monte, a Venetian papal collector who was in England in 1435, dedicated a moral treatise to Duke Humphrey comparing him to Julius Caesar, who waged war and wrote commentaries at the same time.[42] Lydgate's *Fall of Princes* was dedicated to Humphrey. Lydgate addressed his patron as one who was a prince in the mould of Julius Caesar and who:

> Whan the tryumphe he wan in Rome toun,
> He entre wolde the scoole off Tullius
> And heere his lecture off gret affeccioun;
> and natwithstandyng his conquest and renoun,
> Unto bookis he gaff gret attendaunce
> And hadde in stories ioie and gret plesaunce.[43]

Seeing himself in the role of Lucan to a great prince, he described the duke as 'a prince of mighty puissance' who 'loves to be with soldiers and read their books'. According to Lydgate

> this mighti prynce riht manli and riht wis
> Gaff me charge in his prudent auys
> that I sholde in euri tragedie
> Afftir the processe made mencioun,
> At the eende sette a remedie
> With a lenvoie conueied be resoun.[44]

These stories of the fall of princes show great men undone by passion and celebrate stoicism, obedience (the virtue of all virtues) to the laws of nature. The envoys, written by Lydgate, recommend confronting tragedy with a stoic detachment, obedience to fortune and a mastery of passion. Such 'true obedience', bringing prosperity and excluding rebellion, comes, he claimed, from the reading of the works of antiquity. The Duke of Gloucester, he notes approvingly, is a model of such detachment:

> He always continues his studies
> setting aside changes of fortune–
> his courage never doth appalle
> to studie in books off antiquite,
> Thereupon he hath so gret felicite
> vertuously hymself to occupie.

Humphrey's identification with these stories is shown in his decision to name his daughter Antigone after a child of Oedipus.

Humphrey's elder brother, John duke of Bedford, continued Henry V's successful expansion into Normandy. Under his leadership victories such as that at Verneuil in 1424 entered a national mythology that had started at Agincourt. As the ruler of Lancastrian Normandy after the death of Henry V, he used his position to acquire the royal library of Charles V, a collection of 843 books which included the French translations of Livy, Valerius Maximus, Aristotle, Cicero and Lucan which were used by Christine de Pisan.[45] Members of his household therefore had access to these French versions of Roman history and military theory which gave them a sense that they were following in the footsteps in Normandy of the original conquerors of Gaul. It was this dissemination of the literature of antiquity among such men and ultimately into the Yorkist court that was to prove Henry V's most enduring legacy.

The focus of these Roman imperial ambitions after the death of Bedford in 1435 and the political disgrace of Humphrey duke of Gloucester in 1441 was Sir John Fastolf, Bedford's lieutenant in Normandy. One of the most important inspirations for Fastolf was his copy of the military manual of fourth-century Rome, Vegetius's *De re militaribus*,[46] an attempt to save Rome after the first Hun invasions by reviving ancient Roman military discipline. This pragmatic manual for the foot-soldier was little used by the Romans because the infantryman was by then giving way to lightly armed cavalry. But by the fifteenth century, when the long bow was depriving mounted cavalry of its shock-impact tactics, Vegetius's work was becoming the ideal manual. Vegetius favoured prudence, pragmatism and at times ruthlessness ahead of heroism and fair play. For example, he recommended the use of ambushes and starving the enemy.[47] In 1435 Fastolf used his knowledge of such military discipline when he issued a memorandum on how to continue the war effort in Normandy, which shows how his reading of Roman history gave him a new ruthless and secular perspective.[48] Fastolf urged a scorched-earth policy, sending out punishing raids into southern France; his tactics can be compared with campaigns in the Peloponnesian wars and had many classical precedents as well as the more recent precedent of William the Conqueror's harrying of the north. His proposal to starve the enemy through a ruthless destruction of their territory can be found in Vegetius, who recommended the destruction of the infrastructure of the peasants, and is typical of the famous discipline applied by the Romans. Traitors, he urged, were to be mercilessly punished and benefit of clergy was no longer to be allowed. This reveals his ruthless, secular perspective: Normandy was seen as part of an empire to be defended on purely mercantile economic grounds rather than as a fellow Christian country. Fastolf's reading of Vegetius also influenced his disregard for the traditional superiority of the mounted knight of chivalric tradition, and just as Vegetius recommended the importance of infantrymen in defending a decaying empire, Fastolf urged that war against France be fought by foot-soldiers rather than by cavalry, especially by pikemen who could unhorse the French mounted knights.[49]

Although Fastolf retired from Normandy in 1438 he continued to be an inspirational figure for those with imperial vision. He continued to express his identification of English territorial interests in France with those of the ancient Romans in Gaul and he made another report in August 1449 for Richard duke of York urging a greater degree of sacrifice, a mobilization of the 'entire republic' to harness the wealth of private individuals to fight a total war. Otherwise, he pointed out, many English settlers in Normandy would, if it fell, be unable to live up to their accustomed lifestyles when they returned to England and this would cause turbulence 'in our republic'.[50] Fastolf's stepson, Stephen Scrope, whose father Sir Stephen Scrope had served as lieutenant in Ireland, accompanied him to Normandy. Shortly after Fastolf's retirement, Scrope translated the *Epistle of Othea* in 1440 for Fastolf. This work is closely related to Lydgate's *Fall of Princes* in its moralization of classical myths and to the *Troy Book* in its analysis, through a series of letters from Othea to Hector, of the reasons for the tragic fall of Troy. Originally written by Christine de Pisan with the intention of encouraging Louis of Orleans to develop the virtue of prudence so that he could inspire responsible leadership in France, it became in Scrope's version a programme for the reconquest of France through the sort of disciplined leadership that only Fastolf could provide.[51] The very literature that the French turned to and adapted during the second half of the fourteenth century when they were suffering at the hands of the English was now being used by the English in an attempt to turn fortune's wheel in their favour. While many of Christine de Pisan's contemporaries, such as Froissart and Bouvet, saw fortune's wheel being governed by an unstable woman who was to be controlled by male power,[52] Christine instead argued that this could be achieved through the exercise of reason. Scrope argued that there was a need to listen to the advice of older, prudent counsellors such as Fastolf and that it was the Trojans' failure to appoint such men that led to the city's downfall. Othea's advice to Hector is therefore an endorsement of all the qualities Fastolf had shown in his military career in Normandy. Hector is advised not to trust in fortune or her promises, not to rely on his castle in time of war unless it is full of provisions and soldiers, and not to fight with those who are stronger. All of this is pertinent to Fastolf's strategic retreat from superior forces at Beaugeny in 1429, a strategy that caused John Talbot (the 'English Achilles') to bring charges of unbecoming conduct against him, charges that led to Fastolf's disgrace and possibly temporary suspension from the Order of the Garter. Fastolf's response to the rumours spread by Talbot was to implement an enquiry in 1441 into the events of 1429 (in which William Worcester participated) which led to his name being cleared. Scrope's epistle is an exhortation to complete the conquest of Normandy through a redefinition and rejuvenation of chivalry, achieved through the virtue of prudence. In the prologue, addressed to Fastolf, the old knight's martial exploits in France and Normandy are linked to the battle over spiritual enemies in which the aid of the four cardinal virtues, especially prudence, is enlisted.[53] This is a virtue that Hector, for all his heroism, does not possess. A narrative of tragic dimensions unfolds as Hector refuses to listen to counsel and ostentatiously displays his arms, enabling Achilles to identify and kill him.[54] The same moral, imperial message was transmitted in the illustrations commissioned by Fastolf to accompany the original French manuscript used by Scrope. The artist (the Fastolf Master), after illuminating the cardinal virtues, alluded to the bonds of chivalry and respectful memory of Henry V that bound Fastolf, his accountant Spireling and John Paston I (all members of the guild of St George in Norwich),[55] by depicting on the letter handed by Othea to Hector the cross of St George, the patron saint of the English soldiers in France.

The optimistic message in the *Epistle of Othea* was undermined in the summer of 1441 by the trial for witchcraft of Eleanor Cobham, wife of Humphrey duke of Gloucester. She was accused of trying to bring about the death of Henry VI through necromancy and of melting a waxen image of the king. She was imprisoned for life and the astrologer Roger Bolingbroke, a member of Gloucester's household, was hanged and quartered at Tyburn. This case highlighted the widening rift in the English court between those around Henry VI and the duke of Suffolk who wished to negotiate a peace settlement, and those who wished to follow the Roman example and accelerate the English war effort. A new leader of the latter group emerged in the aftermath of the political disgrace of the duke of Gloucester, Richard duke of York (the father of Edward IV), who may have attempted to rescue Eleanor Cobham from prison during the rebellion of 1450.[56] Civil war was becoming a possibility and naturally those in York's circle turned again to the literature of the Romans for comfort and counsel. York was the natural successor to Bedford in France. During his second term as lieutenant in Normandy (1440–5) he was a virtual viceroy in Rouen and he was remembered as a ruler who dispensed justice and showed concern for the welfare of the inhabitants of the duchy. He restored effective authority in a province all but lost to rebellion, and sustained mercantile confidence in a continued English presence. By 1445 York was emerging as a figure with dynastic and imperial ambitions in open conflict with the narrow clique that protected and isolated Henry VI from alternative sources of counsel. This clique was led by William de la Pole the duke of Suffolk and Adam Moleyns the bishop of Chichester and king's secretary. These two men were closely identified with the policy of appeasement with France, the king's marriage to Margaret of Anjou, the truce of 1444 and the running-down of the Norman defences. One writer who saw York as the man to preserve

English honour and dynastic pretensions abroad was the Austin friar Osbern Bokenham (1393–*c.* 1467) of Clare Priory, 15 miles from Bury St Edmunds in Suffolk. Richard duke of York succeeded to the honour of Clare in 1432 and Bokenham incorporated into his legendary of thirteen female saints, composed between 1443 and 1447, a genealogy emphasizing York's title to the Castilian throne, which was further advanced in 1445 in his *Life of St Mary Magdalen*, commissioned for the legendary by York's sister, Isabel Bourchier.[57] Like York's title to the English throne, this came through the female line via his grandmother Isabella, daughter of King Pedro of Spain and sister of Constanza of Castile, who had married Edmund Langley earl of Cambridge and later duke of York. In 1444 York, investigating this claim, gave orders to Sir John Fastolf to procure a copy in Normandy of the original treaty of Bayonne of 1388 for details of the succession. York's imperial ambitions were pressed further in a translation in 1445, probably by Bockenham, of the Roman poet Claudian's *De consulatu Stiliconis*. In this period of English imperial decline and growing domestic instability, York (who had just ended in 1445 his five-year term as lieutenant general of England's forces in northern France) is directly identified with the Roman consul Stilicho, regarded as the last hope of the crumbling Roman Empire in Britain, the representative of Mars in the west confronting the decadent and narcissistic east.[58] In the poem the provinces of Rome, one by one, beg Stilicho to assume leadership of the empire. Britannia in her plea underlines the link between Stilicho and York, the hope for the regeneration of English ambitions in Scotland and France, when she exclaims:

I shulde not fere bataile
Of scotlonde. Ne of picardy. 'ne fro my see banke
I sholde nevir see me for to noye. 'saxon saile with wyndes.
nor fear 'Picts or Picardy.'[59]

Stilicho's consulship of AD 400 is shown to be directly applicable to the conflicts of the mid-fifteenth century. While his rival, Rufinus, is spreading rumours about him in the East, the senate invites Stilicho to rule (Stilicho's claims are strongest through his wife, as York's were through the female line of Anne Mortimer), and this is directly linked to Parliament's exonerating York from the charges brought by Adam Moleyns of financial maladministration and favouritism while serving as lieutenant of France in 1446:

Marke stilicoes life. Whom peoplis preysed
with what labouris. Of the regions wide
And Rome hir selfe. The consulat he upreised
Ffor now the parlement pierys. Wher' thei goo or ryde
Seyen the duke of yorke hath god upon his side.[60]

The poem, which is an exhortation to power, does not counsel rebellion and urges on the duke of York a stoic patience, advising him to trust in his parliamentary peers who, like the senate, have the common good in mind, and to follow the example of this virtuous pagan poet, who, although he could not save, could instruct. The significance of Stilicho for the duke of York lay in his role as the chosen leader of the Roman senate expressing the *vox populi*. Stilicho accepts the people's offer because of his connections with the royal house and because he serves the common weal. In 1445 York had been recalled from Normandy and was seen as Honorarius, the popular military leader committed to the defence of the empire of the child king. The importance of the poem to York can be seen ten years later on 17 November 1455 when he presented articles explaining his assumption of the protectorate which were closely in accord with the *Letter of Stilicho*, drawing attention to the intended benefits of a protectorate sanctioned by Parliament: 'the welfare and honour of the king, the politique and restful rule and govenance of this his land and the entreating of his laws and peace wherein rests his joy'.[61] This translation of Claudian's letter is an eloquent testimony to the impact of classical history on the political and intellectual life of the fifteenth century.

The optimism expressed in the poem and in the Parliament that exonerated York was, however, undermined by two subsequent events that made a peaceful solution to the growing tensions in the English court less likely. In 1447 Humphrey duke of Gloucester died in highly suspicious circumstances while under arrest. Henry VI and his favourite Suffolk were widely held to be responsible. It was probably in the turbulent years between the trial of Eleanor Cobham in 1441 and Gloucester's death that John Lydgate wrote the *Serpent of Division*, a life of Caesar presented in the shape of a sombre sermon for his patron, Humphrey duke of Gloucester, warning of the dangers of civil discord and describing the civil wars of Rome from the days of the triumvirate of Caesar, Pompey and Crassus to the assassination of Caesar, and the impact of these conflicts on the Roman state. Inviting comparisons on the conflict between Gloucester and York and the king's court dominated by Suffolk and Somerset, its popularity was such that it survives in thirty manuscripts.[62] In 1450 there was an expression of popular unrest in the form of a rebellion in Kent led by Jack Cade, in which York's name and the claims of the Mortimer line were invoked. By this time the parallels between the disintegration of the Roman Empire and the collapse of English imperial ambitions in France had become striking and were felt particularly in the circles of the two figureheads of these ambitions, the Duke of York and Sir John Fastolf. Fastolf's secretary, William Worcester (who wrote an account of Fastolf's campaigns in France),[63] began composing the *Boke of Noblesse* around 1451.[64] In the *Boke of Noblesse* he attempted to explain the loss of Normandy as a failure of the English aristocracy to emulate the self-discipline and organization, bravery and moral uprightness, and selfless dedication to the common weal of the Roman governing classes. He defined war as an ennobling experience and advocated the training of the English nobility in arms for the defence of the realm in jousting, running with a spear, handling the bow, axe and sword, skipping and running to make them hardier and ready when they were needed to do humble service.[65] Worcester reflected that all great empires, including those of Athens and Rome, fall when decadence and declining moral standards set in and that this was what had been happening to the English, the descendents of the Trojans, since the time of Henry V: 'Sensualite of the bodie now a daies hathe most reigned over us to our destruccion we not having consideracioun to the generalle profit and universalle wele of a comynalte.'[66] He presented the *Boke of Noblesse* together with a collection of documents illustrating Bedford's regency to Henry VI to induce him to follow his father's policy and renew the war with France.

Worcester was also concerned, in the wake of the Cade rebellion of 1451 and the widening rift between the dukes of York and Somerset, about the possibility that the collapse of the empire would be followed by the disintegration of the realm itself. Roman history provided him with instructive parallels and solutions to this problem. Between November and December 1453 Worcester, using the library that Fastolf had acquired while in Bedford's service in France in 1429, collected extracts from Suetonius and Lucan on the civil war between Caesar and Pompey and from Orosius on the war between Rome under Scipio and Carthage under Hannibal.[67] The lesson Worcester took from his researches was that great Roman leaders, like Julius Caesar and Scipio Africanus, prevented civil war through an aggressive policy of imperial expansion. In December 1453 Worcester copied extracts on the acts of war between Caesar and Pompey from Lucan and Suetonius which he found in a French manuscript that Fastolf had acquired in Paris.[68] He accordingly applied this lesson in the *Book of Noblesse* to the situation in England in the 1450s and urged the reconquest of Normandy as a solution to domestic, political problems. The heroes of his work, apart from the great Roman generals, were those who emulated them like Henry V, Richard duke of York and above all Sir John Fastolf. Worcester by 1453 was applying what he was reading about the internal divisions in Rome to Henry VI's England, compiling notebooks of extracts from these works of Roman history which suggest he was recognizing in England a departure from the virtues of selfless service to the common good and an imperial ideal that had existed under Henry V and the duke of Bedford. He provided examples of self-sacrifice on the part of the Roman senatorial classes, which he thought the English aristocracy should emulate. He recounted senators who reacted to commons complaints about taxation by surrendering their silver and gold and issuing strict restrictions on the amount they were to keep. Similar gestures were made by Bedford when he refused wages, and by the nobility in the Parliament of 1434 when they nominated a graded tax, imposing higher burdens on themselves. An underlying theme of the *Boke of Noblesse* is that the English ruling class had been expelled from Normandy because they were losing this sense of selfless service to the *res publica*. Worcester alluded to the remarks of the commons about poor administration in Normandy and the misappropriation of funds and wages in arrears, complaining that 'through lack of prudence' and 'politique governance' there was no consideration to the 'common wele'.[69] This concern was echoed in the criticisms in Fastolf's circle of the exactions of the duke of Suffolk's officials in Norfolk. Fastolf wrote to the parson of Castle Combe, Sir Thomas Howes, in 1450 complaining about the extortions and maintenance of Sir Thomas Tuddenham, one of Suffolk's officials, and urged those with grievances to approach chief justice Yelverton, adding that the poor of Norfolk and Suffolk because of extortion live their lives in misery.[70]

Later in his *Itinerarium* Worcester would note 'a poor man gets no hearing unless he gives bribes'.[71] For Worcester, concern for the *res publica* was inextricably bound up with service to a sense of imperialistic mission. The *Boke of Noblesse* is in part an apology for Roman military discipline (Vegetius is used to demonstrate the military tactics of conquest and the prudent administration of colonies), and in part an accountant's view of how such conquest and administration could be efficiently achieved through men like Fastolf, who exemplified the necessary qualities. Worcester, like his friend Scrope, advocated that the future conquest of Normandy rested in the hands of older, prudent men like Fastolf who were capable of steering the ship of state. Fastolf had demonstrated during Henry V's campaigns the necessary qualities of discipline and prudence when he stocked his castles and fortresses with sufficient provisions to withstand sieges.[72] Worcester provided illustrations of the Romans' superior qualities of organization and demonstrated how outnumbered Roman armies, like those of Henry V, destroyed the armies of Gaul. He also provided material to facilitate the conquest and occupation of Normandy, such as Fastolf's knowledgeable comments and documents illustrating the success of English military government in Normandy under York in the 1440s. This growing frustration with the collapse of the war effort in France was expressed in the strategically significant garrison town of Calais. A second version of Vegetius was made by a parson of Calais in the late 1450s. The author presented his work to Lord Beaumont, chamberlain of Henry VI, to give to the king.

One of the most enduring legacies of Henry V's reign was a growing self-conscious nationalism celebrated by such writers as John Lydgate, Stephen Scrope and William Worcester. The latter, urging the invasion of France in the 1450s, evoked imperialistic convictions which were especially strong in the household of the duke of York. His ideas contained implicit assumptions about the superiority of an English/British civilization, which it was believed was directly descended from the Romans through the common ancestry of Troy and which culturally was in the process of emulating the civilization of secular Rome; such assumptions had little to do with the crusading ideals that motivated many of the captains of Edward III's armies in the fourteenth century. In 1419 the preacher of the sermon that preceded Henry V's final invasion spoke of the English taking the place of the Israelites. They were described as the chosen people, spreading civilization, the spearhead of which was Oxford University, seen as the font of wisdom giving light to the whole realm, its beacon of wisdom spreading throughout the world: 'As fer as God lay lond Oxon habuit nomen.'[73] The duke of Bedford sustained this idealistic vision of England's imperial mission when he was regent of France (1422–35) and his major domo was Sir John Fastolf. In a roll in which Worcester set down all the offices Fastolf had held while serving overseas between 1412 and 1439, he is credited with the idea of founding a university at Caen in Normandy to train a new class of administrators.[74]

Imperial ideals were also maintained in England's other colony, Ireland. In 1422 James Yonge, a member of an English family that had settled in the Irish Pale, provided his master Sir John Butler, earl of Ormond and lieutenant of Ireland, with a version of *Secreta secretorum* (a standard mirror for princes which, although of seventh-century Arabic origins, was widely believed to have been written originally by Aristotle for Alexander the Great), in which he implicitly compared the administration of the empires of Rome and Henry V.[75] Both empires were ruled by kings who were philosophers, who lived and ruled according to the rules of prudence or reason. Yonge anticipated Scrope in placing especial emphasis on prudence as 'the life lived according to reason'.[76] Yonge upheld the same ideal of a highly trained and educated administration in Ireland that Fastolf's circle held for Normandy: 'estudy of clergi well meynteyneth, is the wyrchyp of Empire, the beauty of the realme the lyght of the lordshippe, the remembraunce of all goodys'.[77] This could involve the application of ruthlessness: Yonge's assumptions of cultural and racial superiority over the Irish led him to identify with his supposed Trojan ancestors and he criticized previous administrators of Ireland who neglected to punish Irish subjects, reminding Butler not to forget Troy's fatal leniency and to execute traitors and enemies who fell into his hands. Yonge described the Greeks and Romans as enlightened civilizations who prized learning above all things. The Romans, he claimed, conquered the world by cunning and study of wise old books rather than battles. Cicero's observation that empires and kingdoms were well governed when kings were philosophers and philosophy reigned was cited. English civilization was regarded as innately superior, like that of the Romans. An illustration of Yonge's prejudices about Irish inferiority occurs when he celebrated Sir John Butler's victories against Art MacMurrough during the reign of Richard II. With Irish polygamy in mind he described these as successful fights against lechery in which God was on the side of the English who, with their restraint, justice and hatred of adultery, scourged the Irish. Such sentiments were not new. They can be found in the works of Giraldus Cambrensis, and they reveal deeply ingrained prejudices about Irish instability and its origins in polygamy.[78] Yonge observed that the Irish needed to be treated with tolerance and understanding because they were capable of loyalty when they saw their conquerors in a position of superiority and strength. He therefore emphasized the need for tolerant enlightened administration in Ireland to secure the willing rather than the forced cooperation of the natives, something tyrants like Nero and Richard II could not achieve. The model imperial administrators were perceived to be Julius Caesar, Augustus and Henry V. Yonge held similar common weal ideals to Worcester's and singled out for praise Stephen Scrope's father, Sir Stephen Scrope, who as deputy lieutenant in Ireland under Thomas duke of Lancaster refused to make extortions in the colony.[79] Yonge's work had a practical influence on Ormond who achieved a pre-eminent position in Ireland. He followed Yonge's advice on avoiding the exploitation of the natives and in 1421 he pledged rents on his own lands as security payment on any debts outstanding at the end of his office. In 1428 he regulated and abolished the coign, the custom of billeting soldiers on the populace in Gaelic lands; this was only to be done on his authority and with the agreement of the community. Ormond died in 1452 after a successful six-week campaign to secure the submission of a number of rebel leaders.

Members of the Fastolf circle shared Irish imperial ideals. As well as praising Sir Stephen Scrope for his efforts against Art MacMurrough, Yonge observed that Ormond in his younger years was a witness to these campaigns. Some continuity can be seen between Yonge, Ormond, Scrope and the duke of York, who presided over the earl of Ormond's political rehabilitation when he arrived in Ireland in 1448 with his wife Cecily. It was in Ireland that York's son, George, was baptised in the presence of the earl of Ormond. During his residence there from 6 July 1449 to 1450 the duke of York secured the submission of forty-two Irish leaders and prepared a major campaign against the Gaelic Irish. York's son, George duke of Clarence, was lieutenant in Ireland, and his deputy, Desmond, passed an act establishing a university at Drogheda. William Worcester, who was himself half-Irish, was at times a victim of English imperial snobbery. Friar Brackley made capital of Worcester's Irish origins, describing him as a swarthy, unstable, thankless Irishman who exhibited all the qualities peculiar to that race. Brackley's sense of racial superiority was also applied to the French, describing Colin the Frenchman, one of Worcester's allies in the dispute over Fastolf's will, as constipated like all his race.[80]

However, the confident, imperialistic assumptions expressed in Yorkist circles belied a deep-seated unease inspired by the disintegration of the body politic in Normandy and England. This was expressed in the form of regrets at the passage of time, and a sense of the loss of a golden age in the reign of Henry V and anxieties about political uncertainties, the turning of fortune's wheel and the possibility of the disintegration of friendships. To alleviate these anxieties members of the governing classes, instead of turning to the traditional consolations of religious literature as their forebears would have done, turned to the literature of antiquity.

One anxiety that had both personal and political ramifications was the disintegration of friendships. The approach of the Wars of the Roses involved the splitting up of families and friends. The quarrels which set in as Fastolf entered senility, and which destroyed his circle once the acrimonious disputes began over his will, came to have a wider symbolic significance, providing a macrocosmic image of the wider fissures appearing in the body politic. These uncertainties were expressed by Friar John Brackley in a letter to John Paston esq., 'his most trusty friend on earth', when he exclaimed in October 1459: 'Be my feyth here is a [unsettled] werld.'[81] In his *Instructions to His Son*, a series of precepts on self discipline and service to the common weal from Seneca, Cicero and Aristotle, written in 1461, Peter Idley cited Cicero's *De amicitia* on the need to unravel friendships slowly rather than tearing them apart.[82] Worcester confronted these concerns with the pragmatic response of the Romans. He copied extracts from Seneca, Cicero and other Roman writers on the theme of friendship and translated for Sir John Fastolf Cicero's *De amicitia*, in which he faced the uncertain world of the 1450s with a stark realism devoid of religious consolations. He asserted the meaninglessness of life, of all experiences, unless you have friends with whom you can communicate; and he maintained that the only mark of a good man was the ability to sustain friendships. This amounted to an explicit rejection of the values of the contemplative and eremitic life (in which experience was regarded as ultimately incommunicable) that had so absorbed the governing class of the fourteenth century and which came to be identified with the discredited Lancastrian king. In Yorkist circles there was a definite shift away from admiration of the eremitic life to an assertion of the importance of social life and communication. For Worcester and his friends there was a special significance in Cicero's words: 'if any bond of kindly feeling were taken from the world no house or city would stand: fields would no longer be cultivated and that where there is internal hatred and division no home or country in the world is strong enough to avoid destruction'.[83]

When Fastolf died one of his executors, his lawyer John Paston esq., produced an alternative will, naming himself as the main beneficiary. Relationships deteriorated in Fastolf's household to the extent that no bill of funeral expenses was drawn up. The prior of St Benet's lamented the dispute and Yelverton referred to it in a letter to Paston as 'the brekyng'.[84] Fastolf's wishes for a collegiate church and chantry at Caister were ignored by Paston, and in the ensuing wrangles Worcester turned to the classics for consolation to reassure himself that it was not the provision of chantry masses that was important but that he should continue to remember Fastolf and work for the interests of his friends and dependents. To a fellow opponent of the nuncupative will, possibly Stephen Scrope (who wrote the *Epistle of Othea*), he wrote: 'the fulfilling of felicite of man is to gete friends'.[85] He also cited Cicero's *De amicitia*: 'A very frende at nede experience will schewe be dede, as wele be auctorite of Aristotle in the Etiques that he made of moralite; also by the famous Reamyn Tullius in his little boke *de amicitia* thanking you for olde contynued frendship stedfastly grounded.'[86] Worcester took to heart Cicero's characteristically secular observation that when he was absent a dead friend could ennoble the existence of those left behind. He tried to maintain the continuity of Fastolf's household by bearing the costs of the funeral, distributing gifts for the next twenty years and in general serving the dead man by rewarding his dependents. He continued to remember his master as late as 1478, noting a poem in a church: 'to love is to fear but the contrary holds not true'.[87]

A concomitant insecurity of this period linked with the disintegration of friendships and affinities was a more generalized fear of the capriciousness of fate, exacerbated by political uncertainties. It is a striking fact that most of the major works of literature of the fifteenth century were written by men in prison: *The Kingis Quair* by King James I of Scotland, the poetry of William de la Pole duke of Suffolk and of Charles of Orleans, George Ashby's *A Prisoner's Reflections on the Active Policy of a Prince*,[88] and Malory's *Morte d'Arthur*. Other literary men and authors such as John Paston, Humphrey duke of Gloucester, William Worcester and Sir John Fortescue all spent time in prison. It is not therefore surprising that many turned to the stoic literature of antiquity which offered the consolations of philosophy and the promise of intellectual detachment from the whims of fortune and political opponents. Charles of Orleans was the grandson of Charles V and his father had owned the works of Aristotle, Ovid, Horace, Lucan and Virgil. From these works Charles imbibed stoic philosophy and while imprisoned in the White Tower he studied Chaucer's translation of Boethius's *Consolations of Philosophy*, procured for him by his friend William de la Pole, the husband of Chaucer's granddaughter. He also studied the source of Lydgate's *Fall of Princes*, Boccaccio's *De casibus vivorum illustrium*. Worcester also studied this work, taking notes from the original Latin version.[89] John Tiptoft the earl of Worcester owned Lydgate's *Fall of Princes* in a manuscript containing Seneca's *Proverbs*.[90] Worcester also took notes from Seneca's letters on the theme of patience in adversity[91] and compiled extracts from Boethius's *De consolatione philosophiae*.[92] The Roman literature of stoic philosophy and the vernacular adaptations, including Lydgate's *Fall of Princes*, Scrope's *Epistle of Othea* and the *Dicts and Sayings of the Philosophers*,[93] Worcester's *Boke of Noblesse* and *On Friendship and Old Age*, and the different versions of the *Secreta secretorum* all had a medical, alchemical dimension with important political implications. All of these works, written for princes and great aristocrats, argued that the prince must rise above passion, that he must achieve a state of balance and equilibrium that renders him immune to the effects of the fluctuations of fortune and offers the best hope for a stable body politic.

There was therefore among the medical and political writers of the 1450s a new sharpening of focus on the psychology of the prince and his counsellors, stimulated by the study of the literature of antiquity. One of the problems facing those arguing for a revitalization of the state through a reinvigoration of its rulers and a revival of England's imperial destiny was that among those who had had the most military experience in France there was a growing sense of inertia, deriving from a nostalgia for the past, for the glory days of Henry V and the Duke of Bedford; this was nowhere more apparent than among Fastolf's circle and his servants. Worcester's *Boke of Noblesse* was full of echoes of Fastolf's reminiscences to the young charges at his households in Rouen, Southwark and Caister. One note recording his account of the defence of Harfleur reads: 'and as for maste and ward yn the wynter nightys I herd the seyd John Fastolffe sey that every man kepyng the scout wache had a masty hound at a lyes, to berke and warne yff any adverse partye were commyng to the dykes and to aproche the towne for to scale yt'.[94] In Fastolf's hall at Caister in the winter of 1444 there were wall-hangings depicting Henry V's epic siege of Calais. By this time such campaigns had attained the status of classical myth. The duke of Suffolk owned a copy of Lydgate's encyclopaedia of mythology, *The Siege of Thebes*, and Sir John Paston loaned Thomas Boyd, the earl of Arran and son of the governor of Scotland, a copy of *The Siege of Thebes* owned by his sister Anne Paston.

Approaching a querulous old age, regaling his followers with stories from his youth, Fastolf may have been searching among the young and among his memories for the elusive elixir of life. This was a search that involved Worcester, his physician, in investigations into alchemy. Worcester may have even seen himself as something of an alchemist. The planetary sign of Saturn, signifying melancholia and the house of scholarship and science, was regarded as the ruling sign of alchemists. Worcester, who admitted to suffering from melancholia, 'all me adversyte, trouble yn my spyryttes, thought, and hevynesse that I susteyn, ye know well',[95] frequently signed himself with the sign of Saturn.[96] Fastolf owned Aldobrandino of Siena's regimen of health, a compilation of Salernitian medicine of the thirteenth century which provided advice on maintaining health by paying attention to the 'nonnaturals': sleep and wakefulness, evacuation and retention, food and drink, motion and rest, the condition of the air and the state of the emotions which would prolong man's life to its natural extent.[97] The key to regulating the state of the emotions was to maintain the balance of the humours, to prevent any one humour (in Fastolf's case choler which caused anger and irritability) predominating, and this is dealt with in the third book.[98] In fact many of Fastolf's books had a medical slant. His 'tract of vices and virtues' was probably his illuminated manuscript of Christine de Pisan's *Epitre d'Othea*. In this manuscript there is an illustration of Prudence, the cardinal virtue that was the key to the health of the individual's physical body and the political and social body alike.[99] Worcester's writings for his master all attempt to show that Prudence was the key to maintaining the humoral balance appropriate for a man of Fastolf's age. Worcester and Stephen Scrope acted as Fastolf's physicians. In Worcester's medical notebook there are many recipes, some for acquaintances 'much vexed with infirmity',[100] others from Stephen Scrope, and yet others from the notebooks of John Somerset, Henry VI's physician. In one place in the manuscript Worcester provided notes on a fever suffered by Fastolf.[101] In Worcester's notebooks there are quotations from alchemical works dealing with the theme of humoral balance, such as Bacon's *Opus maius* and *De senectute*, which dealt with the problems of old age and argued that the ageing process could be postponed through diet and controlling the emotions to restore the balance of the humours.[102] Worcester also copied extracts from Gilbert Kymer's *Regimen sanitatis*, originally written for Humphrey duke of Gloucester but adapted by Worcester for Fastolf. Worcester promises Fastolf contentment and equilibrium in old age if he can maintain good proportion through the achievement of humoral balance with a good diet and exercising control of the emotions; this will purify the humours and prolong life.[103]

Although Worcester also copied alchemical recipes for the philosopher's stone and *aqua vitae*, the main emphasis in his medical notebooks is on a medicine that deals not with cures and drugs but with the leading of a good life and allowing scope for the curative powers of nature. This is accompanied by quotations from Seneca and Cicero relating to the problems of old age, and it appears that Worcester was trying to teach his master to grow old gracefully. He claimed that he had tried to organize his master's affairs in his last years: 'So doon he shall have the better leysur to the plesour of God and the wele of his soule, that all men may say he deyeth a wyse man and a worchepful.' Instead of trying to recapture the lost vigour of his youth Fastolf was being taught how to reach a state of balance, detachment and harmony appropriate to his advancing years. This would be achieved through a moderate lifestyle and stoic detachment which would encourage a preponderance of phlegm appropriate to old age. According to Kymer's *dietarium* each age had an appropriate humour: in youth it was choler (for the young are full of energy and aggression) and in old age phlegm (for old men are sleepy, rheumy and prone to illnesses such as pneumonia, caused by a predominance of phlegm). Fastolf, like Henry V, would in his youth have exhibited the classic qualities of a choleric temperament. But Worcester realized the danger of allowing the choleric humour to predominate inappropriately in old age; it could lead to an imbalance of bile or melancholy – something Worcester himself was personally acquainted with. In Fastolf's case this melancholia could be manifested as compulsive avarice, and Worcester's compilations of extracts from Seneca's *De beneficiis*, Aristotle's *Ethics*, and passages on the themes of friendship, virtue and old age from the writings of Cicero, Seneca and Terence,[104] are full of quotations from Roman writers on this vice. From Seneca he noted: 'wish nothing more to a miser that he should live long', and from Epicurus: 'the miser lacks what he has as well as what he has not'. Worcester, in his translation of Cicero's *De senectute*, which he dedicated to Fastolf, and Stephen Scrope, in his translation of the *Dicts and Sayings of the Philosophers*, a collection of sayings from antiquity relating to philosophical detachment, were both writing to help Fastolf realize that old age was a time for phlegmatic introspection. Scrope described life as the end product of sensuality and lust, and peace as the product of a soul subject to discipline, a self-mastery that resulted from self-esteem, happiness and detachment, that could not be negated by misfortune.[105] Both Scrope and Worcester were interested in sickness of the mind and the question of psychological health and happiness. One of the sayings of Diogenes, translated by Scrope, defined heaviness as a prison for the soul as sickness was for the body. Worcester, in a copy of the *Dicts and Sayings* acquired by him after Fastolf's death, added a note to a saying of Plato about heaviness and sorrow, defining heaviness as a passion for things past and sorrow for things to come.[106] The perspective of these two servants of Fastolf was sceptical and secular, in contrast to the traditional Christian moralistic approach of fourteenth-century writers. In the most popular didactic work of the fourteenth century, *The Prick of Conscience*, old age was regarded as of little account. The emphasis was placed on dying well to secure salvation. *The Prick of Conscience* and other meditations on death remained popular in the fifteenth century, but in these elite Yorkist circles there was a new rational scepticism and an interest in alchemy, medicine and the workings of the mind (what we would term psychology). Worcester's translation of Cicero's tract on old age raises the possibility that age teaches us that death is of no account: either it destroys the soul, in which case it is negligible, or it raises us to eternal life, in which case it is desirable. Death is seen as part of nature, a fire going out of its own accord. Old age is reached if men are prudent, live according to nature, and reach their allotted lifespan. It is a time of tranquillity, a recollection of life and its blessings. A quiet acceptance of the wisdom of nature is advised to make old age as happy and productive as possible. In *Cato's Distichs*, a third-century collection of Latin proverbs and moral observations edited and translated by Benedict Burgh for William Bourchier in the 1440s, there is an emphatic denial of using the certainty of death for any moral, educational purpose:

> drede not deth with ouer besy cure,
> O lyue on erthe is but a jape,
> Yf tho shalt always after deth so gape.[107]

This is a long way from the religious sensibility of devotional writers who taught such a mistrust of nature. The rational study of the humoral balance and psychology of princes became, as we shall see, crucial to an understanding of the tormented politics of the fifteenth century.

Worcester in his writings for Fastolf shows that he was in touch with the practitioners of Baconian medicine at the court in the 1450s. The most crucial question they confronted was the health of the king himself. The Mirrors of Advice, including the different versions of the *Secreta secretorum*, which was presented to both Henry V and Henry VI, and the version adapted by Bacon, all conceived the body politic in organic terms. The king and his realm were one person. The king was the head of the body, which was obliged to rule in harmony with other members. The forces directing the king's head were therefore of crucial importance to theories of government, and this included his mental health and personality. A rational, ordered state therefore depended on the king's thorough grounding in the principles of Roman reason. As the *Secreta secretorum* put it: 'many pepill shall ye well governe, whyle that reyson governeth yow'. This depended on the king's maintaining within himself an equitable balance of humours through a cultivation of the four cardinal virtues of Prudence, Justice, Temperance and Fortitude, with especial emphasis on Prudence. But above all this the health of the realm depended on the will, the personality of the king. This could be managed by good counsel, which mediated the variety of subjects' wills; but strong government and a healthy realm depended on the strength of a personality such as Henry V. Falstaff understood this when he said in 1435: 'The king hath no souerayn in erthe that may be his juge, unless it be his owne pleasure and will.'[108] It was for this reason that alchemy, based as it was on the stoic writings of the ancients, became of key significance in the mid-1450s. When the counsellors of the realm were faced with uncertain leadership, with a king who seemed to lack the necessary will and personality, they needed the assistance of a science that could help them to explore and discover the personality of the king, to diagnose and redress his humoral imbalance and to direct him towards a lifestyle in which he would find the appropriate humoral balance for his age. This would enable him to function, to lead, and put him in touch with the myths and energies that would activate his will, which in turn would restore the nation's sense of well-being. This had wider ramifications. Sir John Fortescue, the chief justice of England, wrote in *On the Law of Nature* of the need for a harmony throughout the social and natural worlds, heat with cold, dryness with moistness. Everything in this world was believed to be held in a fine balance: 'which the chain of this order binds in most harmonious concord'. Fortescue conceived Hell as a state of chaos, of imbalance in the natural world (the elements) and the mind (the humours): 'Hell alone, inhabited by none but sinners, asserts its claim to escape the embraces of this order.'[109] It was in 1456 therefore that a royal commission was issued licensing the court alchemists to find a cure for the sickness of King Henry VI among the writings of the ancients. The activities of Worcester in copying extracts from the stoic writers of antiquity and from the alchemical writings of Bacon and Villanova offer valuable insights into the workings of this commission. Worcester was advising Fastolf and members of his generation to accept that they were old and to allow the phlegm appropriate to their years to take its ascendancy. Instead of living in the past they should enjoy their old age, leaving the redemption of the kingdom to a young king who would have the natural prevalence of blood and choler. Ironically, if the commissioners had consulted Worcester, which they undoubtedly did, they would have had to discuss the problem of Henry VI's lack of choler. Despite being a relatively young man, Henry was diagnosed as suffering from premature senility, an excess of phlegm. Medical and alchemical issues were therefore brought to the forefront of political life and it was beginning to be widely believed that the king and his realm were both sick and in need of redemption.

NOTES

1. *The Middle English Translation of Christine de Pisan's Livre dei Corps de Policie*, ed. from CUL MS K4 1.5 by D. Bornstein (Heidelberg, 1977), p. 99.
2. M. Keen, *Chivalry* (New Haven, 1984), p. 111.
3. A. Sutton and L. Visser-Fuchs, 'Richard III's Books: IV Vegetius's *De Re Militari*', *The Ricardian*, 7 (1987), 541–2; *The Earliest English Translation of Vegetius's De Re Militari*, Middle English Texts, 21 (Heidelberg, 1988).
4. Craig Taylor, 'Handling Defeat During the Hundred Years War: Intellectual and Professional Responses', 36th International Congress of Medieval Studies, Kalamazoo.
5. H.N. MacCracken, 'Vegetius in English', in Anniversary Papers by Colleagues and Pupils of George Ryman Kitredge, ed. E.S. Sheldon and F.N. Robinson (Boston, 1913), p. 389.
6. *Hoccleve's Works, The Regement of Princes*, ed. F.J. Furnivall (EETS, Extra Ser. lxxii, 1897).
7. Bodley MS 649, fos 132r–133r; R.M. Haines, '"Our Master Mariner, Our Sovereign Lord": a Contemporary Preacher's View of Henry V', *Medieval Studies*, xxxviii (1976), 85–96.
8. M.R. James, *The Abbey of St Edmund at Bury*, Cambridge Antiquarian Society (Cambridge, 1894).
9. For the medieval version of the story of Troy see Benoit de Saint Maure, *Troy Story*; N. Griffin 'Un-Homeric elements in the Medieval Story of Troy', *Journal of English and Germanic Philology*, 7 (1903).
10. Lydgate's *Troy Book 1412–20*, ed. K. Bergen (EETS, 1906).
11. Ibid, bk I, l. 104.
12. Ibid, l. 105.
13. Ibid, bk ii, ll. 112–15.
14. Ibid, bk i, l. 36.
15. Ibid, bk ii, ll. 7140–1.
16. Ibid, ll. 166–8.
17. Ibid, ll. 8593–6.
18. Ibid, ll. 145–8.
19. For further reading see *The Roman World, the Oxford History of the Classical World*, ed. J. Boardman, J. Griffin and O. Murray (Oxford, 1988).
20. Lydgate, *Fall of Princes*, ed. H. Bergen, EETS, Extra Ser. cxxi–cxxiv London, 1924 in 4 vols bk ii, ll. 2437–50.
21. Ibid, ll. 2454–5.
22. Ibid, ll. 4473–86.
23. Presumably Maraccus Portius Cato the Roman statesman, republican and opponent of Julius Caesar.
24. Roman emperor and builder of the second century AD.
25. Lydgate, *Fall of Princes*, bk ii, ll. 4488–92.
26. Ibid, ll. 4509–12.
27. Trinity College Cambridge, MS R.14.45 fo. 61. Ibid, bk i, ll. 3023–6.

28. Ibid, ll. 5959–64.
29. Ibid, ll. 5977–85.
30. Ibid, bk ii, ll. 4516–23.
31. Ibid, ll. 4523–7.
32. Ibid, bk i, ll. 6125–6.
33. Ibid, ll. 3432–7.
34. Ibid, bk ii, ll. 54–6.
35. Ibid, ll. 113–16.
36. M. James, 'English Politics and the Concept of Honour, 1485–1642', *Past and Present* Supplement 3 (1978).
37. St Augustine, *Concerning the City of God against the Pagans* (Harmondsworth, 1972), pt 4.
38. J. Hughes, *Pastors and Visionaries: Religion and Secular Life in Late Medieval Yorkshire* (Woodbridge, 1988).
39. *Hoccleve's Works*, ed. Furnivall, I, pp. 14–15, 130; A. Sutton and L Visser-Fuchs, *Richard III's Books* (Stroud, 1997), p. 7.
40. Bodley MS 649.
41. Vickers, *Humphrey duke of Gloucester*.
42. Ibid, p. 404.
43. Lydgate, *Fall of Princes*, bk i, ll. 366–71.
44. Ibid, bk ii, ll. 146–51.
45. *Inventaire de la Bibliotheque du Roi Charles VI*, ed. L. Douet d'Areq.
46. Magdalen College, Fastolf Paper 43, fo. 10.
47. MacCracken, 'Vegetius in English', pp. 389ff.
48. R. Brill, 'The English Preparations before the Treaty of Arras: a new interpretation of Sir John Fastolf's report, September 1435', *Studies in Medieval and Renaissance History*, vii (1970), 211–47.
49. *Letters and Papers Illustrative of the Wars of the English in France during the Reign of Henry VI*, ed. J. Stevenson, 2 vols (RS, London, 1864), Pt ii, pp. 575–98.
50. Ibid, p. 585, items 21, 27 and 77.
51. Stephen Scrope, *The Epistle of Othea*, ed. C.F. Buhler (EETS, 274, London, 1970); J. Hughes, 'Stephen Scrope and the Circle of Sir John Fastolf: Moral and Intellectual Outlooks', in *Medieval Knighthood IV*, ed. C. Harper-Bill and R. Harvey (Woodbrige, 1992), pp. 109–45.
52. Taylor, 'Handling Defeat During the Hundred Years War'.
53. Buhler, 'Sir John Fastolf's Manuscripts of the *Epitre d'Othea* and Stephen Scrope's translation of the text', *Scriptorium*, iii (1949); P.C.G. Campbell, *L'Epitre d'Othea; Etude sur les sources de Christine de Pisan* (Paris, 1924); Diane Bornstein, *Mirrors of Courtesy*, ch. 3.
54. *Epistle of Othea*, XCI, 110.
55. N.P. Tanner, *The Church in Late Medieval Norwich, 1370–1532* (Toronto, 1984), p. 80.
56. R.A. Griffiths, 'Richard duke of York and the Royal Household in Wales, 1449–50', *Welsh History Review*, 8 (1976), 56–69.
57. A. Goodman and D. Morgan, 'The Yorkist Claim to the Throne of Castile', *Journal of Medieval History*, ii (1985), 61–9; Sheila Delaney, 'Bokenham's Claudian as Yorkist Propaganda', *Journal of Medieval Studies*, vol. 22, no. 1 (1996), 83–96; S. Delany, *Impolitic Bodies: Poetry, Saints and Society in Fifteenth-Century England* (Oxford, 1998), 127–43. The legendary exists in a unique manuscript, BL MS Arundel 327.
58. For text see E. Flugel, 'Eine mittelenglische Claudian-Ubersetzung (1445)—', *Anglia*, XXVIII (1905), 255–99, 421–38; BL MS Add. 11814.
59. BL MS Add. 11814, fo. 17.
60. BL MS Add. 11814, fo. 4.
61. J. Watts, '*De consulatu stiliconis*, texts and politics in the reign of Henry VI', *Journal of Medieval History*, 16 (1990), 251–66.
62. *The Politics of Fifteenth-Century England: John Vale's Book*, ed. M. Kekewich, C. Richmond, A.F. Sutton, L. Visser-Fuchs and J.L Watts (Stroud, 1995), pp. 117–21; BL MS 48031A. This work can be dated in the 1440s on the basis of internal evidence, its pessimistic tone. Hammond, *English Verse*, pp. 94, 176–7.
63. See letter of John Davy to John Paston I in 1466, *The Paston Letters*, ed. Davis, vol. ii, p. 201.
64. William Worcester, *The Boke of Noblesse*, ed. J.G. Nichols (Roxburghe Club, London, 1860).
65. Ibid, pp. 76–7.
66. Ibid, p. 52.
67. BL MS Royal 13 C 1, fos 1335–41.
68. Ibid, fo. 143.
69. Worcester, *Boke of Noblesse*, p. 51.
70. *The Paston Letters*, ed. J. Gairdner (Gloucester, 1904), pp. 11, 196.
71. Worcester, *Itinerarium*, p. 250.

72. Worcester, *Boke of Noblesse*, pp. 69–70.
73. Bodley MS 647, fo. 129b.
74. Ms Magdalen College, Oxon, *Norfolk and Suffolk*, 75; K.B. McFarlane, 'William Worcester: a Preliminary Survey', in McFarlane, *England in the Fifteenth Century* (London, 1981), p. 212.
75. *The Governance of Princes* (*Secreta secretorum*), transl. James Yonge, 1422 (EETS, Extra Ser. 74), ed. R. Steele; for another version by Lydgate and Benedict Burgh see Steele (EETS, Extra Ser. 66).
76. Ibid, p. 146.
77. Ibid, p. 144.
78. Ibid, p. 127. See *The English Conquest of Ireland* (*an English translation of the Expugnatio hibernica of Giraldus Cambrensis made by an Anglo Hibernian in the early 15th century*), in Bodley Ms Lib. Rawl B 490, ed. J. Furnivall (EETS, Ord. Ser. cvii, 1896).
79. A. Cosgrave, *Late Medieval Ireland, 1370–1541*).
80. *The Paston Letters*, ed. Davis, vol. ii, p. 212.
81. Ibid, p. 185.
82. *Peter Idley's Instructions to His Son*, ed. Charlotte Evelyn (London, 1935).
83. *Cicero on Old Age and Friendship.*
84. *The Paston Letters*, ed. Davis, vol. ii, p. 333.
85. Stephen Scrope, *The Dicts and Sayings of the Philosophers*, ed. C.F. Buhler (EETS, Ord. ser. ccxi, 1941), p. 172.
86. *The Paston Letters*, ed. Davis, vol. ii, p. 203.
87. Worcester, *Itinerarium*, p. 122.
88. *G. Ashby's Poems*, ed. M. Bateson (EETS, Extra ser. lxxvi, 1899).
89. Magdalen College, Oxford, MS 11198.
90. BL MS Harl. 103.
91. BL MS Royal 13 C1.
92. BL MS Julius VII.
93. Scrope, *Dicts and Sayings.*
94. BL MS Royal B xxii, fo. 32v.
95. Letter to John Berney, 1460, *The Paston Letters*, ed. Davis, vol. ii, p. 539.
96. J. Hughes, 'Stephen Scrope and the Circle of Sir John Fastolf: Intellectual and Moral Outlooks', in *Medieval Knighthood IV*, Papers from the 5th Strawberry Hill Conference, 1991, ed. C. Harper Bill and R. Harvey (Woodbridge, 1993), pp. 103–7; L.S. Dixon, *Alchemical Images in Bosch's Garden of Delights* (Ann Arbor, Michigan), p. 53.
97. Faye Getz, *Medicine in the English Middle Ages* (Princeton, 1998), p. 53.
98. Bodley MS 179. For Inventory see Hist Comm. 8th Report, pt 1, p. 268, and Bennet, *The Pastons and their England*, p. 111.
99. Bodley MS Laud Misc. 570, fo. 9v.
100. BL MS Sloane 4, fo. 56.
101. Ibid, fo. 38v.
102. Ibid; BL MS Cotton Julius F VII; Getz, *Medicine in the English Middle Ages*, pp. 95–7.
103. BL MS Sloane 4, fos 63–78.
104. BL MS Cotton Julius F VII, fos 74–91.
105. Scrope, *Dicts and Sayings*, p. 146.
106. Emmanuel College, Cambridge, MS 1.2 10, fo. 11b.
107. *Magnus Cato*, p. 12.
108. *Letters and Papers, Illustrative of the Wars of the English in France during the Reign of Henry VI*, 2 vols in 3, Rolls Series (London, 1861–4), vol. ii, p. 578.
109. Sir John Fortescue, *Works*, ed. T. Fortescue, lord Clermont (London, 1869), vol. i, p. 322.

CHAPTER 3

The Legacy of Henry VI: The Fisher King

The full moon hath endeavoured the sun to put away the burning of his light.
The Vision of George Ripley[1]

It must be rectified by often distilling, that all this wateriness phlegm which letteth the power and strength of his firmness may be utterly taken from it.
George Ripley, *The Marrow of Alchemy*[2]

In the fifteenth century attention was focused in an unprecedented way on the falling prestige of English kings and the sick state of the institution of monarchy itself. The century had begun with the deposition and subsequent murder of Richard II, a king whose claim to the throne was unimpeachable, and it had all been done with the collusion of a significant section of the baronage. According to Thomas Gascoigne, a leading clerical intellectual writing in the 1450s, the founder of the usurping Lancastrian dynasty, John of Gaunt, when he was on his death-bed, exposed his rotting genitals to his nephew Richard II, to show him the divine retribution for his sexual adventures. Gaunt's son Henry IV was dogged by ill-health, and when he died in 1413 (after surviving numerous plots) rumours were circulating that he had been hideously deformed by leprosy; this was attributed by Gascoigne to divine retribution for the murder of Archbishop Richard Scrope. Henry V, however, was never tainted with accusations of usurpation or with the sickness associated with his father and his son. He was universally praised in Yorkist chronicles. His only misfortune was to have been born in the wrong dynasty, like the virtuous pagans whom he, and the Yorkist courtiers, emulated. His glorious but tragically short reign served only to sharpen the focus on the image of a cursed, diseased and disintegrating kingship, once the intellectual and emotional shortcomings of his son and heir, Henry VI, had become apparent.[3]

Henry of Windsor was mentally unstable, withdrawn and silent, often to the point that he was oblivious of his surroundings, with no apparent energy. Frequently depressed, he was incompetent in dealing with the daily demands of life, never mind kingship. In twentieth-century terms he could be said to have been suffering from either schizophrenia or a manic depressive illness. To contemporary physicians he presented a disturbing example of an imbalance of the phlegmatic humour. Born on 6 December 1421, and thus vulnerable to the influence of the moon, Henry was destined to have a feminine, watery, changeable character, the opposite of the fiery Martian temperament of his father. In John Trevisa's translation of Bartholomeus Anglicus's popular encyclopaedia *De proprietatibus rerum*, made in 1398–9, the truly phlegmatic man is described as listless, heavy and slow, dull of wit and thought, forgetful, soft of body, white of face, fearful of heart, great and slow of pulse, and of little appetite.[4] As he entered adulthood with his pallid, childlike face, Henry grew more phlegmatic, lacking passion, hating violence, withdrawn and forgetful. Most disturbing, his extreme phlegmatic withdrawal threatened to tip him into a state of idiocy, the simplicity of the moon child. In this same encyclopaedia the cause of stupor is ascribed to a superfluity of the phlegmatic humour, a sleepy slumberness, a lethargy and forgetfulness which occurs when 'the fleume is rauished up to the brayne'.[5] The chroniclers John Whethamstede and John Hardynge both commented on this simplicity, and treason trials in 1442, 1444 and 1447 hinged on disparaging references to the king's simplicity and infantile appearance. In 1441 Eleanor Cobham, the wife of the king's uncle, Humphrey duke of Gloucester, was suspected, through casting medical horoscopes with her medical adviser, Thomas Southwell (a canon of St Stephens who died in prison), of forecasting the young king's illness and death, of trying to harness an unfavourable conjunction of watery planets to push the king over the brink. The king's physician, John Somerset, attempted to dispatch an alternative, more optimistic horoscope with the help of another physician, Roger Marshall. Margaret of Anjou retained a foreign surgeon in 1447 to keep an eye on Henry VI's treatment.[6] The popular perception that the problems of the kingdom related to the king's medical condition was demonstrated when the commons petitioned for the removal of the physician, John Somerset, because of the subversive influence he exerted over the king. Somerset was also an exchequer official and widely suspected of using his position to feather his own nest. He was also perceived as being a creature of William de la Pole. Henry's phlegmatic stupor finally occurred at the beginning of August 1453 at the king's Wiltshire hunting lodge at Clarendon. He lapsed into a catatonic withdrawal (or in fifteenth-century terms into an extreme manifestation of phlegmatic feebleness and indifference) in which he had no memory and no control over his limbs; he required constant supervision. In an effort to redress this imbalance of phlegm in the king the administration of 'laxatives, medicines – clysters, suppositories, medicines for clearing the head, gargles, baths, complete or partial, poultices, fomentations, embrocations, shaving of the head, ointments, plasters, waxes, cupping, with or without cutting the skin, and inducements to bleeding' was prescribed.[7]

The first indication of his returning senses did not occur until 22 August 1454 and he probably did not recover his wits until the New Year of 1455. His eventual assertion of active control of government by March 1455 was soon followed by the successful Yorkist rebellion in the streets of St Albans on 22 May 1455 in which Henry VI was wounded in the neck by an arrow. Further mental collapse followed and the distinguished physician and alchemist Gilbert Kymer was urgently summoned to Windsor in June 1455 to tend a king 'occupied and laboured with sikeness', and three surgeons attended him in July. By October fears for his health were being expressed and confirmation that Henry's phlegmatic illness had returned following the Battle of St Albans was provided by the approver who included in his November report 'he (the king) slepeth to myche therto he was hurte at Seynt Albones'.[8] From this point on Henry became an incarnation of the maimed Fisher King of the Grail legends (a sick and wounded king whose lethargy afflicts his kingdom until it becomes a wasteland). Official confirmation of his chronic illness and inability to govern followed on 22 November 1455 when the governance of the realm was formally committed to the council, whose delegated powers remained in force for the rest of the king's reign. There followed no notice of any subsequent return of his health. By the time of the second battle of St Albans on 18 February 1461, when Queen Margaret herself led the Lancastrians to victory over the earl of Warwick's army, Henry, according to the Milanese ambassadors, was so mentally incompetent that during the battle he was placed under a tree a mile away, where he laughed and sang.

By 1456 the king's condition was publicly acknowledged to the extent that there was a concerted attempt to cure him through alchemy. The central place occupied by alchemy in affairs of state contrasts markedly with the situation at the beginning of the reign of Henry IV when a statute of 1403 outlawed the practice. Henry VI's interest in alchemy was in the first instance at least fiscal. After 1436, to finance his campaign against Charles VII, he issued four decrees addressed to the nobility, clergy, university fellows and physicians asking them to contribute their talent to the replenishment of the treasury. Special overtures were made to priests for whom, as he said, it should be easy to change base metal into precious since they daily changed bread and wine into the body and blood of Christ. One doctor of theology, Richard Trevys, obtained a licence to practise transubstantiation but in 1444, 1446 and 1452 eight laymen responded to these requests and obtained licences to transmute metals. The king, in granting a licence to John Cobbe in 1444, even expressed a wish to know the conclusion to the work.[9] The rise in importance of this science was due to the work of a group of royal physicians who made available in court circles the alchemical works of Roger Bacon and the fourteenth-century Catalan writings attributed to Raymund Lull, and applied the theories contained in them to the regulation of the life of the king and his realm. A crucial figure in the popularizing of Bacon's philosophy was John Cokkys (d. 1475). Cokkys was admitted as Bachelor of Medicine on 30 June 1450 and this gave him entry to medical practice and teaching in Oxford (in both of these fields he was prominent) for the rest of his life, and his name appears in another medical manuscript. He transcribed in the mid-fifteenth century Bacon's major medical and alchemical works, *Opus maius, De retardatione senectutis* (a work cited by Bacon but actually by Arnold of Villa Nova) and *De erroribus medicarum*.[10] He transcribed another volume beginning with Bacon's *Opus tertium* in 75 chapters,[11] and also wrote and signed recipes in a manuscript that contains medical recipes addressed to George Neville archbishop of York.[12] Cokkys taught medicine at the university using the standard elementary texts and commentaries of the day as lecture materials. He also practised medicine and between 1467 and 1473 he was a defendant in a case involving the withholding of evidence relating to the death of John Walewyn. His co-defendants were the mayor of Oxford, John Clerk, and the surgeon, John Barbour.[13] Another Oxford fellow with an interest in alchemy and medicine was John Aldeward, fellow of Exeter, who before his death in 1459 donated to the university Pliny's *De natura* and another manuscript containing works on phlebotomy, the quintessence and the philosopher's stone.[14] The interest shown by Cokkys and Gilbert Kymer, another Oxford physician, in Roger Bacon's work on alchemical medicine testifies to the fact that Cokkys and the other alchemists and medical practitioners at court were at the centre of a Baconian medical revolution, placing alchemical science and mythology at the heart of political debate that took place at the onset of the Wars of the Roses. Galenic medicine, scholastic in origins, emphasized the treatment of symptoms by purging excess humours through blood-letting and the administration of emetic drugs. Roger Bacon had advocated a holistic approach to medicine in which the physician acted as a philosopher, teaching the patient to adopt a lifestyle (details of which were provided in his *Opus maius* and his glosses to the *Secreta secretorum*) by which he could achieve a state of balance that would result in equilibrium of the four humours and potency.[15] Bacon paralleled this with the alchemist's quest for the harmony between the humours which would produce the quintessence, the philosopher's stone, described in *De erroribus medicarum* as the ultimate medicine rendering all others unnecessary. For Bacon the source of this medical, alchemical wisdom was the writings of the ancients and in particular the stoicism of the Roman philosophers.

Bacon married the two disciplines of alchemy and classical philosophy (increasingly popular in court circles) in his alchemical glosses to the *Secreta secretorum*, which although

Arabic in origin, drew on antique ideas. He thereby directly applied alchemical teachings on how to live a balanced lifestyle to the mirror for princes.[16] In the *Secreta secretorum* Bacon demonstrated that the balance of the king's humours was intimately connected with the health and well-being of the monarch and of his realm. This was ultimately dictated by the positions of the planets and, citing the *Canon of Medicine* of the Islamic physician Ibn Sina (930–1037), he advised a king, with the help of an exact mathematician, to derive from his precise birthdate a knowledge of his behaviour, his nature, qualities and complexions. Of special relevance to the reign of Henry VI's intimidating father was Bacon's observation that if a king were of a choleric complexion (Henry V's ascendant planet was Mars) he would be naturally inclined to pride and anger and war; his councillors and kingdom would follow in his path and neighbouring kingdoms would also be disturbed. Bacon points out the paradox that all who rule are swayed by their complexions, but if they have good advice from learned physicians skilled in astronomy their evil complexions can be changed for the better and they will be inclined to all good.[17] Of special relevance to the physicians and alchemists treating Henry VI was Bacon's recommendation that sick and insane persons should be exposed to favourable constellations (he warned against the impediments of the moon, especially when in opposition to the sun) and in this way their mental, moral states could be improved. Such a course of action he maintains was especially important for kings, not only for their own good but for the good of their subjects.

The works of Bacon transcribed by Cokkys also supplied medical advice directly applicable to Henry's stupor, which was commonly associated with premature senility. In *De erroribus medicarum* Bacon claimed that the barrier to the study of medicine was ignorance of languages, astrology and alchemy. He defined the duty of the physician in *Opus maius* (a work copied by Cokkys) as regulating the daily regimen, controlling food, drink, exercise and sleep to postpone the ageing process so that the patient could approach the age reached by the prophets. It is claimed in the sixth book of sentences in the *Three Degrees of Sapience* that old age was not natural but a consequence of the corruption of sin passed on from generation to generation until life had shortened to the duration we see in present times. Henry's apparent senility at the age of thirty would therefore be regarded as a sign of his dynasty bearing the burden of the sin of the original illegal usurpation of the throne. In *De retardatione senectutis* the loss of mental qualities associated with old age was described as a dissolution, a slowing of the wits and madness. Bacon was preoccupied with a search for the medicine that could postpone this ageing process, a secret he believed the ancients possessed. He prescribed a number of medicinal remedies to counter the premature ageing caused by phlegm, such as the bone of a stag's heart and rhubarb, which because of its hot properties he had tried on himself for the treatment of excess of phlegm. In the *Compendium Studii Theologiae* Bacon emphasized the restorative qualities of aurum potabile, the medicine derived from alchemical gold, in treating the corruption caused by old age. *De retardatione senectutis* refers to the restorative qualities of theriac, the hot medicine derived from snake-flesh 'that releeveth and repaireth wit enfeebled' and which was a universal application and effectiveness against the disease caused by sin. Known as treacle, it took forty days to make and twelve years to mature, which is why royal alchemists were called to inspect shipments of imports of this universal panacea.[18] It was of particular application to Henry VI because its qualities of heat and dryness made it effective as a means of eliminating phlegmatic or melancholy humours from the body. The image of the spitting serpent accompanying the curative working of choler that occurs on the *Ripley Scrolls* may be an allusion to the effectiveness of theriac in combating Henry VI's phlegmatic imbalance.

At the same time as Cokkys was facilitating a wider awareness of Bacon's alchemical medicine, another parallel philosophical revolution was occurring that served to increase the intellectual respectability of alchemy and to place it at the heart of debates about the king's health. This was achieved through a body of Catalan alchemical treatises erroneously ascribed to Raymund Lull (and henceforth referred to as pseudo-Lullian works). The most influential single work in this tradition in England was the *Testamentum*, which was written in England in the royal hospital of St Katherine, opposite the Tower of London where it faces the Thames, and dedicated to Edward III in 1332.[19] St Katherine's, as a royal institution, was a centre of intellectual life with a good library (John de Hermesthorpe, master of the hospital for forty years from about 1367, spent over £66 on books, chalices and ornaments).[20] It was an appropriate place to conduct secret alchemical experiments. The author upheld the moral objectives of the Baconian tradition, to demonstrate how alchemy could be the means to recover the lost purity and unity that existed before the fall of man. He was presumably in close contact with the king and responsible for his medical care. His *Testamentum* defined alchemical medicine in more directly sexual terms than Bacon's works, and was therefore of relevance to the perceived lack of virility in Henry VI. The quest for the philosopher's stone was depicted in terms of a conjunction between the male *Sol* and female *Luna*, gold and silver. Condemning the physicians and alchemists who founded their art on corrupt medicines such as herbal preparations, the author of the *Testamentum* urged the alchemist to base his art on a knowledge of metals and their ruling planets. Gold and silver were the basis of all cures. After reduction through fire to the blackness of the head of the crow, a resurrection was achieved through pure sulphur and mercury which took the form of any metal put into it. This work was of special relevance to the sickness of Henry VI: the counterbalancing of an excess of phlegm was to be achieved by putting the phlegmatic in *balneo* and nourishing it with *Sol* and *Luna*.

These writings, like Bacon's, reached court circles through the work of another prominent physician and alchemist on the royal commission of 1456, John Kirkeby, chaplain to the king from 1455 to 1457. A manuscript containing several pseudo-Lullian works, including John of Rupescissa's treatise on distillation and the Catalan version of the *Testamentum*, with a Latin translation undertaken by one Lambertus at the Augustinian priory of St Bartholomew (Smithfield) in 1443, was worked on by Kirkeby, who revised the translation and copied it in both languages into a deluxe presentation copy in 1455.[21] Kirkeby went to the trouble to get an illuminator to provide colourful figures to aid understanding of the texts. He also translated other pseudo-Lullian alchemical texts while at St Bartholomew's.[22] Kirkeby was probably practising medicine at the priory: in 1462 he wrote a text on herbal medicine, which included a section on laxatives and clysters for the elimination of excess and corrupt humours. The text concludes: 'I Mr John Kirkeby wrote and copied this book in my own hand.'[23] Kirkeby was also the source for a collation of a miscellany of alchemical treatises variously attributed to Roger Bacon, Arnold of Villanova, Geber, John of Rupescissa and Raymund Lull, with diagrams and texts on magic and medicine, compiled in January 1458.[24] Kirkeby's name also appears in another manuscript as the author of a medical treatise. In this medical collection there is an account of the symptoms of an excess of phlegmatic humour and remedies for the purging of phlegm that may have been written with Henry VI in mind.[25] In 1462 Kirkeby compiled a manuscript of alchemical and medical instructions that included a section on methods of eliminating excess humours. The translation of this Catalan alchemical text is an indication of the growing importance of this pseudo-Lullian branch of alchemy in the treatment of those of high rank. Hospitals, such as the neighbouring St Bartholomew's, were more concerned with the care of the poor and the infirm, and it was in the infirmaries of religious houses that the more theoretical and high-powered branches of medicine were practised by educated clergy on members of the nobility and even kings. St Bartholomew's priory, like

St Katherine's, belonged to this circle of royal practitioners and possessed a library of works of *regimen sanitatis* used by John Mirfield and Kirkeby.

The translation and transcription of the alchemical writings of Bacon and the Catalan treatises of the fourteenth century gave to the practice of alchemy in the mid-fifteenth century a philosophical and academic dignity and made clear its potential in finding a cure for the king's insanity. This lay behind the royal alchemy commissions. On 17 May 1455, a few months before York's second protectorate, a commission made up of prominent London merchants including Thomas Cook and Thomas Davy, the wardens of London Bridge, was instructed to find out the truth behind the rumours of transmutation and report the following July. This report was followed by twelve petitioners applying to the king for permission to practice alchemy. They included Gilbert Kymer, the Baconian alchemist, formerly physician to Humphrey duke of Gloucester; John Kirkeby, principal of St Frideswide's Hall and friend of the duke; John Fauceby, the king's physician; and William Hattecliffe, the queen's physician. The petition refers to the quintessence as a means of prolonging life to its natural term and sustaining the natural virility of body and mind. Two weeks later Kirkeby, Fauceby and Hattecliffe, described as 'learned in natural sciences,' were granted a letter patent to seek out (as Bacon had recommended) the wisdom of ancient texts to find the precious elixir of life that would bring about the transmutation of metals into gold for the well-being of the kingdom. Underlying this statement was the theological belief expounded by Bacon that magic to be effective had to be for common profit rather than private gain. One aspect of their brief, therefore, was to find a means to pay Henry's accumulated debts (they would have been aware of Bacon's observation in the *Secreta secretorum* that when a kingdom continues to finance gifts and expenses more than it may bear, then the king is destroyed). In March and November of 1457 commissions were granted to prominent knights such as Peter Ardene, Brian Roucliffe and Richard Bingham and the friars Thomas Hervei and Robert Glaselay to investigate alchemical means to satisfy the king's creditors.[26] More important, however, was the 1456 commission to Kirkeby and his fellow physicians to cure the king's madness, and in this sense gold became the symbol for the curative properties of the sun which were essential to redress the excess moisture in the king. This search for an ancient alchemical wisdom to cure the insanity of a king had been ironically prefigured in 1396 at the French court when Henry VI's grandfather, King Charles VI, first went insane. According to the chronicle of St Denis Abbey, faith was placed on a book spoken of by the magician Smagorad, holding the secrets of planetary influences, and the harmony of the four elements that had originally illuminated Adam and Abel. The wording of the letter patent makes clear the nature of Henry VI's physical and mental infirmities and alludes to his status as a wounded king. The quintessence or philosopher's stone would, it was claimed, cure the king's infirmities, prolong his life to its natural term, bring him back to health in body and mind, restore him to strength of limb, clearness of memory and keenness of intellect, and heal all curable wounds. Kirkby must have revised the *Testamentum* in 1455, the year of the first alchemy commission and a year before his own appointment as commissioner, with the work of this distinguished body of royal physicians and alchemists in mind, and the elaborate and illustrated Corpus Christi manuscript in particular must have been produced to assist the treatment of Henry VI.[27]

The leading figure behind this project was probably Margaret of Anjou, Henry's assertive queen, for her physician Master William Hattecliffe was appointed to the March 1457 alchemy commission.[28] Around the queen gathered a number of writers who employed alchemical language in the search for a resolution to Henry VI's political difficulties and who saw the interconnection of the health of the king and his realm. Margaret's servant, George Ashby, attempted a defence of the monarchy in his *Dicta philosophorum*. Observing

'How blest is the land that has a wise king', he described the king in alchemical language as the 'water of life' and urged him not to drink too much (a widely recognized cause of an excess of phlegm) and not to sleep too much (a sign of phlegmatic imbalance and one of the symptoms observed in Henry VI).[29] Judge Sir John Fortescue, Margaret's chancellor, was one of those named on the high-powered alchemy commission of November 1457. The influence of Bacon's alchemical writings on Fortescue is suggested by the chief justice's links with the other members of the alchemy commission associated with the transcription of Bacon's works. Thomas Cook the elder, the warden of London Bridge and a member of the November 1457 commission, employed a servant, John Vale, who together with John Multon, a London stationer, produced a manuscript containing Bacon's *Six Books of the Sentences*, *De retardatione senectutis* and an extract from *Compendium Studii Theologiae*, together with Fortescue's *Governance of England*.[30] In his *De natura* Fortescue championed the purity of the Lancastrian line and Henry VI's worth, which would be proved through his suffering, against Yorkist claims to the throne through the female line. He employed an old metaphor of the refiner's fire, used in such homiletic literature as the *Ancren Riwle*, but which may have been given an alchemical slant, to claim that 'the purity of gold, the choicest of metals, though the gold be cleft, cannot be known until it be proved by trial of the fiery furnace'. Fortescue also drew on a long tradition of preachers using humoral/medical analogies to set Henry's monarchy in the context of a political order and a divine alchemical harmony, maintained through the balance of humours, hot with cold, dry with moist, heavy with light. Any interference with this monarchy, such as rebellion, was seen as an infringement against this balance, and hell alone was inhabited by sinners who tried to escape the embraces of this humoral order and who were tortured and punished by their predominant humour. The chief justice maintained the holistic view that this order was guarded by the king whose welfare was intimately bound up with that of the land.

One exclusively alchemical work whose appearance coincided with the first alchemy commission of 1456 was the treatise of Robert Barker. Barker also went by the Latin name of Frumitor and called himself Friar Bungay after his place of origin in Bungay in Suffolk. He probably chose this name in an attempt to identify himself with the fourteenth-century alchemist Thomas Bungay, who was described as an alchemist flourishing *c.* 1315 in a sixteenth-century list of British alchemists. He was not directly involved in any of the alchemy commissions but was subsequently at the centre of Edward IV's court, and he may be identified with the Robert Barker (d. by 1494) who was admitted a fellow of Peterhouse, Cambridge, in May 1456, where there were other Peterhouse fellows with alchemical interests such as John Holbrook, Roger Marshall and King's College Fellow John Chedworth (a member of the alchemy commission of March 1457).[31] Barker's treatise survives in two sixteenth-century copies and begins with a statement by the author that he began his treatise on the second day after the true conjunction of the sun and moon (either a solar or lunar eclipse) in November 1456.[32] Barker too was searching for an elixir that would reconcile conflicting complexions in the human body and the body politic, and 'bring peace between the elements so that they be fixed and steadfast'.[33] He cannot be satisfactorily described as a pseudo-Lullian alchemist. Some of his recipes survive in early sixteenth-century copies, in which he recommends the use of herbs and vegetables, a practice denounced in the *Testamentum*.[34] He also wrote recipes on the fixing of gold and silver.[35] However, like the author of the *Testament*, Barker conceived the philosopher's stone in organic, sexual terms as a living body, the product of a union of male and female that would achieve balance, hardness with softness, heat with cold, dryness with wetness. This reconciliation of opposites, achieved through the medicinal application of gold and silver, had for Barker a psychological component. It represented a miracle of conjunction, a unity between body and soul that was in effect a reintegration of one-sidedness achieved when the stone becomes a living body. Barker also saw the wider holistic dimension of his work in compounding 'the very medicine, through which medicine all thing is fulfilled and cometh to perfect completion'.

Alchemists and physicians at the court therefore used the teachings of Bacon and pseudo-Lull to encourage Henry VI to redress the humoral imbalance in his personality through a variety of ways that included meditation, a carefully moderated diet and daily regimen, and the taking of medicines. John Lydgate, the Benedictine monk of Bury St Edmunds, showed an interest in alchemy and Henry VI's health. He would have had some contact with the young king during his lengthy stay at the abbey of Bury in 1433–4, and just before his death in 1449 or 1450 Lydgate was engaged in translating the *Secreta secretorum* for Henry VI.[36] The physician Gilbert Kymer's acquaintance with Baconian alchemy pre-dated 1424 when he compiled a regimen of health for his patron, Humphrey duke of Gloucester. Kymer promised his patron he would reach the age of Methuselah if he followed his advice about diet, exercise and maintaining a balanced life. According to Thomas Norton, another alchemist prominent at the court of Edward IV, Kymer, influenced by Raymund Lull, was also the author of an alchemical tract in Lullian style on the philosopher's stone.[37] Kymer long occupied a position as chancellor of Oxford and it is possible that he stimulated his fellow chancellor George Neville's interest in alchemy. Humphrey duke of Gloucester shared his physician's interest in alchemy, and was even described as a British alchemist in the sixteenth-century list of British alchemists provided in the *A Lookeing Glasse for Illiterate Alchymists*. Among the possessions of his wife Eleanor Cobham, who was charged with practising the black arts in 1441, was a vial of *aqua vitae*, which implies that Humphrey shared William Worcester's interest in distillation. The alchemical significance of Gloucester's epitaph in St Alban's Abbey (which may have been composed by Lydgate or Kymer) has been recognized by Frank Millard. The strife of the contending four humours (and by implication the struggles of the body politik) have been, for Gloucester, who 'for us all had cure', set at rest in death. The protector, reduced by death to salt, the raw material of alchemy, has 'turned into that thow began/Into the earthe meane I', and is now by God's alchemy 'fforged of thyn hand' into spirit, to become the print of the divine image, crowned in heaven and endowed with 'clearnesse lastyng ay'.[38] Kymer certainly consulted his patron's astrological and medical books. His belief that Bacon's alchemical teaching was the key to the medical treatment of Henry VI was given official sanction in 1456 when he was appointed to the alchemy commission, and between 1448 and 1460 he used his authority and wealth as chancellor of Oxford University and bishop of Salisbury to commission a foreign scribe, Hermanus Zurke de Gretswaldis, to copy a series of elaborate and authoritative medical manuscripts containing the works of Bartholomeus, Anglicanus, John of Gaddesden and Arnold of Villanova (1241?–1311), the French physician and teacher.[39] These manuscripts contain alchemical recipes,[40] and as late as 1459 Zurke was copying for Kymer recipes and treatments for the excess of phlegmatic humours.[41] Baconian medicine was applied by William Worcester and Stephen Scrope to the treatment of Sir John Fastolf, their choleric employer, but it is likely that they applied alchemical experiments to the problem of the king's sickness. Both men were interested in the philosophical writings of the ancients which were supposed to hold the key to humoral balance, and they exchanged medical recipes. Worcester's interest in alchemical medicine seems to have originated in the 1450s and may have been encouraged by the alchemy commission. He spent thirty years travelling around the country, copying recipes and extracts from alchemical and medical works in various libraries (many in 'ancient hands') and meeting physicians. He records having met the remarkable William Johnson, who had been a canon of St Pedroc's church, Cornwall, since 1450. Worcester wrote that Johnson had a great knowledge of medicine and possessed many ancient medical books.[42] Johnson in turn recorded that Botoner (Worcester) had a great knowledge of medicine and found pleasure in it and possessed many medical books.[43] One of Johnson's sources, Friar John Wellys of Bridgwater, was a Cambridge physician who provided Worcester with recipes for the stone.[44] Worcester and Scrope consulted medical recipes lent them by the abbey of Bermondsey, including an 'ancient book of physic'. Around the time of the alchemy commissions Worcester was copying into his medical notebook extracts from Bacon's *Book of Wisdom* on the influence of the planets on humours. He also copied Kymer's *Regimen sanitatis* which, with its advice to the urbane prince on maintaining humoral balance, was applicable both to the problems of Henry VI and to his master Fastolf. Throughout this manuscript there are extracts in Worcester's hand from alchemical tracts of Arnold of Villanova,[45] particularly experiments in the making of the stone. There is also a medicine for a man that has excess of 'fleume'.[46] Worcester also copied extracts from 'an ancient book of Avicenna and Ibn Rushd [Averroes]', the twelfth-century Arab physician, philosopher and astronomer, which he secured from John Inch at St Paul's;[47] from a book of medicine of John Somerset;[48] from Albertus Magnus's *De natura rerum*, which he obtained from the library of Gonville Hall;[49] and from a *Regimen sanitatis* (Kymer's work) which he obtained from a physician called Barber.[50] In addition, Worcester owned a notebook that contained extracts from Bacon's *Book of Wisdom*[51] and an account of sicknesses of men exacerbated by their complexions and caused by constellations in the sky at their nativity.[52] He also owned a collection of the medical writings of Arnold of Villanova.[53] On the flyleaf of another manuscript there is a reference to a copy of Albertus Magnus's *De virtute lapidum preciosorum* made by William Worcester.[54] Given Worcester's expertise in alchemy, classical antiquity and medicine, it is likely that he would have been consulted by members of the alchemy commission.

The work of the alchemy commission was focused on the use of alchemical techniques of distillation of two medicines that, it was believed, held the key to restoring the health of the king and his realm. One, pure gold, the product of distillation of metals, was more elusive. The other, almost pure alcohol, the product of the distillation of wines, was more feasible and had long been practised by Arab physicians. In *c.* 1351 John of Rupescissa had written *De consideratione quintae essentiae* (*On Consideration of the Fifth Essence*), applying the notion of the fifth essence to alcohol, giving various means of distilling the alcohol found in wine and describing how to 'fix the sun in our sky' by treating the alcohol with heated gold to enhance its medical properties.[55] Rupescissa also outlined the procedure for fractional distillation to produce 98 per cent proof alcohol, paving the way for large-scale distillation. Rupescissa recommended this high-proof alcohol (*aqua ardens*) for the treatment of melancholy. William Worcester, a lifelong sufferer of melancholy, included in his medical notebook quotations from Rupescissa and Arnold of Villanova on distillation, a recipe for *aqua vitae*[56] and a reference to a medicine acquired from experiments with the assistance of London apothecaries including Friar John Wellys and Stephen Scrope.[57] Wellys, the physician at Cambridge (1456–80) and a scholar of Henry VI's foundation of Eton in 1454, was the author of medical recipes extant in other manuscripts.[58] In 1458, at the Feast of Corpus Christi, Worcester obtained from John Green, a physician of Bristol (probably the rector of Castle Combe who was an executor of Stephen Scrope and his family), a recipe prescribed by the physician Master Godard for *aqua vitae* (distilled alcohol). The recipe calls for handfuls of bay leaves and the wines of Aquitaine (England's recently lost province), with the statement 'the better the wine the better the water will be'. This *aqua vitae* was to be placed with a powder in a glass limbeck and sealed.[59] The distillation of *aqua vitae* and the quest for pure alcohol (*aqua ardens* or *aqua perfectissima*) were direct concerns of members of the alchemy commission such as John Fauceby and Kirkeby who had been licensed to find the elixir. Nearly pure alcohol would have been seen as a drastic medicine for the king in his state of lethargic depression, and in the short term such treatment would have produced apparently beneficial results.

Linda Voigts has outlined the career and activities of a citizen and vintner of London, Robert Brooke (or Broke).[60] His name occurs in household accounts from 1427 to 1445 and he was important enough to be the recipient of crown grants.[61] He was a king's servant in 1441,[62] and was described with the royal physician Hattecliffe as 'of our privy spicery'. Brook was responsible for producing purifying water for the king, describing himself as 'Master Broke of the kyngs styllatorys and maker of his excellent waters',[63] and was preoccupied with the production of high-proof alcohol. He was the owner of an early fifteenth-century English translation of a practical treatise on distillation, Bernard Gordon of Montpellier's *Lilium medicinae* of 1302, which survives in a unique manuscript.[64] Brook's name occurs with Fauceby and Kirkeby in royal household ordinances of 1454, and there is evidence that he was connected with Fastolf's circle and may therefore have shared his expertise with Worcester. On 7 July 1447 Brook was a witness to a charter of Fastolf's presented to the archbishops of Canterbury and York.[65] Other texts were produced in the 1450s outlining the distillation of wine. One, dated 1454–9, belonged to John Somerset.[66] Another, written in London on 31 May 1461, contains drawings of scales and distillation equipment. The first text, corrected by Roger Marshall, recommends wines as a cure for melancholia, and the ninth text calls for more use of distillation, citing Rupescissa, and praising absolute alcohol as a cure for melancholia.[67] Another manuscript containing references to Kirkeby provides diagrams of distillation equipment and instructions for fractional distillation.[68] The increasing interest in distillation of wines at the court of Henry VI can also perhaps be seen in the earliest version of the *Ripley Scroll*, which features a fountain and the king's bath emerging from bunches of grapes and distillation vessels. On one level the scroll shows the process of distillation of alcohol as well as gold.[69]

All the above measures were concerned with diet, lifestyle and medicine. However, there was another more difficult, obscure and learned side to alchemy concerned with introspection and the reordering of the balance of the mind, will and emotions. The most prolific and influential authority in this branch of alchemy, emerging to prominence in the 1450s, was Sir George Ripley. The alchemical literature that this unprecedented crisis in the English monarchy inspired was primarily influenced by the Baconian tradition. However, Sir George Ripley was more affected by the emblematic, sexual allegories contained in the pseudo-Lullian *Testamentum*, and it is in his writings that we can see most clearly the practical application of the alchemical, medical theories of some of the learned physicians of St Katherine's at the Tower and St Bartholomew's that are contained in the Corpus Christi manuscript.[70] It takes us into an intellectually high-powered theoretical branch of medicine. It is difficult to assess the degree to which some of the alchemists treating Henry VI were able to give practical, medical help to the king. But like the great theoretical physicians of the modern age, Sigmund Freud and Carl Jung, they had a profound cultural impact on their time. St Bartholomew's priory followed the Augustinian rule, and Sir George Ripley was himself an Augustinian canon of Bridlington priory; he entered the service of Edward IV, to whom he dedicated some of his writings, and George Neville, the chancellor and archbishop of York. Most of the manuscripts of Ripley's works survive in sixteenth-century copies of fifteenth-century manuscripts, some owned by the self-styled Welsh wizard and alchemist Dr John Dee. However, there is a surviving corpus of fifteenth-century manuscripts of the *Cantilena* and the *Compound of Alchemy* including a manuscript in a late fifteenth-century hand in which the *Compound of Alchemy* concludes with the date 1471 and an elaborate sigil, like the knot used by Mayre in March 1461 to accompany Rupescissa's treatise on distillation and the quintessence, composed of alchemical symbols and which if it is not by the scribe, may be the signature at Ripley himself. Also surviving from Ripley's lifetime is an emblematic scroll depicting the pursuit of the philosopher's stone, known as *The Ripley Scroll*. Over the next two hundred years Ripley texts proliferated while maintaining a remarkable coherence to the extent that the printed edition of the *Compound of Alchemy* in 1591 coheres closely to the original 1471 manuscript.[71] In 1476, at the age of sixty-three, Ripley revealed in a letter to Neville that he had been studying alchemy from the age of eighteen. Besides being a canon of Bridlington he was a curate of the parish church of Sixforthe (possibly Stickford near Boston).[72] In another letter Ripley refers to himself as the 43-year-old priest of Fax Bulburgh.[73] He was certainly an influential practising alchemist in the 1450s: in his *Compound of Alchemy* he beseeches any man who has met with his experiments from the years 1450–70 to burn them and afford them no credit because he subsequently found them to be false when he finally found the stone in 1470.[74] Ashmole claimed to have seen a similar retraction by Ripley of all his writings from the period 1450–70 in a manuscript in Dr John Dee's library.[75] Ripley also referred to the many men he had seen impoverished in the pursuit of this art. His court connections were such that in 1458/9 he obtained permission from the crown to go abroad to study at a foreign university for seven years.[76] Ripley, in his own words, travelled in Italy – 'Thurgh Roman countrey as I once did passe'[77] – where he learned 'the secrets of the sunne and moone'[78] and 'travelling the coast thereabout, drawing forth (as it were) the marrow of nature'.[79] Only two of Ripley's works are dated, the English poem *The Compound of Alchemy* (in Latin *Liber duodecim portarum* or *The Book of Twelve Gates*) dedicated to Edward IV in 1471 and the Latin prose treatise *The Marrow of Alchemy*, dedicated to George Neville in 1476, but two of his works, the Latin poem *Cantilena* and the emblematic *Ripley Scroll*, may date from this period in the late 1450s; certainly their contents reflect the influence of Catalan works translated by Kirkeby.[80] Exact dating of most of Ripley's works is impossible but the fact that he testifies to a body of alchemical work written between 1450 and 1470 establishes that the characteristic imagery he deploys in his written and visual work would have been formulated with the anxieties over England's kingship in mind. While Bacon and his followers such as Barker recommended that alchemists start their search for gold with the melting down of base metals such as iron filings, faeces and urine, Ripley recommended the reduction of the pure substances gold and silver to base, primitive matter, the primal essence or *nigredo*, represented by the black crow's head (the term used in the *Testamentum*). For Ripley the renewal of gold/sun became the basis of his unique allegories involving *Sol* and *Luna*, mercury and sulphur, which were derived from his reading of the *Testamentum*. These were directly applicable to the search for the political renewal of the kingship. Focusing less on lifestyle and medicines, Ripley envisaged this renewal coming about as the result of a process of introspection on the part of the royal patient meditating on the physical processes of alchemy as a way of understanding his humoral disposition, personality and political potential. At the beginning of a manuscript of alchemical recipes and treatises dating from the 1460s is the motto 'know thyself', and this is the introspective context to Ripley's considerable alchemical output.[81]

A distinctive feature of Ripley's alchemy is his interest in the visual and emblematic side of this art. The nine-foot *Ripley Scrolls*, the earliest dated to *c.* 1450–60,[82] are vivid depictions of the alchemical processes, possibly serving as advertisements in alchemists' shops.[83] There are twenty surviving rolls.[84] They consistently show the distinctive imagery that occurs in Ripley's writings and on his tomb, and have been consistently assigned to him

The tomb of George Ripley. This elaborate tomb with alchemical emblems indicates Ripley's importance at the time of his death. The cross on the top bears a similarity to the arms of George Neville. (British Library Vitellius Ex, *fo. 234v)*

since the sixteenth century.[85] He may have developed this interest in the colourful and highly wrought form of expression during his travels in northern Italy, where images of the Catalan works ascribed to Lull were developed at the turn of the fifteenth century.[86] Other distinctive images on the scrolls such as the black raven (representing the *nigredo*) bearing a horse-shoe (the emblem of the original base matter and associated with the serpent), crossed knives (the cutting instruments that break down matter), and the king holding mirrors containing images of the sun and moon, also occurred on Ripley's tomb. Ripley's tomb, erected at Bridlington Priory in 1490, was decorated with the same cluster of images: the sun and moon, serpents, the *uroboros*, the royal marriage, dragons and birds that occur in the *Ripley Scrolls*. Some of the more individualistic images of the scrolls, such as the black rotten toad, occur in his writings and confirm that he was probably the original author of the scrolls.[87] With this scroll we can see a very different sort of alchemy from the detached, moderate and philosophic contemplation of antiquity espoused by Bacon. Against a background of anxiety about Henry VI's lack of virility and doubts about the legitimacy of his only child, the scrolls celebrate potency and procreation, with their depiction of a copulating couple, a dove shedding semen and fulsome bunches of grapes. A drama unfolds depicting the alchemist, Hermes Trismegistus, holding over a furnace a vessel which represents the human body; the furnace cooks the different elements from which the four humours are derived. Melusine, the serpent woman, slides down the tree of knowledge towards a naked man, on either side of whom are images of the sun and moon. A couple representing the sun and moon are then shown in a bath and underneath them a dragon holds in its mouth a black toad. Below this is the purging fire of choler, on either side of which are two fighting lions in red and green. The eye then travels to the sun in splendour over the bird of Hermes, a great eagle or perhaps falcon with crowned king's head devouring its own feathers, and this leads to an image of the sun and moon in conjunction, three crescent moons around a blazing sun with a union of the four elements of earth, fire, air and water, represented by the four colours gold, red, silver and black. All of this is held in the mouth of a great dragon devouring its own tail, the *uroboros*, perched on a winged globe. It is a war of the elements, dominated by the purging fire of choler that allows the sun to ascend. This is relevant to the attempts to reverse the feminine, phlegmatic condition of Henry VI with fiery humours and also to the rising ascendancy of the sun of York. In this war of opposites there emerges a new king, who in devouring his own feathers, has accepted and integrated all sides of his self; also emerging is a new nation symbolized by images of wholeness like the globe. This celebration of the reconciliation of opposing forces, of masculine energies, fire and sun, of dark, cthonic, primal unconscious forces and of more feminine lunar elements, has disturbing qualities: a pair of sexually rampant lions and a toad

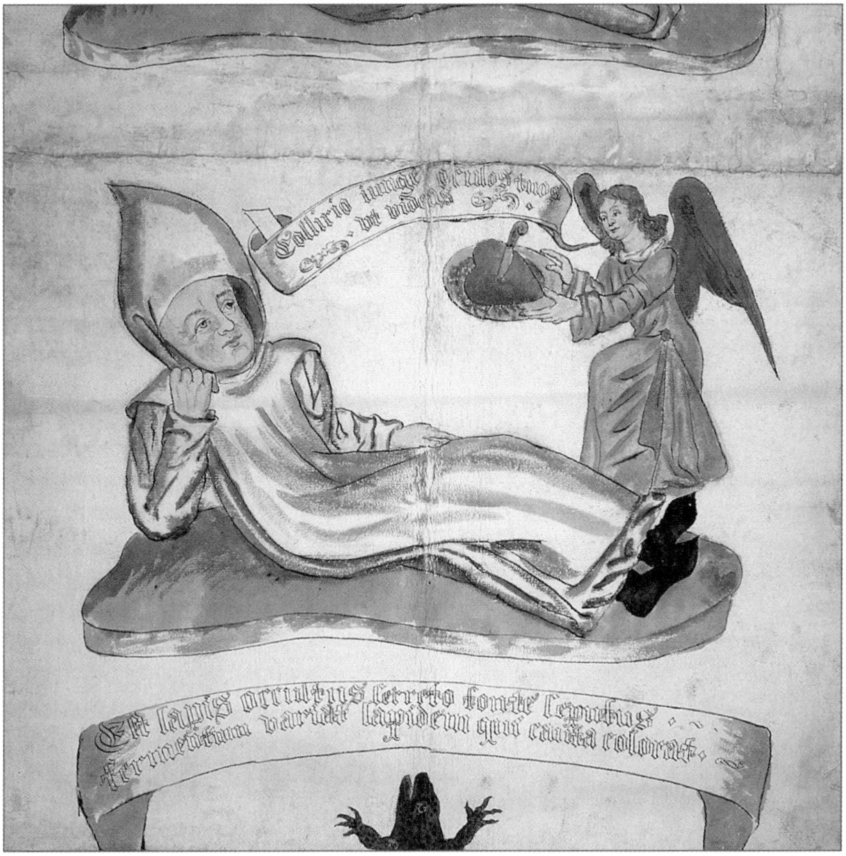

The top of this version of the Ripley Scroll *shows George Ripley in the habit of an Augustinian canon experiencing a vision of an angel bearing a knife and a heart. The knife appears on Ripley's tomb. (Ashmole Roll 53)*

The conclusion to the same copy of the Ripley Scroll *shows the transformation of base matter, represented by the black raven and the horseshoe (which decorates Ripley's tomb), and the reconciliation of opposites, symbolized by the fighting lions. All these symbols had clear political significance between 1450 and 1470. (Bodley Roll 1)*

In the earliest surviving version of the Ripley Scroll, c. *1460, the warring red and green lions preside over the fire of choler, seen as the cure for Henry VI's phlegmatic illness. But the rising sun of York is about to burst through the watery clouds. (Bodley Roll 1)*

The Ripley Scroll *concludes with the appearance of the stone, a globe that may represent the emergence of the nation's soul from the forces of destruction represented by the dragon of chaos. (Bodley Roll 1)*

Above: *Beneath the image of the philosopher's stone is perhaps the earliest known representation of George Ripley holding a staff with the horseshoe that appears on his tomb. Gesturing to the conclusion of the work, the transmutation of base matter represented by the cloven foot, Ripley also brandishes on his pilgrim's staff his original scroll. (Bodley Roll 1)*

In this early sixteenth-century version of the Ripley Scroll, *Ripley faces a king. Above them stands the integrated monarch who will redeem the land. He represents a fusion of opposites, silver and gold, and holds mirrors reflecting the sun and moon, images that occur around Ripley's tomb. (Ashmole Roll 53)* at the foot of a well indicate that all aspects of the self must be acknowledged and integrated.[88] The scroll emphasizes the duality of human nature, man and beast, symbolized by illustrations of Ripley at the base of the scroll holding a staff around which his scroll is furled, at the base of which is a cloven hoof.[89] A contemplation of the scroll could lead to a realignment of the king's phlegmatic, feminine imbalance and may have originally been designed for this purpose. The alchemist, when contemplating the transmutation of metals, could experience visions which were regarded as products of the unconscious; and it is this tradition which has been extensively studied by Jung (the *Ripley Scrolls* are an important source in Jung's *Psychology and Alchemy*). In these scrolls, and in Ripley's writings in general, in contrast to the Baconian tradition, the imbalance in humours is seen in more directly psychological terms with the alchemist acting as a shaman figure, surrendering himself or guiding his patient towards a surrender to the compensatory impulses of the unconscious to redress the imbalance of the humours that could have such a destructive effect on the personality, and if this personality happened to be a king, such a devastating effect on the realm. And so from this scroll there emerge circular mandala images, such as the globe, which represented the totality of the self and the nation. Some later versions of the scroll therefore show Ripley at the foot facing a king who is blessing his nation.[90]

There is a possibility that Worcester's interest in alchemy embraced the pseudo-Lullian tradition. With one exception[91] the earliest *Ripley Scrolls* date from the sixteenth century, but the images are of fifteenth-century provenance. They occur in a number of fifteenth-century medical and alchemical manuscripts,[92] and it seems that Worcester was familiar with such images and therefore the Lullian tradition. In his autograph notebook containing extracts from Bacon and tracts on the virtue of the 'precious stone', there are table headings from Ovid's *Metamorphoses*, which, with its allegories of various forms of transformation, was a valuable source for Ripley's allegorical vision of alchemy as an exploration of the relationship between man and his bestial nature.[93] In the margins, not in Worcester's hand, but with notes by him on the colours of the drawings and folio numbers from the manuscript he was using (perhaps the original), are drawings illustrating various forms of metamorphosis (or transmutation), such as a crowned figure scattering drops of dew or semen on the prostrate figure of a woman holding a sword entwined with a serpent, half man and beast, and a queen holding a sceptre with a peacock at her feet; all these images bear a close resemblance to the emblems on the *Ripley Scrolls*.

An even more direct alchemical reflection on the sickness of Henry VI was provided in Ripley's *Cantilena*, the earliest copies of which survive from the 1470s.[94] There is, in the whole alchemical tradition, no clearer exposition of the illness and healing of a king, and the parallels to Henry VI, whether made in the late 1450s or retrospectively during the reign of Edward IV, are inescapable (Ripley would have been aware of Trevisa's account of phlegmatic madness for he referred to this work in his account of his erroneous experiments). The *Cantilena* focuses on a sick, barren king:

> There was a certaine Barren King by birth,
> Composed of the Purest Noblest Earth,
> By nature Sanguine and Devoute, yet hee
> Sadly bewailed his Authoritie.[95]

Although nurtured under the wings of the sun the king through an original defect has become sterile and senile, awaiting transformation and rebirth. This enfeebled, feminine, phlegmatic king/Sol is senile and must, like the metal immersed in the bath of acid, undergo a death and rebirth. Suckled at his mother's/Luna's breast, hidden under her skirts, he is sexually joined with his mother. During her confinement she eats the flesh of the peacock (George Neville at his enthronement feast as archbishop of York arranged for the consumption of 106 peacocks),[96] drinks the blood of the green lion and sups from the golden bowl of the whore of Babylon.[97] She is delivered of a child who first resembles the moon (perhaps an allusion to Henry VI's phlegmatic birth and condition) and is then changed into the sun. He is suckled by the green lion and resumes his kingly state:

> While from the Bed the Ruddy Son doth spring
> To grasp the joyful sceptre of a king.[98]

The reborn king becomes a victor, a healer and the redeemer of all sins. This is both alchemical and medical drama concerning a sickness that is the result of a conflict of the elements, evoked by ravening beasts and the black waters which represent the primordial chaos of matter and the unconscious. The king/Sol has become weak through one-sidedness: the one-sidedness of consciousness which shuns the darkness, its opposite.[99] The king's one-sidedness is passivity, a phlegmatic femininity. He refuses to acknowledge his shadow, the dark cthonic animal vitality that is essential to his renewal and that of his kingdom, for the land has become unfruitful because like only mates with like and there is no reconciliation of opposites. The disturbing, dream-like sexual visions of the *Cantilena* – incestuous acts, the ravening lions, the feeding off the flesh of the concupiscent peacock and the bowl of the whore of Babylon – all evoke the amoral and animal vitality of the unconscious. The king/Sol, dissolved into the waters of the maternal Luna, undergoes, like the alchemist's metal, a psychic death and resurrection from which he emerges renewed, integrated and balanced.[100]

There is more at stake in the *Cantilena* than the destruction of ego and the rebirth of self. At stake is the destruction and renewal of key cultural dominants of the fifteenth century. Although there are obvious parallels between the alchemical transformation of matter and the transubstantive phenomenon of the Mass, with which Ripley as a monk would have been familiar, the *Cantilena*, in its exhibition of the queen suckling her son and copulating with him, and the feeding of the son from the blood of the wounded lion, displays a series of grotesque distortions or contaminations of the cornerstones of Christian faith: the Virgin birth, the Pieta, the Crucifixion and the Incarnation of the Father in the Son.[101] Carl Jung, the only author to have studied this text, argued that by the seventeenth century these dominants had lost their emotional energy and relevance, ossifying into assertions of religious dogma and authority. They were, according to him, ripe for subversion in such alchemical dramas as Goethe's *Faust*. However, although a number of copies of the *Cantilena* were made in the seventeenth and eighteenth centuries, Jung overlooked the chronological context of this work, which was written in the mid-fifteenth century when religious orthodoxy was under attack from a number of quarters: from devotional writers for whom faith was a personal revelation of mystical experience; from Lollard reformers who placed their faith in the revelation of holy scripture; and from the growing secular, scientific interests of a number of laymen and clergy (a development to which alchemy contributed and which will be discussed later). The visions of the alchemist, especially as depicted in the *Cantilena*, constituted a forthright contribution to these religious developments. They too offered to replace mere acquiescence to dogma and imitation of religious models with a more active participation, applying meditation on alchemical processes to a glimpse into the unconscious self.

This was a more primitive and disturbing experience of self than the associative experiences and memories described by the Yorkshire contemplative writers. Ripley too was a Yorkshireman, and his friend and fellow alchemist George Neville was a member of the family that provided the original patrons of Richard Rolle. This family counted among its members the fourteenth-century visionary John Thweng or St John of Bridlington, and they were patrons of Bridlington priory. Ripley and Neville were therefore in a position to to be well aware of this mystical tradition (Neville even owned a copy of the *Imitation of Christ*, possibly the *Mirror of the Life of Jesus* by the prior of Mount Grace, Nicholas Love). But what Ripley offered in his works was more than an imitation; it was an involuntary realization of the roles represented by Christ and other heroic figures who had undergone a descent into the underworld. Henry VI's religion was characterized as a watery femininity, a one-sided lack of cthonic, masculine sexual energy, and a phlegmatic withdrawal from the roles of active life which had been embraced by his father Henry V, whose religious convictions were always harnessed to the service of the state. Henry VI retreated from the heroic mythic roles important in a king. He presented a disturbing threat to the hopes of his more assertive countrymen because his one-sidedness, his lack of energy, his sexual inertia and his withdrawal from the duties of active life could, despite medical explanations, also be attributed to his excessive religiosity. His devotion to the eremitic life, to daily Mass and to his inner voices and visions received enthusiastic endorsement from one of his chaplains, the Carthusian monk John Blacman, who depicted them as the type of holy manifestation of devotion to the contemplative life espoused by Richard Rolle and his followers. According to the author of the *Great Chronicle*, 'he chose with Mary Magdalene the contemplative life and refused the life of Martha the active which he forsook from his tender age until the last day of his life'.[102] Nevertheless Henry tested the patience of more pragmatic clerical administrators: both John Whethamstede, abbot of St Albans (who was described as an alchemist in the list of alchemists of Great Britain in the sixteenth-century *Lookeing Glasse for Illiterate Alchymists*) and Pope Pius II thought him to be timorous and feminine. Coppini, the bishop of Turin and agent of the duke of Milan, described Henry VI as 'a man more timorous than a woman, utterly devoid of spirit who left everything in his wife's hands'.[103] Ripley, in the *Cantilena*, was suggesting that such one-sidedness, apart from being psychologically harmful, was entirely inappropriate for a king who needed to get in touch with all four complexions within himself, with the warrior (choler), the scholar (bile) and the lover (blood), if he was to bring blessings on his land.

Behind such aspirations for the king lay the towering example of Henry V, that model of piety, martial discipline and masculine energy. To achieve this in the 1450s what was required was the destruction and renewal of another tired dominant of the fifteenth century, the concept of monarchy itself. In the fourteenth and fifteenth centuries English kings had suffered a series of humiliations at the hands of courtiers, the baronage, the common people and fate. This period had witnessed the deposition and murder of Edward II; the senility of Edward III and the illness of the Black Prince; the 1381 Peasants' Revolt; the imposition of a continual council on Richard II in 1386; the deposition of Richard II in 1399; the impositions of councils on Henry IV in 1406; and the degrading illness of Henry IV from 1407 to 1413. The prestige of the monarchy reached its nadir during the mental collapse of Henry VI. In the *Cantilena* the king experiences a series of degrading humiliations, such as his disappearance under his mother's skirts (frequently illustrated in surviving manuscripts). This descent into the darkness of the womb, the earth (like the chemical disintegration of gold and the sun's descent into darkness), is the prelude to a renewal, the rising of the sun. For the old king's descent into the maternal, lunar waters involved, in psychological terms, the surrender of his ego, his conscious self-image (which in the case of Henry VI would be that of the inoffensive Christian, the feminine man of peace), and the recognition of primitive, powerful masculine energies that would bring about the rebirth of a new self. It involved a surrender to collective, heroic warrior archetypes that would allow the birth of a fully rounded hero, a warrior king who would be able to heal the rifts caused by the warring elements in his kingdom and restore her pride and vigour. The alchemist saw political life, history and myth in terms of conflicting personalities

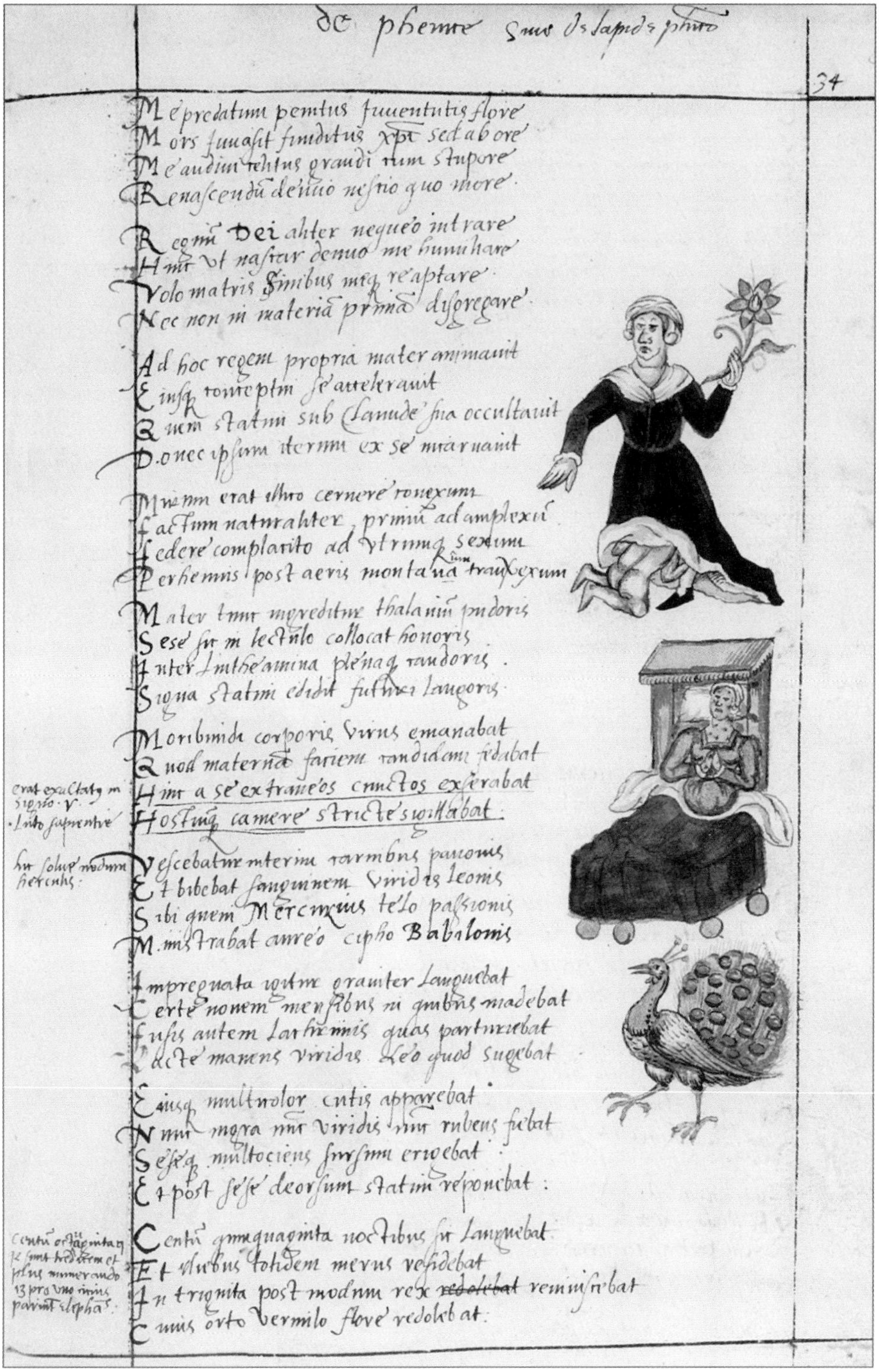

The first of these marginal illustrations to Ripley's Cantilena *shows the incestuous union of the king and his mother, an immersion or death in the maternal depths of the unconscious. The next one showing the queen's confinement refers to the king's gestation and impending rebirth which is heralded by the flourishing of the tincture, the peacock's tail. (BL Add. 11388 fo. 36) Fifteenth-century versions of these images survive in a copy of the* Cantilena, *Trinity College, Cambridge, MS 0.8.24.*

whose antagonisms sprang from the incompatibility of individual humours. A proper balance of choler, phlegm, blood and bile would resolve these conflicts. If the royal patient could learn from the alchemist he would be equipped to perform the multifaceted practical and heroic duties required of a late medieval head of state.The crisis posed by the mental incompetence of Henry VI and the loss of the French empire engendered a crisis in confidence that encouraged the surfacing of a heroic archetype of kingship and an identification of the health of the king with the well-being of the land. The parallels between Ripley's allegories of the sick, senile king and the myth of the Fisher King and his wasted kingdom are striking, and show the alchemist occupying a role in the 1450s as a Merlin-like sage whose intuitive understanding of unconscious forces enabled him to harness these powers in the service of science and myth in such a way that he could emerge as the overseer of the destiny of the nation.

When the problem of the Lancastrian kingship was first officially addressed in alchemical terms in 1456 and alchemists were instructed to search through the writings of the ancients for the secret of redeeming the monarchy, one of the texts they would have consulted was Ovid's *Metamorphoses*, which with its central theme of transmutation was seen as an allegory of the alchemist's art. In the prologue to the French translation of the *Metamorphoses* (owned by Edward IV) and the English translation by Caxton the theme of transmutation is outlined. A delicate balance is said to exist between body and soul and men could, by surrendering to passion, transform themselves into beasts. The alchemical allegory par excellence was Ovid's account of the legend of Jason and the Golden Fleece. According to the myth Chryssomelles, the winged ram sent by Olympian deities, rescues a child from the homicidal plot of his stepmother and carries him to safety on the eastern shores of the Black Sea. There the miraculous ram becomes a sacrifice, its golden fleece hung upon an oak tree in a grove sacred to Aries and guarded by a dragon. Jason sets out from Greece to Colchis to capture the fleece but fearful terms are imposed by its owner, King Aeles. To achieve his quest Jason must yoke the fire-breathing bulls to the plough, till the grove and sow from a brazen helm serpents' teeth which will grow into ghost warriors who will try to kill him; then he must steal past the dragon, the guardian of the fleece. Jason tames the bulls, turns the warriors against themselves and captures the fleece while the dragon is charmed into sleep by the spells of the sorceress Medea, whose magic is so strong she can restore Jason's aged father to youth.

Alchemy in this legend is shown to be a perilous quest. The furnace is represented by dangerous bulls with iron-tipped horns, whose nostrils snort fire and whose chests roar with imprisoned flames like a furnace. The perils of introspection are shown in the warriors, generated by the adept which can turn on and destroy him, and the moral ambiguity of the art is above all things represented by the paradox that the prize, the golden fleece, must be seized from the jaws of the dragon. The alchemical significance of the legend was appreciated by John of Antioch in the seventh century and by the tenth century there was a tradition that the fleece was an alchemical treatise giving instructions on the making of gold and written on sheep skin. By the 1450s the art of Medea that could restore an aged king to youth was seen as the potential solution to England's political problems. William Worcester studied Ovid between 1453 and 1454 in this way and copied out chapter headings and summaries of the *Metamorphoses*, giving instructions for the provision of marginal drawings, some of which have an alchemical theme and are similar to images in the *Ripley Scrolls*. The legend was an allegory of the natural evolution of metals from antimony, the brittle semi-metal perceived as below lead in an infant or childhood state to the fully mature element of gold. It was not difficult to link Henry VI with the infantile metal antimony, which was known as the wolf that devours the king who is buried and reborn by the symbolic ram's horns.

The alchemist was, however, assisted by clergy and military experts who also saw the solution to the political problems of the 1450s in these mythological terms. In 1457 the old soldier, John Hardynge,[104] at the age of seventy-seven, after a lifetime of military service for such warriors as Henry Percy, Hotspur (in whose household he was brought up from the age of twelve), and Henry V (whom he accompanied at Agincourt), presented to Henry VI a chronicle of English history which mirrored the disintegration of King Henry VI's kingdom in the 1450s in the collapse of King Arthur's idealized, mythic kingdom of Britain under the impact of the Saxon invasions.[105] Hardynge depicted Britain in the period between 583 and 689 as a kingdom falling into desolation under a series of weak rulers so that it resembled the wasteland of the Fisher King of the Grail legends:

> Thou understandest full litill theuangilye,
> That every realme within it selfe devide,
> Shall desolate bee (made), as clerkes tell,
> And euery hous an other shall fall and slyde.[106]

These Grail myths were becoming increasingly well known in court circles. According to his inventory John duke of Bedford, the uncle of Henry VI, commissioned thirteen volumes of Arthurian texts including three *Grails*, two *Merlins* and a *de Saint Graal et du Tristan*. This library passed into the hands of Anthony Woodville, lord Scales. Humphrey duke of Gloucester, Bedford's brother, received from this same library the *Queste del Saint Graal* which contained the account of the Fisher King later used by Malory in his *Morte d'Arthur*, and an elaborate manuscript containing this work, later owned by the Woodville family, passed into the hands of Elizabeth, the future bride of Edward IV. Hardynge's chronicle reflects the popularity of these myths. Besides taking Geoffrey of Monmouth as a source, he was the first chronicler to use the account of Galahad's Grail quest from *Queste del Saint Graal*.

Hardynge, who saw himself more as a wise old prophet than a writer seeking patronage, creates out of British myths a holy land called Logres (England), recording its fall as courage and heroism fail with the collapse of Arthur's Round Table, the unity of which was commemorated in the actual table hanging at Winchester where Hardynge located Camelot. The factors that according to Hardynge led to the ruin of Arthur's kingdom, the collapse of law and order and strong government, clearly point in the second version of his chronicle (dedicated to Richard duke of York) towards conditions in the 1450s and the hopes placed on reform under the duke's counsel:

> The cause was of thy disheriteson,
> And of thy realmes desolacion,
> That with lawe aand peaceable consitucion,
> Might haue been saued, with great consolucion.[107]

Hardynge's description of the disintegration of Arthur's world in the face of the rise of baronial unrest, corruption and intimidation, also refers to the circumstances of Cade's rebellion of 1450, and the prominence of such over-mighty subjects as Suffolk and Somerset in the face of Henry VI's incapacity:

> What is a Kyng without lawe and peace
> Within his realme sufficiently conserued;
> The poorest of his realme maye so encrease
> By iniury and force to bee preferred
> Till he his kyng with strength haue ouerterued,
> And sette hym self in royall maieste.[108]

Hardynge makes a direct connection between the two periods when he addresses Richard and warns him that without strong rule the land will be lost as it was under King Vortigern:

> O ye lordes and princes of high astate,
> Kepe well the lawe and peace in gouernaunce,
> Lest your subiectes defoul you and depreciate,
> If peace and laawe been voyed and unytee,
> The floures are lost of all your souerentee.[109]

The most striking connection with Henry VI is made when Hardynge describes in detail the reign of Cadwallader, the king under whom Britain is finally lost to the Saxon invaders. In the second version Hardynge addresses York directly:

> But, O good lorde, take hede of this mischieue
> Howe Cadwallader not kepyng lawe ne peace
> Sufferyng debates and common warrys.

A marginal note to one manuscript of his version of the chronicle emphasizes Cadwallader's falling into 'a great impotence that he moght not govern the land wherefore in fawte of lawe and pees fell baron werre and exile'.[110]

Like Henry VI, Cadwallader is pious, peaceable and God-fearing, a Fisher King who falls 'into a great impotence so that Britons feared no ordinance and took vengeance on each other and each lord made war on the other'. He describes a king who loses touch with heroic martial archetypes so that 'in default of war and peace the common profit was wasted and devoured', and as a consequence of the dissension among the Britons 'God sent vengeance on them that through war, tilth destroyed, and husbandry unoccupied, the people annoyed with hunger'. There was also a great plague and 'a multitude of people lay in heaps like mountains' and many in his kingdom sank into a 'great lethargy' while Cadwallader deserted his wasted kingdom. The medical implications of England's political lethargy for its sick king are implied in the introductory note to the version Hardynge wrote for Henry VI, where he says: 'Who hathe a hurt and will not disclose it to his leche cannot complain of his sorrow'.[111] In the second Yorkist version of the *Chronicle* Hardynge further underlined the parallels between the exiled Cadwallader and Henry VI when he added a chapter heading saying that Henry VI fled into Scotland without cause on Palm Sunday (the day of the Battle of Towton), deserting his kingdom.[112] This theme was taken up in a genealogical chronicle written by Thomas Haselden in 1468, where Edward IV was described as a successor to Cadwallader who was responsible for the loss of Britain and for England becoming a corruption of Britain.[113]

In his analysis of Cadwallader's motives Hardynge blamed religion, the sort of passive withdrawn piety that Ripley and his fellow alchemists condemned and which Cadwallader and Henry VI shared. In all versions of his chronicle, including the first which was presented to Henry VI, Hardynge showed how Cadwallader deserted his kingdom and retreated into religion.[114] Sceptical of Cadwallader's holiness, he did not mention the famous vision of the angel exhorting the last British king to leave Britain and the Britons to their sins, because he wished to stress Cadwallader's implied link with Henry VI, and he suggests that both men deserted their kingdoms and put their hopes in eternity rather than the common weal. Cadwallader went to Rome on a pilgrimage with a section of his court during a jubilee year:

> Through which their land and they were so mischeued,
> That with law kept might wel haue bene acheued.[115]

The defeat of Cadwallader. (British Library Royal 15 E IV, Chronicles of the English, *Jean de Waurin, vol. II, fo. 180)*

During his absence the Saxons took his land and the exiled king died at Rome in 690, buried with an epitaph declaring his conversion 'forsakyng [all] the worlde heuen to haue'.[116] This link between Cadwallader's religion and the collapse of his kingdom was also made in a genealogical roll of the kings of England to Henry VI in which it is said Cadwallader was warned by an angel to go to Rome when he was made a monk and the Saxons invaded his land. In the version he presented to Henry VI Hardynge suggested that after the collapse of the authority of the British king the realm became a wasteland with ineffectual leadership and illness. He wrote of the seven new kingdoms of Britain and the king's falling into a great impotence, with the Britons suffering lethargy and pestilence.[117]

Hardynge was a heroic relic of the glory days of Henry V, and was far too old to have financial motives in mind when writing his chronicle. He was rather a self-appointed prophet with a vision of restoring England to the glory it held under King Arthur. National humiliations and civil unrest made the 1450s a fertile time for prophets: like alchemists they responded to the growing sense of despair by allowing themselves to be guided by heroic myths. Ironically this had already happened in Normandy where the sufferings of the people at the hands of the English invaders caused them to give credence to the visions of Joan of Arc. Two Latin calendars compiled in *c.* 1461 and 1465, probably by a Welsh cleric attached to the house of York, place British and English history in the context of a series of prophecies about the fate of the British nation. They will be referred to frequently, and for the sake of convenience I shall assign to them both the title *The Prophetic History of Britain*.[118] The contents of these manuscripts are very similar. Both contain calendars reviewing British and English history, and a series of prophecies from the time of Cadwallader to the fifteenth century are recorded; these predict a time of civil war and weak

Deaths from famine after the exile of Cadwallader. The realm of the Fisher King. (British Library Royal 15 E IV, Chronicles of the English, *Jean de Waurin, vol. II, fo. 187)*

leadership, comparable to Cadwallader's time, which would presage a return of Arthur's kingdom. Like Hardynge, the author of these manuscripts uses Geoffrey of Monmouth's *Historia regum Britanniae* to depict Cadwallader's kingdom as a wasteland, its people expelled by the Saxons because of a catalogue of sins (including the rapine of magnates and the cupidity of judges) that could equally apply to the reign of Henry VI. The parallels between the two reigns are set up in the calendar which charts the degradation of Henry's kingdom from the onset of the conflict between Humphrey duke of Gloucester and the bishop of Winchester when, according to the compiler, 'the time changeth'. A series of symbolic events are recorded including a great frost from St Valentine's Day 1435; the great dearth of wheat (highlighted in red letters) which fetched as much as 20*s* a bushel throughout 1439; the naming of Eleanor Cobham as a witch in 1441; the death of her husband, the duke of Gloucester, in 1447; the fire in St Paul's steeple in 1445, occurring alongside a note about the coronation of Queen Margaret; and finally, highlighted in red letters, the Battle of London Bridge (the Cade Rebellion), so-called to link it with the prophetic falling of London Bridge into the Thames, calendared in 1437. The concentration in these two calendars on the poor harvests implies that this cleric saw Henry's sickness in terms of vegetative Grail myths: he had become a Fisher King holding on to power for too long in a wasteland. A similar connection was made in a poem composed in 1462/3 and known as *A Political Retrospect*, in which, after commenting on the curse of leprosy falling on the first Lancastrian king, the author claims that under Henry VI all returned 'unto huge langoure' and he likened England

> to a gardayne,
> Whiche that hathe ben overgrowen many yere
> With wedys whiche must be mowne doune playne,
> And than schul the pleasant swete herbes appere.

Edward IV's arrival was heralded as the appearance of the sweet spring flowers that dispel 'the blak cloudys of langoure' so that all in England may sing 'welcom everlastyng joye, and farewal langoure'.[119]

George Ripley was thinking along similar lines. Although his allegories probably originally referred to the need for Henry VI to experience a psychological death and renewal, they were by the end of the decade focused on the youthful redeemer, the earl of March. One vision ascribed to Ripley and John Dastin describes a kingdom afflicted by a contagious leprosy originally caused by a malign constellation and handed down from generation to generation through blood and milk (an explicit reference to the curse of the house of Lancaster). The king and his brethren fell into 'a great langoure', lamenting their infected blood to their mother the queen, who remembers a time when there was no debate, when there was a temperate harmony between the four humours, no infirmity or discord, all well proportioned around a royal king whose unalterable complexion was unaffected by dryness or moistness and who saved imperfect bodies from corruption and cured leprosy. The queen said that the king must die and be born again; though old, he must regain his youth if his brethren were to rise again fresh and well. 'And so the sun in hue of gold rose without war or strife deluging his brethren in a golden rain.' This is how the *Ripley Scrolls* all begin, with the sun bursting through the clouds and the falling of a golden rain. There could be no more eloquent prelude to the emergence of the sun of York.[120]

Today we can attempt to explain Henry VI's affliction in terms of a mental illness inherited from his grandfather Charles VI, king of France. It was most likely to have been a manifestation of schizophrenic withdrawal, the result of a predisposition to this condition inherited from his grandfather, who first exhibited symptoms of extreme paranoid schizophrenic behaviour in 1396 when, suffering under the delusion that he was made of glass, he shot servants who approached too closely. However, it may have been a bipolar manic depressive disorder, which in Henry's case ultimately led to a stuporous and even hallucinatory depression, or it may even have had an organic basis. Contemporaries, however, physicians, alchemists and prophets alike, would have seen it as an inherited curse of a different nature, a wound, perhaps explicitly symbolized in the king's injury at the first Battle of St Albans, which was dealt to the royal family tree when Henry Bolingbroke deposed Richard II. This was conveyed in a prophecy of Edward the Confessor (whose arms Richard II adopted) copied into *The Prophetic History of Britain*,[121] concerning a vision of a fruitful tree cut off from its original trunk and separated from its root by the space of three acres without force of human hand until it is returned to its trunk. The three acres were taken to symbolize the three generations separating Richard II and Edward IV and this prophecy was vividly illustrated in the pictorial roll known as the *Illustrated Life of Edward*

IV, showing the steps by which Edward took the throne. In this roll the lines of York and Lancaster are depicted in terms of a maimed tree, with Henry VI the last representative of an invalid line going back to a severed branch, mended with the arrival of Edward IV.[122] The alchemy commissions of 1456 and 1457, which refer to the search for an incorruptible essence of virtue that could eradicate even mortal sin, would therefore have been set in place with this sin of Henry Bolingbroke's usurpation in mind.

The treatment of Henry VI's illness in mythological terms, comparisons with Cadwallader and allusions to the Fisher King imply that these clerical authors of the genealogical chronicles, together with old soldiers like Hardynge and court alchemists, were beginning to look for a young king of energy and vigour, the 'once and future king Arthur' to restore the kingdom, something Henry VI was too damaged to achieve. This is implicit in the prophecies included in the twenty-seven genealogical chronicles written in the reigns of Henry VI and Edward IV. Many of these prophecies, which were current in the 1450s, include the prophecy of the eagle from Geoffrey of Monmouth's *Historia regum Britanniae*, which was commonly confused with and known as the prophecy of Merlin. Originally intended to apply to the civil wars of the reign of King Stephen, this prophecy was copied into *The Prophetic History of Britain* and headed in red 'A Prophecy of Merlin concerning Henry VI'.[123] It begins 'When the lion of justice is dead' and describes the successor of the lion of justice as a noble but maimed king with a fateful inheritance. This praise for Henry V and his son (Lancastrians in a Yorkist genealogical chronicle) shows how misleading these labels and the term propaganda can be when applied to the political conflicts of this period. These so-called Yorkist propagandists were merely attempting to make sense of the traumas of their time by telling their story in terms of myth. The prophecy goes on to explain:

> There is a white and noble king [originally intended to refer to King Stephen] who will rise in Britain and he will be snared. He will be led through Britain and he will be pointed at with finger and it will be said 'where is the white and noble king', and his followers will all band together and dispossess his people on his behalf [readers would apply this to the Suffolk affinity], and reform will be sought and none will be found and it will be said throughout Britain: he is king and he is nothing. After that he will lift up his head and show that he is king with many deeds but not with healing. And after that it will be the age of strange men, and whatever a man seizes he will hold as his own. Behold the greed and effusion of blood – and the line of few men will remain entire and what is agreed in the evening will be violated in the morn. Everyone will be careful to guard what is his and get what is someone else's. The white and weak king will go west to the place beside the running water. Then his enemies will come running down from all sides. Then the white and noble king will slide into death.[124]

There could be no more eloquent testimony to the fate of a ravaged land, ruled by a sick king who can still act but cannot heal and bless his realm, and this from Merlin, commonly regarded in this period as the first and most insightful British alchemist. His name heads a sixteenth-century list of British alchemists and appears in sixteenth-century verses accompanying the *Ripley Scrolls* as one of the possessors of the secret of the philosopher's stone. And it was the alchemists who, towards the end of the 1450s, were beginning to turn away from Henry VI to look, like Merlin, towards a young vigorous king to redeem the land.

NOTES

1. E. Ashmole, *Theatrum Chemicum Britannicum* (London, 1652), p. 374; Bodley MS Rawl. poet 121, fo. 71.
2. BL MS, 3580 B fo. 13v.
3. A. Gross, *The Dissolution of Lancastrian Kingship* (Stamford, 1996), p. 6.
4. *On the Properties of Things, John Trevisa's translation of Bartholomeus Anglicus De Proprietatibus Rerum*, ed. M.C. Seymour (Oxford, 1975), vol. i, pp. 155–7; Dobbs, *Nebuchadnezzar's Children*, p. 123.
5. Ibid, pp. 350–1.
6. C. Rawcliffe, 'Master Surgeons at the Lancastrian Court', Paper delivered at the 18th Harlaxton Symposium, July 2001, on the Lancastrian Court.
7. C. Rawcliffe, 'More than a Bedside Manner: the Political Status of the Late Medieval Court Physician', in *St George's Chapel, Windsor*, p. 79; T. Rymer, *Foedera, Conventiones, Litterae et cuiusque Acta Publica*, 20 vols (The Hague, 1704–35), vol. v, pt 2, p. 55.
8. Rymer, *Foedera* XI 366; P.A. Johnson, *Richard Duke of York 1411–1460* (Oxford, 1988), p. 167. PRO SC1/43/182; Rawcliffe, 'More than a Bedside Manner'; D. Geoghegan, 'A licence of Henry VI to Practice Alchemy', *Ambix*, 6 (1957–8), 15–16.
9. Ogrinc, 'Western Society and Alchemy', 119; *Cal Pat Rolls*, Henry VI 1441–6, pp. 275, 450, 458; J. Pettus, *Fodinae regales* (1620), p. 27.
10. Bodley Ashmole MS 1475; Bodley MS e musaeo 155.
11. Bodley MS e musaeo 153, fos 1–183.
12. Bodley MS Ashmole 1432, fos 11, 18, 5, 4; L. Voigts, *'Scientific and Medical Books'*, in *Book Production and Publishing in Britain 1375–1475*, ed. Jeremy Grifiths and Derek Pearsall (Cambridge, 1989), pp. 345–402.
13. From information provided by P.M. Jones.
14. St John's College, Oxford, MS 172.
15. E. Brehm, 'Roger Bacon's Place in the History of Alchemy', *Ambix*, ix (23 March 1976), 53–7.
16. *Secreta secretorum cum glossis et Notulis Fratris Rogeri*, ed. R. Steele (Oxford, 1920).
17. Ibid, p. 5.
18. Faye Gete, *Medicine in the English Middle Ages* (Princeton, 1998), p. 54ff; For a mid-fifteenth century copy of *De retardatione senectutis* see Trinity College Cambridge MS R.15.52. For theriac see C. Rawcliffe, *Medicine and Society in Later Medieval England*, pp. 152–3.
19. *Il Testamentum Alchemico Attributo A Raimundo Lullo, Edizione del testo Latino e Catelano del Manuscritto Oxford, Corpus Christi College 244*, ed. M. Pereira and Barbara Spaggiari (Firenze, 1999); Corpus Christi College, Oxford, MS 244, fo. 81 rb; M. Pereira, *The Alchemical Corpus attributed to Raymund Lull*, Warburg Institute Surveys and Texts, xviii; Pereira, 'Quintessenza alchemica', *Kos*, 7 (1984), 33–4; D.W. Singer, 'The Alchemical Testamentum Attributed to Raymund Lull', *Arecheion*, 9 (1928–9), 43–52.
20. C. Rawcliffe, 'Written in the Book of Life: Building the Libraries of Medieval English Hospitals and Almshouses', forthcoming; C. Jamison, *The History of the Royal Hospital of St Katherine* (Cambridge, 1952).
21. Corpus Christi College, Oxford, MS 224, fo. 81 rb; *Il Testamentum*, pp. 512–14.
22. BL MS Sloane, 419.
23. BL MS Sloane, 2948. The date of authorship is on fo. 51. The section on clysters is on fo. 46.
24. BL MS Sloane 1118, fo. 135; see also fo. 36 for a reference to Kirkeby. See Voigts, 'The Sloane Group', 37.
25. BL MS Sloane 2320, fos 1v–2v.
26. *CPR Henry VI 1452–61*, p. 390.
27. *Chronique du Religieux de Saint Denys*, ed. M.L. Bellaquet, vol. 1, pp. 88–92. Corpus Christi College, Oxford, MS 244.
28. *CPR 1452–61*, p. 339.
29. *Dicta Philosophorum*, p. 74; Gross, *Dissolution of Lancastrian Kingship*, p. 42.
30. Trinity College, Cambridge, R.14.52; Gross, *Dissolution of Lancastrian Kingship*, p. 42; C.P. Christianson, *A Directory of London Stationers and Book Artisans 1300–1500* (New York, 1900), p. 136; L. Mooney, *Index of Middle English Prose Handlist XI* (Cambridge, 1995), pp. 61–2; Mooney, 'A Middle English Treatise on Seven Liberal Arts', *Speculum*, 68 (1993); A.I. Doyle, 'English Books in and Out of Court', 177.
31. Emden, *BRUC* (Cambridge, 1963), 309, 38, 133. Anthony Gross, who has been working on Barker, has kindly communicated his knowledge and views which do not necessarily coincide with mine.
32. BL MS Stow 11070, fos 26–32.
33. Ibid.

34. Bodley MS Ashmole 750, fo. 195r.
35. Bodley MS Ashmole 1421, fo. 238; Bodley Ashmole 1408, p. 103; Bodley Ashmole 1485; Bodley Ashmole 750. These recipes are important because the manuscripts in some cases pre-date the two sixteenth-century manuscripts containing Barkers alchemical treatise. The watermark in some of the Ashmole manuscripts is as early as 1520 and the Ashmole 750 manuscript which contains an order for barley (commonly used in medicines) for my master pere (father) Barker (fo. 195b) is a fifteenth-century manuscript.
36. BL MS Sloane 2464.
37. Norton, *Ordinal of Alchemy*, p. 50.
38. F. Millard, 'Epitaphium eisudem ducis gloucestrie: the epitaph for Humphrey, duke of Gloucester, in its cultural and political context', Institute of Historical Reasearch Late Medieval Seminar, 2 November 2001; BL MS Add. 34360. G. Keir, 'The Ecclesiastical Career of George Neville 1432–1476', Oxford Univ. B.Litt, 1970.
39. Bodley MS 361, copied 1453–9; Bodley 362, copied 1448–55; Merton College, Oxford MS 268, copied 1458–9; Bodley MS Laud Misc. 558.
40. Bodley MS 362, fo. 247.
41. Bodley MS Laud Misc. 558, fos 261 and 199.
42. BL MS Add. 5544, p. 15.
43. Ibid.
44. BL MS Sloane 4; Bodley MS Ashmole 1432, fos 155–79.
45. Ibid, fo. 49v.
46. Ibid, fo. 46v.
47. Ibid, fo. 57.
48. Ibid, fo. 8.
49. Ibid, fo. 22.
50. Ibid, fo. 49.
51. BL MS Cotton Julius FVIII, fos 174–85v.
52. Ibid, fo. 180.
53. New College, Oxford, MS 162, fos 1–47.
54. Magdalen College, Oxford, MS 65.
55. Kieckhefer, *Magic in the Middle Ages*, p. 138.
56. BL MS Sloane 4, fo. 37.
57. BL MS Sloane 4, fo. 56.
58. Bodley MSS Ashmole 1432 and Ashmole 1453, fos 155–79.
59. BL MS Sloane 4, fo. 37.
60. The following account of Brook is derived from Voigts' excellent paper 'The Master of the King's Stillatories', delivered at the 18th Harlaxton Symposium on the Lancastrian Court, July 2001.
61. *CCR Henry VI 1422–9*, p. 193.
62. *CPR Henry VI 1436–41*, p. 550.
63. Bodley Ashmole Ms 1505, fo. 245.
64. Eldredge, *The Index of Manuscripts*, pp. 107–8; Bodley Ashmole MS 1505.
65. *CCR Henry VI 1447–54*, p. 229.
66. BL MS Sloane 59.
67. BL MS Sloane 338.
68. BL MS Sloane 118.
69. Bodley Roll 1.
70. Corpus Christi College, Oxford, MS 244.
71. The 1471 manuscript of *The Compound of Alchemy*, BL Sloane MS 2958, is written on paper and contains the *Compound of Alchemy* with the poem in which Ripley describes himself as a canon at Bridlington and recounts his travels in Italy and his exemption from claustral obedience. It also contains the prologue, the preface, and Ripley's retraction of all his writings and experiments before 1471. The sigil with the date of the work's completion appears on fo. 71v. and compares with the sigil of Mayne in BL Sloane 338 fo. 2. This manuscript does not contain the dedicatory letter to Edward IV which, if it contains Ripley's original sigil, would imply that the letter was written separately and after *The Compound of Alchemy*. For comparisons between the 1471 manuscript and the 1591 printed edition see S.L. Linden's edition of *The Compound of Alchemy*, based on the 1591 edition (Aldershot, 2001). The next surviving fifteenth-century manuscript, BL Sloane MS 3747, written *c.* 1475 on vellum, does contain the dedicatory letter to Edward IV (fos 102–5) and the *Cantilena* (fos 84v–7). See G. Keiser, *A Manual of Writings in Middle English 1050–1500, vol. 10 Science and information*, gen. ed. Hartung (New Haven, 1998), which does not mention Sloane 2598. Among other fifteenth-century copies of the *Compound of Alchemy* are Corpus Christi College, Oxford, MS 172, fos 130–78, and Trinity College, Cambridge, MS O.5.31. This is an important text because we have here a fifteenth-century prose version of

the *Compound of Alchemy* with Ripley's authorship 'Explicit Alkimie tractatus philosophie cuius Ripley George canonicus Auctor' acknowledged; Linne Mooney, *Handlist XI The Library of Trinity College Cambridge*, p. 125. Ashmole refers to seeing a copy of Ripley's *Compound of Alchemy* in a vellum manuscript in the possession of John Dee, at the end of which is the date 1471.

72. BL MS Sloane 3580 B. This manuscript was written in 1580.
73. Bodley MS Ashmole 440, fos 209–13.
74. George Ripley, *Compound of Alchemy*, in Ashmole, *Theatrum Chemicum Britannicum*.
75. Bodley MS Ashmole 1457, fo. 276.
76. *Cal. Papal Letters*, vol. xi (1453–64), pp. 530–1.
77. Ripley, *Cantilena*.
78. *Compound of Alchemy*, in Ashmole, *Theatrum Chemicum Britannicum*, p. 108.
79. Ripley, *The Marrow of Alchemy* (*Medulla Philosophorum* in BL MS Sloane 3580 B, fo. 138.
80. For manuscripts of *Cantilena* see Bodley Ashmole 1394, Bodley Ashmole MS 1445 (an English translation of 1539) and Bodley Ashmole 1384. For other manuscripts see L. Thorndike, *History of Magic and Experimental Science* (Columbia, 1934), vols iii and iv, p. 352. Singer, *Catalogue of Alchemical Manuscripts*, nos 322, 324, 810, 813.
81. Bodley MS Ashmole 1448, fo. 1: 'scire teipsum'.
82. Bodley Roll MS 1. The drawings and costumes are mid-fifteenth century. See Pacht and Alexander, *Illuminated Manuscripts in Bodley*, vol. iii, p. 88, and compare the images with the miniature in Bodley MS Rawl A 386, fo. 83. The roll has been retouched in the sixteenth century when the verses were probably added.
83. U. Szulakowska, 'The Tree of Aristotle: Images of the Philosopher's Stone and their Transference in Alchemy from the xvth to the xxth century', *Ambix*, 33 (1986), 53–77.
84. S.J. Linden, 'The Ripley Scrolls and the Compound of Alchemy', in *Glasgow Emblem Studies vol. 3, Emblems and Alchemy*, ed. A. Adams and S.J. Linden (1988).
85. The images occurring on the scrolls also occur in a manuscript containing Ripley's works dated *c.* 1475, BL MS Sloane 37847, fo. 105. These images were to be deployed by Ashmole in his edition of the *Theatrum Chemicum Britannicum* (1652).
86. BL MS Sloane 2523 B. This sixteenth-century manuscript has Ripley's name in verse at the top of the roll and pre-dates Ashmole.
87. Ripley's tomb does not survive but there are two drawings of it. The oldest, in BL MS Vitellius EX, fo. 251v, is incomplete. A later complete copy with notes by Ashmole is in Bodley MS Ashmole 971, 972, fo. 300b. The *Ripley Scroll* which bears the closest resemblance to the tomb is Bodley Ashmole 53 (dated 1530). Ripley is shown at the top of the scroll sleeping in canon's robes and experiencing his vision of an angel bearing a heart and a knife (which appears on the tomb). Also prominent on this roll and on the tomb is the horseshoe.
88. Bodley Roll 1.
89. The image of Ripley bearing a staff with a cloven foot also occurs on the *Ripley Scroll*, Bodley Ashmole Roll 40.
90. Bodley Ashmole Roll 53 (executed in 1530).
91. Bodley Roll 1.
92. BL MSS Harl. 2407 and Egerton 845.
93. BL MS Cotton Julius VII, fos 6–13.
94. For the first translation see F. Sherwood Taylor, *Ambix*, ii, nos 3–4 (December 1946); and C. Jung, *Mysterium Coniunctionis*. For manuscript see BL MS Add. 11388, fos 33v–35r, which is illustrated.
95. Jung, *Mysterium Coniunctionis*, p. 271; *Opera omnia chemica* (Cassell, 1648), p. 421; Sherwood Taylor, *Ambix* (1946). The original *Cantilena* is in Latin. See Bodley Ashmole MS 1394. The sixteenth-century translation used by Sherwood Taylor and Jung is in Bodley MS Ashmole 1445.
96. Keir, 'Ecclesiastical Career of George Neville', 120.
97. *Cantilena*, verses 18–19.
98. Ibid, verse 28.
99. Jung, *Mysterium Coniunctionis*, p. 334.
100. Jung, *Psychology and Alchemy*, pp. 412ff; *Mysterium Coniunctionis*, transl. R.F.C. Hull (Princeton, 1963).
101. *Cantilena*, verses 31–5. For visual representations of these images in *Cantilena* see BL MS Add. 11388, fos 33v–36, and for earlier fifteenth-century representations see the copy of the *Cantilena* in Trinity College, Cambridge, 0.8.24, fos 46–7.
102. For a sceptical view of Henry VI's sanctity see B.P. Wolffe, *Henry VI*, ch. 1. For Blacman's memoir see M.R. James, *Henry the Sixth. A Reprint of John Blacman's Memoir* (Cambridge, 1919). *Great Chronicle of London*, pp. 209–10.

103. 'The Commentaries of Pius II', bks 97–9, transl. F.A Cragg-Smith, *Studies in History*, 35 (Northampton Massachusetts, 1951), bk ix, p. 579.
104. Kingsford, *English Historical Review*, xxvii (1912), 462.
105. John Hardynge, *Chronicle*, ed. H. Ellis (London, 1812); A. Gransden, *Historical Writing*, ii, pp. 274–87. The earliest version presented to Henry VI is BL MS Lansdowne 204.
106. Hardynge, *Chronicle*, p. 154.
107. Ibid.
108. Ibid.
109. Ibid.
110. Bodley MS Arch Selden B 10.
111. BL MS Lansdowne 204, fo. 3v.
112. Hardynge, *Chronicle*, p. 390.
113. Bodley Jesus College MS 114, fo. 32v.
114. BL MS Lansdowne 204, fos 106–106.
115. Hardynge, *Chronicle*, p. 177.
116. Ibid, p. 178.
117. Ibid. p. 106.
118. BL MS Cotton Vesp. E VII and Bodley MS 623. The contents of both manuscripts are similar. BL MS Cotton Vesp. E VII contains the arms of the earl of Northumberland (the Percies were patrons of Hardynge) and is larger and intended for wider use, while Bodley 623 is smaller.
119. Lib. Soc. Antiquaries, no. 101, fo. 78; Wright, *Political Songs*, ii (Rolls Series, London, 1861), pp. 269–70.
120. Bodley MS Poet Rawl., fos 73v–75.
121. BL MS Cotton Vesp. E VII.
122. BL MS Harl. 7353.
123. BL MS Cotton Vesp. E VII, fo. 98.
124. Ibid.

CHAPTER 4

The Alchemy of Kingship: The Emergence of Edward IV

> Such shall be to me a beloved son, behold ye him, beautiful above the suns of men, at whose beauty the sun and moon wonder. For he is the privilege of love and the heir, in whom men trust and without whom they can do nothing.
>
> Anon, *Aurora Consurgens*, early fifteenth century[1]

By abandoning their attempts to heal the sick, prematurely aged king the alchemists placed their faith in a youth, closely identified with the Spring sun, who represented the homunculus in the sense that he had been to some extent schooled in alchemical teaching and who realized his sense of self and destiny in one defining moment during the nadir of his life (the *nigredo*) when he burst into the political arena in the beginning of 1461 like the young Alexander the Great, an eighteen-year-old phenomenon full of self-belief and a sense of destiny. Edward earl of March had spent several years at Ludlow with his brother Rutland, supervising his father's territories in the Welsh marches. He knew the locals well, men like Sir Richard Croft and William Herbert. Given the rout of his father's troops at Ludford Bridge near Ludlow in 1459, the news of the defeat of the duke of York at the Battle of Wakefield on 30 December, which reached him at Shrewsbury, may not have come as a complete surprise.

Despite the execution of his father and his brother Rutland, Edward kept his head, realizing that before he could avenge their deaths he needed to defeat Jasper Tudor, his rival in the marches. He chose the site of the battle carefully, a crossroads on the River Lugg, protected by surrounding hills, and he led his troops to victory there on 3 February 1461 at the Battle of Mortimer's Cross.[2] Undeterred by Margaret of Anjou's march on London and her routing of the army of the earl of Warwick at the second Battle of St Albans on 17 February (when Henry VI was recaptured by the Lancastrians and could be said to have broken the Act of Accord), Edward marched from Hereford towards London on 26 February, and on 4 March 1461 he took the crown. The conflicts which brought Edward to power in 1461 were naturally regarded in terms of the civil wars of the Roman republic. In a letter to the papal legate Coppini, written in April 1461, George Neville described the battles of St Albans and Towton and exclaimed against the civil conflict by quoting the opening lines of Lucan's *Pharsalia*.[3] Edward had emerged to fulfil Roman imperial expectations of kingship. His conquest of the throne had, like Julius Caesar's military intercession, ended the civil wars. Warwick, who was trying to hold things together after the Battle of Wakefield, attempted to negotiate with Margaret of Anjou through Coppini, who sent her a message telling her not to be arrogant on account of her trifling victory for the people were incensed against her and the legate desired peace. The lords with Margaret were told that it was better to make peace after a defeat, as the wise and prudent Romans did. Warwick himself was described by a Milanese ambassador as 'like another Caesar in these parts',[4] but it was Edward who was most commonly assigned the role of the prudent Caesar. John Whethamstede, in a Latin poem written after Towton, referred to Edward's victory over Henry and called him a new Hector and a second Achilles, and hoped he would reign 'more happily than Augustus and better than Octavianus'.[5] Sir James Strangways, the speaker of the House of Commons, congratulated Edward in his first Parliament on 'the wysdome that of his grace is annexed thereunto, and the blessid and noble disposicion and application of youre seid highnes, to the commyn wele and policie of youre seid Reame'.[6] The high expectations that this young king would embody the stoic qualities of the age of Julius Caesar and Augustus and bring stability to the realm were expressed at the top of the roll known as *The Illustrated Life of Edward IV*. A picture celebrating the young king's accession shows him sitting at the apex of fortune's wheel. This wheel had been stopped by a spar thrust through the spokes of the wheel by Reason herself. In the opposite picture, among the prophets anticipating his coming are the four cardinal virtues, and the one that is specifically identified is Prudence, the virtue celebrated by William Worcester. This theme was expressed in a copy of Lydgate's *Troy Book* and the *Siege of Thebes*.[7] Edward, wearing a gold crown and holding a sceptre and orb, is depicted seated on a throne on top of the wheel of fortune. Behind the king there is his badge, the blazing sun on a blue sky. This volume was owned by Edward's chief lieutenant, William lord Herbert, and was subsequently presented to the king. Edward signified his intent to rule through the rational principles of antiquity when on 5 March 1461 on his royal proclamation he took an oath to preserve the common weal, referring to the lamentable state and ruin of the realm of England, the oppression of the nobles and the exile of justice, all of which he associated with the Lancastrian usurpation.[8] In 1462, in an attempt to raise money, he wrote to Alderman Thomas Cook, exhorting his assembled householders within the ward to show zeal for the common weal.

Nothing is known of the state of Edward's mind when he took these momentous steps, but it can be assumed that there was more behind Edward's assumed poise than the confidence of a youthful prodigy and that he was not merely a passive recipient of the projections of intellectuals. He had been prepared for the acceptance of this heroic role and the key to his formulative years between 1456 and 1461 is alchemy. Around 1456, at a time when the alchemists treating Henry VI began to see his condition as incurable, they would have sensed all around them nothing but disintegration. Constantinople had fallen in 1453 to the Turks who were pressing ominously westwards and had already advanced into Macedonia. In October of the same year any hopes of retaining an English empire irrevocably collapsed when the French drove the English out of Guienne. Even within England itself things appeared to be falling apart. Divisions between the baronial factions were highlighted in the summer of 1453 when a feud between Sir John Neville and Sir Thomas Percy engulfed the leading magnate families of the north. The broader north/south feud was to be graphically demonstrated in the six months of dissension between the Battle of Northampton and Margaret of Anjou's march towards London, which the anxious Londoners perceived as a war between north and south.[9] Alchemy was seen as a panacea for these ills, a holistic remedy which, applied to the person of the king and the body politic, could resolve the warring opposites in society around a heroic redemptive king. By 1456 the hopes of the alchemists began to focus on the young earl of March.

Edward's father, Richard duke of York, was closely associated with the failures in France and he was as discredited a figure as the dukes of Suffolk and Somerset. Unwilling to go the full distance and repudiate the rule of Henry VI, York had tried to develop and implement an alternative conception of government that claimed to represent the lords and the interests and attitudes expressed in Parliament, a non-monarchical form of government that appealed to the common weal of the body politic. However, the nobility were inexorably attached to the monarchical ideology and York could only try to recover the initiative by seeking public recognition as the heir presumptive, something the partisans of Queen Margaret of Anjou (who included some with alchemical interests such as Sir John Fortescue and John Ashby) could never accept. Ashby, a servant of Henry VI and Margaret of Anjou, writing in the Fleet prison in 1463, lamented that he could not recognize the authority of Edward of the house of York and held on to the hope that Henry VI could emerge from his troubles purified like alchemical gold:

> And as precyous gold ys thorough puryd
> By foul metall led, and claryfyed
> Right so ys the sowle by trowbyll curyd
> And by humble profe, high glory led.[10]

In his *Dicta Philosophorum* he described the king as a mighty river, the state of mind of his people being determined by whether the river is salt or sweet. The close medical relationship between king and realm is summed up when Ashby advises the king to listen to his physician, who should be prepared to speak the truth, and exclaims: 'How blest is the land that has a wise king.'[11] However, as the possibility of curing Henry VI was so remote, partisans of the house of Lancaster, by employing medical, alchemical metaphors, were merely paving the way for opponents to press the Mortimer claim of the earl of March, who had not made the fatal political compromises of his father and who was freshly minted gold, young enough to be untainted by any associations with military failure. He was therefore able to accommodate the heroic expectations projected on to him and alchemy, replete with the monarchical symbolism of the Sun King, the sun rising from the ocean and illuminating the moon, became much more than an arcane and occult art: it was the means whereby the nation and its king could see 1461 in terms of the *senex* transformed to *puer*, the beautiful youth who emerges as king to heal the body politic. The redemptive, alchemical role of such a charmed youth was dramatized in a window behind the pulpit in St Margaret's church, Westminster, seen by Ashmole in 1652, showing the entire process of the work and a beautiful young man surrounded by bright glory and diverse colours standing upon the earth.

Edward may first have come to the attention of the royal alchemist/physicians at the time of the alchemy commission of 1456. In the preface to the sixteenth-century copy of the alchemical treatise of Robert Barker (Friar Bungay), Barker claims that he wrote his work during the conjunction of the sun and moon in November 1456 for Prince Edward, then aged fourteen.[12] The more prosaic explanation of this dedication is that Barker originally dedicated the treatise to Edward Lancaster, the prince of Wales, and subsequently and retrospectively rededicated it to Edward IV giving him the title prince.[13] However, Barker's commitment to Edward IV was firmly established in 1471 when he was held responsible for causing the storms that delayed Margaret of Anjou's forces before the Battle of Barnet, and it is intriguing to consider the possibility that as early as 1456 he may, like Merlin, have been preparing Edward for his future destiny and in this dedication alluding to the fourteen-year-old earl of March's links through the Mortimers with the princes of Wales, the descendants of the kings of Britain. It is also possible that by 1456, when the commissioners were delving into such ancient texts as Ovid's *Metamorphoses*, Edward earl of March was beginning to be seen as a viable alternative to Henry VI, as a more highly evolved, youthful Jason who could redeem the kingdom. He represented the most highly evolved of the metals, gold. The dull, base and elementary metal, antimony, was, on the other hand, the least evolved of the metals and was used to devour the impurities in gold (like a wolf). It was therefore assigned the house of Aries because this was the house in which the sun begins to be exalted. By the end of the decade the cognomen of *Lupus* (wolf) signifying antimony was applied to Henry VI in Yorkist genealogies. In a mid-fifteenth-century treatise on the four humours antimony is signified by the letter H. The cognomen *Sol* (gold) was applied to Edward earl of March in Yorkist genealogies.[14] Edward later acquired six tapestries showing Jason and the plough with Vulcanus emerging from his ship. These tapestries had been confiscated from Henry Holland duke of Exeter, who was attainted for treason on Edward's orders in November 1461.[15]

In this same year, 1456, John Cokkys was engaged in transcribing Bacon's alchemical writings. Cokkys was responsible for producing the copy of the *Secreta secretorum*, together with medical treatises, and Roger Bacon's introductory treatise and glosses, which has an inscription proving Edward earl of March's ownership and showing that he owned the work in his youth; this inscription may date from 1456.[16] The margin of this manuscript has the same marginal line decorations as those occurring in the Bacon works transcribed by Cokkys in this year and now in the Bodleian Library.[17] The alchemical counsel in Bacon's version of the *Secreta secretorum* was crucial in the formulation of the self-image Edward would adapt when taking the throne.[18] Two alchemists promised to reveal to Edward the alchemical mysteries: George Ripley, in a letter to Edward written in 1471, and Thomas Norton, in his *Ordinal of Alchemy* (1477). However, it was Bacon's adaptation of the professedly secret doctrine of Aristotle to Alexander, with its information on lifestyle and planetary influences, that would have been the first text the young prince turned to for advice on how to create a prosperous kingdom. Edward's motto was 'comfort and joy'.[19] It was a truism of late medieval medicine that laughter was good for the health and Bacon's version of the *Secreta secretorum* prescribed a more relaxed lifestyle for the prince which would foster the state of mind suggested by the above motto and encourage a balance of the humours. This in turn would result in a prosperous reign:

> and moche the more and profitabiler yf he be mery and glad, and yf he myght have resonable glory and honoure, and of his enemyes victorye, hope and trust in the peple, in pleyes and sightes to delyte, to se faire faces and vesages, and to beholde delitable bokes, and to here swete songes and delitable to laugh amonge tham that loven hym, to be clad in the best clothyng of colour and teyntour, and to be wele an-oynted with the best accordyng oynementys delitable to the tyme.[20]

To live according to nature and pursue activities that agreed with the season would, Bacon argued, strengthen rational powers with activities agreeing with the season, and with these things men are made fat.[21] This is advice which, as we shall see, Edward was to follow to the letter. It sets the tone for his reign and was to play a large part in encouraging him to develop his expansive charm, a quality that was in such marked contrast to the asceticism of Henry VI and the neurotic suspicions of his counterpart on the French throne, Louis XI.

This manuscript is the key to Edward's precocious sense of destiny. From it he would learn that the stars and planets controlled all the elements and humours. Bacon claimed that kings needed the advice of wise men to ensure they were not dominated by their ruling humours. Edward III, who also patronized alchemists (notably the author of the *Testamentum*) also consulted a regimen to control his humours, an illuminated copy of the *Secreta secretorum* presented to him as a young man in 1327,[22] and Lydgate was writing a *Secreta secretorum* for Henry VI at the time of his death, 1449–50. In the *Secreta secretorum* the prince is advised to obtain a knowledge of astronomy and to do nothing without consulting an astronomer. He should take careful note of the way his body and soul are affected by the stars and planets, and if a true mathematician were to know his exact birth date he could judge his nature and qualities, for all men follow their complexions. Edward was to employ mathematicians such as Roger Marshall to cast his horoscope. Bacon provided encouragement in the *Secreta secretorum* for Edward's special dedication to the sun, his ruling planet and the most beneficent of stars. This text also provided a justification for the observation of constellations and planetary abnormalities for signs of a profound political change. A comet was regarded as an especially portentous indicator of an imminent change of dynasty. The manuscript contains a reference to the comet of 1264 which preceded the death of Simon de Montfort and frightened many men. These comets, Bacon claimed, were generated in the sphere of fire. In February 1456 John Bocking wrote to Sir John Fastolf, giving him strange tidings of celestial apparitions that accompanied the appearance in Parliament in coats of mail of Richard duke of York and the earl of Warwick: 'And the lords speken this day in the parliament of a greet glemyng sterre that but late hath been seen diverse tymes, mervellous in apperyng.' These words would have taken on an unusual significance when Halley's Comet appeared in June 1456. Most relevant to Edward was Bacon's emphasis on the significance of eclipses, conjugations of the sun and moon, one of which was referred to by Barker in November 1456. Of greater significance, according to Bacon, was the appearance of three suns (parhelia) in the sky, and he suggested that his readers consult Livy or Augustine about the great changes that followed such phenomenon.[23] Parhelia are formed on very cold, frosty mornings when the sun is low in the sky. Falling ice crystals, flat and hexagonal, reflect white light to form images on either side of the sun, creating the illusion of three suns appearing in the sky. Other refracted ice crystals create a rainbow effect of circles of mixed colours of red and green around the sun.[24] Bacon regarded parhelia as potent symbols of political change (one famous instance was the appearance of three suns before Constantine, and a parhelia was observed before the fall of Constantinople in 1453).[25] For Bacon these celestial phenomena were more accurate indicators of future change than astrology because they were based on sound experimental science which considers the way in which the benefit of life is cut off from the world; and this was especially significant in all forms of eclipses.[26]

The significance of the *Secreta secretorum* for Edward was made clear at a crossroads near the River Lugg in the heart of Mortimer country. This crossroads may already have been known as Mortimer's Cross, it certainly was after the decisive and bloody battle that was fought there on St Blaise's Day, 3 February 1461.[27] It was the young earl of March's moment of destiny. On the morning before the day of battle, on the Feast of the Purification of the Blessed Lady or Candlemas Day, three suns appeared 'in the fyrmament shynyng fulle clere', at two hours before none (around 10 a.m.) before Edward and his men, drawn up on the plain at Wigmarsh, west of Mortimer's Cross.[28] Edward was master of the situation:

> Whereof the peple hadde agast. The noble erle Edwarde thayn comforted and sayde, 'bea the of good comfort, and dredethe not; thys is good sygne, for these III sonys betoken the Fader, the Sone and the Holy Gost, and therefore lete us haue good harte, and in the name of Almyghte God go we agayns oure enemyes and put them to flight'.[29]

With this Edward took hope, exhorting his men to victory in honour of the Trinity, and from this time on he bore the sun in full brightness on his badge. After the battle, Edward's first victory without Warwick, he commanded that the badge of the sun would by used by him in commemoration of the three suns that had foretold his triumph.[30] The parhelia were

Above: *Moses before the blazing bush experiences a vision of the Trinity in the form of the three faces of God. In the background and foreground alchemical symbols of conflict between the elements, wrestlers and fighting rams, point towards Moses's importance as the founder of alchemy.*
Below: *Edward, Moses to his people, witnesses the parhelia, three suns shining through the three crowns of the kingdoms destined to be his. Edward interprets this alchemical vision as a manifestation of the Trinity. (British Library Harl. 7353* The Illustrated Life of Edward IV*)*

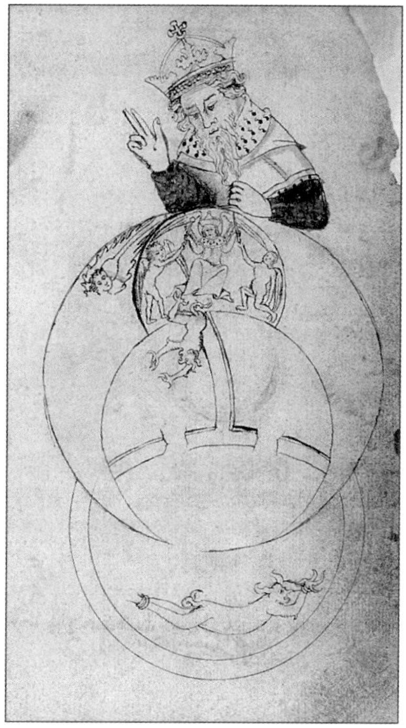

God, like a king blessing his land, creates the four elements from the dragon of chaos. (British Library Egerton 845, fo. 2).

probably first seen from the walls of Croft Castle, which Edward would have used for his advance base as it offered incomparable views across Herefordshire to the Black Mountains of Wales. It was probably at this castle and the adjacent chapel that Edward of Rouen first incorporated the sun in splendour in his self-image. It is likely that the phenomenon of the parhelia was to some extent stage-managed by the alchemists associated with the young prince to enable him to seize the initiative in his quest to take the throne, becoming the embodiment of the new sun emerging out of the *nigredo*, the chaos of civil war. This was the defining moment of the young earl of March's life. The author of the *Illustrated Life of Edward IV* has him employing the words uttered by St Paul when he saw a light from heaven flash about him on the road to Damascus: 'Lord what would you have me do?' Edward was eighteen years old, his youth shattered by the deaths of his father and brother, and his own life was in immediate danger. It was a crisis in which Edward seized something that gave him an exalted sense of his own existence and power as a man of destiny chosen by God. It was appropriate that the moment occurred at a crossroads. It was during the time of the *nigredo*, of the death of the body politic in a destructive civil war and on what must have been one of the coldest days of winter when the land seemed dead. He sees a colourful vision of the golden suns in the sky, representing in alchemical terms the rubedo and tincture heralding the rebirth of the land of his Arthurian ancestors, coinciding with the rising sap of Spring, under a Sun King and saviour who would fulfil the great work of redeeming the nation. The rising sun came to symbolize his self-image as the beautiful boy, the redeemer of his people, an image that was to mesmerize his subjects and later, unfortunately, himself. Croft Castle was the home of Sir Richard Croft, one of Edward's childhood companions. Sir Richard and his brother Thomas had been brought up in the same household as Edward in Ludlow. The brothers were close enough to the young earl to become the subject of a letter of complaint concerning bullying written by Edward and his brother Edmund to their father. Sir Richard Croft became a loyal servant of Edward's and was present at the battles of Mortimer's Cross and Towton. Near the castle, and overlooking the same valley, is the Croft family chapel, the church of St Michael and All Angels (St Michael was a key saint in the creation of Edward's public image as king). The parhelia first appeared in the east and would have been observed in the chancel during the celebration of Candlemas. In the south window of the church, opposite the spot on the battlefield where Edward observed the phenomenon, moving across the southern sky, there can still be seen an image of the sun in splendour, which was placed in the window after the battle, and a window on the opposite northern side shows a distinctively alchemical image of the sun.

The importance of eclipses, especially the parhelia described by Bacon, in the development of Edward's image in 1461 is shown in the *Illustrated Life of Edward IV*[31] which Edward probably commissioned to celebrate his victory at Mortimer's Cross and his triumphant entry into London. It is a genealogy depicting a sleeping king (Henry III) from

At the top of the Ripley Scroll *the alchemist, resembling the divine alchemist shown on page 83, begins the great work. Both images are derived from the alchemical painting in Westminster Abbey, an engraving or which was printed by Ashmole, showing the creation of the four elements. Edward IV was probably crowned before this painting. (Ashmole Roll 40)*

Below: *In Bramley church, Hampshire, a window executed* c. *1471 shows the sun in splendour shining through three crowns. This is an explicit allusion to the illustration in* The Illustrated Life of Edward IV *of the parhelia shining through three crowns before the Battle of Mortimer's Cross (see page 82). (Geoffrey Wheeler)*

whose body springs a flowering rose tree with various branches of the royal family culminating in the earl of March emerging from a tangled rose briar, bearing an upright sword and facing Henry VI. This is followed by a series of cartoons on the right showing the exile of the Yorkist earls in Calais, the victories of Edward of March at the battles of Northampton and Mortimer's Cross, and the coronation of Edward on the wheel of fortune. The illustration of the Battle of Mortimer's Cross features three suns shining on Edward through three golden crowns. A similar image of a radiant sun shining through three crowns can be seen in a stained-glass window in Bramley church, Hampshire, which was probably executed in 1471. The parhelia are also prominently represented in a picture culminating a series of biblical events which foretell the triumphs of Edward. Throned Reason presides over a company of saints and prophets who have predicted Edward's coming. The sky is dominated by an illustration of the blazing golden sun surrounded by three interlocking circles in different colours to represent the parhelia and the rainbow effect that Edward saw at Mortimer's Cross.[32] The Lancastrian star (*Stella*), a symbol for all three Lancastrian kings, is in eclipse.[33] Among the prophets foretelling Edward's coming is a large angel with wings (the same angel who prophesied to Cadwallader, the last British king, that one day another British king would redeem the land).[34] This angel bears a golden sun and above is the word 'Sol', Edward's cognomen. Edward's vision of the three suns had a precise alchemical significance, and the image of Moses' vision of the three faces of God in the flaming bush on this roll (perhaps derived from the *Biblia Pauperum*)[35] is a representation of the experience of the alchemist contemplating the furnace. Also in the sky is an eclipse of the sun. All this amounts to a visual representation of the astrological phenomenon that Bacon used in his version of the *Secreta secretorum* to predict changes of dynasty. It was to be used to powerful effect by Edward IV.

While Bacon's alchemical teaching, and by implication that of such interpreters as John Cokkys, may have played a significant role in encouraging Edward to take the throne, the most important contribution made to the monarchical ideology surrounding this young man was made by George Ripley. His highly individualistic allegories provided an explanation for the disintegration of the body politic over the previous decade and a symbolically charged rationale for the new monarchy, one that developed further the significance of the sun in ascendance. Ripley's close relationship with Edward in the period just before Mortimer's Cross is suggested in the dedicatory letter he wrote to Edward at the beginning of his *Compound of Alchemy* in 1471. Declaring that he is no flatterer, he wishes:

> Unto your Highnes, humbly to present
> Great secrets, which in farre countries I did learne,

and reminds the king that:

> Unto your Lordship, such things I did promise,
> What time you did commaund to send unto me,
> And sith that I wrote it in secret wise,
> Unto your grace from the Universite
> of Louvaine, when God fortuned me by grace to see
> Greater secrets and much more perfite,
> which onely to you I will disclosed be.[36]

This implies that there existed a close relationship between Ripley and Edward through correspondence and secret verbal communications not only throughout the 1460s but also in the period between 1459 and 1460 when Ripley received his licence to leave his convent at Bridlington to study overseas. It is also clear from this dedicatory epistle that Edward had asked for the text and that he was intensely interested in alchemy. Edward's concession revoking the debts of Bridlington in 1468 may be related to his patronage of Ripley.

A key figure in securing this concession for Ripley may have been the papal legate Coppini, who was in England at the time and in close contact with the Yorkists. Coppini supported the claims of Edward of March because he had promised support for a papal crusade against the Turks. He was interested in the alchemical astrological observations concerning the imminent change of dynasty; he had spoken with some astrologers, and in a letter to Francesco Sforza, duke of Milan, he provided the following comment on the Battle of Towton: 'The great chance had come with the victory of Edward and Warwick – Even the stars were favourable.'[37]

An important link between Edward and Ripley was the first Yorkist chancellor George Neville, bishop of Exeter, archbishop of York, and chancellor of Oxford where Ripley returned after his journey overseas. In a letter to Coppini, Neville endorsed his interest in a crusade and described Henry VI as a puppet. Neville was a famous alchemist in his own right: he was described in the sixteenth-century *A Lookeing Glasse for Illiterate Alchymists* as one of England's foremost practitioners, and he was Ripley's closest friend and patron. Ripley certainly respected his learning. A seventeenth-century copy of a text describing a dream of George Ripley includes a meditation on the significance of the dreams of Joseph and Daniel in which Ripley recounts having a fearful dream about going into hell and adds 'I leave the interpretation to the learned prelate'.[38] He was alluding to George Neville, whom he addressed as 'my dear lord and patron'; he even incorporated part of the archbishop's coat of arms, a three-headed axe in the form of a cross, among the alchemical symbols displayed on his tomb at Bridlington.

The bishop of Exeter, who became Edward's first chancellor, made the same sort of impact on the political stage as one of his predecessors as chancellor and archbishop of York, Thomas Arundel. Both men were aristocratic churchmen who intellectually outshone their king-making elder brothers; both were involved in the deposition of kings and the creation of new dynasties; and both were interested in the regeneration of the monarchy – Arundel's solution was political, the renewal of baronial government, while Neville had a more visionary interest in history, myth and alchemy. The philosophical justification that Neville provided for the accession of Edward IV was holistic and alchemical. Margaret of Anjou and her council recognized the gathering of distinguished alchemists around Edward by 1460. On 8 February 1460 a letter from King Henry (in reality from Queen Margaret) complained of 'a report how diverse inhabitants of Coventry since our departing have used unfitting language against our person and in favouring our superstitious traitors and rebels now late in parliament there attainted'. She and her supporters had sought the assistance of alchemists themselves only months earlier (and indeed the Loveday ceremony and processions at St Paul's on 25 March 1458, the formal attempt to bring about a reconciliation between the sons of those killed at St Albans and the Nevilles, sealed by the joining of hands of Margaret of Anjou and Richard duke of York, may have contained alchemical symbolism of renewal). Margaret and her supporters distinguished between magical power legitimately working through the king by sanction of divine providence and misplaced sorcery turned against the justly constituted royal prince.[39] The 'superstitious traitors and rebels' of the letter were presumably alchemists such as Barker, Ripley and Neville.[40]

Another distinguished ecclesiastic who may have had alchemical interests in the renewal of kingship around Edward IV was John Whethamstede, abbot of St Albans. He was described as one of Britain's leading alchemists of the fifteenth century in *A Lookeing Glasse for Illiterate Alchymists*.[41] He was turning to the Yorkist cause in the late 1450s out of respect for Humphrey duke of Gloucester, whose name also appears in this list. Neville's contribution to the accession of Edward was such that he welcomed the Yorkist earls to London in 1460, rode with the earls of March, Salisbury and Warwick to Northampton after the battles of Wakefield and St Albans, and spoke to an assembly of soldiers and citizens at St John's Fields on 1 March, stirring up resentment towards Henry VI and outlining Edward's claim and the prophecies that anticipated his coming. The death and regeneration myths of Neville's friend Ripley, reflecting the influence of the Catalan writings arriving in England in previous decades, appealed at a time of national crisis and were quickly applied to the emergence of the earl of March. Ripley's visions of conflicting humours, conveyed in vivid allegories, were easily applied to the recent political conflicts, and his vision of the regenerating sun and the balance it brought became the key motifs at the start of Edward's reign. Barker too, in his albeit more chemical treatise, described the making of gold and silver in this way: 'Thus we make peace between the elements so that they be fixed and steadfast.'[42]

Most of Ripley's writings are undated, but he hints in the preface to the *Compound of Alchemy* in 1471 that a large body of his work was written in the previous two decades. These works are full of symbols. As Ripley himself put it, 'all secrets are formed from an image'. These verbal and visual symbols represent conflict, which could be applied to the years preceding Edward's assumption of the throne. They include images of fighting lions, the conflict between the sun and moon, choler and phlegm, or water and earth. This conflict results in a disintegration of the four elements into an unresolved primordial chaos, the *nigredo*, represented by such symbols that occur in the *Ripley Scrolls*, as the black raven and the spitting dragon. Ripley's vision, however, is of a vegetative regenerative myth, and from the slaying of the dragon emerges a rebirth symbolized by the *uroboros*, the serpent devouring its own tail. From the slaughter of the dragon of chaos, with its echoes of the fertility myth of St George and the dragon and the civil unrest of the 1450s, emerges the reborn sun. Edward appears to have identified himself with this myth of the king emerging from the death of the dragon of chaos. In a fifteenth-century collection of saints' prophecies proclaiming the coming of Edward occurs St Germayn's prediction of one called Edward who is 'a dragon and he should have wings'. The dragon biting its tail represented Mercury, the beginning and end of the alchemical work. John Cokkys, who copied Edward's *Secreta secretorum*, included marginal line decorations containing alchemical symbols. One of these is an illustration of a crowned, bearded king. Above him there is a scroll with oak leaves and an acorn, symbols of monarchy, but the lower half of the king's body is a serpent's tail, to suggest the philosopher king's emergence from the dragon of chaos.[43]

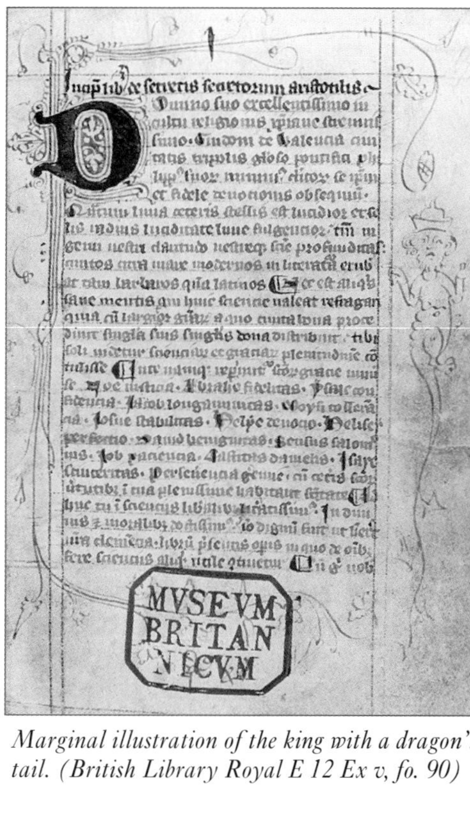

Marginal illustration of the king with a dragon's tail. (British Library Royal E 12 Ex v, fo. 90)

The *Ripley Scrolls* also depict the chemical production of gold. John of Rupescissa had written in the first half of the fourteenth century in *De consideratione quintae essentiae* about extracting the quintessence, the secret of secrets, from antimony, the mercasite of lead, and this was the grey wolf that devoured the impurities from molten gold in the form of a scum called the *balneum regis*, the bath of the king. The bath is shown in the *Ripley Scroll* together with the green and red lions, which, though usually taken to refer to mercury and sulphur, are more likely to apply to antimony.[44] The scroll, on the most practical alchemical level, depicts the conflict between antimony (lupus) and gold (sol), a necessary struggle that produces refined gold, the quintessence. However, given the wide knowledge of the cognomens of *Lupus* and *Sol* for Henry VI and Edward IV, it is likely that the *Ripley Scroll* would be readily interpreted as a depiction of the necessary war between the Houses of York and Lancaster. Out of the *balneum regis* emerged the resplendent gold of the new king of England.

The most important of all these symbols, and the one of most direct political relevance to Edward, was the sun revolving in the sky like a wheel, resolving undifferentiated chaos and the conflicting four elements. Ripley drew circular diagrams showing the sun's path through the heavens, which became known as 'Ripley's wheel': 'Turn around the wheel of the elements. See that thou beest diligent in turning the philosophik wheel, that thou mayest make water out of earth, air out of water, fire out of air, or earth out of fire.'[45] From the turning of the wheel there emerges 'a perfect white',[46] the colour of the Yorkist rose. This wheel of alchemy was the wheel of the four elements turning into the wheel of the sun rolling around the heavens. It becomes identical with the sun god or hero who submits to the arduous labour of the passion of self-creation.[47] In describing the culmination of the alchemical process in terms of the myth of the sun, Ripley employed poetic imagery concerned with youth, the regenerative power of the young spring sun, flowers and springtime, which all had a direct application to the emergence of the young earl of March in 1461 and closely paralleled the imagery of flowers, gardens and spring used in the poetry of this period celebrating Edward's accession. Ripley, like Bacon, described the sun as the most beneficent of the planets, with warm, temperate but not disruptive heat. The sun, he wrote, shines in his own sphere after an eclipse in redness and glory 'as king to rayne upon all metals'. This sun was equated with youthful vigorous kingship. In the *Vision* ascribed to Ripley and Dastin it is written: 'And to comfort his brethren that were doleful the sun hath risen without war and strife. The bright moon when she was at the full to he his mother and his wedded wife in time of ver [spring] the season vegetative yea aright when Titan doth appear.'[48] This sun king is the embodiment of youthful purity and Ripley writes: 'All this I found in the book before me. And in this book I find written as prophets made mention how that there was once a mighty king clear of nature and complexion, devoid of deformity from head to foot.'[49] This is the sun which bestows life and dispels phlegmatic humours. In the *Ripley Scrolls* the sun is shown bursting through dark clouds. This image would become explicitly associated with Edward's badge.

Ripley closely associated the culmination of the alchemical work, the birth of the sun, with the flowering of a garden in spring and this too became closely connected with Edward's public image. In the *Mystery of the Alchemists* he writes:

> in the season of the yeare when the Sun waxeth warme,
> Freshly and fragrante the flowers do grow.

There is also a direct association between the reborn Sun King and spring gardens and the white rose motifs which occur in the poetry of this period. In his *Bosom Book* Ripley writes:

'this is the pleasant and dainty garden of the philosophers, which beareth the sweet smelling roses white and red, abbreviated out of all the work of the philosophers'. In the *Cantilena* he describes the birth of the sun king 'whom God had crowned in Glory, acquell with the sun' as 'fragrant as the prim-rose flower', 'white as the lily flower' and as 'fresh as any flower wyth a mantle of everlasting brightness'.[50] This association of the culmination of the alchemical process and flowers with the young Edward IV was to include the Yorkist white rose itself. In the *Cantilena* the climax of the work occurs when all colours unite in *albedo* (white), when all the colours separated out of the chaos, the *maisa confusa*, are brought back to unity and oneness in the *albedo*, the white rose. Norton in the *Ordinal of Alchemy* wrote

> for everie colour which maie be thought,
> Shall heere appeare before the white be wrought.[51]

The work is finally brought to a conclusion when the white and red sulphur are joined, which is described as the rose of alchemy, red within and white without.

The culmination of the great work of alchemy is the emergence of the sun with all its regenerative power. This virile sun is the product of the union of *Sol* and *Luna* and is symbolized by the emergence of the feathered king from the dragon of chaos, from elemental humoral and political conflict, perched on a globe, a mandala symbol of wholeness that is both psychological and political. The feathered king, in the context of these rolls, contemporary with Edward's emergence, bears a resemblance to the Yorkist falcon.[52] This is the bird celebrated by Ripley in 1476 in his *Marrow of Alchemy*: 'consider the noble bird which when the son is in Aries [Edward was born near the time of Aries] beginneth to fly – not corrupted by mortal man. This is our stone.'[53] This stone or globe represents the reborn and united nation, the stone that Ripley (depicted at the foot of many versions of the *Ripley Scroll* facing a king) would have promised the young Edward.[54] These images of wholeness occurring in Ripley's works – circles, roses and globes – were given Trinitarian significance. In his letter to Edward IV Ripley promised to disclose to him the secret of perfect elixirs red and white, not by writing but by word of mouth, and added: 'I will then worke by grace of the Trinite'.[55] The Trinity of three suns, three kingdoms or crowns, echoes the alchemical trinity of body, soul and spirit repeated throughout the *Ripley Scroll*. This Trinity, when integrated with the sun and the body politic, implies a psychological and political unity:

A sun in splendour bursts through the clouds and the feathered king (resembling the Yorkist falcon) is perched on the philosopher's stone. (Ripley Scroll, *Bodley Roll 1*)

The king, queen and the son. The alchemical Trinity. (British Library Egerton 845, fo. Iv)

A similitude even thereto like,
and according to the Trinity
Our medicine is made of thinges three–
there be persons three made our Trinity:
a similitude like unto our stone.

When Edward IV commented on the threefold Trinitarian significance of the three suns in the sky and thereafter dedicated himself to the Trinity, it is probable that he intended an alchemical significance. The principle of this integration was communicated by Ripley through the symbolism of the incestuous marriage of the sun and the moon. With this marriage there is a harnessing of the warring choler and phlegm, fire and water, which partly refers to the ending of the conflict of 1459–61 and specifically alludes to the balance to be found in the new king, who has all the virility, vigour and capacity to heal, restore and bless his kingdom that were lacking in the one-sided, phlegmatic and feminine Henry VI. The function of the king in reconciling the opposing humours may be commemorated in the royal arms of England: the white lion (nature) and the antelope (spirit),[56] which occur on sixteenth-century wooden panel portraits of Edward IV, the white lion and white hind (Edward V) and the white lion and white greyhound (Henry VII), which face Bishop Oliver's King Chantry in Windsor, Edward IV's foundation. The unicorn counterbalancing the white lion appeared in Scottish arms and was used by James I.

Although the *Ripley Scrolls* were probably first intended to bring about the reinvigoration of Henry VI, they constituted a two-pronged attack. While addressing the possibility of curing Henry VI, they encompassed a new hope in the young Edward.[57] In both the *Secreta secretorum* and the *Ripley Scrolls* there was plenty of material to bolster a usurpation, a change of dynasty, by a young man who identified himself with the sun and the white rose. The *Ripley Scrolls* would therefore soon be reapplied and adapted to Edward IV's arrival and their imagery was assimilated into genealogical histories to provide an alchemical rationale for the new reign. Much of the imagery occurring in the *Illustrated Life of Edward IV* can be seen as an attempt to integrate biblical prophecies with the events surrounding Edward IV's accession from 1459 to 1461, and with Ripley's alchemical allegories of the birth of the sun king, who like the biblical prophets delivered his people from the dark alembic of civil war. Throughout the pictorial narrative showing the exile of the people of Israel, the impending delivery of the chosen people parallels the progress of Edward to the throne, and this is accompanied by images of alchemical conflict. Moses (described by Bacon in the *Secreta secretorum* and by Ripley as the original founder of the science of alchemy) is shown before the burning bush of gold in which shine the three faces of God, opposite the illustration of Edward's vision of the three suns. Moses' rod (Exod. 78–12) which changed into a serpent is echoed in the *Ripley Scrolls* in the staff borne by Ripley, who in some versions of the scroll faces a king, probably Edward. In a diagram of Ripley's wheel appearing in a collection of his writing once owned by John Dee there is a note comparing the alchemist to Moses which says 'he brought water out of the stone and did out the most hard rock'.[58] In the *Illustrated Life of Edward IV* Moses is depicted tending sheep (the traditional pose of Hermes, the first alchemist); behind are two wrestling figures and two fighting rams, symbolizing the conflict between the elements. The series culminates in an illustration of the seating of Reason on a wheel of fortune, surrounded by prophets and saints who had foretold the coming of Edward IV. One is a crowned king with two faces holding in one hand a raven and in the other a serpent. Identified as the cardinal virtue of Prudence it is in fact a composite figure heavily influenced by images in Ripley's writings and the *Ripley Scrolls* of the hermaphrodite king integrating the opposites of male and female, *Sol* and *Luna*, triumphing over the forces of chaos and emerging from the *nigredo*. The sky is dominated by the image of three suns, echoed by the appearance of the angel bearing the word 'Sol', Edward's cognomen and the most important symbol of alchemy. The coronation

The hermaphrodite king perched on a globe, symbol of integrated wholeness, devours his wing to show that like the uroboros, *he is the beginning and end of God's divine plan. (Ashmole Roll 53)*

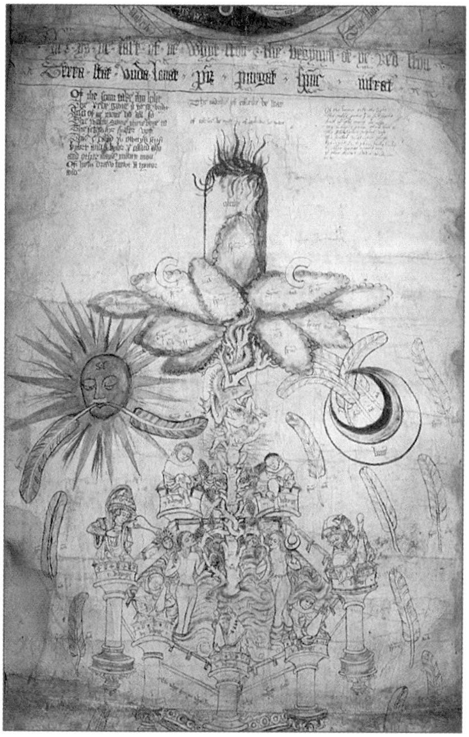

Around the tree of life and Melusine (mercury) occurs the conjunction of the sun and moon. The sun in splendour was to become Edward IV's most important badge, and the image of Luna *in* Sol*'s embrace recurs in such Yorkist texts as* The Prophetic History of Britain. *(Bodley Roll 1)*

of Edward on the throne of reason is therefore the culmination of the alchemical work, the manifestation of gold. The three suns in the sky also represent the Trinity, Edward's other personal motto. The image of the sun and the interlocking circles, apart from representing the parhelia, bear a close resemblance to images in the *Ripley Scrolls* of the crescent moon around the sun symbolizing the conjunction of the sun and moon, the marriage of opposites. The interlocking of three circles in one is also an obvious reference to Edward's other personal emblem, the Trinity, and is a mandala representing integration. These great wheels in the sky may also allude to the wheel of alchemy (Ripley's wheel). In the *Compound of Alchemy* Ripley retrospectively applied in 1471 the turning of this wheel to the circumstances of Edward's assumption, his exaltation into gold. He refers to the turning around of the wheel of the sun as it began its circulation in the west and moved into the south until its exaltation: 'It begins in the west and maketh consummation in the south.' This alludes to the appearance of the three suns in the west and the exaltation of Edward's triumphant entry into London. The victorious voyage of the sun (Edward), Christ and the stone, to ascendancy on the throne of heaven is schematically drawn in Ripley's wheel.[59] It is therefore probable that the wheel of fortune on which reason sits also symbolizes the wheel of alchemy, the revolving wheel of the elements which through the agency of the sun has brought about the fulfilment of the alchemical work, the creation of Edward's kingdom.

Little now remains to convey the impact of the imagery of the sun in splendour, the white rose, the falcon and other Yorkist emblems that dominated the stained-glass windows of churches and domestic buildings in this period. A few fragments of suns, roses and angels remain in Fotheringay's collegiate church, and nearby parish churches such as King's Cliffe, to where the glass was dispersed in the eighteenth century. The most powerful surviving example of this imagery, much of it with alchemical connotations, can be seen in a window in the chancel of Tattershall parish church; this window was originally placed in the nave in 1482 by Bishop Waynflete. The rest of the glass was removed to St Martin's church, Stamford, and Burleigh House in around 1772 but what remains is still an arresting display of the sun in splendour, the angel, the rising sun, the dragon, the eagle and falcon, some in tear-shaped vessels that may be alchemical. The impact of even this mere portion of what once existed is strikingly reminiscent of the imagery of the *Ripley Scrolls*. Edward may have had a special connection with the church and the castle. An anonymous *Lament for the Soul of Edward IV* has the dead king reflecting 'I knew not to whom I purchasyd Tatersayle'.[60]

Alchemical ideas were not just applied to the resolution of the conflicts of the 1450s in the crowning of Edward IV. The political history of Britain recent and ancient was seen in terms

A detail of Edward IV in front of the rose et soleil *in the Royal window of Canterbury Cathedral. (Geoffrey Wheeler)*

of alchemical conflicts. A fifteenth-century collection of fifty-nine alchemical treatises, including the works of Bacon, ends with a genealogy including historical notes of kings of England to Richard III. An astronomical calendar was provided which shows that the compiler of this manuscript saw the whole of recent English history from the humiliation of Richard II in 1387 to Edward's accession as a gradual resolution of the power of the sun.[61]

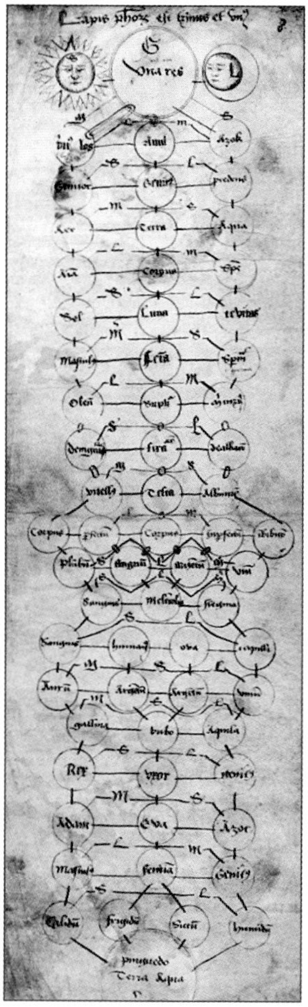

An alchemical table in the form of a genealogy is entitled The Philosopher's Stone. *An evolution occurs from the* nigredo *(representing various combinations of earth, water, sulphur and mercury) through the humours of the different nations to Adam, the first king. The climax occurs with the stone itself, a circle surrounded by the sun and moon. Inside the circle there is a letter, possible E for Edward or more probably G for* genus *(race). (British Library Egerton 845, fo. 21)*

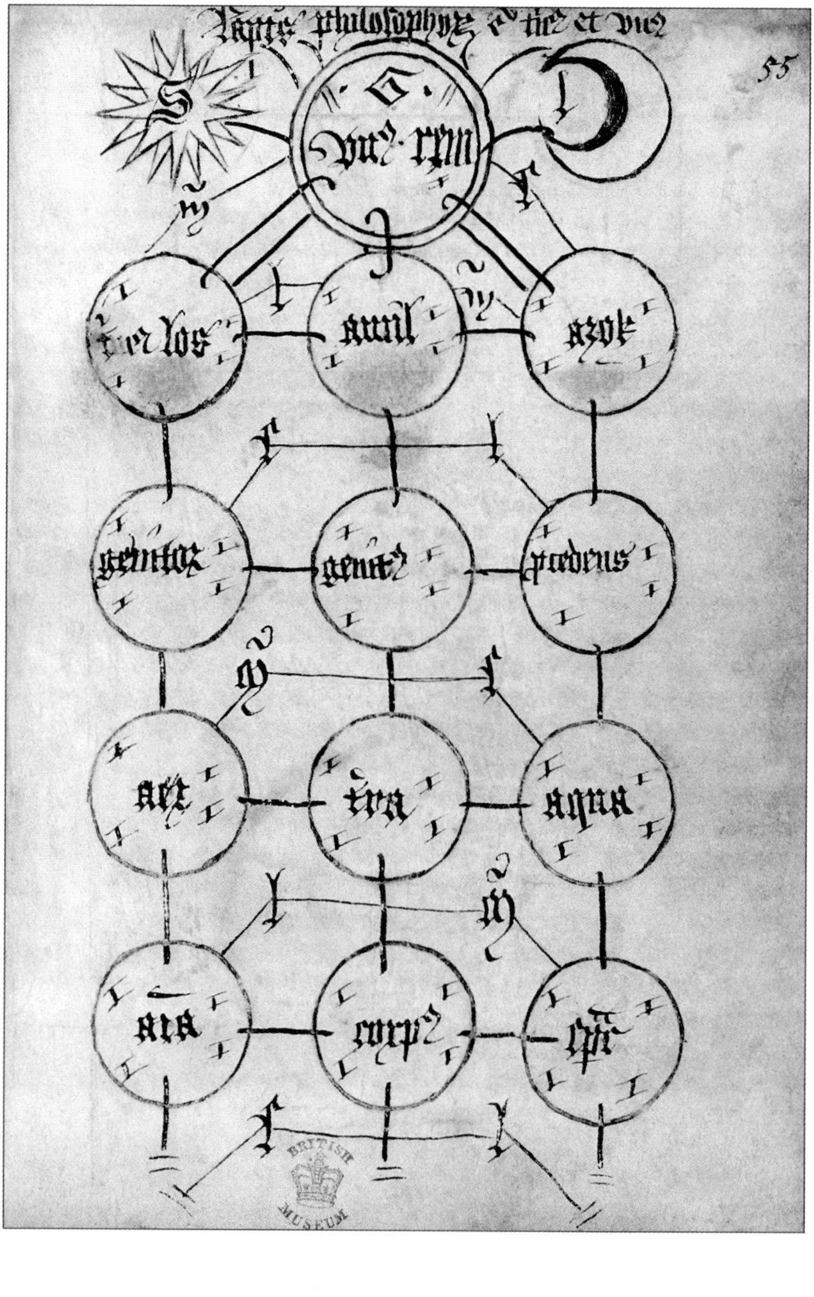

This alchemical/ genealogical table depicts an evolution from the soul, body and spirit, through the elements, to silver and gold, represented by the sun and moon. Inside the circle representing the culmination of the alchemical process (reminiscent of the circle at the foot of Edward's Coronation Roll*) there is a letter, either E or G, and the inscriptions 'one truth' and 'the Trinity three and one'. (British Library Harley 2407, fo. 55)*

Heraldry could reinforce this view, for 'The sonne shyning' was one of the badges used by Richard II. It appears small and inconspicuous on his Great Seal and was emblazoned large on the sail of the ship in which he returned from Ireland. In this calendar there is a table 'to know which particular planet reigns showing the movement of the sun from 1385 to 1461'. The large number of sexual images in alchemy encouraged the perception of a close parallel between marriage, sex and genealogy in alchemical experiments. The long genealogical history of marriages and alliances culminating in Edward's reign was seen in terms of the various combinations of elements and metals that occurred in the alchemist's furnace. Genealogical trees were even constructed in this period showing the evolution of the philosopher's stone out of the four elements. The original inspiration for such trees was probably the manuscript of the *Testamentum* executed for the alchemy commission with the curing of Henry VI in mind, and which had such an influence on Ripley. This manuscript contains a number of tables showing the evolution of elements (each given a letter) from the *materia confusa* to the *materia perfecta*.[62] One late fifteenth-century manuscript of alchemical recipes containing some of Ripley's works includes all the images that occur in the *Ripley Scrolls*, such as the serpent in the tree of knowledge, the birth of the sun, the conjunction of the sun and moon, the sun surrounded by concentric circles of the moon (which also occurs in the *Illustrated Life of Edward IV*), the dove showering golden semen, and the serpent holding the sun and moon in its mouth.[63] It also contains a genealogical tree showing the different stages of alchemical evolution, physical and political. The tree starts with the *nigredo* (undifferentiated chaos) and proceeds to the conflicting four elements through to the various combinations of the sanguine, melancholy and phlegmatic humours, which lead to the three nations France (sanguine), England (phlegmatic) and Britain (melancholy). This leads to the Trinity of body, soul and spirit, the three elements of air, fire and water; and the tree culminates in a circle around a letter that may be a G for *genus* (origin or stock) or an E, the inspiration for many of the prophecies adapted in this period to the coming of Edward IV. Either side of this circle are the images of sun and moon.[64] This tree, the model for an alchemical genealogy in a 1493 manuscript headed 'The philosopher's stone is first and last', culminates in the same circle with the inscription 'One truth'.[65] This manuscript contains a delicate line drawing of an idealized king bestowing blessings, with his queen and their son, the alchemical trinity, and a globe.[66] On another page there is a genealogy from God to the stone showing various alliances of fire, metals and elements. This manuscript too has some extracts from Ripley's works (the *Cantilena*) and diagrams taken from the *Ripley Scrolls*.

If genealogical models were used to demonstrate alchemical processes, the reverse also occurred and the genealogical evolution of families through British history culminating in the arrival of Edward IV was explained in terms of alchemical transmutation. Two genealogical rolls showing the influence of alchemy throughout are the work of the compiler of the *Prophetic History of Britain*.[67] One of the earliest of these rolls was written in 1464 and shows the descent from Adam to Edward IV, whose marriage to Elizabeth, the daughter of a child of St Pol, is mentioned.[68] At the top of the roll, which I shall call the *Genealogy of Edward King of Britain (2)*[69], there is a stylized drawing of seven circles within a larger circle bound by a square formed by four more circles. The meaning of the separate circles is explained: they are representations of the seven days of creation from the primordial chaos, the creation of light from darkness, followed by the creation of the four elements, the sun, moon and stars, and finally the creation of man out of earth in God's image. In the fourth book of Boethius's *Consolations of Philosophy* there is an image of concentric circles explaining the roles of providence and fate. In the margin a fifteenth-century hand has written in French 'this passes understanding'. Surrounding these circles, at the top of the

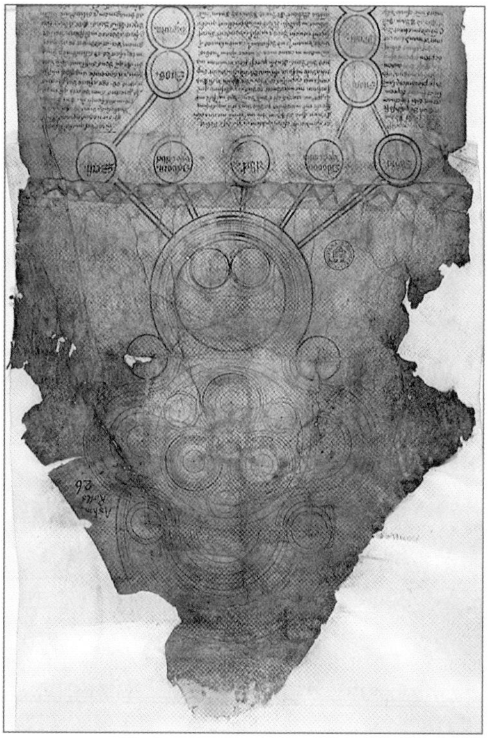

The interconnecting circles revealing the hand of the prime mover which leads to the lines of Seth and Japheth. This shows the hand of God behind Edward's eventual accession. The image is related to the diagram on the floor of Westminster Abbey where Edward was crowned. (Ashmole Roll 26)

roll, are the squares representing the four elements. Squaring the circle is an alchemical image of unity and wholeness in which there is the eternal fellowship of the order of the angels, promised to all men who will be saved. This unity is realized at the foot of the roll in the coming of Edward. A key influence in the execution of these circular alchemical diagrams is again Kirkeby's copy of the *Testamentum*, which has a number of these diagrams of concentric circles surrounded by more circles forming a square to show the working of the divine will.[70] There is a distant echo of this diagram in the representations of the ascendancy of the sun known as 'Ripley's Wheel'.[71] The Welsh compiler of the *Prophetic History of Britain* and the genealogical rolls anticipating Edward's coming compiled another genealogy in *c.* 1471 which I shall entitle the *Genealogy of Edward, King of Britain(3)*.[72] This contains an account of the creation of the world and Adam and Eve, accompanied by a similar diagram with more intricate and interlaced circles. Throughout this roll (which is nearly twenty feet long) the theme is the unravelling of an intricate divine plan from the dawn of the cosmos at the top of the tree through the unravelling of the complex genealogical relationships, the interconnected destinies of the tribes of Israel and the nations of Troy, Saxon England, France and Britain to the consummation of God's 'great work' of alchemy in the coronation of Edward IV and the realization of the British nation in 1461.

This ceremony occurred in the chancel of Westminster Abbey on a Cosmati pavement constructed by abbot Richard Ware as part of Henry III's redecoration of the abbey in preparation for the translation of Edward IV's namesake, Edward the Confessor, in 1269. The fifteenth-century inscription explains how the pattern conveyed a sacred genealogy, a cosmology of the relationship between the elements of the physical and spiritual world and a key to the working of the *primum mobile*, the motivating force of the universe. This is represented in a complex geometric and mathematical diagram of interconnecting circles and squares representing the act of creation and the movement of the planets and spheres around the earth. By the time of Edward's accession in 1460 (according to the Gregorian calendar) and coronation in July 1461 the pavement had acquired complex alchemical significance. Richard Sporley in his 1450 annotations to John Flete's text on the pavement regarded the central disc of Egyptian onyx (veined like the earth) as a microcosm revealing the pattern of the universe as the inscription promised because it contained within itself the colours of the four elements in the undifferentiated form of the *prima materia*. Four was a significant number because it appears in the inscription revealing the date of the pavement's construction and the four elements in the shape of four roundels surround the *prima*

The golden chain, Cathena aurea, *of the four elements and their qualities in harmony found in a fifteenth-century collection of the alchemical writings of the fourteenth-century alchemist, John Dastin. This resembles the circular conclusion to the golden chain of Edward IV's* Coronation Roll. *(British Library Sloane 2476)*

materia. Together before the high altar they form five, the quintessence or Christ manifested in the mass celebrated at the coronation. The other significant number is sixty, also emphasized in the inscription of the date of the pavement. The central circle is surrounded by a ring of sixty lozenges each covering an angle of six degrees. The pavement is bestrewn with hexagrams and hexagons symbolizing God's creation of the world in six days and Capgrave, as we have seen, emphasized the numerological significance of Edward's accession in 1460.

The coronation occurred on the throne of the Confessor in the centre of this squared magic circle surrounded by numerical symbols of the four elements. Either side of Edward as he received his crown above the central roundel of the *prima materia* representing the chaos of the recent civil war was, to the north the element of water, the seven-sided polygon of the moon in her seven phases, and to the south the element of fire, represented by the alchemical symbol of *Sol*, a circle with a black marble disc in the centre, the cognomen of Edward IV himself. The surrounding circles showing the movement of the planets and heavenly spheres represent the *uroboros*, the fulfilment of the Divine plan. This was the alchemical consummation of the age of gold out of the primordial chaos of creation, and through the tangled forces of fortune and history. It was a drama enacted before an alchemical painting showing God, in the form of a king, beginning the great work by creating heaven and hell. This divine king emerges from a sunburst to bless three interconnecting circles and a crescent moon, providing a potent allusion to the parhelion of Mortimer's Cross. The painting, seen by Ashmole in 1652 on an arch in the abbey behind statues of English monarchs and incorporated in the form of a brass engraving in the *Theatrum Chemicum Britannicum* can still be seen in fifteenth-century form in alchemical manuscripts that reveal a close relationship with images in the *Ripley Scrolls* and *The Illustrated Life of Edward IV*.[73]

This ceremony must have left a profound impression on alchemists like George Ripley. Ripley was a frequent visitor to the abbey and wrote ironically in his chapter on putrefaction in *The Compound of Alchemy* on dubious alchemists who congregated in the abbey daily. He was also moved to incorporate the diagram of the pavement into his cosmologically inspired diagrammatic representation of the workings of the Divine primum mobile through the four elements, which became known as *Ripley's Wheel*.[74] The same motif was incorporated, perhaps under Ripley's influence, into the genealogies celebrating Edward's accession and coronation. The circles of the pavement are placed at the head of genealogical rolls depicting archetypal platonic forms, and the subsequent genealogy becomes a focus for alchemical meditation on the Divine mind, the physical processes of creation from chaos, which takes on a political as well as a philosophical and scientific dimension.

The most colourful and eloquent depiction of Edward's descent occurs in a manuscript commissioned by him to commemorate his coronation. This roll, nearly twenty feet long and decorated with gold leaf, is a magnificent sight when unfurled to its full length. Such an impressive object may have fulfilled two purposes: to reinforce the belief and resolve of Edward's followers, but also to win new converts to his cause. Too expensive to be displayed in the open air, it would have perhaps been displayed at council meetings in Westminster Palace or in an ecclesiastical centre where public rituals took place, such as Westminster Abbey or St Paul's Cathedral. The roll shows the whole course of history from Adam and Eve to the coronation of Edward earl of March alongside his family tree, and uses a series of images, some possibly derived from Ripley, to suggest that this vast historical drama had been an alchemical process culminating in the emergence of a united kingdom under the son of York. The pictorial narrative of this roll, which I shall entitle the *Coronation Roll*, even bears a similarity to that of the *Ripley Scroll*. At the head of the roll is an image of God in a blazing sun shining through a tree in the garden of Eden, which is similar to the tree and

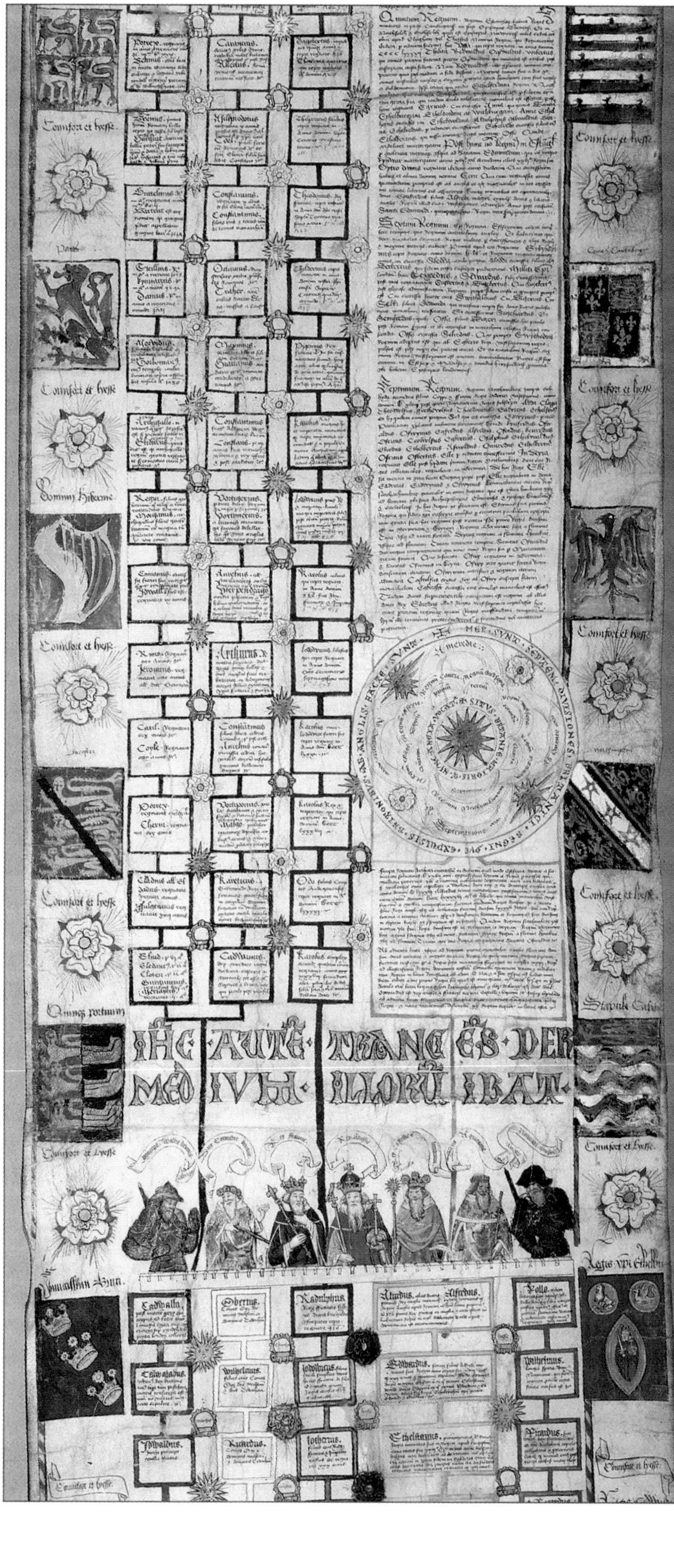

The Coronation Roll *shows the disintegration of Brutus's realm into seven kingdoms after the Saxon invasions. This is represented by a circular diagram of the chaos of the* prima materia, *echoing similar representations in other Yorkist genealogies such as* The Genealogy of Edward King of Britain. *Signs of the eventual fruition of God's divine work in the coming of Edward are provided in the images of the white rose and the sun in splendour within this circle of chaos. Representations of the rulers of the principalities of Wales, the duchies of Cornwall, Normandy and Aquitaine, and the kingdoms of France and England, all of which will be united under Edward IV, follow this. (Philadelphia Free Library E 201)*

fountain (of eternal youth) in the *Ripley Scroll*. Down the tree, on either side of which are a naked Adam and Eve (similar to *Sol* and *Luna*, the royal pair in the *Ripley Scroll*), slides a half-human serpent upside down. Although the half-human serpent is a common image, occurring for example in the *Tres Riches Heures* of the Duc de Berry, this particular representation bears a close resemblance to Melusine, the serpent woman, in the *Ripley Scrolls*. Near the winged serpent is the cross of St George with the Yorkist fetterlock, which Edward assumed after his father's death. Beside this roundel illustrating the fall of man occurs the name St George and his arms, again with the Yorkist fetterlock, perhaps alluding to the dragon-slaying king of the *Ripley Scrolls* (Edward IV himself).

The fall of man is followed by a roundel depicting the flood with Noah and his wife in an ark resembling a fifteenth-century ship above which flies a raven. In alchemical terms this represents a regression to the original chaos, the formless leaden waters before creation alluded to in the text from the beginning of Genesis occurring at the top of the roll, the reduction of God's work to the *prima materia*, the waters of chaos. Alchemists sometimes conceived themselves as Noah floating on the sea of turbulent metals: Ripley in *The Compound of Alchemy* warned 'make fire and beware of the flood of Noah, wherein many men are blind'. He saw the fruition of his work in terms of the receding of the flood and the flourishing of the grapes of Noah's vineyard, which is akin to the flourishing of Noah's family tree in this roll. As the waters recede the raven, symbol of the *nigredo*, flies away only to symbolically return with the disintegration of Britain under the Saxon invasions. This is commemorated in a circular diagram of the division of the ancient kingdom of Britain into seven kingdoms forming a series of interlocking circles. This is very similar to the diagram of seven circles within a large circle that begins the *Genealogy of Edward King of Britain*, which explains the original creation of unity out of chaos.[75] A verbal account of this subject occurs at the top of the *Coronation Roll*. The message is clear in both rolls: the division of the once united Britain into seven kingdoms, like the recent conflicts of the Wars of the Roses, went against the purposes of God. The alchemists were in tune with this divine plan and aspired to realize this original unity. The diagram of the seven circles in the *Coronation Roll* serves another purpose: within this disintegration (the *nigredo*) there are seeds of renewal and rebirth. The circles revolve around a blazing sun, describing a circle that runs back on itself, like the head of the serpent that bites its own tail, the *uroboros*. On either side of this sun occur emblems of the sun, alluding to the parhelia, and a white rose to suggest that despite such disintegration there will be a reconciliation with the coming of Edward.

The role of Edward as a Christlike visionary and redeemer of the land is stressed with the gold letter text around the map of the seven Saxon kingdoms from Luke 4.30. 'But Jesus, passing through the middle of them, went his way.' This refers to Christ's safe passage through a group of hostile Pharisees who had sought his destruction. Its placement between the banners of the Cinque Ports (the ports of south-east England) and Calais would evoke memories of Edward's flight to Calais in 1459 and his return in the summer of 1460 and would suggest that his flight and triumphant return were preordained. The sense that Edward was inspired by religious vision is reinforced by the prominence at the top of the roll, opposite the banner of St George, of a banner of three golden crowns on a red background; the arms of the devout king of the East Saxons, King Sebbi (d. 694 AD). Sebbi was guided into the next world by a vision of the Trinity, three shining men. The depiction of Edward's vision of the Trinity at Mortimer's Cross in the *Coronation Roll*, three golden crowns in the sky, echoes King Sebbi's vision. Another parallel to Edward's vision and his close identification with Christ and the sun is provided in the *Coronation Roll* by the inclusion of the arms of the emperor Constantine, who was told in a dream to place the first two letters of the name of Christ on his troops' shields and who before the battle with his rival Maxentius in AD 312 saw in the sky a brilliant light in the form of a cross superimposed on the sun with the words 'in this sign you will be victor'.[76]

At this point in the roll we are in the realm of prophecy and vision. A series of half portraits introduces Edward's descent from the Prince of Wales, the Duke of Cornwall, the King of France, the King of England, the King of Castile, the Duke of Aquitaine and the Duke of Normandy. Once the united kingdom of Britain has disappeared the lines of descent split between Britain/Wales and the Saxon kings of England until the Norman conquest, which represented another invasion and a further loss of British identity. It may not be too fanciful to suggest that the large black bird perched on the gold Yorkist fetterlock enclosing a rose and a cross of St George may not be an oxidized falcon but a reappearance of the raven that flew from the ark, signifying that the Saxon and Norman conquests have reduced the ancient kingdom of Britain to the primal chaos of the *nigredo*, while holding out the hope of the coming of the age of gold with the son of March.

This theme is played out in the genealogy to the right of the *Coronation Roll* which shows Edward IV's Welsh ancestry. This is celebrated with a pair of roundels containing a red dragon representing the Welsh and a white dragon representing the Saxons, which alludes to the prophecy of Merlin of the defeat of the Saxons by the Welsh achieved under Edward IV and which also celebrates the blending of the Welsh and the Mortimer lines (an alchemical compound) when Ralph Mortimer, Lord of Wigmore, married Gwladys Ddu, daughter of Llewelyn the Great, prince of Gwynedd. Nearly all the images of the sun occur along the Mortimer line. Beside Roger Mortimer the white lion, emblem of the Mortimer earls of March, holds the banner of Constantine and the arms of Edmund duke of York occur with his motto 'without fear' and an image of a peacock with unfolding tail, symbol of immortality, associated with Edmund the Martyr, whose arms occur nearby, but also the alchemical symbol for the tincture, the display of colours that presages the culmination of the work.[77] This is achieved when the Mortimer line converges with that of Henry III in the coming of Edward IV. The links in the chain leading up to this event have been formed from a golden chain (*cantena aurea*) of the four elements made into interlinked circles and squares. This golden chain of alchemy, which links together the four elements, occurs in a fifteenth-century collection of alchemical works by the early fourteenth-century English alchemist John Dastin, once owned by John Dee.[78] The same chain was referred to by Fortescue in *On the Law of Nature* when arguing against the succession in the female line (from Lionel duke of Clarence). He wrote that everything that exists has a cause going back to God and this was the golden chain suspended from heaven to earth that Macrobius spoke about in the *Dream of Scipio*. By such a chain a king and his kingdom hang, and if one descends through the female line the whole chain from this point falls to earth.[79] The chain in the *Coronation Roll*, however, culminates in a square formed by the rose and the fetterlock representing the four elements that have been at war.[80] This is made into a circle by another square formed by four images of the ascendant sun to form the quintessence. The squared circle is the alchemical symbol for the completion of the work. This circle and the arms of Neville interspersed with the white rose and Edward's motto 'comfort and joy' suggest the evolution of an age of joy, of gold, something that Bacon, in Edward's copy of the *Secreta secretorum*, recommended that a prince could achieve through a combination of diet and lifestyle. Such an optimistic anticipation of a time of unity, peace and stability is symbolized in the image of the young king, golden and resplendent on horseback, at the head of this roll above the image of God. Contemplated in its entirety the scroll appears to be a gigantic, intricate golden chain from God to Edward, beginning with a literal depiction of the divine hand of God with the inscriptions 'the right hand of God gives strength' and 'this is the Lord's doing'. Around Edward himself is a gold letter inscription from the first chapter of the Gospel of St John which sums up the divine circular nature of God's great work. 'In the beginning was the word and the word was with God and God was the word. The same was in the beginning.' Around the roundel showing Christ in an ascendant sun (itself an allusion to Edward's messianic destiny) there is the condensation of Revelations 1.8 which sums up the alchemists' sense of Edward's coronation as the fulfilment of the divine wheel or *uroboros*: 'I am the beginning and the end, says the Lord God almighty.' The roll ends with Edward within four blazing suns set in a circle signifying the philosopher's stone. Symbols of the coronation surround the motif, including three crowns and sceptres for the three realms of Britain, France and Spain, ostrich feathers, a badge of the prince of Wales, from whom Edward claimed descent, and garters representing the Order of the Garter. The text within the garters proclaims 'This was the Lord's doing', and nearby is the proclamation 'Edward by the grace of God, King'. In its newly restored state the scroll is illuminated by gold leaf which lights up the images of Edward, Christ and the badge of the blazing sun, showing his coronation to be an alchemical triumph.

The God image of a young king, a beautiful youth and redeemer, is a heroic archetype found by alchemists in the *prima materia* of what we would call the unconscious (what St Augustine in his *Confessions* had called the great mystery of human life, the human memory). They projected this image of the contents of their unconscious on to Edward IV as the search for the transmutation of gold acquired a political significance. In its quest for wholeness and completeness alchemy became a transformative mystery that rescued man from the animal collective psyche dominated in the 1450s by anxieties about chaos and civil war. This was achieved through alchemy's capacity to actualize the soul's potential to form links between the spirit (mind) and matter (body), to initiate a dialogue between the alchemical trinity of spirit, soul and body, which would produce heroic myths and images. An indication of its power can be seen in the beautiful line drawings of the alchemical trinity of the king, queen and their son found in a late fifteenth-century collection of alchemical texts showing the rebirth of the sun king after the incestuous marriage.[81] Alchemy was a flourishing scientific philosophy that explained matter and the soul, the source of the prominent images of the age, all coalescing around the redemptive figure of Edward IV.

The alchemical interpretation of the political life of fifteenth-century England, coinciding with the arrival of alchemical literature at the beginning of that century, was unique and anticipates the way King Charles II, who had his own laboratory, returned to the throne with alchemical concepts of regeneration that were applied to the Restoration. The alchemists who accompanied him maintained that only a king acting as alchemist to a troubled national body could incorporate fire and water into a marriage of opposites to make universal peace. For the seventeenth century as well as the fifteenth, both periods of shifting alliances with conflicting claims to inspire truth, only alchemy provided a language of authenticity to reach the incorruptible gold in men.[82]

The proliferation of alchemical wisdom and symbolism in the political forum demonstrates the way in which the early years of Edward IV's reign represented a golden age of alchemy. His court was a magnet for distinguished alchemists, philosophers and physicians. The Elizabethan alchemist Samuel Norton, in his *Key of Alchemy*, described Edward as a great patron of alchemists in the tradition of Alexander and King Kalide, the patron of Morienus.[83] According to Norton there were seven great alchemists at the court of Edward IV, four religious and three laymen.[84] One of the three laymen was Norton's great-grandfather, Thomas Norton of Bristol. Norton was born in about 1433 in Colne, Wiltshire, and took up alchemy in the 1450s, for which he was probably disinherited by his father, Walter Norton. When Norton reached the age of twenty-eight in 1461 his master agreed to reveal to him the secret recipe for making the stone. Norton soon after gained a prominent position in the royal household as a gentleman of Edward's privy chamber.[85] He was therefore a squire of the household in constant attendance on the king and employed in confidential offices as occasion required. His new position was acknowledged by his father, who restored him to his inheritance in 1466.[86] One of the other lay alchemists may have been Norton's master, who as Samuel Norton pointed out, may not have been George Ripley, for Ripley bequeathed his secret to one who outlived him.

The prestige that the practice of alchemy enjoyed in these years is shown in the way it was accepted at Oxford University, where Ripley and Neville practised, and at Peterhouse College, Cambridge. The four religious alchemists mentioned by Norton included George Ripley, George Neville, archbishop of York, and Thomas Dalton, a monk of Gloucester Abbey. Dalton learned his art from a canon of Lichfield and was a clerk of John Delves, a squire in the confidence of the king and keeper of the royal mint in 1461. Delves had appeared on commissions of the peace in Staffordshire with Richard Bingham, a member of the 1457 alchemy commission. Through him, Dalton, who practised alchemy in Gloucester Abbey, came to the attention of Thomas Herbert, the brother of William Herbert, 1st earl of Pembroke. Delves brought Dalton against his will to Edward's court sometime in the mid-1460s. If the previous decade had witnessed the prominence of Oxford University as a centre for the study of alchemical medicine focused on the illness of Henry VI, the 1460s, with the emergence of the new Yorkist monarchy, encouraged through royal patronage the rise to prominence of Cambridge physicians, many of whom had a sympathetic interest in alchemy. Among those entering Edward IV's service were William Hattecliffe, Roger Marshall, Sergeo James of Frescia, Walter Lempster, Edward Alban, William Hobbes, John Argentine, Lewis Caerleon, and Thomas Denyman.[87] Peterhouse College in particular seems to have been the focus for some of these physicians. Roger Marshall, who was physician to the king in 1468, cast Edward's horoscope in his own hand[88] and donated such alchemical texts as *A Book of Alchemy* of Albertus Magnus and other unspecified alchemical treatises before his death in 1477, including one surviving alchemical collection containing the works of Roger Bacon and John Dastin.[89] Marshall's medical authority was such that he was involved in an investigation into a diagnosis of leprosy in 1468 concerning one Joan Nyghtyngale[90] and in 1471 in an inspection of the quality of a consignment of theriac (treacle) with seventeen apothecaries who pronounced the shipment at the London Guildhall unwholesome.[91] The other physician closest to the king was probably William Hattecliffe, physician to Edward IV from 1461 to 1467 and a member of the alchemy commission of 1456. He was a king's counsellor and secretary from 1466 until his death in 1480. Hattecliffe was rewarded for his medical and secretarial services in 1467 with confiscated Lancastrian estates in Oxford, London and Somerset. James of Frescia, a Cambridge graduate who was physician to Edward in 1461, was admitted a knight of St George's, Windsor, in 1467. He too received a number of confiscated Lancastrian estates.[92] The importance of Edward as a patron of these intellectually distinguished figures is shown by the fact that the two most important alchemical works in English in the fifteenth century, Ripley's *Compound of Alchemy* and Norton's *Ordinal of Alchemy* were dedicated to the king. One manuscript of the *Ordinal of Alchemy* shows the author presenting his book to the monarch. In the border there are the familiar alchemical symbols of the 1460s, the peacock, the white rose and the marriage of the sun and moon.[93]

The idealism and optimism that such alchemists sharing Edward's patronage felt was communicated by Thomas Norton when he described a miracle that happened in 1464/5:

three masters of this science alle
Lay in oon bed nye to Leden halle;
Which hadde Elixers perfite white and redde
A wondir such iii to rest in oon bedde,
And that within the space of dayes tene,
while hard is to fynde oon in Milions of men,
Of the dewkedome of loreyn (oon), I undirstonde,
Was born; that odir ny the mydill of ynglond;
Undir a crosse in thende of shirys three
The iiide was born, the youngest of them is he
Which bi his natyuyte is bi clerkis founde
That he shuld honour alle englishe grounde.
A man myght waalke alle the world a-bowte
And faylle such iii masters to fynde owte.
Tweyn be fletyng, the yongist shalle aabyde,
And do moch good in this londe at a tyde.[94]

The eldest chanted a song for him, saying that after suffering wrongs from those beholden to him and after general troubles a great joy should be had in every quarter of the land which all good men can understand. The younger asked him when this would be and the elder alchemist replied:

– when men shalle se
The holy crosse honouryde both day and nyght
In the land of god in the lond of lyght;
Which may bedo in welle good seson,
But longe delayed it is withowte resone.[95]

According to Norton's great-grandson, the Elizabethan alchemist Samuel Norton, the youngest of these alchemists who was the subject of these prophecies was Thomas Norton himself.[96] The other object of such hopes was of course the patron of these men, Edward IV, who is compared to the mythic kings of antiquity guided by great alchemists:

When that bigynnyth note wel this thinge,
This science shal draw towarde the kynge;
And many mo gracis ye may be bolde,
Mo then of us shulde now be tolde.
Grace on that king shalle descende
– He shal make ful secrete serche
For this science with dowcet sspeche,
And a-monge the solitarie
He shalle haue tidingis certeynle.
So soght king kalide of many men
Til he mett with Morien
Which helpid kalide at his nede.[97]

The optimism of these early years of the new reign was such that there was a degree of megalomania surrounding some of the hopes placed on Edward and his kingdom, the sort of delusions satirized 150 years later by Ben Jonson in his great play *The Alchemist*.

Nevertheless such delusions show the degree of myth building associated with the practice of alchemy at Edward's court. Norton tells of a monk from recently English-occupied Normandy who was determined through alchemy to leave some noble act behind him to immortalize his name. The monk approached Norton, who was initially cautious but interested, wanting a licence from King Edward to purchase enough land to build on Salisbury Plain 'Glorious to be seen' fifteen abbeys every mile. The money for this project would be provided from his alchemical experiments.[98] Another alchemical visionary was the parish priest of a little town near London, who described himself as an alchemist without peer and a part-time physician who, with his fame in mind, desired to build a beautiful bridge across the Thames:

> wherof shulde growe a comone ese
> al the contray there a-bowte to plese.[99]

This bridge he envisaged would be perpetually lit up with gold or precious stones,

> with pynacliss gilte shynyng as golde,
> a glorious thinge for men to beholde

reflecting above and below in the water of the river.[100] Although Norton ultimately came to see this man as a crank, his narration of the incident does illustrate the idealism with which court alchemists were beginning to see the emerging capital of London or New Troy, described by Ripley as 'a noble city'. Bridges were an important alchemical symbol of the conjunction of opposites and, as Norton put it, the bridging of the body and soul through the medium of the spirit (mercury). A number of men with alchemical interests such as Thomas Cook the Lord Mayor were wardens of London Bridge,[101] which was of such symbolic significance in the genealogical histories of the compiler of the *Prophetic Histories of Great Britain*.[102]

There was of course a more hard-headed dimension to alchemical practice in these years, manifested in the search for gold, which was nowhere more apparent than in Edward's growing metropolitan capital. Ripley gives a vivid account in the *Compound of Alchemy* of financially motivated alchemists working at night, bleary eyed and soot stained, seeking the stone in dung, urine, blood, eggs and broken pots. Their houses, he declares (and sounding like Chaucer in the *Canon Yeoman's Tale*), are full of furnaces and glasses and they eloquently converse about the red man and white wife deluding themselves that they are natural multipliers 'whiche naturall philosophie did never rede nor see'. Such men, he wrote, crowded around Westminster prising money from merchants, and when they were cast in prison they gave plausible lies about losing the elixir.[103] Others moved into Westminster Abbey, obtaining money from monks whom they reduced to poverty. This portrait of the confidence tricks of alchemists in a vibrant and exploitative capital was to influence Ben Jonson's satire of the malpractices of an alchemist called Subtle in seventeenth-century London who cites Ripley as his master to give himself more credibility. The dismissive observations of Ripley and Norton of all this alchemical activity testifies to the commercial viability of the practice in the 1460s, and the stimulus was the interest expressed by the crown in procuring gold.

On 21 October 1463 Edward IV granted to Sir Henry Gray of Contenore and his deputies power and authority by the cunning of philosophy for the transmutation of metals so that he shall answer to the king for any profit.[104] Gray was closely associated in commissions of the peace in Derbyshire and Nottinghamshire between 1463 and 1467 with others involved in alchemy including George Neville and Richard Bingham, who served on the alchemy commission of 1457, and William Lord Hastings, keeper of the royal mint.[105] On 7 December 1468 Richard Carter was licensed to practise alchemy with all kinds of metals and minerals for two years in the king's manor of Woodstock (one of Edward's favourite hunting lodges).[106] The alchemist Thomas Dalton was brought from his abbey in Gloucestershire to the court by Edward's squire John Delves, against his will, with financial profit in mind. Delves reported that Dalton had once made him 1,000 pounds 'of as good golde as the Ryalle was' within half a day.[107]

However, even the search for gold had a politically idealistic dimension. Ripley, surveying all this commercial activity, employed a voice of high philosophical seriousness and ironic detachment:

> But if God fortune thee to have
> This Science by doctrine which I have told
> Discover it not whosoever it crave,
> For favour, feare, silver, or gold
> Be no oppressor, letcher nor boaster bold.[108]

The transmutation of iron (the most common of the base matters of the alchemist) into gold therefore represented the exaltation of the soul. One of the alchemical symbols on Ripley's tomb, erected in 1490, was the horseshoe (the emblem of St Eloi, the patron saint of goldsmiths).[109] At the foot of the *Ripley Scrolls* Ripley is shown bearing a staff, like the caduceus of Mercury, entwined with serpents. Ripley's staff has a cloven hoof with a horseshoe at the base to suggest the transformation of base human nature into spirit through a pursuit of the alchemical wisdom represented by the *Rigby Scroll* which is wrapped around the head of Ripley's staff.[110] In some versions he faces a king, the embodiment of gold.[111] Norton too emphasized the religious dimension to the work of transmutation and even suggested that its success depended on the piety of the alchemist's patron, Edward IV himself.[112] Even as intellectually distinguished a figure as Marshall was interested in the transmutation of iron: he was connected with the guild of ironmongers, of which his brother Nicholas was warden.

However, the most telling demonstration of the philosophical dimension to the pursuit of wealth occurs in Edward IV's recoinage. Henry IV legislated against the practice of alchemy to prevent tampering with gold bullion but Edward employed alchemists in the royal mints. In September 1464 Edward gave William Lord Hastings an indenture to produce a new coinage. Hastings' deputy at the royal mint was the London alderman and goldsmith Hugh Bryce, who was granted for life the office of clerk of the royal mint. Their task was to recall all the silver and gold currency in England, especially the noble, first issued by Edward III, because 'many nobles from overseas are unclean and lacking in weight', and to mint new coins.[113] The new coins, the angel and the ryall, were to contain less gold and silver to offset the country's national shortage of gold which was being surreptitiously exported. The amount of gold was reduced in weight from 108 grams to 99.2 grams, and silver was reduced in the same manner. The noble therefore jumped in value from 6*s* 8*d* to 8*s* 4*d*. There are many ways in which the recoinage could be considered a work of alchemy. In a fundamental sense it was a form of transmutation, of multiplication of gold by a sleight of hand, an inflation of the value of the gold found in the currency. The amount of gold and silver bullion in the country was increased and this boosted public confidence. Edward, in issuing Hastings' indenture, proclaimed the recoinage as in the interests of the common good.[114] This same phrase was used by Delves, who was appointed warden of the royal mint in 1471, when Dalton accused him of betraying his confidence and breaking his oath of secrecy. Delves replied that he could break it 'for the kinges wele, and for al his lande'. Norton proclaimed the recoinage of 1464–5 an alchemical miracle on the same level as the appearance of three great alchemists at Leadenhall in the same year:

> Bryce when the change of the coyne was had,
> Made som men sory and som men glad.
> And as to moch people that chaunge
> Semyd a new thing and a strange,
> So that seson be-fille a wondir thinge
> Towchynge this science withowte lesynge.[115]

The London chronicler, Fabyan, connected with Thomas Cook, who also had alchemical interests, proclaimed the issuing of the new coinage of the royal and the angel in the year of Elizabeth's coronation as 'notabyll acts'.[116] The important place occupied by the monarchical symbolism associated with Ripley among officials at Edward IV's mint is demonstrated in William Caxton's translating and printing, at the request of Hugh Bryce, of *The Mirror of the World*, an encyclopaedia of astronomical information. Bryce wished to present the book to his superior at the mint, William Hastings. The sun is compared to the king and described as the patron of all the stars which receive their light from him.

The very act of recoinage could be regarded as an alchemical process and one that even inspired the visions of alchemists such as Ripley. The gathering in of gold and silver coins and reminting them was a form of alchemical marriage of the sun and moon. The melting down of the old gold nobles, with the image of the king in the bath, constituted the form of alchemical death that had been described verbally and visually by Ripley. The appearance of freshly minted new coins bearing Edward's image, was a dramatic emblematic representation of the resurrection of the Sun King, of Edward's emergence as king from the destruction and disintegration of civil war. These bright new gold coins, issued in the interests of the common good, boosted public confidence and testified to the prosperity of the realm.

Given the close parallels that existed between the alchemical process and the symbolic implications of minting coinage, it is no surprise to find alchemists involved in activities at the mint. Norton knew enough about the recoinage to be able to refer to Bryce's work at the mint, and Ripley too referred to the recoinage. George Neville, as archbishop of York, had his own mints in York, Durham and London.[117] Ripley was directly involved in alchemical experiments which involved the melting down of bullion, and it is possible that the distinctive and individualistic visions that appear in his writings and on the scrolls may have been inspired by the process of breathing in fumes and looking intently at the changes of the king's image in his glass alembic and vessels. A number of Ripley's recipes for the multiplication of gold involved melting down the gold from the heavier old nobles in the manner done at the royal mint in 1464. In his sixty-third year Ripley gave George Neville a recipe in which he recommended taking an old Edward noble of fine quality gold, rinsing it with mercury, grinding the two substances together on a stone with vinegar and salt before washing and placing them in a bath and boiling them in a glass over a fire for a day and a night. The dissolved solution is then strained through a linen cloth many times, and the retained gold is reduced to a dry red powder. The next stage of the operation Ripley will only communicate orally, and he then recommends using the temperate heat of the sun to reduce the matter to a red powder, firing it for a day and night, grinding it on a marble stone with saltpetre and dissolving it in balneo (wax). The matter is then multiplied with mercury in the fire, and gold as fine as the gold of the noble is taken out of the furnace.[118] Such experiments with the melting down of the king's image, the symbolic death of the king, the amalgamation with mercury/Melusine, and the redemption of gold, symbolized by the king's rebirth, would have had a powerful influence on Ripley's vivid myths of death, disintegration and resurrection. It is possible that the recoinage, the resurrection of the king's image and the alchemical experiments involving the resurrecting of tarnished gold, reclaiming the king from the dull earth, in turn influenced Edward's own expectations of the resurrection of his spirit in death. In 1475 he left detailed instructions for the building of his tomb, specifying that his body be laid under a monument showing his corpse and a marble stone. Ripley described the grinding down and disintegration of the king's image on a marble stone prior to his resurrection.[119]

However, it also appears that the alchemical symbols on the *Ripley Scrolls* and on the genealogical rolls, which were in part inspired by Ripley's experiments with the coinage, also directly influenced the type of symbols produced on Edward IV's new coins. In 1462 the white rose was introduced on Edward's coinage, and on pennies minted at Neville's archiepiscopal mints at York, Durham and London there appeared the Yorkist rose with a cross and the sun rising. On the new ryall, the highest of the denominations of Edward's new coinage minted in 1464, a large letter E (similar to the letter appearing on alchemical genealogies) was placed on the stern of an image of the ship of state, and a Yorkist rose was placed on the hull. On the reverse side of this coin the device of the fleur de lys gave way to the sun in splendour with a rose at its centre.[120] The noble and groats emerging from the mints in the period between 1461 and 1464 depicted the king bearing a resemblance to the image of a hermaphrodite king with large breasts, as shown on the *Ripley Scrolls*.

The basic currency of Edward's reign, retaining the value of the old noble, was the new angel (perhaps so-called because of the prophecy of the angel about the coming of Edward, and the image of the angel censing Edward at the ceremony of his coronation on 28 July). This coin bore the most significant changes testifying to the impact of Ripley's symbolic art. On one side of the coin there is the ship of state. Either side of the mast, formed by the cross of St George, there is a rose and the sun in splendour. On the reverse side, replacing the image of the king on the ship which Ripley would have contemplated when melting down the noble, there is a new image of St Michael, covered in feathers, slaying the dragon. There is a striking similarity between this image of the feathered dragon-slayer and the feathered king of the *Ripley Scrolls*. This king too is closely associated with the death of the dragon and devours his own feathers to symbolize the *uroboros*, the serpent biting its tail, the mercury which begins and ends the work. This important coin, the denomination of the new reign, expands on the symbolism of the *Ripley Scrolls*. The king emerges triumphant from the dragon of chaos, the *nigredo* of war and civil disintegration. He emerges reborn from the alchemical bath in the royal mint, proclaiming and celebrating the emergence of the reborn nation, identified with the redemptive king; both nation and king are made manifest in the royal coin itself and in the image of the feathered king perched on top of the round globe on the *Ripley Scroll*. Both could be seen as images of the philosopher's stone itself.

The image of St Michael on Edward's angel is also closely related to that other dragon-slayer, St George, established as England's national saint since 1351.[121] This link is firmly established with the cross of St George prominently displayed as the ship's mast on the reverse of this coin. St George was also an ancient fertility god, a sun god who defeated the serpent that tried to prevent the dawning of the new day. As a martyr with pre-Christian associations with the fertility of the land, he was identified with the fight against the outgoing king of the year, placating the spirits through the sacrifice of the king for the good of the community, so that the new king could emerge in the spring, bringing fertility to the land. This cluster of associations placed the cult of St George in a close relationship with the reborn, dragon-fighting king of the *Ripley Scrolls* and the emergent Edward IV (who regularly prayed to the saint) in the spring. Henry V was the first to demonstrate the political potential of this saint. On his triumphant entry into London on 25 November 1415, after Agincourt, he was greeted at the drawbridge by a statue of St George surrounded by angels, and in Cornhill twelve apostles bearing the arms of St George hailed him as part of Christ's lineage of apostolic succession. The close connection between St George the dragon-slayer, the archangel Michael and Edward, and the delivery of the kingdom from chaos was emphasized in a ceremony staged by the city of Bristol on 4 September 1461 to welcome Edward, who was preparing to take Welsh castles from Lancastrian hands. At the Temple Cross he beheld St George on horseback 'upon a tent fighting with a dragon. And at the slaying of the dragon there was a great melody of angels.'[122] This has been seen as a celebration of ordered city life against the chaos and disorder of the uncivilized natural world, represented by the dragon; but it was more likely a pageant of thanksgiving for the new king for delivering the kingdom from the chaos of civil war.[123] Edward similarly had slain the dragon and dispelled the waters of chaos, establishing a new harmony and facilitating the rebirth of the nation, newly emerging like freshly minted coinage. St Michael, merging into St George, brought about on Edward's coinage a conjunction of alchemical symbolism with England's national saint to whom Edward was especially dedicated. In a genealogical roll culminating in Edward's coronation there is an illustration of Edward and his queen kneeling before God the father and the crucified Christ. Behind Edward is St George, prominently displaying the red cross.[124]

The focus for the cult of St George was the chapel of St George at Windsor, originally founded by Edward III in 1348 and rebuilt by Edward IV as the symbolic heart of his new dynasty. This was Edward's supreme achievement as a patron of architecture, a chapel royal intended as a monument to the splendour of the house of York. Unlike France there was in Britain no one place of burial for English kings and Edward was the first king to choose to be buried at Windsor with the sun in splendour depicted in a frieze in the Rutland chapel. In the stained-glass presented by Edward to Canterbury Cathedral in 1482 Edward is shown with his queen in full regalia behind a lectern decorated with St George slaying the dragon. The prominence of relics and representations of St George in St George's Chapel, Windsor, is testimony to the extent to which Edward identified with this national saint. There was a statue of St George and the dragon in the chapel, a rood screen painted with an image of the saint, an altar piece of the life of St George, and a silver reliquary containing three of the saint's bones. In 1417 the Emperor Sigismund brought the chapel the heart of St George in a silver reliquary. John Rous acquired for the Garter chapel at Windsor the head of the relic of St George,[125] (an inventory of the chapel in 1552 refers to a St George's head with a helmet of gold).[126] A cycle of St George was carved in the aisle of the choir of the chapel when the choir stalls were built between 1477 and 1484, including scenes showing St George slaying the dragon and standing astride the beast.

Another important event full of alchemical symbolism occurred in the same year as the appearance of the three master alchemists and the recoinage. The marriage of Edward IV and Elizabeth Woodville took place in secret in May 1464 and became public knowledge when Elizabeth was first introduced to the royal court in the chapel of Reading Abbey on Michaelmas day 1464. The long period of secrecy was understandable, for in many ways the choice of this beautiful widow as a bride was politically disastrous: she was the daughter of 'a simple knight', as the Burgundian chronicler Waurin put it, and a Lancastrian knight who had fought for Margaret of Anjou at Towton at that. A hostile reaction was inevitable from the earl of Warwick, who had been involved in negotiations with Louis XI for a diplomatic alliance to be cemented by Edward's marriage into the French royal family, and from the lords in general who were uneasy about the number of Woodville relatives who would need royal preferment. A key to Edward's motives, apart from Elizabeth's obvious physical qualities, may well be alchemical symbolism. Her mother was Jacquetta of Luxembourg, duchess of Bedford, and through her Elizabeth could claim descent from Melusine the serpent woman.[127] According to the legend, Raymund, the nephew of the count of Poitiers, married Melusine and together they built Lusignan Castle. One afternoon Raymund spied his wife naked and saw her serpent's tail. Realizing her secret was out she resolved to leave her husband and told him their children were descended from a noble race which would reign for ever.[128] The children of Melusine included Anthony duke of Luxembourg and Raymund king of Bohemia. Anthony married Christine of Luxembourg and from them Jacquetta, the daughter of Pierre de Luxembourg, count of St Pol, claimed descent. Jacquetta and Elizabeth's knowledge of this story would have come through the *Tale of Melusine*, compiled by Jean d'Arras between 1382 and 1394 from the chronicles of the duke of Berry, son of the king of France, at the request of Mary, duchess of Bar, sister of the duke. Stephen, a Dominican of the house of Lusignan, developed the work of Arras and made the story so famous that the families of Luxembourg, including Jacquetta, altered their pedigrees to be able to claim descent from Melusine.[129] Jacquetta of Luxembourg may have read this account of the legend when she married John duke of Bedford in 1433 at a ceremony officiated by her uncle, Louis of Luxembourg and bishop of Therome. Bedford, who was in command of the English administration in Normandy, acquired the royal library at the Louvre and left all his possessions, including possibly the *Tale of Melusine*, to his wife in 1435.

By the fifteenth century Melusine the serpent woman had become an important symbol in the alchemical process. A metaphor for the feminine spirit of nature, the primeval mother of being that led to the production of the philosopher's stone, she stood for the perpetual cycle of generation and regeneration that eventually led to the balance between the four humours.[130] She was a manifestation of the earth mother that devours the dead and regurgitates the new born. From her body in a sealed vessel the waters of creation rose, and through her agency the sun and moon conjoined in marriage. Melusine was used this way in the *Ripley Scrolls*, where she was depicted as the maternal serpent woman winding her way down the tree of knowledge between the sun and moon, presiding over their marriage. Melusine, as ancestor of Elizabeth Woodville, was therefore an appropriate figure to preside over the marriage of Edward (the sun) and Elizabeth (her descendant, the moon), and alchemists around the king, especially Ripley, must have been excited at the alchemical possibilities raised by this marriage. Norton commented on the significance of the royal marriage when he wrote:

Yet once this science I understand
shall greatly honor the throne of England
When in this Land shall raigne a king,
Which shall love god above all thing.
The which I most desire to come to pass
By the fortune and by the grace
Of a woman faire of face.

Norton's great-grandson, in his *Key of Alchemy*, took advantage of the Christian name of Edward's bride and applied the prophecy to Elizabeth I.[131] There is little doubt that Edward, with his intense interest in alchemy, was excited by his bride's genealogy. The marriage ceremony itself, coinciding with the recoinage, further publicized the alchemical symbolism of Edward's kingship, and in particular Elizabeth's descent from Melusine. In January 1465 Edward sent envoys to Philip of Burgundy informing him that Elizabeth would be crowned on the Sunday before Pentecost and inviting him to send a delegation, since Elizabeth's family was descended from the kings of Bohemia and the emperors of Germany. He further requested that Philip send to his wife's coronation kinsmen and friends of Jacquetta of Luxembourg, especially her brother Jacques de Luxembourg, and he was indeed present when she was crowned in Westminster Abbey. This ceremony was preceded by a procession towards London Bridge, where a pageant was staged with a display of peacock feathers, the alchemical symbol of the approaching climax of the work.[132] Further contacts with the court of Burgundy may well have had an alchemical dimension. The Burgundian Order of the Golden Fleece, to which Edward was elected at the chapter of 1468, had alchemical significance, and Ripley had close connections with Burgundy by virtue of his studies at the University of Louvain, where John Dee was to study mathematics in the sixteenth century. These connections between the two courts were strengthened by a marriage alliance between Edward's sister Margaret of York and Charles the Bold, duke of Burgundy, in 1468; and it is possible that Ripley, if his studies abroad covered this period, may have been involved in the marriage ceremonies.

In this version of the Ripley Scroll *Melusine, the ancestor of Edward's queen, initiates the process of disintegration (represented by the dragon and toad) necessary for rebirth, in the alchemical bath. (Ashmole Roll 53)*

The conjunction of opposites, the union of conscious and unconscious, depicted in alchemical writings of this period, were of significance in encouraging the integration and development of the true self. However, it was also of national, political significance, as demonstrated in the public displays of alchemical symbolism and myth in the recoinage and the marriage of 1464. Melusine was seen as the transforming agent taking the student of alchemy on an inner journey that involved considerable alteration (transmutation) of his self-image as he discovered, deep within himself, within his memory (or what we today may perhaps term the unconscious), deeply buried archetypes that if assimilated could encourage the birth of the true self. But these archetypes were not just of personal significance. With alchemy occupying such a central place at the court and in the political affairs of the nation, introspection took on a broader, more historical and mythological dimension, as the inner journey became a meditation on British prehistory, what some twentieth-century scientists may perhaps call the 'collective unconscious'. Alchemy, with its graphic enactments of the descent of the king into the collective *nigredo* and the surrender of his ego, was a search for the national identity in the early childhood of the nation, and at this level the conjunction was a source of powerful energy, of masculine archetypes that would energize the new-born king. The prehistorical source for this inspiration was the age of King Arthur, the heroic king whom alchemists regarded as an integral part of their national history. The philosopher's stone, the gold they sought, was to be found in the age of Lancelot, the Round Table, and the marriage of Arthur and Guinevere. It is now time to examine the Arthurian ethos that grew up around the earl of March as he became king. He was young, flexible and confident enough to allow these archetypes to be projected on to him as he instituted, with the encouragement of alchemists, the rebirth out of a disintegrating realm of the nation's true self, its soul: Arthurian Britain.

NOTES

1. *Aurora Consurgens*, transl. R.F.C. Hull and A.S.B. Glover (London, 1966), p. 63. George Ripley was influenced by this work in his use of biblical quotation and in writing some of the allegories in the *Compound of Alchemy*. *Aurora Consurgens*, p. 25. Sometimes attributed to Thomas Aquinas, *Aurora Consurgens* is thought to have been written in Austria at the beginning of the fifteenth century. Barbara Obrist, 'Les debuts de l'imagerie alchemique xiv–xv siecles' (Paris, La Sycamore, 1982), Review.
2. G. Hodges, 'The Civil War of 1459 to 1461 in the Welsh Marches. 2. The Campaign and Battle of Mortimer's Cross', *The Ricardian*, vi, 85 (1984), 330–43.
3. *Cal. State Papers Venetian*, 99–101.
4. *Cal. State Papers of Milan*, vol. i, p. 46.
5. T. Wright (ed.), *Political Poems and Songs*, Rolls Series, 2 vols (London, 1859–61), vol. ii, pp. 264–5.
6. J.S. Roskell, *The Commons and their Speakers in English Parliaments 1376–1523* (Manchester, 1965), pp. 80–1.
7. BL MS Royal 18 Dii.
8. *Cal. Milanese Papers*, vol. i, p. 57; Keir, *Ecclesiastical Career of George Neville*, p. 193.
9. The Croyland chronicler, reflecting on this march, perceived the real enemy to be the men of the north. *Crowland Chronicle*, vol. I, pp. 421–3. See also Watts, *Henry VI, The Politics of Kingship*, p. 360.
10. George Ashby, *A Prisoner's Reflections AD 1463* (EETS, Extra Ser. 76, 1899).
11. *Dicta Philosophorum*, p. 74.
12. Bodley MS Ashmole 1490, fo. 42; BL MS Stowe 1070, fo. 26.
13. Problems of interpreting this introduction are compounded by the fact that both manuscripts are sixteenth-century transcriptions.
14. BL MS Add. 18268A. BL MS Sloane 965, fo. 109v. The author of the *Prophetic History of Britain* reveals his knowledge of astrology (everywhere apparent in Bodley MS 623 and Vesp E vii) by assigning to Henry VI the cognomen of Anti Lupus as well as lupus. In all respects he shared the qualities of antimony except being born in December far away from the warm sign of Aries so closely associated with Edward IV. See Bodley MS 623 fo. 71v.
15. S. McKendrick, 'Edward IV: An English Royal Collector of Netherlandish Tapestries', *Burlington Magazine*, cxxix (1987), 521–4.
16. BL MS Royal 12 Ex V. The inscription 'this book owned by Edward earl of March, son of Richard duke of York' is on fo. 2b.
17. Bodley MSS e Mus 155 and Bodley e mus 153.
18. Other fifteenth-century copies of Bacon's version of the *Secreta secretorum* include the Latin version Bodley Rawl c 274 and Bodley Lyell 36 and an English version in Bodley MS Ashmole 396. For the edition based on Ashmole 396 see M.A. Manzalaoui, *Secreta secretorum* (EETS 276, 1977). See L. Thorndike, 'Some Medieval Texts', *Ambix*, vii (1959), 1–24.
19. The *Secreta secretorum*, though purporting to be Aristotle's advice to Alexander, was originally written in Persia between the seventh and ninth centuries and translated into Latin in the thirteenth century. Bacon's version was completed in 1220. All copies are derived from a thirteenth-century manuscript in the Bodleian Library.

20. *Secreta secretorum*, ed. Manzalaoui, p. 36.
21. Ibid, p. 59.
22. BL MS Add. 47680. This manuscript contains images of the sun and moon that may reveal the ancestry of some of the images in the *Ripley Scrolls*.
23. Parhelia are described by Pliny in his *Natural History*.
24. Anne Geneva, *Astrology and the Seventeenth-Century Mind* (Manchester, 1995), pp. 95ff.
25. Thorndike, *History of Science*, vol. iv, pp. 98–9.
26. *Secreta secretorum*, ch. 5.
27. According to Prospero Carmalio writing to Ludovico Sforza duke of Milan on 11 March (*Cal. State Papers Milan*, ed. A.B. Hinds (London, 1912), vol. 1, p. 74; and John Benet, G.L. and M.A. Harris, *Camden Miscellany, 24*, Camden Society, 4 ser., 9 (1972), 229.
28. Parhelia are not unusual in polar regions but rare in England. Two were observed in the cold winters of 1940 and 1947 when temperatures reached minus 10 degrees Fahrenheit in north Herefordshire. From notes by Geoffrey Hodges, kindly supplied by Geoffrey Wheeler.
29. Davies, *English Chronicle*, p. 111; *Three Fifteenth-Century Chronicles*, ed. J. Gairdner (Camden Society, 1880). From Lambeth Palace MS 306.77; *Gregory's Chronicle in a London Chronicle* ed. J. Gairdner (Camden Society, 1876), pp. 211–12; *A Chronicle in the Reigns of Richard II, Henry IV and Henry VI*, ed. J.S. Davies (Camden Society, 1865), p. 111. The parhelia was also noted by Abbot Whethamstede, *Register Abbatiae Johannis Whethamstede* (Rolls Series, 2 vols, 1872–3), p. 386.
30. Hall, p. 251.
31. BL MS Harl. 7353.
32. Geneva, *Astrology in Seventeenth-Century Mind*, p. 99.
33. College of Arms Roll 9/9.
34. See this book, ch. 5.
35. *Biblia Pauperum*, ed. Schreiber, 8 (Munich, 1961).
36. Ashmole, *Theatrum Chemicum*, pp. 109–10.
37. Scofield, *Edward IV*, p. 178
38. Bodley MS Ashmole 1485, fo. 53. This is a seventeenth-century copy, a translation of a dream of Ripley's that is different from the version printed in Ashmole, *Theatrum Chemicum Britannicum*. There is a Latin version in Cassell's 1449 edition.
39. Gross, *Dissolution of Lancastrian Kingship*, pp. 23ff; *Coventry Leet Book* (EETS, 1907–8), part 1, p. 309.
40. Commines referred to the superstitiousness of the English.
41. BL MS Sloane 2218, fos 20v–21, 23v–24.
42. BL MS Stowe 1070, fo. 29.
43. *A Lookeing Glasse for Illiterate Alchymists* BL MS Royal 12 Exv, fo. 19.
44. R.I. McCallum, *Antimony in Medical History* (Edinburgh, 1990), pp. 36ff; Dobbs, *The Foundations of Newton's Alchemy*.
45. Ashmole, *Theatrum Chemicum Britannicum*, p. 34.
46. Ibid, p. 136.
47. See Jung, *Psychology and Alchemy*, pp. 376–406.
48. Bodley MS Laup. poet 121, fo. 74.
49. Ibid.
50. *Cantilena*, verse 20.
51. Ashmole, *Theatrum Chemicum Britannicum*, p. 54.
52. Bodley Roll 1; BL MS Add. 40742, fo. 5c. 1466–70
53. Bodley MS Ashmole 1480, fo. 15.
54. Bodley Ashmole Roll 53.
55. Ashmole, *Theatrum Chemicum Britannicum*, p. 108.
56. Jung, *Psychology and Alchemy*, p. 463.
57. For *Ripley Scrolls* see Laurence C. Witten II and Richard Pachella, *Alchemy and the Occult: a Catalogue of Books and Manuscripts from the Collection of Paul Mary Mellor*, 4 vols (New Haven, 1968–77), vol. iii, pp. 271–85.
58. Corpus Christi College, Oxford MS 172, fo. 42.
59. Ibid.
60. R. Kinsman, 'A Lament for King Edward IV', *Huntingdon Library Quarterly*, 29 (1966), 95–108.
61. Bodley MS Ashmole 1448, fos 213–38.
62. For heraldry of the son and Richard II see H. Stanford, London, 'Royal Beasts' Norfolk Herald Extraordinary, *Heraldry Society* (1956). Corpus Christi College, Oxford, MS 244, fos 58v, 84r.

63. BL MS Harl. 2407.
64. Ibid; cf BL MS Egerton 845, fos 14v, 15v, 16, 17v.
65. BL MS Egerton 845, fos 19v, 21v.
66. Ibid, fo. 14v.
67. College of Arms MS 20/25 and Bodley Ashmole Roll 26, both the work of the compiler of the collection of prophetic writings relating to Edward IV in BL MS Cotton Vesp. E VII and Bodley MS 623. Ashmole 26 is incorrectly labelled Ashmole Roll 27 in the 1845 catalogue and the summary catalogue (Madan) should be followed.
68. College of Arms MS 20/20. No children are mentioned.
69. I have called this roll 2 because there is an earlier version to which I shall refer later.
70. Corpus Christi College, Oxford MS 244, fos 46–58 and esp fo. 55r ff bis r. *Il Testamentum*, Pereira, p. cxlv.
71. Corpus Christi College, Oxford, MS 172, fo. 42.
72. There are references to the births of Elizabeth, Mary, Cecily and Edward.
73. F. Hervey, *Holbein's Ambassadors: the Picture and the Men* (London, 1900); R. Foster, *Patterns of Thought: the Hidden Meaning of the Great Pavement of Westminster Abbey* (London, 1991); John North, *The Ambassador's Secret: Holbein and the World of the Renaissance* (London, 2002) pp. 154–61. For the alchemical painting in Westminster Abbey see Ashmole, *Theatrum Chemicum Britannicum*, p. 210, and for fifteenth-century representation of the picture see BL MS Egerton 845 fo. 15. The fact that Ashmole attributes the commissioning of the painting to the legendary fourteenth-century Abbot Cremer, supposed patron of Lull implies that the painting predated Edward's coronation; but it is possible that it was executed to celebrate this event. For a fifteenth-century drawing of this picture see above, p. 83.
74. An image of *Ripley's Wheel* appears at the end of the 1591 printed edition at *The Compound of Alchemy*. The printer, Ralph Rubbards, testified to the 'diversitie of copies' of this wheel. It was copied into the Corpus Christi manuscript of *The Compound of Alchemy* (MS 172 fo. 42) by a former owner, Brian Twyne. See Linden's edition p. 97.
75. Philadephia Free Library MS E 201; College of Arms MS 20/20.
76. For King Sebbi see Bede, *A History of the English Church and People*, transl. L. Sherley-Price (Penguin, 1955), pp. 223–5. L. Blanchard, *The Edward IV Roll* (Free Library of Philadelphia).
77. Philadelphia Free Library MS E 201.
78. BL MS Harl. 2476, fo. 10v; G. Roberts, *The Mirror of Alchemy. Alchemical Ideas, and Images in Manuscripts and Books* (London, 1994).
79. *Works of Sir John Fortescue in 2 vols*, ed. T. Fortescue, Lord Clermont (London, 1869), pp. 295–6.
80. There is a prevalence of diagrams of the four elements in alchemical manuscripts and they relate to the search for wholeness, integration and the balance of the four humours in the individual and the kingdom. In BL MS Add. 10764, fo. 12v, these elements are shown in a square made of the four qualities of heat, cold, moistness and dryness.
81. BL MS Egerton 845.
82. J. Andrew Mendelsohn, 'Alchemy and Politics in England 1649–65', *Past and Present*, 135 (1992), 30–78.
83. Bodley MS Ashmole 1421, a Latin translation of the Arabic revelations of Morienus to Kalide, was an important influence on Ripley. For text see L. Stavenhagen, *A Testament of Alchemy* (New Hampshire, 1974).
84. Norton, *Ordinal of Alchemy*, p. 45.
85. *A collection of Ordinances and Regulations for the Government of the royal Household* (Society of Antiquaries, London, 1770), pp. 13–86.
86. J. Reidy, 'Thomas Norton and the Ordinal of Alchemy', *Ambix* (December 1457), vol. vi.
87. L. Voigts, 'A Doctor and his Books: the manuscripts of Roger Marshall d. 1477', in *New Science out of Old Books*, ed. R. Beadle and A.J. Piper (Aldershot, 1995).
88. BL MS Harl. 267, fo. 235r; C.H. Talbot and E.A. Hammond, *The Medical Practitioners in Medieval England: A Biographical Register* (London, Wellcome Institute, 1965).
89. Gonvill and Caius College, Cambridge MS 181/214.
90. *CCR 1468–76*, p. 30.
91. Voigts, 'A Doctor and his Books'.
92. *CPR 1461–7*, pp. 77, 168, 270; *CPR 1467–9*, p. 50; *CPR 1476–8*, pp. 251, 430; Rawcliffe, 'The Profits of Practice'.
93. BL MS Add. 10302. Norton's name appears as an acrostic in the text of the *Ordinal of Alchemy*.
94. Ashmole, *Theatrum Chemicum Britannicum*, p. 32.
95. Norton, *Ordinal of Alchemy*, p. 45.
96. Bodley MS Ashmole 1421.
97. Norton, *Ordinal of Alchemy* ll. 1423–35.

98. Ibid, p. 21.
99. Ibid, ll. 635–6.
100. Ibid, p. 23.
101. C.P. Christianson, *Memorials of the Book Trade in Medieval London* (Cambridge, 1987), p. 12.
102. BL MS Cotton Vesp. E VII; Bodley MS 623.
103. Ashmole, *Theatrum Chemicum Britannicum*, p. 152 ff.
104. *CPR Edward IV 1461–7*, p. 285.
105. Ibid, p. 569.
106. C.G. Mathews, *The Royal Apothecaries* (London, 1967), p. 47.
107. Norton, *Ordinal of Alchemy*, p. 31.
108. *Compound of Alchemy* (Linden), p. 56.
109. BL MS Vitellius E x, fo. 235v.
110. Bodley Ashmole Roll 40.
111. Bodley Ashmole Roll 53.
112. Bodley Ashmole Rolls 40, 54.
113. *CPR Edward IV 1467–77*, p. 425; *CPR Edward IV–Henry VI 1461–7*, pp. 147, 482, 546, 551, 556, 586; T.E. Reddaway, 'The King's Mint and Exchange in London', *English Historical Review*, cccxii (1967), 16–17.
114. C. Oman, *The Coinage in England* (Oxford, 1931), pp. 175–92, 219–21; C.E. Blunt and C.A. Whithorn, 'The Coinages of Edard IV and Henry VI (Restored)', *The British Numismatic Journal*, 3rd series, vol. v (1945–8).
115. Norton, *Ordinal of Alchemy*, p. 45.
116. *Fabyan's Chronicle*, p. 198.
117. Oman, *Coinage of England*, p. 220; Blunt and Whithorn, 'Coinage of Edward IV', p. 7.
118. Bodley MS Rawl. poet 121, fo. 77; BL MS Sloane 3580 B, fos 173v–175; Bodley Ashmole MS 1426. (This manuscript is dated 1500.)
119. For Edward's will see *Excerpta Historica*, ed. S. Bentley (London, 1833), pp. 366–76; W.H. St John Hope, *The Architectural History of Windsor Castle* (London, 1913), pp. 376–7.
120. Oman, *Coinage in England*, p. 220.
121. Samantha Riches, *St George: Hero, Martyr and Myth* (Stroud, 2000), p. 21.
122. Nancy Bradley Warren, *Spiritual Economics: Female Monasticism in Later Medieval England* (Philadelphia, 2001), p. 115; *Gesta Henrici Quinti*, ed. F. Taylor and J.S. Roskell (Oxford, 1975), pp. 105–7; Ricart's Calendar, p. 43; *Three Fifteenth-Century Chronicles*, pp. 85–6; Warkworth, *Chronicle*, p. 32; Riches, *St George*.
123. Riches, *St George*, p. 123.
124. Jesus College, Oxford, MS 114, fo. 34.
125. John Rous, *Historia regum Angliae* (Oxon ii, 1716), p. 711.
126. Riches, *St George*, p. 17.
127. D. MacGibbon, *Elizabeth Woodville* (London, 1938); A.F. Sutton and L. Visser-Fuchs, '"A Most Benevolent Queen": Queen Elizabeth Woodville's Reputation, her Piety and her Books', *The Ricardian*, x, 129 (1995), 214–45.
128. Sabine Baring-Gould, *Myths of the Middle Ages* (1996); *Melusine*, compiled 1382–94 by Jean d'Arras, translated in 1500 edn. From BL MS Bibl. Reg B11 (EETS, London, 1895).
129. The first to do so was the emperor Henry VII, count of Luxembourg from 1288 and emperor in 1312; C. Ray, *Melusine* (Ligage, 1898); J. Baudot, *Melusine* (Paris, 1908); *Rotuli Parliamentorum*, vol. vi, p. 993.
130. Paris, Bibliothèque Nationale MS fr. 14765, fo. 135; L.S. Dixon, *Alchemical Imagery in Bosch's Garden of Delights* (Ann Arbor, 1981), pp. 43–5.
131. Bodley MS Ashmole 1421, fo. 171v.
132. C. Strouff, 'Essai sur Melusine Roman du XIVième siècle par Jean d'Arras' (Paris, 1930). In April 1474 Queen Elizabeth visited Coventry where she was welcomed by an elaborate pageant of her royal ancestors and saintly protectors including the three kings of Cologne; Christianson, *Memorials of the Book Trade*, p. 12.

CHAPTER 5

The Redeemer of Great Britain: Edward IV, the King of Myth and Prophecy

Myths are things that never happened but always are.

Attrib. Herodotus

Hotspur: 'He said he would not ransom Mortimer,
Forbade my tongue to speak of Mortimer,
But I will find him when he lies asleep,
And in his ear I'll holla "Mortimer!"
Nay, I'll have a starling shall be taught to speak
Nothing but "Mortimer", and give it him
To keep his anger still in motion.'

William Shakespeare, *King Henry IV Part I*

Alchemy in 1461 represented far more than the search for gold. It provided Edward with his sense of destiny and a belief that he was the man to redeem the fragmented realm. The sources of this inspiration were familiar to him as the heir of a great family: the genealogies and prophecies of the house of York. This material was mobilized with any change of dynasty. The house of Lancaster deployed it in 1399, as did the Tudors in 1485. A flurry of activity in the production of genealogical rolls and the revising of prophecies concerning the arrival of a new king would therefore have been entirely expected and conventional in 1461. It was a legalistic approach to the claims of the new dynasty based on the genealogy of the eldest male heir, and it was backed up by prophecies issued in the previous millennium that were vague enough to be applied to most candidates. This activity has been studied in the valuable work of Sydney Angelo, Allison Allan, Anne F. Sutton and Livia Visser-Fuchs.[1] However, something new and unusual was happening in 1461 and the following decade. At the time of Edward's accession there occurred a convergence of the personal trauma of Edward earl of March and a national trauma – the outbreak of a civil war which had split families and friends after years of popular unrest, national humiliation and incompetent leadership. The Battle of Wakefield must have been a terrible moment for an eighteen-year-old youth entrusted with the care of his father's territories in the Welsh marches. His father and younger brother had been killed, their corpses desecrated and their heads placed on York city walls; indeed his own life was in immediate danger. Yet it was also a time of exciting opportunities. He was now the heir to the kingdom, and it was during this period of intolerable stress that he turned to genealogies and prophecies. These traditional sources need to be taken out of the library and placed in the great cathedrals and baronial halls, and this is the context in which they will be studied here. The labels of Lancaster and York are misleading. A great family was splitting apart and its members turned to their family trees, which harboured ghosts and crimes but which also contained inspiring tales that were great sources of energy. Edward appreciated this. He personalized them, using them to chart the evolution of his own destiny and self-image, placing on them alchemical symbols that were his own badges, such as the ascendant sun, the red dragon and the falcon, and cognomens such as 'Brutus' and 'Sol', to provide a unique and compelling vision of the evolution of a sense of identity and inflation of a sense of self, on a personal and national level, that would lead to a sense of heroic and epic destiny for the king and his people.

The background to this unique and powerful vision was conventional enough: the genealogical and prophetic traditions of the Houses of Lancaster and York. The genealogical tree was a powerful symbol for the nobility of this period. It was to be found on Latin rolls which were probably of clerical authorship, although as they were closely related in content to Hardynge's *Chronicle*, it is possible that laymen with military and heraldic knowledge may have had some impact. Lancastrian genealogies were commissioned in 1438–40 to reflect the king's assumption of royal power in 1436–7. But it was at the point when the internecine rivalry between the dukes of York and Somerset erupted in battle at St Albans, and the king was wounded and taken captive by York, that Henry's kingship and title had to be symbolically reaffirmed by a formal crown-wearing in June 1455 and the production of scrolls in London in support of the house of Lancaster. These were attributed to Roger of St Albans, a Carmelite monk of London, though he is not identified in any of the surviving manuscripts.[2] These genealogies combined historical narrative derived from the *Brut* and religious history derived from the beginning of the twelfth-century compilation *Historia in Genealogia Christi* of Peter of Poitiers and English chronicles, and served to demonstrate the antiquity of the royal house of England. Elaborately decorated, up to forty-two feet in length they were probably designed for hanging in great baronial halls, courts and cathedrals. Henry VI's claim to the throne of France was hung in Notre Dame in Paris at the order of John duke of Bedford and consisted of a poem with a picture.[3] Such works were produced in considerable numbers by craftsmen, possibly in a secular workshop. They were certainly treasured possessions and remained in noble archives. Some were commissioned by great magnates. One was written 'at the instance of my most powerful lord, Henry [Percy], second earl of Northumberland [1416–55]'.[4] The Beauchamp earls of Warwick and the Botelers of Sudeley Castle commissioned their own rolls.[5] While they may have served as reference works, they were also intended for public display and had a wider educational purpose. One Hansa merchant sent a letter to his principal in Lubeck in November 1468 enclosing records of recent events in England and a tree of King Edward 'heir to the crown and nearer to it than Henry VI'; he advises the recipient to 'have it explained to you by doctors and clerks'.[6]

The house of Lancaster also attempted to reinforce its legitimacy by the utilization of prophecies.[7] English kings and their subjects had traditionally shown an interest in prophecy. One English knight had told the French chronicler Creton, when discussing the deposition of Richard II, that the king's downfall fulfilled the prophecies of Merlin. Creton remarked that the knight held this prophecy to be true 'for such is his nation that they very thoroughly believe in prophecies'. Henry V made a pilgrimage to the shrine of St John of Bridlington, a famous fourteenth-century prophet, and Edward IV himself was supposed to have consulted prophecies when in doubt.[8] Howard, the earl of Northumberland, remarked in 1583 that when the civil war between York and Lancaster was at its height, the *Book of beasts and babies* was exceeding rife and carried in every quarter and corner of the realm.

The prophecies were responses to crises in the English past that had parallels to the situation in the mid-fifteenth century. They were originally reactions to the Norman invasions, the civil wars of Stephen and Matilda, the continental ambitions of Edward III, and such recent events as the deposition of Richard II and the precarious position of Henry VI. Some were adaptations of continental prophecies concerning the coming of a last world emperor who would defeat evil and take the world into an age of happiness. By the fifteenth century these prophecies were being circulated more widely on cheap, paper manuscripts and among laymen.[9] The Oxford burgess Nicholas Bishop owned a collection of extracts of the *Brut* and the prophecies of Merlin dated 1432,[10] and Robert Thornton included political prophecies in his paper volume of literature. However, after the outbreak of the king's first bout of illness in 1453, and the birth of his son Edward of Lancaster, the prince of Wales, on 13 October that same year, attention turned to the issuing of prophecies originally written for Edward the Confessor, Edward I and Edward III and now adapted for Henry VI's son. In a collection of astrological and historical extracts and genealogies of Prince Edward of Lancaster and a list of English kings culminating in Prince Edward,[11] there is a group of prophecies concerning a prophetic hero; they include the prophecy of the Holy Oil of St Thomas, the Last of the Kings of the English, and *Lilium regem*. In the accompanying genealogy Prince Edward is described as *verem heredem anglie*, perhaps in riposte to attempts by the house of York to challenge his right to inherit.[12] In the correspondence of Thomas Beckington, Henry VI's secretary, and Margaret of Anjou (1445–56), there are letters addressed to Prince Edward as the hero ruler who will continue Henry VI's conquests.[13]

Edward earl of March would have grown up with the house of York's own perspective on these genealogies and prophecies. His was a family with a unique and exotic history. Edward's father laid claim to the throne of Castile through the female line of Isabella, the daughter of King Pedro the Cruel of Castile and the wife of Edward's great-grandfather Edmund of Langley. In July 1444 Richard duke of York paid for a copy of the Treaty of Bayonne of 1338 between John of Gaunt and his Castilian father-in-law, providing for a reversion of the throne of Castile to descendants of Isabel in the absence of Constanzia's line. In the following year he obtained a copy of the agreement made between John of Gaunt and Juan Count of Trastamara. His negotiations with Charles VII in this year for the betrothal of his son and heir, Edward, to the French king's infant daughter were preparations for Edward's possible occupation of the throne of Castile. As earl of March Edward bore the arms of Castile, the lions gules (or purpure).[14] As Henry VI's incompetence and sickness became more manifest, the house of York's link with the house of Mortimer and the claim that the Lancastrian kingship was based on a wrongful usurpation was first raised. The Mortimers were a Welsh marcher family, joined in marriage to the princes of Wales when Gwladys Ddu, daughter of Llewelyn ap Iorwerth prince of Gwynedd 1200–40, married Ralph Mortimer (d. 1246). Anne Mortimer, daughter of Roger Mortimer earl of March (d. 1398) and sister of the young Edward Mortimer earl of March, married Richard duke of York in a clandestine ceremony in early 1408. Because the two parties (Edward IV's grandparents) were too closely related a papal dispensation was subsequently sought to validate their secret union and legitimize their future issue. Popular awareness of the Mortimer claim to the throne through Lionel of Antwerp, second son of Edward III, was shown when Jack Cade, leading the rebellion of 1450, called himself Mortimer 'for to have the favour of the people'.[15] York himself began to use on his seal the white rose of Mortimer (which had been deployed by Edmund Mortimer as a badge, and a rose bush in flower from which his arms were suspended),[16] and he wore a collar of white roses worth £2,666.[17] Edward would have seen depictions of the Mortimer claim in the parish church of St Laurence in Ludlow, his beautiful childhood home. In the misericord of the choir in the chancel and on the roof bosses there were placed in the 1450s emblems that were to demarcate the ensuing idealogical conflict between the two houses. Richard II's emblem of the white hart therefore appears, to signify that he was the last legitimate king. In the same choir appears the antelope, an emblem of the usurper Henry IV, and in the choir-stalls and in the roof are the Yorkist emblems of the angel, and the falcon in a closed fetterlock, first used by that hunting enthusiast Edmund of Langley and increasingly used by York in the form of a falcon in an open fetterlock (perhaps to symbolize the releasing of the family's dynastic claims). Some vestiges of the Yorkist heraldry still remain in the collegiate church of Fotheringay, including a falcon with outspread wings perched on top of the fetterlock.

It was at the time of the outbreak of the Cade rebellion that Edward's father, Richard duke of York, emerged as a plausible alternative to Henry VI. The prophecies that had been used by the Lancastrians were accordingly adapted for the house of York. One set of prophecies and poems, occurring in a manuscript with pardons for the Kent rebels of 1451, heralds the emergence of a new hero, a British descendant of Cadwallader, chosen by the people; this refers to Richard duke of York, a Mortimer descendant of the Welsh princes, and his emergence as a political force in 1451. One of the prophecies refers to the emergence of a man of might and the people choosing a new king in Parliament. Another refers to the city of London 'Troy untrew', trembling 'to hear a dead man speak'. This may have been a reference to the prophecy the angel delivered to Cadwallader about the return of a British king (Cadwallader's statue was supposed to have protected the city), or perhaps to the return of King Arthur:

> Then shall Troy untrew tremble that dayes,
> Ffor drede of a dede man when they here hym speke
> Then shall Saxons chese theym a lord,
> That reconcile them rightfully, and bryng hem under
> A dede man shall make bytwene hem acorde
> He that is ded and buryed in sight
> Shall ryse agayn, and lyve in lond.[18]

By October 1460 the Yorkist claim was proclaimed in public by Richard duke of York, who maintained his hereditary right to rule before Parliament.[19] The basis of York's claim was that Bolingbroke had unlawfully entered upon the crown, ignoring York's ancestor Edmund Mortimer; and this theme was taken up in the Commons' petition to Parliament in 1461, which treated Bolingbroke as a usurper who had desecrated the state of kingship. Richard duke of York was described as the heir of Brutus in many genealogies.[20] Edward himself was probably involved in studying genealogical matters by the time he arrived in Calais on 2 November 1459. As a seventeen-year-old he had shaken off the tutelage of his father and emerged as an independent political figure. In March 1460 Edward sent Warwick to Ireland on 'a jeopardes a grete viage' to meet with the duke of York. The following June he brought back to Edward news which the young king later mentioned when making a grant to the earl as 'oure grettest joye and consolacion'. This must have been that York intended to depose Henry VI and advance openly for the first time the Yorkist claim to the throne.[21] The three earls arrived in England fortified by this news and intent on pressing their dynastic claims. Edward's promise was such that when news of his victory at the Battle of Northampton reached Bruges at the end of June 1460 it was thought that Warwick intended to depose Henry VI and replace him with the earl of March. Warwick's (and apparently Edward's) subsequent distancing himself from York's claim to the throne in September 1460 may have been due to the failure to enlist support at court to depose God's anointed (the failure commemorated in an illustration of the Battle of Northampton in the *Illustrated Life of Edward IV*[22] (where York is notably absent) showing the victorious Edward, like David, pledging his support to his prisoner, Henry VI), but it may also indicate that Warwick's ambitions were beginning to focus more on the earl of March.

The period between 1456 and December 1460 was an awkward time for those hoping for a new dawn with the earl of March. Hardynge, even when rededicating his *Chronicle* to Richard duke of York, seems to have seen Edward as the true stock of Brutus, and advised York to instruct his son on the need to establish the sort of national unity that Cadwallader and Henry VI were not able to maintain:

> Wherefore, good lord, thynke on this lesson nowe,
> And teache to my lorde of Marche, your heire,
> While he is yong, it may be for his prowe
> To thynke on it, when that the wether waxeth faire
> And his people unto hym dooeth repaire –.

Employing the horticultural images that associated the earl of March with a young and fruitful stock, he advises York that a graft in a garden savours of the stock from which it comes:

> Wherefore graft nowe the wand while it is grene
> Endowe hym with noble sapience,
> Bay whiche he may the wolf were (bete) from the gate.[23]

The wolf was the cognomen for Henry VI and the metal antimony. Although Henry VI was not viable as a king, the nobles were bound to show him loyalty. They were also bound by ties of loyalty to Edward's father Richard duke of York, who did not convince as the new hero king. The Battle of Wakefield on 30 December 1460 and the death of the duke freed the house of York from this dilemma, and this explains why it was not the great disaster it appears to have been to historians, and why Edward responded to the death of his father and younger brother with such decisiveness.[24] Their uncharismatic former leader could now become a prophet to the cause, and Edward himself could compensate for the emotional confusion he must have been feeling by employing all the genealogical, prophetic, historical and mythological material at his disposal to assert his position as unchallenged head of the house of York. Henry VI's involvement in the battle, although he was not personally present, also freed Edward and Warwick from the shackles of the oath of loyalty to Henry VI that they took at the Parliamentary accord of 31 October 1460: 'eache bore trew feythe and lygeaunce to the Kynges persone'.[25] They could now fight against a king who had turned against them without being accused of making a false oath to him and thereby perjuring themselves. This was the very crime, they maintained, which underlay the original Lancastrian usurpation in July 1399: Henry Bolingbroke arrived in England from exile pledging (according to the testimony of the Percies in 1403) his loyalty to King Richard and merely claiming his confiscated duchy of Lancaster. Perjury was definitely committed in the next month during negotiations with Richard II when Bolingbroke sought reinstatement and the summoning of a Parliament to reform the government; however, after entering London in triumph on 1 September (as Edward IV was to do) Bolingbroke made himself king, acceding to the throne as Henry IV. The other crucial date for the flowering of Edward's genealogical and mythological claims was 3 February 1461, the date of the Battle of Mortimer's Cross. This victory, presaged by the phenomenon of the three suns, convinced Edward and his followers that God had given them a sign of his approval of their cause, and that Edward was the heroic king foretold in prophecies. The *Receuil des Chroniques d'Engleterre* narrates how Edward, in the subsequent Battle of Towton that secured the kingship, when he saw the earl of Northumberland carrying the banner of King Henry, 'rode his horse along his army where all his nobles were and told them how they wanted to make him their king and he reminded them that they were seeing the next heir to the throne which had been usurped by the Lancasters a long time ago'.

Between the Battle of Mortimer's Cross and Edward's coronation as king on 28 July 1461, there was a hasty compilation of genealogies showing Edward's descent from the Mortimer line. The earliest surviving rolls, pre-dating Edward's coronation, emphasized the legitimacy of the Mortimer line and the crime of Henry IV's usurpation. The standardized family of rolls derived from Peter of Poitiers and Roger of St Albans were adapted for Edward IV to show the legitimacy of the Mortimer claim and to prove that the Lancastrians were usurpers. They replaced the list of popes found on the right-hand side of the Lancastrian rolls with Edward's descent from the Mortimers, and described Henry of Lancaster as a usurper who deposed and incarcerated the rightful king Richard II and named himself as Henry IV.[26] Another roll, from a separate source, which concludes with Edward's public acclamation on 4 March 1461, was hastily written before the coronation on 28 June and is contemporary with the *Illustrated Life of Edward IV*. This roll claimed that Henry IV incarcerated Richard II (after voluntarily agreeing to meet Henry, then earl of Derby, at Flint to discuss his proposals for reform, Richard II found himself placed under an armed guard). The roll also maintained that Henry IV violently deposed King Richard (he was imprisoned in Pontefract Castle and murdered in March 1400).[27] The Welsh author of the *Prophetic History of Britain* started producing genealogies before the coronation. The earliest is a seventeen-foot roll giving a detailed genealogical descent of Edward through the Mortimers to the Welsh kings and Cadwallader. This roll was issued in such a hurry there was not even time to illuminate with coloured letters the gaps left in the account of Edward's acclamation as king. The haste is explained by the wish to use it for public display. As Gloucester and Clarence are only mentioned as lords, this roll must have been executed before the coronation in July.[28] A more finished and polished work produced around this period (perhaps immediately after the coronation) was the *Illustrated Life of Edward IV* in which Edward is still referred to as the earl of March.[29] This genealogical tree is accompanied by a series of cartoons of the crucial events leading up to Edward's entry into London, emphasizing the way Warwick and Edward obeyed their oaths to Henry VI at the Battle of Northampton, and the importance of the parhelia at Mortimer's Cross as a divine sign that Edward was now free to make his bid for the throne.

Edward's formal coronation in June 1461 was accompanied by more genealogies and prophecies stressing the link between Edward earl of March and the legitimate Mortimer line. They attempted to show that the Lancastrian deposition of Richard II was a crime because it had interfered with the natural succession, which was through Richard II's nearest kin and named heir Roger Mortimer, earl of March and son of Philippa, daughter of Lionel duke of Clarence, second son of Edward III. Hardynge's *Chronicle*, revised and adapted for Edward IV in 1463, shows the royal line in the margins and includes prologues to Edward IV; it could be described as an extended family tree, tracing the royal line all the way from Adam and Japheth. Hardynge suggested that although Henry IV had the integrity to feel some remorse for the crimes on which his dynasty was based (he reburied Richard II at Westminster, allowed pilgrims to Scrope's tomb and restored the Percies to their lands), he lacked true repentance because he did not recognize the validity of the claims of the

Mortimer line: 'for all his rightwisnes and justice that he did he had no conscience of usurpement of the croune'.[30] Hardynge posed the question why God did not allow such a just king as Henry V (whom he had served at Agincourt) to live longer and fulfil his desire to conquer the Holy Land; his answer implied that this was because, despite all his formidable qualities, he belonged to the line of usurpers. A vision of St Bridget on the rightful succession through the older brother (Lionel of Antwerp) rather than the younger brother (John of Gaunt) was included in the *Prophetic History of Britain*, together with an evocation of the desolation and affliction that would affect a kingdom if the elder brother were to be disinherited.[31]

Prominent among these genealogies was the work of the Welsh author of the *Prophetic History of Britain*. In this year he produced hasty versions of his *Genealogy of Edward, King of Britain*.[32] Most go back to ancient Britain or even to Adam, but one starts with Henry III.[33] None of these rolls contains any reference to Edward's marriage and as they were produced rapidly they probably date from the period around the coronation. However, this same author produced more lavish, finished genealogical chronicles and prophecies for public display, and probably for the king's own use. The earliest of these more expensive and illuminated genealogies is the *Prophetic History of Britain*, executed soon after June 1461.[34] A smaller version of this work was produced in 1465.[35] One genealogy adapted for Edward IV early in his reign (there is no mention of Edward's children) that survives only in a seventeenth-century copy shows the line of Henry VI, and the line of England on the left is shown to be false and sterile by being crossed out at the earl of Derby. The true line is shown to be established when the lines of England and ancient Britain merge with the marriage of Anne Mortimer and Richard earl of Cambridge, Edward's grandparents. This is depicted in the form of a cross made out of rose-briars. This could be an allusion to the crossroads where the decisive Battle of Mortimer's Cross was fought, and may also draw a parallel between Edward's origins from his maternal grandmother Anne and the origin of the redeemer, the son of man, from his grandmother St Anne.[36] BL MS Egerton 1076

An important prelude to establishing the superiority of Edward's Mortimer line was to establish the legitimacy of the succession through the female line of Anne Mortimer, Edward's maternal grandmother, who may have become an idealized figure in part because of her early death around 1412, shortly after the birth of Richard Plantagenet, 3rd duke of York and future father of Edward IV on 22 September 1411. Edward's succession has parallels with the succession of Jesus through St Anne. In England the cult of St Anne received a political stimulus in 1382 when her feast was officially promulgated to celebrate the marriage of Richard II to Anne of Bohemia on 26 July. Richard II was regarded by the house of York as the last legitimate king of England who nominated the Mortimer line to succeed him, thereby highlighting the connection between St Anne and Anne Mortimer. Attention to St Anne increased with the promulgation of the doctrine of the immaculate conception of the Virgin at the Council of Basel in 1439. The link between St Anne mother of the Virgin and Anne Mortimer was suggested by Bokenham at the time he was exhorting Richard duke of York to press his dynastic claims in 1445. Bokenham wrote a life of St Anne for Katherine Clopton (d. 1466) of Long Melford and her husband John Denston, a coroner and justice of the peace of Deniston, a village between Clare and Bury. This story of the miraculous birth of a child to a barren couple had particular relevence to Katherine and John Denston, whose only child Anne is portrayed in Long Melford parish church. Bokenham used the life of St Anne to emphasize the parallels between the transmission of the thrones of the kingdoms of heaven and England through the female lines of St Anne and Anne Mortimer. The descent of Jesus from King David had been traced back through the male line of Joseph, despite the absence of a blood line, in the same way as the kings of the house of Lancaster were traced through the male line. Although neither St Anne nor Joachim make an appearance in scripture, Bokenham, using the Greek apocryphal Protevangelium of James and such patristic writers as St John of Damascus, followed Jesus's links to David through St Anne and Joachim. Bokenham referred in his English life of St Anne to a Latin verse account of the life of the saint and her three daughters. Edward IV capitalized on this by emphasizing his ancestry through Anne Mortimer back to King David. Edward's much-vaunted devotion to St Anne, whose feast is prominently signalled in large red letters in the calendar accompanying the *Prophetic History of Britain*, therefore had precise genealogical significance.[37] In the *Prophetic History of Britain* Edward's claim to the throne via Anne Mortimer is compared to the claim of Jesus of Nazareth to the throne of heaven through the female line of his mother the Virgin Mary and his grandmother, Anne.[38] Edward's right to the thrones of France through Isabella, the French wife of Edward II, and to Britain through Anne Mortimer, is supported by a citation of Moses's judgement concerning the daughters of Salphad who went to him because their father's estate had been denied them.[39] At God's command Moses decided they would inherit, and so would all daughters from that time on if their fathers had no son. In the margin to one copy of Hardynge's *Chronicle* this judgement is repeated, together with Jesus of Nazareth's inheritance through the female line.[40] In the *Coronation Roll*[41] a passage is quoted from the *Revelations of St Bridget* which states that a kingdom shall not return to the original prosperity it enjoyed unless the rightful heir was set up through succession of the father's side or the mother's. St Bridget, one of Edward's patron saints, asserted in the *Revelations* that a king could not be forced to alienate part of his crown, just as an amputated finger could not be said to belong to any man but he who lost it.[42] This statement underlies the depiction of the crime of Henry IV's usurpation in the *Illustrated Life of Edward IV*,[43] compiled soon after the coronation. This roll shows a tree sprouting from the navel of a recumbent Henry III (perhaps inspired by the tree of Jesse in the east window of the Lady Chapel of Ludlow parish church, executed *c.* 1330), and is dominated by an image of King David, with whom Edward is identified in this roll. Moses stands on an adjacent branch to the family tree of Henry VI and Edward IV, at the point where Richard II is severed from the tree with a stroke of Henry Bolingbroke's sword. The prophet condemns this violent alteration of the succession by referring to the inheritance of Salphad, 'Zelophehad', which had passed to his daughters and so to their heirs.[44] The crown is still the property of Richard's heirs and the tree is healed by Edward IV, the descendant of Lionel duke of Clarence and Anne Mortimer. The care with which the visual narrative of Edward's possession of the realm in the *Illustrated Life of Edward IV* was constructed is shown by the way emphasis is placed on his wielding the sceptre rather than wearing the crown; and this echoes the ceremonies for the coronation in the Great Hall of Westminster in March 1461 when Edward sat in the King's Bench, sceptre in hand, before going to Westminster Abbey to receive the crown of Edward the Confessor, representing possession of the kingdom.

Edward's active interest in his family history was shown in March 1461, when, according to Abbot John Whethamstede, he personally addressed the crowd at St John's Fields and St Paul's, stating his claim.[45] Once he became king he displayed his knowledge of his ancestral pedigree by giving a statement to Pope Pius II on his genealogy.[46] The same language was employed in official proclamations and correspondence following his accession. The phrase describing Henry VI as 'a king in deed but not of right' was used in a variety of documents and letters.[47] In the proceedings of the 1461 Parliament the commons' petition attacking the Lancastrian dynasty makes no allusion to Henry VI's unfitness to rule but emphasizes the usurpation of his ancestor, Henry IV.[48] The parliamentary petition concentrated on the hardships and self-sacrifices endured by Edward for the common weal, his putting away personal sorrow and the customary mourning for his father in order to speed towards London. Above all, though, it emphasized Edward's naturalness, his inherent qualities and the rightness of his accession.[49] The second parliamentary petition directly employs the language of the genealogical chronicles and prophecies, linking the Lancastrian usurpation with national ill-fortune and divine retribution. The claim that leaders in ancient times were universally admired but had fallen into sorrowful decline after the usurpation was in part an allusion to the decline of England's chivalrous reputation from the time of Edward III.[50]

This judicial approach to Edward's accession went beyond dynastic considerations to establish his moral superiority. The *Illustrated Life of Edward IV* was intended for public persuasion. Nail-holes can still be seen at the edges of the roll where it was publicly displayed on a wall or door. The two rivals Henry VI and Edward IV are shown in armour stepping out of their floral cups, their relative positions made clear from the lines of the *Gospel of St Luke*. Edward's scroll says:

> What is that I hear about you? Turn in the account of your stewardship, for you can no longer be steward.[51]

Above Henry VI, the unworthy steward of the realm, are the words:

> What shall I do, since my master is taking the stewardship away from me?[52]

All this amounts to a conventional, legalistic attempt to give moral weight to a military seizure of the throne. It had been done before in 1399 and would be done again in 1485, but something different was happening in 1461. Edward, through his interest in alchemy, used these genealogies and prophecies to reach above and beyond mere title. The accession and the early years of his reign were accompanied by a mobilization of the kingdom's leading alchemists (the scientists of their day) as one aspect of an impressive gathering of the leading intellectuals of the time: alchemists, genealogists, historians, physicians, poets, illuminators, scribes and heralds, all focusing on the problems of the kingdom and the role of the monarch. A consideration of the cooperation between the experts in these different disciplines on the subject of the nature of Edward's kingship is not without its pitfalls. The appearance of the *uroboros* or knot on a heraldic roll or royal genealogy can be taken as an illustration of such cooperation. In the two forms in which it appears in the Coronation Roll it can also allude to the knots of the Staffords and Bourchiers, families who intermarried with the house of York and who employed such an image as an obvious heraldic symbol of the permanence and fruitfulness of an ancient baronial line stretching into infinity. Similarly Edward would have used the peacock's feathers in a heraldic sense alluding to the bird's well-known symbolism of immortality to stress the infinity of his family line. There are other alchemical symbols on genealogical rolls that have a heraldic, poetic tradition, such as lions, falcons and eagles (all royal badges). However, such confusion between the symbols of the alchemist and the herald or the poet is in itself a significant indication of the way many different intellectuals focused their attention in this period on the nature of kingship and the question of the redemption of the nation. The most important alliance was between alchemy and the related sciences of genealogy and history.

By 1461 the alchemists had come to the conclusion that the true gold they were seeking could only be found in the young earl of March, who was from a separate genealogical line. To justify such a switch of allegiance they needed the cooperation of the country's historians, prophets, chroniclers, heralds, genealogists and astrologers to demonstrate in genealogical, legal and medical terms that the Lancastrian line was a non-British line of usurpers and that this explained the illness and misfortune dogging the house of Lancaster, culminating in the madness of Henry VI. They also needed such experts to show, through the explication of the nation's myths and prophecies, that a radical treatment of England's malaise, involving a change of dynasty, was justified.

This search for inspiration, for the source of identity, took the same path in the Yorkist rolls that it took in the alchemical scrolls and writing of the period: it was an inner journey. The alchemist meditated in his laboratory on the origins of matter, the creation of the four elements. When George Ripley and his fellow alchemists observed the changes within their alembic retorts they saw branches and twigs blossoming so that they 'may grow within the glass like a tree'.[53] Ripley advised his followers to concentrate on the growth of such trees, which he called oak trees or vines, and to reinforce this with active imagination. The tree, with its bronchi and vessels, was for the alchemist a projection of the organic growth of the self towards completion, and while it was seen in psychological terms as the embodiment of the individuation process, it also acquired in the mid-fifteenth century a profound cultural and political dimension. Through heraldry, colour symbolism and historical narrative, the genealogical tree demonstrated the growth of the nation towards selfhood. One genealogical roll culminating in Edward IV begins with an alchemical illustration of the sun and moon.[54] Alchemy, in its psychological, religious dimension, involved the contemplation of the individual adept's past, the deeper recesses of his being within the darkness of the unconscious, but the metaphor of the tree of life was also applied to genealogical rolls to enable a meditation on the nation's past, its soul, where the core of its identity was to be found.[55] Ripley in his visions saw the descent of the king and his nation into the primal substratum of the nation's prehistory and myths, on to which Christianity was a mere gloss, and their rebirth in splendour like the rising sun or the newly minted coins of the Tower. Some of Edward's genealogies went back to the beginning of time to show the prime mover at work initiating the process of creation that would bring order out of the chaos of the *prima materia* and ultimately lead to the accession of Edward IV. The author of the *Prophetic History of Britain*[56] and the *Genealogies of Edward King of Britain* executed at least six other genealogical rolls known to me. Three of them begin with concentric and interconnecting circles that resolve into Edward's line of descent from Noah's son Japheth. Ripley saw the tree of life as inverted, with its roots in Paradise with God, and this pattern was adopted by the compilers of genealogical trees. In the *Coronation Roll* the line of Edward commences under an illustration of Christ in Paradise and the Garden of Eden, before unfolding into the various branches of the royal families in the fallen world.[57] The more standardized genealogical rolls, those derived from Peter of Poitiers and Roger of St Albans, which survive in twenty-seven Latin and English copies, were all written by the same scribe in this period of the Wars of the Roses and adapted for Edward IV. Two long versions in particular were adapted for Edward IV around 1467[58] and between 1469 and 1470.[59] These two genealogies also go back before this idealized period of ancient Britain to the creation of Adam and Eve. They show the evolution of early British history alongside biblical events to suggest the parallels between the Hebrew and British races and to imply that the British descendants of the Trojans were a chosen people awaiting deliverance. The flattering allusions to Edward IV in the long English versions of these rolls[60] indicate that he may have commissioned them. The fact that they were in English suggests that the king was attempting to reach a wider audience. They show the evolution of the line of Japheth to 'kings of Bretayn that nowe is called England'. An epic of national determination is revealed, showing the birth of the Hebrew and British nations and the Christian church. In a 1467 roll[61] one line depicts the founding of Troy by Tros while the other line shows Joshua, the successor to Moses (a figure whose prominence echoes that of Joshua in the *Illustrated Life of Edward IV*), leading 'the chylder of Israel' over the River Jordan bearing the ark of the covenant.[62] At the same time that Joshua destroys Jericho, according to the accompanying historical narrative, Troy too is destroyed. The destruction of these cities prepares the way for the founding of Jerusalem, Rome and New Troy. The Trojans (a captive people like the Jews and the Britons under the Saxons) made their way towards the promised land, led by a goddess to an island called Logres, and their leader Brutus was told by a goddess in a dream to go west of France where he would find an island called Albion. When Brutus around 1170 BC slays the giants of Albion, David slays Goliath.[63] The victory of Brutus is preparation for the founding of the British equivalent of Jerusalem, the city of New Troy or London (in the margin a fifteenth-century hand has added New Troy for special emphasis). In another genealogy[64] there is an account of the conquest of Britain by Brutus which praises the island's great beauty and includes the statement that for a thousand years the Britons ruled the land of the red dragon when Wales, England and Scotland were under the one name of Britain and shared one language.

The genealogies compiled by the author of the *Prophetic History of Britain* between 1461 and 1471[65] similarly show Edward's descent from Noah. At Noah the line of Israel divides into two, the lines of Shem and Japheth. On the right the line of Shem leads to David, described as King of the Hebrews, who prefigures Christ and is identified with a large circle and crown. This line climaxes at Christ. The line of Japheth goes to Brutus, who is highlighted in a similar manner to David and shown almost adjacent to him to make explicit the comparison. The description of Brutus as King of the Britons therefore implies that, like David, he is king of a chosen people. As David heralds the arrival of Christ, Brutus heralds the arrival of Edward IV; at the point where Christ's line ends the line of Japheth crosses over to the right-hand side (facing the viewer) and ends in a similar manner with Edward. The four figures of David, Jesus, Brutus and Edward dominate these scrolls. The same author, in the genealogical chronicles written to accompany the prophecies of the coming of Edward,[66] draws comparison between Joseph's exile in Egypt and the in-habitants of Troy searching for their promised land. The calendar therefore gives special emphasis to the birth of Brutus and the founding of New Troy; the reign of King David, the building of Solomon's Temple and the foundation of New Troy are all shown to occur within the same fifty years.[67] The building of New Troy was also paralleled by the construction of Rome by another group of the survivors from Troy.

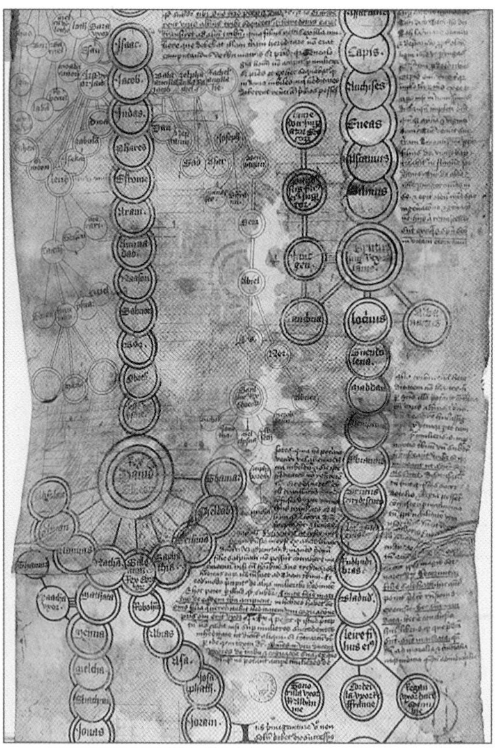

In The Genealogy of Edward King of Britain, *Edward's ancestors King David and King Brutus are represented by blue circles in close proximity to one another to demonstrate their close relationship as leaders of the chosen people of Israel and Britain. (Bodley MS Ashmole Roll 26)*

This represents a radical departure of outlook in the production of royal genealogies.

In the family of thirteenth- and fourteenth-century Anglo-Norman rolls derived from Mathew Paris and Peter of Poitiers (which have been studied by Olivier De Laborderie) there is a geographical and legalistic assertion of the legitimacy of the preceding English kings, all (with the exception of Edward the Confessor) usurpers or descendants of usurpers. In an attempt to consolidate the Plantagenet monarchy, the question of conquest and usurpation was avoided. Tracing the dynasty to its Anglo-Norman roots, these genealogies emphasized the continuity of the English kings (in a manner more appropriate to the French royal house) by exalting royal function rather than blood. The true king was one who ruled righteously. His legitimacy was emphasized in the contractual oath and neither blood nor unction were regarded as significant. With so many different lines of descent and conquests accompanied by bloodshed, including the conquests of the Giants, the Britons, the Romans, the Angles, the Saxons and the Normans ('the plagues of the English' as Mathew Paris

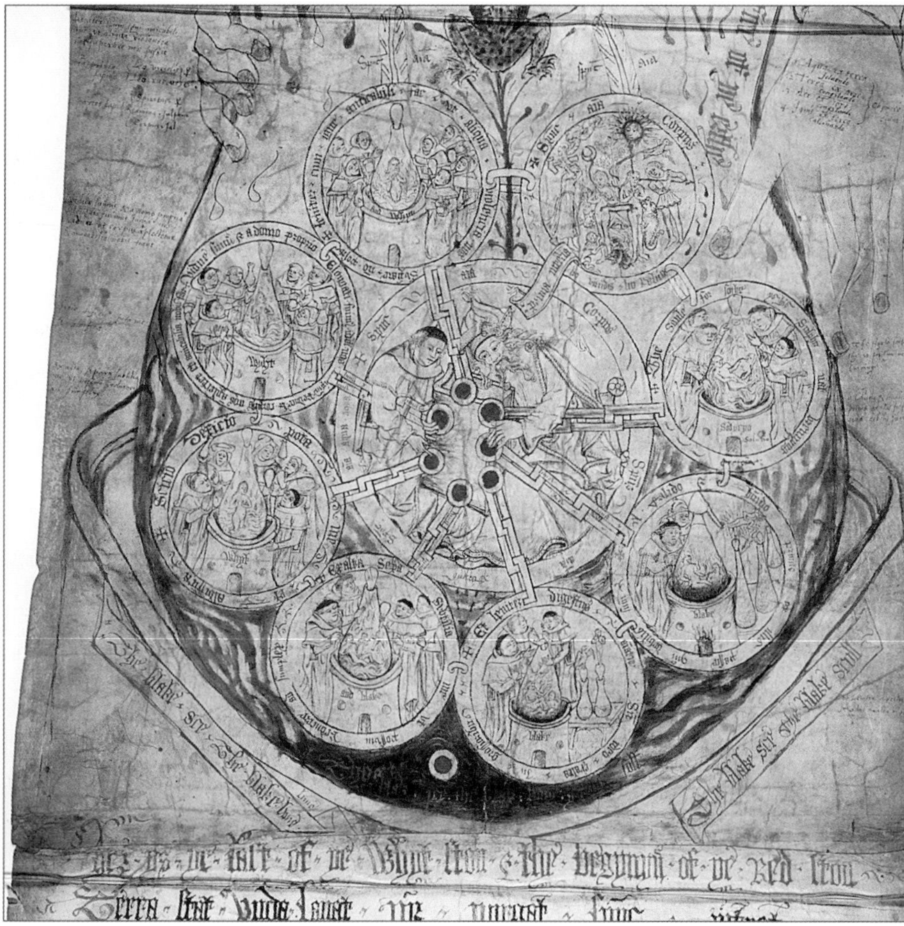

The Ripley Scroll *begins with an image of the alchemist holding an alembic. Within the vessel are seven axles of a wheel representing the seven stages of the alchemical process. At the centre of this wheel there is a great book containing the secrets of alchemy within seven seals. The diagram of the Saxon heptarchy in the* Coronation Roll *(which represents the* nigredo*) also emphasizes the division of the kingdom into seven. The work of generating the unity of the nation is just beginning. (Bodley Roll 1)*

called them), the only solution was to demonstrate that the English were the chosen people, not ethnically defined but chosen rulers of a land promised them by God: 'The fairest of all the islands blessed by God.' The Holy Land was promised first to the Jews and later to the English. But the English were not a race like the Jews. They were a nation of many races and therefore defined as the chosen people by their devoted service to God (in Pope Gregory the Great's pun they were the *angeli*). Their status as the chosen people was also geographically determined by their occupation of this 'blessed island' and their acknowledging the lordship of the king of England. The foundations of this nation were traced back in these Anglo-Norman rolls to a circular heptarchy representing the division of Britain into seven kingdoms and the imposition of a formal political organization of the monarchy.[68]

This imposition of order and continuity on the Plantagenet line was to be turned upside down during the political turmoil caused by the onset of the Wars of the Roses. The genealogical rolls produced by the house of York, including those derived from the same sources as the twelfth- and thirteenth-century Anglo-Norman rolls, emphasized the disorder, discontinuity and lack of unity brought about by the various conquests and usurpations from the time of the Saxon heptarchy until 1461. This heptarchy, as we shall see, was shown in Yorkist rolls to mark the destruction of the British nation. Alternatively the foundation and birth of this nation were to be explored in a more distant past and defined in ethnic terms of race. The heptarchy, in an alchemical sense, represented the return of chaos, the *nigredo*, and the purpose of the alchemists was to use their precious stone (the new king Edward IV) to restore this lost national unity by re-establishing the true British king on the throne of England. It is significant that in the earliest of the *Ripley Scrolls* the beginning of the work, which culminates in the establishment of the stone (or the united kingdom), is represented by a secret book of alchemy enclosed within seven seals, a deliberate echo of this heptarchy. The reign of Edward IV ushered in a new type of genealogy distanced from the French antecedents by being written in Latin and English, which emphasized the status of the new king as the head of a chosen people defined by their pre-Saxon British origins.

The primal core of the nation's soul was perceived to have been conceived with the destruction of Troy, an event that is described in detail in the Yorkist *Prophetic History of Britain*[69] and begins the calendar by the same author.[70] The *Percy Roll*, a colourful genealogical roll nearly forty feet long, completed just after Edward's death, and covering the period from Noah to Edward, is dominated by an image of Brutus in armour on horseback[71] (bearing some resemblance to the equestrian image of Edward in the *Coronation Roll*[72] and to the idealized drawings of the city of Troy and its descendant New Troy). In Hardynge's revised *Chronicle*, dedicated to Richard duke of York,[73] the arms of Brutus, a red shield with two rampant lions and a crown, are prominently displayed. The standard history of Britain, the *Brut*, commences with the mythical Trojan foundation of the British kingdom. Contemplation of the destruction of Troy, the precursor of London, amounted to a stripping back of layer upon layer of myth to get to the origins of British identity. John Lydgate, who had alchemical interests, described in his *Troy Book* the birth of British civilization out of the *nigredo* of war. This was of particular relevance to two owners of the *Troy Book*, Edward IV and William Herbert, and to Edward's courtiers, who had just witnessed the emergence of their nation from the alembic of war in the apocalyptic Battle of Towton. Troy, in Lydgate's work, embodied all the chivalric qualities to be found in the vision of Arthurian Britain upheld by Hardynge and Malory, and which the defeated Trojans had brought to their new land.

The genealogical rolls asserting and celebrating Edward's rise represented therefore a journey from a fragmented country into a prehistoric past, a period between the first British king, Brutus, to the last British king, Cadwallader, when the nation was undivided. This idealized period represented the time when the nation's selfhood was intact and it was believed that the soul of the nation could be found in these times. The genealogies, which bore such a marked resemblance to alchemical scrolls, were designed to harness the powerful energies to be found in such a past. The alchemical trinity of body, soul and spirit also had a political dimension. The body was represented by the people of England, the soul (or to use modern parlance the unconscious) by the mythical prehistoric past of Britain, and the spirit or the head by the king. Edward was regarded as the Sun King who would perform the feat of transmutation that would integrate these three to generate the philosopher's stone, the British nation.

In all these accounts of the early history of the land ruled by Brutus and its descendants, this island is known as Britain and it reaches the height of its power under King Arthur, variously described as the mighty, the miraculous, the famous and the doughty. It was Hardynge who did most to mythologize the lost golden age of Britain, especially in the version of his *Chronicle* presented to Richard duke of York and in the final version presented to Edward IV in 1463, bearing the coat of arms of Brutus 'formerly of Troy'.[74] Using the first book in the great Vulgate cycle of Arthurian legends, the *Estoire del Saint Graal*, written in France between 1215 and 1230, Hardynge described how Joseph of Arimathea collected the blood from Christ's wounds in a vessel called the Grail and took his family to Britain, establishing a Christian community at Glastonbury soon after the crucifixion and building a church dedicated to the Virgin in AD 64. This version of British history had been propounded by the English delegation at the council of Constance in 1417 in response to French claims that England was too small to be a nation, unlike the German nation that incorporated so many different peoples. The English delegation replied that there were many kingdoms under the English: Scotland, Wales, Ireland and the Isle of Man, and a multiplicity of languages, unlike the single Gallic language, all asserting a harmony that proclaimed the importance of the British nation.[75] Thomas Poulton at this council maintained the superiority of the English nation over the French on account of the greater antiquity of its faith stemming from the conversion of the British by Joseph of Arimathea. The 'matter of Britain' was asserted at subsequent councils at Siena and Basel in the first half of the fifteenth century. Hardynge located the Grail Castle of King Pellas, the repository of the lance of Longinus and the Grail, in Wales, and gave an account of the life of Galahad, the descendant of Joseph of Arimathea and discoverer of the Grail, whose heart was buried at Glastonbury by Perceval. He described Arthur as 'the worthiest and wisest [king] in the world, the hardiest and most courageous, in whom there was no drop of cowardice or avarice, one who was like a lion in the field and a lamb of mercy'.[76] Using the *Queste le Graal*, Hardynge endowed Britain with a special spiritual authority during the reign of Arthur by suggesting that the Round Table served as the table that Joseph of Arimathea originally created for the grail knights. Hardynge was a fifteenth-century Geoffrey of Monmouth, creating out of the civil war and confusion of his time a myth of a golden age when Britain was whole. In this period of civil war between 1450 and 1461, when England suffered the humiliation of expulsion from France, many intellectuals urged a retreat inwards to find reasons for such failures, and to find the point in the past at which it all started to go wrong. This led to the radical conclusion that England had always been a conquered nation in exile and that, as with the troubled history of the Jews, there was a divine purpose to all this. Alchemists, genealogists and historians all shared a vision of a mythical time before the Saxon invasions when Britain was an integrated, prosperous and holy land, and that God's purpose was to restore their homeland to His people.

Hardynge weaves a haunting myth that evokes a sense of the lost holiness of his fragmented country. In the version of his *Chronicle* presented to Richard duke of York and subsequently to Edward IV, he describes how Joseph of Arimathea put in the north door at Caerleon (which was Camelot according to Geoffrey of Monmouth) a crucifix 'just like to Christ that after yere abide'.[77] Afterwards Agnastes, King of Wales, cast it into the sea in the River Usk and it washed up where the waves beat on St Paul's wharf in London. King Lucius, with a solemn procession, set it up in St Paul's Cathedral on the north door, where it stood while the kings of Britain ruled. Besides giving divine sanction to all British kings from Brutus to Cadwallader, this narrative bestowed a mythic dimension on the nation's capital, London, or New Troy, which for all these years had the face of God on its cathedral. In the margin to the Yorkist version it was claimed that Joseph also converted Arveragus and made him a shield of arms by making a red cross out of his blood to signify Christ's passion.[78] This was done long before St George was venerated in this land and these were the arms adopted by Constantine, the first Christian emperor, who was also a Briton, the son of Constantius and Helen, finder of the True Cross and daughter of King Coel of Britain, when he experienced his vision of the cross in the heavens.[79]

For Hardynge there was a mystic significance in the original name of Britain 'that nowe is Englande' and he repeatedly referred to it as 'Great Britain' when describing the reigns of Arveragus and Constantine. The heart of this holy land was England, then known as Logres. Hardynge associated the name England, or Anglia, with the Saxon invaders, and maintained that it was first used when King Vortigern allowed the Saxons into his country. Logres attained its zenith in the reign of King Arthur, the most feared conqueror and most regal of kings:

> Eche day came newe, that then more like it semid,
> An heuenly life, then erthely, as menne demid.[80]

For Hardynge, the death of Arthur spells the end of this season of May when the heart flowered, and the onset of a long winter. Arthur was buried in the isle of Avalon and the forsaken nation has ever since awaited the return of 'the once and future king'. With Arthur's death Great Britain's hegemony was eroded by waves of Saxon invaders and the Britons, because of their sins, were finally driven from their heartland of 'Logres' westwards into exile during the reign of King Cadwallader.[81] According to the genealogical rolls accompanying Edward's accession there fell over Britain, after the reign of Cadwallader, a sort of a dark age.[82] The single unbroken line of British kings ends and is replaced with a conglomeration of regional kings. There is no single line, king or country and no Christianity. The line is reunited with King Egbert, the first king of all the realm after the Romans, and he commanded that it be given the name England. However, there is no Britain, and indeed the last British king was told by a prophetic angel that the Britons would never inhabit their homeland until their Saxon supporters were guilty of the self-same sins, and then a British king would reconcile the land. Until that time the refuge of the chosen people living in exile, like the Israelites awaiting their redeemer, was the frontier region of Wales.[83] These myths of Britain's status as a holy land and of the British race as a chosen people awaiting the return of their messiah Arthur (and ultimately Edward IV), have a long Welsh ancestry that pre-dates the writing of the *Estoire del Saint Graal* and ultimately perhaps derive from the emigration of Britons to Brittany in the wake of the Anglo-Saxon invasion. In Brittany (Armorica) the hopes for the return of a messiah such as Arthur to win back the ancestral home were preserved in Celtic tales that ultimately influenced the composition (probably in Champagne) of the Vulgate Arthurian cycle.[84]

The importance of Edward's Mortimer inheritance was that the young king represented the link to this idealized time, this source of national identity. In the centre of London a stone of great antiquity (which still survives in Cannon Street), popularly believed to be the stone of Brutus, was the objective of the Kent rebels in 1450 and Jack Cade touched it with his sword, exclaiming 'Now is Mortimer'. This 'London stone' symbolized the core of British identity and Fabyan seems to have attached to it the sort of alchemical significance usually reserved for the Grail or the Round Table when he celebrated the religious properties of a stone so pure that 'though some have it thrette – Yet hurt had none'.[85] The British identity of the Mortimer line enabled Edward and his advisers to assert in genealogies and public pronouncements that the Lancastrians, far from being legitimate monarchs of England, were merely the last in a series of invaders who had stifled the identity of the British, the direct descendants of the Saxons. In an address to Richard duke of York Hardynge wrote:

> Gracious Lord and true heir in right
> Of Great Britain enclosed within a sea
> O my heir of Logres that now England hight
> Now also of Wales, Scotland
> Which all thre of Bretagne so hight of olde antiquite.

Hardynge was also among the first to identify the house of Lancaster with the invading Saxons who destroyed the integrity and identity of Britain (he noted the arrival of Julius Caesar in Britain 'that nowe is Englande').[86] This had a powerful influence on those who compiled the genealogies and chronicles that accompanied Edward's campaigns for the throne. One version of Hardynge's *Chronicle* produced in the 1470s probably by Sir Thomas Burgh, a member of Edward's household, was presented as a genealogy.[87] Hardynge, and the authors of the other genealogies and chronicles written at this time, linked the Lancastrian crown with the original Saxon invaders and identified the Lancastrian monarchy as a kingship of the Saxons. This link had been first suggested by Henry VI himself in his attempts to have the Saxon king, Alfred the Great, canonized in 1445. The cause was promoted at St Bartholomew's Hythe Abbey, Winchester, where King Alfred was buried. The details borne by Adam Moleyn, bishop of Chichester and the king's secretary, to the Pope stressed that this was being done (for the first time) under the personal initiative of King Henry VI and emphasized that Alfred was the first king of the English.[88] Edward distanced himself from this Saxon pedigree by showing how he was directly linked to the British kings in exile in North Wales and therefore to Cadwallader and the kings of Britain, including Arthur, through his descent from Gwladys Ddu (d. 1251), the daughter of Llewelyn the Great, who married Ralph Mortimer.

Another Yorkist genealogy, concluding with the arrival of Edward the red dragon (and which I shall call the *Genealogy of the Red Dragon*), which must have been compiled between the creation of George as duke of Clarence in June 1461 and Richard as duke of Gloucester in November 1461 (he is not given this title), describes the conquest of Britain by Brutus and praises the island's beauty.[89] It gives three lines of descent. The lines of England from Ethelred on the left (facing the viewer) and France in the centre are interconnected and intercrossed with alternating colours of pale and dark green during the reigns of Henry III and Edward III to show the close relationship between these two realms as a result of intermarriage and foreign invasions such as the Norman conquest. The implication is that Henry VI's Lancastrian line is French, through his mother Katherine, who represents the last in a series of intrusions of French blood. The impact of this roll is to suggest that the recent disasters in British history were genealogical, and that the Lancastrians, far from being a conquering English dynasty, were in fact French, posing a further violation of

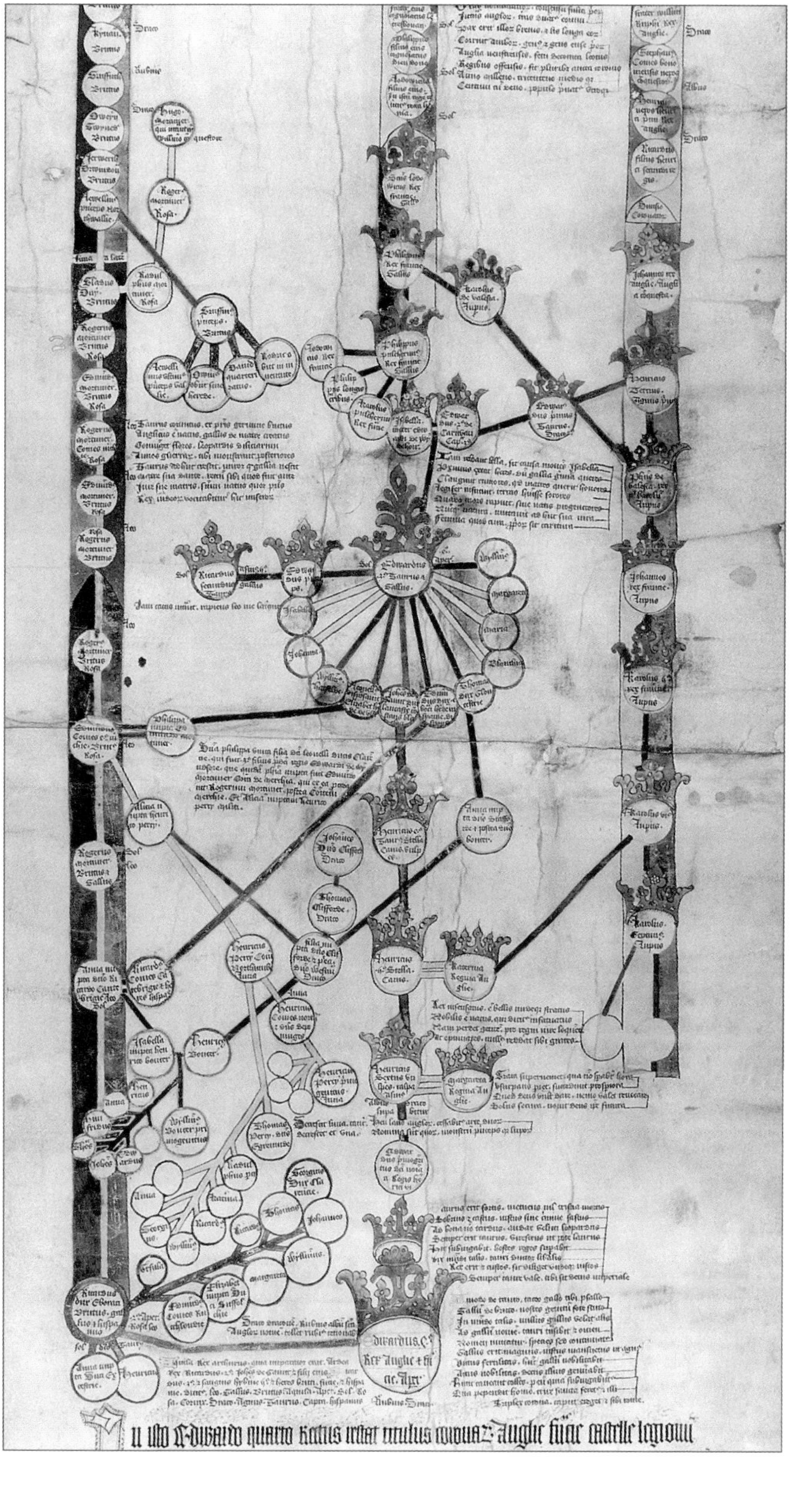

In The Genealogy of the Red Dragon, *demonstrating the king's British descent, Edward is shown with three crowns. His ancestral line of Mortimer is coloured purple, red and gold and accompanied by his cognomens Brutus,* Leo, Sol, Rosa *and* Red Dragon. *(BL Add. MS. 18286 A)*

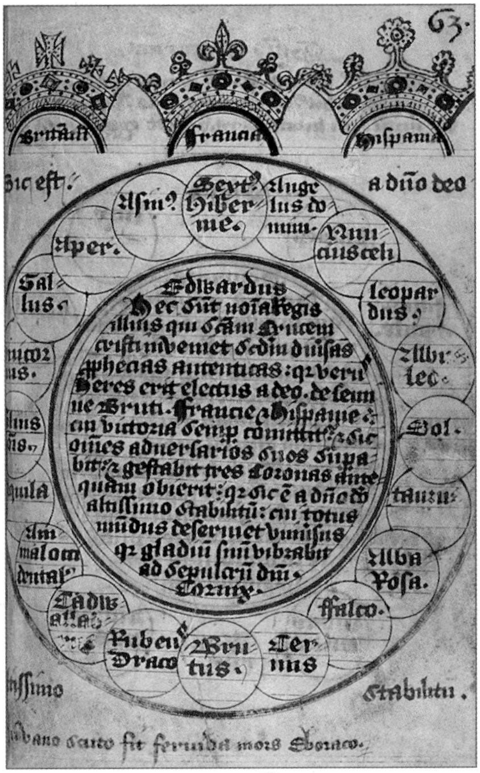

The calendar in The Prophetic History of Britain *culminates in an account of Edward's accession represented by this circle surrounded by various cognomens assumed by Edward, including: Red Dragon, Brutus,* Sol, *Falcon, the Angel of the Lord, Cadwallader and the Eagle. (Bodley MS 623)*

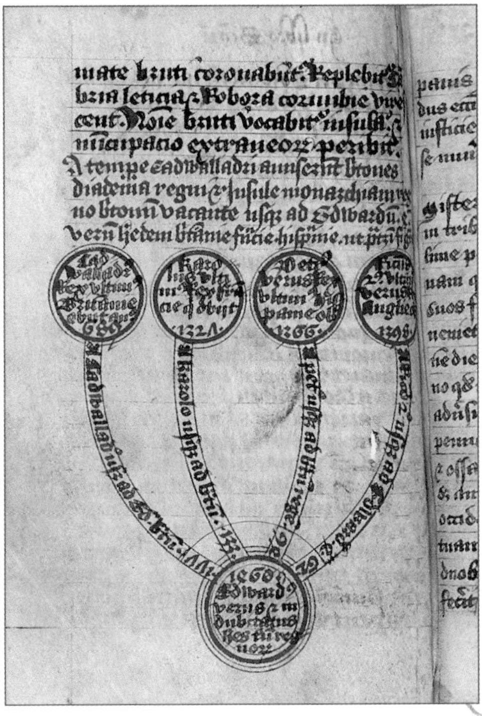

In The Prophetic History of Britain, *the state of sickness and crisis facing monarchies throughout Europe is demonstrated in this representation of the deaths of the last true kings in Europe: Cadwallader of Britain in AD 689, Pedro of Spain in 1264, Charles IV of France in 1321 and Richard II of England in 1399. All will be resolved in 1460 with the accession of Edward IV, who will unite all these realms.*

British identity. The line of Edward IV from Brutus through Cadwallader to Llewelyn, is kept clear of all this: prominently displayed on the right-hand side in red and gold, it becomes the line of Mortimer, and Edward, as a Mortimer, becomes the first truly British king since Cadwallader. The lines of France and England in this genealogy are represented by the white dragon and the line of Britain by the red dragon.[90] These two dragons feature in Merlin's interpretation of the significance of the fighting dragons in Geoffrey of Monmouth's *Historia regum Britanniae*, compiled between 1120 and 1135 and recounted in the *Prophetic History of Britain*.[91] The fight between a red dragon and a white dragon in a pool under a castle that King Vortigern was attempting to build was interpreted by Merlin as representing the conflict between the Saxon and British nations, a conflict that would be finally resolved with the defeat of the white dragon by the red. The *Ripley Scrolls* employed the same colour symbolism, showing the evolution of the philosopher's stone through the colours red, gold and black, and using the same images of conflict, fighting lions and dragons. The compiler of the *Genealogy of the Red Dragon* maintained that this resolution occurred in 1461 when a British king, Edward, defeated the Saxon Lancastrians.[92]

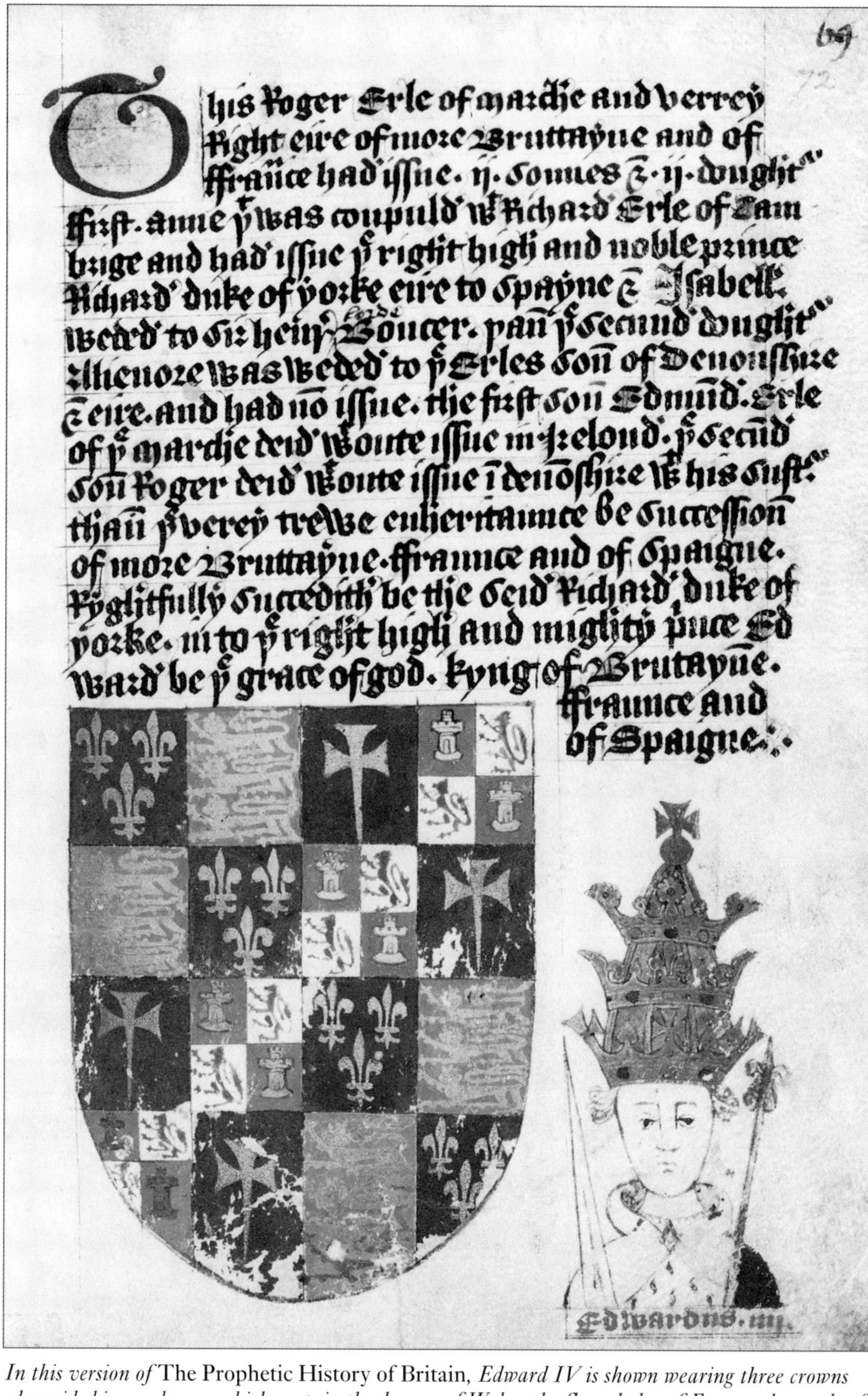

In this version of The Prophetic History of Britain, *Edward IV is shown wearing three crowns alongside his royal arms which contain the dragon of Wales, the fleur de lys of France, the castle of Spain and the arms of Cadwallader, the last king of Britain. (BL Vespasian E VII)*

The most detailed exposition of Edward's British claim to the throne occurs in the earliest version of the *Genealogy of Edward King of Britain*, compiled before June 1461 by the Welsh author of the *Prophetic History of Britain*.[93] A later version of this was compiled in 1471.[94] Edward's descent from Noah is shown and the tree is dominated by the British line. Brutus, Arthur and Cadwallader[95] are all depicted with golden crowns and symbolically linked with Edward who is shown with three golden crowns. The British line on the right is shown in red, with the Saxon, English and Lancastrian lines on the left in black, and there are no crowns alongside the rulers in these lines. Next to Cadwallader there is a representation of the prophecy of the angel who predicted that the Britons would be expelled by the Saxons, and Merlin's prophecy of the return of the British rule in 1460. The most detailed exposition of Edward's British claims to the throne occurs in the *Prophetic History of Britain*,[96] which contains a detailed genealogical discussion of the links between Cadwallader, the last British king, Llewelyn, the last prince of Wales, and Edward IV, who is shown with the arms of Cadwallader, a blue shield with a gold cross and a shield with the red dragon of Llewelyn.[97] There is also a discussion of Edward's links to the thrones of France and Castile, commemorated in illustrations of his coat of arms. A specific connection is made in the later and shorter version of this *Prophetic History* between the deaths of Cadwallader in 687, Pedro of Spain in 1264, Charles of France in 1321 and Richard II of England in 1399 to show that monarchy was in a state of crisis throughout Europe.[98] A portrait of Edward IV wearing three crowns is accompanied by his description as the true heir of all these realms.[99] The calendar accompanying the *Prophetic History* concludes with a sermon declaring that the rightful rulers of Britain, because of their sins and the sins of their people, were driven out in 689; and now the wrongful rulers of England, because of their sins and the sins of their people, have been expelled from this land by the rightful descendants of the ancient kings of Britain in the year 1460/1.[100] This event is celebrated in the calendars of both manuscripts and the coming of Edward in 1460/1 is commemorated with the reintroduction of the name 'Britain' in large red letters.[101] 'Britain' was last used in the calendar for King Cadwallader.[102] Succeeding kings until Edward were described as 'kings of Anglia'.

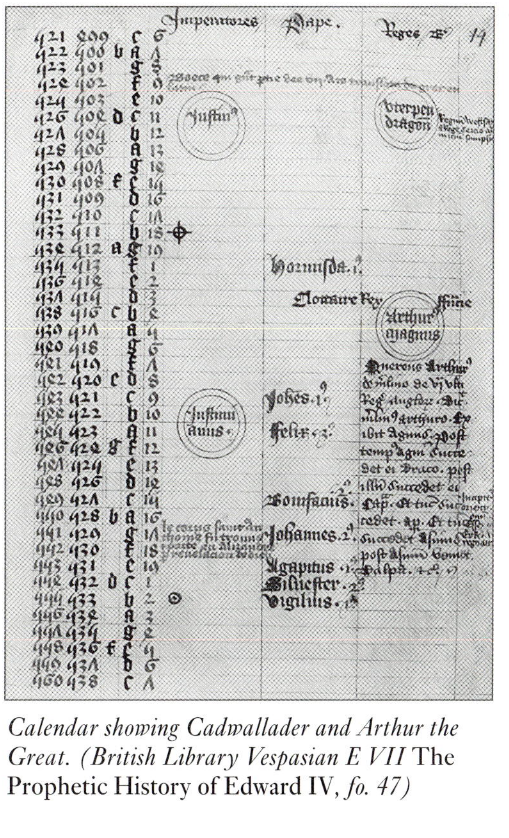

Calendar showing Cadwallader and Arthur the Great. (British Library Vespasian E VII The Prophetic History of Edward IV, *fo. 47)*

The genealogies and chronicles produced for Edward around the beginning of his reign varied in their assessments of the Lancastrian kings. Most praised Henry V and some even recognized Henry IV's virtues, but they all made it clear that they were usurpers, set against the wishes of God, and some even crossed out the Lancastrian line to invalidate it completely. They also went further and suggested that the invasion of Bolingbroke from France in 1399 was no more than the last in a series of foreign invasions, including the Norman conquest and the Saxon invasions, which deprived the British people of their rightful king and name. With this comprehensive approach, Edward and his supporters were able to invalidate the most politically damaging of the house of Lancaster's achievements, the French conquests of Henry V, for Henry himself was depicted as merely the representative of a foreign power.

The source of this British identity was perceived to be Wales. Between the death of Cadwallader in AD 649 and the reign of Llewelyn the Last of Gwynedd, Wales west of the marches was never conquered and remained untouched by the successive waves of foreign invaders – Saxons, Angles, Vikings and Normans – who overran the renamed England. Llewelyn the Great (d. 1240) and Llewelyn the Last tried to create a feudalized Welsh state to counter the Norman advance. With the death of Llewelyn the Last in 1282 Gwynedd became a crown possession and a dynasty that had ruled in Wales since the departure of the Romans became extinct in the male line in 1378. The royal Welsh title then passed to the Mortimers. Hardynge was one of the first to identify the house of York as the heirs to the rulers of this holy island.

What was at stake in the mid-fifteenth century was the salvation of a nation splitting apart through the divisions of Lancaster and York, and north and south. Henry VI and Margaret of Anjou, whose peripatetic childhood in the courts of Europe had given her little sense of national integrity, were even prepared to give Berwick to the Scots in return for their help. But the English, with their precocious sense of governmental unity and their integration into the new European cultural orbit, had no professional literary class who could preserve historical mythology in the manner of the bards of Ireland, Wales and Scotland. As England began to split apart from Europe in the wake of the Hundred Years War and the dissolution of the Lancastrian empire in northern France and Gascony, and her people became more aware of their vernacular language, the English compensated for their lack of professional remembrancers by turning to the myth-makers of the Welsh marches, where Edward and the Mortimer line had originated.[103] The author of the *Prophetic History of Britain* and the *Genealogies of Edward King of Britain* was in all probability Welsh, but he was no marginal figure and he was as central to Edward's cause as William Herbert. Considering the Welsh origins of the earl of March's family (Edward himself was brought up in Ludlow in the Welsh marches), the Welsh interests and probably origins of the author of the *Prophetic History of Britain* and the *Genealogies of Edward King of Britain*, and the Welsh origins of many of the myths and prophecies associated with the new king, it is no surprise that the impetus for Edward's campaign was more than merely theoretical. Welsh poets, with the decline of crown authority in Wales in the 1450s, hailed the coming of this 'royal' (or privileged) Welshman. The main influence in enlisting the support of the Welsh poets was Edward's closest companion of these years, the Welshman William Herbert of Raglan. Lewis Glyn Cothi (d. 1490) saw Edward as a descendant of Gwladys Ddu, daughter of Llewelyn the Great, and a man who heralded the beginning of an era when 'Saxons will no longer be found presiding over the Welsh or holding an official position among them'.[104] Lewis put himself at the disposal of Edward after 1461, praising his descent from Gwladys Ddu and emphasizing how closely the king and Herbert worked together. Guto'r Glyn (d. 1493), a man of the marches where Mortimer influence was strong, was a steady supporter of the Yorkist cause. He asserted Edward's British origins and asked him to descend on the deceits and wrongs of Wales.[105] He wore Edward's badge and sang to him as a descendant of Gwladys Ddu, calling on the Yorkists to restore order: 'come thyself valiant Edward and check the oppressors'.[106] Edward's association with Wales goes back to 1452 when, aged ten, he appeared as the nominal head of an army approaching London from Wales while his father was in the Tower. The army that provided the military sanction for Edward's installation as king in Westminster Hall was largely recruited from the Mortimer lordships of Wales and the marches. From the same area came the Welsh troops who fought at

Agincourt and wore the red dragon of Cadwallader. William Herbert was a key military commander and he was at Edward's side when the apparition of the three suns appeared at Mortimer's Cross. The name of this battle had great symbolic significance for Edward's Welsh supporters, for it alluded to the marriage of Anne Mortimer and Richard earl of Cambridge, which was commemorated in the form of a cross in a genealogical roll compiled in 1461. Edward and Herbert turned the growing Welsh nationalism, noticed by Hardynge, on its head, using it as a springboard to political power. In doing so they were appeasing the emerging Welsh gentry, who did not desire the national independence that Owain Glyndwr had fought for but wanted rather a long-term champion of their political interests within the English political system.[107]

It was on the *Coronation Roll*,[108] probably commissioned by Edward himself to commemorate his coronation, and executed between the coronation and his marriage, that the importance of the Welsh Mortimer line was most eloquently demonstrated and linked with alchemical images to show how Welsh blood and myth contributed to the rebirth of the nation in an alchemical sense. This twenty-foot roll, intended for public display, uses the colours of the different lines to complement the alchemical motifs discussed earlier to show the evolution of Edward's family tree as the culmination of the alchemical process. The tree, representing both organic and psychological growth, embodies the individuation process in a collective sense, the coming to fruition of a nation. In collective, cultural terms the unconscious strives for recognition and acceptance by the spirit or intellect, and this issue coheres around a redemptive king who represents the spirit, and who must integrate the nation's head and body (the king and his people) with its soul, the instinctive emotions that in cultural terms are represented by such myths and archetypes as those of Brutus and Arthur; these are the sources of the energy and power to be found in the prehistoric past of the nation. The arms of Brutus, three gold crowns on a blue shield impaling those of his wife Pandrasus, daughter of the King of Greece, are prominently displayed near the top of the roll. Geoffrey of Monmouth is faithfully followed as the line of England, incorporating the Lancastrians and Saxons, is therefore shown in gold, because this is the spirit or head of the country, the source of kingship. The Welsh line of Brutus which goes from Llewelyn ap Gruffyd, Prince of Wales (whose banner is displayed opposite that of Brecknock, mother of Edmund first lord of Wigmore) through to the Mortimer dynasty (whose banner is also displayed) and Edward IV is shown on the right in red, the colour of the heart, of the Passion. These two opposites have to be integrated if the nation is to attain the wholeness it possessed before the division of Britain into seven kingdoms. These seven kingdoms are depicted on the roll as a series of circles forming an image of a rose, at the centre of which is a gold, blazing sun. As the work approaches culmination, the red and green lines of Wales, the blue line of France and the gold line of England all merge to form the tincture, represented by the appearance of a peacock displaying its tail at the appearance of Richard duke of York. This rainbow of colours symbolized the imminence of the appearance of the stone and refer back to an image at the top of the scroll of Noah's ark. This is immediately followed by the appearance of the squared circle containing an account of Edward's accession and coronation. Within this circle there is a description of Edward's entry into London and his proclamation as king by popular will of the people on 4 March 1461 through the grace of God, and his crowning at St Paul's in July before a great gathering of people. Edward's popular acclamation (his election by a small body of Yorkist lords and acclamation by the people of London) was a reassertion of a dormant elective principle which, prior to the establishment of primogeniture, played an important part in succession to the crown. This formal expression of popular consent gave structure and character to the usurpation of Edward IV.[109] As George Neville expressed it in a letter to Coppini: 'He took

In the Coronation Roll *the approach of the accession of Edward IV is presaged by heraldic images that also serve as alchemical symbols of the imminence of the achievement of the quintessence, the philosopher's stone. The Yorkist falcon and fetterlock may represent the raven or* nigredo, *the Percy moon and the Yorkist suns can also represent the alchemical conjunction of the sun and moon, and the Stafford knot is also the symbol of the* uroboros, *the* Alpha et Omega, *the completion of God's plan. (Philadelphia Free Library E 201)*

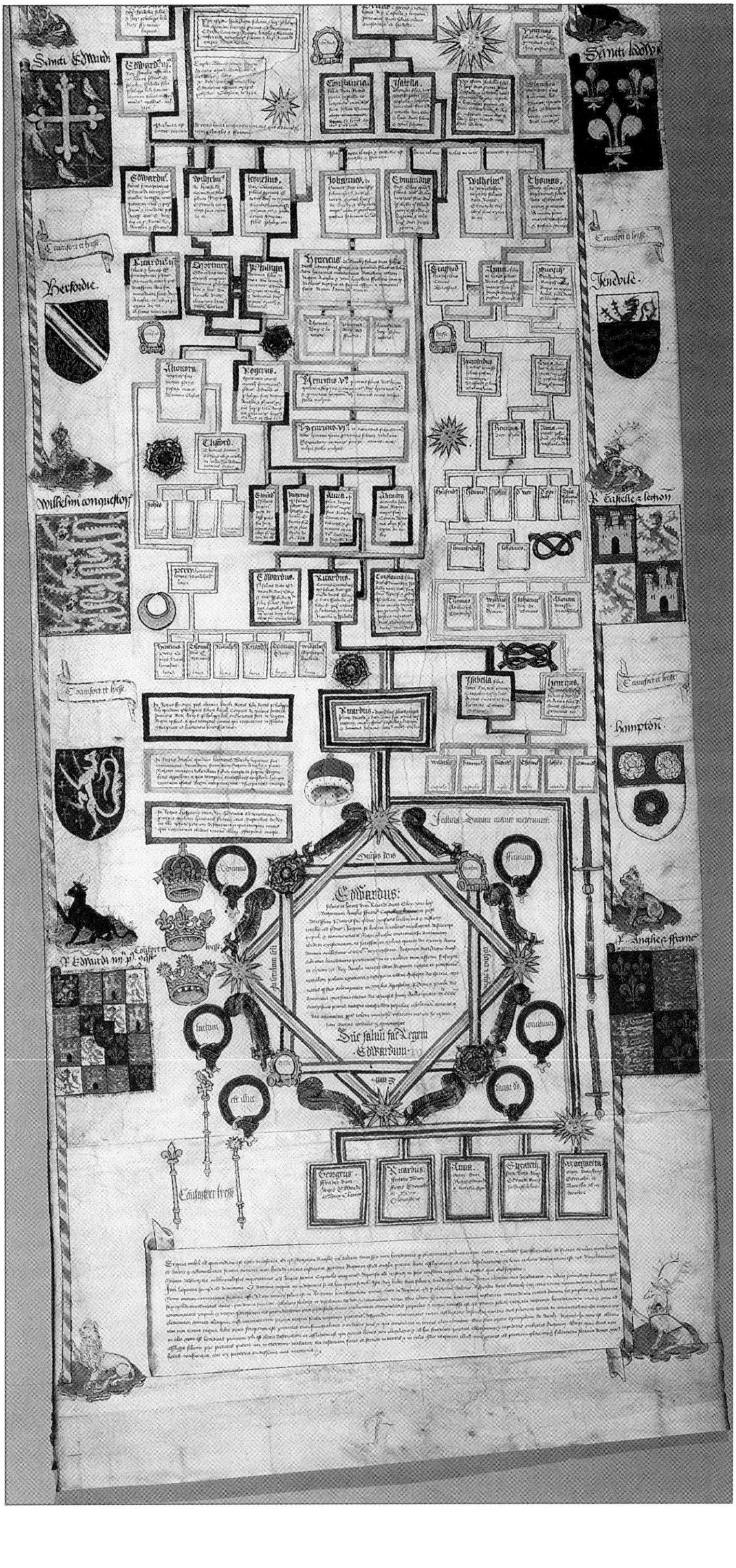

*The perfection of the 'Great Work' of alchemy, the squaring of the circle occurs with the coronation of Edward IV. (*Coronation Roll, *Philadelphia Free Library, E 201)*

upon him a crown of England by advice of the lords spiritual and temporal and by election of the commons.'[110] In alchemical terms the people represent the body of the nation. The alchemical trinity of the spirit (the king), the soul (the ancient British past) and the body (the common people) is complete within a circle of shimmering gold leaf. This gold leaf is also used in the images of Edward on horseback and Christ in heaven at the top of the roll, and thanks to the recent conservation of the roll it shines brilliantly. This is the true alchemical gold, in contrast to the more insipid yellow ochre with which the Saxon and Lancastrian line of England is depicted. This completed circle, suspended from a golden chain of heaven, is the culmination of the alchemical work, the philosopher's stone, the holy grail, a nation's selfhood.

Another way that Edward was able to inflate his own sense of power and confidence and to harness energy was through the use of prophecy. Previous kings of England had used prophecy but Edward was to take it to new and imaginative heights as he took on the mantle of heroic redeemer of the British nation, to whom was assigned a number of prophetic names, some of which had alchemical significance. If Henry VI had been bypassed as the prophetic king in favour of his son, it is possible that the same thing happened to Richard duke of York. Bound as a separate quire after the letter book of William Swan, a canon lawyer to Pope Gregory, is a collection of nineteen political prophecies, including the prophecy of Merlin, about a heroic crusader who will be king of France.[111] These prophecies culminate in a list of the prophetic names of the king who will recover the Holy Cross, and his opponent. The prophetic names for the heroic redeemer include Edward, Brutus, the Red Dragon, Cadwallader, the Eagle, the White Rose, the Bull and Jupiter – all recognized cognomens for Edward earl of March and the house of York. The cognomens White Dragon, the Pretender, the Usurper, the Antelope (Henry VI's badge), rex insensibilis and Saturn were all widely employed by the Yorkists for Henry VI and the house of Lancaster. Coote wrongly dates this collection of prophecies to the late 1440s, to coincide with Swan's letter collection and a section on events in the period between 1419 and 1444, before either of the two Edwards was on the scene. But they were clearly written later, probably in 1460 after the death of the duke of York, but it is just possible that they date to the mid-1450s when Edward earl of March was emerging as a young hopeful and his father was beginning to be bypassed in the same way as Henry VI. Confirmation of this appears in the form of a gold cross, around which there seems to be a *uroboros* on top of an ascendant sun, after an account of Brutus' conquest of Albion.[112]

After the death of the duke of York at Wakefield, the utilization of prophecies in favour of Edward earl of March intensified. His campaign, from the beginning of 1461 through to his accession in March 1461 and his coronation in June, was fuelled by the belief that he was the one chosen by God and spoken of by a series of prophets over the preceding thousand years. Many of these prophets heralding Edward's arrival are shown in the *Illustrated Life of Edward IV*, which documents the steps taken by Edward until his accession in March 1461. On the top left-hand section of the roll, after captions illustrating Edward's victory at Mortimer's Cross and his entry into London, Edward is shown crowned on a wheel of fortune, wearing royal robes and holding the sceptre and sword of state, while the Lancastrian kings are shown descending the wheel. The revolutions of this wheel have been stopped with the thrust of a spoke by the figure of Reason (*Ratio*) wearing a judge's coif and robe.[113] Opposite this scene, on the right of the scroll, are the prophets who have predicted the coming of Edward. They include the angel who promised Cadwallader that the British would one day have a king again (this angel bears a blazing sun with the word 'Sol' overhead). In the centre of these prophets, holding the host, is the archbishop of York, Richard Scrope, who was martyred outside York in 1405 for rebelling against Henry IV (he was trying to bring about the Mortimer succession). Another conspirator in this rebellion, executed alongside Scrope, Thomas Mowbray, the Earl Marshal, is depicted in armour wearing a coronet and bearing the inscription 'Northffulk'. The other figures are more problematic but probably include St Apollonia in the form of a crowned woman holding pincers; Joshua carrying a model of a city, Jericho or perhaps New Troy; Edward the Confessor, and two figures associated with the Confessor's prophecy, St John the Evangelist, in the guise of an old man who was reputed to have received a ring as alms from King Edward, and a pilgrim who received this ring from St John in the Holy Land and heard a prophecy about Edward's imminent but holy death; an angel with a trumpet; the martyr St Vincent; and the cardinal virtue, Prudence. Above Scrope, in the sky alongside the three suns, is depicted a comet, possibly an allusion to the comet that according to the author of the *Prophetic History of Britain* and the *Brut Chronicle* appeared after Bolingbroke's usurpation in 1402, foreshadowing Scrope's martyrdom.[114]

Some of the vaguer prophecies, such as those of a last world emperor who would defeat evil and take the world into an age of happiness, were easily adapted for Edward's motto 'comfort and joy', but most of these prophecies, such as those of the angel and the eagle, were derived from the Welsh trust in ancient prophecies drawing on history and myths of a

An illustration of Edward IV on Fortune's Wheel from the king's copy of The Troy Book. *In the background are suns in splendour. The image is closely related to that of Edward crowned on the Wheel of Fortune stopped in its rotation by Reason in* The Illustrated Life of Edward IV. *(British Library Royal 18 D II, fo. 6)*

redeemer of the Celts. The largest body of Welsh political poetry of this period, the prophetic, is still unpublished. This redeemer was by 1460 seen to be Edward IV and his lieutenant William Herbert. Herbert's involvement in the *Illustrated Life of Edward IV* is implied in an illustration to the opening of one of Edward's books, Lydgate's *Troy Book*, which shows the king sitting on the stationary wheel of fortune in an identical manner to the image in the *Illustrated Life of Edward IV*.[115] At the foot of the wheel Herbert and his wife kneel before the king. Behind them on a blue sky are images of blazing suns. Further Welsh involvement in this roll is suggested by the prominence of a prophetic cognomen for Edward, the black bull of the Mortimers (a beast which will deliver the Celts) in the illustration of Edward's vision of the three suns and the Battle of Mortimer's Cross. Guto'r Glyn, in a poem addressed to Edward, referred to the bull as the badge of the king, asking 'where is the great bull of the Mortimers?', and another poem addressed to Sir Walter Herbert referred to Edward IV as the bull. The possible Welsh origin of the *Illustrated Life of Edward IV* is also implied by the fact that it records Henry III's foundation of the Dominican House at Gloucester.[116] This may indicate that the roll was owned by that same house, which was sufficiently close to the Welsh marches.

Another Welshman close to the king, and presumably to Herbert, who was the leading authority on these prophecies, was the author of the *Prophetic History of Britain* and the *Genealogies of Edward King of Britain*.[117] The earliest of these, compiled before June 1461, contains Bede's prophecy of an alliance of the Celtic peoples against the Saxon English (applied in this genealogy to the Lancastrians), together with an explanation of the significance of some of the prophetic names used to signify the coming of Edward, such as the Red Dragon, Sol and Taurus. This genealogy shows the fragmented British line joining again with Edward IV represented by a large circle containing a celebration of Edward's fulfilment of the prophecy of the angel and the return of the British island's identity, the loss of which since the exile of Cadwallader is recorded in a unique lament, 'lost out of mynde'. This hastily executed roll was intended for public display and proclamation. It begins with the following statement: 'Let it be known to all men how this lande called the realm of Anglia was first and formerly inhabited with Britains.' A hint that the Welshman Edward is the 'once and future king' is provided by the account of the reign of King Arthur and his burial in the isle of Avalon.[118] Another hurriedly executed roll by the same author and originating in 1461 goes back to Henry III and includes the prophecies of Merlin, the angel, St Gildas, St Bridget and Richard Scrope, all foretelling the coming of Edward, and this roll too has an account of the reign of King Arthur.[119] The British line is dominated by Brutus, Arthur, Cadwallader and Edward himself, all shown with golden crowns, noticeably absent from the Saxon line of Henry VI. This points to a close relationship between these works and the *Illustrated Life of Edward IV* which would have been completed with the knowledge, approval and probably sponsorship of Edward himself.

The *Prophetic History of Britain*, the most authoritative account of these prophecies, contains fifty-six prophecies relating to Edward, preceded by a calendar showing the evolution of British history culminating in Edward's kingship. The last entry in this calendar records the coronation of Edward IV and the beginning of the pontificate of Pius II. As Pius died in 1464 the composition of this work must date from before then and may be as early as 1461.[120] Soon after, the same author compiled a smaller version of these prophecies in which the calendar includes the beginning of the pontificate of Pope Paul II in 1464, and there is a calculation of the number of years from the original creation to the fifth year of Edward IV in 1465.[121] He also includes some of these prophecies in his *Genealogies of Edward King of Britain*. One, written in about 1464 in Latin and English, has the prophecy of the angel to Cadwallader and on the verso there are extracts from the *Revelations of St Bridget* relating to the joining of the thrones of England and France, adapted to Edward IV's claim to the French throne.[122] A simplified version of this roll was written in about 1470 and contains the prophecy of the angel and the prophecy of Merlin to Arthur on the return of the Britons.[123] His most ambitious version of the *Genealogy of Edward King of Britain* was written in the same year[124] and contains the most famous of the prophecies from the *Prophetic History of Britain*. The crucial prophecy in this volume was that of the angel, taken from Geoffrey of Monmouth. The angel told Cadwallader, the last king of Britain, that his race would be driven out of England because of their sins, and that the Celtic nation would flourish again in this island and its ancient name of Britain be restored only when the Saxon invaders had become as sinful as the Britons they replaced. This *Prophetic History* also contains an English sermon on the importance of these prophecies as proof that Edward's coming was God's will.[125] In the sermon in the *Prophetic History of Britain* that may have preceded Edward's march to Towton, the congregation was asked to devote itself to the fulfilment of God's will and to beware of the Devil. Recent history is seen in terms of a Corpus Christi cycle play, conflict between good and evil, between the witnesses of God's will and those tyrants who oppose it. Men, it is claimed,

> are unable to comprehend fully the will of God and the devil can subtly deceive people. To prevent men walking into evil ways, God has revealed his wishes to certain blessed servants and holy saints who then informed men through prophecy what they needed to know. No man should ignore or deny the messages of these divinely inspired orators. These prophetic revelations are made in order that the people might eschew great vengeance that shall fall for sinful wrongs done in old times by disinheriting of rightful kings. Men should guard against the sin of disrupting the divine succession and all will be revealed to certain virtuous men who are able to distinguish good from evil.[126]

The author of this sermon was suggesting that the true succession, the rebirth of the British line, long denied because of the people's sins, 'Right for synne was put owte anno 689 and now againe wrong for syne be ryghte is flemed oute of the land for evere, anno 1460', had been prevented by Bolingbroke's usurpation, and a number of prophets from prehistoric times to the present had spoken out to ensure that God's will would prevail.[127]

A similar sermon accompanying the prophecy of the angel was recorded in a four-foot genealogical roll, the *Genealogy of the Red Dragon*[128] executed in Edward's reign. This roll emphasizes the various codenames contained in prophecies that referred to Edward. The sermon gives an account of the conquest of the island by Brutus, praises the island's great beauty and claims that for a thousand years the Britons ruled the land of the red dragon when Wales, England and Scotland were united under the common name of Britain and spoke one language. The author laments that:

> since the reign of Cadwallader this land has been dissevered by many nations through conquest; but one day, when the supplanters of the British are guilty of the same sins as the people they drove out, an heir of Cadwallader shall claim and recover the lands of his ancestors and there will be a final destruction of the Saxons and Normans and all other strangers of this land. He who shall conquer will be called the red dragon and the ancient name of the island, Britain, will be restored. For though we have no knowledge of the secrets of God yet these truths have been revealed to holy men and women by the Holy Ghost.[129]

A form of this sermon on the fulfilment of the prophecy of the Angel (probably the one occurring in the *Prophetic History of Britain*) may have been the one preached by George

Neville on behalf of Edward's claim to the throne on 1 March 1461 in St John's Fields to three to four thousand people and at St Paul's Cross.[130] Edward, in a proclamation in 1471, referred to these sermons delivered by Neville in diverse places. The detailed form of the prophecies in the *Prophetic History of Britain* celebrating Edward's Welsh, British ancestry, which were alluded to in the *Genealogies of Edward King of Britain* and the *Illustrated Life of Edward IV* produced between March and June 1461, would have provided powerful backing to Edward's campaign which started in Wales. Reservations about identifying the sermon in the *Prophetic History* with Neville's sermon seem to rest largely on the Welsh preoccupations of the compiler of this manuscript and these prophecies,[131] but they were central to Edward's campaign and according to the *Brief Latin Chronicle* Neville set out his master's claim with abundant evidence refuting hypothetical evidence against it.[132]

The author of the *Prophetic History of Britain* and the related group of manuscripts made elaborate provision for the explanation of the significance of the various prophetic codenames by which Edward IV was known. In the *Prophetic History* and in the 1470 version of the *Genealogy of Edward King of Britain*, circular diagrams of Henry VI and Edward IV are surrounded by various cognomens.[133] In these manuscripts, and in other genealogies containing prophecies, Edward was described as *Sol*/sun (possibly under the influence of alchemists such as Ripley, who may have been consulted on the production of the *Coronation Roll*[134] and the *Illustrated Life of Edward IV*), *Rosa*/rose, *Rubeo Draco*/red dragon, the Falcon, the Eagle, the Son of Man (another cognomen with alchemical associations), the heir of Brutus, Cadwallader, and the Bull with the Golden Horns. His opponent, Henry VI, the last representative of a long line of foreign opponents of the attainment of British destiny and fulfilment of God's will, was described as *alba rosa*/white rose, *albino draco*/white dragon, the wolf and the ass. The same cognomens for Edward and Henry (including David and Saul) were applied in the rolls adapted from the genealogical chronicle of Peter of Poitiers.[135] They also appear in a similar collection of prophecies (which I shall call the *Yorkist Prophecies*), written by a different scribe on cheap paper around the same time, and probably compiled between Edward's entry into London in March 1461 and his coronation in July. The date 1460 appears next to the prophecy of St Gildas.[136] The manuscript contains the prophecy of a king who will find the Holy Cross, identified by the cognomens the Son of Man, the Eagle, the Boar, the True Dragon, and the delicate rose of Britain prophesied by Mahomet. The importance of prophecies in Edward's campaign for the throne and in his subsequent campaigns against Lancastrian resistance in Wales and Northumbria between 1461 and 1465 is shown by the appearance of these

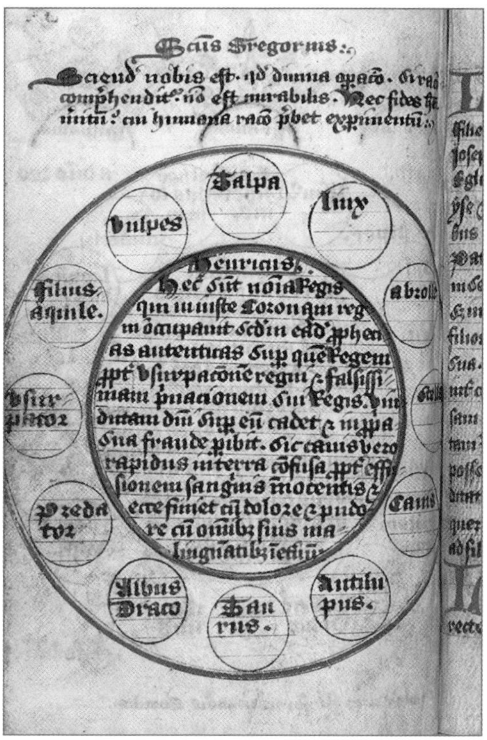

In The Prophetic History of Britain, *Henry VI is commemorated with a circle surrounded by the cognomens assigned him by Edward and his supporters, including: Saul,* Vulpes *(fox), predator and* albus draco *(white dragon). (Bodley MS 623, fo. 71v)*

prophecies in a number of other manuscripts dating from Edward's reign.[137] It is likely that these terms were used outside the genealogical rolls. Prophecies favourable to Edward IV in commonplace books, such as the one written by J.R. Herryson in about 1464, a collection of the prophecies of the six kings, the angel, Bridlington and Merlin, transcribed with a genealogy of Edward IV, and the commonplace book of John Benet, which also contains a chronicle for the years 1400–62, indicate a receptive audience for such prophecies. A burgeoning literacy led to a popular awareness of these prophecies and a number of favourable chroniclers of the early years of Edward's reign.

Despite their appearance in a wide variety of manuscript sources, these prophecies shared common themes, the most important of which was that of Edward as the heir of Brutus and Cadwallader who would defeat the usurping Saxons, the descendants of the Norman and Saxon invaders, and who, in healing the shattered line of Brutus, would restore the ancient name and hegemony of Britain. The key prophecy was that of Merlin, Britain's original alchemist, delivered to King Vortigern and found in Geoffrey of Monmouth's *Historia regum Britanniae*. The castle which King Vortigern was trying to build was being continually swallowed by the ground because, as Merlin pointed out, there was a pool there in which two dragons were sleeping, and when the pool dried the dragons started fighting. Merlin predicted the eventual triumph of the red dragon, symbolizing the Britons, over the white dragon representing the Saxons, and this was interpreted by the author of the *Prophetic History of Britain* as the triumph of Edward IV over Henry VI. Ripley presumably had this prophecy in mind when he experienced a vision while contemplating the fires of his furnace: 'It makes white and makes black, it burneth and maketh cold, it beginneth and performeth, here are two dragons fighting together in the flood of Galatea that is to say the white stone and the red stone.'[138]

These prophecies were applied precisely to the contemporary political situation. The prophecy of the angel to Cadwallader, taken from the last section of Geoffrey of Monmouth's *Historia*, includes a list of the sins for which the British king and his race were driven from England. They include the cupidity of judges, the negligence and evil life of the clergy, the rapine of magnates and abominable luxury, and they bear a close resemblance to the catalogue of complaints outlined in the manifesto delivered by Edward earl of March and the earls of Warwick and Salisbury in the summer of 1460 to the archbishop of Canterbury and the commons of England on their return from Calais to Ludlow.[139] These, along with the original Lancastrian usurpation, are the hidden and unpunished sins referred to in the *Prophetic History*.[140] This indictment of the government of Henry VI (also compared to Cadwallader by Hardynge) included ineffectiveness, abuse of the judicial system, the poverty of the king, extortion, murder, perjury, violence unpunished, lack of a fear of God, disregard for the king and his laws, and the corruption of the law practised by those who should most love the law. Henry VI was also charged with unpatriotic behaviour in planning to give back Calais and putting the realm of England into the hands of foreigners. According to the angel's prophecy, a Celtic king would defeat the Saxons and redeem the land. Edward's position as the heir of Cadwallader was asserted by the appearance of Cadwallader's shield, a white cross on a blue background, in the *Prophetic History of Britain*, the *Genealogy of Edward King of Britain* and the *Coronation Roll*.[141] Richard Beauchamp, the bishop of Salisbury (who was closely associated with the dean of Salisbury, the alchemist Gilbert Kymer), echoed the themes of these genealogical rolls and prophecies when he expressed to Coppini 'the hope that God who has permitted a sinful race to be scourged with dire strokes under an unhappy prince, being now appeased by our tears and prayers, has at length sent us this saviour'. Chroniclers related the appearance of omens before the Battle of Wakefield as portents of divine retribution on a sinful people, reporting the appearance of a two-edged sword in the heavens over Norfolk pointing towards the earth in imitation of God wielding the sword of vengeance against the people. In Bedfordshire a bloody sun appeared to show that blood would flow like water.[142] The angel was an important symbol at the start of Edward's reign. It was prominently displayed at the top of the *Illustrated Life of Edward IV* among the prophets foretelling his victory. When Edward addressed the crowd at St Paul's to state his claim, a representation of an angel descended and censed him. The use of the new coin, the angel, to celebrate the start of Edward's reign was probably a deliberate allusion to this prophetic angel.

Also originating with Geoffrey of Monmouth was the story of a prophetic eagle who spoke while the walls of Shaftesbury were being built; at the end of the *Historia* he made this prophetic eagle an authority to be consulted on the angel's advice to Cadwallader to retire to Rome, leaving Britain to the conquering Saxons until the time when the red dragon would rule again. A group of texts known as the prophecy of the Eagle became attached to this bird. Derived from bardic texts found by Gerald of Wales, they included the prophecy of the white king which was applied to the impotent Henry VI, and the Vision of King Edward the Confessor or the Vision of the Green Tree. A fruitful tree, cut from its original trunk, will be separated from its own root by a space of three acres. Without force of human hand, and without any command, it is returned to its trunk, that is to Kambrius and Kambria. When it has restored itself to its trunk and regained its sap it will flourish again and the affairs of the country will prosper. Originally written to apply to the division of the royal line with the Norman conquest and the return to the original line in the person of Henry I, it was adapted (probably from Aelred of Rievaulx's *Vita Sancti Edwardi Regis*)[143] for Edward IV who healed the wound caused by Bolingbroke's usurpation. The prophecy was incorporated into the *Illustrated Life of Edward IV* alongside the illustration of the rose tree at the point where Henry IV severed the branch of Richard II with his sword. It was applied to Edward IV, who had come to the throne after the three usurping kings (the three acres) to restore the line of Mortimer to its original trunk. Edward the Confessor is one of the prophets gathered around Richard Scrope at the top of the roll. An echo of the Confessor's vision of a dead tree regenerated and bearing fruit through the line of Mortimer occurs in a fifteenth-century tomb embrasure at the east end of the north choir aisle of Salisbury Cathedral, showing a sunburst and a tree stump with a branch to one side. Also appearing among these prophets is the prophetic eagle itself. The eagle became one of Edward's cognomens, together with the falcon, derived from the falcon forced to leave Britain (like the earl of March) but which according to the *Prophetic History of Britain* would return to build its nest high and take the crown of Britain from the Saxon lynx. Then the Welsh would rise.[144]

Another group of prophecies circulating at the time of Edward's accession consisted of those of near-contemporary confessors and martyrs. These tended to be politically more pointed and were important in enabling those around the new king to interpret recent history in radically new ways. Henry V had capitalized on the prophecies of St Bridget of Sweden in 1336 to justify his claim to the French throne through the female line of Isabella wife of Edward II and his invasion of France in 1415 (which coincided with his founding of the Brigettine order at Syon). The prophecies of St Bridget of Sweden in 1336 were recorded in the calendar of the 1465 version of the *Prophetic History of Britain*.[145] Bridget had recommended the joining of the English and French crowns and noted that it was vital for the well-being and survival of a kingdom that it be ruled by its rightful heir. Both these statements were applied by the author of this manuscript to Edward IV. In the *Genealogy of the Red Dragon*, Edward's succession was justified with the assertion: 'if the rightful heir is disinherited the realm will suffer desolation'.[146] Bridget's prophecies regarding succession through the female line were also included in the *Coronation Roll*.[147] St Bridget also prophesied the appearance of a last emperor who would overcome evil and bring happiness, and these words were commemorated in Edward's motto 'comfort and joy'. Edward's special devotion to St Bridget and his identification with her prophecies was shown by his interest in Syon abbey. He was regarded as Syon's second founder. In 1480 he and Elizabeth named their daughter Bridget and another daughter was professed as a nun there. At the outset of his reign he restored to the abbey much of its original property, the original endowments of which had been taken from Syon by Henry VI in the 1440s and given to his foundations of Eton and Kings. In 1462 Edward granted a charter of protection for all Syon's possessions. He stayed in the abbey in February 1463 on his march from Durham to London after Warwick's successful recapture of the Northumbrian castles in Lancastrian hands. Here he would have witnessed a Brigettine divine service emphasizing Mary's place in the tree of Jesse from David and the process of the Incarnation and role of St Anne and the Virgin Mary in the female lineages through which all mankind would be saved, and would have reflected on the messianic role he was playing within his own family lineage in redeeming the nation.[148]

The most recent prophecies available to Edward IV were those of John Erghome, written in the late fourteenth century. Erghome, to give his vague utterances more weight, had foisted them on to John Thweng, the saintly prior of Bridlington, and by the mid-fifteenth century they were widely known as the prophecies of St John of Bridlington. The author of the *Prophetic History of Britain* began his work with a line from these prophecies about the dog and star, both prophetic names for Henry VI, which signified this king's malediction. He also gave an exposition of section three of the Bridlington prophecies, detailing the events that would befall the kingdom because of bad government, including pestilence and destruction through fire and water, and he blamed King Henry. He also transcribed some lines from the ninth chapter of the prophecies applying to Edward IV the glorious career promised the Black Prince, and in the 1465 version of his work after a Bridlington prophecy he described Edward as the heir of Brutus.[149] The *Yorkist Prophecies* and a Yorkist genealogical roll of the same period applied John of Bridlington's words to Edward, quoting from his prophecies promising the emergence of Taurus as a king of British line.[150] And in another genealogy it was claimed that Robert the scribe of Bridlington called Edward the cock of the true Brutes.[151] Bridlington's significance as a source of symbolic prophecies was probably enhanced by Ripley's membership of the house, and Edward granted special concessions to the priory.

The most contemporary and politically most powerful of these holy prophets and patrons of the new king was the unofficial Yorkshire saint Richard Scrope, the archbishop of York. Scrope's martyrdom at the hands of Henry IV in 1405 was commemorated in the calendar in the *Prophetic History of Britain* in large red letters.[152] A lengthy account of Scrope's opposition to Bolingbroke's landing in 1399, his leading of a rebellion of Yorkshire gentry against Henry IV in 1405, the articles he published criticizing his government, and his martyrdom and its aftermath was produced by the author of this manuscript, who adapted them into condemnations of the illegitimate destruction of Richard II's line, the Mortimers, and prophetic anticipations of the coming of Edward IV.[153] In the margin by an account of the Battle of Shrewsbury in one copy of Hardynge's *Chronicle* there is a reference to the 'Holy archbishop Scrope'.[154] In one genealogy roll it was asserted that Henry earl of Derby violently, against his oath, took the crown, 'as it appears in the articles of Master Richard Scrope'.[155] In another, belonging to the family of rolls derived from Peter of Poitiers, it was claimed that 'Richard Scrope, the holy bishop of York, called Edward the true blood of the nativity'.[156]

Scrope was the unofficial patron saint of the new Yorkist dynasty, and this position was endorsed in the roll commemorating his accession, the *Illustrated Life of Edward IV*, where

Scrope dominates the illustration showing the prophets who predicted Edward's coming. The Scrope cult was important to Edward because the shrine, which flourished at York Minster in a way that rivalled Becket's shrine at Canterbury, could be harnessed to support the Yorkist dynasty. The cult also enabled the intellectuals at Edward's court, the genealogists, writers and alchemists, including the author of the *Prophetic History of Britain*, to impose a sense of divine order on the many political conflicts of the preceding fifty years and to make sense in ways hitherto unimagined by twentieth-century historians of such events as the enigma of the rebellion of Richard Scrope in 1405 and the rebellion of Henry Lord Scrope of Masham in 1415.

Richard Scrope, the archbishop of York and chancellor of England, becomes an inspired prophet rather than a politically naive cleric loosely related to the Percy family, the prime movers in the rebellions of 1403 and 1407, through the marriage of his sister. One genealogy executed for the Percy family stresses the joining of the lines of Percy and Mortimer, and gives even Scrope's connection to this family a prophetic significance.[157] In Hardynge's words the archbishop was 'one for whom God almighty hath showed many miracles sith that time he dirwarde'.[158] As Richard II's key adviser, Scrope saw the king's childlessness as a chance to bring about the fulfilment of the prophecy of the angel (prominently displayed opposite Scrope and another martyr to the Mortimer cause in 1405, Thomas Mowbray, the Earl Marshal, in the *Illustrated Life of Edward IV*). As Richard II's chancellor, he had naturally opposed the arrival in England of the exiled duke of Lancaster, Henry Bolingbroke. But Bolingbroke deceived Scrope, swearing on oath that he did not intend to take the throne. Scrope soon came to realize that this was an act of perjury when Bolingbroke usurped Richard's throne and became Henry IV. He saw this as a crime all the more heinous because it was an attempt to thwart the divine will, which was that the throne of Britain would at last revert to its rightful owners, the descendants of the original British kings in the Mortimer line.

Henry IV's crime thrust England into conflict with the Celtic neighbours which had once formed a united kingdom, and he subsequently found himself at war with Wales and facing the possibility in 1405 of being opposed by a tripartite Celtic alliance of Wales (under Owain Glyndwr), Scotland (under the future James I) and Ireland (under Ard Mac Murchada). This was seized on by the author of the *Prophetic History of Britain* because of Edward's Welsh origins and was seen as the beginning of the Celtic resistance to this last in a line of invaders and usurpers who had ruled Britain for over seven hundred years. Even Hardynge explained the Welsh wars as an attempt by Glyndwr to fulfil the prophecy of the angel and return the name of Britain, which he thought would occur with the arrival of Yorkist rule.[159] Scrope was martyred because, as a leader of the northern church, he advised the king to atone for his crime in usurping the throne by restoring it to the rightful Mortimer heirs and then published articles defending the liberties of the church against the crown's encroachments, leading a rebellion in Yorkshire that attempted to depose the king and restore the throne to the Mortimers. Henry IV's subsequent papal excommunication has additional force as punishment for his going against the original vision of the angel to Cadwallader. To undo Bolingbroke's crime, graphically depicted in the axing of the tree of Jesse in the *Illustrated Life of Edward IV*, he was prepared to die. Scrope's martyrdom was described in detail in the *Prophetic History of Britain*:[160] he chose to be beheaded with three blows in honour of the Trinity. The Trinity was also prominently displayed on the *Illustrated Life of Edward IV*, and also served to symbolize the joining of the different nations of Britain into one realm. God's disapproval was manifested in Henry IV's reputed leprosy, which was noted in the 1462 poem 'A Political Retrospect', describing Scrope's martyrdom,[161] and in the many miracles reported at Scrope's tomb in York Minster, including an old man's miraculous removal of the barriers placed around Scrope's tomb by Henry IV. The plot of 1415, involving Edward's grandfather Richard earl of Cambridge and Richard Scrope's kinsman Henry Lord Scrope of Masham, could be viewed in the same idealistic way, and was compared by the author of the *Prophetic History of Britain* to the beheading of Roger Llewelyn in his struggle against the Saxons.[162] He emphasized in his calendar the national disasters of the first half of the fifteenth century, such as the fall of London bridge into the Thames in 1437, to show God's continuing disapproval of the Lancastrian dynasty. It was at Edward IV's prompting that the dean and chapter of York Minster began to consider the possibility of Scrope's formal canonization in 1462. His efforts failed for the dean and chapter, more concerned with the local significance of the cathedral's saints, resolved after prolonged consideration to raise the celebration of the Minster's dedication to a double feast and to improve the existing celebrations on the Feast of St William. This did not discourage Edward from issuing a proclamation on 27 April 1471 in an attempt to bolster his reconquest of the kingdom which referred again to Scrope's role as the martyr who sacrificed his life in defence of the Mortimer heirs: 'for the right and title of our Auncestire, whose estate we now bere and love, died and suffered deth and martyrdom'.[163]

The most radical implication of the new Yorkist government's assertions of the uniqueness of the British identity and destiny was that England was no longer to be part of Europe but of Britain, an island nation with a separate identity forged in a distant past before this insularity had been lost. Edward was able to make sense of and resolve the divisions of the present and the invasions of the past by asserting his role as a saviour of biblical proportions, the leader of an exiled and suffering people awaiting the redeemer promised them in prophecies. The history of Britain was one of invasion and struggle for identity that would be resolved by recapturing a long-lost identity through myths as powerful as those of the Jewish people.

Throughout the genealogies, chronologies and prophetic literature of this period there was an assertion that the British were a chosen people like the Israelites (they were described as 'Ebrues' in one Yorkist genealogy), emerging out of a long period of exile towards deliverance.[164] Their history could therefore be closely paralleled with biblical history. The genealogical histories of Edward IV were typologically constructed like the fourteenth- and early fifteenth-century Corpus Christi plays of the north of England with their martyrs and prophets who anticipated the divine will and tyrants who frustrated it. Edward IV was therefore seen as a visionary king in the Old Testament mould, the leader and deliverer of the chosen people. This powerful idea was expressly conveyed between March and July 1461 in the pictorial biblical narrative in the *Illustrated Life of Edward IV* which provided a typological accompaniment to the sequence of pictures showing Edward's progress to being acclaimed king in March 1461. The model for this technique may be the late medieval pictorial accounts of the New Testament juxtaposed to their prefigurations in the Old Testament, the *Biblia Pauperum*, such as the one produced in the Netherlands around 1470.[165] The first in the series shows Edward departing for Calais with the earl of Salisbury and the earl of Warwick (who had to steer the boat). This occurred after the rout at Ludford (12–13 October 1459) when York, to preserve the Yorkist dynasty, separated all his heirs. This sense of danger to the heir of the chosen people was expressed by juxtaposing this picture with an illustration of a swaddled infant Moses in the River Nile among many drowning infants. The journey to Calais in this illustration takes on an epic quality as Edward is shown to be like Moses, the leader of captive people in exile.

The next picture on the left-hand side of the roll (the viewer's right) shows Edward kneeling before Henry VI, who has just been defeated at the Battle of Northampton. The illustration to the right shows David, with Saul at his mercy, refusing to kill God's anointed. Edward, like David, is the king chosen by God, biding his time, waiting for a signal from the

Lord. In David's tent is the ark of the covenant and Edward, armed in the same manner as David, is similarly posed before his tent, depicted as the guardian of the destiny of his people. The next scene in Edward's life is the morning of the Battle of Mortimer's Cross when he is given a sign from the lord, the three suns in the sky, which, according to chronicle sources, he interpreted as the Trinity, emphasizing his claims to the crowns of England, France and Castile[166] (at the foot of the family tree lie Henry III of England and Peter of Castile and Leon). In the opposite right-hand column is an illustration of Moses tending his sheep before the blazing bush containing the three faces of God, the Trinity (Exod. 4). The Lord said to Moses: 'I have seen the affliction of my people who are in Egypt, and have heard them cry because of their taskmasters and I have come down to deliver them out of the land of the Egyptians, and to bring them up out of that land to a good and broad land flowing with milk and honey.' There could be no more effective way of capitalizing on Edward's vision at Mortimer's Cross. He was the inspired leader and deliverer of his people out of bondage.

The next scene shows the aftermath of the Battle of Towton, where the bodies are piled high (some three thousand casualties were reported at this battle). Heralds blow their trumpets and the Yorkist standard of the black bull is displayed. Opposite there is a depiction of the Battle of Jericho with Joshua ordering the blowing of the trumpets which at the command of God would destroy the city walls. Clear parallels were drawn between Joshua and Edward. Like Joshua, the great biblical general, Edward was severely outnumbered, especially before the arrival of Norfolk. Both men were great military leaders and quick, decisive generals (Joshua marched his men all night) and both were greeted with astrological phenomena foretelling their victories. Joshua in the sight of Israel said:

> Sun, stand still at Gideon
> and Moon in the valley of Aijith
> And the sun stood still and the moon stayed,
> Until the nation took vengeance on their enemies.

Bellicose extracts from the psalms confirm divine approval:

> You shall break them with a rod of iron,
> and dash them in pieces.[167]

And Edward's position as the divinely inspired leader of his people:

> Prove me, O Lord, and try me;
> test my heart and mind.[168]

Behind the victorious Edward there is shown a city. This may represent London, which fell to him without a fight after his rapid march from the battlefield of Mortimer's Cross, its walls useless like Jericho's.

The parallel destinies of the Hebrew and British nations shown in the *Illustrated Life of Edward IV* were demonstrated in closer detail in the genealogical rolls prepared around the time of Edward's accession. Two rolls, written in English and intended for a secular audience, trace the line of Japheth to 'kings of Bretayn that nowe is called England'.[169] Alongside Joshua is Tros, the founder of Troy, and the defeat of Jericho is paralleled with the conquest of Troy. The devastation of Jericho prepares for the emergence of Jerusalem, and Troy's destruction is followed by the founding of Rome and New Troy by Aeneas and

Brutus. Parallels were implied with the destruction of Jericho and Edward's liberation of London from the threat of Margaret of Anjou and her French troops. Joshua charged his followers: 'nothing to take thereof as for their own use', and this is echoed by Edward's orders to his troops not to pillage when in London. As Jericho makes way for Jerusalem in this roll, Troy makes way for New Troy or London, and in 1461 this becomes the embodiment of the New Jerusalem, a familiar motif in fifteenth-century civic pageants. Echoes of the *Illustrated Life of Edward IV* also occur in these rolls' accounts of the founding of New Troy by Brutus who, like Edward, is shown leading his people to the promised land. This is paralleled genealogically by an account of David's leadership of the Israelites. The account of David slaying Goliath is shown opposite Brutus's defeat of the giants. As Edward journeyed around England after he became king he was welcomed into cities such as Bristol with giant-slaying pageants to stress his links with these two leaders. Guildhalls in London and Norwich contained statues of Gog and Magog, the giants slain by Brutus.

The same interaction between the lives of Edward IV and those of the biblical prophets occurs in the group of works written by the author of the *Prophetic History of Britain*, who probably had some part to play in the production of the *Illustrated Life of Edward IV*. In the calendars accompanying the *Prophetic History of Britain* Edward is given the cognomen David and Henry VI is given the cognomen Saul.[170] This pattern is developed in this author's later *Genealogies of Edward King of Britain*.[171] David, Jesus Christ, Brutus, Arthur, Cadwallader and Edward IV are the only rulers shown with crowns. Both Edward and David are commemorated by identical red and gold circles. The cognomen David is also inserted at the foot of the 1470 version of the *Genealogy of Edward King of Britain* alongside the circle commemorating Edward's coronation.[172] Henry VI on the other hand is given the cognomens Saul and Lupus. The two lines of Israel from Noah to Abraham and from David to Christ, and the British lines from Japheth to Brutus (whose name occurs alongside David's) and from Arthur to Edward, are given special prominence. All these texts place great emphasis on the conflict between David and Saul and this suggests their close relationship with the *Illustrated Life of Edward IV*. Alongside the name of Saul there occurs in all of them the statement that King Saul went against the mandate of God and that 'king Saul wickedly erred wishing to make war on David whom God chose to be king of Israel'. Alongside David are the words: 'David king in the judgment of God', a phrase echoed in the Coronation Roll.[173]

Another recurring image in these rolls is the Ark of the covenant, alluded to in the *Illustrated Life of Edward IV*. This is perhaps symbolically represented in the *Coronation Roll* with Noah's Ark itself and Edward, through his identification with these biblical prophets, was seen as the guardian of the covenant, identified with the hopes of the nation.[174] This was made explicit in the celebration of the obsequies for his father, Richard duke of York, at St Paul's in February 1461. These were planned by Edward and Warwick at their meeting at Chipping Norton after the victory at Mortimer's Cross to serve the added purpose of acclaiming Edward as king. They belong to the same period that saw the production of the *Illustrated Life of Edward IV* and the prophecies and genealogies recorded by the author of the *Prophetic History of Britain*. The duke of York's hearse, displayed at St Paul's on 4 March to reinforce Edward's claim, resembled the illustration of the ark of the covenant in the *Illustrated Life of Edward IV* and the *Coronation Roll*.[175] The hearse had an elaborate wooden roof and eight pillars and was made by John Talbot, the king's chandler, at a cost of £75 17*s* 7*d*, with £44 worth of candles supplied by London grocers. A white angel (the angel that appeared to Cadwallader) held a crown behind the effigy's head. The king's painter, John Stratford, provided 51 gilded wax images of kings and 420 wax angels decorated the pillars of the hearse. The structure was painted with silver roses and gilded

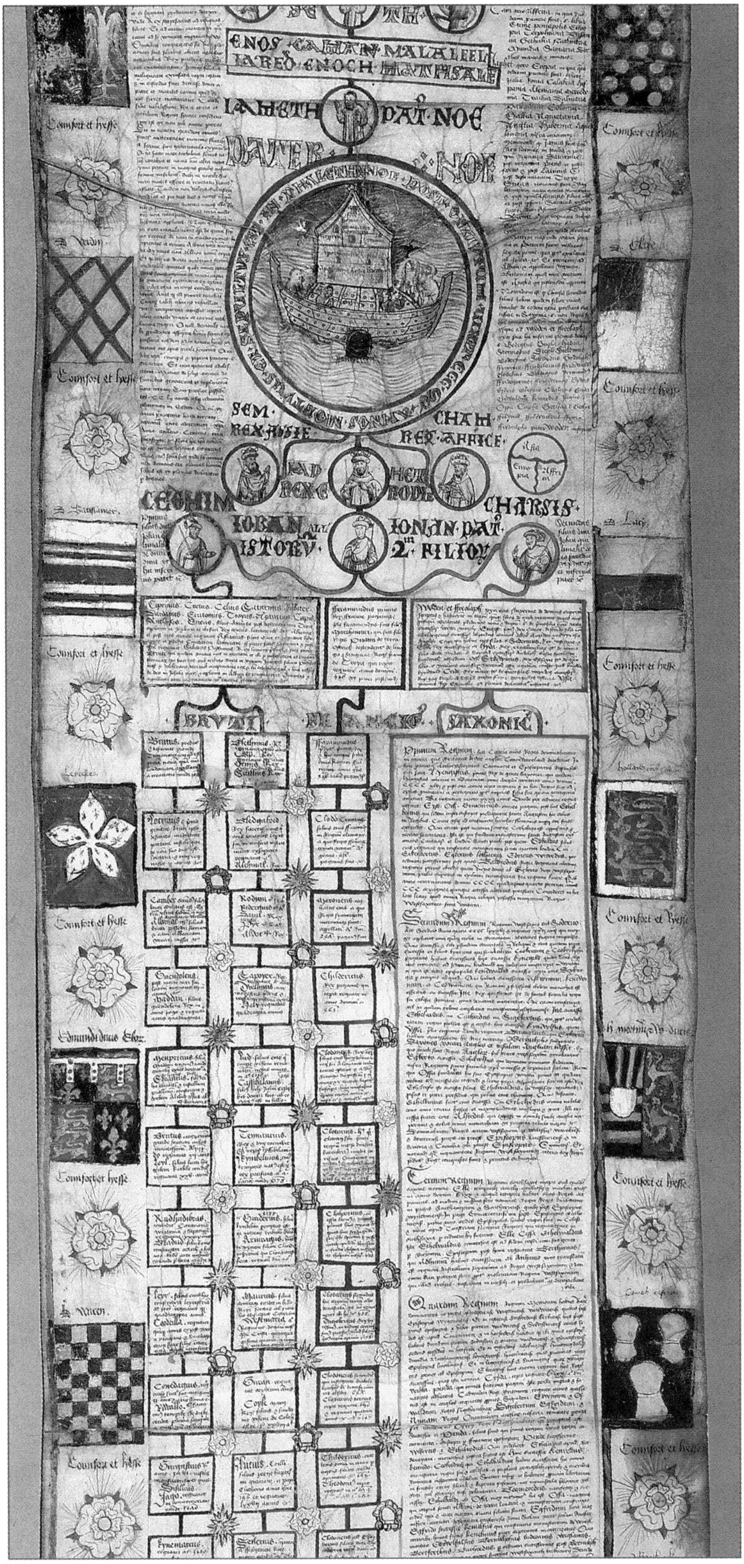

The Coronation Roll *begins with the origin of the line of Edward from the time of the great flood. Noah's ark is also a symbol of the alchemist, afloat on the leaden, primeval waters of chaos, beginning the task of transmutation. (Philadelphia Free Library E 201)*

with a great sun. On the majesty cloth Christ was depicted sitting in judgement on a rainbow, an allusion to the covenant between God and his prophets.[176] Such imagery of Noah's covenant with God occurs at the head of many of Edward's genealogies. The clear message from the ceremony would be that the duke of York was a prophetic leader who took his people to within sight of the promised land like Moses and Joshua, but it was Edward who delivered them. This hearse was used on 20 January 1463 when Edward, to celebrate his father's anniversary, sent for the hearse to be transported from London to Fotheringay.[177]

In attempting to create for Edward a heroic persona as a deliverer of his people, his followers naturally did not stop at Moses and David, but drew parallels with the most powerful of heroes, Jesus Christ. In the 1465 calendar of the *Prophetic History*, the nativity of the Virgin and Christ are both commemorated with blazing suns, an implicit allusion to the coming of Edward.[178] It must have been especially tempting for the alchemists associated with Edward IV to make such connections. For them the symbol of the son of the king, or the son of man, was an integral part of their experiments. Edward was their homunculus created in imitation of God the alchemist, the creator of Christ the son. Some of the prophecies retain messianic, alchemical language, such as the prophecy of Marlyn, the abbot of Ireland, who called Edward the fifth lion which shall be engendered by no man but by God himself.[179] The most propitious time for the alchemist's work was during the conjunction of the sun and moon, the integration of opposites. Robert Barker began his treatise for Edward earl of March during just such a conjunction in November 1456. The new moon for this month occurred on 28 November at eleven minutes after midnight.[180] Rarely, a perfect conjunction occurred during a solar or lunar eclipse, but more commonly it took the form of the appearance of the new moon, when the two planets were perceived to be directly opposite each other on either side of the earth. Christ's Passion was supposed to have occurred in March like Edward's accession, and much was made of this by the author of the *Prophetic History of Britain*, who calculated in circular diagrams in both of these manuscripts the time when the sun and moon were in conjunction in this month at the time of the Passion. The image he used to illustrate this conjunction, the sickle-shaped moon in the embrace of the sun, is similar to the representation of the con-junction in the earliest version of the *Ripley Scroll* showing the same image in the mouth of the dragon. The *Percy Roll* begins above Adam and Eve with a circular diagram of the heavens showing at opposite sides of the circle the conjunction of the sun and new moon. The roll ends with the accession of Edward in the month of March to suggest that this is the culmination of an alchemical process beginning and ending with the conjunction of sun and moon.[181] Christ's Incarnation and Passion, which figure so prominently with images of the

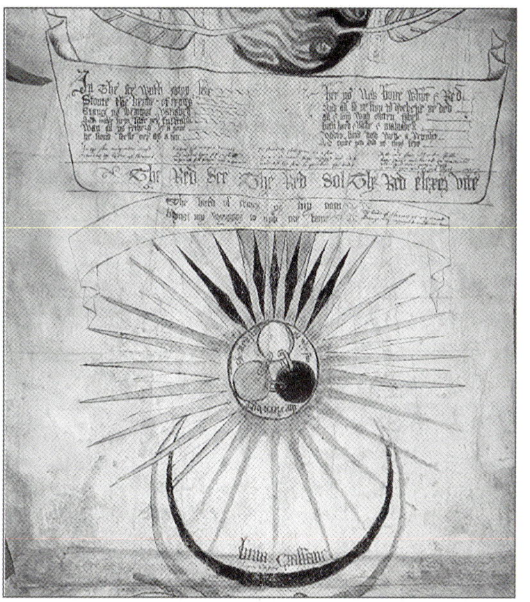

The conjunction of the sun (containing a symbol of the alchemical Trinity) and the moon in the Ripley Scroll. *(Bodley Roll 1)*

sun and moon in the *Prophetic History of Britain*, are seen in similar astrological terms.[182] Edward's redemptive Christ-like role was demonstrated in the *Illustrated Life of Edward IV*. The image in the sky above the prophets of a dark planet with a fiery annulus may represent a conjunction in the form of a partial eclipse signifying the arrival of the redeemer.

The last scene of the historical pictures shows Edward enthroned at the top of Fortune's wheel, watched by a group of armed men and clerics led by a mitred abbot. Above their heads are biblical quotations from the *Book of Acts* affirming Edward's position as the chosen messiah:

> who by the mouth of our father David,
> thy servant, didst say by the Holy Spirit –
> The Kings of the earth set themselves in array,
> and the rulers were gathered together,
> against the Lord and against his Anointed.[183]

And from the Psalms:

> He who sits in the heavens laughs; –
> I have set my King
> On Zion my Holy Hill.

Although many of the genealogical rolls hint at the relationship between Christ and Edward, representing both of them with triple, golden crowns, it is not surprising that it is in the *Coronation Roll*, with its precise alchemical imagery, that the connection is strongest.[184] It is possible to discern in the recent restoration of the scroll the features of Edward's Christ-like face as he sits astride his horse; the use of gold leaf establishes a connection between this image and the circular image denoting his coronation, and the golden image of Christ in a blazing sun. The alchemists called the stone animate, because at the final operation a dark red liquid, like blood, sweated out of their material, and they prophesied that in the last days a most pure man, through whom the world will be free, will come to earth and sweat bloody drops of a rosy red hue, whereby the world will be redeemed from its fall. Edward the redeemer, identified by the prophets, is represented in this roll by the dark red centres to the white roses (blackened with oxidization) which appear in a circle around his name at the foot of the scroll. He represents the attainment of the stone, the redemption of his nation, the culmination of a process started by Moses.

This concept of the arrival of a redemptive saviour who was closely identified with the land and its people was conveyed in the Latin poetry probably commissioned by Edward himself in 1460–1. The themes, symbols and images of these poems are closely related to those of the genealogies and prophecies first executed in this period. The two earliest poems, the 'Canterbury Ballad' and the 'Twelve Letters that Would Save England' (a poem fixed on the gates of Canterbury purporting to be a meditation on the letters sewn by a woman on a vestment and their significance for England), were written after the Battle of Wakefield.[185] Richard duke of York is seen in these poems as the prophet who delivered his followers to within sight of the promised land, like his Old Testament forbears, an image suggested in the funeral celebrations organized by Edward in this same year. He was depicted as a Job-like servant of God 'that be grace of God and gret revalacion the which for oure sake suffer vexacion'. The author of the 'Twelve Letters', influenced by the prophecy of the angel, attributed the unhappy condition of England to the corruption into which the nation had fallen. Because of its wickedness, God's merciful hand had been withdrawn from all subjects. In contrast to the perfidy of the Lancastrian courtiers, it was claimed that the virtues of York and his adherents were inspired and guided by heavenly grace.[186] A poem on the Battle of Northampton comments that God heard the people crying for mercy and sent Edward 'young of age', and concludes with the declaration that appears under the illustration of the newly crowned Edward IV in the *Coronation Roll*: 'If God is with us who is against us?'[187] This poet was preoccupied with the role of the Trinity in Edward's campaign, a central theme in the visual images in the *Illustrated Life of Edward IV*: 'Blessed be God in trinite which kepith his servants in adversite – save the king and his – illumine hym with the holy ghost.'

The poems written in this period also employ some of the cognomens used in the prophecies, especially the rose. One verse pedigree created or copied for the city of Coventry, reciting Edward's position as heir of Brutus, ends with a celebration of 'the rose of gret plesaunce in which ros alle the worlde schalle Ioye now the lion [of March] has torn up the thorns and briars stunting its growth, and the fox [Henry VI] has fled'.[188]

A poem on the Battle of Towton declares: 'Had not the Rose of Rouen been all England be destroyed.' The poet attributes to Edward the qualities of this flower, freshness, beauty and vigour, and each verse ends with the refrain 'blessed be the time when ever God spared that flower'. The rose also dominates the *Illustrated Life of Edward IV*. The genealogical tree which grows out from the navel of Henry III and is severed by Bolingbroke is a rose-briar, which is regenerated by Edward IV. This theme is echoed in a poem called 'Deo Gracias', which celebrates the vigorous growth out of a stock long dead to restore the true line. The rose, with its connotations of Christ's Passion, becomes at this time a powerful symbol of the redemption, with links with the motif of the wasteland awaiting redemption from a vigorous king. An even more direct link with the regenerated rose in the *Illustrated Life of Edward IV* is made in a poem written to commemorate Edward's entry into London in March 1461:

> Out of the stock that longe lay dede
> God hathe caused thee to sprynge and sprede
> Sith God hath yeven the thorough his myghte
> Oute of that stoke birede in sight
> The floure to springe and rosse so white.

The young Edward in these poems attains the status of the virginal pure knight, the Galahad who will redeem the land ruled by a sick king:

> Thou vergyne knight of whom we singe
> Undeffiled sith thy begynyng.[189]

'A Political Retrospect', composed in 1462/3, stressed further the idea of Edward as the redeemer of a wasteland. Paying homage to the martyred prophet, 'the holy bishop Scrope', the poet emphasizes the sickness of the Lancastrian usurping line, the presumed leprosy of Henry IV, and the huge languor around Henry VI. He urged all true Englishmen to pray for Edward of Rouen to clear the garden. The vigorous growth of the white rose would save the garden and dispel the black 'cloudys of langoure'. Referring to the prophets who 'saith there shal dire hym noo thynge', the poet invokes St George as the protector of Edward and ends with an exclamation that echoes Edward's motto and sums up his role as the vigorous redeemer of a sick land: 'Welcome everlasting joye, and farewel langoure.'[190]

The genealogies, chronicles and prophecies composed for Edward IV were not just retrospective attempts to gloss a new dynasty. In their original form they pre-dated the coronation, and the ideas contained in them were certainly circulating before the accession. They have previously only been analysed as propaganda. Such a term is misleading and anachronistic. Edward's genealogies are in fact very fair-minded. They, in common with the alchemical literature of the period, express the search for a way of reviving the monarchy, and therefore there is universal respect and praise for Henry V, the lodestar of knighthood, the lion of justice, as he is described in the *Prophetic History of Britain*.[191] Even Henry IV, the original usurper, earns some respect. The compiler of one of Edward's genealogies expresses admiration for the way Henry IV, despite all his problems, used his talents to retain the throne. The real purpose of the intellectuals around Edward, whether they were alchemists, soldiers or clergy, was to instill in the young man a sense of self-belief and destiny. The Celtic myths and prophecies were sources of energy, powerful archetypes emerging at a time of collective crisis.

Such emergence of myth and heroism occurred in the war-torn and humiliated districts of northern France in 1428, where a local peasant girl, inspired by her divine visions, led the French to victory over the previously invincible English troops at Orleans and inspired the coronation of Charles VII at Rheims. These ancient British archetypes explain why an eighteen-year-old was able to react to the death of his father and younger brother at the Battle of Wakefield in such a courageous, brilliant way (the original question which inspired this book). The young man who so ably capitalized on the parhelia at Mortimer's Cross, who led his troops personally into battle, who marched into London to popular acclaim and to sermons celebrating the arrival of the redeemer foretold by prophecy, and who postponed his coronation to march north to engage Margaret of Anjou was an inspired man who inspired those around him. Much of this had been noted in the first Parliament of November 1461 when the speaker, Sir James Strangways, delivered a congratulatory address to the king, dwelling on the king's progress at Mortimer's Cross and his rapid march to London when Margaret of Anjou threatened the city. The Three Chronicles, which end in 1465 and were written shortly after these events, convey this sense of a young leader impelled by a powerful sense of self-belief and great energy.[192] The earl of March was at Gloucester when tidings reached him of the deaths of his father and brother at Wakefield. He marched with three thousand men into Wales to encounter the force from France, Brittany and Ireland raised by Jasper Tudor; on Sunday, at Candlemas, he saw the three suns ascending in the east and 'anone freshly and manly he toke the felde upon his enemyes and put them to flight, and slew then 112 men'. James Joyce, in *The Portrait of the Artist as a Young Man*, satirized the way Jesuit teachers divided a classroom into the red and white roses of York and Lancaster in an attempt to encourage competition and group fellowship. Such party identification was inimical to the young hero's dawning sense of self, the process of individuation on which he was embarking. Such labels are just as inappropriate to the emerging sense of nationhood of the fifteenth-century body politic. This was a nation divided because a family was tearing itself apart. Those close to the court were searching for a way to heal these wounds, which is why alchemists were becoming increasingly interested in politics. There was an intellectual dimension to the Wars of the Roses, hitherto, with the exception of the work of John Watts[193], barely recognized by historians who have placed too much emphasis on the participants' identification with feudal affinities. What was at stake was the process of individuation for the nation. This explains the ferocity of the Battle of Towton, the bloodiest conflict fought on English soil. This was a civil war like the American Civil War. The stakes were very high: the nation's very identity and selfhood.

NOTES

1. S. Anglo, 'British History and early Tudor Propaganda', *Bulletin of John Rylands Library*, 44 (1961); A. Allan, 'Yorkist Propaganda: pedigree, prophecy and "the British History" in the reign of Edward IV', in *Pedigree, Patronage and Power in Later Medieval England*, ed. C. Ross (Gloucester, 1979), and A. Allan, 'Political Propaganda employed by the house of York in England in the mid-fifteenth century, *c.* 1450–71', PhD thesis, Swansea, 1981; A. Allan ' Royal Propaganda and the Proclamations of Edward IV', *Bulletin of Institute of Historical Research*, 59 (1986), p. 19ff; A. Sutton and L. Visser-Fuchs, *Richard III's Books*, ch. 8; A. Sutton and L. Visser-Fuchs, 'The Prophecy of the Eagle', *The Ricardian*, 8 (1989–90), nos 107–10; A. Sutton and L. Visser-Fuchs, 'Richard III's Books: Ancestry and True Nobility', *The Ricardian*, ix (1992), 119, 355; R.A. Griffiths, 'The Sense of Dynasty in the Reign of Henry VI', in *Patronage, Pedigree and Power*, pp. 13–37.
2. J. Bale, *Scriptores*, xii, no. 71; C.L. Kingsford, *English Historical Literature in the Fifteenth Century* (Oxford, 1913), pp. 164–5; G. Harris, intro to *The Scroll Considerans (Magdalen MS 248) Giving the Descent from Adam to Henry VI* (Oxford, 1999), p. 3; St John's College, Oxford, MS 23; BL MS Harl. Roll T. 12.
3. B.J.H. Rowe, 'King Henry VI's claim to France in picture and poem', *The Library*, 4 ser., 13 (1932–3).
4. Bodley MS Marshall 135.
5. *The Rous Roll*, ed. C. Ross (Gloucester, 1980); A. Gransden, *Historical Writing in England*, 2 (London, 1982), p. 253.
6. A. Sutton and L. Visser-Fuchs, *Richard III's Books*; E.D. Kennedy, *Chronicles and other Historical Writing.*
7. R. Taylor, *The Political Prophecy in England* (1967).
8. Martin de Belles, *Memoirs.*
9. See Bodley MS Hatton 56.
10. Cambridge University Library MS Dd xiv 2.
11. Bodley MS Digby 196, fo. 35r.
12. Coote, *Prophecy and Public Affairs*, p. 211.
13. BL MS Add. 46846; *Letters of Margaret of Anjou*, ed. Munro, pp. xv–i.
14. A.C. Fox Davies, *The Art of Heraldry* (London, 1904).
15. T.B. Pugh, *Henry V and the Southampton Plot of 1415* (Southampton, 1988), p. 90. *An English Chronicle*, ed. J.S. Davies, p. 64.
16. J. Ashdown-Hill, 'The Red Rose of Lancaster', *The Ricardian*, x (1966), 133; Delaney, *Impolitic Bodies*, p. 132.
17. K.B. McFarlane, *The Nobility of Late Medieval England* (Oxford, 1973), p. 98.
18. BL MS Cotton Rolls ii 23; *Historical Poems*, ed. Robbins, p. 117; Coote, *Prophecy and Public Affairs*, pp. 199–200.
19. *Rot. Parl.*, vol. v, pp. 375, 378.
20. College of Arms MS 20/20.
21. M.K. Jones, 'Edward IV, the earl of Warwick and the Yorkist Claim to the Throne', *Institute of Historical Research*, vol. 70, 173 (1997), 342–51.
22. BL MS Harl. 7353.
23. Hardynge's *Chronicle*, p. 181.
24. For an account of the battle see *The Short English Chronicle* ed. J. Gairdner (written soon after 1465, when it ends), pp. 76–7.
25. Lander, *Crown and Nobility*, p. 101.
26. Bodley MS e mus 35; Bodley MS Lyell 33.
27. BL MS Lansdowne 456.
28. College of Arms MS 20/6; another roll hastily executed and concluding with Edward's public acclamation as king on 4 March was BL MS Lansdowne 456.
29. BL MS Harl. 7353.
30. Hardynge's *Chronicle*, p. 387. The tradition that Richard II nominated Roger Mortimer as his heir is probably false. The source *Eulogium Historiarum* is a later interpolation. It was not mentioned by Richard duke of York when he made his claim, nor by Edward IV in his first Parliament in November 1461. See Allan, 'Yorkist Propaganda', 401.
31. BL MS Cotton Vesp. E VII, fo. 116v.
32. College of Arms MSS 20/6, 9/9, 3/2.
33. Ibid, 9/9.
34. BL MS Cotton Vesp. E VII.
35. Bodley MS 623.
36. BL MS Egerton 1076.

37. Pugh, *The Southampton Plot*, p. 94; for birth of Richard duke of York see BL MS Cotton Vesp. E VII, fo. 55; Delaney, *Impolitic Bodies*, pp. 82–5, 160–2; Osbern Bokenham, *A Legend of Holy Women*, transl. Sheila Delaney (Notre Dame, 1992).
38. BL MS Cotton Vesp. E VII.
39. Bodley MS 623, fo. 70v.
40. Bodley MS Selden B 10, fo. 6.
41. Philadelphia Free Library MS E 201.
42. *The Revelations of St Bridget, The Liber Celestis of St Bridget of Sweden*, ed. R. Ellis (EETS, 1987), vol. I, pp. 252–3.
43. Ibid.
44. *Book of Numbers*, 36.
45. C.A.J. Armstrong, 'The Inaugural Ceremonies of the Yorkist Kings and the Title to the Throne', *TRHS*, 4 ser. xxx (1948), 51–77.
46. H. Ellis, *Original Letters*, 2nd ser. (London, 1827), vol. i.
47. *CPR 1461–7*, p. 19; Rymer, *Foedera*, vol. v, pt 2, pp. 66, 106, 114, 139; Allan, 'Yorkist Propaganda', 331.
48. *Rot. Parl.*, vol. v, pp. 462–3, 463–7; Allan, 'Yorkist Propaganda', 331.
49. *Rot. Parl.*, vol. v, pp. 461–4; Allan, 'Yorkist Propaganda', 348.
50. *Rot. Parl.*, vol. v, p. 464.
51. Luke 16.2.
52. Luke 16.3.
53. Ripley, *Opera*, p. 146.
54. Bodley MS Lat. Misc. b2 (R).
55. Jung in *Psychology and Alchemy* argues that man is naturally not a self and needs transformation mysteries to rescue him from the chaos of the collective psyche. The same argument could apply to the identity of the nation.
56. BL MS Cotton Vesp. E VII; Bodley MS 623.
57. Philadelphia Free Library MS E 102. In the long Bodley Roll 5 the line of Edward begins with the garden of Eden.
58. Bodley MS e mus 42.
59. Bodley MS Lyell 33; Sam Fogg, *Text Manuscripts of the Middle Ages and Renaissance*, Catalogue 15 (London, 1992); K. Scott, *Later Gothic Manuscripts 1390–1490*, vol. 6; C. Ross, 'Rumour, Propaganda and Popular Opinion', in *Patronage Crown*.
60. Bodley MS e mus 35; Bodley MS Lyell 35.
61. Bodley MS e mus 35.
62. Ibid, fo, 4v.
63. Ibid, fo. 6v.
64. BL MS Add. 18268 A.
65. College of Arms MSS 3/2, 20/6 and 9/9. The earliest of these rolls (College of Arms 20/6) describes Edward's brothers George and Richard (who were created dukes of Clarence and Gloucester respectively in June and November 1461) as lords and therefore must have been written between June and November of this year. Later rolls by the same author (College of Arms 20/20) refers to Edward's marriage but mentions no children, and Bodley MS Ashmole Roll 26 refers to four children, Elizabeth, Mary, Cicely and Edward prince of Wales.
66. BL MS Cotton Vesp. E VII and Bodley MS 623.
67. Bodley MS 623, fo. 35v.
68. For the above account of the Anglo-Norman Plantagenet rolls see Olivier De Laborderie, 'Royal Genealogies in England in the XVth century', a paper delivered at the Histoire Medievale Comparee: France, Angleterre, Pays Bas, organized by Jean Philippe Genet, Universite de Paris 1and M. Vale. The paper was based on De Laborderie's forthcoming PhD thesis, University of Paris.
69. BL MS Cotton Vesp. E VII.
70. Ibid; Bodley MS 623.
71. Bodley Roll 5.
72. Philadelphia Free Library MS E 201.
73. Bodley MS Arch. Selden B 10, fo. 11.
74. Bodley MS Arch. Selden B 10, fo. 11; Kingsford, *English History Review*, 27 (1912), pp. 422–82; BL MS Harl. 661.
75. See the paper by Alfred Hiatt, 'Lancastrian Forgers', delivered at the eighteenth Harlaxton Symposium of *The Lancastrian Court*, July 2001.
76. Hardynge, *Chronicle*, p. 48.

77. Bodley MS Arch. Selden B.10, fo. 34. This is not in Ellis's edition.
78. Ibid, fo. 35.
79. Ibid. The account of Vespasian endowing Joseph of Arimathea with Avalon and the subsequent account of the cross of Joseph is not in the manuscript edited by Ellis and can be found in the Harleian and Selden manuscripts.
80. *Hardynge's Chronicle*, ed. Ellis, p. 126.
81. Ibid, p. 154.
82. See especially Bodley MS e mus 42.
83. For the prophecies of the coming of the British king see S. Anglo, 'British History and early Tudor Propaganda'; A. Allan, 'Yorkist Propaganda'; and A. Allan, 'Political Propaganda Employed by the house of York'.
84. R.S. Loomis, *The Grail from Celtic Myth to Christian Symbol* (New York, 1963), p. 13ff.
85. P. Ackroyd, *London: the Biography* (London, 2000), p. 16.
86. Hardynge's *Chronicle*, p. 76.
87. Felicity Riddy, 'John Hardynge's Chronicle and the Wars of the Roses', *Arthurian Literature* xii (1935), 91–108.
88. See the paper delivered by Nicholas Rogers, 'Henry VI and the proposed canonization of King Alfred', delivered at the eighteenth Harlaxton Symposium on *The Lancastrian Court*, July 2001.
89. BL MS Add. 18268 A.
90. Ibid.
91. BL MS Cotton Vesp. E VII.
92. Bodley MS 623, fo. 18v.
93. College of Arms MS 20/6. Edward's brothers George and Richard, who were created dukes of Clarence and Gloucester in June and November 1461 respectively, are named as lords.
94. Bodley Ashmole Roll 26.
95. The date 1460 is used because according to the Gregorian calendar March, the time of Edward's accession, falls just within the previous year.
96. See BL MS Cotton Vesp. E VII and Bodley MS 623.
97. BL MS Cotton Vesp. E VII, fo. 70. Cadwallader's arms also appear on the *Coronation Roll*, Philadelphia Free Library MS E 201 and the *Genealogy of Edward King of Britain*, Ashmole Roll 26.
98. Bodley MS 623, fo. 23.
99. Bodley MS 623, fo. 23b; BL MS Cotton Vesp. E VII, fo. 71.
100. BL MS Cotton Vesp. E VII, fo. 22.
101. Ibid, fo. 60.
102. Ibid, fo. 39v.
103. R.R. Davies, 'The People of Britain and Ireland 1100–1400. IV: Language and Historical Mythology', *TRHS*, 6 ser. vii, 5.
104. H.Evans, *Wales and the Wars of the Roses* (Cambridge, 1915).
105. W. Gamon Jones, 'Welsh Nationalism' in *Transactions of the Honourable Society of Cymmrodorian* (1917–18).
106. M.P. Siddons, *The Development of Welsh Heraldry* (Aberystwyth, 1991), vol. 1, p. 121.
107. G. Williams, *Renewal and Reformation. Wales c. 1415–1642* (Oxford, 1993), pp. 179ff; D. Rees, *The Son of Prophecy* (1985).
108. Philadelphia Free Library MS E 201.
109. C. Armstrong, 'Inauguration Ceremonies of the Yorkist Kings and their title to the throne', *TRHS* (1948), 51–6.
110. Gregory's Chronicle, in *Historical Collections of a Citizen of London*, ed. J Gairdner (Camden Society ns xvii, 1986), p. 215.
111. BL MS Cotton Cleopatra CIV.
112. Ibid, fo. 116v.
113. Reason featured in the debate about the succession. Fortescue in his *De natura legis naturae* claimed that it worked for the Lancastrian cause. *Works*, ed. T. Fortescue, pp. 137–8. I am grateful for the help of Margaret Kekewich on this and subsequent points and for letting me see her unpublished article on this roll. See also Sutton and Visser-Fuchs, *Richard III's Books*, p. 209.
114. *Brut*, ed. Brie (EETS, London, 1908,) p. 136; Gross, *Dissolution of Lancastrian Kingship.*
115. BL MS Harl. 7353; BL MS Royal 18 Dii, fo. 30b.
116. Sutton and Visser-Fuchs, *Richard III's Books*, p. 206. A Dominican friar features among the clerics at the foot of Fortune's Wheel, and another Dominican priory at Thetford had received the body of John Mowbray, duke of Norfolk, the descendant of the martyr for the anti-Lancastrian cause. M. Kekewich, 'A Yorkist Propaganda Roll: British Library Harleian Mansucript 7353', unpublished paper.

117. BL MS Cotton Vesp. E VII.
118. College of Arms MS 20/6.
119. College of Arms MS 9/9.
120. There are references to Edward's children but these are in a faint, additional hand.
121. Bodley MS 623.
122. College of Arms MS 20/20.
123. College of Arms MS 20/25.
124. Bodley Ashmole Roll 26.
125. BL MS Cotton Vesp. E VII, fos 21b–22, 18v.
126. Ibid, fos 21b–22.
127. Ibid.
128. BL MS Add. 18268.
129. BL MS Cotton Vesp. E VII and the English poem concluding BL MS Add. 1826A.
130. Armstrong, 'Ceremonies of Yorkist Kings', 51–73; Fragment published by J.D. Halliwell in *Archaeologia* (1842); Storey, *The End of the house of Lancaster*, pp. 190–4.
131. Armstrong, 'Ceremonies of Yorkist Kings', 51–73.
132. *A Brief Latin Chronicle*, p. 173.
133. BL MS Cotton Vesp. E VII, Bodley MS 623, fos 71–71v and on the verso of Bodley Ashmole Roll 26.
134. Philadelphia Free Library MS E 201.
135. See Bodley MS Digby 82; Bodley MS Lyell 35, fos 17v–18v.
136. Bodley MS Hatton 56, fo. 34. The Bodleian Library Catalogue wrongly dates this manuscript to 1450–3 and Coote, following this dating, gets into a muddle trying to apply these prophecies to Henry VI and the period of Cade's rebellion. She tries to get around the problem of the incorporation of Edward's name in the prophecies by applying them to Edward of Lancaster and ignores the date of the manuscript, which is written by the same scribe in the same ink as the rest of the text. This demonstrates the danger of using the content of prophecies to date manuscripts. Prophecies by their very nature are vague and can be applied to many different situations.
137. Cambridge Trinity College MS R.3.21; Bodley MSS Digby 82, Digby 181; Bodley MS e mus 42, in which the births of Elizabeth and Mary are recorded and which therefore was completed before 1467; and the identical Bodley MS Lyell, which also records the birth of Cicely.
138. Ripley, *Cantilena*.
139. BL MS Harl. 543, fos 164–5; Allan, 'Yorkist Propaganda', 51–66; BL MS Cotton Vesp. E VII, fo. 49r, pp. 659–98.
140. Bodley MS 623.
141. BL MS Cotton Vesp. E VII, fo. 70; Ashmole Roll 22; Philadelphia Free Library MS E 201.
142. See also College of Arms MSS 20/20 and 20/25 for similar catalogues of sins in the prophecy of the angel.
143. Aelred of Rievaulx, 'Vita Sancti Edwardi Regis', *Patrologiae*, ed. J.P. Migne, 195 (1885), pp. 738–90.
144. Bodley MS 623.
145. Ibid.
146. BL MS 18268 A.
147. Philadelphia Free Library MS E 201.
148. Scofield, *Edward IV*, vol. i, p. 269; Warren, *Spiritual Economics*, pp. 123–4, 129–30; *The Myroure of Oure Ladye*, ed. J.H. Blunt, EETS Ex. Ser. 19 (London, 1873), p. 238.
149. Wright, *Political Poems*, 1, pp. 203–5. BL MS Cotton Vesp. E VII; Bodley MS 623.
150. BL MS Egerton 1076 (a seventeenth-century copy of a fifteenth-century roll); Bodley MS Hatton 56.
151. Cambridge Trinity College MS R3.
152. BL MS Cotton Vesp. E VII.
153. Ibid, fos 96v–100v.
154. Bodley MS Selden B10, fo. 192.
155. BL MS Egerton 1076.
156. Bodley MS Lyell 35.
157. Bodley Roll 5.
158. Hardynge, *Chronicle*, p. 351.
159. Ibid, p. 178.
160. BL MS Cotton Vesp. E VII, fos 96v–11v.
161. Wright, *Political Songs*, ii, p. 268.
162. BL MS Cotton Vesp. E VII, fos 96v–11v.
163. Ibid and Bodley MS 623; Simon Walker, 'Political Saints in Later Medieval England' in *The McFarlane Legacy*, ed. R.H. Britnell and A.J. Pollard (Stroud, 1995), p. 95.

164. BL Lansdowne MS 456.
165. *Biblia Pauperum*, ed. Schreiber, 8 (Munich, 1961).
166. *Three Fifteenth-Century Chronicles*, ed. J. Gairdner (Camden Society, ns 28, 1980), p. 77.
167. Psalm 2, v. 9.
168. Psalm 26, v. 2.
169. Bodley MSS e mus 42 and Lyell 33.
170. BL MS Cotton Vesp. E VII and Bodley MS 623.
171. College of Arms MS 20/25 and Bodley Ashmole Roll 26.
172. Bodley Ashmole Roll 26.
173. Philadelphia Free Library MS E 201.
174. Ibid.
175. Ibid.
176. A. Sutton and L. Visser-Fuchs, with P.W. Hammond, *The Reburial of Richard Duke of York, 21–30 July 1476* (London, 1996).
177. M.K. Jones, review of the above in *The Ricardian*, xi (September 1997).
178. Bodley MS 623, fo. 55v.
179. Cambridge Trinity College MS R.3.29.
180. Herman H. Goldstire, *New and Full Moons 1001 BC to AD 1651* (American Philosophical Society, Philadelphia, 1973), vol. 94, p. 205.
181. Bodley Roll 5.
182. BL MS Cotton Vesp. E VII and Bodley MS 623.
183. Acts 4, vv. 25–6.
184. Philadelphia Free Library MS E 201.
185. *An English Chronicle*, pp. 91–3; Allan, 'Yorkist Propaganda'.
186. Robbins, *Historical Poems*, pp. 218–21.
187. Philadelphia Free Library MS E 201.
188. C. Louis, 'A Yorkist genealogical chronicle in Middle English verse', *Anglia* (1991), 1–20.
189. BL MS Lambeth, fo. 136.
190. Wright, *Political Songs*, p. 267.
191. BL MS Cotton Vesp. E VII.
192. Edited from BL MS Lambeth 306.
193. Watts, *Henry VI and the Politics of Kingship*, pp. 1–80.

CHAPTER 6

The Rise of Camelot

Hit was a worlde to se hym ride aboute
Throughout his land and that was day by day.

Anon, *The Death of Edward IV*[1]

The poems and laments composed on Edward's death all associate the king with the sun, beauty, joy, dancing and flowers, a spring time of happiness for England.[2] The optimistic idealism of the prophetic, genealogical and alchemical literature at the time of Edward's accession was reflected in the atmosphere of the early years of his reign. There was a widespread perception that a redeemer had arrived. The cathartic Battle of Towton was widely known as the Battle of Palm Sunday (and described as such in a copy of the *Brut*[3] and in the calendar of the *Prophetic History of Britain*). The *Recueil des Chroniques d'Engleterre* captures Edward's heroism and inspirational leadership during the battle: 'He suffered his troops and knights to help him now to recover his inheritance and they all assured him of their desire to help and said that if any wished not to fight they should go their own way. So all of them hearing this good request by the young king, shouted in unison that they would follow him until death if need be. Hearing this good support, the king thanked them and he jumped down from his horse and told them, sword in hand, that on this day he would live or die with them in order to give them courage. Then he came in front of his banners and waited for the enemy which was marching forward with great noise.'[4] The Burgundian chronicler Jean de Waurin's report on Edward's accession and first battles reads like a chivalric romance, with the young king behaving like a hero: mourning his father and his friends, haranguing his troops before battle, and most importantly dismounting to fight on foot with his men to encourage them. Warwick too fought on foot and even killed his own horse at Towton to make the possibility of flight from the field less feasible. Coppini, writing to George Neville, bishop of Exeter, about this battle, described 'how a merciful God has granted a glorious victory to the renowned Edward and the devout sons of the holy church', and in a letter to Pope Pius II he evoked Edward's entry into London 'incredibly beloved by all' welcomed with embraces and kisses. 'These things I saw – they seemed wonderful and well nigh impossible.' In Edward's first Parliament the speaker expressed the conviction that success in the field was the seal of divine approval.[5] The coronation was a religious ceremony occurring over a weekend, like an Easter festival. On Friday 28 June twenty-eight knights of the Bath were created; on Saturday afternoon there was a royal procession from the Tower to Westminster with thirty-two knights of the Bath wearing blue gowns with white roses on their left shoulders and white hoods 'like priests'. According to Waurin, the young Edward before the coronation expressed his gratitude to Warwick and his other supporters, and he certainly looked the part: 'fair and a pleasure to behold, his whole body well proportioned, as good as anyone you could find in the whole of England'.[6] The coronation followed on Sunday at Westminster Abbey, and on the Monday Edward wore his crown three times at St Paul's while an angel censed him.

In his role as the heir of Brutus, Edward was also seen as the liberator of New Troy from the foreign troops of Margaret of Anjou.[7] The identification of the citizens of London with a king who claimed to be a descendant of Brutus was something new. The last king to identify with New Troy was Richard II (the last legitimate king according to the Yorkists). Richard II's favourite, the one-time mayor of London Richard Brembre, was arrested in 1387 and charged by Richard's opponents (the Appellants) with attempting to change London's name to New Troy. John Gower referred to his meeting Richard on the Thames on the banks of New Troy. Richard's court witnessed the continuation of the Arthurian pageants started by Edward III. In 1390 Richard held a great tournament at Smithfield with sixty courses of jousts. However, the Londoners themselves, as Caroline Barron has shown in a recent paper, never took to this concept in the fourteenth century, regarding it as a courtly affectation.[8] Brembre was seen as an upstart and his unpopularity was so great that the Londoners failed to come to the king's help when Brembre tried to raise troops in support of him. The Appellants and the Lancastrians who eventually deposed the king were therefore identified with the opposition to the 'matter of Britain'. Henry IV continued to resist the blandishments of Arthurian myth and established a more austere liturgical and classical court which Henry V upheld. Jousting ceased to be a part of court life. However, Edward IV revived the great Arthurian pageants that had enlivened the courts of Richard II and Edward III. The citizens of London, far from being hostile to a court-directed revival of the identification of their city with New Troy and the matter of Britain, embraced it. This is to some extent a measure of Edward's popularity in the capital: he would go hunting with London citizens, knight them and bed their wives. His popularity would be celebrated in Heywood's play. One prophecy identifies Edward in the following manner: 'the rose shall rise that shall win London'.[9] Edward was king by popular acclamation. Initially elected by a small body of Yorkist lords, he sought and obtained from the Londoners an acclamation that legitimized his claim. Gregory's *Chronicle* describes the rapturous reception he received in London, 'the city that sometimes cleped was New Troye', ten days after the second Battle of St Albans, and exclaimed: 'Let us walk in a new vineyard, and let us make a gay garden in the month of March with this fair white rose and herb the earl of March.'[10] In the beginning of Edward's reign there were a number of civic ceremonies in which Brutus's slaying of the giants was commemorated. A poem transcribed in the reign of Richard III and occurring in a manuscript of Yorkist prophecies captures the optimism surrounding Edward's capital in these years.[11] Using the refrain 'London thou art the flower of cities all', the poet praises the beauty of the town imperial, its rivers and,

> borial stremys under the lusty walls
> where many a swan swimeth with wynge fayre
> where many a ship resteth with top royall.

He depicts London as the direct heir of New Troy, a city the equal of Rome, a great centre of mercantile life and culture:

> Upon thy lusty bridge with pillars white
> Ben merchants full froyall to be
> Upon thy streets, goth many a semely knight
> In velvet gowns and chayns of gold
> – strong be the walls about the standing
> wise be the people that with thee dwells

fresh thy river with lusty strands
Blyth be thy churches well sounds thy bells
Rich be thy merchants in substance that excels
fair thy wives right livesome white and smal.[12]

Once the religious rituals surrounding the coronation had finished it was the image of Edward as a hero, an embodiment of the divine image, that continued to mesmerize his subjects. In the above manuscript there is a description of Edward as 'A prince excellent and pure and loved very devoutly by true reputation with divers grete battayls.' As the epitome of martial vigour and purity he attained the status of a golden youth who would redeem the land. In this he resembled Sir Galahad, the son of Sir Lancelot and descendant of Joseph of Arimathea, a pure youth destined to discover the Holy Grail. There was more to this than literary conceit. Edward was undoubtedly a very charismatic and attractive youth. In 1787, when his skeleton was discovered alongside Elizabeth Woodville's in the vault in the north aisle near the high altar of St George's chapel, Windsor, it measured six feet three and a half inches in height and was broad in proportion. Spectators even took strands of his chestnut hair.[13] He must have towered over most of his subjects. The German visitor, Gabriel Tetzel, described Edward in 1466 as 'a handsome upstanding man', and according to the Croyland continuator 'when in the flower of his age' he was both 'tall of stature' and 'elegant of person'. Philippe de Commines, when he met Edward in 1470, had reservations about his character but declared he was a 'very handsome prince, more handsome in fact than any other I ever saw at that time and he was very courageous'. Thomas More, who spoke with Edward's mistress Jane (Elizabeth) Shore in her old age, described his courage in adversity, his joy in prosperity, his fierceness in war, his clemency and his strong, clean-made body. He also described him as one 'favoured by way of nature with his wisdom and manhood'. The Milanese ambassador at Edward's court, Count Ludovico Dallugo, wrote to Francesca Sforza duke of Milan that on his departure Edward accompanied him to Sandwich, and Dallugo felt the inhabitants of the towns through which they passed loved Edward like a God.[14] The most sincere and public compliment to the young king was made by the speaker of the House of Commons, Sir James Strangways, in Edward's first Parliament on 12 November 1461. Strangways, who had been imprisoned after the Battle of Wakefield, where his lord, Richard Neville earl of Salisbury, was executed, and released after Towton, gave thanks for the king's victories in the field, praising 'the noble and condigne merites, Princely and Knyghtely corage – the beaute of personage that it hath pleased Almighty God to send you'.[15] By way of contrast Henry VI was not only mad but shabby, badly dressed and indifferent to appearances.[16]

The embodiment of all these heroic redemptive qualities projected on to Edward was the mythical Arthur, king of Britain at what was believed to be the height of its military and spiritual greatness. It must have seemed to many, carried away in the initial enthusiasm of Edward's triumphant uniting of this divided country, that he was the returning king who it was widely believed had never died. This belief was derived from Geoffrey of Monmouth's ambiguous statement that Arthur, after his last battle, was taken to Avalon (the isle of the blest) for the healing of his wounds. John Lydgate, in his *Fall of Princes*, reported the Britons' belief in Merlin's prophecy that Arthur will come again to reign in England and reconstitute the Round Table. He also asserted:

His epitaphie recordeth so certayn:
Heer lith kyng arthour, which shal regne ageyn.

The dying Arthur slays Mordred in Edward IV's copy of Boccaccio's De Casibus Illustrium Virorum. *(British Library Royal 14 E V fo. 439v)*

This was echoed by the author of the 1470 version of the *Genealogy of Edward King of Britain* when he described Arthur as the one-time king of Britain sleeping with his knights. At the conclusion to the *Morte Arthure*, composed between 1399 and 1402 and copied by Robert Thornton, lord of East Newton in Ryedale, Yorkshire, between *c.* 1420 and 1450, perhaps while looking back to the conquests of Henry V, there occurs in a later hand, but not Thornton's, in Latin the inscription 'Here lies Arthur once and future king', which reflects this particular reader's sharing of the genealogists' expectation of the return of a British king. This *Morte Arthure* was one of Malory's sources and as the inscription appears to pre-date Malory's 1469 works on the death of Arthur it may have inspired his observation that 'Men say in many parts of England that King Arthur is not dead but led by Lord Jesu into another place and men say that he will come again. Many men say there is written on his tomb "here lies Arthur, king once, king to be".'[17]

Nearly all the genealogical chronicles provided glowing accounts of Arthur's reign and refer to his many virtues and his conquest of the Saxons. He is styled the fierce,[18] the magnificent, the famous, the marvellous and the miraculous.[19] In the calendars accompanying the *Prophetic History of Britain* special emphasis is placed on the reign of Arthur, styled Arthur Magus.[20] In another Yorkist genealogy there is an account of Arthur's rule of the realm of Britain, his conquest of Europe and his burial on the isle of Avalon.[21] Hardynge in his *Chronicle* implies a link between Arthur, the opponent of the Saxons, and Edward, the opponent of the Lancastrians, when he describes Arthur's vow to defeat the Saxons 'who have done us much annoy'. He specifically connected Edward's Mortimer ancestors with Arthur when claiming that in 1279 Sir Roger Mortimer, 6th baron of Wigmore, began the Round Table at Kenilworth for a hundred knights and ladies to exercise discipline of young men in tournaments and jousts, and that Edward I bestowed the earldom of March on him after a forty-day joust. In fact Edward, growing up in the Mortimer heartlands in the marches around the duke of York's chief citadels of Wigmore and Ludlow which dominated mid-Wales, would have been aware of the strong Arthurian traditions among his ancestors. According to the author of the *Brut* Roger Mortimer held a round table at Wigmore in 1328, and at Wigmore Abbey (a Mortimer foundation located in the area where Edward assembled his troops before the Battle of Mortimer's Cross) there was a manuscript containing a *Brut*, a genealogy of English kings, and a Mortimer genealogy prepared by the family after 1376 to advance their claim to the throne by emphasizing Mortimer descent from Arthur and Cadwallader. The Mortimer lands contained many sites of Arthurian legend – Caerleon on the river Usk in Monmouthshire became a Mortimer possession in the fourteenth century. In this ancient city of the Roman legions where (according to the *Brut*) he was crowned, Arthur was supposed to hold court.[22]

Certainly in the genealogical reconstructions of British history there was an attempt to link Edward, the son of the prophecies and the last British king since Cadwallader, with King Arthur through heraldry and cognomens. The author of the *Genealogies of Edward King of Britain* ensures that the dominant figures, the only ones marked with three-tiered crowns, are Brutus, Arthur, Cadwallader and Edward IV.[23] Hardynge in his account of the reign of Arthur has him crowned emperor with three crowns, and described his various banners: an image of Our Lady of Gold, the Trinity, St George, the arms of Brutus, three gold crowns, and a red and gold dragon, all of which were arms used by Edward.[24] In the *Illustrated Life of Edward IV* the triple suns shine on Edward, passing through three golden crowns, the coat of arms of Arthur, and in the illustration commemorating Edward's entry into London after the Battle of Mortimer's Cross the banner of the black bull with golden horns, one of Arthur's standards, is displayed. The *Coronation Roll*,[25] produced soon after the *Illustrated Life of Edward IV*, depicts Edward galloping on horseback in a very Arthurian posture. The links with Arthur are strengthened through a prominent display of Arthurian heraldry. Two of King Arthur's banners occur on the roll, a cross fleury on a green background with a gold image of the Virgin and child (described as Arthur's arms in Hardynge's *Chronicle*) borne by the Black Bull of the honour of Clare. Edward could trace his pedigree back to the De Clare earls of Gloucester (whose shield occurs on the roll) through Lionel of Antwerp's wife Elizabeth de Burgh. The Bull of Clare was significant for

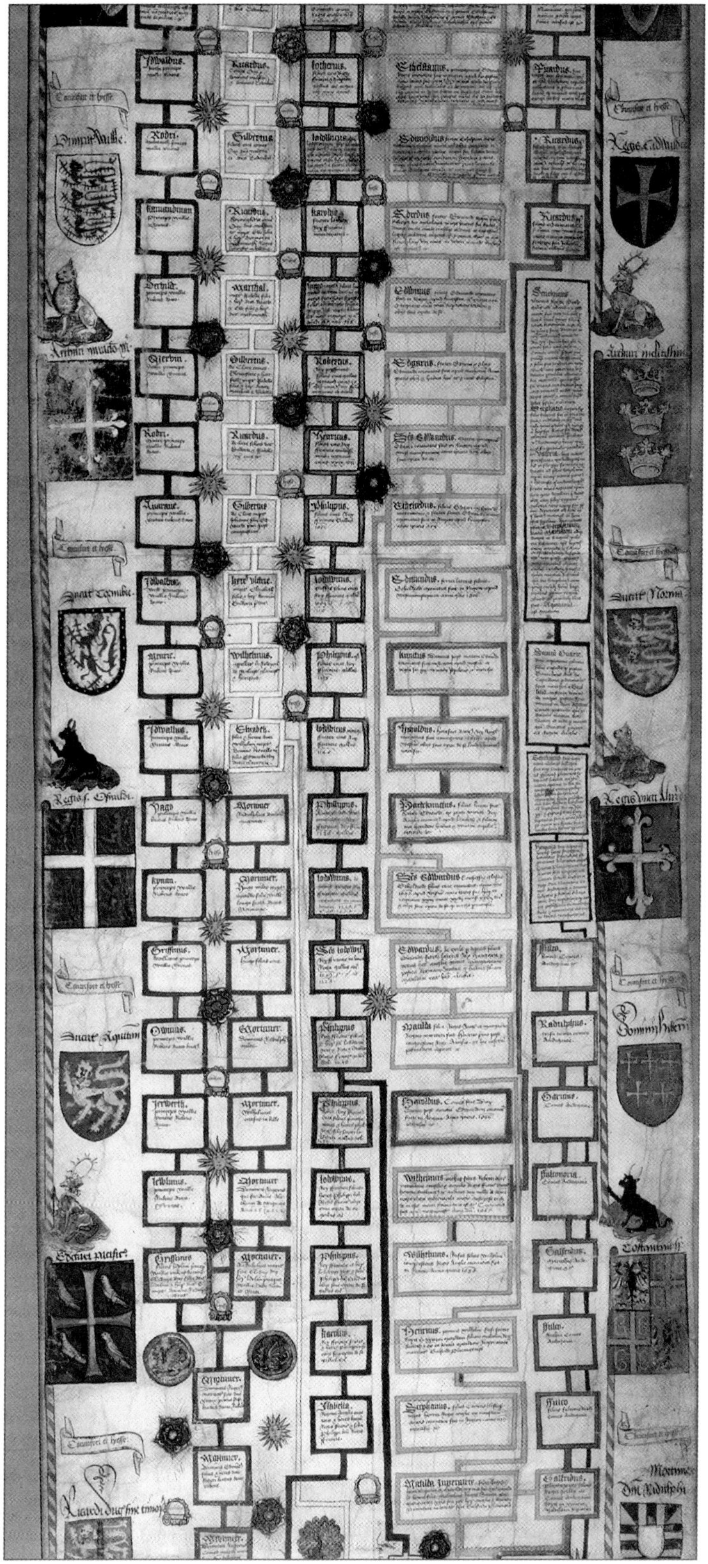

The arms of Edward IV's ancestors in the Coronation Roll *include: the shield of Cadwallader, a gold cross on a blue background (which occurs in* The Prophetic History of Britain*), and the banner of Arthur, three gold crowns on a red background. (Philadelphia Free Library E 201)*

Edward's links with Arthur because it was the intermarriage of the Clare and Mortimer lines that allowed Edward to claim to be the upholder of the British heritage of Brutus, Arthur and Cadwallader. Another of Arthur's banners to appear on the *Coronation Roll* is the three gold crowns on red borne by the white lion of March, which also bears the standard with the royal arms of England quartered with the arms of Castile and Leon with a central shield bearing the three crowns, the arms of Brutus/Arthur. Edward frequently used the three crowns (associated with the three suns at Mortimer's Cross) on other genealogies and his linking Arthur's arms with the badge of the Mortimer earls of March is suggestive for it was the badge he used throughout his life. The gold livery collars of alternating links of suns and roses, bearing a single white lion at the centre, were worn by his attendants. Another prominent banner on the *Coronation Roll* associated with Arthur was the banner of the duchy of Cornwall. According to Geoffrey of Monmouth, the duke of Cornwall was one of King Arthur's most trusted supporters. Among the various cognomens used for Edward in the *Genealogy of the Red Dragon* are King Arthur and Taurus.[26]

Although none of the genealogies for Edward IV disguises the fact that Arthur's line ceased with him, they all emphasize Edward's descent from Arthur's father, Uther Pendragon, and capitalize on the similarities between these two young men who came to their thrones to popular acclaim. In one there is an account of the coming of Arthur heralded by the appearance in the sky of the dragon-tailed star and he is described as young and fair of body, well beloved of all the people.[27] One way of achieving this identification of Edward IV with Arthur was through the symbolism of the sword: Arthur's claim was legitimized by his ability to remove Excalibur from the stone. In another Yorkist adaption of a traditional genealogy, there is a drawing of Excalibur in the margin alongside Geoffrey of Monmouth's prophecy of the eagle which predicts the coming of Edward.[28] In the *Illustrated Life of Edward IV* Edward emerges from the branch of the rose wielding an upright sword and facing Henry VI whose sceptre is inverted. The coronation ceremony also focused on this Arthurian symbol: £4 was expended on a new sword to be displayed on 28 June 1461.[29]

Another significant Arthurian image popular at the beginning of Edward's reign was the circle in its various manifestations: the wheel of fortune, the Round Table and the philosopher's stone. At the top of the *Illustrated Life of Edward IV* the crowned Edward sits on top of Fortune's wheel which has been permanently halted. This alludes to the Trinity Sunday dream of Arthur sitting in a chair on a wheel. The roll seems to be saying that this time the turning of the wheel with all its attendant political ills has stopped permanently. Edward at the top of the circle bears a strong similarity to images of Arthur at the top of the Round Table. The grail can mean many things but one of its associations is with the table of the last supper which, according to legend, was at Glastonbury and transformed (in the version of Hardynge's *Chronicle* dedicated to Edward) into Joseph of Arimathea's table created for the grail knights. The Round Table at Winchester, described by Hardynge as

> the rounde table at Wynchester beganne,
> And there it ended, and there it hangeth yet[30]

can also be interpreted as an image of the philosopher's stone, for it represented a state of happiness that had been long lost: a healthy body politic with political unity and humoral balance that had once existed in ancient Britain under King Arthur and which had been rediscovered under Edward IV. The Round Table at Winchester, founded (Lydgate claimed) on the advice of Merlin, was possibly first hung on the wall of Winchester Palace as a relic at the beginning of Edward's reign. Hardynge, in his rededication of his *Chronicle*, suggests that

The coronation of King Arthur who bears a resemblance to the portrait of Edward on fo. 4. (British Library Royal 15 E IV, Chronicles of the English, *Jean de Waurin, vol. 1, fo. 141v)*

Arthur's final battle was fought with Mordred near Winchester and that the table had remained there ever since, but he is the first writer to suggest that the table was hanging in display.

Another manifestation of the grail and the philosopher's stone was the comet, the lance-shaped ray of light that could blight a land or bring salvation. Such astrological phenomena were of interest to the alchemists who provide the most intellectually productive link between Arthur and Edward through their formulation of the public image of these kings. Merlin, who guided the destinies of Uther Pendragon and Arthur, was regarded as the original founder of alchemy in Britain.[31] One fifteenth-century alchemical work was written in the form of instructions given by Merlin to his son.[32] Another recipe for the elixir attributed to Merlin occurs in a collection of Ripley's letters and writings.[33] Edward's path to the throne was similarly guided by court astrologers including Robert Barker, George Ripley, John Kirkby and George Neville. Merlin was also an astrologer who interpreted to Uther Pendragon at Stonehenge the significance of a comet with two tails, shaped like a dragon, which he said presaged the death of a king and the rebirth of a dynasty, a time of joy and bliss.[34] This evokes Edward's own motto 'comfort and joy' (which was a bold contrast to the martial and virtuous mottos of his peers) and his reign was similarly presaged by astrological phenomena that were interpreted by alchemists occupying Merlin-like roles. The most important was the parhelia, which in Edward's copy of the *Secreta secretorum* was interpreted like Merlin's prophecy to Uther as portending a change of dynasty. An even closer link existed with the dragon-tailed comet observed by Merlin. In June 1456 Halley's Comet appeared over England and was widely seen in London. It is possible that the astrologers and alchemists at the Yorkist court made the connection between this comet and the comet that preceded the reign of Arthur. Appearances of comets in the reign of Edward IV were also reported in John Warkworth's *Chronicle*. The comet is possibly depicted at the top of the *Illustrated Life of Edward IV* in the form of a dark planet with a fiery tail in the heavens alongside the three suns above the various prophets predicting Edward's coming. The author of the *Prophetic History of Britain* was also an astrologer and in both these manuscripts he provides volvelles (two-dimensional astrolabes used to calculate the movement of planets through time). Alongside the prophecy of St Gildas concerning a sixth monarch who will become king of Britain and another of Merlin concerning the return of the name of Britain on the second day of November, there is added in the margin the words 'Britannia, 1456'.[35] It is very likely, given the astrological nature of these manuscripts, that this observation was inspired by some planetary phenomenon (apart from the monthly conjunction of sun and moon), such as the appearance of Halley's Comet, interpreted as a revisitation of the heavenly body heralding the start of the original Arthurian age. It is interesting that Robert Barker began his alchemical treatise dedicated to the fourteen-year-old Edward in November of this year. For these alchemists the parallels between the accessions of Edward and Arthur were striking. Two young attractive kings (in one Yorkist genealogy Arthur is described as crowned when he was 'yong of age' but 'fayr of body' and 'doughti of manhood')[36] attained their thrones to a popular acclaim that overrode the selfish ambitions of the baronage. This was accompanied by celestial phenomena indicating divine approval and guided by alchemical wisdom showing that Britain was about to regain its aura as a holy land.

The alchemist, with his knowledge of astrology, occupied the role of Merlin in this period, the source of prophetic and wise counsel behind the emerging Arthur. Edward's

Vortigern consults the magicians. This perhaps gives an indication of the appearance of fifteenth-century alchemists. (British Library Royal 15 E IV, Chronicles of the English, *Jean de Waurin, vol. 1, fo. 93)*

alchemists frequently evoked Merlin as their mentor and a source of authority in their recipes. Ripley quoted Merlin in one of his recipes for the elixir[37] and John Sawtry, a monk of the fenland abbey of Thorney (Cambridgeshire), who was prominent around 1477 according to the sixteenth-century list of British alchemists, cites Merlin as an authority in a recipe for a marriage of the red and white man (a potent allusion to the political reconciliation of 1461: 'Yf the whole world be married to the red man they are combined together they that were two shall be made one.'[38] An allegorical work of alchemy in the form of a dialogue between Morien the father and Merlin the child was composed in the latter half of the fifteenth century.[39] In a medical collection containing the works of Arnold of Villanova, which Roger Marshall, who described himself as King Edward's physician, received from John Somerset, there is a recipe for making the wine-based drink methaglyn, which was supposed to have come from Merlin.[40] Another of the court alchemists, John Kirkby, the transcriber of the works attributed to Raymund Lull which were such an influence on Ripley, was the author of a recipe that provided instructions on how to mend a broken sword (which had clear symbolic, political implications).[41] The Welsh Herbert family, who had benefited so much from Edward's rise, may have appreciated the fusion of Welsh Arthurian myth, history and alchemy. William Herbert's brother attempted (sometimes by force) to bring alchemists into Edward's court. For these alchemists the divisions of Britain represented an unhealthy humoral imbalance. The sickness of Britain under Edward's predecessor, the phlegmatic Henry VI, is demonstrated in an alchemical genealogical table showing the combinations of the different elements leading ultimately to Edward IV. The grail in these alchemical genealogies becomes the blood line linking the ancient kings of Britain to Edward. A diagram of the three elements shows the sanguine humour leading to France, the melancholic to Britain, and the phlegmatic to England. The alchemists, poets and genealogists saw Edward as a young man who was able to draw on the power of the heroic image of Arthur to unite his kingdom and achieve an alchemical trinity of the body politic, three kingdoms in one, England, Wales and Scotland, which was symbolized by the philosopher's stone or the grail. The arms of Brutus, Arthur and Edward, the three crowns, underlined the significance of the trinity.[42] Another of the royal arms, two lions, is a recurring image in the writings and the scrolls of George Ripley. The alchemists at Edward's court believed they had the key to the grail's elusive secret, the link between the health of the king and his land. In a manuscript containing alchemical recipes and prophecies of the coming of Edward there is a prayer for Henry VI, adapted to apply to Edward IV, in which Edward is compared to Arthur. Running through the poem is the recurring refrain,

> long ever preserve under thy mighty hand
> the king, the queen, thy people and thy land.[43]

The author of this adapted poem and the owner of the manuscript, Roger Thorney, a mercer of London, was interested in the wider dissemination of knowledge about British history. He was a patron of the printer Wynkyn de Worde, who published at his request the *Polychronicon*, the most popular work of history in late medieval England, in 1495.[44]

The early years of Edward's reign showed him attempting to live up to this Arthurian ideal. He had a son by Lady Elizabeth Lucy, his mistress from 1461 to 1464, whom he called Arthur (another chivalric hero of the Yorkists, Humphrey duke of Gloucester, had called his own illegitimate son Arthur, perhaps in acknowledgement of the ambiguous circumstances of the legendary Arthur's conception). In 1477 payment was made by the king to George Lovekyn, tailor and yeoman of the wardrobe, for a coat of black velvet for Arthur, described as 'My lord the Bastard'.[45] Edward's identification with King Arthur was encouraged by writers associated with his cause. Hardynge, a veteran of Agincourt and Verneuil, who used Geoffrey of Monmouth and *La queste le Graal* in compiling his British history, rededicated his history to Edward at Leicester in May 1463. He described Arthur as the worthiest, wisest, hardiest, most courageous man, in whom there was no drop of cowardice or avarice, a celestial, bounteous ruler, a lamb of mercy and a lion in battle. Recounting the disintegration of Logres, its religion and chivalry, he saw around him the ruins of Caerleon and Glastonbury and Stonehenge, relics of Britain's lost holy legacy and its potential for renewal around a king of sufficient courage and energy. The purpose of Arthur's Round Table, he wrote, was to move young knights to seek arms that otherwise would be at home in idleness. He called on Edward to establish the old British unity by bringing Wales and Scotland under his control and England would then be made 'Albion'. William Worcester also rededicated a work to Edward, the *Boke of Noblesse*, a call to the knighthood of England to rediscover the chivalric ethos and masculine energies and sense of imperial destiny shown by Henry V, a ruler admired by Hardynge. Worcester too saw Arthur as an inspirational figure, and on his travels around Britain in 1479–80 he visited such sites as Glastonbury (where Henry V planned a royal visitation to uncover the relics of Joseph of Arimathea, the discovery of which had been announced by Richard Fleming, bishop of Lincoln, at the council of Siena in 1424) and Tintagel seeking information on early British history. Edward's association with Arthur, and therefore with Glastonbury, may have been encouraged in this region. The arms of Edward IV, with a white lion and black bull, surrounded by roses and the sun in splendour, occur in a fifteenth-century carving in front of St George's Inn for pilgrims in Glastonbury, built in 1475. Worcester's interest in astrology and alchemical medicine, which he used to treat Sir John Fastolf, was probably induced by the old knight's search for a lost youth spent in the campaigns of Henry V when he felt the power of participating in a heroic military quest. Given Fastolf's notorious love of money it is possible that Worcester's master may also have had a more pragmatic interest in the stone.

These Arthurian myths emphasized the importance of adventure and danger, of having a sense of quest in the search for self-realization and destiny. In the years surrounding his accession Edward gained self-confidence and empowerment by acting out the role of Arthur. He was probably exposed to Arthurian literature early in his life. His mentor and father figure, Richard Neville earl of Warwick, was married to Anne Beauchamp whose ancestor Guy Beauchamp had donated forty books to Bordesay Abbey in 1305 including the *Book of Lancelot*, a volume of romance, and *Joseph of Arimathea and the Holy Grail*, and a volume on the death of Arthur and Mordred. He stipulated that he and his heirs should have access to them and that they would never be sold. The Beauchamps illustrate the shared interest of the aristocracy and the court in the myths of chivalry and the grail. They claimed descent through Rohandus, the first Saxon earl of Warwick, from Eneas the knight of the swan, the fifth of six twin brothers born of a nymph with collars of gold and transformed by enchantment into swans when their gold chains were removed. All recovered their human form when their chains were returned except one whose chain had been melted down to mend a broken cup. Eneas would not leave his enchanted brother, who towed his boat. The legend, known in England since the twelfth century, has close parallels with the myth of Melusine. Eneas eventually married Beatrice and they had a daughter Ida, from whom the Beauchamps, Staffords and Bohun families all claimed descent through Eustace count of Boulogne. When Beatrice broke her promise to Eneas never to question him about his origins he departed in a boat with his swan brother and was never seen again. The story, occurring in the crusading cycle *Chevalier au Cyne*, was copied and illustrated in a collection of romances also containing the statutes of the Garter, which was commissioned by John Talbot earl of Shrewsbury for his wife Margaret, eldest daughter of Richard

Beauchamp earl of Warwick (who in 1417 had brought what was reputed to be the heart of St George to Windsor). Talbot and his wife took part in bringing Margaret of Anjou over to England in the spring of 1445 and later they presented the Shrewsbury book to her as a wedding present.[46] Edward's connection with the myths of this family is suggested by his marriage and plight-troth to Eleanor, the daughter of John Talbot and Margaret Beauchamp, sometime before 1464. Margaret of Anjou was so influenced by the legend that she adopted a chained swan as the livery badge of her son Edward, the prince of Wales (a swan with a gold chain – the Dunstable Jewel – was excavated at Dunstable, ten miles from the site of the first Battle of St Albans). However, it was the Beauchamps who most closely identified with this mysterious grail knight, who was introduced by Wolfram von Eschenbach as Loherangrin (Lohengrin), Parsifal's son, and was celebrated by Edward I in the Feast of the Swans in 1306, and by Edward III, the founder of the Order of the Garter and self-styled man of 'the wythe swan'. John Rous, the chantry chaplain of Guy's Cliff near Warwick, recorded the deeds of Eneas in his history of the Beauchamp family, the *Rous Roll*, written between 1478 and 1483, and claimed that the gold cup made from the chain of the swan-brother of Eneas (which had been bequeathed by Thomas Beauchamp earl of Warwick to his son Richard in April 1400) was kept in the Beauchamp's treasury in Warwick Castle and that he had drunk from that very cup. Rous also drew on oral tradition to claim that the derivation of the badge of the earls of Warwick, the bear, was derived from the first syllable of the name of one of the knights of the Round Table, Arthgal, which in Welsh means bear.[47]

Edward's acquaintance with such myths would have intensified with the adventurous circumstances of his first extended contact with the family of Richard Woodville, Lord Rivers, who was given the job of preventing Edward from using Calais as a safe haven in 1459. It was from Calais, the base from which Edward was preparing to invade, that the abduction of Earl Rivers, his wife, the duchess of Bedford, and their son Anthony Woodville, was organized. They were seized by Warwick at Sandwich and shipped to Calais, where they were berated by the earl of March. This family was steeped in the Arthurian myths. Jacquetta, Lord Rivers' wife, had previously been married to John duke of Bedford, who had acquired the royal library of the kings of France at the Louvre in 1425. According to an inventory he commissioned, he obtained eighteen volumes of Arthurian texts including two *Lancelots*, three *Grails*, a *Tristan*, two *Merlins*, a *Saint Graal et de Tristan*, *Tristan and Lancelot*, and a romance of the Round Table. All of these were prose works; in addition there were two copies of *Perceval de Galtres* in verse. Over the next forty years this library (parts of which may now be in the Bodleian Library) passed into the hands of his widow Jacquetta and her second husband Sir Richard Woodville, Lord Rivers.[48]

Edward's contact with this family was soon on a more friendly footing when he began to court in secret Anthony Woodville's sister, the beautiful widow Elizabeth Grey. Presumably before her first marriage to John Grey, Lord Ferrers of Groby, Elizabeth had acquired the volume of the cycle of legends written in France, possibly Champagne, between 1215 and 1230, dealing with the arrival of the Grail in Britain, the development of the Round Table and the discovery of the Grail. Because of its popularity and the number of surviving manuscripts and of redactions in other languages, this was known as the prose Vulgate cycle. Elizabeth's early acquisition of this work is suggested by the inclusion of her signature in the form of her maiden name on the flyleaf of an illustrated manuscript containing the *Estoire del Saint Graal*, dealing with the history of the Grail from the time of Christ to Merlin and its removal from the Holy Land to Britain; the *Lancelot*, dealing with the adventures of the knights of King Arthur's time and Lancelot's love for Guinevere; and the *Queste del Saint Graal*, a Cistercian work showing Galahad's arrival at Camelot, his vision of the Grail, his discovery of the Grail Castle and his healing of the maimed king.[49] Elizabeth Woodville must

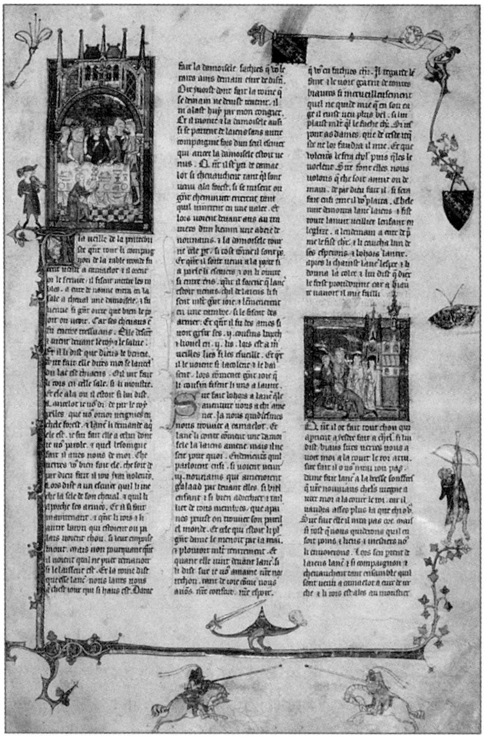

Arthur's table during the feast of Pentecost at the time of the arrival of Sir Galahad. (British Library Royal 14 E III The Saint Graal, Oueste du Saint Graal *and* Morte Arthure, *fo. 89)*

have acquired this book from her mother Jacquetta, Bedford's widow, and it was in turn handed on to her daughter Elizabeth of York, whose inscription 'Elysabeth the Kyngys dowter' appears at the beginning of the book.[50] Elizabeth Woodville was a very beautiful woman (whose features can be seen in a contemporary illustration of the king and queen before St George)[51] and her influence in encouraging Edward to live out these Arthurian ideals is shown by the circumstances of his controversial marriage, which could have been lifted from the pages of a romance. En route to York to meet the threat of the Lancastrians in Northumberland, the king stopped at Stony Stratford on 30 April 1464. That night, probably in the early hours of the morning, Edward slipped away from his entourage and rode alone to Grafton Regis, five miles away, to the home of Richard earl Rivers and his wife, Jacquetta duchess of Bedford. There, the next morning, 1 May, in the presence of Elizabeth's mother, a priest and two gentlewomen, Edward was married to Elizabeth. Immediately afterwards the king, presumably with his bride, went to bed for a short time, then returned to Stony Stratford, explaining to his attendants that he had been out hunting; complaining sorely of fatigue, he went to bed again. Soon afterwards he returned to Grafton for three (possibly four) days. Elizabeth was brought secretly to his bed each night. He then continued on his journey north from Northampton.[52] The marriage remained secret for three months.

During his reign Edward was a patron of romance and chivalric literature. He owned the *Chemin de Vaillance or Song Dore* (the *Road to Courage or the Golden Dream*), written by the Norman nobleman Jean de Courcy in the 1420s. This was a manual for knights, a dream vision of a knight's guidance by Lady Courage. In the manuscript are the royal arms with a white rose and the arms of Cadwallader, a blue shield with a gold cross. Edward also owned a copy of the French text of Raymund Lull's *Ordre de Chevalerie*[53] in which he would have seen outlined his role as patron of chivalry, mirrored in the concept of knighthood as a sacred vocation. A king sends for many nobles because he would hold a great court and a squire on his way falls asleep in a hermit's house. The hermit teaches him from a book of chivalry and tells the squire to present the book to the noble king. When Caxton translated this work and presented it to Richard III he lamented that there were no heroes in England to compare with Arthur's time and recommended that knights read the noble volumes of *Saint Graal*, Camelot, Galahad, Tristram, Percival and Gawayn (the sort of literature that was read in the household of Edward's queen): 'there shall ye see manhode, courtesye and gentylesse'. Edward certainly envisaged the reading of such texts at his court. His household ordinances envisaged a common court culture for a group of between twenty and forty squires of the household and a number of magnates and their retinues at court (totalling about 600). They reveal that the esquires of the household were accustomed to withdraw in the winter and in the afternoons and evenings to the lord's chamber within court, and there to keep honest company, talking of chronicles of kings, harping and singing. An elaborate ritual and pageant was maintained in this court, probably in imitation of romance. Edward sat in the King's Bench and, assisted by his chancellor, like a king in romance literature, heard the case of a distressed widow.[54] In 1466 Gabriel von Tetzel, on a diplomatic embassy from Bohemia, thought England had the most splendid court that could be found in all Christendom. Tetzel described the elaborate rituals when Elizabeth dined in unbelievably costly apartments; the lords and ladies who served her were all of noble birth and had to kneel for three hours.[55] The Croyland chronicler described Edward keeping Christmas at the palace of Westminster, dressed in a variety of costliest clothes of different styles with full sleeves and sumptuously furred robes. The prince, he noted, always stood out because of his elegant figure, an incomparable spectacle before onlookers. In those days you might have seen a royal court such as befitted a mighty kingdom filled with riches and men from almost every nation. Such conspicuous displays of wealth and hospitality may have been a conscious attempt to emulate the rich Fisher King of Welsh myth, who was the origin of the legends of the Grail recorded in the queen's Vulgate cycle. The Celtic Welsh myth of a Rich Fisher, who possessed a horn and a dish of plenty with which he entertained his guest, and the more recent legend of Joseph of Arimathea placing a fish on the Grail table of the Fisher King[56] were perhaps commemorated in an illustration in Edward's *Black Book*, compiled in 1471–2 laying down the new regulations for the royal household. The illustration shows the king dining in state before a table on which are conspicuously displayed a dish and a fish.[57]

The most significant evidence of a conscious attempt to emulate the court of Arthur occurs in the revival of jousting under Edward IV.[58] Tournaments had all but died out in the first half of the fifteenth century. When it was suggested to the austere Henry V that he hold jousts after his marriage to Catherine of France in 1420, he replied that the knights who proposed the jousts would do better to prove their prowess by laying siege to Sens where they could joust to their hearts' content for a worthwhile cause. Needless to say Henry VI was not interested in them. Their revival may have been due initially to Edward's father-in-law, Richard Woodville, an enthusiastic tourneyer who held the first recorded joust in England for thirty years at Smithfield in 1440, engaging in individual combat against a Spanish knight. The lists at Smithfield had to be newly made for the occasion. Richard's son Anthony Woodville held jousts in March 1458 following the reconciliation between Henry VI and the earl of Warwick. Henry Beaufort duke of Somerset, Anthony Woodville and four others jousted before the king and queen at the Tower against three esquires of the queen, and again at Greenwich. Through the influence of the Woodvilles and another experienced tourneyer, Sir John Astley (who had killed an opponent in the lists before the king and queen of France), jousting was revived and became a significant activity at Edward's court during his first reign. By 1461 Sir John Astley had compiled a collection of chivalric and heraldic treatises including texts concerning knighthood, military affairs and ceremony. Astley added to it accounts of his own exploits and instructions for the heralds announcing jousts and procedures to be followed when they took place.[59] Another member of Edward's jousting fraternity, Sir John Paston, borrowed this book and commissioned a scribe, William Ebesham, to bring it up to date with additional material in 1468 to form a manual of chivalry in a volume subsequently known as John Paston's *Grete Boke*.[60] Paston's interest in jousting was closely tied to his interest in Arthurian literature. In an inventory of his books taken in 1469 there are the following items: 'A boke had off myn ostesse at the George . . . off the Dethe off Arthr', *The Green Knight* and *La Belle Dame Sans Merci*'.[61] Edward's personal interest in the formalization of the rules for jousts was shown in 1466 when he commanded the constable of England, Sir John Tiptoft, to draw up in English formal rules for the holding of jousts in England.[62]

One of the first jousts in Edward's reign resulted from a diplomatic mission to Duke Philip of Burgundy in October 1461; led by John Lord Wenlock the purpose of the mission was to negotiate a marriage for the new English king. A Burgundian knight came to England asking for safe conduct for Louis de Gruuthuse, the Burgundian envoy, who was renowned for his prowess in the lists and wished to come to England to tilt with Sir Ralph Grey.[63] Following the coronation of Elizabeth Woodville, a tournament was held on 27 May 1465; judging from the preparations, it was intended to be a grand mêlée. Some £84 was spent on horses, saddles and shields for the king's use, all delivered to Thomas Burgh the master of the horse.[64] On the Thursday before the event John Wadden was given a writ for the immediate payment of £34 10*s* for a bill of items needed for the tournament including 200 spears and 150 pronged tips to prevent lances penetrating armour. Twenty-four carpenters were employed for two days. Edward created fifty knights of the Bath in his queen's honour and the tournament took place on the Monday following the coronation at Westminster. Some of the knights of Burgundy who were sent to the coronation with Jacques of Luxembourg appeared at Edward's request in the lists, which was won by Lord Stanley, who received a ring set with a ruby. Edward's personal interest in jousting is shown by his involvement in a joust at Eltham in late March 1467. John Paston the younger reported: 'My hand was hurte at the tournay at Eltham upon Wednesday last. I would that you had been there and seen it. For it was the goodliest sight that was sene in Inglande this forty yeares of so fewe men. There was upon the one side within the kinge, my lord Scales, myselfe, and Sellynge and without my lord chamberlain, Sir John Woodville, Sir Thomas Mountgomery and John Aparre.'

There was certainly something in the air in the 1460s. The men of Edward's court sought to find a mythic quality to their lives, proving their courage in the lists, emulating their heroes, the knights of the Round Table. The equivalent institution that allowed them to express and celebrate these ideals was the Order of the Garter. This had been founded in 1348 by Edward III, himself something of an inspiration as a chivalric king who was praised in the household ordinances. But Edward IV saw himself as the second founder of the order, to which he became patron, so much so that William Lord Hastings would refer to the Garter as Edward IV's Order in a letter in 1477. Under Henry VI the Garter had become a largely ceremonial religious order used by the king and Margaret of Anjou as an instrument of political control in which elections were restricted to those foreign princes and magnates who were supporters of the Lancastrian dynasty. The raison d'être of membership of the Order, as a means of honouring individuals who had given outstanding military service, largely disappeared after the end of war with France in 1453. It can be argued that Henry VI's lack of interest in military affairs and the deterioration of his relations with his nobility affected the cohesion of the body of the Order, evidenced by poor levels of attendance at meetings of the chapter between 1445 and 1460.[65] Edward IV, who was admitted sometime in 1461, elected thirteen new knights of the Garter in 1461 and 1462, the largest group of new elections in the Order's history. They included Sir John Tiptoft, William Lord Hastings, John Neville Marquess Montagu, William Lord Herbert, John Lord Scrope of Bolton and Sir John Astley. They were soon followed by Anthony Woodville Earl Rivers.[66] Edward's vision was for a revived Order imitating Arthur's Round Table and the original Order of Edward III. He even reorganized the Order's collegiate establishment and provided it with a home in his new chapel of St George at Windsor. In February 1473 Edward instructed Richard Beauchamp bishop of Salisbury to choose the carpenters and masons to work on a new chapel that was to replace the old chapel of Henry III.

Construction began in June 1475, and between 1478 and 1483 over £7,000 was spent, bringing craftsmen from all over the country to work on the chapel. This location of the headquarters of the Garter in the heart of Windsor Castle (which even today seems to be an evocation of Camelot when viewed from the River Thames) can be seen as part of Edward's impressive programme of rebuilding castles in a specifically English style. Eltham Palace in south London was a case in point, but it was St George's chapel, with its exclusively British, Arthurian associations, that was Edward's most personal project. The Cross Gneth, said to be a portion of the true cross on which Christ died, was closely associated with Edward's image as the returning British king. This relic had belonged to the last of the princes of North Wales, Llewelyn the Last, until his capture in 1283 and Edward III had given it to the Chapel of the Order of the Garter at its foundation in 1348. Edward IV transferred it to the new chapel and it was represented on the vault in the south choir aisle on a boss together with Edward's personal badge, the sun rising, in the background; before the cross and the sun Edward IV and Richard Beauchamp kneel in prayer. Other relics transferred to the new chapel included the heart of St George (presented by the Emperor Sigismund in 1415), a piece of his skull and a bone of King David, a saint with whom Edward closely identified.[67] The chapel even possessed a near-contemporary equivalent of Excalibur, Edward III's two-handed battle sword, 6ft 8in long, which can still be seen near the Oliver King chapel. The badge of the sun rising can also still be seen carved in many parts of the building, in three-dimensional relief on the outer walls and in the lower levels of the choir and aisle (which were the first parts of the chapel to be built). In the will Edward made before setting out for France in 1475, he left specific instructions for the building of his tomb, begun in his lifetime, on the north side of the high altar. He also ordered the construction of a chantry chapel with a tomb in the upper chapel.[68] But although the chantry was constructed there is no evidence that the memorial tomb was ever built. Instead he was interred under the marble touchstone he had requested (marble was the stone on which alchemical preparations were made,[69] but Edward was also perhaps alluding to the marble chair on which he had been crowned at Westminster). What does survive, however, is the beautiful and uniquely delicate wrought-iron gates made by John Tresilian which probably originally contained the king's royal arms and which may have been designed to give his tomb the appearance of a tabernacle. Perhaps modelled on Henry V's chantry at Westminster, they form two polygonal towers topped by miniature lamps and linked by buttressed gates; they were originally covered in gold gilt. There is no doubt that he intended this area of the chancel to be the symbolic heart of his new British dynasty and the burial place of his descendants. On 10 February 1480 additions were even made to the oath of all Garter knights, new and old, that 'they will aid, support and defend with all their power the royal college of St George within the castle of Windsor, as well in its possessions, as in all other things whatsoever'.[70]

The Order of the Garter was above all intended to be the Yorkist monarchy's equivalent of the Round Table, an institution that channelled men's violent instincts into a courteous and civilizing institution. The Arthurian ideals of the Order of the Garter were eloquently expressed by John Russel, later bishop of Lincoln and chancellor of England, on 4 February 1470 to Charles the Bold, duke of Burgundy, when he was presented with the insignia of the Garter. The speech was printed by Caxton in 1475, possibly at the insistence of the king, who wished to advertise the Burgundian alliance. Russel, after praising this third bond between Charles and Edward (who were already brothers of the Golden Fleece and brothers-in-law), forged, he believed, by the Holy Trinity and unbreakable, maintained that the orders of knighthood were not idle or superfluous but were one of the 'strong societies' or 'holy friendships' which support and unite nations. Man had emerged from his 'silvan huts' and 'bestial life' because he realized the advantages of social ties and 'from this fountain of social sense welled up all order, all faith and all community of people'. Russel went on to say that military men 'who are by nature very fierce' become restrained, obedient and devout in their way of life, 'excelling all others both in – courage in battle and devotion in the church'. The greatest examples of such orders were the Round Table of King Arthur, the Garter of Edward III, and the Golden Fleece of Charles's father.[71] The speech captures the way knighthood in the Arthurian myths, especially in Malory's work, was a feat of delicately balancing aggressive and protective instincts.

Hardynge described how the Round Table met every year at Whitsunday to tell of their adventures. Its purpose was to move young knights to seek arms who otherwise would be at home in idleness

> for better is with honour for to dye,
> Than with (lyfe ay) ashamed for to be.

This sums up the mentality of Edward's household and his Garter knights in these years. The household ordinances describe how esquires of his household of old were accustomed to perform virtuous service in the afternoons and in the evenings they withdrew to their lord's chambers within the court to keep honest company in talking of the chronicles of kings, harping and singing. They were adventurers. Knights and even squires could be admitted to the Order because of their chivalric prowess. When they met to take their stalls in the chapel they would have exchanged anecdotes about their chivalric adventures. Most of them accompanied Edward on his Northumbrian expedition in 1462, taking part in the sieges of the Lancastrian castles of Dunstanburgh, Alnwick and Bamburgh. Astley, who was put in charge of the garrison at Alnwick, was captured and taken to France when his second-in-command, Sir Ralph Grey, betrayed Alnwick to the French in May 1463. For three successive years his stall at the Garter remained empty because he was a prisoner in France. Anthony Woodville, too, was an expert in single-combat jousting and a crusading knight who later made pilgrimages to France, Compostela and shrines in southern Italy. He is represented, along with other participants in the conquest of Granada, on the choir stalls of the cathedral of Toledo.[72] Like Lancelot he had an ascetic streak and wore a hairshirt under his armour. In 1477 he jousted at a tournament in the guise of a hermit. Warwick was a charismatic personality who had created a reputation for himself as a skilled mariner and a pirate in the 1450s. He was the only one capable of steering the ship that took Edward earl of March and Richard Neville earl of Salisbury safely to Calais in 1459. Another knight to embody the Arthurian ideal was William Herbert, who was Welsh on both sides of his family. When Edward elevated him to the peerage he became the first Welshman to enter the ranks of the aristocracy, and he held more power than any Welshman since the conquest. He was the virtual ruler of west Wales, responsible for driving the Lancastrians out of the area, a feat he achieved by 1468. The poet Lewys Glyn Lothi, emphasizing how closely Edward and Herbert worked together, described Herbert as the great ear of Wales in London, Edward's master lock in Wales, the Gawain to his Arthur. And above them all shone Edward himself, who was seen as the embodiment of Arthur. Hardynge, exhorting Edward to invade Scotland in 1463, wrote:

> By small hackenays greate coursers men chastise,
> as Arthure did by Scottes wanne all fraunchese.[73]

Among a collection of prophecies concerning the coming of Edward there occurs Roger Thorney's poetic tribute to Edward IV's Arthurian reputation:[74]

> of a more famous knight I never read
> Syn the tyme of Arturs dayes
> he that loveth not I hold hym mad –
> Lorde haue eke in remembrance
> On King Edward the fourth thy own chosen knyght.

Poetry commissioned for Edward's funeral has an elegiac sense of nostalgia for this period of his reign when his court seemed the reincarnation of Camelot. In one Latin lament Edward is described as an Arthur to his enemies and as beautiful as Absolon, and the rose of the world, the son of triumph.

The power that these myths exerted over Edward, his queen and the knights of the Garter is shown most forcefully in an incident that could have been lifted out of the pages of the *Book of Lancelot* or the *Tale of Gawain and the Green Knight*, and which was witnessed in April 1465 by Jacques de Luxembourg on a visit to the English court. Edward and his household were at Shene when Lord Scales was speaking with his sister, the queen, kneeling before her with his bonnet doffed and lying on the floor beside him. The fair ladies of the court gathered around him, tying around his thigh a collar of gold and pearls with 'a noble flower of souvenance enamelled and in manner of an emprise'. They then dropped into his bonnet a little roll of parchment tied with a thread of gold. Being wise in such matters, Woodville at once understood that he was being asked to win the flower of souvenaunce by some deed of chivalry, a challenge to some 'noble man of four lineages'. After thanking the queen and ladies for the honour they had done him, he carried the roll of parchment to the king who broke the thread of gold and commanded the articles to be inscribed and read aloud. Edward approved of the exploit the ladies had chosen for his brother-in-law, a two-day encounter to take place in London the following October. The man chosen for Scales's challenge was Anthoine Count of La Roche, the illegitimate son of Duke Philip the Good of Burgundy; known as the Great Bastard of Burgundy, he was a famous warrior and jouster. Chester Herald travelled to Brussels to deliver the challenge to the Bastard, who had just returned from an abortive crusade, and was entertained for two days at the Burgundian court, which was regarded as the source of inspiration for the revival of jousting. The Bastard gave the herald letters to be delivered to Scales in which he promised to be in London on the day appointed for the tournament. On 23 May Chester Herald appeared with gifts before Edward at Greenwich and by the king's command the emprise was fastened on Lord Scales's collar of gold. Scales was very much Edward's champion, his Lancelot; he had previously fought in a tournament at Edward's new palace at Eltham, partnering John Paston the younger and the king himself in April 1467. The contest finally took place at

Smithfield on 11–12 June 1467, with Sir John Astley acting as Woodville's counsel. The event has been described by four eye-witnesses, two from the English side – Chester Herald and the author of the *Great London Chronicle* – and two from the Burgundian – the Burgundian master of ceremonies Olivier de la Marche, and an anonymous observer, the author of the most thorough description of this tournament.[75] The combat was theoretically planned as a single combat to the death 'and this dedys of armys was for lyffe or dethe,' unless one of the combatants yielded. The joust was to consist of one course with sharp spears, run without tilt or barrier and to be followed by a tourney on horseback with swords. Up to thirty-seven strokes could be delivered, including thrust and edge strokes, and the tourney would end when either party was borne out of the saddle or injured so badly they could not continue. The foot combats were to be fought with axes and daggers after each knight had cast one spear at the other, and the struggle would continue until one warrior bore the other to the ground or disarmed him.

On the face of it this was a celebration of chivalry, eagerly awaited throughout Europe for two years. The lists built at Smithfield cost £91 5*s* 1*d*. The royal gallery was on the east side (with its associations with the rising sun). In the middle was the king's throne, covered with a cloth of gold, in a pavilion surmounted by a golden eagle holding a banner of Scales's arms. On the first day the two men charged at each other before the king, trying to make 'direful contact' but they missed, bringing the perilous tilt to an end. The knights cast away their jousting armour and tourneyed with swords, Scales crying St George as was his custom. The contest on horseback was stopped by the king after the Bastard's horse was fatally injured in a collision. On the following day, 12 June, the two champions fought on foot with axes and daggers, Scales using the head of his axe and the Bastard the haft. There was some confusion and discrepancy between the four witnesses' accounts of this fight and whether Scales or the Bastard had the advantage. According to the two Burgundian observers it was the fiercest axe fight they had ever seen and the spectators never saw such thick and heavy blows. The king stopped the fight and the two men were parted with difficulty. Subsequent examination of the armour revealed Scales's suit to be broken in several places and the third piece of the Bastard's shoulder plate was hacked away. The two fierce warriors shook hands before the king, lunched together and then attended a reception given by the king when they partnered Edward, John Tiptoft and four other sportsmen in the *jeu de paume*. The following week was punctuated by further feasts and deeds of arms performed by two members of the Bastard's entourage, Jehan de Chassa and Philippe Boutin, against two Gascons in the English service, Louis de Bretalle, a member of Scales's retinue, and Thomas de la Lande, an esquire of Edward IV.[76] They first fought on foot, exchanging thirteen blows, on 13 June and jousted on 15 June, completing nineteen courses at the king's pleasure. Festivities were finally brought to an end on 19 June with the news that the Bastard's father, Philip the Good, had died.

Edward was clearly concerned with providing his court with a theme of Arthurian chivalry closely in tune with the accounts of tournaments in the Vulgate cycle of Arthurian legends. However, this theatrical showpiece for the Yorkist court masked a large gap between theory and practice. The tournament also had a political dimension. Edward was courting the friendship of Burgundy and sought a marriage alliance between his sister Margaret of York and Charles the Bold, the heir to the dukedom of Burgundy. An indication of the wider political ramifications of the Smithfield tournament was provided by Edward's secret visit to the bishop of Salisbury's house in Chelsea, where the Bastard of Burgundy was staying. Edward was accompanied by William Lord Hastings and Scales's father Richard Earl Rivers, both of whom had been busy during Warwick's absence in France trying to further the Burgundian alliance. Edward and the Bastard strolled together alone in the garden for half an hour. It was imperative for the success of these negotiations that the tournament was a success but also that neither of the two stars of the event, the brother of the queen of England and the brother of the future duke of Burgundy, was seriously injured or killed. This explains Edward's repeated interventions in the combat, politics not chivalry being his main priority. It was on Edward's order that the Bastard was freed from his horse after it had fallen on him, and when the horse collapsed again he ordered the cessation of the mounted combat. On the following day at the commencement of the foot combat he forbade (ostensibly at the request of the ladies) the casting of sharp spears. When the axe fight appeared to get out of control he again intervened.

But there was a further dimension to this gap between theory and practice. There is strong evidence that Scales, the Lancelot of the English court, the champion of the king and queen, cheated. The regulations of the mounted combat required that neither horse wore any sort of armour such as daggers or harness and neither horse should be used to hurt the other. The Burgundian counsel members were very precise on this matter, even ascertaining whether Scales's horse had been trained to bite. Scales answered in the high tones of chivalry that he never intended to have any advantage by means of a horse that bit but by his own hands and by means of knighthood, and if he had any such horse he would refuse it. Yet when the two horses crashed into each other the Bastard's horse was mortally wounded. According to the London chronicle, Scales's mount had a spike of steel mounted on its nostril and according to Olivier de la Marche, the Bastard's horse's head struck a projection from Scales's saddle. The suspicion of foul play was reinforced by the way Scales (according to Chester Herald) rode over to the king to show he had no chanfron or perser of steel. But according to the anonymous Burgundian chronicler, a post mortem revealed a piece of metal that showed Scales's sword had been rammed down the horse's throat at the point of collision. Sir Thomas Malory was no doubt a spectator at this tournament and may have consulted the details of the joust recorded in Sir John Paston's *Grete Boke*. In the *Morte d' Arthur* written two years later he retains the chivalry, bravery and brutality of this conflict, and even the failure of his heroes to always live up to the chivalric ideals they espoused. Sir Palomydes, one of the noblest knights of the Round Table, while jousting at a tournament at Lonzep, 'wyth his swerde he smote off his horse nek that Sir Launcelott rode uppon' and the two men subsequently fought on foot. The ensuing scandal may well have been intended by Malory to echo the rumours that must have been whispered after the Smithfield tournament:

> Than was the cry huge and grete, how sir Palomydes bycause he had done that dede, and helde there ayenste hit, and seyde hyt was unknyghtly done in a turnemente to kylle an horse wylfully, othir ellys that hit had bene done in playne batayle lyff for lyff.[77]

Whatever happened between Scales and the Bastard, they continued, just like Malory's two heroes, to maintain the solidarity of brothers in arms. In the following year Scales accompanied the king's sister Margaret to Bruges where she married the Bastard's brother Charles the Bold, duke of Burgundy. Scales again jousted with a Burgundian champion, but as John Paston related to his mother Margaret 'not with the Bastard for they mad promyse at London that non of them bothe shold never dele with othyr in armys', but the Lord Bastard was 'one of the lords that browt the lord Scalys in to the field'.[78] John Paston the younger described the Bastard in April 1468 in the following terms in a letter to his mother Margaret: 'I trow God mad never a mor worchepfull knight', and he was so overcome by this spectacle and its parallels with the Camelot of his imagination that he exclaimed: 'And as for the duke's court, as of lords, ladys and gentylwomen, knyghts, sqwyers, and gentylmen, I hert never of non lyk to it, save Kyng Artourys cort'.[79] Charles the Bold himself was a great reader of Arthurian literature and used to speak of his desire to emulate the knights of chivalrous romance. He had his court at Dijon decorated with tapestries depicting the siege of Troy and King Arthur.[80]

There was more to these Arthurian ideals than a love of adventure. Behind them lay aspirations of unity after a period of civil war. This was expressed by Hardynge in his elegiac appeal to the young Edward to bring home the exiled Henry VI:

> O righteous prince bring home the scatred men
> To theyr pasture forsaken and forlorne,
> For of your breste shulde greate foyson ren,
> To nedy men of grace and help euermore,
> Consyder howe God hath you set therfore,
> And ouer the flocke to seke the scatered shepe,
> And laye them in your folde surely to slepe.[81]

The high value Edward placed on jousting as the ultimate knightly pastime reflected this ideal. Like Arthur, Edward attempted to bring together feuding barons in jousts of peace where in sharing danger they formed bonds of friendship. In this he was following the examples set by previous monarchs who had promoted the cult of Arthur at their courts. Henry III presided in 1282 over the exhumation of what was claimed by the monks of Glastonbury to be the bodies of Arthur and Guinevere. Edward I had made the vast wooden disc known as King Arthur's Round Table as the centrepiece of a feast held at Winchester in 1290 after a tournament to mark the culmination of the king's plans for the dynastic arrangements of his children. Edward III announced his intention in June 1344 to found at Windsor a Round Table 'in the same manner and form as Lord Arthur once King of England had established it, namely for the number of 300 knights'. His plan was abandoned under pressure of the war with France, but he did begin to build a Hall of the Round Table at Windsor in 1344 and probably set up the Round Table made under his grandfather's orders on the wall of this hall. He also instituted the Order of the Garter, a fellowship of twenty-four knights, in 1348 and promoted an Arthurian tournament at Smithfield.[82] Edward IV in 1463 held jousts in London. According to the collections of one London citizen, the king, for a great love, 'made a grete justys at Westemynster, that he shulde se sum maner sporte of chevalry after hus grete labur and hevyness', and to the great astonishment of the assembled tourneyers he introduced a rather surly Henry Beaufort, duke of Somerset, who started his jousting career at the Tower of London during Whitsun week in 1458 when he was accompanied by Lord Scales as co-challenger. Somerset had a few months previously held Dunstanburgh and Bamburgh castles for the Lancastrians against Edward, 'and at great instans the kyng made hym to take harnys uppon hym, and rode in the place – and prayd hym to be mery – and – to ronne fulle justely and merely'.[83]

Another important feature of the Arthurian myths communicated by Hardynge and of the romances read by the queen (which he adapted) was the role of the king as a defender of the Church and a Christian king of a holy land who was dedicated to the recovery of the Grail. The prophecies foretelling the coming of Edward emphasized his role as the recoverer of the true cross and the crusader who would recover Jerusalem. One such prophecy occurring in the *Yorkist Prophecies* of 1461, taken from Geoffrey of Monmouth's *Historia regum Britanniae*, concerned a certain Sextus (counted down the Mortimer line to Edward IV), who was preceded by a lynx (Henry VI), who would bring about the downfall of his race. This Sextus would restore the kingdom and the Church to its original dignity. A prophecy of David in the psalms concerning the coming of the son of honour and worship was applied to Edward, and Alpha the patriarch of Jerusalem called him the western beast who will come from the west and free the Holy Land. A prophecy of the lily, the lion and the son of man predicted that he (the king of England) would undertake a crusade for the Holy Land, and a prophecy of Mahomet foretold a delicate rose of Britain called Edward of Rouen who would recover the Holy Land. There was also a prophecy of the Sybil regarding Albion concerning one so worthy and mighty that the realm of God would belong to him.[84] Images of the true cross allegedly discovered by St Helen, Edward's reputed ancestor, occur frequently in his genealogies,[85] and in the *Prophetic History of Britain* it is claimed that Edward would recover the true cross.[86]

Around the time of Edward's accession the Ottoman Turks were moving towards the Danube and the Adriatic, and in 1459 Pope Pius II sent Francesco Coppini, bishop of Turin, to England to attempt to reconcile the factions and preach a crusade against the Turks. So convincing was Edward's role as the successor of Arthur, the Christian king of the holy Celtic kingdom, that Coppini was converted to his cause and endorsed the identification of the Lancastrians with the pagan Saxons when he excommunicated them before the Battle of Northampton, offering Yorkists absolution and plenary remission of sins and giving the subsequent campaigns the dignity of a crusade.[87] Coppini took part in a procession from Northampton to London with George Neville and the captured king, and he corresponded with the Pope suggesting that a strong Yorkist regime was the best hope for a crusade. In a letter to George Neville on Edward's victory Coppini noted 'how a merciful God had granted a glorious victory to the renowned Edward and the devout sons of the church' and he remembered how in his last conversation with the bishop and the king they expressed their desire to use all their good and strength for the glory of God, the church and the Pope.[88] The alchemists at Edward's court were also attracted to the idea of a crusade, possibly because of its attendant ideals of unity. George Ripley corresponded with George Neville on the subject, and he also had connections with the crusading order of the Hospital of St John of Clerkenwell. There is a strong tradition that Ripley visited the knights of St John at Rhodes and lent them money for their campaigns against the Turks. In 1461 Philip of Burgundy, ambitious to be leader of the crusade, entertained Edward's ambassador Sir John Clay, wearing the king's new collar of the 'sun and white roses'.[89] The possibility of Edward's direct involvement in a crusade became strongest in October 1463 when France, England and Burgundy reached a peace agreement in the truce of Omer. Edward promised to send English archers to accompany Philip of Burgundy in his proposed expedition against the Turks, and George Neville offered to accompany him with three hundred men. In the following year Edward was toying with the idea of sending archers to join Burgundy on a 'blessed viage', and when Pius II announced the papal alliance with Burgundy in Venice Edward authorised a crusade grant. His identification with the crusading ideal in these years is commemorated in an illustration at the end of a genealogical roll written by Thomas Haselden soon after the royal marriage, which shows Edward and Elizabeth kneeling before the crucified Christ and the Trinity praying for a fruitful marriage and flanked by St George with the red cross and St Margaret with the Greek cross.[90]

The identification of Edward with Arthur as recognized by genealogists and chroniclers was given most powerful expression by the one writer of unquestionable genius in the fifteenth century, Sir Thomas Malory of Newbold Revell in Warwickshire. The debate that swirled around the identity of the author of the *Morte d'Arthur* in the twentieth century has now been satisfactorily resolved by P.J.C. Field.[91] Elected as knight (or member of parliament) for Warwickshire in 1445, and a retainer of Henry Beauchamp earl of Warwick, Malory spent the last decade or so of Henry VI's reign as a misfit, an adventurer and knight errant looking for good lordship, but in the government's eyes he was a criminal. He spent most of the 1450s imprisoned on various charges of rape, forcible entry and theft (the most serious of which was the attempted murder by ambush of the duke of Buckingham in 1450) in various London gaols including the Marshalsea, the Tower, Newgate and the Fleet. He had support from the Yorkist lords and the duke of York himself unsuccessfully tried to grant him a pardon. He eventually found patronage from the Nevilles: William Lord Fauconberg, Warwick's uncle, bailed him out of the King's Bench in 1458 and he was released from Newgate during the Yorkist invasion after the Battle of Northampton.

This release by Edward IV, after ten years of Lancastrian captivity, was a defining moment in Malory's life. A pardon granted by Edward in January 1462 was taken by Malory to the King's Bench in the same year and all charges against him were dismissed. He found help from one of Warwick's closest associates, John Lord Wenlock, whom he met in July 1460, and he entered the service of Edward IV (Warwick had Wenlock elected to the Garter on 3 February 1461). Malory's son, Robert Malory esq., became a lieutenant of the earl of Warwick in October 1461 and a lieutenant of the tower. Malory himself served in Edward's army. He was possibly at Mortimer's Cross and probably at the Battle of Towton. He was certainly in the army that accompanied Edward on the Northumbrian campaign of October 1462 to January 1463, as his name occurs in a Yorkist chronicle in a list of knights and peers accompanying Edward in November 1462 to besiege the Lancastrian-held castles of Alnwick, Bamburgh and Dunstanburgh.[92] It was on this expedition that he would have encountered the Garter knights living the Arthurian myth, such as Anthony Woodville, Sir John Astley, John Paston the younger and Warwick. Malory was named as one of the fifteen knights at the siege of Alnwick (1462–3) at which Anthony Woodville was second-in-command.[93] Malory also had connections with Astley, whose estates were in Warwickshire and who was part of a faction in the 1440s with Malory's father. He would also have had the opportunity to associate with such men at court and at the numerous jousting tourneys. The last official notice of Malory as a free man in this decade occurs in September 1464 with his attendance at a betrothal. Sometime between this date and April 1468 he lapsed into his former violent ways. By 29 April 1468 he was in Newgate gaol again.

A document among the records of the Mercers Company of London shows that he was one of twenty-one men gathered around the deathbed of Thomas Mynton, a gentleman in Newgate gaol, hearing a declaration that he would, if he lived, perform all his past promises made to Sir Thomas Cook and cease to vex him in any way.[94] Malory was specifically excluded from the second general pardon of Edward IV's reign on 14 July 1468. The fact that he was imprisoned in Newgate establishes that he was already in gaol at the time of the June plots of the Nevilles and Robin of Redesdale involving Sir Thomas Cook and his patron Wenlock. He was not in the state gaol, the Tower, but in a gaol for criminals, and as he was not sentenced to death and did not plead benefit of clergy it is likely that he was charged with a misdemeanour rather than a felony, such as assault, and that he was serving a specific sentence or a custodial sentence until he paid a fine. His failure to secure sureties in his own locality of Warwickshire in the last decade of his life suggests he was regarded as a public nuisance.[95] He was probably sentenced before July 1468 and he was still serving his time on 22 February 1470 when he was excluded from Edward IV's third general pardon.

The evidence of the Winchester manuscript of the *Morte d'Arthur* suggests that Malory wrote the whole of this work in prison and he must have taken up writing this epic in response to the knowledge that he would be in gaol for a set period. He completed the work about two years later, in his own words 'in the nineteenth year of the reign of King Edward IV' (between 3 March 1469 and 4 March 1470). He was not a political prisoner so it is wrong to assume he was released by Henry VI during the Readeption, and he probably remained in custody until his death in early 1471. On 14 March he was buried across the road in the cemetery of Greyfriars in Newgate Street, which contained the tombs of a number of eminent convicts. Newgate gaol, rebuilt in 1423–32 by the executors of Richard Whittington, would have offered a prisoner of some social standing like Malory the privilege of easy access to two well-lit day rooms on either side of the chapel. This relative comfort may well have contrasted with some of Malory's confinements under the Lancastrians. He had access to books, including the eight texts used for the writing of *Morte d'Arthur*, including the three books of the Vulgate cycle, *Estoire del Saint Graal*, the *Lancelot* and the *Queste del Saint Graal*, the English alliterative *Morte Arthure*, the French *Merlin*, the first two books of the prose *Tristram*, and probably Hardynge's *Chronicle*, including a revised shorter version presented to Edward in 1464 and which was widely circulated. Malory may have owned some of these texts, like the courtier Sir Richard Roos who owned the *Estoire de Saint Graal* and the prose *Lancelot*, and he could have purchased or hired books through a servant from the booksellers outside the gaol in the shops of Pater Noster Row. Although there is no specific evidence, it is possible that Malory may have received encouragement in his enterprise from Anthony Woodville, Lord Scales, his former brother in arms in the Northumbrian campaigns, and he may have had access to Woodville's books including possibly the Vulgate cycle owned by Woodville's sister the queen.[96] Malory used these texts to produce a complete Arthurian cycle in English which gave the legends an unprecedented coherence, producing an epic creation of Arthurian England which closely mirrors his own world at the time of Edward's accession. *Morte d'Arthur*, as it became known in Caxton's subsequent edition, established Malory as the most important in a line of writers who used these Arthurian romances to compare Edward to the mythic British king.[97] Edward IV is the only contemporary to be mentioned by name in this work. Woodville realized the significance of Malory's achievement when he persuaded Caxton to print the work. He was, in Caxton's own words, one of the 'many noble and diverse gentlemen of England' who 'often demanded of me to make a print of the noble history of the grail and the renowned king Arthur'. Woodville may even have made the Winchester text available to Caxton.

The *Morte d'Arthur* begins with the 'Tale of Balin' and the two swords, a tragic story of a fierce but well-intentioned knight whose attachment to a fateful sword causes him to inadvertently slay his brother, and unwittingly, in Merlin's words, to strike the dolorous stroke that would render King Pellas, a descendant of Joseph of Arimathea, into a frail Fisher King and render three kingdoms into a wasteland awaiting redemption from Arthur and his knights, which will come when Galahad finds Balin's scabbard. This powerful tale evokes the crisis facing Edward's kingdom and the expectations placed upon him. Malory, after his release in March 1461, would have been familiar with the genealogical rolls and prophecies surrounding Edward and especially with the *Illustrated Life of Edward* and it is possible that Balin's fateful sword was inspired by the sword wielded by Bolingbroke at the foot of this scroll to cut off the Mortimer line. This was the blow which inflicted the fatal wound on the Lancastrian dynasty, leaving Henry VI a maimed king and bringing the three kingdoms of England, Wales and France to the wounds that Edward was pledged to heal.

The restoration of a sick kingdom lay for Malory in the assertion of male energy. He had little time for the passive religiosity of Henry VI. Hermits, such as the one displayed in an illustration in Edward IV's copy of Lull's *Manual of Chivalry*, have an important role in guiding Arthurian knights, but they were usually former soldiers. This was a role played by Woodville and Lancelot. Malory alters the ascetic, monastic tone of one of his sources, *Le queste le Graal*, so that Lancelot becomes the real hero of this epic: his adulterous passion comes in for less censure, and he almost achieves the Grail. Penance and self-examination are less important to Malory than courage and loyalty, and these qualities Lancelot shows in loving Guinevere and serving Arthur; and they are the qualities celebrated at Arthur's Round

Table. He celebrated male sexual energy whether active in the case of Lancelot or withheld as in Galahad's chastity. This he held to be an essential part of the religion of Arthur's knights. It is possible to read the *Morte d'Arthur* as a condemnation of Henry VI's piety, which had such a negative effect on the kingdom, and a celebration of the martial vigour and sexual male energy of Edward and his Garter Knights, which for a time seemed to promise the regeneration of the kingdom. With the 'Tale of Lancelot', Malory's work changes from history to romance and he produces an epic journey into the subconscious, like the visions of contemporary alchemists. As a prisoner forced inwards on himself, like Charles of Orleans, Malory produces an imaginary world of the dark forest where things happen the way they do in dreams; Malory's dream is the product of the particular personal and political conflicts of the period in which he lived. This tale, like the alchemical texts, celebrates primal energies and adventurousness that allows courage and individuality to surface. Camelot embodies these qualities, the willingness to ride off into the dark in search of honour and God: 'Ayn Lancelot rode ouerthwarte and endelong a wylde foreyst and hylde no path but as adventure led hym.'[98] The ultimate adventure was the crusade and this too is an addition that Malory brings to his sources from his observations of Edward's court. He has Arthur pledging to go on a crusade and to recover the true cross, echoing the prophecies applied to Edward IV.

Malory was a violent, adventurous man, and these were the qualities he admired in Edward IV. However, he also welcomed the opportunity that the revival of Arthurian myths and especially the concept of the Round Table at Edward IV's court offered for knights to harness their aggressive instincts into a protective and chivalrous attitude towards women and the Church. Edward struck an Arthurian pose in his proclamation to Parliament on 6 March 1461 giving his reasons for taking the throne. The dukes of Somerset and Exeter, he claimed, were moved by the spirit of the devil to destroy England and its people, and to this end they rode through the country committing horrible treasons, robbing churches and religious houses, taking goods hallowed and dedicated to God, and cruelly oppressing wives, maidens and women of religion with a cruelty not shown even by Turks. Echoing the orders Henry V gave to his army in France, Edward IV added the command that on pain of death no man should rob or spoil any church or person of the church, or deflower any woman, whether wife, maiden or widow. The same language was used in the chivalric orders of Edward's court. Among the heraldic material in Astley's volume and Paston's *Grete Boke* is the ceremonial for making knights of the Bath (Edward made fifty in honour of Queen Elizabeth). The king's steward exhorted these knights to love God and defend the Church, to be true to their sovereign, to sustain widows and virgins and their rights, and succour them with goods, and to sit in no place where a wrong judgement was given against anybody. This influenced a unique passage in Malory's *Morte d'Arthur* where the knights of the Round Table swear an oath after Arthur's marriage to Guinevere to meet every Pentecost and never to do outrage, to flee treason, to give mercy to he who asks for it on pain of forfeiture of King Arthur's worship and lordship, and to always succour ladies, damsels, gentlewomen and widows, to uphold their rights and never to force them, and never to take battle in a wrongful quarrel or to love worldly goods.[99]

An important aspect of this chivalrous attitude towards the Church was the crusading ideal upheld in Edward's court in the early 1460s and incorporated into the plot of the *Morte d'Arthur*. With the arrival of Sir Galahad at Camelot the Round Table begins to look less like a secular Order of the Garter and to resemble more closely a sacred order of warrior monks, like the Templars (on whom Wolfram von Eschenbach modelled his Parsifal) or the Hospitaller knights of St John of the Cross, who were devoted to the capture of the holy sites of Jerusalem. Malory may have been specifically inspired by the Hospitallers, whose headquarters in England were at Clerkenwell Priory in London. By the 1460s the

Hospitallers were specifically concerned with the care of sick and poor pilgrims to the Holy Land and in their formidable fortress on Rhodes they were the last realistic bulwark against the advance of the Turks. Malory's uncle Sir Robert Malory was prior of the priory of the Hospital of St John of Jerusalem in England from 1432 to 1439 (or 1440). When the Sultan of Egypt threatened Rhodes, Sir Robert Malory organized and commanded the Hospitaller contingent that sailed from Britain to help ward off the attack. The danger subsided and he returned to England in 1438 with oriental wines and rugs. Another member of the family, John Malory, possibly Sir Thomas's younger brother or son, was also a Knight Hospitaller who served in Rhodes in 1469. He became a senior knight of the priory at Clerkenwell where he was buried. He presented the newly elected prior to Edward IV in 1474 and he may have died a prior of the order. The faith and courage of the military order was to be demonstrated in the heroic defence of the island of Rhodes in 1480. Even by this time there was still considerable interest in the fate of Rhodes at Edward's court and a first-hand account of the siege, *Obsidionis Rhodie urbis descriptio* by the vice-chancellor of the order, Guillaume Caorsin, was translated by John Kaye, the poet laureate, in 1480 and dedicated to 'the redoubtable Christian king Edward IV'. This work was printed soon after by Wynkyn de Worde.[100] Caxton translated and printed Godfrey of Bouillon's *Siege and Conquest of Jerusalem* in 1481, dedicating it to Edward IV, [101] with the purpose of inspiring his readers to avoid evil and to remind princes of their responsibility to recover the Holy Land 'which our blessed Lord Jesus Christ hath hallowed and the relief of Eastern Christendom'.[102] So in 1469, when Malory was in gaol writing his epic, at a time when his son or younger brother was on this strategically crucial mission to the island of Rhodes, he may have had these warrior monks in mind when deviating from his sources to give Arthur's court considerable crusading zeal. He has Sir Tristram obeying a papal summons to go on a crusade to Jerusalem and the climax to this book is the conversion of the Saracen knight, Sir Palomides, which is not in the sources. The work concludes with a claim that the surviving knights – Sir Bors, Sir Ector de Maris, Sir Blamor and Sir Bleoberis – 'went into the Holy Land there as Jesu Christ was quick and dead'.

Another peaceful outlet for aggression was the joust, and the prevalence of tournaments in the *Morte d'Arthur*, influenced by the tournaments held by Edward, is another important innovation in Malory's work. For Arthur's Round Table and for Edward's court, the joust was an opportunity to reconcile tensions. After Lancelot accepts Guinevere's apology for having suspected him of disloyalty over the lady of Shalot, jousts and tourneys were held, bringing many great lords who every day would joust for a diamond. At the end of the episode in which Lancelot healed the wounds of Sir Urry, Arthur organized a mêlée of 200 knights jousting for a diamond. In these accounts Malory was probably influenced by the chivalric handbooks of Sir John Astley and John Paston, where a diamond is specified as a first prize in a joust of peace. Malory's King Arthur, like Edward, has an at times naive belief that the chivalry and courage displayed in the joust could bring men together and heal the personal and political rifts of the realm.

The imaginative power of this work rests, above all, in the way Malory, in meditating in prison on events of Arthur's reign, provides an eye-witness account of the exciting events of the early part of Edward's reign. His repeated journeys across the Thames from imprisonment in Ludgate and Marshalsea gaols to the court of the King's Bench at Westminster Hall covered the stretch of river across which Lancelot rode when he attempted to rescue Guinevere. While he was in Newgate, he witnessed the siege of the Tower at the time of the Battle of Northampton when guns were used and this goes into his description of Mordred's use of firearms in besieging Guinevere. The Battle of Northampton marked Malory's release from gaol, and he alludes to Edward's command that while lords and knights were to be killed the commons were to be spared in the scene when Arthur has his enemies at this mercy and he suggests abandoning the infantry because he does not wish to hurt footsoldiers. The circumstances of Edward's popular acclamation as king were fresh in Malory's mind when he described the crowning of King Arthur. The feuding barons selfishly procrastinated: 'Then stood the realm in great jeopardy long while, for every lord that was mighty of men made him strong, and many wende to have been king.' In the end it is the commons (who have no part in Malory's source) who forced the barons to accept Arthur as king and this recalls the popular acclamation of Edward as king in St John's Fields in March 1461.

After this acclamation Malory entered Edward's military service and the carnage he witnessed at Towton inspired his account of Arthur's last battle, where survivors saw by moonlight the pillaging and robbing of the dead knights of jewellery and the slaying of the wounded for their harness and riches. Malory fought under Anthony Woodville at the sieges of Alnwick and Bamburgh and Woodville may have inspired his depiction of Lancelot as a combination of chivalric adventurousness and ascetic piety. The close relationship between the two men is symbolized by their wearing of a hairshirt under their armour, and by Malory's decision to make Bamburgh Castle, overlooking the North Sea, the home of Lancelot, 'Joyous Garde'.

However, the imaginative power of this epic is mainly derived from the autobiographical impetus given to it by its author. Malory closely identified with Sir Tristram, a fellow prisoner incarcerated through no fault of his own but through the corruption of King Mark's government. Malory, reflecting on his own experiences, writes of Sir Tristram's imprisonment:

> So sir Trystram endured there grete payne, for sykness had undirtake hym, and that ys the grettist payne a presoner may have. For all the whyle a presonere may have hys helth of body, he may endure undir the mercy of God and in hope of good delyveraunce; but when syknes towchith a presoners body, than may a presonere say all welth ys hym berauffte, and than hath he cause to wayle and wepe. Ryght so ded sir Trystram whan syknes had undirtake hym, for than he toke such sorow that he had allmoste slayne hymselff.[103]

Tristram, like his creator in the 1450s, was a figure on the fringes, looking for good lordship in the corrupt kingdom of Cornwall that mirrored Henry VI's England in the decade before Edward's accession, a place of constant feuding. The euphoria Malory must have felt when he was released from gaol into Edward's service was expressed in the 'Book of Tristram' when Tristram moves from the fragmented world of Cornwall to Logres and the Round Table where all conflicts are resolved and where all good knights go. In Cornwall Tristram aggressively and restlessly asserted himself, pursuing honour and ladies, questing for the beast in the forest in an anarchic world, and like Malory frequently suffering imprisonment. As he gravitates from the fragmented fringes of King Mark's corrupt kingdom to Logres to join Lancelot at Joyous Garde and the Round Table, places of noble idealism in contrast to the cynicism of Cornwall, all conflicts are resolved and he feels calmer and becomes more optimistic. No longer an outsider, he is brought into the fold of a society where discordant elements are resolved in jousts and fellowship. The Round Table resolves all conflicts and all good knights such as Palomides, Gareth, Lancelot and Galahad gravitate towards this sacred place which is at its zenith when Galahad is welcomed to the Round Table and jousts are held. Malory, too, was released from gaol and welcomed into Edward's service to enjoy the camaraderie in battle and the jousts of Anthony Woodville, Sir John Astley, William Herbert and the earl of Warwick. The nostalgia and gratitude that Malory felt for this period of his life are reflected in the way he conveyed the two worlds (the England of Edward IV and

Arthur) in his imagination. Malory located Camelot at Winchester (the site of the 1449 parliament) and was the first writer to do so. He located the Grail Castle of King Pellas precisely in North Wales in 'the land of the two marchys', the land from where Edward took his ancestry and title. He introduces Welsh knights, contrary to his sources, locates the 'Tale of Sir Gareth' in Wales, has his hero, Sir Tristram, visiting Wales and describes Arthur as 'the Welsh king'[104] and notes his arms, the 'doleful dragon'. Malory's nostalgic remembering of these early years of Edward's reign is shown in the way he describes Lancelot's love for Guinevere, recalling this time at Camelot as a perpetual May time, a golden age, which recalls the gardens and flower imagery associated with the poems about Edward IV.

NOTES

1. John Rylands University Library MS Eng. 113, fos 3r–4v, printed in A. Sutton and L. Visser-Fuchs, 'Laments for the Soul of Edward IV', *The Ricardian*, xi, 145 (June 1999), 516–18.
2. Bodley MS Rawl. C 86, fo. 74; A. Sutton and L. Visser-Fuchs, 'Laments for the Soul of Edward IV', *The Ricardian*, xi, 145 (June 1999).
3. BL MS Add. 10099, fo. 8.
4. W. Hardy and E. Hardy, eds, *Receuil des Chroniques d'Engleterre*, vol. 5 (London, 1891), p. 348. BL MS Cotton Vesp. E VII.
5. *Rot. Parl.*, vol. v, p. 463a; see also Edward IV writing to Thomas Cook, alderman of London, on 13 March 1462. Ellis, *Original Letters*, vol. ii, p. 130.
6. Jean de Waurin, *Receuil des Croniques et Anciennes Istories de la Grant Bretaigne, a present nomme Engleterre*, ed. W. Hardy (Rolls Series, London, 1864–91), vol. v, p. 349.
7. New Troy was traditionally identified with the Mortimer line.
8. Caroline Barron, 'The Lancastrian Court and London', paper delivered at the 18th Harlaxton Symposium on the Lancastrian Court, 23–7 July 2001.
9. Bodley MS Hatton.
10. Scofield, *Edward IV*, vol. ?, p. 148; *Cal. State Papers Milan*, ed. A.B. Hinds (London, 1912), vol. i, p. 54; *Gregory's Chronicle* (Camden Society, 1876), p. 215.
11. BL MS Lansdowne 262.
12. Ibid.
13. One lock is in the muniment room of the chapel, another in the Ashmolean Museum.
14. *Cal. Milanese Papers*, vol. 1, pp. 101–2.
15. *Rot. Parl.*, vol. v, pp. 462–3; J.S. Roskell, *The Commons and their Speakers in English Parliaments 1376–1532* (Manchester, 1965), pp. 80–1, 274.
16. See *Henry VI: A Reprint of Blacman's Memoir*, ed. M.R. James (Cambridge, 1919).
17. Lincoln Cathedral Library MS 91; L.D. Benson, 'The Date of the Alliterative Morte Arthure', in J.B. Bessinger and R.K. Raymo (eds), Medieval Studies presented to William Heslands Hornstein (New York, 1969), pp. 19–40; Lydgate, *Fall of Princes*, bk viii, ll. 3121–2.
18. Bodley MS 623.
19. Philadelphia Free Library MS E 201.
20. BL MS Cotton Vesp. E VII and Bodley MS 623, fos 638, 616.
21. BL MS Lansdowne 456.
22. M.E. Giffin, 'Cadwallader, Arthur and Brutus in the Wigmore Manuscript', *Speculum*, 16 (1941), 111; J. Vale, 'Arthur in English Society', in W.R.J. Barron, ed., *The Arthur of the English* (Cardiff, 2001), 193–4; Hardynge's *Chronicle*, p. 289.
23. College of Arms MS 20/20 and Ashmole Roll 26.
24. Hardynge's *Chronicle*, p. 121.
25. Philadelphia Free Library MS E 201.
26. BL MS Add. 18268 A.
27. Bodley MS e mus 35, fo. 29.
28. Bodley MS Lyell 35.
29. Scofield, *Edward IV*, p. 178.

30. Hardynge, *Chronicle*, p. 146.
31. See the *A Lookeing Glasse for Illiterate Alchymists* in the sixteenth century which places Merlin at the head of a chronological list of British alchemists.
32. BL MS Add. 15,549.
33. Bodley MS Ashmole 440, fo. 205.
34. Comets were commonly described as dragons. According to M. Baillie, in *Exodus to Arthur: Catastrophic Encounters with Comets* (London, 1999), there was considerable comet activity around the time of Arthur, AD 540, when there were reports of fighting dragons in the sea (a fall-out of comets). This may explain the origin of Merlin's interpretation of the significance to Vortigern of the fighting dragons in the pool. Hardynge, *Chronicle*, p. 116.
35. BL MS Cotton Vesp. E VII.
36. Bodley MS e mus.
37. Bodley MS Ashmole 446, fo. 205.
38. Bodley MS Ashmole 1459.
39. BL MS Sloane 3747.
40. Trinity College, Cambridge, MS 0.8.31, fo. 112b.
41. BL MS Sloane 1118, fo. 27.
42. The three crowns were variously interpreted. In Bodley MS Lyell 35 it was England, Ireland and Wales; in Trinity College, Cambridge, it was England, France and Spain.
43. Trinity College, Cambridge, MS R 3.21, fos 242ff. Composed between the deaths of Henry VI and Edward IV (a reference to Henry's burial at Chertsey).
44. G. Bone, 'Extant Manuscripts Printed by W. de Worde with notes on the owner Roger Thorney', *The Library*, 4th ser. 12 (1931), 284–306.
45. John Stow, *A Survey of London*, ed. L.L. Kingsford (Oxford, 1908), 433; Edward Hall, *Hall's Chronicle*, ed. H. Ellis (London, 1809), 367; Stow 433; Hall 367; More, *History of Richard III*, pp. 61–2; Scofield, *Edward IV*, vol. ii, pp. 56, 161.
46. A.R. Wagner, 'The Swan Badge and the Swan Knight', *Archeologia*, cxcvii (1956); BL MS Royal 15 E vi, fos 273–92.
47. Wagner, 'The Swan Badge', 127–8; John Rous, *Rous Roll*, ed. W.H. Courethope, 2nd edn (Stroud, 1980), ch. 18; BL MS Add. 48976.
48. C. Meale, 'Readers and Patrons in 15th Century England: Sir Thomas Malory and Arthurian Romance', *Arthurian Literature* (1983), vol. iv, 93–127. Anthony Woodville's father, Richard Woodville 1st Earl Rivers, owned an early fourteenth-century *Alexander*, Bodley MS 264.
49. Loomis, *The Grail.*
50. BL MS Royal 14 E iii.
51. Jesus College, Oxford, MS 114, fo. 18v.
52. Ross, *Edward IV*, p. 185.
53. BL MS Royal 14 E ii.
54. C.H. Wilkins, 'A fifteenth-century Lawsuit', *Law Quarterly Review*, XI (1934), 354–66.
55. *Travels of Leo of Rozmital*, ed. and transl. M. Letts (Hakluyt Society, 2nd ser. Cambridge, 1957), p. 45.
56. Loomis, *The Grail*, pp. 239, 243.
57. BL MS Harl. 642, fo. 4; *Household Book of Edward IV*, ed. A. Myers (Manchester, 1959).
58. Richard Barber, 'Malory's Le Morte d'Arthur and Court Culture under Edward IV', *Arthurian Literature*, xii, ed. J.P. Carley and F. Riddy (Cambridge, 1993).
59. *Sir John Paston's Grete Boke*, ed. G.A. Lester (Cambridge, 1984), pp. 92–3.
60. BL MS Lansdowne 285; *Sir John Paston's Grete Boke*, ed. Lester, p. 61, footnote.
61. *Paston Letters*, vi, ed. Gairdner, p. 65.
62. Tiptoft's rules are printed in E. Cripps-Day, *The History of the Tournament in England and France* (London, 1918).
63. Scofield, *Edward IV*, vol. i, p. 214; Rymer, *Foedera*, vol. xi, p. 481.
64. Burgh was possibly the one who commissioned Hardynge's revised chronicle.
65. Diana Dunn, 'Margaret of Anjou, Chivalry and the Order of the Garter', in *St George's Chapel, Windsor*, p. 53; J. Anstis, *The Register of the Most Noble Order of the Garter*, 2 vols (London, 1724), vol. i, pp. 174–5.
66. Barber, 'Malory's Morte d'Arthur'.
67. John Rous, *Historia regum Angliae*, p. 211.
68. For Edward's will see *Excerpta Historica*, ed. S. Bentley (London, 1833), pp. 366–76; W.H. St John Hope, *The Architectual History of Windsor Castle* (London, 1913), pp. 376–7.
69. *Marrow of Alchemy*, Bodley MS Ashmole 1480, fo. 12v.

70. For Tresilian's altar canopy see Jane Geddes, 'The Search for John Tresilian Master Smith to Edward IV', *History Today,* May 2002. Sutton and Visser-Fuchs, 'Chivalry and the Yorkist Kings', 128.
71. Ibid, 129; Scofield, *Edward IV*, vol. i, pp. 485, 507; Russel's speech is printed in *Proposito Johannis Russel, printed by William Caxton circa A.D. 1476*, introd. H. Guppy (Manchester and London, 1909).
72. J.R. Goodman, *Chivalry and Exploration 1298–1631* (Bury St Edmunds, 1998), p. 170.
73. Hardynge, *Chronicle*, p. 419. *Gwaith Gutor Glyn*, ed. I. Williams and J. L. Williams (Cardiff, 1939), p. 63; G. Williams, *Renewal and Reformation Wales,* c. *1415–1642* (Oxford, 1993).
74. See note 101.
75. For a subsequent account of this tournament see S. Anglo, 'Anglo-Burgundian feats of Arms Smithfield June 1467', *Guildhall Miscellany* (September 1960), 271–83.
76. Barber, 'Malory's Morte d'Arthur'; Fabyan, *Chronicle*, p. 203.
77. *The Works of Sir Thomas Malory*, ed. E. Vinaver (Oxford, 1947), vol. ii, p. 739.
78. Gregory's *Chronicle*, p. 236.
79. *Paston Letters*, ed. Gairdner, pp. 4, 298.
80. R. Vaughan, *Charles the Bold* (London, 1973).
81. Hardynge, *Chronicle*, p. 412.
82. M. Biddle, *King Arthur's Round Table: An Archaeological Investigation* (Woodbridge, 2000); Vale, *Edward III and Chivalry*, pp. 67–8; Barber, *The Tournament in England 1100–1400* (Woodbridge, 1986).
83. *Historical Collections of a Citizen of London*, ed. Gairdner, p. 219; and *Three Fifteenth-Century Chronicles*, ed. Gairdner, p. 65.
84. Bodley MS Hatton 56.
85. BL MS Lat. Misc. b2.
86. Bodley MS 623.
87. G. Baskerworth, 'A London Chronicle of 1460', *EHR*, xxviii (1913), 125.
88. *Cal. Milanese Papers*, pp. 78–81.
89. G. Chastellain, *Oevres*, ed. K. de Lettenhove, 8 vols (Brussels, 1863–6), iv, 164–6; Waurin, *Chronicles of England*, vol. ii, p. 313.
90. Jesus College, Oxford, MS 114, fo. 34.
91. The identification of the Newbold Revell knight was first made by G.L. Kittredge in the 1890s; A.T. Martin, 'The Identity of the author of the Morte Darthur', *Archeologia*, vol. xlvi, 176, 179; G. Whitteridge, 'The Identity of Sir Thomas Malory, Knight-prisoner', review in *English Studies*, ns xxiv, 257–65; A.L. Baugh, 'Documenting Sir Thomas Malory', *Speculum*, xlvii, 3–29; W. Mathews, *The Ill Framed Knight* (Berkeley and Los Angeles, 1966); R.R. Griffith, 'The Authorship Question Reconsidered. A Case for Thomas Malory of Papworth St Agnes, Cambridgeshire', in *Aspects of Malory*, ed. Toshiyuki Takamiya and D. Brewer (Cambridge, 1981); P.J.C. Field, ' Sir Thomas Malory, MP', *BIHR*, xlvii (1974), 24–35; P.J.C. Field, *The Life and Times of Sir Thomas Malory* (Cambridge, 1993); P. Field, 'The Malory Life Records', in *A Companion to Malory*, ed. E. Archibald and A.S.G. Edwards (Cambridge, 1996).
92. Kingsford, *English Historical Literature*, p. 161.
93. Sir Thomas Malory owned the Northamptonshire property which contributed to the support of an honour that later merged with Woodville's lordship of Rivers.
94. For the discovery of this document and the following account see Anne F. Sutton, 'Malory in Newgate', *The Library*, 7 Ser., vol. 1, no. 3 (September 2000).
95. C. Carpenter, 'Sir Thomas Malory and Fifteenth Century Local Politics', *BIHR*, 53 (1980), 41–2.
96. The debate about Woodville's possible patronage of Malory is unresolved. The case for has been stated by R.R. Griffith, 'The Political Bias of Malory's Morte d'Arthur', *Viator*, 5 (1974), 365–86.The case against is argued by C. Meale, 'Readers and Patrons in Fifteenth Century England: Sir Thomas Malory and Arthurian Romance', *Arthurian Literature*, 4 (1985), 93–126. Sutton agrees with Meale but her discovery of the Mercers document excluding Malory from political involvement in the plots of 1468, so ruthlessly opposed by Richard Woodville Earl Rivers, actually strengthens the case for the involvement of Earl Rivers' son Anthony with Malory.
97. *The Works of Sir Thomas Malory*, 3rd edn, ed. E. Winaver and rev. by P.J.C. Field, 3 vols (Oxford, 1990).
98. Malory, *Morte d'Arthur*, p. 893.
99. Barber, 'Malory's Morte d'Arthur'.
100. *The Siege of Rhodes*, transl. John Kaye 1482, facsimile repr. (New York, 1975), the English Experience no. 236.
101. E.G. Duff, *Fifteenth Century English Books* (Oxford, 1977); William Caxton, *Godfrey de Boleyn*, ed. M.N. Colvin (EETS, London, 1893).
102. Tyerman, *England and the Crusades.*
103. Malory, *Works*, p. 540.
104. Meale, 'Sir Thomas Malory and Arthurian Romance', p. 131.

CHAPTER 7

The Disintegration of Camelot

Full many a glorious morning have I seen
Flatter the mountain-tops with sovereign eye,
Kissing with golden face the meadows green,
Gilding pale streams with heavenly alchymy;
Anon permit the basest clouds to ride
With ugly rack on his celestial face,
And from the forlorn world his visage hide,
Stealing unseen to west with his disgrace.

William Shakespeare, *Sonnet xxxiii*

When Edward was crowned in July 1461 he epitomized the hero king, a man from whom power and charisma emanated, because he was perceived to hold within his youthful form a near perfect balance of the four humours, like Christ with whom he was frequently compared. In the book of the guild of barber surgeons of York, made in 1486, there is a diagram of the four personified humours around Christ, the quintessence, who is shown with a halo and the sun in ascendancy (Edward's badge) rising behind his head. Edward was identified in 1461 with this life-giving, solar warmth, but despite the optimism of the early years of his reign and his Arthurian aspirations, there were signs that he could only summon his considerable reserves of courage and energy (or in fifteenth-century medical terms to act by mobilizing all four humours) when he was faced with great danger. As he settled into the rule of his kingdom, his energies were dissipated in hedonistic pleasures in which the humours of phlegm and blood predominated in an indulgence in ease, food, drink and sex. The planetary influences of the moon and Venus were being increasingly courted instead of those of the sun and Mars. This meant that Edward was ceasing to act under the influence of choler and he all but lost sight of the warrior within him. The king therefore could no longer be identified with the sun blessing his land.

Misgivings were first expressed by the ambassador of the duke of Milan, Pietro Legnola, who wrote after the death of Charles VII that Edward, after Towton, rode to Windsor to go hunting: 'the king's desires seem to me to be directed towards some kind of pleasure'.[1] The consolidation of the conquest of the kingdom in Wales and Northumbria was left largely in the hands of the Nevilles, and Hastings wrote to the Burgundian envoy, Jean Lannoy, on 7 August 1463 from Fotheringay praising Warwick's accomplishments, including raising the siege of Norham and forcing Margaret of Anjou to take to sea. However, Hastings observed that while Warwick had the situation well in hand 'the king was at his sport and entertainment of the hunt without any fear for his honourable person or any of his subjects'.[2] In this same year Parliament had imposed restrictions on the import of wine from Gascony and other places, but two years later, as the summer hunting season approached, Edward wrote to his chief butler Lord Wenlock ordering him to 'lay at our servant Nicholas

Gaynesford's house a tun of good Gascon wine that we in sporting which we make in hunting for the hare at this season may have it ready there for our drinking'.[3] In 1466 Edward gave a fifty-course dinner for visiting Bohemians.

The most urgent concern was Edward's sexual excesses, something on which all the chroniclers commented, and associated with him from youth. In Gregory's *Chronicle* it is claimed that men marvelled that our sovereign lord was so long without any wife and were even fearful that he might not have been chaste in his living.[4] The Croyland chronicler observed that Edward was much given to passion, and Polydore Vergil described him as a man who readily cast his eye on the ladies. Before his marriage to Elizabeth Woodville, Edward had sired an illegitimate son and had secretly pre-contracted to marry Eleanor Butler. Commines perceived a pattern in Edward's life in which he was unable to sustain the energy he deployed in facing a crisis; when the danger was past this energy was dissipated in sexual excesses. But given the heterosexual excesses of other fifteenth-century rulers, such as Louis XI, it is hard to understand why Edward was singled out for censure, unless his sexual energies led him into more unorthodox sexual practices. Contemporaries were preoccupied with his extraordinary beauty (most surviving copies of his portrait capture his androgynous features), and it was Commines, the most perceptive of Edward's observers, who explicitly suggested there was something effeminate about his good looks and his pleasures: 'As soon as he had overcome all his difficulties, he began to give himself up wholly to his pleasures, and took no delight in anything but ladies, dancing, entertainments and such like effeminate diversions; and in all this voluptuous course of life, if I mistake not, he spent about sixteen years until the quarrel between him and the earl of Warwick.' In the fifteenth century women were perceived as libidinous and more sexually predatory and given to pleasure than men; an effeminate man was one who indulged himself indiscriminately, and in Edward's case perhaps with women and men. Edward's narcissistic confidence in his own charm and ability to win people over may have manifested itself in bisexuality (the image of the hermaphrodite king (an important manifestation of the power that came from the fusion of opposites in alchemy) was proclaimed in the *Ripley Scrolls* and indeed in the king's image on Edward's new coinage). This would explain his extraordinary and politically disastrous indulgence of Henry Beaufort, the Lancastrian duke of Somerset. The author of Gregory's *Chronicle*, in describing how Edward introduced a sulky Somerset, wearing a straw hat, to his incredulous court at the Westminster jousts in 1463, employs the language of courtly love with Somerset in the role of the king's champion: 'The kynge lovyd hym well, but the duke thoght treson undyr fayr chere and wordys, as hyt apperyd. And for a grete love the kyng made a grete justys at Westemynster.' The duke and Edward's knights refused to joust until: 'The kynge prayd hym to be mery and sende hym a tokyn and then to runne fulle justely and merely.'[5] According to the author of Gregory's *Chronicle*, Edward made Somerset his close companion. They lodged together and shared the same bed many nights. At this time sharing beds was relatively common and would not necessarily have had the connotations it has today. When Edward rode to Yorkshire he was accompanied by Somerset and two thousand of his men, 'for the kyng hadde the duke in moche lovyn and trustyd hym welle'.[6] At Northampton the commons, seeing Somerset and his men forming the king's guard, would have slain him in the king's palace, but Edward, with 'fair speed and great difficulty', saved his life and sent him in secret to Newcastle to guard it. On 10 May 1463 Edward granted Somerset a general pardon and an annuity of £220.[7]

Edward seems to have been alone in trusting Somerset, who betrayed him at Christmas 1463 by stealing out of Wales with his men and making towards Newcastle. According to the Gregory chronicler, Edward's folly in favouring Beaufort caused the deaths of many of Lord Montagu's men at the battles of Hedgeley Moor and Hexham in April 1464 when Somerset was captured.[8] The attainder of 1465, which was probably written by Edward himself, is personal in tone with its emphasis on hurt and betrayal. In Gregory's *Chronicle* the account of Somerset's rebellion is followed by a paragraph describing Edward's marriage to Elizabeth Woodville. The two paragraphs are linked with the following statement: 'Nowe take hede what love may doo, for love wylle not nor may not caste no faute nor perelle in noo thing.'[9] Such is the author's literary skill and subtlety that this judgement could be applied equally to both relationships. In the period between Beaufort's betrayal and Edward's secret marriage the kingdom seemed to be falling apart. Edward left London many times with the intention of crushing the Lancastrians in the north – but always came back without engaging in battle. Many suspected he was using his campaigns in the north as an excuse for demanding money. By February 1464 there were hangings in Gloucestershire and Cambridgeshire, and risings in Cheshire and Lancashire. Parliament assembled in this month and was adjourned because the king was unable to attend because of the risings. In the early months of the year the Lancastrians captured Norham and Skipton-in-Craven. The news took Edward, feasting with his lords in London, wholly by surprise. It was at this critical time, during the expedition north to take Bamburgh Castle, that Edward made a detour on the pretence of going hunting to marry Elizabeth Woodville. Gregory's chronicler described the marriage in courtly love language similar to that he had used to describe the Somerset affair, and it had even more disastrous political consequences. Edward's failure to marry and the nature of his sexual life had occasioned concern: 'Lords movyd hym and exhorted him in God's name to marry and live under the law of God and church and they would send him overseas to find a queen of good birth among his dignity.' To this end the earl of Warwick had been working towards a marriage with the sister-in-law of Louis XI, Bona, daughter of the duke of Savoy, to cement a Franco-English alliance. The king did not disclose his marriage to a widowed daughter of a mere gentleman until three months later, on All Hallows Day at Reading. His secrecy and his decision to go behind Warwick's back bear the hallmarks of a son's rebellion against the influence of a father figure. Indeed Commines claimed that the earl of Warwick 'could almost be called father of king Edward in respect of rearing and servants'.[10] The Croyland chronicler thought Edward was provoked by the ardour of youth and did not consult the nobles; Commines believed it was a love match; Vergil commented that the king was led into marriage by blind affection rather than reason; and More suggested that Elizabeth refused him until he married her to satisfy his desire.

The marriage represented a humiliation for Warwick, and by 1468 he was fostering popular discontent with Edward's government. In the spring of 1469 Neville agents were at work in Yorkshire exploiting popular grievances, culminating in the rebellion of 'Robin of Redesdale' (Sir John Conyers) in June 1469. Edward made a leisurely progress north to meet the threat and lingered three weeks in Nottingham awaiting the Welsh forces of William Herbert earl of Pembroke. All this time he seemed sluggish, out of touch and complacent. Unlike Henry VI, Edward certainly had the intellectual capacity to keep in touch with what was going on in his kingdom. The Croyland chronicler, a chancery official in a position to know, observed that the king possessed such a retentive memory that he knew of all the affairs of his leading subjects in all corners of his kingdom. But he was reluctant to acknowledge the treachery of his friends and members of his family, including Richard Neville, earl of Warwick, George Neville the archbishop of York, and George duke of Clarence, who were all in Calais for the wedding of Clarence and Isabel Neville, Warwick's daughter. Edward's inertia can perhaps be explained as a narcissistic over-confidence in his own charm, his ability to win people over. Like Joseph approaching the brothers who would throw him down the well, complacent in his position as the charmed and favoured son,

Edward feared and suspected nothing from his kinsmen until 12 July, when Warwick and Clarence declared their association with the rebels. They landed in England on 16 July. While Edward stayed at Nottingham for three weeks, William Herbert's Welsh army was decimated near Banbury on 25 July at the Battle of Edgecote. This was a humiliating blow to a king whose image depended on his links with the mythic Welsh kings. Herbert, lodging at Edgecote Manor, had euphorically buoyed up his troops before this battle by invoking the prophecy of the angel to Cadwallader of a future great victory for the Welsh descendants of the ancient Britons. The poet Gutor Glyn warned Herbert about Warwick: 'Let not the Saxon rule in Gwynedd and Flint.'[11] During the battle some two thousand Welshmen were slain, including a significant section of the Welsh nobility. It was a disaster for the Welsh people. The poet Hywel Gwerdad implored Edward to come to Wales to rekindle the nation.[12]

Further humiliation was to follow when Edward, heading for Northampton, was deserted by almost all his men. Arrested by George Neville, appropriately while he was in bed, he was taken as a prisoner to Warwick Castle. Warwick now took his revenge on the Woodville family, executing the king's father-in-law Lord Rivers, Edward's treasurer, and his brother-in-law John. He also executed William Herbert, 'the Gawain to Edward's Arthur'. The king was moved to Pontefract Castle. Warwick planned to have Edward declared a bastard and to rule through Clarence, but this policy failed because the earl could not maintain order and he was forced to release Edward. In August 1469 Edward reasserted his royal authority. He briefly regained some of his old decisiveness and vigour in March 1470 when, invigorated as always by hardship, he reacted resolutely to the quarrel in Lincolnshire between Sir Thomas Burgh, Master of the King's Horse, and Richard Lord Welles, marching into Lincolnshire in person. This sparked off the revolt of Welles's son, Sir Robert Welles, guided by Warwick and Clarence, but Edward successfully routed the rebels at the Battle of Lose-cote Field near Stamford in March 1470.[13] In the words of the Croyland chronicler, quoting Caesar's conquests, 'he came, saw and conquered'.[14] By 27 March 1470 Warwick and Clarence had fled to Honfleur, seeking asylum from Louis XI, with whom they intrigued to bring about a reconciliation between Warwick and Margaret of Anjou. This was to culminate in a French-assisted invasion of England in September that year.

The alliance between Warwick, Margaret of Anjou and Louis XI was cemented on 25 July 1470 with the betrothal of Margaret's son Edward prince of Wales to Warwick's daughter Anne. In a plan coordinated from France and relying on residual support for Henry VI, Warwick organized another northern rising in Richmondshire and Cumberland. This rebellion, led by Henry Lord FitzHugh, Warwick's brother-in-law and lieutenant on the west march, took place early in August. Edward had little choice but to march north with his household. The rebels withdrew before him, submitted and sued for pardon – but while Edward delayed in Yorkshire Warwick slipped past the blockading fleet, scattered by storms, and invaded England, landing on the Devonshire coast. On 13 September Warwick arrived in Dartmouth and Plymouth with an army assisted by sixty of Louis's ships. In only three weeks Edward lost his throne. He stayed in Doncaster, waiting for Montagu to come to his assistance, but he soon learned that Montagu, resentful of losing the earldom of Northumberland to Henry Percy, was intending to capture him. When he heard of Montagu's defection, Edward had no alternative but to take flight across Lincolnshire and the Wash to Bishop's Lynn, whence he sailed to the Low Countries on 2 October 1470 with only a small band of followers. Edward had once again been too complacent. His charm, confidence in his own luck, charisma and bravery stood him well in battle and hardship but they could also be his undoing in situations requiring more prosaic political virtues. This was understood by the perceptive Commines and by the Burgundian court chronicler

Georges Chastellain. According to Commines, the duke of Burgundy gave Edward precise information about Warwick's impending invasion and urged him to put his kingdom in a posture of defence.

> But he never was concerned at anything, but still followed his hunting. – King Edward was by no means a man of superior capacity but a most handsome prince – very valiant. He did not worry nearly so much about the earl of Warwick making a landing in England for he had no fear, which seems to me the worst kind of folly and having no fear on one's enemy and even refusing to believe any warnings despite knowledge of the enemies' preparations.[15]

Chastellain pointed out that Edward's bravery – 'he believed that Warwick was a coward who would not oppose him in the field' – was inappropriate over-confidence in the political arena.

These astonishing events cannot be explained in purely political terms. They also have an important fifteenth-century cultural and indeed scientific, medical dimension. Contemporaries would have seen a disempowered and enfeebled king, one who, with the brief exception of the Lincolnshire expeditions of 1470, had lost his energy and vigour, dissipated in lust, eating, drinking and idleness. Perhaps he was the victim of unrealistic expectations. He was certainly no longer able, through the force of his personality, to hold together the various factions of his court.

Just as the origin of the feud between Edward and his Neville supporters lay in the marriage to Elizabeth Woodville, so a popular explanation for Edward's decline was the malign influence of his queen. During the height of the king's troubles in August 1469, when Warwick was purging the court of Woodville influence, the mother of the queen was brought before Warwick at Warwick Castle (where Edward was held captive) and accused by Thomas Wake and Clarence of sorcery. It was alleged that she had made a finger-length leaden image of a man at arms broken in the middle and made fast with line, and had used witchcraft to cause the king to fall in love with her daughter.[16] Warwick had clearly been biding his time ever since the royal marriage that had so antagonized him and seized this opportunity to bring this descendant of Melusine to trial. But there may have been more to this case than political opportunism. As the disastrous political consequences of the marriage became apparent and Edward's reputation as a voluptuary grew, the demonic aspects of the king's falling into the clutches of these two descendants of Melusine would have preoccupied those prosecuting the charge of witchcraft. Edward had stolen away from his entourage to meet these two women in the middle of the night of 30 April, St Walpurga's Eve (or Walpurgisnacht), one of the four grand sabbaths of the witches' year. It was a night when decent, country folk stayed within doors as celebrants were supposed to give homage to the devil with dancing and orgiastic rites, presided over by a queen of the sabbath.[17] The marriage the following morning was not a church wedding and was popularly believed to have taken place by an oak tree known as the queen's oak (although it is possible that a secret yet consecrated place was found, the chapel at the hermitage at Grafton Regis which was subsequently refloored with alternating tiles showing the arms of Woodville and York). There were of course other irregularities such as Edward's pre-contract with Eleanor Butler and Edward, not as wise as his grandparents Richard duke of York and Anne Mortimer, failed to get a papal dispensation from the diocesan bishop. In 1484 Richard III revived the charge of witchcraft against Jacquetta to include her daughter, and the Act of *Titulus Regis* claimed that the marriage took place in a profane place, contrary to the laws of God's Church, through sorcery and witchcraft. Even the fatigue (strange in such a young man) that Edward succumbed to on his return may retrospectively have been seen as a consequence of his lone night ride on the witches' sabbath and subsequent encounter with the two serpent-women.[18] The case did not proceed any further, however, for Jacquetta had been very popular in London since she had persuaded Margaret of Anjou not to enter the city with her army in 1461, and she was cleared of the charge after appeals to the mayor and aldermen of the city. Nevertheless, attacks continued to be made against her during the Readeption. In November 1470 Henry Stafford and his wife Margaret countess of Richmond were granted the keeping of Jacquetta's lordships which she had held in dower since the death of her husband John duke of Bedford.[19] During the period of Edward's release from captivity in February 1471 she lodged a complaint before the king and council for having been brought before 'a common noise and slander of witchcraft'.

Nevertheless, this accusation demonstrates how women (who occupied ambiguous roles in the literature of courtly love and chivalry as both empowerers of the knight errant and evil temptresses) could be seen, in times of political upheaval, as serpents and witches who undermined and disempowered the hero. The dragon vanquished by St George was often depicted as female with prominent pudenda, sometimes offering herself sexually in an effort to save her life. As Edward's old friends and family drifted towards civil war, his court increasingly resembled Camelot disintegrating around Guinevere and an enfeebled king, undone by the negative, malign power of the mother and daughter who were the descendants of Melusine the serpent-woman. This was a view that would have been endorsed in the Arthurian romances read at court and by the alchemists who were keenly aware of the dual nature of Melusine as the agent of transformation and rebirth of the king and as the venomous serpent. Fortescue, a member of the 1456 alchemy commission, considered Yorkist England to be inflamed with a fever caused by the machinations of Melusine. He probably had the activities of Eleanor Cobham, Jacquetta of Luxembourg and Elizabeth Woodville in mind when he argued against the female succession, the basis of Edward's occupation of the throne. He declared in *De Natura*: 'This was the crafty serpent nurtured on the poison of ambition which, insinuating itself into the minds of princes, poisoned them so with malice of its virus that there was scarce a king, who inflamed by the angry venom growing therefrom, did not betake himself to the clash of arms by which he thought to appease the fever of that venom.'[20]

The decline of Edward's powers was naturally of concern to the court alchemists and physicians. To some extent Edward's hedonism was endorsed in the alchemical text he used to prescribe his daily regimen, Bacon's version of the *Secreta secretorum*. This recommended that after defeating his enemies a prince should lead a merry, sociable life with good food and daily baths to attain a state of plumpness which would lead to humoral balance and a state of psychological equilibrium. However, there are also indications that with Edward's rising consumption came concerns about the king's health and hypochondria, dating back to the early years of the reign, which are revealed in the increasing expenditure on drugs. The royal apothecary John Clark, a personal friend of Roger Marshall, who had been appointed king's physician for life in February 1462, presented a bill for drugs in 1462 which amounted to £40. In 1464 he was paid the substantial sum of £87 18*s* 7*d* for certain physic supplied for the use of the court.[21] Some of these medicines would be administered to the king under the advice of his six physicians. Many other payments were made to Clark, who was responsible for making the medicines and ensuring they were taken in the early years of Edward's reign, and they show that the king's health was a cause for much attention from the physicians who accepted important positions at the court.[22] They included John of Frescia, who was granted an annuity of £40 a year, property in several confiscated Lancastrian holdings and lodgings in Westminster Palace and the royal free chapel of

Windsor, and William Hattecliffe, physician and secretary to the king, who occupied several confiscated crown holdings in 1467.

The alchemists, and those physicians with alchemical interests, were concerned with Edward's psychological and spiritual well-being. In the period following his successful conquest of the throne he needed to retain his heroic energies to unify his kingdom, a goal regarded as a Grail-like quest. Most alchemists believed that a crusade was the best way to restore a sense of purpose and holiness to the nation. George Neville, the chancellor and archbishop of York, was devoted to the ideal of the crusade. The Turks were threatening western Europe and Rhodes, guarded by the knights of St John, was in the front line of defence. A threat to the island led to calls for a crusade against the Saracens.[23] Edward, despite coming to the throne professing his commitment to the crusade, was showing little inclination to invest in an expedition, and by the middle of the decade there was increasing concern that Edward was no longer interested in alchemy as a means of transmuting himself into the focus of the heroic aspirations of his nation, but was following the narrower pursuit of the transmutation of metals, the procuration of gold, to support his hedonistic lifestyle and narcissistic self-image.

The first signs of the growing rift between the ideals of the alchemists and the performance of the king appeared in 1465, according to Norton's account of the three masters of alchemy lodging in Leadenhall, London. The eldest prophesied that the youngest of them would do much good in the land,

> but synn of princes shal left or delay
> the grace which he shulde do on a day.

He would furthermore,

> – soeffre much wronge
> Of theym which were to him gretely beholde;
> – After trowbles grete ioy shalle be
> In euery quarter of this londe,
> – The holy crosse honouryde both day and night
> In the land of god in the lond of light
> until great days would fill every quarter of the land
> when the holy cross is honoured in the land of light.

This would, however, only occur, according to the eldest of the three alchemists, when

> – grace on that king shall descende
> when he old manes shall amende.[24]

This prophecy shows that Norton was identifying in 1465 a dissatisfaction with Edward's lack of a religious vision that could lead to the transformation of his kingdom. According to the alchemist's great-grandson Samuel Norton, the recipient of this prophecy was Thomas Norton.[25]

By 1468 the assumption that Edward had abandoned any pretence to a sense of religious destiny for his realm was becoming widely held. Not since 1456 had there been such widespread disillusionment among alchemists with the reigning monarch. Edward's reputation for avarice was growing and his search for bullion was intensifying. Any hopes that this would finance a crusade were permanently dashed in May 1468 with the announcement of plans for war against France. Edward's commitment to alchemy was now limited to finding the secret of the transmutation of base metal into gold. In the letter to Edward IV beginning the *Compound of Alchemy*, Ripley reveals that he had been corresponding with the king from the University of Louvain on the secret of the red and white elixir, a reference to the transmutation and multiplication of metals. This correspondence may have taken place in July 1468 towards the end of Ripley's seven-year period of overseas study around the time of the marriage of Margaret of York in Burgundy. In this year Ripley may have come under increasing pressure to produce gold for Edward, in return for which the king revoked the debts of Bridlington Priory. The correspondence from Louvain does not survive, but the contents appear to have been alluded to in the cautionary advice provided in the introduction to the *Compound of Alchemy*, where Ripley expresses his concern about Edward's loss of focus, urging the king to serve God devoutly using his gifts of grace, fortune and power to God's pleasure:

> Most especially intending over all thing,
> To your power and cunning his precepts ten
> So to observe, that into no danger
> But that you in glory may see him.[26]

Ripley was aware of Edward's ability to tap into myths, but he was also aware of his weaknesses, particularly his pride and avarice, and pointed out that many kings have been undone because they have lost wisdom.

This same sense of unease was expressed in 1468 by Ripley's friend and fellow alchemist George Neville. Stephano Trento, bishop of Lucca, was in England with a licence to raise a papal tenth for the crusade, and on 20 June 1468 he wrote to his friend George Neville, who had advised him to leave England because of an outbreak of plague. Stephano pointed out that there was another kind of disease, a moral illness affecting all those around him, and in the face of this courage was required: 'In this age of display and royal wantonness people must cultivate the right way of life surrounded by every kind of deceit and impiety.'[27] Alchemists, as we have seen, showed an idealistic, holistic approach to politics and were beginning to express their sense that a moral unease was settling on and around Edward, and that the land and its king were falling into a sickness.

The immediate cause of their disillusionment was the pressure Edward was bringing to bear on them to transmute base metals (in December 1468 Edward granted a licence to Richard Carter to practise the art of alchemy with all kinds of metals and minerals for two years). This pressure can be most clearly demonstrated by an incident that occurred in this same year and which was observed by Thomas Norton. Thomas Herbert, a squire of the body of Edward IV's household[28] and brother of William earl of Pembroke, took one Thomas Dalton, against his will, from an abbey in Gloucestershire and brought him before the king. Dalton, whose name occurs in the sixteenth-century list of prominent alchemists, was described by Norton as a good man who served God night and day and had a great store of the red medicine.[29] The abduction was probably done at the instigation of John Delves, a squire in the king's household, who was often in the royal presence and who had served as the king's clerk. Delves claimed that Dalton had once made £1,000 'of as goode golde as the Ryalle was, within halfe a day'. A precedent for this attempt to control an alchemist had been set around the time of Edward's accession in an incident recorded in an undated petition to the chancellor concerning one Thomas Crop, a London grocer, who took Thomas York who had transmuted plate into silver which had been tested by London goldsmiths, into his house, kept his instruments and elixir, and, with the collusion of others, caused York to be imprisoned in Newgate.[30]

Delves, playing on Edward's desire for gold bullion 'to speed his name and prosperity', announced that he was prepared to break his oath of secrecy 'for the king's wele and for al his lande' and boasted that Dalton could provide gold for more royals.[31] A shocked Dalton asked Delves how he hoped to enjoy the king's trust after perjuring himself. He then pointed out that he had been troubled in many places for this medicine and to prevent it hurting anyone in the abbey he had, before being seized by Herbert, thrown it from a privy into a ditch leading into a tidal river, thereby destroying as many nobles as would

haue seruyd to the holi lande
for twenty thousand men upon a bond.

Until that time he had preserved the medicine:

I kept it longe for oure lorddis sake,
To helpe a kyng which that Iournay wold make.[32]

This gesture of throwing the secret of the stone into the river echoes the throwing of Excalibur into the lake, and Dalton was explicit in his condemnation of Edward's unworthiness to possess the Grail, and his disappointment with the king's failure to show any interest in the crusade or other higher ideals. This disillusionment had probably been triggered by his kidnapping. Edward did not respond to the accusation:

Alas Dalton, then seide the kynge,
It was fowle done to spille such a thynge.
He wolde haue Dalton to make it agayne.[33]

Dalton replied that this could not be because he had obtained the entire stock of the medicine from a canon of Lichfield in return for keeping his works diligently until his death. Edward then allowed Dalton his freedom, presenting him with a gift of four marks, 'sad at heart that he did not know him earlier'.

This incident is important because it shows the king's obsessive personal interest in alchemy and his growing impatience with the alchemists' inability to provide him with immediate gratification, emotional or material. Herbert lay in wait for Dalton at Stepney and took him first to the royal castle at Gloucester, where he was constable (which implies that Edward was behind this abduction), and then to the family seat in Monmouthshire where he was imprisoned for four years. At the end of this period Herbert brought him out to execute him. The alchemist prayed:

Lord ihesu blessid thu be!
Me think y haue be to longe fro the.
A science thu gave me with ful grete charge,
which I haue kepte with-owte owtrage;
I fownde no man yet apte therto
To be myn heyre when I am go.
Wherfore swete Lorde now am I fayne
To resigne this thi gifte to thee agayne.[34]

Herbert, listening to these fervent prayers and recognizing Dalton's willingness to die, was moved to tears; realizing that neither death nor imprisonment would force Dalton to reveal the secret of his art, he released him.[35] Norton's concluding remarks about this affair probably reflect his opinions about events of the time to which he was an eye-witness. They also show the degree to which court alchemists were involving themselves in direct expression of political dissatisfaction with Edward's government. Norton asserted that a noble man had been treated like a felon when patience and grace might have obtained the great solace for the king and the commons of the land:

> But wondire not that grace do not falle,
> For synne regnyth in this londe ovir alle.[36]

Here at hand, Norton maintained, was the grace to procure easing of taxes and levies from the land, which would ensure that there was,

> – moch love and grace wolde haue be
> Bitwene knyghthoode, prestehode and comynalte.[37]

Certainly within Norton's family the tradition persisted that he was at this time disenchanted with Edward and that he withheld from him such secrets as he possessed. According to Samuel Norton, Thomas accompanied Edward to Burgundy but did not impart the secret 'because of some great faulte in the king'.[38]

Another tradition relating to Edward's increasingly notorious avarice is the story of the imprisonment of the alchemist Ramon Lull, by a King Edward. Variations on this legend were recorded in the beginning of verse commentaries of the *Ripley Scrolls* in the sixteenth century. The most common form of this legend is that Abbot Cremer of Westminster (of whom there is no record among the abbots of Westminster) persuaded Lull to visit England where he met Edward III, who asked him to make gold. Lull agreed on condition that the king used it for pious purposes such as fighting crusades rather than attacking fellow Christians. According to the story the king had rose nobles struck from the metal but then he broke his promise and made war on France, imprisoning Lully.[39] All the key elements of this legend pertain to the events at Edward's court between 1465 and 1468, including the popularization of the body of writings attributed to Ramon Lull under the auspices of George Ripley; the imprisonment of a devout and serious alchemist who appears to have been a follower of Ripley; the devotion of Edward's alchemists, including Dalton, Neville, Ripley and Norton to the crusade; the minting of new coins; and Edward's reneging on his promise to support the crusade, signified by the declaration of his intent to make war on France.

The reservations and warnings expressed by Norton in the *Ordinal of Alchemy* and by Ripley in his correspondence indicate the way court alchemists towards the end of the decade were becoming increasingly concerned about the political health of the kingdom, and this was beginning to be manifested in actual rebellion. One of the first to be accused of treason was Thomas Cook, the stationer and former mayor of London, who was interested in both the crusade and alchemy. In early June 1468 an emissary of Margaret of Anjou, bearing letters from Lancastrian exiles to friends in London, was captured by Sir Richard Woodville. Under torture he accused several prominent Londoners of complicity in correspondence with Margaret including John Hawkins, who in turn implicated Cook. Arrested for misprision of treason, Cook was sentenced to payment of £8,000, including an arras depicting Godfrey of Bouillon's siege of Jerusalem which was coveted by Jacquetta of Luxembourg. (Bouillon was the grandson of Eneas the Swan knight who, according to a prophecy, would be the ancestor of the future conqueror of Jerusalem.)[40] Cook had been connected with the alchemical search for a solution to the kingdom's problems as a member of the 1457 alchemy commission with Sir John Fortescue, and he was also involved in the production of a manuscript of alchemical writings (including works of Bacon) and recipes copied by his servant John Vale and the London scrivener John Multon, who was responsible for disseminating the works of Fortescue. The prime mover in this attempt to spread Margaret of Anjou's influence in England would have been her chancellor Sir John Fortescue; as well as serving on the 1457 alchemy commission, he was also the author of the *Governance of England*, a copy of which was owned by Cook. The increasing opposition to Edward's government among those dedicated to the higher ideals of alchemy, and especially the crusade, became much more dangerous when it spread beyond the Lancastrian circles to include members of the Neville affinity who had previously been the main supporters of the Yorkist dynasty. The leader of this new focus of opposition to the king was George Neville, archbishop of York, who can be regarded in intellectual terms as the real kingmaker of England, for he brought an alchemical dimension to kingmaking.

The rift between Neville and Edward became public in 1467 when Edward visited him in his house at Charing Cross and took away his chancellor's great seal. In September he bestowed the cardinal's hat on his kinsman Thomas Bourgchier, and in spiteful mockery, or perhaps in an attempt at making a distasteful joke that went badly wrong, he sent the Pope's letter of appointment to George Neville. It was an immature gesture that showed how inappropriate Edward's youthful charm and high spirits were in a king. Now simply archbishop of York, Neville played his hand in 1468 by presiding over the marriage of Warwick's daughter Isabel to George duke of Clarence in the presence of five knights of the Garter. The news of the defeat of Pembroke's Welsh army at Edgecote, which reached Edward at Olney near Nottingham, must have completely demoralized the king. Neville may have seen alchemical significance in the circumstances in which he arrested Edward: he was in bed, like the enfeebled king depicted in Ripley's *Cantilena* and the accompanying illustrations, deserted by his men. A contemporary portrayal of the scene in Jean de Waurin's *Chronicles of England* (owned by Louis de Gruuthuse) shows George Neville betraying a languishing, frail, bedridden Edward while in the background the king is taken prisoner by the earl of Warwick.[41]

Among Neville's allies in this northern insurrection, sharing his more idealistic, alchemical motives, were members of the Order of the Knights of St John. One of their duties was to care for sick and needy pilgrims (a large hospital was built on the island of Rhodes in the fifteenth century) and it is likely that the knights of St John developed an interest in alchemical medicine. There is a strong and persistent tradition that Ripley had specific links with the order. Elias Ashmole claimed that he resided for some time with the knights in Rhodes, and in a note to the 1652 edition of his *Theatrum Chemicum Britannicum* he claimed that an acquaintance of his, 'an English gentleman of good quality and credit', observed in his travels abroad in Malta a 'record which declared that this Sir George Ripley gave yearly to those knights of Rhodes £100,000 towards maintaining the war against the Turks'.[42] Malta became the home of the knights of St John after the fall of Rhodes in 1523. Despite the obvious exaggeration, the story accords with the letters Ripley wrote to George Neville in which he prescribed 'medicine, a quintessence of gold, a precious portable liquid to help pilgrims that travel into fair countries'. He also expressed his wish to 'visit the holy places of Jerusalem where Christ walked, lived and died'.[43] Another alchemist, Bernard of Treves, who is said to have stayed in England for four years, retired to Rhodes where he died in 1490, spending the last of his fortune on a laboratory.[44] The link between these two alchemists is suggested by the occurrence of a treatise of Bernard of Treves dated 1453 in a manuscript containing the works of Ripley.[45] William Worcester was also interested in the

Order of St John. In 1478 he compiled a list of the islands lying between Rhodes and Venice from a book once belonging to Fastolf, and in his *Itinerarium* he records the details of a temple church in Bristol explaining the foundations of the hospitallers.[46] Some of the priors of the order may have had similar alchemical interests. Sir John Langstrother, who was appointed warden of the mint in the Tower with John Delves (the man responsible for bringing the alchemist Dalton before Edward IV),[47] was a knight with an outstanding record of service in the Mediterranean. He served as a castellan of Rhodes in 1454–6 when he helped to coordinate a crusading indulgence for the defence of Rhodes, and was elected prior in 1469 when he was closely associated with Sir John Fortescue. Now in exile, Fortescue made several appeals to the papacy for a crusade.[48] Robert Multon, prior of the order in 1474–6, was a member of the family that had founded the hospitallers' house at Skirbeck on the outskirts of Boston, where Ripley retired. Multon's relatives John and Robert Multon, stationers and scribes in Pater Noster Row, London, produced in the late 1450s, perhaps in cooperation with Fortescue and other members of the alchemy commission, the *Somnium Vigilantis* and a compendium of Bacon's alchemical treatises.[49] Multon was also firmly attached to Fortescue and George duke of Clarence (who owned the Honour of Richmond, which contained the house of Skirbeck),[50] and the priory at Clerkenwell became the headquarters for preparations for risings against Edward. The voices of Langstrother and George Neville can be heard in the manifesto issued by Warwick and Clarence in 1468 which was aimed at rallying opposition to Edward. The king was accused of spending the goods of the holy father which had been given for the defence of the Christian faith and of taking portions of land without payment to him (a reference to the 1463 licence of indulgences). On 1 September, against the imprisoned Edward's wishes, Langstrother was elected prior of the order on the basis of his outstanding record of service in the Mediterranean in order to maximize the order's contribution to the defence of Rhodes. Given the alleged involvement of Ripley with this order and with Rhodes, it is likely that there was some connection between these two men. Langstrother was also appointed by Warwick as treasurer in place of the executed Rivers.

George Neville became a key figure in this period. When Edward was released Neville accompanied him from York to London on 7 October 1469. Together with Warwick and Langstrother (who was in correspondence with Richard Lord Welles), he took the opportunity afforded by the feud between Burgh and Welles to join the latter in fomenting a rebellion in Lincolnshire against the king; their object was to replace Edward with Clarence. After Edward's decisive victory at the Battle of Lose-cote Field near Stamford in March 1470, Warwick and Clarence escaped to France but George Neville was placed under guard at his home, The Moor, while Langstrother went to the Tower. Their attempts at replacing Edward with his younger brother had failed, and they now concentrated on the restoration of the Lancastrian monarchy. Henry VI would be a puppet king, with real power lying in the hands of his son Edward of Lancaster, who was approximately the same age as the earl of March when he had taken the throne. The alchemical significance of this plan, redeeming the land through a freshly minted Edward, would not have escaped George Neville, Langstrother and Cook. The driving force behind it was Fortescue, Margaret's chancellor, who since Henry's deposition had been the devoted tutor of the exiled prince. Fortescue gave an alchemical rationalization to this scheme in *De natura* when he argued for the by-passing of a monarch and finding the essence of gold in another, and in 1470 he had pressed Margaret of Anjou's credentials as a daughter of the king of Jerusalem. When London capitulated to the earl of Warwick, George Neville, shaking off his guard at The Moor, took control of the Tower on 5 October; together with Langstrother he knelt before Henry VI. George Ashby, Margaret of Anjou's servant, also wrote a justification of the Lancastrian monarchy employing alchemical imagery, describing the king as the water of life.[51] During Henry's Readeption those with an interest in alchemy who had rebelled against Edward IV, with perhaps a degree of idealistic motives, prospered. George Neville retrieved his great seal, the treasurership was restored to Langstrother and Thomas Cook regained his aldermanship. Another man with alchemical interests who seems to have deserted Edward and prospered during the Readeption was John Delves, who in February 1471 was appointed (with Langstrother) to the office of warden of the exchange and mint within the Tower of London and custodian of coinage in gold and silver within the realm of England and the town of Calais. The crucial figure was George Neville, who performed the same role for the young Edward of Lancaster, waiting with his mother in France until Warwick had secured the kingdom, as he had done for Edward earl of March in 1461. He gave the opening address to Parliament that was summoned in Henry VI's name on 24 November. The parallels with 1461 are striking and raise the possibility that Neville's friend Ripley, whose writings most explicitly alluded to the making of the Yorkist monarchy, was somehow involved. Ripley's disenchantment with Edward was perhaps strong enough to explain the conversion he underwent around 1469–70, alluded to in 1471 in the prologue to the *Compound of Alchemy*, in which he repudiates all his writings of the previous twenty years. Ripley referred in this prologue to the sufferings of his neighbours and kinsmen in 1470. Ties of family and friends may have implicated him in the Yorkshire rebellions of 1469: in the *Marrow of Alchemy*, written in 1476 for George Neville, Ripley addressed his friend in the preface, revealing that: 'he had divers kindred gentlemen of Yorkshire and Lincolnshire as Yevesall, Ripley, Medley, Willoughby and (notably Welles) who were by the conquering sword of Edward IV (God so permitting) lamentably destroyed'.[52] This implies that Ripley was at the very least implicated in the Neville-inspired rebellion of Lord Welles, and that he would have shown at least some interest in George Neville's political, alchemical experiments of this period.

And this is what the Readeption was. Viewed from the most optimistic perspective it was the period of the *nigredo* when nothing was resolved. The alchemical transformation was far from complete. On 13 October 1470 Neville led Henry VI in a procession from St Paul's through Cheapside, Cornhill and Watling Street to Westminster Palace. The bewildered King Henry VI, wearing a shabby blue gown, clung to Neville's hand like a frightened child. Observers must have been struck by the contrast between the readepted king's pathetic, dishevelled appearance and the glory of Edward IV in his heyday. Henry's medical condition, his imbalance of phlegm and premature senility, had deteriorated. The author of the *London Chronicle* described the procession as a play featuring an old and impotent man.[53] The completion of the work depended on the arrival of Edward of Lancaster, and Langstrother was entrusted to meet the young prince in February 1471. The elements in this alchemical work were to undergo many more metamorphoses thanks to the workings of fate, bad weather and the rejuvenation of Edward IV. In the meantime it represented an extraordinary period in England's history. Between 1468 and 1471 the kingdom disintegrated in a way unparalleled since the civil wars of Stephen and Matilda.

The alchemists were not alone in seeing these years as a period of anarchy and unresolved chaos. John Warkworth, master of Peterhouse and chaplain to William Grey bishop of Ely, reflected in his chronicle between 1478 and 1483 on the events of 1468–71, lamenting: 'Whenne kynge Edwarde iiii regnede, the peple looked after alle the foreseide prosperytes and peece, but it came not; but one batayle aftere another, and moche troble.'[54] He paints a picture of a reign disintegrating into inertia, cruelty and division, which reached its nadir when Edward tried to establish order after the Lincolnshire rebellion of 1470 by allowing the earl of Worcester to butcher twenty men captured from Warwick's escaping force at

Southampton. These men were hanged, drawn and quartered, and then hung up by their legs with their heads placed on sharpened staves thrust between their buttocks.[55] The chronicler conveys a sense of the Fates deserting the king with such portents of divine disapproval as the appearance of a blazing star shining for five or six weeks preceding the hanging, drawing and quartering in January 1469 of Henry Courtenay, esquire, brother and heir of the former earl of Devon, and Thomas Hungerford, son of the rebel Lord Hungerford executed after Hexham. On slender grounds both men were charged with involvement in the conspiracies of July 1468 and with plotting with Margaret of Anjou the death of Edward IV. Warkworth further observed that when Clarence and Warwick were in France in 1470 a blazing star appeared in the west with a flame-like spear which was seen by many men of the king's house, and they were afraid.[56]

The events of these times fired the imagination of Sir Thomas Malory. During his imprisonment between April 1468 and March 1470, he learned about and remembered a series of traumatic events. These included the disintegration of the court through the influence of a beautiful woman who was regarded as both a source of chivalric inspiration and also a beguiling water-witch; the decline of a great king into an indecisive baffled figure alternating between clemency and compassion and malicious cruelty; the break-up of families and friends and the spread of civil war; the simultaneous imprisonment of two kings; the destruction in one battle of a large section of the Welsh gentry, around whom Edward had built the myths that sustained his self-image; and the failure of the transformative magic of the alchemists who had guided him to the throne. All this has the qualities of a dark myth, and it was Malory who saw the striking parallels between the events of his own time and the Arthurian legends of the disintegration of Camelot. It was this view that enabled him to stamp indelibly on these myths the unique pessimism and pathos to create his memento mori, the *Morte d'Arthur*.

Malory identified most closely with Sir Tristram, a violent, adventurous man who spent a great deal of his life in prison on the fringes of the charmed world of Camelot until he became a member of the Round Table. Malory similarly was admitted to Edward's court in those halcyon years of the early 1460s. He had plenty of time to reflect in Newgate gaol on the tumultuous events of the years 1468–70, a period that saw the first betrayals of the king in the Thomas Cook affair, the northern rebellions of the following year, the fleeing of Warwick and Clarence to Harfleur, the Yorkshire rebellions they inspired, and the battle of Edgecote. Malory was in a unique position to reflect with regret on the disintegration of Edward's court, on the betrayals of a king who had shown his opponents a degree of clemency and kindness. He may even have felt a degree of guilt because of his association with Warwick and Wenlock (and perhaps through his connections with the hospitaller knights led by Langstrother). His son Robert Malory, a lieutenant of Warwick from 1461 to 1464 and lieutenant of the Tower, was implicated in the deaths of earl Rivers and his son, according to the testimony of Jacquetta of Luxembourg. Both were beheaded on Warwick's orders in Coventry in August 1469. All of this influenced Malory's sympathetic portrayal of Arthur, primarily undone by betrayal, and his plangent lament for the passing of Camelot.

Malory, as a member of Warwick's affinity, was in a unique position to appreciate the ambivalent role Queen Elizabeth occupied among Edward's courtiers: a beautiful woman, she was the owner of Arthurian romances and the inspirer of a code of chivalry at the court; however, she was also the descendant of Melusine the water-witch, and the unwitting agent of the downfall of the king and his court through the feud between her family and the followers of Warwick, the buttress of Edward's power. Malory observed how women who had power over key men in the kingdom easily attracted accusations of exerting malign influence and practising witchcraft, in effect using their sexuality to rob men of their power and further their own ambitions. Even Henry V, that model of chivalry, accused Joan of Navarre, his father's widow, of witchcraft.[57] Eleanor Cobham, wife of Humphrey duke of Gloucester, was tried for witchcraft in 1441, accused of using necromancy to hasten Henry VI's death and fulfill her ambition to become queen. Margaret of Anjou, described by Shakespeare as the

> She-wolf of France, but worse than wolves of France,
> Whose tongue more poisons than the adder's tooth

(which echoes the appellation of Isabella, wife of Edward II but may also perhaps allude to the alchemical cognomen of Henry VI), seemed to get stronger as her husband grew weaker. The scandal closest to Malory during his imprisonment concerned the accusations levelled against Jacquetta of Luxembourg, and by implication against her daughter Elizabeth, of using witchcraft to capture the heart of Edward.

The significance of the Melusine legend for Elizabeth and Jacquetta was underlined by the prominent position given by Malory to water-witches who attempt to destroy the Round Table. Merlin warns Balin that the sword he obtained from the messenger of the Lady of the Lake will cause him to give the dolorous stroke that will render the kingdom a wasteland; with this sword he will kill himself and his brother, and Merlin says to the messenger: 'God wold ye had not come here, but ye came never in felyship of worshipful folke for to do good but always grete harm.' The Lady of the Lake, Viviana Nineve, who brought up the infant Lancelot, uses magic to trap Merlin. Morgan le Fay, Arthur's half-sister, who can transform herself into a serpent, obtains from Arthur the scabbard of Excalibur: 'She wythstoyth with her for to destroy all his knights at Kyng Arthure lovyd.'[58] Malory's attitude to women was ambiguous. They could empower men and inspire them to show great courage and heroism, but they could also rob men of their power through their sex or through sorcery. He therefore set against this unsettling and subtle influence images of uncomplicated male energy: the figure of the questing knight alone in the forest resisting the enchantments of women and keeping his power, his sexual energy, for deeds of knighthood. Lancelot, in reply to a maid who asks him why he is wifeless, replies:

> But for to be a weddyd man, I thynke hit nat, for then I muste couche with her, and leve armys and turnamentis, batellys and adventures. And as for to sey to take my pleasaunce with peramours, that woll I will refuse: in prenciple for drede of God, for knyghtes that bene adventures sholde nat be advoutres northir lecherous, for than they be nat happy nother fortunate unto the werrys; for other they shall be overcom with a sympler knyght than they be themselves, or else they shall sle by unhappe and hir cursednesse bettir men than they be hemself. And so who that usyth peramours shall be unhappy, and al thynge unhappy that is aboute them.[59]

There is a concern with the correct harnessing of sexual energy in Malory that has much in common with the alchemists' views on the balancing of humours. Most physicians argued that moderate sexual activity was essential for balance, and in Edward's copy of the *Secreta secretorum*, the prince is advised to use young women to restore his humoral balance. But the emphasis was always on moderation and Edward presented an example of the loss of energy, power and a sense of heroic purpose through sexual dissipation. Malory was a misfit whose masculine ideal was not easily integrated into the English society of the 1460s. He demonstrates in the *Morte d'Arthur* that it was an impossible ideal in Arthur's kingdom. The Round Table collapses because masculine bonds of loyalty are severed once the adulterous passion of Lancelot and Guinevere becomes public: 'Her beauty and falsehood caused such discord that caused all Arthur's court and his princes to be slain.' After the Grail has been seen by Galahad, emotional tensions increase and the knights of Camelot find that their world is now dominated by feminine wiles more baffling than the spells of witches: the growing mistrust between Lancelot and Guinevere is accompanied by quarrels, deception and game playing. When Guinevere is accused of poisoning an apple none of the twenty-four knights will defend her. As Guinevere's unpopularity mirrors Elizabeth's, so too the growing rift between the affinities of Gawain and Lancelot mirrors the feud between the Woodvilles and Nevilles. Lancelot, like Warwick, has French interests, and as Malory was concluding his work in March 1470 with Lancelot building his power-base in France, Warwick was planning to use his connections with Louis XI to subvert Edward's kingdom. It is appropriate that the final apocalyptic battle between Arthur and Mordred was triggered by the hiss of a snake.

In the later books of his epic, Malory directly mirrored that baffling period of insurrections between 1468 and 1470 that undermined Edward's kingship. In August 1469, when Malory was in the middle of compiling his work in prison, he was aware that two anointed kings were also imprisoned under Warwick's control and this must have contributed to his description of the wasted lands of the Fisher King and the confusion in his narrative over the existence of two maimed kings besides Arthur himself. Both Edward and Arthur were impotent in the face of the deep-seated and unresolved feuds and rivalries that ran like fault-lines beneath their kingdoms. Just as the Wars of the Roses were dominated by family feuds, especially those involving the Nevilles, so too were the conflicts of the knights of the Round Table essentially family quarrels, and all the more bitter for it: 'for hit ys an old sawe "there ys harde batayle thereas kynne and frendys doth batayle ayther ayenst otheer" for there may be no mercy but mortall warre'.[60] When Arthur welcomes Palymedes and Lanerocke to the Round Table all are glad except Gawain and his brethren, and Gawain says:

> Fayre bretherne, here may ye se: whom that we hate Kynge Arethur lovyth, and whom that we love he hateyth. This Sir Lanerocke wil neveyr love us, because we slew his fader, kynge Pellynor, for we demed that he slew oure fader, Kynge Lothe of Orkenay, and for the deth of Kynge Pellynor Sir Laneroke did us a shame to our modir. Therefore I will be revengyd.[61]

Paying more attention to the civil wars than to his sources, Malory focuses on the jealousies and betrayals of the knights, in the face of which Arthur is an innocent man unjustly betrayed by Lancelot in the same way that Edward was betrayed by Warwick. He is a baffled, enfeebled and defeated human being who manages occasional displays of force. An increasingly impotent figure, faced with the disintegration of families and friendship, he can no longer hold it all together as he used to through his charismatic rule or the holding of tournaments. In all this he bears a close relationship to the naively credulous Edward of 1469–70. Malory's sympathy for Arthur and Edward may stem from his own guilt, his association with those who have betrayed the king, or simply because he had let him down and had been unable to help him. Edward nevertheless showed him more compassion than his Lancastrian captors had done, allowing him comfortable imprisonment with access to books, possibly the Arthurian romances belonging to the king's brother-in-law Anthony Woodville. Some sense of the personal impact on Malory of the desertions of Edward in 1468–9 can be seen in a passage at the end of his work and therefore dateable to late 1469 or early 1470, when he interjects:

> Lo ye all Englysshemen, se ye nat what a myschyff here was? For he that was the moste kynge and nobelyst knyght of the worlde, and most loved the felyshyp of noble knyghtes, and by hym they all were upholdyn, and yet myght nat thes Englyshemen holde them contente with hym. Lo thus was the olde custom and usayges of thys londe, and men say that we of thys londe have nat yet loste that custom. Alas! this ys a greate defaughte of us Englysshemen for there may no thynge us please no terme.[62]

Malory's sense of guilt and ambivalence is reflected in the way he admires men on both sides of the civil war in Camelot such as Gawain and Lancelot; in the same way he would have admired men on both sides of the Neville–Woodville feud, such as Anthony Woodville, Wenlock, Warwick and Sir Humphrey Neville, under whom he had either served or fought against.

However, Malory did not just intend his readers to relive the collapse of Edward's kingdom in his unmitigatingly bleak account of the destruction of the Round Table. There is also a poignant nostalgia for the golden days of Camelot, the period covered by the Book of Tristram, when the order was growing; this period reached its zenith just before the appearance of the Grail, when the fellowship of knights including Sir Tristram, Sir Lancelot, Sir Gawain, Sir Lanerocke, Sir Gareth and Sir Perceval welcomed Sir Galahad. Malory, as he sat in prison, felt the same nostalgia for those days in the early 1460s when he served alongside Edward's Garter Knights. He closely identified with Lancelot, exiled from Camelot in his madness and cared for by King Pellas and Elaine: 'He wolde onys every day loke towarde the realm of Logarys, where kynge Arthure and quene gwenyvere was, and then wolde he falle uppon a wepyng as hys herte shulde to-brest.'[63] The magic had gone, Merlin was dead and the Order had lost its sense of purpose and mission, its quest. The realm therefore ceased to be the holy land of Logres where the Grail was kept and honoured at Carboneck. Now the Grail has to leave Logres and Galahad is told to go because the lord is no longer served in the realm of Logres and will never more be seen here: 'for hy ys nat served nother worshipped to hys ryght by hem of thys londe, for they be turned to evyll lyvyng, and therefore I shall disenherite them of the honoure whych I have done them'.[64] As the fellowship disintegrates, and the number of Round Table knights is reduced by feuds to twenty-four (the number of Edward's Order of the Garter), Malory substitutes the place-names of Edward's realm for those of Arthur's kingdom. Logres becomes England, Camelot Winchester, and Ascalot Guildford. The Grail Castle is located in North Wales near the English border, and when Lancelot crosses a bridge to leave Logres Malory evokes the English bridge at Shrewsbury facing Wales, the land of exile.[65] This is 'the landys of the two marchys', the border regions where royal authority is weakest and where Edward grew up and took his title, and it becomes 'a wasteland for that dolorous stroke'.[66] As Camelot disintegrates with the feud between Lancelot and Gawain, Arthur and his party return from Winchester to London, increasingly the centre of his kingship, like Westminster in the 1460s. These geographical echoes of Edward's kingdom reinforce the sense that there is a similar loss of a sense of quest in the Yorkist court as the call for a crusade is ignored and the magic of the alchemists no longer succeeds in transforming the king and his kingdom. As Camelot declines a sense of mortality pervades as the apocalyptic confrontation between Arthur and Mordred approaches. Malory, writing this section around March 1470, must have anticipated that the gathering momentum of Warwick's opposition in the north-east and in France would lead to a final bloody battle like Towton.

The dominant tone of this work is therefore tragic[67] and there is no apportioning of blame, apart from the general recognition of the fallibility of human nature and the gradual intrusion of the dark powers revolving around Morgan le Fay and Mordred. The adultery of

Lancelot and Guinevere is minimalized and if there is a penitential theme it is the disruption to the fellowship of the Round Table caused by the various manifestations of the sin of envy. This is in accord with the outlook of the penitential manuals of the fourteenth and fifteenth centuries. Sin was defined as an act of hostility that threatened the harmony of communities, and confessors usually traced such acts back to envious impulses. Edward's conventional will, in which he makes restitution to those he has wronged, is in accord with the teachings of these manuals.[68] There is also an emphasis in the *Morte d'Arthur* on private mysticism, which is in conflict with this communal emphasis on religion, and this reflects the devotional trends of the mid-fifteenth century which were exemplified in the lives of many at Edward's court. Ironically it is this individualistic piety, the search for a personal revelation of God, which initiates the break-up of the Round Table, and this is symbolized by Galahad's decision to seek the Grail.[69] Arthur clearly sees the implications of this decision:

> 'Alas!' seyde kynge Arthure unto Sir Gawayne, 'ye have nygh slayne me for the avow that ye have made, for thorow you ye have beraufte me the fayryst and the trewyst of knghthode that ever was sene togydir in ony realme of the worlde. For whan they departe frome hense I am sure they all shall never mete togydir in thys worlde, for they shall dye many in the queste.'[70]

Malory reluctantly abandons the hope of a collective pursuit of an ideal of holiness because of the fallibility of men (writ large in Edward IV) and focuses instead on the successful attainment of the quest by the austere, single-minded Galahad, a practitioner of the contemplative life. It is ironic that Malory, who through much of his life and in this work rejected the contemplative ideals of Henry VI as inimical to the interests of the nation, comes to accept them when he is in prison meditating on the failures of Edward's kingship and embraces them himself. The survivors of the final battle therefore all embrace the contemplative life: Guinevere retires to a nunnery; Lancelot becomes a hermit; and Sir Bors, Sir Ector, Sir Blamor and Sir Bleabens 'wente into the Holy Lande, thereas Jesu Cryst was quycke and deed – And there they dyed upon Good Fryday, for Goddes sake.'[71]

Malory identifies with these knights and ends his work with the following prayer: 'Jesu helpe hym to hys grete myght, as he is the servaunt of Jesu both day and night.' Malory was perhaps intuitively identifying this individualistic asceticism of the disintegrating Camelot with the devotional trends at Edward's court. Ripley, probably in the later 1470s, would take up the life of an anchorite at St Botulph's in Boston. The king's own mother Cicely became increasingly pious and withdrawn as she grew older, and at Berkhamstead she was to follow a near-monastic routine of prayer and meditation. Anthony Woodville, in the face of Edward's opposition, sought permission to go on a crusade to Portugal in 1471/2.[72] Steps had been taken to install Woodville as a knight of the Order of St John, and the Grand Master of the Order described him as 'wearied with the vanities and vicissitudes of the world'.[73] Like Lancelot, Woodville became increasingly religious: he wore a hairshirt and insisted on leaving court to go on a crusade to Portugal in 1473 (annoying Edward, who maintained that he was leaving at a time when he was most needed).[74] Elizabeth, Edward's queen, like Guinevere, became more pious with age. After his death she developed close links with the Carthusians of Sheen and appointed the prior, John Ingilby, as her executor.[75]

Malory, like Hardynge, cherished the ideal of a united holy land of Logres. He was intuitively aware of the power of myths to harness energy and to forge a community, a nation. He was also aware of the weaknesses of men and his great work is an allegorical lament on the great potential and the failure of King Edward. The collective myths of ancient Britain are reluctantly laid aside at the end of his work and he embraces the individualistic myth of Jesus, the new fashionable devotional piety of his age. As Warwick was planning to bring about the Readeption of Henry VI, Malory must have felt that this king's rejection of the world was being validated. However, what he was not to know, as he spent his last few months in Newgate gaol, was that shortly after his death in March 1471 life would outdo art and Edward would reinvent himself, rediscovering his connection with myths that he had enjoyed in 1461, and would recapture his kingdom. Some of these myths of antiquity that he employed in the reconquest would serve to create a community, a state: a construct less individualistic and destructive and more rational than either his first kingdom or Arthur's Camelot, and immune to the disruptions of either chivalric pride or religious asceticism.

NOTES

1. Scofield, *Edward IV*, vol. i, p. 188.
2. Ibid, pp. 461–2.
3. Ibid, p. 287.
4. Gregory's *Chronicle*, p. 226.
5. Ibid, p. 219.
6. Ibid.
7. *CPR*, *Edward IV 1461–67*, vol. i, pp. 261, 263; Scofield, *Edward IV*, vol. i, p. 274.
8. Ibid, p. 223.
9. Ibid.
10. Philippe de Commynes (Commines), *Memoirs: The Reign of Louis XI 1461–83*, trans. M. Jones (Harmondsworth, 1972), p. 181.
11. Williams, *Renewal and Reformation in Wales*, p. 199.
12. Ross, *Edward IV*, p. 131; *Crowland Chronicle*, p. 446; Warkworth, *Chronicle*, pp. 6–7, Hall, *Chronicle*, pp. 273–4.
13. Ross, *Edward IV*, p. 140; *Chronicle of the Lincolnshire Rebellion*, pp. 6–16; Warkworth, *Chronicle*, pp. 8–9; Kingsford, *Chronicles of London*, pp. 180–1; Vergil, *English History*, pp. 126–8.
14. *Crowland Chronicle*, p. 121.
15. Commines, *Memoirs*, p. 114.
16. Kitredge, *Witchcraft*, p. 84; *Rot. Parl.*, vol. vi, pp. 232, 241; H.A. Kelly, 'English Kings and the fear of sorcery', *Medieval Studies*, vol. 39 (1977), 206–38.
17. Montague Summers, *The History of Witchcraft* (London, 1926).
18. Geoffrey Parker, 'The Medieval Hermitage of Grafton Regis', *Northamptonshire Past and Present*, vi (1878–83), 247–52; W.E. Hampton, 'Witchcraft and the Sons of York', *The Ricardian*, v, 68 (1980), 170–8.
19. *Cal. Fine Rolls, 1461–71*, LHMSO (1949), p. 281.
20. *Works of Fortescue*, ed. Clermont, p. 331; Gross, *Dissolution of Lancastrian Kingship*, p. 44; Riches, *St George*, p. 141.
21. Rawcliffe, *Medicine and Society*, p. 164.
22. Myers, *Household of Edward IV*, p. 245.
23. *Paston Letters*, vol. v, p. 128.
24. Norton, *Ordinal of Alchemy*, p. 46.
25. *Key of Alchemy* (1577).
26. *Compound of Alchemy*, ed. Lindon, p. 90.
27. Keir, 'Ecclesiastical Career of George Neville', 207; Stephani Baluzii, *Tutelensis Miscellanea – opera ac studii Johanis Dominici Mansi Lucensi* (Lucca, 1961), pp. 494–50.
28. *CPR Edward IV and Henry VI 1467–76*, pt ll, pp. 116, 422.
29. Norton, *Ordinal of Alchemy*, p. 31.
30. *Select Cases in Chancery*, ed. W.P. Baildon, Selden Soc. vol. 10 (1896), no. 134. One of the officials investigating the affair, William Scott, was active in a judicial capacity betweeen 1459 and 1462; Norton, *Ordinal of Alchemy*, ll. 933–4.

31. Ibid, p. 31.
32. Ibid, ll. 954–9.
33. Ibid, ll. 938–95.
34. Ibid, ll. 989–95.
35. The likely date of Dalton's interview with Edward is in the period 1467–8. He was imprisoned for four years. Herbert was dead by 1478 and Delves was executed at Tewkesbury in 1471.
36. Norton, *Ordinal of Alchemy*, ll. 1023–5.
37. Ibid, ll. 1025–6.
38. Bodley MS Ashmole 1421, fo. 131v.
39. The sources of the legend are *The Testament* of Abbot Cremer, which appears in Bodley MS Ashmole 1512, fo. 443 and Ashmole's preface to his *Theatrum Chemicum Britannicum*.
40. *Chevalier au Cyne* in BL MS Royal 15 E.vi, fos 273–92; A. Sutton, 'Sir Thomas Cook and his troubles: an investigation', *Guildhall Studies in London History*, 3 (1978); A. Sutton and L. Visser-Fuchs, '"A most benevolent queen": Queen Elizabeth Woodville's reputation, her piety and her books', *The Ricardian*, x, 129 (1995).
41. See Paris, Bibliothèque nationale, MS fr 85, fo. 277; reproduced in Sutton and Visser-Fuchs, *Richard III's Books*, p. 181.
42. E. Ashmole, *Theatrum Chemicum Britannicum* (London, 1652), p. 458; F. Sherwood Taylor, *The Alchemists.*
43. BL MS Sloane 2580 B.
44. C.J. Thompson, *The Lure and Romance of Alchemy* (New York, 1996).
45. Bodley MS Rawl. poet 121.
46. C. Tyerman, *England and the Crusades 1095–1588* (Chicago, 1988).
47. *CPR Edward IV*; *CPR Henry VI*, p. 239.
48. M. Harvey, *England, Rome and the Papacy 1417–64* (Manchester, 1993), pp. 187–223.
49. Trinity College, Cambridge, MS R 14. 52.
50. There is a funeral monument to a knight of the Order of St John in St Botulph's parish church, Boston.
51. Ed. Bateson (EETS, London, extra ser. 76, 1899); Gross, *Dissolution of Lancastrian Kingship*, p. 39.
52. Bodley MS Ashmole 1480, fo. 15v; BL MS Sloane 3580 B, fos 165v–6v.
53. *Great London Chronicle*, p. 215.
54. *Warkworth's Chronicle*, in *Three Chronicles of the Reign of Edward IV*, p. 12.
55. Ibid, p. 9.
56. Ibid.
57. A.R. Myers, 'The captivity of a royal witch: the household accounts of Queen Joan Navarre, 1419–21', in his *Crown, Household and Parliament*, pp. 93–133.
58. Malory, *Morte d'Arthur*, p. 597.
59. Ibid, pp. 270–1.
60. Ibid, p. 1,098.
61. Ibid, p. 597.
62. Ibid, p. 1,229.
63. Ibid, p. 827.
64. Ibid, p. 1,030.
65. R.R. Griffith, 'The Authorship Question Reconsidered', in T. Takamiya and D. Brewer (eds), *Aspects of Malory* (Exeter, 1981), p. 163.
66. Malory, *Morte d'Arthur*, p. 985.
67. Felicity Riddy, 'Contextualizing Malory', in *Companion to Malory*.
68. J. Hughes, 'The Administration of Confession in the Diocese of York in the Fourteenth Century', in *Studies in Clergy and Ministry in England*, ed. D. Smith, Borthwick Studies in History, York (1991).
69. F. Riddy, *Sir Thomas Malory* (Leiden, 1987), pp. 112–38.
70. Malory, *Morte d'Arthur*, ed. Vinaver, vol. ii, p. 866.
71. Ibid, vol. iii, p. 1260.
72. *Paston Letters*, vol. v, no. 778; Tyerman, *Crusades*.
73. Gross, *Lancastrian Kingship*, p. 129.
74. Anthony Woodville's father, Richard Woodville, owned Rolle's *Emendation Vitae* (Bodley MS 456).
75. *Testamenta Vetusta*, ed. N.H. Nicolas (1826).

CHAPTER 8

The Rebirth of the King

> They saw a Fog rise, and pass over the whole face of the earth, they also saw the impetuosity of the Sea, and the streams over the face of the earth, and how these became foul and stinking in the darkness – Night enveloped all things. The day after they saw over the King an apparent Morning Star, and the light of Day clear up the darkness, and bright Sunlight pierce through the clouds, with manifold coloured rays of brilliant brightness and a sweet perfume from the earth, and the Sun shining clear. Herewith was completed the Time when the King of the Earth was released and renewed, well apparelled, and quite handsome, surprising with his beauty the Sun and Moon. He was crowned with three costly crowns.
>
> Salomon Trismosin, *Splendour Solis, c. 1490*[1]

On 29 September 1470 Edward fled from Bishop's Lynn. His small fleet was scattered across the Channel by hostile ships and storms, but they landed on a stretch of coast in the Low Countries, where Edward spent the next five months in relative poverty and hardship. This was an exile, an epic, spiritual journey with a small band of followers, a period of self-discovery and renewal that saw the rejuvenation of Edward as a heroic, charismatic leader and general. During the 1450s alchemists had been concerned with the symbolic death of the old king (Henry VI) to effect his rebirth through the integration of his four humours. In 1461 they had supervised the emergence of a homunculus, 'the son of March'. Now in 1471 they faced the symbolic death of Edward and witnessed and supervised his rebirth, the recapturing of his youth. Always at his best under pressure, he found himself back in the sort of situation he had faced at the beginning of 1461. His confident self-belief in his own luck and charm (such a handicap when he was in power at court, surrounded by sycophants and temptations) became his greatest asset as he planned the epic reconquest of his realm. The self-image he had fashioned during the crises of 1461 did not serve him well in the performance of his responsibilities as a ruler. Losing the throne was a blessing. It enabled Edward to return to the sources of his inspiration and sense of self: the leading of an army, theatrically performing, exercising his charm and demonstrating his courage.

It was the alchemists, many of whom doubted Edward in 1469, who saw the possibilities presented by this exile for the king to rediscover and renew himself. Thomas Norton may have expressed reservations about Edward, but he was still in his service in 1477 (the year he dedicated his *Ordinal of Alchemy* to the king), and according to his great-grandson he accompanied the king into exile. George Ripley may also have been with the king in Burgundy, despite the involvement of his friend George Neville and other friends and neighbours in the rebellions of 1468–70. He was certainly on Edward's side in 1471 when he dedicated to him his *Compound of Alchemy*, and it is in this work that he refers to his correspondence with the king from the University of Louvain. It is possible that his seven-year period of study abroad (and it could have been longer) covered the period between 1465 and 1471, during which time Margaret of York was married to the duke of Burgundy. Also in Edward's service during this period of exile were two alchemists with definite political interests. One was 'Friar Bungay' (Robert Barker), who was held responsible for practising a form of weather magic to aid Edward at Barnet in 1471, and the other was Robert Marshall, a Peterhouse fellow who owned fourteen manuscripts associated with alchemy, including the works of John Dastin. Marshall, who was appointed Edward's physician in 1468, also owned an alchemical manuscript containing Petrarch's *De remediis utriusque fortunae*, written in his own hand. He noted specific passages for signs and comment, singling out chapters on the misery of civil war and the misery of *infauso prelio*.[2]

These alchemists were aware of the failure of the Readeption, the sad spectacle of Neville leading Henry VI around London. They may also have had reservations about Edward of Lancaster. One Yorkist genealogy, executed in 1468 (Bodley, Jesus College MS 114), has an illustration of the Lancastrian prince in the pose of a vain, cruel-looking young man. But what was of most interest to them were the signs of Edward's rejuvenation. Sharing an exile with warriors such as Richard duke of Gloucester and old companions in arms like Anthony Woodville and Lord Hastings, he was becoming leaner and fitter, emotionally and physically. In the library of his host, Louis de Gruuthuyse, he was perusing literature about the epic campaigns of antiquity. There is no evidence that Louis had a particular interest in alchemy beyond the legend of the Golden Fleece, but Ripley's sojourn in the University of Louvain gives a hint that there may have been a flourishing alchemical scene in Burgundy. The alchemists and physicians accompanying the king in exile must have seen it as a chance to redeem Edward from the waste of the previous few years: in alchemical terms his exile represented a death that would bring about his submission to the mythic archetypes and a rebirth, a rediscovery of the identity he had enjoyed in 1461 as the redeemer of his nation.

This process was visualized in experimental, alchemical terms in the recipes for the stone, the medicine of transmutation and multiplication, that Ripley wrote for his friends, including George Neville. The recipient was advised to take 'an old Edward noble of fine gold' and grind it upon a marble stone with water and sulphur until cleared. The contents are then placed in a glass box in a round, lead case and left standing in a brass pot and boiled a day and a night. They are then strained through linen cloth in a marriage with mercury, and the gold, dissolved in mercury, will pass through the cloth. After repeated strainings the gold is placed in balneo and strained through linen cloth until dry, placed in a glass and reduced to a red powder with the temperate heat of the sun. The creation of this medicine, which will purge all misfortunes and leprosy and restore the king to his old vigour, is depicted in terms reminiscent of the events of 1468–71. The king's image is tarnished and reduced and he is symbolically buried in a coffin, only to be resurrected as pure gold: 'In the world's plan your brother must die to be reborn. And though he be old to be renewed suffer poison – you rise again right fresh and well – with these words the king began to breathe life.' Ripley's role as the physician Mercurius, who brought about the transformation of the king, is emphasized in the symbols for mercury on his tomb at Bridlington, displayed in the form of crosses indicating the year of his death CMXXXXIX[3] Around the base of the tomb occur images of the king in various stages of resurrection. It is easy to see how Ripley and his fellow alchemists in Edward's service would have been able to rationalize the king's humiliations and sufferings and use them to restore him to his original lustre of 1461. In fact the alchemists advising Edward during his exile would have turned to the imagery they had employed in 1461 to show that his fall heralded a new dawn. In Ripley's *Cantilena* and Norton's *Ordinal of Alchemy* there are references to the chaos, the *massa confusa*, which could be applied to the situation in 1468–71, and the restoration of unity heralded by the appearance of many colours as the work approaches its fruition in the *albedo* could be applied to the white rose of York:

for every colour which mane thought,
Shall here appeare before the white be wrought
– I herde my noble Maistre saye
How many men, pacient and wise,
Fownde oure white stone with exercise.[4]

The master Norton was referring to may have been Ripley. Edward's personal badge, the sun in ascendancy, was also subjected to alchemical analysis. The loss of royal authority between 1469 and 1471 could be explained from the *Cantilena* in terms of the chaos caused by the sun's eclipse (the reduction of gold to the state of undifferentiated base matter) and the reassertion of Edward's power by the *rubedo* (the appearance of a red glow in the materials in the furnace) which signified the rosy hue in the sky just before sunrise, the beginning of the sun's ascendancy. In the alchemical process in the *Cantilena* this was accompanied by the expectation of the birth from matter of the *homunculus* (the son) and this would have had added relevance with the announcement of the birth of Edward's son in the sanctuary of Westminster Abbey on 2 November 1470. This association of images occurs in a stained-glass window completed soon after Edward's successful reconquest of the realm. In Bramley church in Hampshire a radiant sun in splendour is shown emerging from the clouds in an image very similar to that occurring at the top of some of the *Ripley Scrolls*. Around the borders of the window are prince of Wales feathers, celebrating the birth of Edward's son.[5] These feathers also dominate many of the *Ripley Scrolls* and may reflect the alchemist's celebration of this event.[6] Some sense of the way Ripley and his fellow adepts would have consoled and inspired Edward during these five months can be seen in the dedicatory letter to the king which appears in the preface to the *Compound of Alchemy*. Ripley begins by asserting: 'As God knows and people bear witness I am no flatterer.' He promises to reveal the secret of transmutation of metal into gold, but it is clear he was writing in symbolic terms and more is at stake than the transmutation of metals. Ripley meant no less than the transformation of Edward, and the treasure he had in mind was the kingdom. As a key adviser to the king, Ripley was aware of Edward's strengths and his ability to tap into myths, and as he witnesses this happening again in 1471 he warns the king to use his gifts of grace and fortune to please God. The close identification of Ripley's alchemical instructions with the recipient of his work, the king, is underlined when Ripley provides Edward with the following prayer: 'Suffer me teach me be my governor – and this beginning [enterprise] be nigh me with grace and enforce my will grant to fulfill my plan.' In discussing the marriage of the red and white elixirs, the reconciliation of opposites which had the same political implications in 1471 as in 1461, Ripley employed the alchemical symbols that were to characterize Edward's reconquest. Invoking the Trinity, he referred to the wheel of the elements, turning towards summer where there is disport and delight 'and your work becomes a perfect white'. The Trinity, the motto 'comfort and joy', the white rose and the ascendant sun were to be as crucial in the campaigns of 1471 as they were in 1461.

The alchemical myth that would have had the most significance for Edward during his Burgundian exile was the legend of Jason and the Golden Fleece. As we have seen, Edward's connection with this myth dates back as early as 1456. His familiarity with the legend can be assumed from his ownership of texts where the story occurs, such as Stephen Scrope's translation of the *Epistle of Othea*. Practically his first action on regaining his freedom from Warwick's captivity, when he was led to London by George Neville on 7 October 1469, was to take the oath of the Order of the Golden Fleece. But his Burgundian exile would have sharpened his awareness of the legend and encouraged him to conceive of the reconquest of his kingdom in terms of the setting out of Jason's argosy. Burgundy was a particularly fruitful place to make the connection between this legend and the alchemical transformation of Edward into a hero in the mould of Jason about to undertake a daunting task. The Order of the Golden Fleece was a Burgundian order modelled on the Garter, and Edward's host for most of the five months when he was in Burgundy was Louis de Gruuthuyse, who had been a knight of the Order since May 1461.[7]

Louis de Gruuthuse. Groeningemuseum (Bruges). (Geoffrey Wheeler)

Burgundy was the focus of literary representations of the legend. Louis de Gruuthuyse owned a manuscript of Lefevre's *Histoire de Jason*, written in two versions in 1460 and 1467 for Philip the Good. By 1467 Philip the Good also acquired from the ducal library one of the sources of this work, the *Ovid Moralized*. Between 1468 and 1473 Guillame Fillostre produced the *Troesis de Jason* at the instigation of Charles the Bold, who was inspired by Fillostre's sermon as chancellor of the Order of the Golden Fleece at the chapter meeting in 1468. In the following year Caxton began translating Lefevre's *Receuil des Histoires de Troie*, which featured the story of Jason and Hercules; he completed it in September 1471 at the instigation of Margaret of York, to whom he presented it. Caxton later followed this up with a translation of Lefevre's *Continuation of the Receuil des Histoires de Troie*, the *Book of Jason*, which he completed in 1477 and which became the first book to be printed in Westminster.

The Burgundian court also provided opportunities for Edward to contemplate artistic representations of Jason's quest. One of the tableaux set up for the entertainment of the wedding party at the marriage of Margaret of York and Charles the Bold at Sluys in 1468 was said by English eye-witnesses to have been of Medea, and at the court of Burgundy a tapestry of Jason's expedition to gain the Golden Fleece was commissioned by Philip the Bold. (Burgundy had also been very active earlier in promoting crusades with such institutions as the feast of the Golden Pheasant.) At Margaret of York's castle of Hesdin, where the exiled King Edward stayed in December 1470, he would have been able to contemplate a painting described by Caxton in his prologue to his translation of Lefevre's *Histoire de Jason* as 'craftyly and curiously depeynted on the conquests of the golden fleese by the sayd Jason'.[8] This painting was in a room equipped for the production of special effects such as thunder, snow and rain in remembrance of Medea and her 'cunning science'.

It is likely that those with vested interests in the invasion of England would have encouraged Edward to see the impending invasion in terms of Jason's argosy. Caxton would have been one of them. As the head of the merchant adventurers in Bruges he met Edward IV, Richard duke of Gloucester and Lord Hastings during their exile, and he may have been a key figure in financing the king's return. Edward's Burgundian hosts seem to have recognized his heroic potential. Commines met Edward in 1471 and commented on his great beauty and presence. Jean Mielot, the most influential of the Burgundian popularizers of classical myth and a member of Charles the Bold's entourage, wrote a poem for Edward

IV in which he compared the impending invasion of England to the quest of Jason and the Argonauts for the Golden Fleece.[9] Edward himself, contemplating this risky invasion with a mere four ships supplied by his brother-in-law and a further fourteen hired from the Hanseatic League, must have taken comfort and inspiration from allowing himself to be convinced that he and his followers were a select band of Argonauts about to embark on an argosy in a quest across the sea. An indication of the way Edward saw his kingdom as the cherished Golden Fleece can be seen in the manuscripts he commissioned from Burgundian scribes and illuminators after 1478, once he had re-established his kingdom, all of which depict heroic deeds of conquest. In his copy of the Burgundian Waurin's *Chronicle*, which emphasizes Brutus's conquest of Britain, the author praises Edward's ancestry and justifies his succession by referring to his opponents as usurpers. Waurin is shown presenting his work to Edward, who is wearing the collar of the Order of the Golden Fleece.[10] In Edward's copy of *Ovid Moralized* there is an illumination of Jason yoking the bulls before the fleece. Most significant is the way Edward chose to identify his conquest of Britain with Caesar's conquest of the same island. In Edward's copy of *Le Grande Histoire Cesar*, the fleece is shown hanging under the Garter belt at the foot of Edward's arms in a full-page illustration showing the birth of Caesar. The fleece on the same Garter belt appears in Edward's copy of a biblical history, Josephus's *Jewish Wars*.

There was a very specific alchemical and medical dimension to the perception of this classical legend which shows the interfacing of medicine and politics in Edward's campaign of conquest, and this was demonstrated in Mielot's use of alchemical symbolism. Charles the Bold, Edward's ally, is compared to Jason, and Edward, because of his great height and beauty, is compared to the giant Alcides (Hercules). The labours of Hercules had been staged at the marriage festivities of Margaret of York and Charles the Bold. It was appropriate for the poem that Jason made Hercules a knight given that Charles and Edward exchanged Orders of the Golden Fleece and the Garter. It was also appropriate that Hercules was connected with sheep given the importance of English wool to Burgundian cloth-weavers. According to the poem Jason will help Hercules regain his island:

> In the vast ocean of the world lies a large island:
> England at first by Brutus called Britannia:
> – in the old days knew no snakes and savage wolves.
> Today it is infested with them and grim dragons,
> By which the woolly sheep are scattered and torn up.
> Now Hercules, the shepherd of the harmless sheep, ventures
> To catch them with his tight net and with strong hounds
> By Jason's help; a golden race will spring up in the land:
> Let Jason and Hercules go again to Aetes's Colchis;
> Then anger is kindly, grief burning their hard bones.[11]

This poem exhibits an awareness of the alchemical significance of this legend to Edward's campaign. The wolves devouring Hercules's sheep refer to Henry VI's cognomen *Lupus* or antimony. The ancient name of the kingdom is evoked and the plight of Britain is likened to that of Colchis. England under Margaret of Anjou has become the home of Medea, a land once free of snakes but which now brings forth the fiery dragon. Ripley too was fully aware of the significance of the legend in the reconquest. In his vision he warned that if the king were to regain his youth he had to face the dragon, and he added that the old king if he was prepared to die could be 'made young by Medea with her drink and her potions'.[12] The personal and political significance of the alchemical allegories of this poem to Edward at this crucial time of his life can be seen in the vision of a land afflicted by leprosy awaiting redemption from its king. This widely circulated tract attributed to Ripley (but also in two fifteenth-century manuscripts to John Dastin) would have been well known to Edward and his alchemists (including Marshall who owned Dastin's works) and may have been included in the *Bosom Book*. In the surgical treatise written by John Bradmore and translated around 1450[13] leprosy is defined as *lupus*: 'that which is a contagious kanker that devoureth and corrupteth all the meat that it feasteth on. And right so leprosy devours all the members of the body.'[14] The term *lupus* was also applied to any suppuration of the flesh, particularly the genitalia, and was often thought to be venereal in origin, but it may also have included cancers, carbuncles and other eczematous afflictions (of the type which plagued Stephen Scrope), which were often treated with dead flesh. Bradmore also applied the term *lupus* to herpes (probably gonorrhoea), a hardness and softness of the lower members. He used alchemical language to describe the black corrosiveness and putrefaction (an allusion to the *nigredo*) to which the flesh was reduced when the 'foul matter of *lupus* was fretted and chafed away';[15] the treatment – the application of dead flesh to devour the disease – also had an alchemical rationale. Thus in Mielot's poem, Henry VI's cognomen was identified with the sexual diseases imputed to John of Gaunt, the founder of the house of Lancaster, and with the leprosy imputed to Henry IV, the founder of the Lancastrian dynasty. The diseases covered by the term *lupus* were seen as cancers that attacked the limbs of the body politic and they could only be cured by the application of mercury and gold (the cognomens for Ripley and Edward IV). The vision of Ripley and Dastin can best be understood in the context of *The Bosom Book of George Ripley* which survives in a sixteenth-century copy of alchemical treatises. A note in the margin explains: 'This book seemeth to be his bosom book, or his book he daily used.' Originally written in Latin it was translated by Samuel Norton on 5 February 1573 and was copied from 'an old booke, which is thought to be in the handwriting of Mr George Ripley, Canon'. It is likely that Ripley's original autograph manuscript passed from Thomas Norton, who accompanied Edward in Bruges, to his great-grandson. The *Bosom Book* was probably written in 1470 during the Burgundian exile for it contains a genealogical table of the process for making the 'Great Work named the Elixir' and the table begins with Edward's crown decorated with the sun in splendour, and ends with George Ripley's name (perhaps a copy of his signature) under an alembic and the date, 1470. The vision if applied to the genealogical evolution of the great work, the recapture of Edward's crown, reflects the advice the alchemist would have given to the exiled king. Edward, now aged twenty-eight and overweight, had to recapture his youthful energy and confidence. According to the vision the king, if he is to die and be reborn as the golden youth who will heal his suffering realm, must encounter the dragon that, as Mielot's poem expressed it, now plagues his kingdom. Ripley, no doubt reflecting on the challenge facing his king, poignantly expressed Edward's desire to redeem the lost courage and energy of his golden youth: 'To save my brethren I have so great delight from darkness to illumine. And for I dread the venemous serpent my tender youth I must now win.'[16] Ripley was also responsible for designing a wheel tracking the paths of the planets, especially the sun, around the earth, describing Christ as the sun ascending into the heavens to shine on his throne, renewing the glory of the stone, curing leprosy (the disease specifically associated with the house of Lancaster) and restoring youth (probably King Edward's): 'As Christ ascended to heaven, so his throne shines on our sun, and so is made our stone to glow again with the power to cure lepers and renew youth.'[17] Edward's identification with St George added to his lustre as the curative gold for a sick leprous kingdom because of the association with a martyrdom that involved the escoriation of his skin (vividly presented in the great stained-glass cycle in St George's church in Stamford).[18] St George was widely regarded as a patron saint against leprosy.

Alchemists advising Edward had, since 1460, been aware of the significance of the ancient British myths in the pursuit of the goal of national identity and this included the most distant origins of the nation in the siege of Troy. Jason was responsible for the fall of the first Troy, and this legend served to focus Edward's mind on the ultimate goal of his quest, which in 1471 was no different than it had been in 1461: the capture of London or New Troy, the city founded by Brutus. Lydgate had first established the centrality of the Trojan myth in the origins of Britain, and Edward in 1471 capitalized on this and assumed the role of the heroic British king. The myth was even more potent in 1471 than in 1461 because this time Edward would proclaim himself as the king in exile, delivering his people from bondage. In a commonplace book of alchemical recipes and prophecies about the coming of Edward, the British king, there is an account of the childhood of Brutus: like Oedipus who inadvertently killed one parent, Brutus accidentally kills both his parents and flees to Italy where he delivers the Trojans from bondage. Edward's position as Brutus preparing to invade his island was reinforced in expatriate circles in Bruges in this period. Caxton started his translation of the *History of Troy* in 1467 but decided not to go on with it because it had been translated by Lydgate from a different source. However, at the insistence of Edward's sister Margaret of Burgundy, he completed it in 1471. One of Caxton's associates in the production of this work was Johannes Veldener, who matriculated in the University of Louvain in July 1473. Caxton was aware of the political significance of his translation fitting in with Edward's ambition to reunite Britain, and he identified the times in which he completed his translation as 'the time of the trobbelous world of the grete tenysions and reygnyng as wel in the royames of England and France'. Completed in Bruges under the protection of Edward, it became in 1473 the first book to be printed in English. It was dedicated to Edward's recently born son, the prince of Wales 'because no doubt his grace has a copy in French'. Edward was also familiar with Lydgate's version, which was owned by William Herbert and which, after Herbert's death in 1469, passed into his hands.[19]

The myths of Edward's descent from the British kings and the prophecies of his return became as important in 1469–71 as they had been in 1461, meeting as they did the need for reassurance in these turbulent and uncertain times. John Benet, vicar of Harlington in Bedfordshire, had a passion for British history and compiled his own chronicle. This he transcribed into a manuscript containing prophecies of the king who will win the Holy Cross.[20] Benet turned to his volume during times of political uncertainty, signing his name in it in 1461, 1468 and 1471, taking comfort from the expectation that the will of God would prevail. The Yorkshireman John Herryson (d. 1474), chaplain to the nuns of St Radegard and a medical graduate of Cambridge, compiled a chronicle for the period 1377–1469[21] and a collection of historical writings including Geoffrey of Monmouth, Higden's *Polychronicon* and historical prophecies. This manuscript, completed around 1464, contains the following prophecies: the Bridlington prophecy; the last kings of the English; the Holy Oil of St Thomas; the Cock of the North; *Arbor fertilis*; and the King who will find the Holy Cross.[22] All these present Edward as a prophetic hero. The fly-leaves of the manuscript are dated 1469–70, and there is a note of panic in the way Herryson began to record prophecies and portents in 1469. The copying of texts ceases when the political crisis passes. One text shows Herryson's concern that after eight years of peace the civil wars were returning and he blamed the malign influence of Margaret of Anjou. He noted an eclipse of the sun in July 1467 and warned of upheavals to come: 'And dyuerse astatys schall dye thys yere. And women schall be cawse of dyuerse insurreccions. Stabyllnesse non schall be thys yere in thys regine. And euery man schall be fayne to save and provyde for hym selfe and for the iiij partys off thys regine schall be gyffen to insurreccions – And olde trowbyll schall sprynge newe.'[23] Like Benet, Herryson was not using the prophecies in any retrospective sense. He was not sure what was going to happen, noting in his manuscript that 'on September 1470 King Edward was driven out and took ship at the town of Lynne'. He did not know when the king would return and turned for solace to these prophecies about the returning British king. Before one text beginning 'Videbunt iusti et timebunt' the writer addresses 'ye comyns and trewe comynalte off Ingelande', urging them, if they wished for peace and stability, to support King Edward and his badges: the lion, the eagle and the falcon. If they chose not to support him then, the author warned, 'your rysyngs and steryngs will be to your confusion'.[24]

The same anxiety can be found in prophecies from Merlin, adapted around 1470, which occur in a bundle of legal documents relating to the priory of South Creake in Norfolk.[25] Edward's rightful inheritance, claimed in 1461, is seen as the culmination of a divine plan that included the conquest of Britain by Brutus, the exile of Cadwallader and the expulsion by God of the sinful Saxons through Edward's conquest of the throne: 'In the year of our Lord 1460 schall re—— [redeemed?] by the meryts of hys feyth be all londes what so euer his Auncesters hath before owt of myhnde.' The prophecy of the angel to Cadwallader is moreover adapted to fit the circumstances of Edward's expulsion in October 1470. The Lancastrians of the white dragon, repeating the sins of their Saxon ancestors in the reign of Cadwallader, have driven the rightful king of the Britons from his land, but Edward, the heir of Cadwallader, bearing the red dragon, will return, and there will be 'a fineall distruccion of the Saxons and Normands. And all other straungers of this lond.' This will be carried out by he who merits that honour because of his faith and lineage:

> This lord with his children eyres that wer dreuyn – of this land be oure lawis of conquest. Contrys to goddis lawis yet God hath don as the Aungell seyd trusted – the seyd Relikes and Eyres of Cadwaladrus bodi from Rome by the Pope is power. And blessed all tho that helpeth hym in his right. And cusseth all them that doth contrary. And allys they scall be browght into wyld desert – to owre final distruccion. And the lond shall be called Bretayn a gen dowtless.[26]

The author concludes with the threat that God will curse all those who do not support Edward for they will have little influence on the outcome as God's will is inescapable.

Edward was quick to capitalize on his subjects' need for reassurance from the prophecies, and the genealogical chronicles and prophecies that he had used to capture the throne in 1461 were revised at the time of his invasion; this time Edward's position as the heir of Brutus and Cadwallader and the opponent of the Saxon invaders was given added significance by the alliance between Henry VI and the earl of Warwick, with the French princess Margaret of Anjou and Louis XI, king of France. In one large and colourful genealogical tree, executed after Edward's death, it is claimed that the many people who inhabited the northern part of the world – the Saxons (barbarians from Germany, beyond the bounds of the Roman Empire), Norwegians, Danes, Goths, and Vandals – were jealous of the Britons because of their superior civilization and their links with Troy and Rome.[27] The production of the family of chronicle rolls derived from Peter of Poitiers's biblical chronicle that had been adapted for Edward IV in the 1460s continued in London and Westminster during Edward's exile. One roll, executed between March and November 1470, shows the parallel evolution of the lines of David and Brutus to reaffirm Edward's position as the exiled leader of the chosen people and shows the loss of Britain's name and identity when the angel commanded Cadwallader to go into exile in Rome, precipitating the Saxon invasion and the division of Britain into seven kingdoms.[28] The issuing of this genealogy at this crucial time was tantamount to asserting that this exile of the British kings was about to end with Edward's return. This chronicle also stresses Edward's descent on the right-hand side (facing the viewer) through the Mortimer line, and suggests that Henry IV was a usurper who deposed King Richard, 'which was the trewe inheritance of the crown of England and named himself Henry IV'. Other biblical genealogies issued in this period stress Edward's descent from Brutus.[29] In all this revisiting of the rhetoric of 1461, the most ornate and elaborate attempt to validate the reconquest of the realm was made in the 1470 version of the *Genealogy of Edward King of Britain* by the compiler of the family of genealogies and chronicles containing the prophecies of the coming of Edward from Geoffrey of Monmouth and other sources. This roll was made in 1471, perhaps during Edward's exile.[30] It has many of the prophecies that are found in this author's earlier *Prophetic History of Britain*, including the prophecy of the angel to Cadwallader concerning the arrival of a British king who will finally defeat the Saxons.[31] Throughout the genealogy Edward's identification with such prophetic cognomens as Brutus and David is stressed to emphasize his role as the exiled leader of the chosen people and Henry VI is identified with Saul and the foreign invaders of Britain. The manuscript has alchemical symbolism, especially in a drawing of the process of Creation, the manifestation of God's divine order from the chaos of undifferentiated matter at the beginning of time, and it is significant that two of the cognomens for the kings destined to meet in battle again are drawn from alchemy: Henry VI was described as *Lupus*, the wolf, the semi-metal antimony that corresponds to the infancy of metalline evolution, while Edward was given the cognomen of *Sol*, the sun or gold, the perfection of the alchemical work.

Apart from the Lancastrian alliance with the French royal house and Edward's status as an exiled leader of his people, another aspect of the political situation in 1471 not present in 1461 was Edward's alliance with the Percies. Apart from securing control of the north, this added a new dimension to Edward's mythology. In 1469 the earl of Northumberland had been released from the Tower, and in March 1470 he was restored to his family earldom, an event that precipitated Marquess Montagu's desertion from Edward to join his brother Warwick, bitterly complaining that the king had compensated him for the loss of this earldom with 'a pie's nest'. Henry Percy's cooperation was essential to the success of Edward's invasion (he was in correspondence with Edward prior to the invasion), and this was symbolized by Percy's acquisition (probably in 1469) of the *Prophetic History of Britain*, to which his arms had been added.[32] In the 1470s he also acquired a manuscript of Hardynge's *Chronicle* in which the Percy family is described as descended from the line of March.[33] Some time later the Percy Roll was commissioned by this family, with the Percy badge prominently displayed.[34] This roll allowed the Percies to integrate their family history and connections with those of the Mortimers and therefore with Edward's genealogy. On the left-hand side there is a descent from William Percy, the presumed original founder of Whitby Abbey, which emphasizes the joining of the families at the beginning of the fifteenth century. Further mythologizing of the recent past now became possible. Bolingbroke's perjury in 1399 could be emphasized and the Percies, through their involvement in the rebellions of 1403, 1405 and 1407, could appear, like Richard Scrope, as persistent opponents of the original Lancastrian usurpation and as key elements in the gathering alliance of the Celtic peoples against these invaders of foreign blood, symbolized in 1405 in the Tripartite Indenture – a Celtic alliance of Owain Glyndwr of Wales, the Earl Douglas of Scotland and the Irish – against Henry IV. Edward's concern to assimilate Scotland into this vision of a Celtic conquest of the kingdom is shown in his concern over the Lancastrian alliance with Scotland in 1470 and his attempt to secure agreement with the Scots involving a repudiation of the Lancastrian monarchy. Prophecies found in the *Prophetic History of Britain* concerning Merlin's forecast of an alliance between the Britons and the Scots against

Edward, the conqueror and redeemer of Britain, wearing the collar of the Order of the Golden Fleece, receives his History of Britain. *On the left is perhaps Richard duke of Gloucester with the Garter. (British Library Royal 15 E IV,* Chronicles of the English, *Jean de Waurin, vol. 1, fo. 14)*

the English therefore became increasingly relevant.[35] Edward's assumed role as the British king, the focus of the hopes of the Welsh, had added significance with the death of William Herbert after the Battle of Edgecote in 1469.

Edward's exile in Burgundy was therefore an extremely fertile time for the rediscovery of his public image and his self-image as an inspirational leader of the nation. On his return to England he commissioned the copying at Bruges of books that were in part inspired by his encounter with texts in the libraries of his Burgundian hosts. They included works of ancient history such as biographies of Julius Caesar and Caesar Augustus, all of which would have reinforced his image as the conqueror. One such text, the compilation of which may date to his time in Burgundy, was Xenophon's *Cyropoedia*, translated by Fr Vasco Fernando de Lucca. Illustrated throughout with the white rose and sun blazing, this shows Edward identifying with Cyrus the Great (590–529 BC), a Moses-like figure brought up by shepherds, who founded the Achaean Empire in Persia and liberated the Jews.[36] The work of history produced in Burgundy that was most relevant to Edward's quest was the first volume of his *Anciennes et*

Nouvelles Croniques Angleterre; the work of the Burgundian chronicler Jean Waurin, it was executed between 1472 and 1475. This book, having much in common with the *Brut*, has a preface dedicated to Edward praising his ancestry by linking him with Jason and such heroic figures of British history as Brutus and Arthur, and referring to his opponents as usurpers. The work opens with a miniature showing the author presenting his work to Edward who wears the collar of the Order of the Golden Fleece.[37] It is likely that at the end of his five-month exile Edward had become leaner and fitter, much more like the young man of 1461, and the symbolism of the genealogies, stressing his links with Moses, David and Brutus, now had even more power as he prepared to lay siege to his kingdom from exile and against a largely foreign enemy. The reputation of the house of Lancaster as a foreign institution was confirmed on 6 February 1471 when a ten-year truce was signed between Henry VI, the English Parliament and France in an alliance against Edward and the Duke of Burgundy.

The impression that the reconquest of England was a theatrical epic led by a man who had rediscovered his decisiveness and self-belief was conveyed in all the contemporary accounts of the invasion, especially in the official account, the *Arrivall*, written by one of Edward's servants in 1471.[38] The author, a Peterhouse fellow, probably encouraged Edward to see the invasion as a key moment in the destiny of the British nation. He owned a copy of Caxton's second version of the *Brut*, which he presented to his college[39] along with another chronicle. When Edward started out from Flanders on 19 February 1471 he chose to walk the short distance from Bruges to Damme instead of going by boat as planned, so that he could be seen by as many of the citizens as possible and could thank the friendly people of Bruges for their support. On 2 March he set out from Zeeland in a ship called the *Anthony*, followed by a force of two thousand Englishmen. A poem composed by a Londoner in 1471 opens in an epic style:

> The coming of King Edward, and of his good spede,
> Oute of Docheland unto England over the salt sea
> In what perell and trowbill in what payne was he.

Edward arrived off Cromer on the Norfolk coast only to be told that it was in hostile hands and he set out to sea again and: 'sailed north and on the 14 March fell great storms, wyndes and tempests upon the sea, so that the said 14th day in great torment, he came to Humberland.'

All his ships were scattered but eventually Edward landed in Ravenspur. Gloucester was four miles away with seven hundred men and Earl Rivers was fourteen miles away with three hundred more. Edward was in an even more desperate plight than he had faced in February 1461. His forces were pitifully small and needed to be reinforced by Hastings and his men. Everything depended in the meantime on Edward keeping his confidence. Instead of reboarding his barge he walked ashore so the people could touch him and, according to the author of the *Arrivall*, by 15 March the remnants of his scattered argosy, 'the rage of the tempest somewhat appeasyd, landyd and alwaye drewe towards the kynge',[40] and from every landing place 'the felowshipe came hoole toward hym'. Retracing the steps made by Bolingbroke in 1399 Edward too depended on the inaction of his new ally the earl of Northumberland, with whom he had been in communication since landing. Trusting in the love that the local people bore towards the duke of York, his father, he maintained, like Bolingbroke before him, that he was claiming not the throne but only the duchy that had been rightfully his father's. Showing great courage and confidence, Edward proclaimed his loyalty to Henry VI and, sporting the ostrich feathers of the prince of Wales, entered York with only sixteen men. By that evening he had persuaded his hosts to open the gates to his army.[41]

His subsequent march south to Coventry was a testimony to his self-belief, mental courage and powers of leadership. His small army could easily have been crushed by Montagu, and he relied on new men coming to his cause as he marched, drawn by his charisma and military reputation. According to the author of the *Arrivall*, the people of Yorkshire, though outnumbering his small army, 'durst not take upon them to make hym any manifest warre, knowynge well the great curage and hardiness that he was of, with the parfete asswrance of the felowshype that was with hym'.[42] Fortunately for Edward there was tension between John Neville and Henry Percy over the earldom of Northumberland (Montagu still bitterly resented the loss of this earldom). Crucially, however, Neville, perhaps wary of Northumberland's intervention on Edward's side, did nothing to stop him, because, according to the *Arrivall*: 'They were so habiled, and so well piked men, and in theyr werke they hadd on hand so willed, that it had bene right hard to right a great felawshipe, moche greatar than they.'[43] Edward's courage and decisiveness, which had been so apparent at Mortimer's Cross in 1461, were just as clear in 1471. Warwick, according to the author of the *Arrivall*, was reluctant to meet Edward in the field because 'he lacked the hardiness and courage so to do' and by 29 March Edward's army had swelled in numbers as he arrived before Coventry to challenge his old friend to open combat.

On Friday 5 August Edward left Coventry, spending the weekend at Daventry. By this time he had a huge following. The crowd pressing into the abbey church for divine service on Sunday was so thick that it probably caused vibrations in the pillars, causing the boards of a tabernacle covering an image of St Anne to spring open, so that: 'All thos, also, that were present and sawe this worshippyd and thanked God and Seint Anne, there, and many offeryd; takyng of this signe, shewed by the power of God, good hope of theyr good spede for to come.'[44]

Fifteenth-century alabaster figure of St Anne teaching the Virgin to read, East Barsham, Norfolk. It would have been an image similar to this, within its wooden housing, which opened miraculously before Edward IV at Daventry. (Geoffrey Wheeler)

This popular enthusiasm was in marked contrast to the apathetic spectacle played out in London, where George Neville, in an attempt to stiffen opposition to Edward's approach, paraded Henry VI around the city in shabby clothes. The rulers of the city, at council, noted that the power of Henry VI and his adherents was so feeble 'they cowld thereby take no corage to draw to them ne to fortefye theyr partye'.[45] Edward's entry into the capital was as triumphant and unopposed as it had been in 1461. He was met by the archbishop of York, who presented him with Henry VI as a prisoner. However, this time the city had to be immediately defended. By now Edward's energies were fired by the mythic dimensions of his campaign. On the Thursday evening before Good Friday he took the advice of great lords 'for the adventures that were lykely for to come'.[46] The armies of Edward and Warwick clashed at Barnet near London on Easter Sunday, 7 April. Warwick hoped to surprise Edward by attacking on this the most holy day, but Edward was no longer the inert, passive figure of 1469. He had ridden out of London on the preceding Saturday evening, camping near Warwick's force at Barnet. Warwick's fire-power was superior and the might of his guns bombarded Edward's troops, but the discipline in the Yorkist army was such that they kept close and quiet and the guns overshot their mark. At four or five in the morning a heavy mist descended, and under cover of this Edward, 'commytted his cawse and qwarell to Allmyghty God, avancyd bannars, dyd blowe up trumpets, and set upon them firste with shotte, and than and sone, they joyned and came to hand-strokes'.[47] The fog was crucial to the outcome of the battle, because it enabled Edward to surprise Warwick and get close enough for hand-to-hand combat, thereby negating Warwick's superior artillery. The east of Edward's line overreached Warwick's and the west of Warwick's line overreached Edward's at a point where the earl of Oxford's men routed the Yorkists three or four hours into the battle. Oxford's men, who wore as their livery the badge of a star with streams, pursued the Yorkist army but Oxford was eventually able to turn them around and return them towards the field. His intention was to attack Edward from behind, but the battle lines had swung round so far that their positions were reversed and so Oxford's men fell upon Warwick's rear instead. Warwick's men, dimly seeing Oxford's star with streams advancing through the fog, mistook it for Edward's sun in splendour. Believing Oxford's men to be Edward's they opened fire and Oxford and his men fled with shouts of treason.[48]

Barnet was probably Edward's finest hour and he seems to have played a direct, heroic role in a battle of furious hand-to-hand fighting where his superior height and strength inspired those around him. According to the author of the *Arrivall*, while the east and west lines were overreaching and manoeuvring, Edward held the centre:

> The kynge trusting verily in God's help, our blessed ladyes, and Seynt George, toke to hym great haries and corage for to surprise the falsehode of all them that so falsely and so traytorously had conspired agaynst hym, where thurgh with the faytheful welbelovyd and myghty assystaunce of his felowshipe, that in great nombar diseveryd nat from his parson, and were well assured untu hym as to them was possyble, he mannly, vigorowsly, and valliantly assayled them, in the mydst and strongest of theyr battaile, where he with great violence, bett and bare down afore hym all that stode in hys way, – and so bet and bare them downe, so that nothing myght stande in the syght of hym and the welle asswred felowshipe that attendyd trewly upon hym.[49]

No quarter was asked or given in this battle. Edward no longer gave orders to spare the common people as he had done at Northampton and 1,500 men died, although in a characteristic gesture he did try, unsuccessfully, to find in the mist his old friend and father figure, Warwick, before his troops slew him.

Another crucial factor in Edward's victory at Barnet was the failure of Margaret of Anjou and Edward of Lancaster to join forces with Warwick. Langstrother had been waiting for them at Harfleur as she embarked on 24 March, but storms drove the ships back to the port. She did not manage to land in England with her precious son until the very evening that Warwick was killed. On 19 April Edward was informed that Margaret was making her way to Wales to join Jasper Tudor, and on 24 April he rapidly moved westwards to intercept her. The sense of energy and momentum in Edward and his army, raised from fifteen counties, and the contrast with the weary fatalism of Margaret of Anjou and her troops, disheartened by the news of Warwick's death, was captured by the author of the *Arrivall*. Margaret's army travelled thirty-six miles 'in a fowle contrye all in lanes and stonny wayes, betwyxt woodes without any good refresshynge'.[50] Even the horsemen and the horses were tired and 'they therefore determyned t'abyde th'aventure that God would send them in the qwarrel they had taken in hand'.[51] By contrast Edward, that same Friday morning, marched out from Windsor along the ancient road running high over the western scarp of the Cotswold ridge, over the champaign country of the Cotswolds, some thirty miles in a rapid march without stopping for food, his men suffering from heat and thirst, and crossing only over one water source, a brook soon muddied by the horses' hooves. He rode all that day until he came within five miles of Margaret of Anjou's army at Tewkesbury. He placed an ambush in the wood.

On the morning of 4 May the king 'aparailed himselfe and all his hoost, set in good array – displayed his bannars, dyd blowe up the trompets; commytted his caws and qwarell to Almyghty God, – the glorious martyr Seint George avaunced directly upon his enemyes – full manly, set for the even upon them'.[52] According to contemporary chronicles and newsletters, Edward of Lancaster was either slain in battle or taken prisoner and killed. According to the author of the *Arrivall*, he died fleeing the field (like the earl of Warwick), and this is the most widely accepted view. However, in an illumination of the Battle of Tewkesbury, in a Burgundian copy of the short version of the *Arrivall*, completed some ten years later, Gloucester and Clarence are shown manhandling the prince while their brother strikes him.[53]

The sense of Edward's invincibility was such that further planned rebellions in the north collapsed when the Lancastrians 'heard the certeynte of his great vyctories, – and they sore dredyng his good spede, and great fortunes'.[54] However, there was still one campaign left to fight. While Edward was in Coventry, Warwick's half-brother Lord Fauconberg, with an army drawn from Kent and the Cinque Ports, marched on London, ostensibly to free Henry VI. Anthony Woodville refused them admission to the capital and the rebels intended instead to encounter Edward who, learning of their advance, was preparing to march towards London. Fauconberg was informed of the size of the royal army and 'greatly fearinge his highe corage and knyghthood'[55] he returned to London and laid siege to the city. On 12 May they attacked London Bridge and tried to cross the river, bringing guns to the south bank. By 18 May they learned of Edward's approach 'with great puissance whereof they greatly adred',[56] and the rebels retreated to Blackheath. On 21 May the king's army triumphantly entered London, led by Gloucester, with Hastings and the king following, and with Margaret of Anjou and Clarence at the back of the party. According to Warkworth, Henry VI was put to death between eleven and midnight on 21 May while Gloucester was in the Tower.

The author of the *Arrivall* sums up Edward's campaigns, completed in a mere eleven weeks, as an astonishing feat of endurance, inspired leadership, sense of mission and discipline:

> by his full noble and knightly cowrage, hathe optaynd two and right great, and crwel and mortall battayls; put to flight and discomfeture dyvars great assembles of his rebells, and riotows persons, in the many partyes of his land, the whiche, thowghe all they were also rygorously and maliciously disposed, as they myght be, they were, netheless, so affrayde and afferyd of rthe verey asswryd courage and manhod that restethe in the person of our seyd sovereigne – Whereby it apperithe and faythfully is belevyd, that Almyghty God, which from his begynning hitherto hathe not fayled hym.[57]

This servant of the king was not merely writing propaganda; he was aware that the king had recovered something he had lost. Edward in 1471 was as charismatic and decisive a military leader as he had been in 1461 and just as popular in London, where he was again acclaimed king by the people. Edward found sustenance, inspiration and power from the same sources, a potent combination of religion, myth, genealogy and alchemy.

As in the 1461 campaign allusions were made to Edward's Christ-like status as the saviour of his people. John Warkworth, a Northumbrian scholar of Peterhouse in 1473, wrote an account of the invasion between 1478 and 1483 in which Edward followed the path of 'a most marvellow blazing star' that first appeared just before Christmas and was then seen in the east at the beginning of January 1471. Rising in the east fully at midnight it moved westwards over all of England for fourteen nights. It then seemed to expire before suddenly burning fervently again until 22 February when it appeared again in the firmament in the east before descending with great smoke and blazings a mile high.

An important aspect of Edward's messianic role was his image as the redeemed sinner, the Job-like man of sorrows restored by God's grace to the position of His chosen one through suffering. This had the advantage of giving a mythological dimension to the king's years of inertia. The poem 'On the Recovery of the Throne by Edward IV', written by a Londoner, depicts the journey from Holland as a purgatorial punishment for the king's sins:

> the wynde, the water spareth nodyr priynce ne kyng
> Haply that trowbill was for wykyd lyvyng.[58]

At Coventry he was 'beaten with the scourge of God', punished for his sins, shunned by the people and short of food.

The crucial turning point, when Edward was given a sign that he was God's chosen one, occurred at the abbey church at Daventry on Palm Sunday when 'Seint Anne schewyed a fayre miracle; a goode prognostique of good aventure that aftar shuld befall unto the kynge by the hand of God, and mediation of that holy matron Seynt Anne.'[59] The image of Edward's patron saint had been kept behind closed, painted doors; according to the custom for all images in churches, they were to remain hidden from Ash Wednesday to Easter Monday. In front of the throng of people pressed around the king the doors of the tabernacle opened and closed and opened again without human agency (like the doors in Camelot which admitted the Holy Grail)[60] and 'So the ymage stode open and discovent in sight of all the people there beynge.'[61] Edward mastered the situation the same way he did at the appearance of the parhelia before the Battle of Mortimer's Cross. He thanked and honoured God and St Anne, taking it 'as a good signe and token of a prosperous aventure that God wold send hym in that he had to do and remembrynge his promyse he honoured God and Seynt Anne in that same place and gave his offerings'. The promise, Edward would have explained to his followers, referred to his recent perilous voyage from Burgundy:

> The Kyng being out of his realme, in great trowble, thowghte and heviness, for the infortwne and adversite that was fallen hym, full often, and specially upon the sea, he prayed to God, our Lady, and Seint George, and amonges othar saynts, he specially prayed Seint Anne to helpe hym.[62]

In this way Edward was able to show that at times of crisis, in a storm at sea, he was able to tap into sources of great power within himself, and that he was assisted by higher powers. St Anne's name was therefore invoked along with the Virgin's before and after the subsequent battles of Barnet and Tewkesbury. Edward's identification with St Anne was to be commemorated in his copy of *La Fleur des Hystoires*, an historical collection by Jean Mansel containing a history of the Incarnation from the birth to the Assumption of the Virgin. A large illumination of the birth of the Virgin shows in the distance the meeting of Joachim and St Anne at the Golden Gate. In the border are the arms of Edward with his Garter and badge, the white rose and sun in splendour.[63]

The birth of the Virgin. This shows Edward's interest in the cult of St Anne. In the distance occurs the meeting of Joachim and St Anne at the Golden Gate. In the border are Edward's arms with the Garter, the Yorkist sun and white rose. (British Library Royal 18 E VI La fleur des Hystoires, *vols I and III, A Historical Collection by Jean Mansel containing a history of the incarnation from the birth to the Assumption of the Virgin, fo. 8)*

Another crucial point when God revealed his favour to Edward was the night before Barnet, and this too has strong echoes of the early morning appearance of the three suns at Mortimer's Cross. The author of the poem 'On the Recovery of the Throne by Edward IV' depicts a Job-like Edward at prayer on the Saturday night before the battle on Palm Sunday, like Christ in the garden at Gethsemane:

> God lett never prynce be so hevy in his hert
> As kynge Edwarde was all that hole nyghte.

There then appeared to the king in his darkness a sign of his resurrection:

> And aftur that shone a ster over his hede full bryghte,
> The syght of whiche made his enmys woo;
> It was a tokyn of victory, Goddis will was soo.[64]

Edward's skilful handling of the event enabled him to convert his past lapses into a source of strength, to mythologize his personal past and project himself as a returning prodigal, God's favoured son, who, after chastisement by God, has come back stronger than ever:

> Then sodenly uppone his knes the prynce did falle,
> Besechyng the good lorde and his seyntes alle
> His ryght hym to sende, and defende hym of his foo,
> And said ever, 'Goode Lorde, thy will be doo.'

He then asked God to send victory to the righteous side:

> And I promesse the, good lorde, my lyffe to amende,
> I knolege me a synner wrappid in woo.
> And all said with one voyse, 'Lord thy will be doo.'

The consequence of this prayer is the emergence of a formidable and empowered warrior:

> 'Avaunce baner,' quod the kynge, 'passe forth anone.
> In the name of the Trynyte and oure Lady bryghte,
> Seynt Edward, seynt Anne, and swete seynte Johan
> And in the name of seynte George, oure Ladis knygte,
> This day shew thy grett power and thy gret mygte,
> And brynge thy trew subjectes owte of payne and woo.'[65]

All stages of Edward's campaign were marked by religious processions and prayers. Services were held in Daventry parish church on Palm Sunday, in Westminster Abbey on 21 April on Edward's entry into London and on the Easter Monday after Barnet, when he presented the abbey with a banner riddled with arrow holes; and in Tewkesbury Abbey, where, despite the violence perpetrated in his name, Edward 'was received with procession and so conveyed through the church and the quere, to the high autre with grete devocion'. Before each battle Edward committed his cause to God and all the saints, in particular the Virgin, St Anne and St George. All his victories were dedicated to God and attributed to His intervention. A proclamation after Barnet referred to 'the God-given victory at the feast of the Passion', so that not only by descent and assent of Parliament but by diverse victories in battles 'the truth right and well for God appears evident to every person'. Before Tewkesbury Edward issued a proclamation condemning Margaret of Anjou as 'a Frenchwoman born, daughter of our adversary', and condemning her army as largely composed of Frenchmen levying war against a king whose title to the throne had been solemnly approved by Parliament and by 'God in diverse battles'. By the time Fauconberg's force had dispersed on hearing of the approach of Edward's army and of 'the great victories that God had sent him', it must have seemed that God was truly on Edward's side. He had fought in the six major battles of the Wars of the Roses: Northampton, Mortimer's Cross and Towton in 1461, Lose-cote Field in 1470, and Barnet and Tewkesbury in 1471 – and he

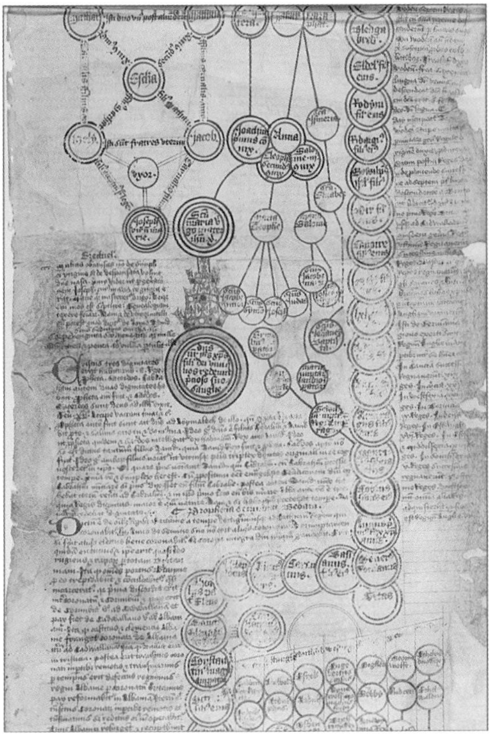

In the Genealogy of Edward King of Britain, *Christ, like Edward, is represented with three crowns. (Ashmole Roll 26)*

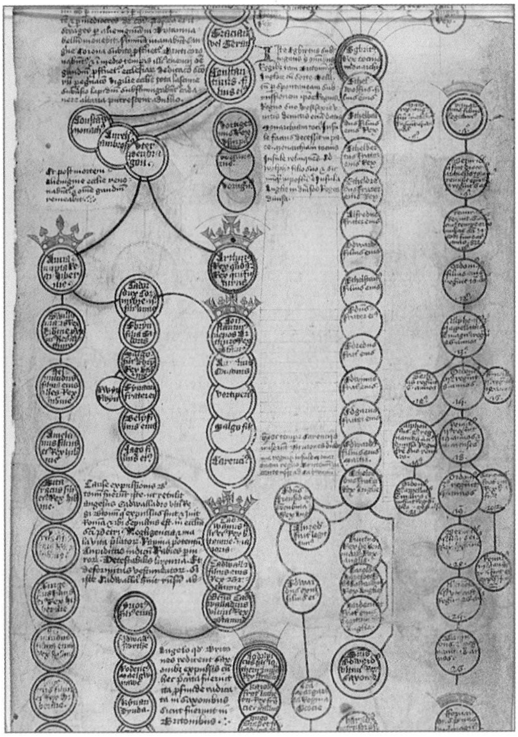

In the same genealogy, Arthur and Cadwallader are distinguished with gold crowns. (Ashmole Roll 26)

had never been defeated. The image of Edward as God's chosen knight and king was encouraged in poems such as the 'Balet of the King', which emphasized his recovery of his rightful title through God's help and his reluctance to shed Christian blood, an emphasis that was retained in the short version of the *Arrivall* that Edward sent to the Duke of Burgundy in 1472. Edward's redemptive role and his close links with David, God's chosen king, and even with Christ, were proclaimed in the reissuing of the prophecies and genealogies such as the *Genealogy of Edward King of Britain*. In this work King David, Christ and Edward are all prominently displayed, the latter two represented by three crowns.[66]

Edward's reconquest was also sustained by his identification with the heroes of antiquity. The other key figure in the 1471 version of the *Genealogy of Edward King of Britain* was Brutus, which was one of the cognomens assigned to Edward. Edward's arrival from exile in Burgundy enabled him to pose as the descendant of Brutus who would unite Britain. Once again the focus of his campaign, politically and symbolically, was therefore London, or New Troy, the city supposedly founded by Brutus. In the poem 'On the Recovery of the Throne by Edward IV', composed in 1471, the poet, thanking God for Edward's recovery of the throne, ignores Tewkesbury and concentrates on Barnet, which he depicts as the successful defence of New Troy, redeeming the original tragic fall of Troy, from which the British nation had evolved. Special praise was given to Richard duke of Gloucester, who commanded a division at this battle, as the husband of fortune, a Hector in his defence of the city.[67] Soon after the city was besieged by Fauconberg, and the poet singled out Clarence, Anthony Woodville and Hastings for similar praise:

O that nobill prynce and emperour flouere,
To sitt at London resorte he than.

It must have seemed that Edward was indeed the returning Arthur, and the poet, describing the victory procession led into the city by Gloucester, Edward, Hastings and Woodville, exclaimed:

Nothur Alisaunder ne Artur, ne no conqueroure
No better were acompenyd with nobill men.
Like none of the rounde tabulle were besyn,
Ryally horsid and aparelde in the fere of thayr foo.[68]

Edward's position as the Welsh king, enhanced since the death of Herbert at Edgecote in 1469 when Dafyd Llwyd described Edward as 'sprung from the trunk of alle old stocks', was confirmed with this victory. Guto'r Glyn interpreted Barnet as a revenge for Edgecote. With the redemption of New Troy the nation's soul, the Round Table, was restored.[69] Edward had always had a special relationship with this city; he seems to have understood its mythic significance, and in 1478 he gave orders for the rebuilding of its walls.

Another ideological factor that was as important in 1471 as in 1461 was the genealogical issue of Edward's descent from the house of Mortimer and the ancient kings of Britain. The reconquest was therefore seen as the fulfilment of God's will, the final extirpation of the Lancastrian usurpers. When Edward's ships were prevented from landing at Cromer and found their way to Ravenspur after a violent storm, it must have seemed that God was orchestrating things so that Edward would retrace Bolingbroke's footsteps. Edward's official chronicler, echoing the language of a genealogy of 1470,[70] noted that Edward was forced to land 'even in the same place where sometime the usurper Henry Derby, after called King Henry IV, landed, after his exile, contrary to and to the disobeyance of his soverayne lord, King Richard the II'. Edward capitalized on this. By retracing Bolingbroke's steps, even to the extent of repeating the assertion that he was merely claiming his father's duchy, and relying on Percy's cooperation, he had become God's instrument, eliminating all traces of the original act of violence against the divine will which had been revealed to the Yorkist prophet Richard Scrope. The Percies were integrated into this divine drama. Their genealogy was given new focus and their links with Edward's Mortimer line were stressed in the production of such works as the Percy Roll, which emphasized the joining of the lines of Percy and Mortimer at the beginning of the fifteenth century,[71] and the acquisition of the *Prophetic History of Britain* in 1469.[72] Although the Percies were involved in the deposition of Richard II in 1399 they could claim to have attempted to bring about the fulfilment of the Yorkist prophecies once they had joined the Mortimer line.

The miracle of the disclosure of the image of St Anne on Palm Sunday 7 April must have seemed another manifestation of God's interest in the restoration of the Mortimer line. Edward's nurse Anne Devereaux bore the same name as St Anne, but more importantly it was the name of his maternal grandmother. Anne Mortimer was the link to the line of Welsh princes. In the genealogical chronicles in the *Prophetic History of Britain* produced in the previous decade[73] and in the 1471 version of the *Genealogy of Edward King of Britain*,[74] there is a detailed rationalization of the descent of the crown to Edward through his grandmother Anne Mortimer, which is compared to the succession of Jesus Christ as King of Heaven through his maternal grandmother St Anne, Edward's patron saint.[75] *The Revelations of St Bridget* are also used to justify his succession through the female line. Edward was therefore able to suggest that this phenomenon was the latest in a series of divine interventions going back to the appearance of the angel to Cadwallader (Cadwallader was one of the cognomens assigned to Edward on this roll). Popular awareness of Edward's links to the Mortimer line were further encouraged by the production of the Yorkist version of the genealogical chronicle derived from Peter of Poitiers[76] and after the reconquest shorter versions of this roll in English, which omitted the biblical history, stressed the Lancastrian usurpation of the Mortimer inheritance. Another important saint invoked in the reconquest was Edward's namesake Edward the Confessor, whose vision of the healing of the severed green tree was applied to the restoration of the Mortimer line cut by Bolingbroke. This vision was copied on to the 1471 version of the *Genealogy of Edward King of Britain*.[77] Edward invoked the Confessor's name at all the battles in 1471 and on 21 April, after Neville had delivered Henry VI to his custody, he gave thanks to Edward the Confessor. On 27 April Edward invoked the name of Archbishop Scrope, who had sacrificed his life in defence of the crown's true heirs: 'for the right and title of our Auncestire, whose estate we now bere and have, died and suffered deth and martyrdom'.

There was clearly the same sophisticated, intellectual dimension to the reconquest as there had been in 1461, and again it was probably the alchemists in Edward's service, men like Robert Marshall, George Ripley, Thomas Norton and Friar Bungay, who encouraged him to see things in terms of myths and patterns, the unfolding of a great work. Thomas Norton, according to his great-grandson, accompanied Edward on his Burgundian exile, and a measure of the sort of advice he may have given his king when he was a near-penniless fugitive in Bruges can be seen in the work he later dedicated to Edward, the *Ordinal of Alchemy*. In the alchemist's retort, the place of the secret work, the ingredients must first be black and inert, forming the *nigredo*, but then, through the alchemists' art, life returns to the decayed corpse: through purification of the corrupt and brittle bones the work begins anew with distillation and redistillation, moving towards the goal of transmutation, or the re-emergence of the king. Ripley too may have remained in Burgundy and accompanied Edward on his return. For Ripley Edward's rejuvenation, his emergence from the years of sin and inertia, was an alchemical experiment, 'the secret process of the making of the red and white elixir', found with the help of the Trinity (which Edward evoked in all his successful campaigns).[78] The heart of this was the resurrection of the king from the *nigredo*. The process in 1471 was the same as it had been in 1461 and involved the surrender of the king's ego to the mythic dominants of the hero on a quest. Ripley was inspired by Edward's courageous voyage from Burgundy to use the motif of the alchemical work as a sea voyage towards a castle with the alchemist at the helm in *The Compound of Alchemy* which he dedicated to the king in 1471. However, he also referred to the king's wisdom undone by sin and compared him to David. In the Fifth Gate of Putrefaction he promised that from the blackness would come the strong colours of the rainbow. The sun rose from the waters of Noah's flood after 150 days and Noah planted a vineyard which brought forth grapes. Likewise the soul, after the darkness of purgatory, passes into paradise and the elements are joined without strife and the red king is reborn rejoicing in the wholeness and beauty of his white queen. By evoking images of the subsiding of Noah's flood, the rainbow and the emergence of the king from darkness, Ripley was recalling the alchemical motifs that occurred on the *Coronation Roll* commissioned for Edward's coronation in 1461,[79] and reapplying them to his triumph in 1471. He alluded to the squaring of the circle by advocating turning the elements so they did not strive to form a circle from a quadrangle.[80] He also alluded to the reunion of Edward and his queen and possibly the birth of their son, the *homunculus*: in alchemical terms this represented the stabilization of the warring elements and in political terms the birth of a male heir secured the succession, ensuring stability and peace in the kingdom.[81]

Edward's alchemists would therefore have encouraged the king and his supporters to read alchemical significance into the events surrounding the reconquest of the kingdom. The

This detail of the White Lion of March occurs on the brass of a Yorkist livery collar of suns and roses from the Memorial of Joos de Bul (d. 1484) which was formerly in the Hospital of St Juisse in Bruges, Belgium. (Geoffrey Wheeler)

triumph of Edward's badge of the rising sun in the mist of Barnet is a very alchemical image, and the confusion caused among Warwick's men by the similarity between Oxford's streaming star and Edward's ascendant sun suggested to contemporaries the operation of some kind of alchemical weather magic. Robert Fabyan, who was apprenticed to Sir Thomas Cook, who had served on the alchemy commissions, recalled that this mist had been conjured by Friar Bungay, who may have been regarded in Yorkist circles as a Merlin figure, using white magic to bring back his king.[82] Edward's alchemists may have seen Margaret of Anjou as a Medea practising the black arts. Describing the bad weather that prevented Margaret crossing the channel to join forces with Warwick, Fabyan commented that those ill-disposed to her explained the unfavourable wind which detained her in France as a heavenly injunction against her return to a land which she had already harmed so much. Those well-favoured interpreted it as a trick of the mysterious sorcerer Friar Bungay.[83]

Some of the symbols Edward used to celebrate the reconquest of the kingdom were alchemical. Naturally considerable use was made of the badge of the sun in splendour which appeared on ceilings in Tewkesbury Abbey and in such churches as those at Rainham in Kent, Bramley in Hampshire and Tortworth in Gloucestershire. The badge of a six-rayed sun, gilded with an amalgam of gold and mercury, was worn on the belts, livery collars and necklaces of the king's followers, and can be seen on the effigies of those who fought at Barnet and Tewkesbury, such as the monument of William Lord Saye in Broughton church, Oxfordshire. Edward's prayers to St George before Barnet and Tewkesbury and in the services of thanksgiving may be related to the alchemical conceit of seizing the gold, the kingdom, from the jaws of the dragon. His gratitude to this saint, who was his mentor, was such that he presented a relic in the form of a skull of St George to St George's chapel,

In Rainham Church, Kent, a wooden ceiling vault originally forming a canopy of honour above the rood screen, is decorated with the Yorkist rose en soleil *of King Edward IV. Sir Thomas de Leger who lived in the parish and married the king's sister Anne probably installed the ceiling. (Geoffrey Wheeler)*

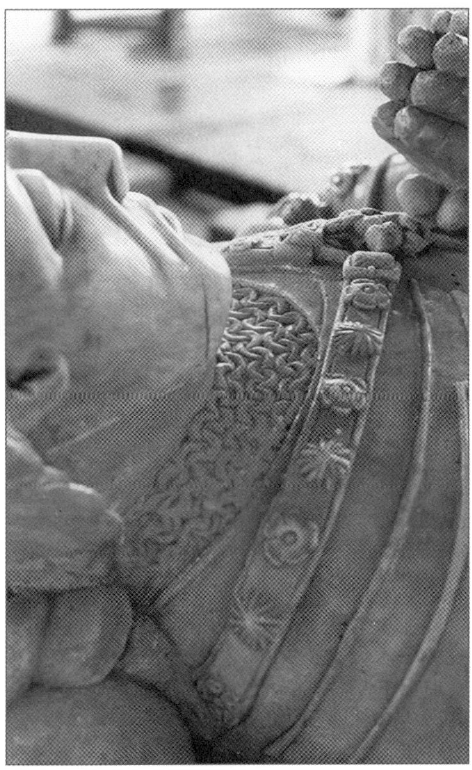

A Yorkist collar on the effigy of William Lord Saye (d. 1471) of Broughton in Oxfordshire. (Geoffrey Wheeler)

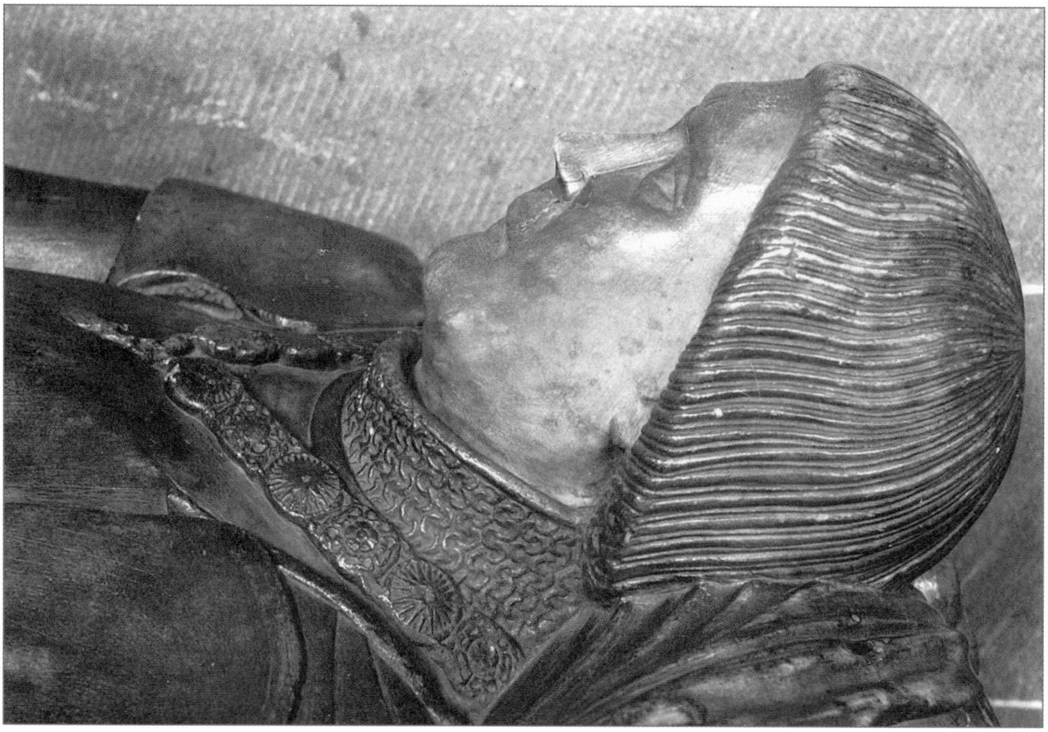

Sir John Savage (d. 1495), Macclesfield parish church, Cheshire. Around his neck he wears the Yorkist livery collar of suns and roses. He was knighted on the battlefield of Tewkesbury in 1471 by Edward IV. (Geoffrey Wheeler)

Windsor, and when he undertook the rebuilding of the chapel in 1475 a cycle of St George images, including the slaying of the dragon, was carved on the choir. Edward, as we have seen, also conceived of the reconquest of his kingdom in terms of the capture of the Golden Fleece, and this was symbolized by the way he had the fleece hanging from the belt of the Garter in a number of the manuscripts he commissioned in Burgundy, especially Waurin's *Chronicles of the English*.

The alchemists were also aware that their task was not over once the reconquest of the kingdom was complete. Ripley was at pains to point out to Edward that with the acquisition of this treasure came responsibilities. He began the *Compound of Alchemy* with a personal letter to the king, urging him to use his victory as an opportunity to use alchemy to heal the nation's wounds, and to create a new golden era of national peace and reconciliation:

> O honourable Lord, and most victorious Knight,
> With grace and vertue abundently endewed,
> the safegard of England and maintainer of right;
> That God you loveth, and indeed he hath well shewed:
> Wherefore I trust this lond shalbe renewed
> With joy and riches, with charitie and peace,
> So that olde ranckors new understrewed,
> Tempestuous troubles, and wretchedes shall cease.[84]

However, this hope of a new beginning and a reconciliation of opposites depended, Ripley thought, on Edward's showing clemency to his political opponents:

> And therefore sith I see by tokens right evident,
> that God you guideth, and how that ye be vertuous,
> Hating sinne, and all such as be insolent,
> How that also manslaughter to you is odious,
> Upon the judgement also that ye be piteous,
> Me seemeth ruthe it were but that you should live longe:
> For of your great fortune you are not presumptous
> Nor vengeable of spirit to revenge you of each wrong.[85]

Apart from the executions of those who sought sanctuary in Tewkesbury Abbey, Edward followed this advice. There were only two executions in Kent after the Fauconberg rebellion. Perhaps Ripley had in mind Edward's treatment of his fellow alchemists, many of whom found themselves on the wrong side in the fluctuating political situation of 1468–71. John Delves and Langstrother, as members of Margaret of Anjou's entourage, could expect no mercy and they were executed after Tewkesbury. The prior of St John's beheading was depicted in a Burgundian copy of the short version of the *Arrivall*.[86] George Neville was pardoned a few days after Tewkesbury, and Fortescue and Thomas Cook were pardoned in February 1472, partly on the intervention of Margaret of York. Fortescue in particular, with his combination of political, theoretical skills and alchemical interests, would have been regarded by Ripley as a key figure in creating this new order. His attainder for treason was reversed, and he became a member of Edward's council in 1474. In his *On the Law of Nature*, Fortescue pronounced his sentence on the question of the Yorkist title through the female line and Edward's triumph through adversity 'the purity of gold, the choicest of metals, though the gold be cleft, cannot be known until it be proved by trial of the fiery furnace'.[87] William Worcester too obtained a general pardon.[88]

Ripley of course was right to issue these words of caution in 1471. There was a need to rebuild the nation and this would require different myths than those that had sustained Edward during the conquest and reconquest of his kingdom. Malory died in March 1471, just before Edward's invasion, and even he realized that myths of courage and loyalty would not hold together the court. What was needed were more pragmatic, rational, scientific principles that could be deployed to build a community, when service to the state became more important than the Arthurian ideal of service to a lord; and to this end Edward and his advisers would turn to the myths and history of Rome which they had inherited from Henry V and which they had also encountered during their Burgundian exile and which would guide them in the creation of a more rational, impersonal political order, one in which men such as Fortescue would play their part.

NOTES

1. Salomon Trismosin, *Splendour Solis*, ed. J.K. Jordon (1920).
2. All Souls College, Oxford, MS Gg1, fos 1–223.
3. For Ripley's recipes see Bodley MS Rawl poet 121 fo. 77; Bodley MS Ashmole 1426; BL MS Sloane 3520 B fos 173v–175. For Ripley's tomb see BL MS Vitellius EX, fo. 251v; Bodley MS Ashmole 971, 972, fo. 300b.

4. Norton, *Ordinal of Alchemy*, ll. 2584–6.
5. Photo supplied by Geoffrey Wheeler.
6. Bodley Ashmole Roll 40.
7. On the order see D.J.D. Boulton, *The Knights of the Crown* (Woodbridge, 1897), p. 394.
8. McKendrick, 'Classical Mythology and Ancient History', 31.
9. Kekewich, *MLR*, 66 (1973).
10. BL MS Royal 15 E IV; BL MS Royal 14 E IV, vol. 1, fo. 14.
11. For text see C.A.J. Armstrong, 'Some Verses by Jean Mielot on Edward IV and Richard earl of Warwick', *Medium Aevum*, 8 (1939), 193–7; and for translation of the poem see L. Visser-Fuchs, '*Sanguinis haustor*: Drinker of Blood. A Burgundian view of England, 1471', *The Ricardian*, vii, 92 (1986), 213–19.
12. Bodley MS Poet Rawl. 121, fo. 74.
13. BL MS Harl. 1736; S.J. Lang, 'John Bradmore and His Book *Philomena*', *Social History of Medicine*, vol. v (1992), pp. 121–30.
14. BL MS Harl. 1736, fo. 133. For fifteenth-century manuscripts attributing this vision to Dastin, see Bodley MS Ashmole 1486 fos 74–5 and Cambridge, Trinity College Library MS 1122 fos 158v–159r.
15. Ibid, fos 94v–96.
16. See BL MS Sloane 3667, a paper manuscript. *The Bosom Book* occurs on fos 124–59. The note referring to Norton's translation of *The Bosom Book* is on fo. 124. The alchemical table with Ripley's name and the date occurs on fos 23v and 146. Also in this manuscript in the same sixteenth-century hand is Ripley's *Epistle to King Edward IV* on fos 157b–160 which may have been copied from the original manuscript in Ripley's hand. *The Vision* of Ripley also occurs in Bodley MS Ashmole 1480 pt 1 fo. 36 which is also a sixteenth-century manuscript, and Bodley MS Poet Rawl. 121, fo. 73 and Bodley MS Ashmole 1459, p. 34.
17. Corpus Christi College, Oxford, MS 172, fo. 42.
18. The cycle now survives only in the coloured drawings of Dugdale; Riches, *St George*, pp. 73–7.
19. N.F. Blake, *William Caxton and English Literary Culture* (London, 1991), 82–4; BL MS Royal 18 D ii.
20. Trinity College, Cambridge, MS 516.
21. J.J. Smith, C.A.S Quarton Series (1846), Cambridge Antiquarian Series.
22. Gonville & Caius College, Cambridge, MS 249.
23. Ibid; L. Coote, *Prophecy and Public Affairs*, p. 227.
24. Gonville & Caius College, Cambridge, MS 249, fo. 246v; Coote, *Prophecy and Public Affairs*, p. 227.
25. Norfolk County Record Office MS Bradfer Lawrence Xa/15; Coote, *Prophecy and Public Affairs*, p. 228.
26. Norfolk County Record Office MS Bradfer Lawrence Xa/15; Coote, *Prophecy and Public Affairs*, p. 228.
27. Bodley Roll 5.
28. Bodley MS Lyell 33.
29. Trinity College, Cambridge, MS G3, a Latin roll issued around May 1471; Lambeth Palace, 1176; and Queens' College, Cambridge, written between November 1470 and April 1472.
30. The death of Edward of Lancaster is mentioned but this may have been added later.
31. Bodley MS 623 and BL MS Cotton Vesp. E VII.
32. BL MS Cotton Vesp. E VII.
33. Bodley MS Arch Selden B.10.
34. Bodley Roll 5.
35. BL MS Cotton Vesp. E VII and Bodley MS 623.
36. BL MS Royal II G XL, fo. 42.
37. BL MS Royal 15 E IV, vol 1, fo. 15.
38. *The Historie of the Arrivall of Edward IV*, ed. J. Bruce in *Three Chronicles of the Reign of Edward IV*, intro. K. Dockray (Sutton, 1988). For the short prose version by Nicholas Harpsfield, clerk of the signet, see L. Visser-Fuchs, 'Nicholas Harpsfield, Clerk of the Signet, Author and Murderer', *The Ricardian*, x, 125 (1994). C. Richmond and M. Kekewich, 'The Search for Stability 1461–83', in *The Politics of Fifteenth-Century England*, pp. 43–67.
39. Peterhouse College, Cambridge, MS 190.
40. *Arrivall*, p. 149.
41. Ibid, p. 7.
42. Ibid, p. 5.
43. Ibid, p. 7.
44. Ibid, p. 14.
45. Ibid, p. 16.
46. Ibid, p. 17.
47. Ibid, p. 19.
48. Ibid, p. 16.

49. Ibid, pp. 18–19. See also *Croyland Chronicle*, p.125.
50. *Arrivall*, p. 27.
51. Ibid, p. 28.
52. Ibid, p. 29.
53. Besançon Bibliotheque municipale MS 1168; L. Visser-Fuchs, '"Edward IV's Memoir on Paper", to Charles, Duke of Burgundy, the so-called short version of the *Arrivall*', *Nottingham Medieval Studies* (1992), p. 36; R.W. Hammond, *The Battles of Barnet and Tewkesbury* (Stroud, 1990), p. 213, App. 2.
54. *Arrivall*, p. 32 (176).
55. Ibid, p. 32 (178).
56. Ibid, p. 37 (183).
57. Ibid, p. 39 (185).
58. Wright, *Political Songs*, pp. 271–82. BL MS Reg. 17 D xv, fo. 327.
59. *Arrivall*, p. 13 (159).
60. Hardynge's *Chronicle*, p. 130.
61. The church no longer survives. Between 1752 and 1758 it was replaced by the present church of the Holy Cross.
62. *Arrivall*, p. 13 (159).
63. BL MS Royal E VI, fo. 8.
64. BL MS Royal D xv, fos 327–32v. Also in this manuscript is Fortescue's declaration giving up his old opinions against the Yorkist succession, copied by John Multon, stationer; Wright, *Political Songs*, pp. 271–82; Rymer, *Foedera*, xi, pp. 709–11.
65. Wright, *Political Poems and Songs*, p. 275.
66. Ashmole Roll 26.
67. BL MS Royal 17 D xv, fo. 327; printed T. Wright, *Political Songs*, 2 vols (Rolls Series, 1859–61), vol. 2, pp. 271–87.
68. Wright, *Political Poems and Songs*, vol. 2, p. 279.
69. The family seat of the Herbert family in Monmouthshire was called Troy House.
70. Bodley MS Lyell 33.
71. Bodley Roll 5.
72. BL MS Vesp E VII.
73. BL MS Vesp E VII and Bodley MS 623.
74. Ashmole Roll 26.
75. In Ashmole Roll 26 this discussion of Edward's succession through the female line occurs on the verso of the roll.
76. Bodley MS Lyell 33.
77. Verso of Ashmole Roll 26.
78. Ashmole, *Theatrum Chemicum Britannicum*, p. 110.
79. Philadelphia Free Library, MS E 201. U. Szulakowska, 'The Pseudo-Lullian Origins of Geroge Ripley's Maps and Routes as developed by Michael Maier', *Cosmos* 9, Edinburgh, 1993, p. 108.
80. Ibid.
81. This image also occurs in the *Ripley Scrolls*, especially the tree bearing grapes.
82. Fabian, *Chronicles*, p. 661.
83. A.H. and I.D. Thornley (eds), *The Great Chronicle of London* (1937), p. 214. The chronicle was probably by Robert Fabyan. See A. Sutton, 'Sir Thomas Cook', in *Guildhall Studies in London History*, iii (1978), p. 36; Gross, *Dissolution of Lancastrian Kingship*, p. 23; 'The Great Chronicle', Guildhall Library MS 3313, fo. 187.
84. Ashmole, *Theatrum Chemicum Britannicum*, p. 109; *Compound of Alchemy*, ed. Linden, p. 89.
85. *Theatrum Chemicum Britannicum*, p. 109; *Compound of Alchemy*, p. 89.
86. Ghent Universiteitsbibliotheck MS. See Visser-Fuchs, 'Edward IV's Memoir'.
87. Fortescue, *Works*, ed. Clermont, p. 331.
88. *Rot. Parl.*, vol. vi, p. 69.

CHAPTER 9

Ancient Rome and the Cultural Foundations of Edward's Second Reign

> We are not born for ourselves alone –, but our country claims for itself one part of our birth, and our friends another. – Men are born for the sake of men, so that they may be able to assist one another. Consequently, we ought in this to follow nature as our leader, to contribute to the common stock the things that benefit everyone together, and, by the exchange of dutiful services, by giving and receiving expertise and effort and means, to bind fast the fellowship of men with each other.
>
> Cicero, *De officiis*, *Bk I, 22*

Until 1471 the dominant impression of Edward is of an inspirational, erratic king who at his most impressive, usually in times of danger, was motivated by powerful archetypes from Britain's largely mythical past, imaginative forces that galvanized his leadership. There was, however, another important source of inspiration, especially after his reconquest of the kingdom, that determined his public self-image and even more crucially influenced the actions and political outlook of his courtiers. This was the political, military and philosophical outlook of the ancient Romans, which had begun to make an impact during the reign of Henry V. Edward's court in the second reign was characterized by a proliferation of images of the king as a Roman emperor, and his courtiers emulated the public and private lives of Rome's leading senators. This was facilitated by the literary activities of some of these courtiers, who made the literature of Rome available to the governing classes in vernacular translations, and the printing enterprises of William Caxton, all of which encouraged the development of an informed and broadly based educational system modelled on that of the Romans.

The interest in antiquity at Edward's court went deeper than the transmission of popular myths. There was a real scholarly dimension to the discovery of Roman culture among the clerical officials who trained in the 'studia humanitas' in Italy to further their diplomatic and administrative careers. Edward valued the services of men trained in classical rhetoric, but it is important not to draw an arbitrary distinction between these so called 'humanists' and the translators and adaptors of classical history and myth who cannot be dismissed as crude popularizers. All were concerned with the image of the king and were employed to this end. The more technically accomplished classicists were employed on an ad hoc basis as proctors at the papal Curia in Rome. Robert Fleming, who studied at Padua in 1441 and at Ferrara University (1447–50), where he learned Greek, and who transcribed Cicero's *De officiis*, became a royal proctor in 1455, and although the Lancastrian affiliations of his family prevented him securing royal preferment in Edward's first reign, he was in Edward's service in the 1470s, and even wrote a poem in his honour, describing him as the embodiment of the classical virtue of prudence.[1] John Shirwood, a protégé of George Neville, learned Greek in 1455 under Emmanuel of Constantinople. He had an extensive library and eventually became a papal notary in Edward's second reign.[2] John Gunthorpe completed a copy of Seneca's *Tragedies* in August 1460, and studied poetry at the University of Ferrara and Greek under Guamino da Verone. At Ferrara he became acquainted with Worcester's friend John Free, whom he followed to Rome where he became a papal chaplain in 1462. Gunthorpe left for England with Free's library in 1462. In 1467 he became secretary and chaplain to Queen Elizabeth Woodville and the king's chaplain. In the same year he was appointed envoy to the king of Castile and in 1468 he attended Margaret of York at her marriage to Charles duke of Burgundy, giving two orations. His library of twenty-three manuscripts reflects the Latin curriculum of the *Studia humanitas* and contained Cicero's *Dream of Scipio*, *De amicitia* and *De officiis*, Plato's *Timeum* and a Latin translation of Homer's *Odyssey*. Gunthorpe had other intellectual interests relevant to Edward's kingship and owned a *Polychronicon* and Albertus Magnus's *De animalibus libri*, which may indicate alchemical interests.[3] John Tiptoft, earl of Worcester and constable of the court of chivalry, went to Rome in 1461 on a commission to carry the king's obedience and congratulations to Pope Pius II on his accession. Tiptoft, like Humphrey duke of Gloucester, was a collector of the writings of antiquity. He owned an English manuscript containing Seneca's *Proverbs* and two tracts on medicine; but like Humphrey duke of Gloucester he was also a collector of Italian manuscripts, including: Suetonius's *De Claris Grammaticus Rhetoribusque*, Tacitus's *Dialogus de Oratoribus Claris*, completed in 1462,[4] Lucretius's *De rerum natura*, made in Florence[5] and the *Astronomicum* of Bosinio of Parma, containing under Aries a digression on the Golden Fleece.[6] Tiptoft's gifts of rhetoric were such that after one speech the Pope (according to his friend John Free) claimed Tiptoft to be 'above all princes of his age' and 'one worthy to be compared in virtue and eloquence with the greatest emperors of Greece and Rome'. George Neville, a patron of many of these scholars, was himself a student of antiquity. One manuscript displaying his coat of arms has a collection of the sayings of philosophers such as Diogenes and the dramatists Sophocles and Euripides, expounding on the virtuous life, and a prologue addressed to Neville, extolling his great fame and virtue.[7] This classical ideal of the good life was something Neville cultivated with the papal legate Stephano Trento, bishop of Lucca, who visited England in 1466 to collect a papal tenth for a crusade. On 20 June 1468 Stephano wrote to Neville on the subject of cultivating this life, exhibiting the sophisticated Italian's horror of Neville's enjoyment of such English rustic diversions as hunting.[8]

These scholars were infatuated with Italy, with the soil that had nourished the Roman civilization and its ancient language. Tiptoft explored the whole of Rome at around the time that Pius II issued a bull designed to protect the ancient monuments.[9] Anthony Woodville undertook his Italian tour in 1475–6, and with his companions John Lord Scrope and John Butler the sixth earl Ormond he visited Rome (where they were robbed of their jewels).[10] These 'humanist' diplomats had a sympathy with the cruder popularized versions of ancient culture. They too were enamoured of the myths of antiquity and their applicability to the king they served. Tiptoft also owned Lydgate's *Fall of Princes* and he was the author of the *Declamacion of Noblesse*, sharing Lydgate's vision of imperial Britain. He wrote the chancellor a letter from Padua referring to the great benefits he had gained from studying at Oxford, 'our second Athens'.[11] William Worcester shared Tiptoft's scholarly interest in classical languages: he owned Free's manuscript of the plays of Euripides but he also wrote the *Boke of Noblesse*, which was concerned with the assimilation of ancient myths and history in the British monarchy. Worcester recorded in his notebooks much of the history, philosophy, tragic drama and poetry of the ancient world. His particular heroes were Cicero, whose works he listed[12] and whose death he recorded in his *Itinerarium*, and Seneca, whose letters he copied.[13] Even the cultivated George Neville was closely involved in the proliferation of myths around Edward in the early years of his reign. However, their popularization owes much more to Burgundian than Italian influence, and in this the court of the dukes of Burgundy carried on the role previously fulfilled by that of Charles V in facilitating the availability of French translations of the classics and didactic and chronicle adaptations of Roman history and philosophy. These were to play an increasingly important role in determining the character of Edward's reign after the marriage of Margaret duchess of York to Charles the Bold in 1468, and especially after Edward's exile to Burgundy in 1471, when classical myths and ancient history were to play an increasingly important part in the king's image and policies. The real Romanization of Edward's court was to take place after his return from exile following the collapse of his Camelot, so poignantly captured by Malory. In the aftermath of the disintegration of his Arthurian dream, there seems to have been an increasing dependence on the myths and history of antiquity to rejuvenate the dynasty.

Edward and his courtiers, as the generation which succeeded Henry V, Bedford and Lydgate, were brought up on the myths and history of antiquity derived from the French court culture of the late fourteenth century. Lydgate, Worcester and Stephen Scrope had studied, copied, adapted and translated the story of Troy in Ovid's *Metamorphoses* from Italian translations of writers such as Christine de Pisan. Lydgate was also the author of an encyclopaedia of mythology, the *Siege of Thebes*. But during the 1460s there occurred in Burgundy an intensification of interest in antiquity in the seamless band of myth and history from stories of Thebes, Troy, Aeneas, Alexander and Rome to the time of Julius Caesar.[14] Unlike the Italian humanists, the Burgundian nobility read their classics in French translations, as did the English. Charles the Bold kept his secretaries busy translating Caesar, Xenophon, Cicero and Sallust. He ordered Valerius Maximus and Titus Livy to be read to him at his camp at Neuss.[15] The dukes of Burgundy, as patrons of the Order of the Golden Fleece, had a special interest in the story of Jason. The Burgundian Raoul Lefevre drew on the *Ovid Moraleaux*, the *Genealogia deorum* and the prose *Roman de Troie*, found in *Histoire Ancienne*, for his *Histoire de Jason*, the first version of which was dedicated to Philip the Good and completed in 1460, and the second in 1467.[16] Lefevre claimed in his introduction that the duke 'all his time inclined to hear, live and see the ancient histories from his singulere passetymes'. Also at the Burgundian court and at the instigation of Charles the Bold, Guillame Fillostre produced his *Troison de Jason*, after he had delivered a sermon as chancellor of the Golden Fleece at a chapter meeting in 1468. One of the most important translators of classical myth at this court was Jean Mielot. In 1460 he revised Christine de Pisan's *Epitre d'Othea* for Duke Philip, and in 1468 he translated into French Boccaccio's *Genealogia deorum*, a scholarly reference book on classical myth. This work was the source for the *Receuil Histoire des Troie* which wove the story of Hercules around the fall of two Troys and was produced in 1464.

The contents of the Burgundian ducal library reflected this interest in classical mythology. By 1467 Philip the Good had acquired an *Ovid Moralized* in two volumes, an *Othea*, two copies of *Des casibus*, four manuscripts of *Epitre d'Othea*, Seneca's *Tragoedia*, Lefevre's *Histoire de Jason*, and an allegorical poem on the Golden Fleece, addressed to Philip shortly after 1454. Lord Louis de Gruuthuyse, the governor of the Netherlands, was another collector of translations of the works of antiquity in manuscripts. Of the 175 volumes he owned, which included the standard collections on Troy and the history of Rome and works by such authors as Aristotle, Livy, Caesar, Ovid and Valerius Maximus, only five were in Latin; the rest were translations. In the 1460s Gruuthuyse had two manuscripts made of books one and three of Lefevre's *Receuil* and another of Christine de Pisan's *Othea*, and around 1471 he acquired Lefevre's *Histoire de Jason* with its dedication to Louis.

In this same period the dukes of Burgundy and their leading courtiers were commissioning and collecting French translations of Roman history. In 1454 Jean Mansel's *Histoires Romains*, which used Bersuire's French translation of Livy's History of Rome, *Ab urbe condita*, was dedicated to Philip the Good. The most important manifestation of the Burgundian court's interest in the world of ancient Rome through intermediary adaptations and translations of early humanist texts was the work of Jean Mielot, who was in the service of Philip duke of Burgundy from 1448 to 1467. In 1460–3 he translated into French for Duke Philip the *Romuleon*,[17] Livy's History of Rome, the main source for accounts of early history and the Republican period, and Suetonius's *Lives of the Caesars* for the account of the emperors from Augustus to Domitian. Unlike the *Faits des Romans*, this text was not in any original French compilation from Latin sources but was a close translation of a Latin text of Italian origin, prepared in Bologna between 1361 and 1364. A manuscript of Valerius Maximus's collection of anecdotes of ancient Rome, the *Memorabilia*, was executed for Philip the Good in the second quarter of the fifteenth century. Another vernacular adaptation of Roman history, the *Faits des Romans*, originally composed in 1213–14 as a history of the twelve Caesars, became popular in Burgundy by 1470 in the form of a biography of Julius Caesar which drew on the works of Lucan, Suetonius, Sallust and Julius Caesar himself. It was after 1450 that the ducal library of Burgundy made its greatest number of acquisitions of Roman history, including the *Historia Ancienne*, three copies of the *Faits des Romains* and three of Lebeque's translation of Bruni's commentary *De primo bello*, composed in 1415. Some of these arrived from the library of Charles V via Anthony Woodville, including an illuminated manuscript of Bersuire's translation of the *Faits des Romains* made for Charles V, which had been owned by John duke of Bedford.[18]

This interest in antiquity had an important visual dimension. From 1460, when Mielot's translation of *Romuleon* was illustrated for the Philip the Good, until 1480 Netherlandish artists produced luxury volumes of translations of the *Memorabilia*, the *Faits des Romains*, the *Romuleon* and the Commentaries for the Burgundian court, illustrated with scenes from Roman history. Such events were also depicted on tapestries. Charles the Bold acquired a tapestry showing Hannibal's struggle with Rome just before his accession in 1467, and in May 1470 he obtained another showing the early part of the story of Rome, the struggle between Albus and the Romans during the reign of Tullius Hostilius. Charles the Bold's adviser, Philippe de Commines, wrote that 'one of the surest means to make a man wise is to have him read ancient history and learn how to conduct and guard himself and how to manage his affairs wisely, according to histories and examples of his ancestors'.[19]

Burgundian illuminated books and tapestries enabled the duke of Burgundy and his entourage to live imaginatively in the world of ancient Rome. During Margaret of York's residence in Bruges for her marriage celebrations in July 1468 her dressing chamber was adorned with a tapestry which, according to a contemporary chronicler, showed 'the histoire de la Bonne Lucresse' as an example of the ultimate sacrifice of a noblewoman and as a witness to her fidelity to her husband. In 1472–4 Jehan de Chesne translated the *Commentaries of Caesar* into French, peppering the text with comparisons between Caesar and the duke of Burgundy to dissuade Charles from rash action. In 1474, while on campaign, Charles the Bold had read to him Valerius Maximus, Titus Livy and a book about

Alexander the Great and his battles.[20] Charles took his copy of the *Romuleon* with him on his campaigns, and had it with him when he was defeated at Neuss in 1477.

Once Edward was settled in his kingdom again, he established himself as a collector and patron of the historic and didactic literature of antiquity popular in the Burgundian court.[21] In this he was no mere slavish imitator of his brother-in-law and his courtiers but a discerning observer of the history and myths of antiquity which were playing an increasingly important role in the self-image of the king and his court. As early as 1462 Edward signified the importance of the royal book collection when an officer with the status of yeoman of the crown was put in charge of the king's books. This is described in the *Household Book of Edward IV*, compiled in 1471–2, when the library was part of the inner chamber of the king's household.[22] Edward was the first English king for whom there is evidence of serious, formal collecting of books; in a sense he was the founding father of the present British Library. Thirty volumes of elaborate copies of historical and literary works collected by Edward formed the core of the royal library which was made over to the newly instituted British Museum in 1757 by George II. The surviving volume of Wardrobe accounts for the summer of 1480 suggests that Edward was in the habit of carrying this library of large manuscripts around with him from palace to palace.[23]

Most of Edward's collecting was done in the period between 1479 and 1483, thanks to the financial security offered by his pension from Louis XI in 1475. Edward's library was strikingly similar to those of Charles the Bold and Louis de Gruuthuyse, and the impact of Edward's six-month sojourn in the Netherlands and the subsequent cultural contacts between the two courts, including the visits to Edward of Louis de Gruuthuyse in 1472 and Margaret of York in 1480, cannot be discounted. However, Edward was more narrowly focused on the literature of antiquity than any of these other collectors.[24] Among the royal manuscripts in the British Library are twenty-one large illuminated volumes from the South Netherlands which are shown by their heraldry to have been owned by Edward IV. Some are dated 1479, and this coincides with a payment made to a foreign merchant, Philip Mais, for books brought for the king from foreign parts in that year. The manuscripts were illuminated in the Netherlands and dispatched to England singly or over a couple of years. They are not straightforward copies of standard Burgundian texts, haphazardly or passively acquired. Fifteen of the twenty-one surviving works bearing Edward's arms contain historical texts with historical lessons, most from antiquity.

The manuscript that most evocatively shows Edward's interest in ancient Rome and his identification with these times is *La Grande Histoire Cesar*,[25] which bears the arms of Edward IV and his sons, and his devices the rose et soleil. The colophon says it was compiled from Lucan, Suetonius, Sallust and Caesar at the command of Edward IV in 1479. Throughout the text, accompanying scenes from Caesar's life and conquests, occur Edward's badge, the white rose and sun in splendour. The main text, *Le Fait des Romains*, or *Le Fait de Julius Cesar*, is a biography of Julius Caesar, subsequently revised for the king. It is followed by a brief account of the character of subsequent emperors in the west up to the death of Frederick II in 1256. Unlike other manuscripts of the *Faits des Romains*, this manuscript was specifically revised and illuminated for Edward IV. Another copy of this work contains the same colophon, mentioning the king.[26] In seeking a comprehensive mirror of Roman history, Edward commissioned in 1480 the production in the Netherlands of *Le Livre Romuleon continant les fais des Romans*. Edward's copy, accompanied with lavishly illustrated scenes from Roman history, also has the date of Mielot's original translation, 1463.[27] Mielot, who celebrated the invasion of Britain in terms of the conquest of the Argonauts, probably entered Edward's service through the connections of Elizabeth Woodville (her uncle Louis of Luxembourg, owner of four tapestries of Julius Caesar and two manuscripts of Bersuire's translation of the *Faits des Romains*, was Mielot's patron) rather than through Burgundian channels. Edward's copy of the *Romuleon* contained his arms, the rose et soleil borne by an angel and the Garter belt with the Golden Fleece. It is symbolically significant that this occurs in the border of a full-page illumination of the birth of Rome showing the wolf suckling Romulus and Remus. In the background is the idealized city of New Troy.[28] The text covers the story of Rome from Romulus and Remus to the reign of Domitian. Suetonius is the main source for the accounts of the Caesars from Augustus to Domitian, and Livy's History of Rome provides most of the information for the early Republican period.[29] Edward also owned a manuscript entitled *Titus Livius*, which may have been Bersuire's translation of Livy's History.[30] The *Romuleon* and the Livy were complemented by Edward's ownership of Valerius Maximus's collection of stories from Roman history, *Dicta et facta memorabilia*, which also bears his arms, the white rose with the Garter belt and Golden Fleece, in the border of an illustration showing the translator at work.[31] Broader works of ancient history acquired by the king included Jean Mansel's *la Fleur des Hystoires* (a universal history popular in Burgundy and illustrated for Edward between 1470 and 1480 in Flanders with his arms and the badge of the blazing sun),[32] Xenophon's *Cyropoedia* (containing the royal arms), translated into French by Vasco de Lucerna in 1470,[33] and Josephus's *Antiquities judaiques*, a French translation from the end of the fourteenth century.[34]

Edward did not just surpass his brother-in-law as a purposeful collector of French versions of the historical and didactic literature of antiquity; he was the patron of and focus for English translations and adaptations of such literature. Of most importance for Edward in his second reign was the didactic literature that applied the wisdom of antiquity to social and political life. Tiptoft, before his death, had translated *De controversia de nobilitate* into the *Declamacion of Noblesse*. This used the learning of antiquity as a basis for guides for the behaviour of the nobility. Chief Justice Fortescue, after his return from exile in 1471, while in the service of Edward, addressed his reflections on the English political system in *De laudibus legum Angliae* (*In Praise of the Laws of England*), which was heavily influenced by his expressed admiration for Roman government. William Worcester rededicated and adapted his *Boke of Noblesse* for Edward IV in 1474–5. One of Worcester's sources was *Le Quadrilogue Invectif*, originally written in France in 1424 by Alan Chartier, a French diplomat who analysed the decline of French chivalry using ancient Rome as a model of military virtue, and who called on his countrymen to use the example of the Romans to revive courage and virtue. *Le Quadrilogue Invectif* was translated in the 1470s, probably by one of Edward IV's courtiers, and was intended, like Worcester's work, to encourage the king to revive the glories of Henry V's reign.[35] The most important translator and adapter of didactic teachings based on Roman literature was the king's brother-in-law Anthony Woodville. During this decade he translated into English Christine de Pisan's *Livre du Corps Policie*, a mirror for princes drawn largely from Roman history, which he probably intended to present as a gift to his executor, Richard Haute. A copy of the original *Livre du Corps Policie* appeared in the royal library, probably through Elizabeth Woodville. Christine de Pisan's *Epitre d'Othea*, together with Lull's *Book of the Order of Chivalry* and Jean de Courcy's *Chemin de Vaillance*, appears in another of Edward's manuscripts containing his arms, an invocation to the Trinity and an illustration of the Golden Fleece hanging from the Garter belt.[36] Another copy of the *Epitre d'Othea* occurs in Edward's collection, together with that quarry of the alchemists, Ovid's *Metamorphoses*.[37] In 1477 Woodville completed his translation of the *Dicts and Sayings of the Philosophers*, probably as a Christmas presentation to Edward IV, as shown in a miniature in one copy of the work.[38] In the following year he translated Christine de Pisan's *Book of Proverbs* into English. William Caxton translated such literature for members of the court. In 1475 he translated *The Book and Game of Chess* into English for George duke of Clarence. In the spring of 1480 he turned Ovid's *Metamorphoses* into French. In 1483 he translated and dedicated to the city of London *Cato*, a book of advice written by a citizen of Rome for his son. Pietro Carmeliano, who came to England in 1480 and found employment as a chancery clerk, dedicated his copy of Cicero's *De oratore* to Edward IV.[39]

Edward's patronage may have facilitated the greater availability of the culture of ancient Rome and antiquity through English translations, but even more important were the printing enterprises of William Caxton, which started in Edward's second reign under his protection and patronage and which were dominated by the publishing of ancient history and didactic teaching. Caxton, an English merchant in Bruges and a servant of Margaret of York, may have been one of the key figures financing Edward's return. In 1476 Caxton moved his printing press to England, establishing it near the royal court at Westminster, where the sanctuary afforded him protection and where he could cater for the tastes of the courtiers and nobility. The first work he printed in England in 1477 also related to Edward's reconquest. Entitled *Jason*, it was his translation of Raol Lefevre's *Continuation of the Receuil des Histoires de Troie*. He especially linked this work to Edward, stating that he did not presume to present it to the king because 'I doubt not his grace hath it in Frensh which he wele understandeth', and he dedicated it to the prince of Wales. Edward did indeed possess the work in French. His manuscript of the *Receuil des Histoires de Troye* contains an illustration of the building of Troy which bears some similarity to Edward's capital, New Troy.[40] Caxton's interest in popularizing the early history of Britain, such an important feature of Edward's campaign to regain the throne, was shown in 1480 when he printed the first English history, his *Chronicles of England*, an edition of the standard history of Britain, the *Brut*, which concludes with a prayer for the welfare of England's most recent king, Edward IV.[41] Through this edition the legend of Troy became even more widely known. It was reprinted in 1482,[42] in which year Caxton also printed Higden's *Polychronicon* with a prologue derived from a dissertation by the Greek historian Diodorus Siculus on the value of history.

Caxton's main interest, however, was didactic, to provide the moral teaching of antiquity for a wider audience. In 1477 he printed Woodville's *Dicts and Sayings of the Philosophers*. In February he wrote the epigram at Woodville's command and completed the edition by 24 March 1477. In the same year he printed Benedict Burgh's translation of the *Distichs of Cato*. A further reprint was issued in 1483. In 1478 Caxton printed Woodville's translation of Christine de Pisan's *Moral Proverbs*, and in 1480 Chaucer's translation of Boethius. Also in this year the encyclopaedia known as the *Mirror of the World* was published for Hugh Bryce, an alderman, who intended to give it to Edward's close friend William Lord Hastings. This was reprinted in 1481. In the same year Caxton produced a comprehensive volume of three works which he decided had a thematic unity: Worcester's translation of Cicero's *Old Age and Friendship*, published under the titles of *Tullius on Friendship* and *Tullius on Old Age*,[43] and Tiptoft's *Declamacion of Noblesse*. These three, Caxton wrote, he was publishing under the protection of Edward IV, to whom the volume was dedicated. Worcester's resurrection of Roman senatorial life and Tiptoft's redefinition of the English nobility along Roman senatorial lines were integrated into a single volume. For Caxton, as much as for Worcester, Cicero was a hero, and in the prologue to this edition of *De senectute* he describes him as one who took great thought for the governance of the common profit, keeping Romans prosperous and defending them from adversaries.[44] Like Worcester he saw Fastolf as a fifteenth-century equivalent of a Roman senator who devoted his life to exercise of arms and the administration of justice in the service of the public weal.

Caxton too acknowledged his admiration for Roman civilization and recounted the trouble he went to to obtain these works of Cicero and make them available to a select audience of state servants, for those great lords, noblemen and merchants who have heard of the noble policy and prudence of the Romans and who 'have been daily occupied in matters touching the public weal'.[45] Also in this year he prepared for print the *Metamorphoses*.

This production of vernacular versions of the myths of history and the philosophy of antiquity in manuscripts and printed editions was of great cultural significance, indicating as it did the spread of literacy and political moral awareness among the merchants and the gentry and among courtiers, especially in London; more specifically it also had profound implications for the self-image of Edward IV and the governing class and their attitude towards the exercise of political office in domestic and foreign policy.

The stoicism that was implicit in many writings of Cicero, Seneca, Boethius, Boccaccio and in such recent adaptations of the stoic philosophy of the ancients as the *Dicts and Sayings of the Philosophers*, all of which were so strongly represented in Edward's library, provided an important model for those on both sides of the political divide for an appropriate, dignified response to the turmoils of the years 1468–71. In 1469, during the height of these troubles, Sir John Paston quoted a phrase attributed to Socrates from Scrope's *Epistle of Othea*: 'Thou art a man, thou shouldst not be to hevy ne to mery for no cause.'[46] The medical dimension to the stoic teachings of antiquity, especially important in the circle of Sir John Fastolf, was not forgotten. Tiptoft owned a manuscript containing the proverbs of Seneca and tracts on health.[47] Anthony Woodville emerged as a key figure in the restoration of Edward's kingdom. Once the situation had stabilized Woodville, 'moved by grateful remembering of many perils safely passed during the late civil wars', determined to undertake a voyage in a jubilee year to the shrine of St James of Compostela. On the ship he met the Gascon knight Louis de Bretalle, one of Edward's spies in Spain well known at the English court, and borrowed from him Guillame de Tignonville's version of *Les dicts morleaux des philosophers*, recently printed at Bruges.[48] The book so pleased the earl that he studied it at some length. This work, previously translated by Scrope for Fastolf, offered Woodville some solace from the tribulations of civil war and he translated it, adding a prologue saying every human creature is in thrall to the storms of fortune. He offered these sayings of the pagans 'which is a glorious fair mirror to all good Christian people' and which provides 'the virtue and knowledge that enables princes kings and people of all estates to suffer misfortune with patience'. This work of thanksgiving for his deliverance reflects the thinking man's experience of the Wars of the Roses and provides the context for the exile in Burgundy of Woodville's brother-in-law Edward IV.

The God Woodville contemplated was closer to Athena or Othea than the interventionist Old Testament God or the suffering redeemer of the New Testament, an image of detached rationality and wisdom. In his meditation on the last four days, the *Cordyale*, which was printed by Caxton in 1478, Woodville expounded an ideal of contemplative retirement inspired by the example of antiquity. This he offered to those who were really only in public office through a sense of duty, and whose real love was study. Such people, he argued, longed to be released into solitude to enjoy the consolations of a detached contemplation of fortune's wheel.[49] In the epilogue to this work, Caxton noted of his friend: 'It seemeth that he conceiveth well the mutabilite and the unstableness of this present lyf.' The supreme authority for counselling on the triumph of stoic rationality over political misfortune was Boethius, to whom Charles of Orleans, Louis de Gruuthuyse, James I, Philippe de Commines (who wrote his *Memoirs* in prison in 1487) and later Sir Thomas More all turned for solace during periods of imprisonment. Worcester studied Boccaccio, the original model for Lydgate's *Fall of Princes*, in the original Latin and took notes from it.[50] He also owned a manuscript containing Lydgate's *Fall of Princes* and the proverbs of Seneca. In 1478 Caxton printed Chaucer's translation of the *Consolations of Philosophy*, and in the prologue he wrote that one 'can see what this transitory, mutable world is and where every man living in it is going'. He was less interested in Boethius's Christian martyrdom than the fact that in exile he was a senator of Rome who worked for the common weal. He printed it in the hope that it would 'profit people for the wele of their souls to have better patience in adversity.' Georges Chastellain, chronicler of the court of Burgundy, who described fortune as a formidable goddess alternately serving Edward IV and Henry VI,[51] saw Margaret of Anjou as an exemplar of stoicism and composed for her *Le Temple de Bocace*, a dialogue between the queen and Boccaccio, who offers her consolation in the face of her many misfortunes.[52] Elizabeth of York owned a verse translation of Boethius's *De consolatione philosophiae*, which has her motto 'I do not change'. The appearance of her signature, without the title princess or queen, and the motto of Richard duke of Gloucester near the end of the manuscript, which also contains the *Book of Tristram*, suggests she owned this work at a time of upheaval and accepted with resignation her change of fortune and the coronation of Richard III.[53] William Worcester was engaged after 1471 in a trawl through the stoic writings to find the consolations of philosophy, and he recorded in his notebook extracts from Seneca's letters on patience. In Edward's copy of the *Epistle of Othea* there is an illustration which contains both his arms and those of Cadwallader and depicts Prudence, the most important of the cardinal virtues and the key to philosophical detachment, wisdom and health.[54] Edward IV must have used his library to reflect on the fluctuations of his own political life. He would have taken to heart the statement from the *Fall of Princes*:

> fortune hath no domynacioun
> when noble prynces be gouerned be resoun.[55]

He would have seen his own life and the turbulent lives of his friends and political opponents mirrored in his lavishly illustrated copy of Premierfaits's French translation of Boccaccio's *De casibus illustrium*. All the illustrations in this manuscript, accompanied by Edward's coat of arms, show scenes from antiquity illustrating the mutability of fortune and the violent deaths and dismemberment of kings and princes, with recurring images of the mutability of fortune.[56] These, combined with the illustrations of his device, the white rose, must have served as sources for meditation on Edward's past and possible future, a reflection on his violent and uncertain times.

There was a political dimension to the stoic philosophy expressed in the literature copied and printed at Edward's court. Stoic detachment relied on an obedience to the laws of nature, but in the writing of this period it also involved obedience to the state. The concept of the state as a source of order and stability, a civilized and rational construction, was formulated as a reaction to the chaos and uncertainties brought about by years of civil war. Worcester expressed this by quoting from the opening of Aristotle's *Metaphysics*: 'Wisdom is the utmost perfection of reason, whose perfection is recognizable order.' Such order depended on the rationality of the prince who placed himself above the vagaries of fortune. This concept of the prince as the embodiment of reason had been portrayed in the image in the *Illustrated Life of Edward IV* celebrating Edward's crowning by depicting the enthroned Reason, dressed as a judge, opposite the enthroned Edward on the wheel of Fortune, sinister symbol of mutability, stationary through the intervention of Reason, and converted into a mandala, a symbol of peace and integration. The model of the rational, ordered state was the secular society of ancient Rome. In Rivers' *Book of Policy*, his translation of Christine de Pisan's *Livre de Corps de Policie*, it is asserted that 'the glorious time of the Romans' produced an advanced civilization in which wisdom, the exercise of arms, and military and intellectual discipline went hand in hand.[57] There was no doubt that this civilization was perceived to be superior: 'we may wele thenke that the Romayns were better men and mor worthy than othre', and that it was one to be emulated: 'the noble Romayns whiche wer paynemys, and mysbeleuers, yet they gouerned theim so well that it ought to be example to us, Valere saith'.[58] According to Rivers the dicts and sayings of these pagans, which he translated, were 'a glorious fair mirror to all good Christian people'.

Rome was perceived to be at the height of its influence as a source of order and stability in the world during the reign of Augustus, and obedience to the world monarch was elevated to a religious principle, so much so that there was special significance attached to the appearance of Jesus of Nazareth in this reign. Stephen Scrope, in the conclusion to his *Epistle of Othea*, delivered the following encomium:

> Cesar Augustus was emperoure of the Romaynes and of alle the worlde, and because that in the tyme of his reigne thes was in alle the worlde, and that he regned pesibelly, lewde peopil aand mysbeleves thougt that the pes was because of his goodness; but it was not. For it was Christ Jesu, the which was borne of the Virgine Marie and was that tyme on the erthe.[59]

Caxton expressed this in his translation of the lives of the saints, the *Legenda aurea*: 'There was so greete pees in the erthe that alle the world was obeyssant to hym, and therefore our lorde wold be born in that tyme.'[60] In this single sentence Caxton linked the Christian principle of obedience with conformity to the authority of the state. He suggested that the Christian civilization was contingent on the stability and order established by the Romans. Conformity to nature, to the divinely instituted order of things and to the state as a manifestation of this order amounted to a secular religion for Edward's courtiers. Tiptoft, Rivers, Caxton, William Worcester and other writers of this period were naturally reacting to the political turmoil and party strife of the time, and they sought pragmatic guidelines that would help them to bring order to political life by moralizing politics and religion, bringing passions under control and exorcizing fate. The ruling class of the previous hundred years, the higher clergy and lay nobility, shared an interest in the eremitic life and devotional literature and a conviction that there was a religious significance in the lineages of noble families.[61] Such outlooks were inevitably accompanied by individualistic mysticism, heresy, aristocratic self-assertion and feuds, all of which threatened the social order. Consequently the state was weakly conceived in the fourteenth century. The Church was a separate institution, and the king's writ did not apply in the sanctuaries of major abbey churches, or in the palatinates of the Prince Bishops of Durham and the duchy of Lancaster. The aristocracy had their own courts and armies, and usually relied on these to seek justice. Henry V did much to create a strong state, purging the Church of heresy and forcing the barons to accept his justice. But this achievement was undermined by his son, whose withdrawn piety showed that a combination of ineptitude and religious extremism in the monarch could threaten the health of the body politic. During the Wars of the Roses the prestige of the state under the monarchy had sunk to such a low level that Warwick, the epitome of the overmighty subject, put two kings, Edward IV and Henry VI, in prison and was plotting to place on the throne in their place both George the duke of Clarence and Edward of Lancaster. This must have represented the abyss for intellectuals of the period looking for political order, and after the Readeption such men, who like Tiptoft, William Worcester and Fortescue represented both sides of the political divide, sought to elevate the secular state around the king to an almost religious principle. Rome was the healthiest body politic known to them, and so became the model for a rational world order. The alchemists had got it right. The 1456 commissioners recognized the crisis and searched the writings of the ancients to solve the problem of the king's illness, and the answer was found in these writings: the creation of a rational, secular state following the example of the most political order known to them, ancient Rome. The prince, at the head of this state, was to embody the balance that the stoic philosophers counselled, and under him there would consequently exist a balanced rational society, immune to the fluctuations of passion and fortune.

The emphasis placed on the political, didactic literature of the 1470s, on stoic obedience, was accompanied by a new definition of the nobility. The ruling class was now defined not by the aggressive pursuit of family honour or ordination and the possession of the keys of heaven through administration of the sacraments but through obedience and service to the state, the collective good or the common weal. The Roman senatorial class, it was believed, pointed the way to such selfless service. William Worcester, in rededicating his *Boke of Noblesse* to Edward IV in 1474, was upholding the king as the hope for the establishment of a state founded on the principles of common good. He provided illustrations of the way the Roman governing classes sacrificed themselves to the good of the state. He cited Cicero's *De officiis* on the need for every officer to advance the cause of the common weal and gave examples of great servants to the common good. One was Cato, who:

> that was son manlie, prudent and of holsom conseite, whiche in his yong daies occupied the office of a knight in exersising armes, another season he occupied the office of tribune as a chief juge among the Romayns, another season was a legat as an ambassatoure into ferre contreis, yet anothir tyme in his gret ancien age, that he might not gretlie laboure, was made counsul of Rome.[62]

Another was Fabricius who, according to Cicero in *De senectute*, battled with Hannibal 'to kepe the conquest of Romayne contreis, and to see theire libertees and fraunchises observed and kept for the wele of alle maner peple; whiche Fabricius despraised renamee and vayne glorie, but onlie gafe his solicitude thoght and his bisy cure about the common profit of Rome'.[63]

In Edward's copy of the *Romuleon* there is an illustration of the Yorkist hero Scipio issuing forth over a bridge to defend Rome. In the border conspicuously displayed are Edward's arms and his badge, the rose et soleil.[64] Worcester exhorted the English nobility to emulate the Roman senators who, when faced with commoners complaining about taxation in market places, brought forth their silver and gold and issued legislation restricting the amount of jewellery that could be kept. This recalls Bedford's gesture in refusing a salary. Woodville, around the same time, in his *Book of Policy*, placed the knight's duty to the common weal before his love and fear of God: 'The right worthy Romayn prynces seithe hye [Aristotle in his *Poetics*] had their hartis so moche in the loue of the common wele' and it is maintained that 'every man entendid for the proffyte of the common wele and not for his owyn singuler wele'.[65]. In the translation of Chartier's *Quadrilogium Invectif*, he similarly argued that 'after the bonde of the feith Catholike, nature byndeth yow to fortefye the common wele of the londe wherin ye ever borne'. An indication of the way devotion to the common wele had become an official part of the Yorkist monarchy's programme is shown in Caxton's prologue to his translation of Jacques de Cessoles's study of the social duties of different classes, *The Book of the Game and Play of Chess*. Caxton printed this in Bruges in 1474 and revised it for George duke of Clarence in 1475. He wrote:

> For as moche as I haue understand and knowe, that ye are enclined unto the comyn wele of the kinge oure sayd saueryn lord. his nobles lordes and comyn peple of his noble royame of England, and that ye sawe gladly the Inhabitans of ye same enformed in good, vertuous, prouffitable and honeste maners. In whiche your noble persone wyth guydyng of your hows haboundeth, gyuyng light and ensample unto all other. Therefore I haue put me in deuour to translate a lityll book late comen in to myn hands – In which I fynde thauctorites, dictes and stories of auncient Doctours pilosophers poetes and of other wyse men whiche been recrecunted applied unto the moralite of the publique wele as well of the nobles as of the comyn peple after the game and playe of the chess.[66]

The forum where the governing classes could gather and make their contributions to the common good was Parliament and the king's council, and this was compared by Chief Justice Fortescue to the Roman senate. Fortescue first raised this theme in articles he addressed to Warwick in 1470 when attempting to install Henry VI on the throne. He advised Warwick to avoid making the mistake of neglecting the common weal which had lost Henry the throne in 1461.[67] These articles were later incorporated into the *Governance of England*, which was presented to Edward IV. Fortescue perceived a close relationship between fifteenth-century political history and that of ancient Rome. The key to successful rule in the fifteenth century was good counsel such as had existed during the infancy of Henry VI. For Fortescue a continual counsel of distinguished advisers was the equivalent of the Roman senate, and it was the wisdom of the Roman senators that explained Rome's imperial greatness: 'through wisdome and manhood' the Romans 'gate the lordship and monarchie of the worlde'.[68] Fortescue explained how, after the civil war, Caesar and Octavian rose to the status of emperors, but it was still the senators who steered Rome to greatness 'while lordship and monarchie themperor kepte all the while they wre reuled bi the counsele of the senate'. Rome's decline set in, he claimed, when emperors such as Nero and Domitian slew the greater part of the Senate and were advised by private counsellors. The decay of Rome was so complete that in Fortescue's own time only the Holy Roman Empire survived as a relic of this empire.[69] Analogies were drawn with the decline in the fortunes of English kings of the fifteenth century. While Henry V listened to wise counsellors, which enabled him to gain military success over the Welsh and the French, kings such as Richard II and Henry VI were ruled by private counsellors and this resulted in a loss of overseas territories and civil strife:

> We have had civil wars amongst ourselves as had the Romans when they had not one head but many governors and our realm is fallen into decay and poverty as was the empire when the emperor left the counsell of the Senate. But if our kings be counselled by such wise established counsellors as before devised and do as did the first emperore who obtained the monarchy of the world, we should first have unity and peace within our land, riches and prosperity, and be mightieste and most welthe reaume of the world.[70]

Fortescue's analysis of the consequences of the factionalism of the 1450s and his historical perspective indicate how intellectually advanced political life was compared to the late fourteenth century, and how thoroughly infused it was with Roman values. When Thomas Woodstock duke of Gloucester and Richard FitzAlan earl of Arundel tried to dispose of the court favourites and impose a continual council on Richard II, they had no intellectual justification other than naked ambition and their own resentment at their exclusion from office; the only political philosophy that Gloucester, the constable of the court of chivalry, embraced was the one he shared with the Black Prince and Edward III, the code of chivalry that sustained the French campaigns. Richard II rejected this code and attempted to establish an autocratic form of monarchy in the 1380s, based on the concept of the divine right of a king anointed by God. Drawing on ideas in John of Salisbury's *Policraticus*, Richard saw himself as the head of a body politic with its members acting together in order. However, apart from his marital links with the Holy Roman Empire, Richard and his court had little interest in the practical, political ideas of the ancient Romans. By the fifteenth century therefore the ruling class, influenced by the Roman political literature made available from the library of Charles VI after the conquest of Normandy, proved hostile in their judgements on Richard II, who was regarded as a tyrant who had failed to measure up to the Roman ideals of Augustus. For James Yonge he was like Nero.

The celebration during Edward's reign of the king's council (and to a lesser extent Parliament) was accompanied by an assertion that the basis of crown authority and justice was English common law, itself a rational code that served the interests of the common weal because these laws were made with the consent of the public and defined by custom. Expounding on a case in 1468, Chief Justice William Yelverton asserted that English common law, or natural law, sprang from the great law of Rome and that, when dealing with cases for which there was no existing law, a judge must resort to 'the law of nature, which is the ground of all laws', and whatever was decided on such criteria must be beneficial to the common weal.[71]

Between 1472 and 1475, when William Worcester was revising his *Boke of Noblesse*, he also presented to Edward IV a collection of documents dating from Bedford's regency that were originally in Fastolf's possession.[72] During this period the common explanation for the loss of empire was the neglect of the common good, the selfishness of the aristocracy and their failure to pledge themselves to a higher good. It was during the late 1470s that Lydgate's account of the Roman civil wars, the *Serpent of Division*, was copied to illustrate Lydgate's theme that history repeats itself and to suggest parallels with the conflicts between Edward IV and Warwick and Clarence.[73] Reflecting on the loss of Normandy, Worcester, pursuing a similar circular notion of history, observed that it was not that planetary influence caused adversity, but 'lak of prudence and politique governance and having no consideracion to the common wele, but rather to magnifie and enriche our selfe by singuler covetise'. The translator of *Le Quadrilogue Invectif*, probably a courtier of Edward IV, was intent on encouraging Edward to revive the glories of Henry V's reign and, like Worcester, he used Rome as a mirror of what was happening in England. Rome started to lose its empire when its ruling classes became less disciplined and militaristic, and selfishly put their own ease and peace above the common good: 'But now speke we of Rome, which was last in souerayne mageste and excellent vertu, and note we the woorde of Lucane, that seid that the seid citee shuld be cause of his own dekay and rune, for the to grete and heuy burdon causeth the grete and greuous falle.'[74] Referring to the corruption and softness of the nobility in their respective counties, who are compared to the inhabitants of Babylon when it fell to vice, he extolled the virtues of Scipio Africanus, who commanded that any man inclined to 'voluptuosite within his legions' was to be thrown out of the army.[75] By contrast, the nobility of England, the translator reflects, spend their days in the fields and woods, hunting and hawking, refusing to put themselves in danger by defending their natural lordships.[76]

The epitome of service to the common good therefore was perceived to be preparedness to give one's life to the service of a higher ideal, the empire, and here too Rome was the obvious inspiration, providing the intellectual justification for Edward's plans for the invasion of France. Preparations began in 1472. Parliament provided Edward with four fifteenths, close to the sum obtained by Henry V in 1413–17. In giving assent to the first taxes, the commons specifically referred to a declaration delivered among them in this

Parliament inducing them for 'reasons of the weal and surety of this your said realm inward and defence outward to assist your royal estate'. This declaration was delivered by John Alcock, bishop of Worcester, who was deputizing for the indisposed Robert Stillington on 30 November 1472. Alcock employed medical metaphors referring to the 'long disease of this lande' and the 'unhealed wounds'. The cure for this illness of the body politic was perceived to be the application of a Roman imperial rationale.[77] In contrast to the ideology of Henry V, who emphasized his rightful claim to the throne of France, Alcock broadened the appeal beyond feudal dynastic ambitions and, while barely mentioning the claim to the crown, emphasized the need for territorial expansion for younger sons. He praised Edward for ending the civil war, but observed that ever since the loss of Normandy England had been stuffed with younger gentlemen and men of war (the descendants of the dispossessed English nobility in France) who cause internal dissension, extortion and robbery. The rigid application of justice would, he claimed, only exacerbate the internal problems of the realm, for these are the very men needed to defend the realm against outward enemies in France, Scotland and Denmark, all willing to take any opportunity to invade. It was claimed that the violent perpetrators of crimes in England are the members of the ruling class, whose aggressive instincts would be best served in foreign conquest, after which landless gentlemen and younger sons could be reunited with land and settled in garrisons, which would provide employment for the mischievous and ports for mercantile interests. For it is a political fact, Alcock maintained, that never since the conquest, had justice, peace and prosperity continued in this land, except during the reigns of kings who made war: Henry I, Richard I, Henry II, Edward I, Edward III, the usurper Henry V and even, despite his simplicity, Henry VI. The king, he argued, should show courage and a tender affection for the common weal by appearing at the head of his army to inspire his subjects.[78] This rhetoric recalled the success Henry V had in defusing internal problems by achieving overseas military victories, and also echoed the arguments employed by William Worcester in his *Boke of Noblesse* which he revised for Edward IV. Alcock, like Worcester, employed the same arguments about the Punic wars to point out that internal stability was best preserved by foreign conquest. The jeopardy that Rome stood in when Hannibal came out of Carthage was offset by Scipio's aggression, but this policy was not maintained:

> Right so it happened in olde daies at the citee of Rome, for after Carthage was clerly overthrown and distroied, the residue of the world, obeying the Romayns, they not havyng were with any contre outwards, where they might sett theyr warrely purpose in occupacion, fell amongs them selfe to such division and inward battalle, that finally they were brought to ruyne and desolacion.[79]

This speech reflects Alcock's classical learning, the common admiration for Henry V's achievements in securing internal order through conquest, and an imperialistic ideology that sought outlet for underemployed and aggressive younger members of the nobility in an empire. It also reflects the influence of writers such as Worcester and Fortescue, both enthusiastic readers of Roman history and alchemy, who knew each other. Fortescue, whose pardon was granted in the third session of this Parliament, revised his *Governance of England* for Edward IV. He also wrote a pro-Yorkist declaration from Scotland which was owned by Edward's daughter, Cecily, and her husband Viscount Lord Welles.[80] Fortescue reflected on the decline of Rome and England and called for a revival so England would 'be the most mighty and wealthy realm in the world'. Worcester, a probable inspiration for Alcock's sermon, also used the Punic wars, which he read about in Fastolf's copy of Livy, as a historical exemplum, and he held Scipio in especially high regard. His notebooks show that between 1469 and 1472 he was copying extracts from classical authorities to support his argument for a reconquest of France, and he went even further than Alcock in his analysis of the younger sons of governing classes, suggesting that they were abandoning their chivalrous heritage by turning to the study of law. This call for a revival of military traditions among the young also occurs in Lull's *Book of the Order of Chivalry*, which was printed by Caxton in 1484, a version of which was owned by Edward IV.[81] William Worcester saw war as ennobling and invigorating, and he provided practical advice on how to achieve conquest, citing Vegetius, and even providing some of Fastolf's papers to assist in the occupation (in the same way Hardynge provided maps to facilitate Edward's conquest of Scotland).[82] Worcester also exhorted Edward to invade France and regain his ancestral glory and status and urged the king to follow in his predecessors' footsteps. He was alluding to the militaristic, imperial traditions upheld by the heroes of the *Boke of Noblesse*, including Henry V, John duke of Bedford, Humphrey duke of Gloucester, Sir John Fastolf and Richard duke of York, who were all pledged to the conquest of France and the ennobling effects of war. Edward's awareness of this legacy was made apparent in the reburial of Richard duke of York in 1476. Richard duke of Gloucester's heralds paid tribute to York's martial prowess, and recalled that during his governorship of Normandy he passed the river at Pontoisie and drove into the army of Charles VII, creating the last occasion when the English had any real chance of turning the tide against the French. Edward's awareness of the common weal rhetoric employed by Alcock, Fortescue and Worcester is shown in the radical new measures he employed to raise money, using a new decree for the voluntary contribution of benevolences.

Roman history and mythology were also incorporated into the genealogical chronicles copied around 1471, which served the purpose of assimilating the reconquest of the throne with Edward's British pedigree as the descendant of Brutus, the reborn Arthur. In the translation of Claudian's poem in honour of Stilicho, Edward's father Richard duke of York is identified with Stilicho, the hero of the conquest of Britain, to whom the Britons appealed to defend them and their empire against the Scots, Picts and Saxons. This identification of the Britons with the Roman Empire and the Saxons with the northern European barbarians, including the Lancastrians, was developed in the genealogies produced in Edward's second reign. The Percy Roll emphasizes Edward's descent from the classical world of Brutus, and provides a detailed account of the founding of Rome by Romulus and Remus, and idealized portraits of New Troy and London.[83] The special status of Britain as joint descendant of Troy with Rome is emphasized in an account of the barbarian nations of northern Europe, which include Saxons, Norwegians, Danes, Goths and Vandals, who, it is claimed, were all jealous of Britain. In this same roll the lines of Roman emperors and kings of Britain are shown to be one and the same, with Constantine the last Roman king of Britain. This was the context for the treaty made with Scotland in October 1474 and ratified with the marriage of Edward's daughter Cecily to James III, which was an important prelude to the invasion of France, and where reference was made to the peace which would preserve the wealth and prosperity of this noble island of Britain. The Scottish campaign of 1481–2, when Richard duke of Gloucester took Berwick and advanced as far as Edinburgh, was accompanied by a degree of imperial rhetoric. Hardynge attempted to facilitate the conquest by providing maps, and Sir John Howard, a diplomat of Edward's court in the 1470s, took with him when he went to fight the Scots his copy of the *Dicts and Sayings of the Philosophers*.

The fusion of Roman and British imperialism occurred in the myths surrounding King Arthur. Geoffrey of Monmouth had Arthur carving out a North Sea Empire containing Ireland, Iceland, Sweden, the Orkneys, Norway, Denmark and Gaul; he was about to be crowned as Roman emperor when he was recalled to Britain to deal with Mordred's usurpation of his throne. This interpretation was followed in the fourteenth-century alliterative romance *Morte Arthure*, which occurs in the Thornton manuscript. Hardynge considerably enlarged on Arthur's Roman pedigree. After conquering France, Arthur is challenged by the emperor Lucius to pay tribute and he replies that Britain was humiliated by Julius Caesar through a treaty, and he intends to defend the freedom of the realm and 'all that longeth to themeralite' as it was in the time of Brutus, and furthermore, to claim Rome and its empire as held by his ancestor Constantine. Arthur defeats and kills Lucius in battle and sends his body to Rome. Arthur comes to Rome at the request of the senate, and at the capitol, in the see imperial, he is crowned with three crowns of gold and feasts with the Pope.[84] This was a vision endorsed in Malory's version of the Arthurian myth. He follows Hardynge in having Arthur crowned Roman emperor long before Mordred's usurpation, and emphasizes his dedication to the recovery of the Holy Land.

Edward IV, in his identification with Arthur, chose to give special emphasis to these three crowns. They appear alongside both Arthur's name and Edward's in the genealogical rolls tracing Edward's British ancestry, including the *Coronation Roll*. The three crowns represent for Edward, England, France and Spain, and he laid claim to them at his coronation in 1461. After Edward's victory in 1461 a poet celebrated by proclaiming his dynastic and imperial claims:

> King of England and France I say
> it is your own who can say nay
> And so is Spain, that fair country
> fffy on sloutful countenaunce
> where conquest is a plesaunce,
> And registered in old remembraunce.

Hardynge stresses the parallels between Edward and Arthur, both imperial conquerors in Scotland:

> By small hackneys greater coursers men chastise,
> As Arthure did by Scottes wonne all fraunchise.[85]

He directly appealed to Edward IV to realize his imperial destiny: 'If you could add Scotland to Wales and England who have power to resist you in any maner and my lord England then be kept securely in your absence and make it Albion.' These imperial pretensions were broadcast in the prophecies occurring in the poems and genealogies that accompanied Edward's accession and which were copied and disseminated following his reconquest of the throne. One such prophecy was that of Almayn who 'calleth hym a lyon of the ayre, the which shall take hys wynges and flee to Rome. And there be made Emperor.' Another was the prophecy of the Patriarch of Afric who 'calleth hym a western beeste that shall wynne the grete part of the world', and another the prophecy of Peter of Baldewele in Almayn 'who calleth hym the Egyll the whiche shal overcome vi kings'. In the *Coronation Roll* the imperial Roman eagle occurs on a banner that is probably intended to represent the arms of the Holy Roman Empire to indicate Edward IV's descent from Frederick II of Hohenstaufen. In a Yorkist genealogy executed in Edward's second reign, there is a prophecy concerning 'he that is lord above alle thynge save Edward our king'.[86] London was depicted as an imperial city in a poem that appeared in a manuscript containing prophecies of Edward's greatness. The poem captures the sense of London as a great centre of trade for merchants, its many beautiful municipal buildings with white pillars and its Roman origins stressed in the line 'By Julius Caesar thy tower founded of old'.[87] In the second half of the fifteenth century there would still have been considerable remains in cities like London with Roman origins. Remnants of city walls, pillars, and the remains of temples and bathhouses would have served as evocative reminders of Britain's imperial Roman past. A fifteenth-century handbook of London customs even asserted as a well-known fact that London was founded before Rome, and that the city enjoyed the liberties, rights and customs of the ancient city of Troy and possessed its institutions. Although the story was doubted by John Whethamstede, abbot of St Albans, it was retold by Caxton in his edition of the *Eneydos* in 1490. Edward, by closely identifying with Roman and Arthurian imperial ambitions, lent the Wars of the Roses an ideological dimension, claiming to represent the island of Britain, its Roman ancestry and Celtic Christianity, against the pagan Saxons whose descendants, the Lancastrians, were Germanic and northern European in outlook, lacking any sense of a vision of imperial Britain.

Edward's invasion of France was also preceded by a fusion of the Romano-British imperial myths and history with the more recent and tangible heroic exploits of Henry V. Malory linked Arthur's Roman imperial ambitions with those of Henry V by deviating from the route given in the Thornton romance, so that instead of turning south Arthur moved towards Flanders and Brabant, recalling the itinerary followed by Henry V on his way from Felong to Agincourt. The triangle of Soissons, Luxembourg and Flanders is an exaggerated replica of the triangle of Amiens and Calais in the route chosen by Henry V. When Edward invaded France he was probably inspired by both Henry V and Arthur. In the period between 1471 and 1475 he was able to sustain the sense of inflation derived from his successful invasion of Britain by drawing on Roman history and British mythology. He set out with an invasion force even larger than Henry V's and headed towards a meeting with the French army near Agincourt. The seriousness of his intent was signalled by the employment of craftsmen to construct a portable wooden house covered in leather for his use on campaign. His ally and brother-in-law, Charles the Bold, who accepted the Order of the Garter from the king of England and wore it for the rest of his life,[88] was an avid reader of Arthurian romances and was aware of the Arthurian, imperial dimension to Edward's quest. According to Chastellain, Charles used to speak of his desire to emulate the knights of chivalrous romance. His court at Dijon was decorated with tapestries depicting the voyages of the Argonauts and King Arthur.[89] The Croyland chronicler described how the duke met the king's council at Calais to discuss routes, and commented on the numbers Edward had brought over: 'It was enough to meet any attack and supposed that if the men had been his, he would not have wished for more to carry his conquest right through France even as far as the gates of Rome and he said these very words in public.'[90]

However, it is important not to overemphasize the influence of Arthurian literature on the behaviour of Edward and his governing class in the second reign. The emulation of Roman political life entailed the adoption of Roman theories of education and a new definition of the nobility, defined in terms of their knowledge of Roman history and literature and their skills in the practical application of Roman political philosophy. Woodville's *Book of Policy* maintains that the Roman Empire was the product of an advanced civilization in which wisdom, the exercise of arms, and military and intellectual discipline went hand in hand, 'for it is no doubt that the exercise of arms and of wisdom togedir helped theim gretly in their conquests'. The key to this 'glorious time of the Romans' was education: 'They maintained the schools that produced the Cesars.' Christine de Pisan, and Woodville following her lead, advocated the development of a professional civil service where officials were not appointed through favour and the help of patrons; instead they advised following the example of the Romans who governed the city and their empire with the common weal in mind and changed their officials annually. The overall philosophy of this education system was militaristic and imperialistic, integrating military and intellectual discipline. William Worcester, in a note in his *Itinerarium* recording the death of Chief Justice Richard Newton, observed 'the hand of Julius Caesar was no less fitted for the pen than the sword'.[91] Woodville, presumably with Henry V's triumphant processions in mind, even advocated a revival of Roman state processions as a means of encouraging the nobility to serve the state, anticipating chariot rides, salutes and the presentation of laurel wreaths and jewellery for deeds of valour in emulation of the triumphs of Caesar and Scipio: 'wherefor and it was pleasyng to our blessed lorde Jhesu I wolde that Englond, which is one of our noblest realmes of the worlde, wolde use this coustome'.[92] He suggested that the aim of education was to inculcate a military mentality: Aristotle's recommendation that young children should be hardened by exposure to the cold was endorsed. Lydgate devoted a section of his *Fall of Princes* to the role that Cicero played in the political life of Rome and the defence of its liberties:

> Lik a sunne he dude hem enlumyne
> Bi hih prowesse of knihtli excellence;
> And thoruh the world his bemys dede shyne
> Of his rethorik and his elloquence,
> In which he hadde so gret experience.
> Bi circustaunces that nothyng dede lakke,
> He transcendid Polityus and Grakke.[93]

In his translation of the *Book of the Game and Play of Chess* Caxton advocates the teaching of letters and quotes Suetonius's remarks about Augustus educating his sons in military skills. This attitude to education was summed up by Worcester in the *Boke of Noblesse* when he called for a revival of jousting, wrestling and other martial sports for the young; by Caxton in his call for a return to a chivalric military education in his translation of Lull's *Book of the Order of Chivalry*; and by Tiptoft, who observed that men who were utterly ignorant of letters were rarely excellent in arms. According to Commines, it was an advantage to a prince to have studied history in his youth, and he remarked that on the basis of what he had seen in eighteen years or more of close experience with princes 'one of the surest means to make a man wise is to have him read ancient history and learn how to conduct and guard himself and how to manage his affairs wisely, according to histories and examples of his ancestors'. He added that one can learn more in three months from reading a book than twenty men living successfully could observe and understand by experience.

Ancient Roman society gave the highest value to participation in the political life of cities, and vested power in a widely based citizen class (rather than priests). This class controlled and participated in priestly functions, ensuring that religion was subservient to the interests of the state, and this was a model that was beginning to be adopted during Edward's second reign. Many of the clergy who were prominent in public life were those who were mastering the rhetorical skills outlined by Cicero. They included John Alcock; John Morton, archbishop of Canterbury, king's chancellor and keeper of the Privy Seal in 1473, who owned Seneca's letters;[94] Roger Marshall, the king's physician and owner of the works of Pliny and Plato; John Whethamstede, who compiled a dictionary of classical myths; John Argentine; and John Russell, bishop of Lincoln, who owned two copies of Cicero's *De officiis*. However, they were being joined by common lawyers such as Thomas Kebell of the Inner Temple, a leading member of the bar and protégé of William Lord Hastings. Kebell's inventory of printed books included Worcester's translation of *De senectute* and *De amicitia*; Chaucer's translation of Boethius's *De consolatione philosophiae* and Cicero's *De officiis*.

Kebell bequeathed his books to his son Walter, 'to the intent that he should further apply him to virtue and cunning'. More importantly, the ranks of the nobility, defined as servants to the common weal and empire, were being joined by members of the landed aristocracy who were adding to their military skills and ancestral pedigrees a knowledge of classical literature in translation. John Tiptoft[95] (whose execution in 1471 became a stoic parody of a Christian martyrdom when he asked to be beheaded with three strokes in honour of the Trinity and declared that all he had done was in the service of the state) gave more formal definition to this more broadly defined ruling class in his *Declamacion of Noblesse*, which he wrote just before 1471, and which was printed by Caxton in 1477. To Tiptoft the ruling classes were those who drank from the well of Greek and Roman learning and took their pleasure in their libraries rather than in their meadows.[96] In a debate between two Romans on the definition of nobility he satirizes the potentially unstable forces in the state represented by such insular barons as the Percies who refused to acknowledge that there was any difference between them and the king. The new breed of nobleman for Tiptoft (and Woodville) was not defined by possessions of inheritance but rested in cunning and 'vertu' which were applied to the 'seruyse for the comyne weale'. The best way to advance noble status, Tiptoft writes, is to devote oneself from earliest years to the study of philosophy, and he has his ideal nobleman boast: 'There is no day I spent in idleness and no night without study and learning.' This learning was consequently applied to the service of the public good of the city of Rome.[97] The same theme was expounded in the 1470s translation of Chartier's *Le Quadrilogue Invectif* where the Roman aristocracy are praised for recognizing the importance of intellectual skills rather than military prowess: 'for the penne and the tongue of oratours enhauncid as moche the glory of Rome as did the fighters'. The ruling class of this society asked to be judged not for glory but 'for compassion and necessite of the common wele'.[98] In *Le Quadrilogue Invectif* there was an implicit condemnation of the aristocratic familial pride of knights who had little knowledge of 'vertu' (the mental skills Machiavelli was to regard as crucial to the service of the state), and an exhortation to learn from Livy to put civil obedience before family honour.

This vision of an aristocracy defined in terms of a broad education in classical literature and history was expressed by William Caxton in his prologue to his printed edition of the *Mirror of the World*, which he translated for William Lord Hastings, one of the courtiers responsible for the welfare of the prince of Wales, and for the London alderman and mercer Hugh Bryce. Caxton maintained that:

> Writyngs duelle permanent and the ffaites and dedess of Anncyent menn ben sette by declaracion in fair and Aourned volumes, to thende that science and Artes lerned and founden of thinges passed myght be had in perpetuel memorye and remembraunce, ffor the hertes of nobles in eschewyng ydlenes at suche tyme as they haue none other vertuous ocupacion on hande ought texercise them in redyng, studyng the noble faytes and dedes of sage and wysemen somtyme trauillyng in prpuffytable vertues, of whom it happeth ofte that some men ben encllyned to visyte the bookes treatyng of sciences particule. And other to rede visyte bookes spekyng of faytes of armes, of loue, or of meruailous histories.[99]

This entailed a new vision of educational institutions. The university, formerly monopolized by clergymen studying theology and canon law at the higher levels, was beginning to be seen as the focus for the study of antiquity and the spiritual heart of the empire. As early as 1419, in a sermon delivered on the departure of Henry V to France, it was claimed: 'As fer as God has land Oxon habuit nomen.' It was the hope of Bedford and Fastolf that a university would be established at Caen to train the administrators of this new English empire.

Humphrey duke of Gloucester made a gift of 120 volumes of classical texts (with some medical and scientific treatises) to the University of Oxford and they were brought to the university in November 1439 by his physician Gilbert Kymer.[100] Tiptoft, in presenting to Oxford his collection of 500 volumes of classical literature, including the proverbs of Seneca and the *Dialogues of Tacitus*, wrote a letter to the chancellor from Padua, referring to the great benefits he had gained from studying at Oxford, which he referred to as 'my second Athens'. Rivers' educational ideals can be seen in his will where he bequeathed money to Whittington College.[101] Classical ideals were also being imported in the grammar schools founded from the mid-fifteenth century, such as Hull, established by John Alcock in 1479, and Magdalen College School, founded in Oxford in 1480 by William Waynflete. The first headmaster, John Anwykyll, published a compilation of model sentences in Latin and English taken from the plays of Terence.[102] In the curriculum of these schools, medieval texts were being replaced by classical texts, especially Cicero's *De officiis*.[103] The educational ideals they would have espoused can be seen in the outline provided by John Dowden, founder of Pocklington Grammar School in 1514, for 'the zeal and love that he had for his country and to the education and upbringing of youth in virtue and learning'. The most complete exponent of these educational ideals was written two generations after Edward's reign by Sir Thomas Elyot in the *Boke Named Governor*. According to Elyot, the nobility were those who learned the duty of serving the prince and the governance of the common weal.[104] From reading Cicero they learned eloquence, from Caesar strategy. The aristocratic household itself, and especially the royal household, became an important educational institution and importer of the ideals of antiquity. Fortescue, in *De laudibus legem Angliae*, praised the system that took boys from small households and rustic backgrounds and placed them in the households of lords of higher rank. The best of these households, from an educational point of view, was the king's. This was, Fortescue claimed, in the supreme academy for nobles of the realm, a school of behaviour and manners. The importance of antiquity in the royal household is demonstrated in the ordinances for the education of Edward, prince of Wales, issued by Edward IV in 1474 to accompany the appointment of Anthony Woodville, Earl Rivers, as governor and ruler of the prince. Until he was ready in the morning none but Earl Rivers, his chamberlain or his chaplain was to enter the prince's chamber: 'No one was to sit at his table but such as the earl Rivers would allow, and there would be read to him noble stories as behoveth a prince to understand and all that be communicated to him at all times in his person be of virtue, cunning, wisdom, and deeds of worship, and nothing that would move him to vice.' After breakfast there would be one hour of school and after dinner a further two hours of school, and the curtains of his chamber were drawn at 9 o'clock.[105] The regimen of Roman discipline and the content of the uplifting literature were Rivers' responsibility, and the latter would have featured the type of classical literature he was engaged in translating, such as the *Dicts and Sayings of the Philosophers* (a version of which had been translated for the previous prince of Wales, Edward of Lancaster, by George Ashby). That Edward approved of such a classical education is further shown by his saying of Sir John Butler earl of Ormond that he was 'the goodliest knight' and 'if good breeding, nurture and liberal qualities were lost in the world they were to be found in this earl of Ormond'. An indication of the importance of the cult of antiquity in the princes' household at Ludlow is shown when Carmeliano in 1482 dedicated to Edward prince of Wales his Latin poem 'Ver' ('Spring'), which both displayed the author's knowledge of mythology and assumed the same from the recipient.[106]

A classical education was also available for the nobility of Edward IV's kingdom outside such educational institutions as the university and the household, thanks to the activities of translators and printers who made classical texts available in vernacular literature of instruction[107] to the entire literate class, thereby facilitating the development of the cultivated amateur. Their achievement can be compared with Cicero's. He transmitted in a more accessible form the content of Greek philosophy to the Roman governing class. Members of Fastolf's circle, especially William Worcester, transmitted the Roman culture of Cicero and his contemporaries to the governing class of England. Worcester's awareness of his place in this educational tradition was shown when he acknowledged in his *Itinerarium* the debt fifteenth-century culture owed to the Greco-Roman civilization: 'I find all the theory of all eloquence and every kind of study that shines with the light of wisdom has been derived from Greek sources and practised in their tongues by the Latins, and I see that in all the Liberal arts they have followed in their [the Greeks'] footsteps.'[108] Caxton was even more influential in broadening the appeal of such literature in his quick perception of the educational potential of the printing press. In 1481, in his prologue to Worcester's translation of Cicero's *Old Age and Friendship*, he addressed the work to noblemen, gentry and merchants who were 'daily occupied in the common weal', and claimed that the work was not suitable for the simple or for those who had not heard of the Romans' prudence and noble policy. Caxton's educational ambitions were further revealed in December 1483 when he decided that the citizens of London had lived upright lives when he was a boy but today hardly any tended to the common weal as they did in cities abroad and above all in ancient Rome:

> O when I remembre the noble Romayns
> That for the comyn wele of the Cite of Rome
> They spente not only theyr moueable goodes
> But they put theyr bodyes lyues in Iopardy to the deth.[109]

To correct this he was printing Benedict Burgh's translation of the *Distichs of Cato*. This collection of proverbs and moral observations, advice given by a citizen of Rome to his son, was originally translated by Burgh in the 1440s for the young nobleman William Bourchier, and Caxton dedicated his edition to the citizens of London, of whom he was a proud and grateful member.

The dissemination of vernacular, printed versions of the classics represents the final breakdown of the professional mysteries of the medieval ruling classes. These classes had been divided into two exclusive groups: the lay aristocracy, defined by lineage, coats of arms and estates, and the upper clergy, who were still defined by the sacrament of ordination, although many served as episcopal bureaucrats. Together they represented the twin pillars of St Augustine's vision of the two cities, the earthly city of Rome and the heavenly city of Jerusalem; this vision was becoming increasingly irrelevant during Edward's second reign. Now Cain's earthly, secular city was perceived to be the source of all moral and political philosophy for a nobility defined in terms of their knowledge and practical application of the political theories of Roman civilization.

The focal point for the nobility's emulation of Roman military ambition, education and institutions was the king himself. Edward's private collection of books is testimony to the extent to which he identified himself and his kingdom during his second reign with the Rome of the Caesars. His copy of the *Romuleon*, depicting the history of Rome from Remus to the division of the empire between Galerius and Constantinus in AD 306, was lavishly illustrated with miniatures showing the evolution of this civilization. The identification of the evolution of the Yorkist dynasty with that of the Roman emperors is established from the opening illustration of a wolf suckling Romulus and Remus in a medieval setting with an idealized New Troy in the background. In the borders are Edward's arms and banners, the white rose and the sun, supported by angels.[110] Edward could find in his library parallels between his role in ending the civil wars in 1471 through the conquest of England, with Julius Caesar's intervention in the civil wars of the Republic. Edward's copy of the biography of Caesar, *La Grande Histoire Cesar*, opens with a full-page illustration of the emperor's birth. This is surrounded by Edward's royal arms and his device, the rose et soleil, executed in Bruges according to patterns supplied by the king.[111] The author of the *Arrivall*, at the point of Edward's entry into York, commented: 'The kinge may say as Julius Cesar he that is nat agaynst me is with me.'[112]

The history of Rome (the Romuleon, *translated by Jean de Mielot) begins with an illustration of the birth of Rome symbolized by a wolf suckling the founders Romulus and Remus. In the border are Edward's arms, the* rose et soleil, *the garter belt and the Golden Fleece. (British Library Royal 19 E V, fo. 32)*

By July 1475, when Edward's bloodless invasion of France was concluded with a treaty with Louis XI, cemented with a lucrative annual pension, it was no longer appropriate for Edward to identify with heroic, martial figures, and the Roman leader of most significance for the period from 1475 to 1483, when Edward had the peace and prosperity to acquire the bulk of these elaborate versions of classical literature, was Augustus, who represented the Roman Empire at the height of its stability and wealth, culture and power. The parallels between the two rulers could be observed in Pliny's account in his *Natural History* of the appearance of parhelia when Augustus entered Rome after the death of Julius Caesar. Abbot John Whethamstede, in a Latin poem written immediately after Towton, referred to Edward's victory over Henry VI and compared Edward to Augustus, whom he surpassed. Even Edward's copy of the biography of Caesar, *La Grande Histoire Cesar*, gives special emphasis to the reign of Augustus, an account which is followed by a list of subsequent emperors, to suggest that an important part of Edward's self-image was that of a ruler who ended the civil wars and established a long, secure succession. This point was reinforced with the repeated occurrence of Edward's arms and those of his two sons in this manuscript.

There was a messianic dimension to Edward's identification with Augustus, for in the 1470s much was made of the fact that it was during the time of universal peace established by Augustus that Christ was born. In Edward's genealogies the link between Augustus and the coming of Christ was frequently stressed. Fortescue, after his return from exile in 1471, addressed his *Governance of England* (*De Monarchia*) to Edward IV, and it is in the sixteenth chapter of an alternative version occurring in two manuscripts[113] that he urged the king and Parliament to follow the example of Augustus and the senate who, after a period of civil war 'when many were slain and exiled, commanded, at the time of Christ's birth, the whole world'. In Edward's copy of Josephus's *Jewish Wars*, written in Bruges around 1470, the coming of Jesus was linked to the reign of Augustus and Edward: in one miniature the king is shown wearing an identical jewelled crown to the one shown in an illustration of Augustus in the same manuscript.[114]

In the conclusion to the *Epistle of Othea*, which Edward owned and which Stephen Scrope translated into English, there is an account of the coming of Christ during this time of universal peace in the reign of Augustus, and a description of this Caesar being led by the Sibyl to a mountain outside Rome, where he experiences a vision of the Virgin and child.[115] The Sibyl explained to him that this was the one God that should be worshipped. The standard guidebook to Rome from the twelfth to the fifteenth century popularized the legend (recounted in Higden's *Polychronicon*) and may have encouraged the popular perception of Edward as an embodiment of Augustus when it described the circumstances of the emperor consulting the Sibyl. He was compelled to do so by the Sibyl because the senate, seeing in him such great beauty that none could look into his eyes, and thinking that the great peace and prosperity that existed all over the world was due to his goodness, wished to render him tribute and to worship him.[116] In Edward's illustrated history of Rome, the *Romuleon*, where his arms and devices are prominently displayed, the account of the vision of Octavius (found in the *Epistle of Othea*) is accompanied by a full-page illumination of Octavianus (Augustus) as an old man, kneeling by a river. In the sky above there is an apparition of the Virgin and child and over the river there lies a wooden bridge, recalling the cross of St Helena. (The tradition that St Helena, the allegedly British mother of the Emperor Constantine and ancestor of Edward IV, guided by an angel, discovered the Holy Cross at Golgotha, was alluded to in many of Edward IV's genealogies.) The persistence of the identification of Edward with Augustus, and of the latter part of his reign as an Augustan age of peace and prosperity, was maintained by Thomas More between 1514 and 1518 in the *History of Richard III*. Influenced by his reading of Suetonius and Tacitus, More drew comparisons between the reigns of Augustus and Edward as periods of peace, with the exception of a single prestigious military campaign, that had followed periods of civil war. Edward had secured Berwick, pacified Scotland and faced no foreign threats. Nearly all Henry VI's supporters were dead. More's idealized vision of the 1470s as an Augustan age had been influenced by the way Edward and his court adopted Roman values and assimilated Roman political wisdom, but it was also reflected in More's reading of the

Octavius's vision of the Virgin and child. (British Library Royal 19 E V The Romuleon, *translated by Jean de Mielot, fo. 336v)*

idealized republic of Plato: 'This realm was in quiet prosperous estate, no-feare of outeward enemeyes, no warre in hande, nor no contrayned feare, but a wyllyng and louyng obedyence; amonge them selfe, the commons in good peace'.[117] Just as Augustus's reign was to be followed by the cruelties and excesses of Tiberius, so too, in More's eyes, Edward's reign was followed by that of Richard III.

This was of course a rationalization, and to leave Edward at this point would create the misleading impression that his second reign was an Augustan age of tolerance, rationality and enlightenment. He had successfully harvested the energies of youth to recapture his throne and certainly everything was in place for him to grow into a mature man and monarch like Henry V or Augustus, following the counsel of the stoic writings in his library and the advice of his alchemist physicians. However, Edward and his court were to succumb to darker, more irrational forces, especially after 1475.

NOTES

1. Emden, *BRUO*, p. 699; Weis, *Humanism in England in the Fifteenth Century*, p. 191. For Fleming's 'Lucubratiunculae', see Weis, *Humanism*, pp. 102–3, 191. The poem was printed in Rome in 1477. A presentation copy, prepared for Thomas Rotherham, then bishop of Ely, is in Bodley MS BB Art Selden 4.
2. Emden, *BRUC*, pp. 524–5; P.S. Allen, 'Bishop Shirwood of Durham and his Library', *EHR*, xxv (1910), 445–56.
3. Emden, *BRUC*, pp. 275–6.
4. R.J. Mitchell, *John Tiptoft, 1427–1470* (London, 1938), p. 153; BL MS Harl. 103; BL MS Harl. 2639.
5. Bodley MS Auct F1. 13; Bodley MS 646.
6. R.J. Mitchell, 'A Renaissance Library: the Collection of John Tiptoft, Earl of Worcester', *The Library*, xviii (1937–8), 66–83; MS 138.
7. BL MS Harl. 3346, fo. 4v.
8. Keir, 'Ecclesiastical Career of George Neville', 207; Stephani Baluzii, *Tutelensis Miscellanea – opera ac studii Johanis Dominici Mansi Lucensis* (Greca, 1761), vol. I, pp. 494–501.
9. Vespasiano de Bistichi, *Vite dii uomini illustri del secolo XV*, ed. L. Frati (1892), vol. 1, p. 322.
10. For a description of this visit see the letter written by John Paston II to his mother Margaret. *Paston Letters* ed. Davis, vol. ii, p. 494.
11. Mitchell, *John Tiptoft*, pp. 64–79.
12. BL MS Julius VII, fos 67–9.
13. Ibid, fos 48–8v, 74–91v.
14. Scot McKendrick, 'Classical Mythology and Ancient History in Works of Art at the courts of France, Burgundy and England, 1364–1500' unpublished PhD thesis, Courtauld Institute, London, 1988.
15. G. Kipling, *The Triumph of Honour*, p. 18; J.H. Hexter, 'The Education of the Aristocracy in the Renaissssance', *Journal of Modern History*, xxii (1950), 1–20.
16. McKendrick, 'Classical Mythology and Ancient History', 19ff.
17. Ibid, 232ff.
18. Ibid, 239ff; Scott McKendrick, 'The *Romuleon* and the Manuscripts of Edward IV', in *England in the Fifteenth Century: Proceedings of the 1992 Harlaxton Symposium*, ed. N. Rogers (Stamford, 1994).
19. Commines, *Memoirs*, p. 169.
20. R. Vaughan, *Charles the Bold* (London, 1973), p. 16.
21. L. Visser-Fuchs, 'Choosing a Book', in C. Barron and N. Saul, *England and the Low Countries in the Later Middle Ages* (Stroud, 1995); J. Backhouse, 'Founders of the Royal Library: Edward IV and Henry VIII as Collectors of Illuminated Manuscripts', in *England in the Fifteenth Century, Proceedings of the 1984 Harlaxton Symposium*, ed. D. Williams (Woodbridge, 1987), pp. 23–41.
22. *Household Book of Edward IV*, ed. Myers.
23. BL MS Harl. 4780, ed. Nicolas; Backhouse, 'Founders of the Royal Library', 23.
24. Scott McKendrick, 'Louis of Gruuthuyse and the Library of Edward IV', in *Lodewijk van Gruuthuyse mecenam en European Diplomat ca 1427–1492*, ed. M.P.J. Martens (Bruges, 1992).
25. BL MS Royal 17 F ii; Scott McKendrick, '*La Grande Histoire Cesar* and the manuscripts of Edward IV', *English Manuscript Studies*, vol. ii (1990).
26. Paris, Bibliotheque nationale MS na Fr 11673.
27. BL MS Royal 19 E V.

28. Ibid, fo. 32.
29. Ibid.
30. BL MS Royal 15 D vi.
31. BL MS Royal 18 E III and IV, fos 143–174v.
32. BL MS Royal 18 E VI.
33. BL MS Royal 16 G ix, fo. 42.
34. Sir John Sloane MS 1.
35. *Fifteenth-Century Translations of Alain Chartier's Traite de L'Esperance and le Quadrilogue Invectif*, ed. M.S. Blayney (EETS, 1974); Bodley MS Rawl. A 338; E.J. Hoffman, *Alain Chartier, His Work and Reputation* (New York, 1942).
36. BL MS Royal E II.
37. BL MS Royal 17 E IV.
38. Lambeth Palace MS 265; M.R. James, *A Descriptive Catalogue of the Manuscripts in the Library of Lambeth Palace* (Cambridge, 1932). For a printed edition in 1477 see Piershall, *Scriptorium*, vol. xxiii (1969).
39. This book used to be in the library of Ely Cathedral but has disappeared. See Weiss, *Humanism*, p. 171; Tanner, *Bibliotheca Britannico-Hibernica* (repr. 1963), p. 155.
40. BL MS Royal 17 E II, fo. 250.
41. A.F. Sutton and L. Visser-Fuchs, 'Richard III's Books Observed', *The Ricardian*, x, 120 (1993).
42. N.F. Blake, *William Caxton and English Literary Culture* (London, 1991), p. 167; Gransden, *Historical Writing*, vol. ii; Sutton and Visser-Fuchs, *Richard III's Books*, p. 178.
43. *Cicero on Old Age and Friendship*, W. Caxton, 1481, The English Experience Facsimile, no. 861 (Amsterdam, 1977).
44. Crotch, *Prologues*, 10–18. An inventory taken by John Paston II before 1479 shows that he owned Cicero's *De amicitia* and *De senectute* (the latter certainly Worcester's translation), along with Scrope's *Epistle of Othea*, Burgh's *Governance of Princes* and Vegetius's *De re militari. Paston Letters*, ed. Gairdner, vol. 6, pp. 65–6; *Sir John Paston's Grete Boke. A Descriptive Catalogue with an introduction to British Library MS Lansdowne 285*, ed. G.A. Lester (Cambridge, 1984).
45. Ibid, pp. 41–4.
46. N. Davis, review of B.J. Whiting, *Proverbs, Sentences and Proverbial Phrases from English Writings Mainly before 1500*, *Medium Aevum*, xli (1972), 164–6.
47. BL MS Harl. 103.
48. Stevenson, vol. ii, pp. 497–9.
49. *The Cordyale by Anthony Woodville*, ed. J.A. Mulders (Nijmegen, 1962).
50. Magdalen College, Oxford, MS 198; H.G. Wright, *Boccaccio in England from Chaucer to Tennyson* (London, 1957).
51. Chastellain, *Ouvres*, ed. K. Lettenhave (Brussels, 1884), vol. iv, pp. 155–60.
52. Ibid, vol. vii, pp. 73–143.
53. BL MS Royal 20 A xix; L. Visser-Fuchs 'Where did Elizabeth of York Find Consolation?', *The Ricardian*, ix, 122 (1993); A. Sutton and L. Visser-Fuchs, 'Richard III's Books: X the Prose Tristran', *The Ricardian*, ix, 112 (1991).
54. BL MS Royal 14 E II, fo. 274.
55. Lydgate, *Fall of Princes*, bk ii, ll. 54–6.
56. BL MS Royal 14 E v.
57. *The Middle English Translation of Christine de Pisan's Livre Du Corps De Policie*, ed. from Cambridge University Library MS K.K1.5 by Diane Bornstein (Heidelberg, 1977). Woodville's authorship is implied by the appearance of the coat of arms of Haute-Woodville on a manuscript of *Livre de Corps de Policie*, probably belonging to Sir Richard Haute, son of Joan Woodville, an aunt of Queen Elizabeth. Anthony Woodville was nominated overseer of Richard Haute's will. P.W. Fleming, 'The Hautes and their Circle', in *Culture and the English Gentry in the Fifteenth Century*.
58. Christine de Pisan, *Livre du Corps de Policie*, pp. 63–4.
59. Stephen Scrope, *Epistle of Othea*, pp. 119–20.
60. Caxton, *Legenda aurea*, fo. 4b.
61. See Hughes, *Pastors and Visionaries: Religion and Secular Life in Late Medieval Yorkshire*.
62. Worcester, *Boke of Noblesse*, p. 61.
63. Ibid, p. 59.
64. BL MS Royal V, fo. 196.
65. *Book of Policy*, p. 116.
66. *Prologues and Epilogues of William Caxton* (EETS, OS 176, 1928), pp. 10–12.
67. *The Politics of Fifteenth-Century England*, pp. 122–6; BL MS Add. 48031A, fos 146–8.

68. BL MS Add. 48031A, fo. 148v.
69. BL MS Add. 48031A, fo. 183.
70. Ibid.
71. E.W. Ives, 'The Common Lawyers', in *Profession, Vocation and Culture in Later Medieval England. Essays dedicated to A.R. Myers*, ed. C.H. Clough, p. 192; Year Books Mich 9 Edward IV, pl. 9 ff. 12–13.
72. Lambeth Palace MS 506; BL MS Royal B xxii.
73. *The Politics of England: John Vale's Book*, pp. 120–1.
74. *Fifteenth-Century Translations of Chartier's le Quadrilogue Invectif*, p. 139; cf Worcester, *Boke of Noblesse*, p. 52.
75. *Fifteenth-Century Translations of Chartier's le Quadrilogue Invectif*, p. 156.
76. Ibid, pp. 156–8.
77. *Rot. Parl.*, vol. vi, p. 8. For text see *Literae Cantuariensis: the Letter Books of the Monarchs of Christchurch Canterbury*, 3 vols (Rolls Series, London, 1839), vol. iii, pp. 27–85; Gross, *Dissolution of Lancastrian Kingship*, p. 91.
78. *Letter Books of Christchurch Canterbury*, vol. iii, pp. 27–85.
79. Lander, *Government and Community in England 1450–1507*, p. 285.
80. BL MS Royal D XV; Gross, *Dissolution of Lancastrian Kingship*, pp. 91ff.
81. BL MS Royal 15 E IV; *The Book of the Order of Chivalry*, translated by William Caxton, ed. A.T.P. Byles (EETS, OS 168, 1926).
82. BL MS Harl. 661.
83. Bodley Roll 5.
84. Hardynge's *Chronicle*, pp. 138–45.
85. Ibid, p. 419.
86. Bodley MS Lyell 33.
87. BL MS Lansdowne 762, fos 7v–8v.
88. Commines, *Memoirs*, p. 143.
89. D. Waley, *Later Medieval Europe* (New York, 1985), p. 125.
90. *Crowland Chronicle*, p. 135.
91. Worcester, *Itinerarium*, p. 325.
92. *Book of Policy*, p. 116.
93. Lydgate, *Fall of Princes*, vol. vi, ll. 3080–8.
94. Bodley MS Laud. Lat 70.
95. Weis, *Humanism in England*, pp. 120–1; Mitchell, *John Tiptoft*, pp. 26–35.
96. For the increasing importance of the concept of service to the state at the expense of familial loyalties see J. Hughes, *Richard III*, pp. 49ff.
97. Mitchell, *John Tiptoft*, pp. 176–8; for the text of the *Declamacion of Noblesse* see appendix, pp. 215–41.
98. Chartier, *Quadrilogium Invectif*, p. 246.
99. *Prologues and Epilogues of Caxton*, pp. 50–2.
100. Emden, *BRUO*, vol. ii, p. 1069.
101. *Excerpta Historica* (London, 1831).
102. A.B. Cobbam, *The Medieval English Universities* (Aldershot, 1988), p. 250; R.S. Stannier, *A History of Magdalen College Grammar School* (Oxford, 1958).
103. Ibid.
104. Kipling, *Triumph of Honour.*
105. Fortescue, *De Laudibus legem Anglie*, ed. Chrimes, pp. 108–11; N. Orme, *From Childhood to Chivalry* (London, 1984), p. 48. BL MS Sloane 3479; Scofield, *Edward IV*, p. 15; N. Orme, 'The Education of Edward V', *Bulletin Historical Research*, lvii, 136 (1984).
106. BL MS Royal 12 A xxix.
107. James, 'English Politics and the Concept of Honour', 358.
108. Worcester, *Itinerarium*, p. 251.
109. *Parvus Cato Magnus Cato*, translated by Benedict Burgh, ed. from William Caxton's first edition by F. Kuriyawa (Tokyo, 1974), p. 77.
110. BL MS Royal 19 E V, fo. 32.
111. BL MS Royal 17 F II.
112. *Arrivall*, p. 7 (153).
113. BL MS Add. 37801, fo. 183; Yelverton MS 35.
114. BL MS Sloane MS 1.
115. BL MS Royal E V, fo. 336b.
116. Stephen Scrope, *The Epistle of Othea*, ed. C.F. Buhler (EETS, London, 1970), p. 120.
117. *The Complete Works of St Thomas More*, ed. R.S. Sylvester, vol ii, *The History of Richard III* (Yale, 1963).

CHAPTER 10

The Death of the King

All he admires that all admire in him,
Himself he longs for, longs unwittingly.
'Narcissus and Echo', from Ovid, *Metamorphoses, Bk iii, ll. 423–4*

Utterly perished is the flower of youth
Through all my veins there courses naught but death.
George Ripley, *Cantilena, verses 11–12*

To leave Edward at this point would be to create an artificially rational view of a Yorkist England that had more in common with England in the Augustan age of the eighteenth century. There is no gainsaying the achievement of Edward, an essentially instinctive ruler, in assimilating, with the help of courtiers such as Anthony Woodville, pragmatic, scientific Roman values in government and education, and in creating out of the civil war thirteen years of relative peace and prosperity. This is certainly how Thomas More, influenced by Suetonius and Tacitus, regarded Edward's reign. He saw Edward as Augustus, the bringer of peace, who created a family that would be decimated by his Nemesis, his younger brother Richard duke of Gloucester, a cruel Tiberius. (Tiberius also killed members of Augustus's family and like Gloucester created a sorrowing widow and children.) It is easy to see how More arrived at this conclusion. Edward is unique among English medieval kings in the images he helped to project in the early 1470s of a royal family and of his role as a husband and father, evoked by the author of the *Arrivall*'s account of Edward entering the sanctuary of Westminster, comforting his queen and hearing the news of the birth of his son, 'to the kyngys great joy'.

This image of a royal family is captured in Bluemantle Pursuivant's account of the visit of Louis de Gruuthuyse to Westminster in 1472 to discuss an alliance between England and Burgundy. This visit gave Edward an opportunity to show his gratitude for Gruuthuyse's hospitality during his exile. Bluemantle captures Edward at his finest in peacetime, in the role of the returned hero at rest with his family, the complete man. The hospitality meted out is reminiscent of Arthur's Camelot. Gruuthuyse (perhaps an important model in the chivalric cultivation of the learning of antiquity and service to the common weal, in acknowledgement of which he had been created earl of Winchester in 1472)[1] was led by Hastings into three chambers where Edward was with his queen in the apartments hung with cloth of gold arras. The queen was playing morteaux and Edward was dancing with his eldest daughter Elizabeth. The following day the king hunted in Windsor deer park. He gave his guest his own horse to ride and dinner was served in a lodge in the park. After dinner the king hunted again, and then he showed his guest his garden, a vineyard of pleasure. The queen ordered a great banquet in her own chamber where there was a rich table 'with a good view of the ladies'. After dinner the king and queen took Gruuthuyse to three chambers of 'plesaunce' hung with silk and linen and with diverse colours. He was given a bed with sheets of Bretayne cloth and a gold counterpane. In the third chamber there was a bath with tents of white cloth where Gruuthuyse and Hastings bathed, supping on green ginger and diverse syrups. On the following day, 13 October, St Edward's Day, after the speaker had commended the queen's courageous behaviour while her husband was overseas, they went to St Edward's shrine in Westminster Abbey to make offerings.[2] This is Edward at his most attractive, the open, generous and charming man who can bring people together in an atmosphere of courtesy and chivalry. At this moment it must have seemed as if Arthur had returned.

However, Edward was no simple Abel to Richard's Cain. He was just as complicated and he had a dark side which emerged as the decade unfolded. There was consequently a less rational, mythic dimension to his second reign. Edward had regained his throne riding the energy of powerful myths, and these myths were not simply to be laid aside once he became king. He continued to be associated with prophecies. When the Irish Parliament asked Edward in 1474 for help against rebellious Scots settled in Ireland they referred to the prophecies of the coming of Edward known as Sextus Hiberniae, and the prophecy of the white lion who would win the land of Ireland. His quest was not completed. There was one further task he had to fulfil if he and his new nation were to attain full selfhood and measure up to the myths he had tapped into. That task was the conquest of France, the completion of Henry V's work. This was the only way to lay to rest the ghost of the one truly heroic figure of the house of Lancaster. If Edward could complete what Henry, through the intervention of fate, had failed to do, then he could once and for all establish that he and not Henry V was the divinely ordained king, the hero anticipated in the prophecies and in the epitaph at the conclusion of Malory's *Morte d'Arthur*.

The invasion of France in 1475 was therefore preceded by the reissuing of prophecies concerning the destiny of a British king who would acquire an empire. After the death of William Herbert, hopes in Wales were even more forcefully pinned on Edward. As the king of prophecy he was perceived to be the British king who once again ruled in London and through the creation of the prince of Wales's council at Ludlow he gradually extended the direct influence of the crown over the whole of Wales.[3] Guto'r Glyn addressed a poem to the king when he was preparing for the campaign in France in 1474–5. He appealed to Edward to look to his grandmother's Welsh kinsmen for support in Wales, reminding him of Mortimer's descent from the ruling house of Gwynedd, and exhorted to him to free the Welsh from all the deceit and oppression under which they laboured.[4] Prophecies relating to Edward III's continental ambitions were reapplied to Edward IV. The prophecy of Six Kings contained a passage on the boar (Edward III) whetting his tusks in four lands and at the gates of Paris, where he would receive three crowns. Many countries would tumble before him, and he would regain all the lands lost by his ancestors. Edward IV alluded to this prophecy in the letter he wrote to Louis XI predicting the overrunning of France with various animals, including the boar. A frequently copied text was the prophecy of the lily, the lion and the son of man. The son of man (the king of England) would, in alliance with the emperor, overcome the lily (the king of France and usurper) and assume his crown. The son of man would then undertake a crusade to the Holy Land.[5]

For the alchemists, too, the search for gold was accompanied by dreams of empire, as it would be at the beginning of the seventeenth century.[6] Ripley, commenting on the alchemists of London with their houses full of furnaces and glasses of diverse shapes, paints and oils, thought of their dreams of making enough gold to help the king 'Fraunce for to wyn, a wondrous thyng', and to pay his ransom if he were captured. It is doubtful if alchemists as high minded as Ripley were committed to the conquest of France per se; they were more interested in the crusade, but a quest such as the French invasion may have been enough to convince them that King Edward was still capable of heroic deeds. In alchemical language (or at least in the terms that would be understood by such twentieth-century interpreters of alchemy as Carl Jung), the king, in showing a willingness to invade France, was prepared to surrender his egoistic, selfish comforts and to allow himself to be led into danger by a heroic mythic dominant. Just as Edward had landed at Ravenspur in 1471 to follow in Bolingbroke's footsteps and to overcome the legacy of the Lancastrian dynasty established when Bolingbroke landed at Ravenspur in 1399, so too in August 1475 he landed in France with the largest invasion force ever assembled to follow in Henry V's footsteps and to surpass him. Edward therefore pointedly marched from Calais to the historic site of Agincourt where he spent two nights. The plan was then to march into Champagne to meet with the Duke of Burgundy and head for Rheims where he would be crowned, something his predecessor had not been able to achieve.

The boastful letter that Edward wrote to Louis XI, giving a list of the animal emblems – including the black bull (Clarence), the boar (Gloucester) and the dragon (Edward) – with which he would hunt through France, is both an allusion to the prophecies and an emulation of Henry V. Henry was supposed to have received from the Dauphin the insulting gift of a tennis ball, while Edward received from Louis a donkey. Edward like Henry responded defiantly: 'I shall blow my horn follow my beestes and my beestes must follow the chase ye shall we hunt through all the parties of France. And I trust to our Lady that your moche shall turn to shame for you must wot right wel I am master of the game.'[7] However, the game he was beginning when he decided to open negotiations with Louis XI was one he could not hope to win. Edward's relationship with the French king went back to 1461 when, after a quarrel with his father, Louis sent from the court of Philip of Burgundy troops under Seigneur de la Barde bearing the banner of Louis the Dauphin.[8] The two men were complete opposites. Even after all the betrayals of 1468–71, Edward remained an essentially open, tactile person. Polydore Vergil certainly perceived his warmth: 'By reson – of humanity which was bred in him abundantly, he would use himself more familiarly among private persons than the honour of his majesty required.'[9] According to Dominic Mancini, the Italian cleric in England on a papal mission and writing in 1483, he was easy of access to his friends and to others, even the least notable:

> Frequently he called to his side complete strangers, when he thought they had come with the intention of addressing or beholding him more closely. He was wont to show himself to those who wished to watch him and seized any opportunity occasion offered of revealing his fine stature more protractedly and more evidently to on-lookers. He was so genial in his greeting that, if a newcomer was bewildered at his appearance and royal magnificence, he would give him courage to speak by laying a kindly hand on his shoulder.[10]

Above all Edward had charm, the ability to make people feel good. His retentive memory, so powerful 'that the names and circumstances of almost all men, scattered over the counties of the kingdom, were known to him just as if they were in the habit of seeing him daily, even if, in the districts where they lived, they were reckoned to be of rather inferior status',[11] might perhaps seem obsessive and needy in an ordinary person but for a king it was a formidable weapon in his charm offensive. When he placed 'a kindly arm on the shoulder'[12] of a nervous newcomer to the court and displayed this memory he was able to make that person feel special. He employed this warmth and charisma to spectacular effect in raising money for his French campaign. In his address to Parliament in 1473 he argued that his expedition would occupy riotous malefactors and secure internal peace. The lords and commons voted a novel income tax of 10 per cent which, it was calculated, would raise over £118,000 (nearly four times a single tenth and fifteenth tax). All this was to be held in special repositories until the king mustered his army, which he undertook to do by Michaelmas 1474. By the spring of 1473 Parliament had also agreed to a conventional tenth and fifteenth to be paid into the same repositories.[13] By July 1474, however, little progress had been made in gathering the taxes voted a year earlier, and to raise the cash to meet the first instalments of his troops' wages Edward devised a way of testing his subjects' goodwill. Besides costing for subsidies, three-and-a-half lay subsidies amounting to £118 62s, and three-and-a-half clerical subsidies amounting to £48, he devised in 1474 the extraordinary method of raising benevolences – free gifts in lieu of military service. An Italian visitor described how Edward went from place to place summoning likely contributors who would be cajoled and charmed into promising payments. What surprised the Italian observer was that every one gave willingly: 'I have frequently seen our neighbours here who were summoned before the king. When they went they looked as if they were going to the gallows, when they returned they were joyful, saying they had spoken to the king, and he had spoken to them so benignly that they did not regret the money they had payed.'[14] According to *The Great Chronicle of London*, a rich Suffolk widow liberally granted the king £10 and decided after he 'took her till him and kissed her, the which kiss she accepted so kindly, that for that great bounty and kind deed he sould have £20 for his £10'. By such methods at least £20,000 was raised.

Louis could not have been more different. Ruling from deep within palaces, shunning personal contact, he was never present in battle. He spent his last days in a state of paranoia, fortifying his residence with iron bars, so that Commines commented: 'The king who kept others in cages 8ft square had imprisoned himself in a cage, afraid even of his own children.'[15] In his pursuit of power he was isolated at the centre of a web of men, money and iron which held together the state and earned him the epithet the 'universal spider' (a phrase first used by the Burgundian chronicler Chastellain). However, Commines, who served Charles the Bold and joined Louis's service in 1472, understood Louis in a way he could never understand Edward. Commines saw politics as a chess game that would be won by the coolest player rather than the most aggressive, one who outwitted his more emotional opponents. Louis embodied the qualities of the remote, passionless intelligence that Commines attributed to God and the ideal monarch. Commines had a rational view of God and history as a series of checks and balances. France balanced England so neither became too powerful. For this Burgundian writer the power that worked was the commonsensical, unwearying pursuit of the practically obtainable, the sort of power he attributed to God. He therefore had little understanding of Edward's more emotional dependence on the energizing power of myth. He did comment on the size of Edward's army and reflected that it was the largest since King Arthur's, but sniggered at the way Edward's chancellor began the peace talks with a reference to a prophecy, probably Merlin's. He also cynically observed that at the conclusion of the talks the English excitedly observed a dove perching on the king of England's tent and took it as an apparition of the Holy Ghost, a ratification of the peace, and added that Louis was at pains to prevent his men laughing at them. The French delegation's explanation was that this white pigeon had been caught in an earlier shower and was perched in the sun drying herself. Commines was undoubtedly affected by Edward's warmth, charm and attractive looks when he met him in 1475: 'He was a good-looking tall prince, although he was beginning to get fat and I have seen him on previous occasions looking more handsome. Indeed I do not recall seeing such a fine-looking man as he was when my Lord Warwick forced him to flee from England.' Yet he never understood him. As an intellectual he was horrified by Edward's reliance on his instincts and the motivation of powerful emotions generated by myths and his own personal charisma and charm.

So when this brave, open, and at times generous, man approached the bridge erected across the River Somme near Amiens for the peace negotiations, it must have seemed to onlookers as if he was entering a very alien world, a spider's web. Edward was forced to approach along a causeway two bow-shots in length, with marshes on either side, on to a bridge. Louis XI, anxious to avoid a repeat of the assassination of Jean sans Peur, the duke of Burgundy, on the bridge of Montereau on Sunday 10 September 1419 (a crime perpetrated with the connivance of Louis's father, the then sixteen-year-old Dauphin), ordered the construction of a strong wooden lattice, such as those used for making a lion's cage, but large enough to hold twelve men on either side. Each gap between the bars was only wide enough to permit the thrust of a man's hand. Even Commines was moved to comment as Edward approached: 'The English do not manage their treaties and capitulations with so much cunning and policy as the French do – but proceed more ingenuously, and with greater straightforwardness in their affairs.' The extrovert Edward, in every way a contrast to the neurotic Louis, approached the contraption, pulled off his feathered, velvet cap with its jewelled fleur de lys and bowed to within six inches of the ground. Louis then embraced him through the bars of his cage.[16]

The terms of the treaty of Picquigny were, on the face of it, very favourable to England. Louis agreed to pay Edward 75,000 gold crowns (a crown being a silver coin worth 5 shillings) for expenses in preparation for the war and afterwards a yearly pension of 50,000 crowns for the surrender of Margaret of Anjou. Edward was furthermore promised a future marriage for his eldest daughter with the Dauphin of France, with a jointure of £60,000 yearly provided by King Louis. Edward's leading counsellors were also given pensions. Thomas Montgomery received 1,200 crowns, Bishop Thomas Rotherham 1,000 crowns and John Morton £600. Hastings received an annual fee of 2,000 crowns and John Lord Howard a pension of 1,200 crowns and gifts amounting to 24,000 crowns. Sir Thomas More, seeing Edward's reign in terms of the world of Plato's *Republic*, a harmoniously ordered, rational society, saw this treaty as a triumph of reason: 'thys realm was in quiet prosperous estate; no feare of outeward enemyes, no more in hande, nor not toward – the people toward the prynce, not in a constreyned fear, but a wyllyng and louyng obedyence/ amonge them selfe, the commons in good peace'. The treaty, according to More, embodied what he perceived to be Edward's Augustan values, for More shared his friend Erasmus's mistrust and dislike of heroic myths. In his *Instructions* in 1516, Erasmus commented on romances, observing: 'We see so many people these days who enjoy the stories of Arthur, Lancelot and others of their kind. These stories are not only about criminals, they are also coarse and sentimental.' This judgement ignores the importance of such myths to the self-image of Edward and to his people. The fact is that the perceptive Louis began the process of breaking Edward's spirit with this offer, which was nothing more than a bribe deliberately aimed at appealing (as Commines admitted) to Edward's principal weakness, his avarice. He cold-bloodedly set about corrupting Edward and his men, draining from them their sense of mission and destiny. It represents the same betrayal of the higher ideals of alchemy that Edward showed when he tried to force Dalton to transmute base metal into gold.

It began as Edward's army approached Amiens. Louis sent them 300 cart-loads of the finest French wine as a token of the truce. When Edward's troops entered the town they were greeted by long tables set on either side of the street laden with food and wine, 'the richest that France could produce'. Wherever Edward and his men went in the town, they had to pay for nothing, including the alcohol consumed in the town's nine taverns; this feasting at Louis's expense lasted three or four days, with the English army getting uncontrollably drunk. After the two kings had sworn to observe the treaty on the bridge, Louis, according to the *Memoirs* of Commines, told Edward:

> in a jocular way, he should be glad to see his majesty at Paris; and that if he would come and divert himself with the ladies, he would assign him the Cardinal of Bourbon for his confessor, which he knew would willingly absolve him, if he would commit any sin by way of love and gallantry. The king of England was extremely pleased with his raillery, and made his majesty several good repartees, for he knew the cardinal was a jolly companion.

What Edward did not know as he turned back to England was that Louis was jesting that he had easily driven the English from France with venison pasties and fine wines.

Edward was permanently damaged and tarnished, but he did not know it. He attempted to depict this treaty as a triumph: carvings showing him and Louis on the bridge at Picquigny were placed on the sovereign's stall in St George's chapel, Windsor. It would not have fooled anybody. A defeat would have been more honourable than the army's ignominious return to England with gold, gifts and hangovers. Instead of stories of deeds of heroism, all they could recount were anecdotes about their French debauch. Louis de Bretalle, a Gascon in the service of Earl Rivers, told Commines that Edward had won nine victories and lost only one battle, the present one, and that the shame of returning to England in these circumstances outweighed the honour he had gained from the other nine. Some soldiers chose to remain in the service of Charles the Bold, who was disgusted with his brother-in-law's behaviour.[17] The Milanese ambassador at the Burgundian court wrote to the duke of Milan that 'the king of England, to the great disgust of his kingdom', had returned with his army to England after apologizing to the duke of Burgundy. He claimed

Centre section of the carved misericord on the Sovereign's Stall, St George's Chapel, Windsor. King Louis XI (headless left) meets King Edward IV to sign the peace treaty of Picquigny, August 1475. (Geoffrey Wheeler)

that in the opinion of intelligent persons there was likely to be a disturbance in England because the king enacted a great truce and did nothing.[18] Hostility towards the returning army in England was considerable, because so much money raised in taxes had been wasted, and even the Croyland chronicler, who attempted to defend the treaty, had to admit that many people openly murmured at the king's avarice and threatened with public vengeance the ministers who had allowed themselves to be bribed by the French king.[19]

Picquigny was a watershed in Edward's life, the counterbalance to Mortimer's Cross; in terms of the values he had stood for it was a self-destructive act of betrayal. He threw away the chance to emulate and surpass Henry V and to complete the quest he had embarked upon. Henry V and Edward IV were both impressive young men around whom myths cohered. But Henry V (as Shakespeare so perceptively understood) grew up and left his princely persona behind. No act demonstrated this more clearly than the execution of a companion of his youth for stealing on the Agincourt campaign. Prince Hal became the stern and disciplined martial general about whom his troops complained in letters in 1419 because he campaigned through the winter months. Edward, if he were to succeed in this French expedition, needed to show the same qualities, but he did not have the patience and self-discipline for a long uncomfortable campaign that would dissipate his energy. He was happiest in short, decisive enterprises where he could feed off the adulation of his men and the heady brew of alchemy and myth. He needed excitement and applause. We can see this in the way he paraded himself before leaving Burgundy and in the drama and pageantry of his raising benevolences. Perhaps he was in love with his youth, a narcissus mesmerized by his own beauty and charm. The power and the terror, the sorrow and the beauty of that February day in 1461 may have been too much for him, a trauma from which he could never recover. His life seems to have circulated in a coil of negative restless energy (and therefore no *uroboros*) around that defining moment: the assertion of courage and decision in response to a crisis followed by narcissistic self-indulgence and inertia, inflation and deflation. But after Picquigny there would be no more rising of the sun. For the rest of his reign he would prove that he had never grown up to embrace the sort of mature, masculine energy that Henry V displayed in his short but eventful life. The alchemist more than anyone was aware of the dangerous nature of strong emotional energies, especially the dangers of self-inflation. Norton's *Ordinal of Alchemy* is full of illustrations and warnings about it. Ripley, when he wrote about the king reclaiming his tender youth from the jaws of the dragon, must have been aware of the potentially self-destructive tendencies of his talented and narcissistic sovereign.

Picquigny also marked the beginning of a rift between Edward and his enigmatic younger brother, Richard duke of Gloucester, which was to have momentous repercussions for the future of his dynasty. Richard idolized his older brother. At the age of eight, Richard had lost his father at Wakefield, and Edward had taken his place as a heroic paternal figure. Richard was an introvert, lacking his brother's good looks and charm, but he became a dedicated soldier and played a crucial role in the reconquest of the kingdom in the battles of Barnet and Tewkesbury. As warden of the Marches in 1475 he was critical of the peace policy towards Scotland: his failure to hold regular days of the March, redress infringements of the truce, and his implication (as lord admiral) in illegal piracy earned the rebuke of Edward IV.[20] He soon became a leading member of the war party against France. In the winter of 1472 it was rumoured that he would cross to Normandy at the head of an English army. The expedition never took place, but Gloucester took personal responsibility for the dispatch of English archers, sent in support of the Burgundian cause.[21] He also contributed more to the 1475 invasion than anyone else. His boar badge was prominent after the Clarence bull on the 1475 muster roll for Edward's invasion.[22] He was the only high-ranking councillor opposed to the treaty. He took no part in the negotiations on the bridge and instead inspected the French army and its commander. The treaty represented for him a grubby betrayal of his father's martyrdom at Wakefield and all that he had stood for in France. Richard duke of York had written a letter from Ludlow on 3 February 1452 to the city of Gloucester lamenting the losses in France which he regarded not just as a loss of territory, a slight on the king's honour, but a blow to English standing abroad: 'What praise, lordship, honour and manhood was ascribed by all nations to people of this realm while the king, our sovereign lord possessed the realms of France and Normandy, and what derogation, loss of merchandise and destruction and villainy reported to the English nation from the loss of the same.'

Richard of Gloucester, contemplating the shameful sell-out at Picquigny in the light of this letter, must have seen it as a betrayal of all his father had stood for, and from this point his father the duke of York, the dead war hero, would have taken Edward's place in Gloucester's affections. Eloquent testimony to this was provided by Chester Herald's account of Richard duke of York's reburial the following year. The hearse, which had been ordered in 1461, resembled a house with a pitched roof. Candles enclosed the duke's effigy, with a white angel holding a crown. It symbolized the ark of the covenant[23] borne by a divinely chosen leader of God's people, who had a vision of the promised land but died before reaching it. Gloucester would have received encouragement in holding on to this idealized image of his father from such poems as 'The Twelve Letters to Save England', which describes the duke of York as a prophet 'that be grace of God and gret revalacion – the which for our sake suffer vexacion'.[24] The procession went from Pontefract to the family home at Fotheringay on 27–30 July 1476, and it was Richard duke of Gloucester, not Edward, who was the principal mourner, assuming his brother's position as leader of the tribe, the heir to his father's vision.[25] Galling for him must have been the presence of two ambassadors from Louis XI who had come to pay the first instalment of the pension.

The genealogical rolls produced in 1470–1 would, in the context of this ceremony, assume new importance in Gloucester's eyes. Two rolls emphasize the symbolically significant Yorkist family tree of the younger son David, chosen by God to assume leadership of the tribe of Moses: the *Yorkist Prophecies* has a prophecy of David of the coming of the son of man (one of Edward's cognomens which Gloucester would later usurp for himself),[26] and the other contains the lines 'David the best of hys brede was chose of God by Samuel the prophet'.[27] In the 1471 version of the *Genealogy of Edward King of Britain* David's name occurs beside Edward's in red, but it is also just underneath Gloucester's, who has a prominent place in the genealogy and is described as the son of Richard duke of York.[28] Both genealogies symbolically link David, king of the Hebrews, with Brutus, king of Britain, for their names occur almost opposite one another in parallel lines. Richard duke of Gloucester owned Guido delle Colonna's *History of the Destruction of Troy* and Geoffrey of Monmouth's *Historia Regum Britanniae* and a composite text of the *Prophecy of the Eagle* with a commentary in a single manuscript in which he signed his name and described himself as a descendant of Brutus.[29] The 1471 version of the *Genealogy of Edward King of Britain* provided further inspiration for Richard's identification with the chosen younger son for it contains discussion of primogeniture and claims that this should not be the sole factor determining succession, and cites the examples of Jacob and Joseph.[30] Richard was not only the youngest son, he was also much smaller than the giant-like Edward, like David to Goliath. Gloucester's quiet disapproval of Edward's abandonment of the heroic ideals and his patient waiting-in-the-wings is perhaps captured in some of the illustrations in Edward's collection of chivalric literature. He is thought to be shown in a presentation miniature to the left of Edward who wears the Golden Fleece and receives from Waurin, the author, a copy of *Anciennes et nouvelles*

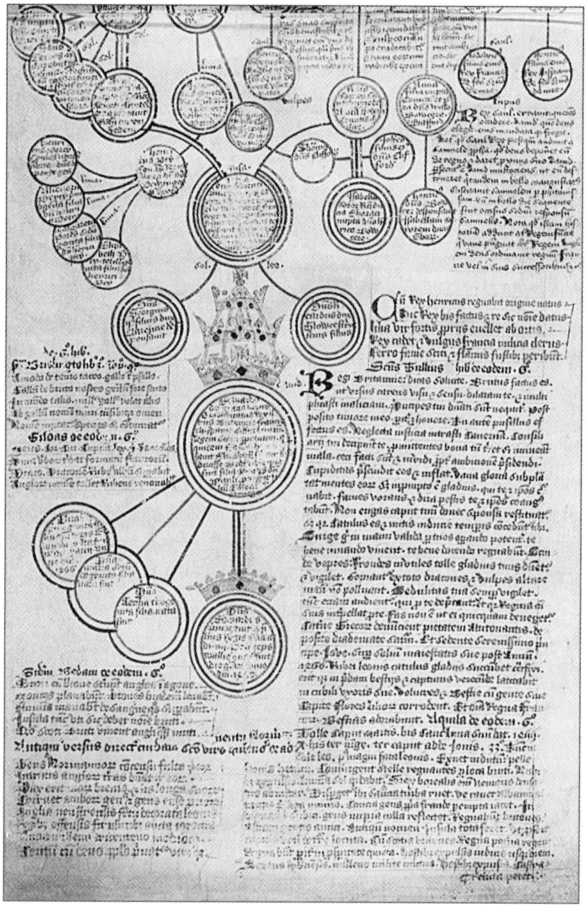

Near the conclusion to The Genealogy of Edward King of Britain, *Edward is represented with three crowns. Next to him but also close to Richard, Duke of Gloucester, occurs the cognomen David. Gloucester would capitalize on this ambiguity. Above them both, next to Henry VI, appears the cognomen Saul. (Ashmole Roll 26)*

croniques d'angleterre.[31] This figure, in an admittedly stylized posture, can perhaps be identified by the Garter on his leg and a crudely individualized portrait of a face with a prominent chin.[32] This surly figure does show a striking resemblance to the portrait of the squire sent for by a king who wishes to hold a great court, and who falls asleep in the forest and receives from a hermit, a retired knight, a book about the chivalric ideals that form the teaching of Edward IV's copy of Lull's *Book of the Order of Chivalry*,[33] teachings that Edward fails to observe and which Gloucester believed he was the man to fulfil. It is possible that the rumours of the king's illegitimacy, which Cicely duchess of York had first threatened to expose at the time of his marriage to Elizabeth in 1464 and which Clarence was accused of circulating in 1477, may have started to spread at the time of this funeral.

The period between the treaty of Picquigny and the reburial of the duke of York may also have been the time when Gloucester started to apply some of the prophecies found in his copy of Geoffrey of Monmouth, in the *Prophetic History of Britain* and in other Yorkist collections of prophecies executed in the 1460s[34] to his growing conviction that only he remained true to the original vision of the house of York. At the head of the muster roll of Edward's 1475 expedition, underneath the bull of Clarence, is the white tusked boar of Richard duke of Gloucester. Many of the prophecies in the above collections stress the boar's ferocity in his conquest of France. Most relevant to the brothers' different attitudes to

At the beginning of Lull's Book of the Order of Chivalry, *a hermit instructs a knight, who bears a resemblance to images of Richard duke of Gloucester that appear in other manuscripts in Edward's library, about the principles of chivalry that have been abandoned at Picquigny. (British Library Royal 14 E II, fo. 338)*

the treaty of Picquigny was the Thomas Becket prophecy that occurred in the *Yorkist Prophecies*.[35] A tower was being built by the king of France and two boars came from England to ruin the tower. One of the boars (Richard) charges the king and puts him to flight, but the other (Edward) merely positions himself in the choicest fields of the kingdom. The prophecy of the Six Kings, originally directed to Edward III, refers to the boar of prophecy coming out of Windsor, whetting its tusks against the gates of Paris, wearing three crowns and going to the Holy Land. Gloucester, unlike Edward, never lost his dedication to the ideal of the crusade. The prophecy most relevant to Gloucester because it symbolised his taking the place of Edward as the favoured chosen son was the prophecy of the son of man found in the *Yorkist Prophecies*: 'The Realm of Gaul shall rise and the son of man shall take the name of the bore and do battle against Gaul. There shall fall great effusion of blood – The Bore shall speak the words of truth.'[36] It would of course have been especially convenient for Gloucester, in his imaginary bond with his absent father, if he could believe in the illegitimacy of his elder brother. Rumours were already circulating to this effect at the time of Edward's marriage to Elizabeth Woodville. Gloucester, during the reburial of his father, may have found special comfort in the verification of these prophecies from the prophecy that 'a bastard shall come, not in England born shall he be, and he shall win the victory and all the land after Britain shall be'.[37] Edward, who restored Britain's identity in 1461, was of course born in Rouen.

From 1476 until his death in April 1483 Edward moved even further away from the heroic ideals he had once embodied and in which his people believed, and sank ever deeper into the web spun by Louis XI; it was Gloucester and Hastings who increasingly stood for these patriotic values. They stood alone among Edward's councillors in refusing to be bought by Louis. Gloucester received no payment at Picquigny, and although Hastings did receive a pension he suspected that Louis was gloating over the proofs he was laying by of the number of English lords who were in his pay, and he refused to give a receipt for his payment, declaring he had not asked for the money and did not intend that anyone should have the chance to say that the lord chamberlain of England had become a pensioner of the king of France. A sense of the inertia that gripped Edward at this time can be seen in Chastellain's commentary on Edward's reactions to the advice of the duke of Burgundy concerning Louis's intentions: 'He never knew how to put into effect what would be for his salvation. He promised many things and said he would do them, but he never did any of them.'

On 5 January 1477, Edward was informed that Charles the Bold, the duke of Burgundy, had been killed while besieging Nancy. This caused a crisis in foreign relations and Burgundy's northern dominions were now vulnerable to invasion from Louis XI. Charles's twenty-year-old daughter Mary was heiress to the duchy, and her stepmother Margaret of York, Edward's sister, requested military assistance to protect her lands and to safeguard a marriage alliance for Mary with an English husband. On 30 January 1477 a letter from Mary told how her stepmother was 'fully occupied in dealing with the very high and mighty prince our well beloved lord and cousin, the king of England, to persuade him to come to our aid and to uphold the everlasting alliances and treaties which were signed between him and our late lord and father'.[38] A popular ballad, the *Complainte d'Arras*, written shortly after the death of Charles the Bold, caught the mood of expectation of help from the house of York. Arras invoked the protection of Margaret of York because the fragrance of her flower, the marguerite, would attract the rose of England. Margaret was presented as a recipient of the chivalrous support of the white rose of England:

> Let all the men who make war be afraid,
> since the rose of England
> is of our party now:
> he will be there soon.[39]

The council meeting called by the king on 14 February 1477 was a response to Margaret's call for help, her appeal to Edward to answer the Arthurian call of chivalry to defend a helpless widow, and a reminder of his moral responsibilities. Margaret had sent word to Edward that Mary was virtually a prisoner of the burghers of Ghent and that Louis was trying to force her to marry the Dauphin. Margaret and Mary may even have tried to strengthen Edward's resolve by giving his servant John Donne (whose portrait, showing him wearing the sun and roses collar, can be seen in the Memlic Diptych) a copy of the *Life of Alexander the Great.* The letter Sir John Paston wrote in excitement to his brother in Norwich conveys this mixed sense of fear and expectation raised by these events: 'It seemeth that the world is all wavering, it will reboil somewhere, so that I deem young men shall be cherished, take your heart to you.' Sir John was anticipating a major campaign in Flanders in which his younger brother Edmund (a member of the Calais garrison) would participate. Sir John Paston and many others at the court envisaged rapid military action. The Calais garrison was to be reinforced by William Lord Hastings in 'a great company'. This was to be followed by a major expedition to Flanders, commanded by the dukes of Clarence and Gloucester. The death of Clarence's wife the previous Christmas offered for many a chance for a permanent resolution to the threat posed by Louis's ambitions in Burgundy (and Clarence's in England). The ultimate objective of English military intervention would be to secure for the lady Margaret a marriage between her stepdaughter Mary of Burgundy and her favourite brother George duke of Clarence. As the Croyland chronicler related: 'It was common knowledge that – the duchess, Lady Margaret, who was more fond of her brother Clarence than anyone else in the family, devoted all her effort and all her attention to uniting in marriage Mary, the only daughter and heiress of the deceased Duke Charles, and the Duke of Clarence, whose wife had recently died.'[40] This marriage would solve the problem of Clarence's ambitions in England and present a permanent English interest in Burgundy. For Gloucester it represented a chance to augment the military glory he had won at Barnet and Tewkesbury. Edward's consent and the provision of military aid were essential for the fulfilment of all these objectives. According to the Croyland chronicler, the king, who was becoming increasingly estranged from his brother George, was resolutely opposed to the marriage. This opposition was fuelled by Louis XI who persuaded Edward that Margaret had made remarks to great lords about the things Clarence would do when he gained possession of Burgundy. Edward offered instead Anthony Woodville, Earl Rivers, the queen's eldest brother, as a husband for Mary, despite the fact that, as Commines observed, Woodville 'was only a petty earl, and she the greatest heiress of her time'.

For many at the great council meeting of 14 February the more immediate issue was the threat to English political and mercantile interests in Calais. Gloucester, according to John Paston, arrived at this meeting in haste. If Louis invaded Artois, Picardy and Flanders, the English stronghold at Calais would be threatened and trading connections with the Netherlands disrupted. Vigorous measures were therefore recommended to prevent Louis overrunning Mary's inheritance. However, Edward was concerned about the risk of losing his French pension and a marriage alliance. In previous months he had been soothed by payment of this pension and reassurances about the marriage between his daughter Elizabeth and the Dauphin, and the promise of the 60,000 a year dowry. This marriage was strongly sought after by Queen Elizabeth Woodville and members of her family.[41] Their influence prevailed. On 16 February instructions were given to English ambassadors to seek further guarantees over payment of the pension and the marriage as the price for English non-intervention in Burgundy. Edward could only inform his sister: 'I fear I cannot be excused but I shall forth with my lord Hastings over the seas.'[42] Hastings was to be sent with 514 archers and 16 spearmen. But instead of being told what he could do to shield Mary he was instructed to keep the peace with the French king. His troops were only to be used to reinforce the Calais garrison and Edward's ambassadors had come to an agreement with Louis to this effect on 4 March.

This attempt to preserve the terms of the treaty of Picquigny ran counter to the chivalric ideals of many of Edward's subjects. As Commines put it, if Edward had followed his subjects' wishes he would have offered Duke Charles's widow Margaret of York an English army for her protection. Most importantly it was against the wishes of the two leading opponents of the treaty of Picquigny, Richard duke of Gloucester and William Lord Hastings. On 6 March 1477 Louis XI wrote from Arras that Edward's object in sending Hastings with so many men was to carry off Mary of Burgundy and that the dowager Duchess Margaret was directing the whole enterprise. Louis overestimated the number of men brought over at a thousand or twelve hundred.[43] Michael K. Jones has uncovered two pieces of evidence suggesting that Louis was reacting to genuine fears that Edward was not in charge of his own foreign policy and that Hastings, with Gloucester's support, was intent on military action to preserve Burgundy. In April Louis chose to communicate with Hastings rather than with Edward, and offered a division of the Burgundian territories of Holland, Zeeland and Brabant should England acquiesce to the French invasion of Picardy and provide financial assistance. This proposal was sent first to Hastings in mid-April.[44] A formal approach to Edward was not made until late June. Hastings rejected the offer out of hand.[45] Louis's offer of Artois had been preceded by military action. At the end of March he had attempted the conquest of Flanders and Picardy. He captured Hesdin (Margaret's castle, where Edward had been entertained with an enactment of Jason and the Golden Fleece) and then approached the port of Boulogne from the south. On the evening of 13 April the main French army under Louis de Bourbon arrived. All communications to the port were cut off. Sir John Paston, who had arrived in Calais in Hastings' retinue, expressed the feelings of the garrison: 'The French king hath gotten many of the towns of the duke of Burgundy including Hesdin one of the most royal castles in the world and is laying siege to Boulogne, and at this day it is said the French king "shall come thither".' Paston conveyed the anxiety about the siege in his account of 'a vysion seyne aboute the walls of Boleyne, as it hadde ben a woman with a mervylowse lyght; men deme that Our Lady ther will shewe hyrselff a lover to that towne. God fforfende that it weer Frensche, it weer worthe £40,000 that it wer Englyshe.'[46] Boulogne submitted to the French king on 19 April 1477 after a six-day siege, and Hastings' frustration at being prevented by his king from doing anything to help the town can only be guessed at.

Another document unearthed by Jones suggests that with Gloucester's support he did try to do something, against Edward's wishes. On 3 May 1477 Louis XI's newly recruited commander of Boulogne ordered an enquiry into reports that Lord Hastings had offered the garrison help and attempted to bring English troops into the town.[47] Jean Marchat, mayor of Boulogne, informed Louis that on the evening of Saturday 12 April, with the French army in the suburbs, two English soldiers appeared outside the town, prominent in their red crosses of St George, wishing to speak with the town's captain to offer him 200 English soldiers as reinforcements. The deputy mayor, Robert Legaignon, added that Lord Hastings was negotiating with Mary of Burgundy to provide ships for an ambitious military operation to carry to Boulogne a force of soldiers from England. All this activity ran directly counter to Edward's instructions to his ambassadors on 16 February to demand prompt payment of the French pension and to seek confirmation of the marriage alliance. Hastings could only have defied the king's wishes with the powerful support of Gloucester (Clarence was out of favour). The man employed in the negotiations with Boulogne, Reginald Clifton, had been a member of the Calais garrison for ten years and the proposal of a seaborne operation bringing troops from England would have required Gloucester's assent as admiral. Evidence of a broader military agreement between Hastings and Margaret emerges from the Calais victuallers' account which lists pieces of artillery being illicitly transported to Margaret of York on the express orders of Hastings.[48] The enquiry into this affair allowed the French king to justify his delaying tactics over the marriage alliance between the Dauphin and Elizabeth of York. On 1 June Louis told Edward that the ample powers for a new French embassy had only been withheld because of an agreement between Margaret of York and Lord Hastings. Louis insinuated that Hastings was not operating alone within the English court, alerted Edward to Clarence's ambitions, and alleged that Margaret had made remarks to great lords about the things Clarence would do when he gained possession of Burgundy.[49] This explains why Edward recalled Hastings later in the same month. Sir John Paston, in a letter of 23 June, reported Hastings' sudden departure from Calais to attend the king at Windsor to answer the charges of Louis's ambassador. Hastings was able to convince Edward of Margaret's innocence but Clarence was arrested in June 1477, and this left Gloucester as the only man with the necessary influence to save Hastings. Gloucester's involvement in this chivalric attempt to save Boulogne is suggested by the career of one of his Yorkshire followers Sir Thomas Everingham, who was with Charles the Bold at his death in Nancy. Sir Thomas fought for the Burgundians in the following months, establishing a reputation for martial valour with the tacit support of the Calais garrison. On his return to England Everingham became one of the duke's chief advisers in the war against Scotland.[50] Above all this incident shows the contrast between the energy and sense of military purpose displayed by Hastings (and probably Gloucester) and the inertia of the king who had led and inspired them in 1471.

With Hastings' wings clipped, the advance of Louis's troops into Flanders was virtually unopposed. By 17 August Edmund Bedingford was writing of the ongoing destruction: 'The French king is besieging St Omers and ravaging Cassel which is our lady of Burgundy's jointure.' He reflected that Margaret had lost a great part of her livelihood 'and that is a shrewd token that he meaneth well to our king [Edward] our sovereign lord that he intendeth to destroy her'. Hastings, openly fulminating against Louis to Tiger Pursuivant and 200 of his followers, could only watch as the French king got closer to Calais, and he ordered the destruction of all passages except Newham Bridge. After the burning of her town of Cassel, Margaret, in a desperate attempt to preserve Burgundy, arranged a marriage between her stepdaughter Mary and Maximilian, archduke of Austria, son of the emperor, on 17 August. However, Maximilian was not powerful enough to protect his new bride and mother-in-law. Nevertheless Mary and her family were grateful to Hastings for all he had tried to do. Mary sent one of her most trusted servants to Calais shortly after Hastings' arrival, to assure him that she was well informed of his endeavours. In 1478 she and Maximilian sent him, in secret, a special token of their appreciation. The magnificent gift consisted of five specially commissioned Bruges tapestries. But Margaret had nothing but contempt for her brother, the one man who could have helped her. After the burning of Cassel she openly reproached him, describing how she had been left 'one of the poorest widows, deserted by everyone, especially by you'.[51]

Margaret and her beleaguered court still continued to hope for help from Edward. After all, Arthurian ethics, which emphasized above all things the protection of helpless women of rank, were not entirely dead at Edward's court. The king was in the process of rebuilding St George's chapel at Windsor, and had even made provision for his sepulchre in the chapel. In January 1478 the wedding of his younger son Richard duke of York and Anne Mowbray had been followed by a tournament at Westminster with jousts, royal jousts in harness, and jousts armed with swords, at which Earl Rivers appeared in the field horsed and armed in the habit of a hermit (like the hermit instructing the knight in the illustration to Edward's copy of Lull's *Book of the Order of Chivalry*), bringing with him his hermitage walled and covered in black velvet.[52] Margaret appealed in April 1478 to what remained of her brother's Arthurian values when she requested him to protect her, 'a poor widow separated from all my kindred and friends, from the king of France, who is doing all in his power to make a beggar of her'. She assured Edward that Louis had robbed her of property worth 3,500 marks a year in rents. One hope for Margaret was an alliance between Maximilian and Edward, cemented by marriage between Mary's new-born son and one of Edward's daughters. It was a strange irony that just at the moment when Edward was abandoning all vestige of his Arthurian ideals he had the opportunity of forming an alliance with a young man who lived in an imaginative Arthurian world. Maximilian later gave an account of his life in three biographies cast in the form of Arthurian romances, one of which, *Theuerdank*, published in 1517, is an encoded and fictionalized account of his journey to the land of his future bride Mary of Burgundy and his eight years as ruler of the duchy. The underlying theme of these works – the knight finding moral and ethical renewal for himself and his society in his struggle against allegorical adversaries (accompanied with 255 woodcuts revealing the chivalric exploits of his life) – shows that Maximilian regarded his entire life as an Arthurian quest.[53] He chose to have cast for his funeral monument in the Hofkirche at Innsbruck in 1513 a magnificent statue of King Arthur.[54] How hopeful he must have been about his alliance with Edward, and how disappointed in the outcome.

Edward's obsession with Louis's pension was such that he required Maximilian to pay the equivalent sum if this was lost as a consequence of any alliance with Burgundy. At the same time, however, Edward was entertaining Louis's envoy, the bishop of Elne, who was so unpopular in England that he feared for his life. The bishop's job was to prevent Edward interfering in Louis's war with the Flemings, and this was done by the usual tactic of leading Edward by the nose with the instalments of his pension and the promise of the 60,000 crowns dowry for Elizabeth, and promises that Louis would protect Margaret and her dower lands and revenues in conquered territories. Throughout 1479 Edward continued to press Louis for the marriage and for the commencement of the payment of the jointure now that Elizabeth had reached the marriageable age of twelve. Edward's frustration was compounded, according to Commines, by Louis sending different men on each embassy to England, so that when Edward complained of some promise made by one set of ambassadors but not kept, the next group of ambassadors could plead ignorance. By 1480 he had achieved none of his goals. Louis continued to overrun Flanders and Edward had not succeeded either in being allowed to mediate a truce between Louis and Maximilian, or in bringing any nearer the marriage of the Dauphin and Elizabeth or the payment of the dowry. Margaret's plight was such that she visited Edward in England in an attempt to seal an alliance between Burgundy and England with the marriage of Maximilian's son and Edward's daughter Anne, and to secure immediate military aid in the form of 2,000 archers. Maximilian had even agreed to pay Edward's pension and offered him the same prospect of the conquest of Champagne and coronation in Rheims that Charles had offered him.

Louis, faced with a repetition of the 1471 alliance of England, Burgundy and Brittany, distracted Edward by fomenting trouble in Scotland. Edward's invasion of Scotland in 1481 prevented him from accepting Maximilian's proposals and providing military aid and gave him an excuse to explain to his subjects his continued refusal to take aggressive action against Louis. Throughout 1482 Maximilian continued to attempt to persuade Edward to join him in invading France, and while Edward gave him promises of assistance he also renewed with Louis the truce of 1477, and Louis promised no further interference in Scotland. On 27 March 1482 Maximilian's plight was intensified when Mary of Burgundy died after a riding accident and Louis pushed closer to Calais, despite the fact that a year earlier he had assured Edward he would not touch the least village around Calais. Hastings had to repair the fortifications and drown much of the surrounding land. Louis distracted Edward by releasing James III of Scotland's rebellious brother the duke of Albany, and encouraged Edward to help him take the throne of Scotland. Maximilian was near breaking point and close to accepting a humiliating truce with France, but Louis's devious plan failed, thanks to Gloucester's military successes in Scotland. By August 1482 Gloucester had taken Edinburgh and Berwick, and forced James III to sue for peace and a reconciliation with Albany, thus freeing Edward to come to the aid of Maximilian at the last minute. It looks as if Gloucester's rapid military exercise was done with the relief of Calais in mind. Hastings gave orders for a general procession and firing of guns and bonfires in every doorway in Calais in celebration. This would explain Gloucester's haste in bringing the peace negotiations between James and Albany to a speedy conclusion and his rapid march out of Scotland (and perhaps also might explain Edward's annoyance with Gloucester). However, with impeccable timing, Louis sent Edward on 25 August the latest instalment of his pension and Edward again did nothing to help Maximilian. According to a poem written on Edward's death, the king after the capture of Berwick 'came riding home and hym-selfe to sporte and pleye'.[55]

On 29 September Louis played his trump card, giving orders for the publication of the truce he had made with Edward the previous year. It was enough, combined with the death of Mary of Burgundy, to bring Maximilian to his knees and he entered into negotiations with Louis: on 23 December Louis and Maximilian signed the treaty of Arras, by which Maximilian's infant daughter Margaret was pledged to marry the Dauphin. The countries of Artois and Burgundy were to be regarded as her marriage portion, swallowed up by

France. Edward was crushed, his foreign policy in ruins. The sense of disenchantment in these last months of the reign was captured by Dominic Mancini: 'that by his [Edward's] inactivity the Flemings, ancient friends, had been permanently estranged from him, whereas his foes, the French, had been made the stronger, so that his own subjects were disaffected, supposing that it was owing to his meanness that the Flemings had received no help from him'.[56] Gloucester persuaded Edward that the only thing he could do was pursue further victories in Scotland. To prevent a popular outbreak in England, Edward therefore made Gloucester warden of the West Marches in January 1483, with Palatine rights in the county of Cumberland and all lands he conquered in Scotland. With the creation of this hereditary principality with a degree of independence from England, Edward had demonstrated how completely his judgement had deserted him. He had squandered the chance to create such a state in Burgundy with Clarence and had fostered a potentially similar state within his own borders under the rule of the much more dangerous and formidable Gloucester.

On 9 April 1483 Edward died after catching a chill while boating on the Thames. The circumstances of his death were mysterious. No one was sure of the cause. It may have been pneumonia, a stroke brought on by excessive eating and drinking, or a water-borne illness such as typhoid. Poisoning was even advanced as a theory. What was generally acknowledged was that Edward's spirit was broken and that a deep depression probably contributed to his premature death.

Even during these later years Edward never entirely lost his charisma and charm, his ability to radiate light and warmth, and this emerges in the sincere compliments and expressions of grief seen in the poetry written immediately after his death.[57] Most affecting is the 'Death of Edward IV', written by someone close to the king, perhaps a member of his household. Searching for his lost lord, the poet expresses the conviction that there was something blessed about this king:

> the rose, the sonne-beme,
> which was full fortunate,

who gave a sense of well-being to his realm:

> Hit was a worlde to see hym ride aboute
> Throughout his land, and that was day by day.

His death moreover made his subjects acutely aware of the confidence and optimism that he emitted in his finest moments:

> What may we wrecches say,
> That nowe have lost the lanterne and the light?

It also makes the poet aware of the aspirations towards a better life that Edward's reign embraced:

> I see his lordis, I see his Knyghtes all;
> I se his plasis made of lyme and ston;
> I see his servauntes sittyng in the hall.

All of this reminiscence serves to accentuate the sense of loss and emptiness that accompanied his death and the long funeral procession with his coffin draped in a pall of cloth of gold, bearing the banners of St George and the Trinity, from Westminster Abbey to Syon on 17 April, and from Syon to Eton and Windsor on 18 April:[58]

I met his men wepyng in clothis blake
Not oon not tweyn, God wote, many oon,
Which daily wayleth and sorowth for his sake
Hit to endur hit maketh my hert quake,
When I remembre he was here yesterday.[59]

Another poem expresses the grief that must have been felt by Edward's many female admirers. The poet, walking on a May morning after Edward's death in an attempt to cheer himself up with the sound of birds singing, can only write:

I herd a wofull lamentinge
Of ladyes tht were clothed in blake
Wept for king Edward's sake.[60]

Even the more formal author of the Latin epitaph (possibly Carmeliano) expressed the sense of aspiration that Edward evoked: 'He reached for the sky but now has left his castle high' and laments the passing of

Castles full of dancing, of people singing in the gardens
That is past now they are weeping and can hardly speak.[61]

Fifteenth-century politics were played out in an arena that required patience and cynicism. Edward was intelligent and he played this game well, but he was no match for Louis and ultimately it did not suit his character. He was at his best when facing challenges requiring courage and leadership, when the imagination and the emotions were fully engaged. He was an Othello of noble ideals, humiliated when he fell into the web of a Iago 'bound to thee forever'[62] and led down a path of self-betrayal and betrayal of his family and his people. The calculated payment of the pension, the thirty pieces of silver, took on the diabolic quality of Desdemona's handkerchief; it always served to undermine Edward when he was on the point of shaking free from Louis's grasp and rediscovering his own powers. Even the pragmatic Commines saw that Louis had broken Edward's spirit with promises always just beyond reach. The treaty of Arras in particular, he maintained, had killed Edward:

> He thought himself deluded and baffled in danger of losing his reason; he feared it rendered him contemptible and despised at home – the prospect of rebellion at home and of the king of France encroaching upon and ready to invade his dominions had made such a deep and lasting impression upon his spirits he fell sick upon it immediately and died not long after, though some say of cattarh. But let them say what they please, the general opinion was that it was the consummation of the marriage that killed him in the month of April 1483.[63]

Another first-hand witness to these events was the Croyland chronicler. According to him 'the spirited prince now realized that in the end he had been tricked by King Louis and was deeply troubled and grieved'.[64] He too thought Edward had been drained of his vital force by the 'spider king'. For him, Edward's end was an unimaginable tragedy. He had become a diminished figure, duped, vengeful, impotent, vindictive and vain, who died because he had lost the will to live: 'the king, though he was not afflicted by old age nor any known type of disease which would not have seemed easy to cure in a lesser person, took to his bed about Easter time and gave up his soul to his maker'. He died, according to this first-hand witness, 'the most penitent of men for all his sins and those who were present at his death bore witness to his meek and humble end after so much human frailty'.[65] In his last years Edward had become the disempowered Fisher King, and contemporary speculations about the malaise, the depression, that contributed to his early death raise questions about his health, physical and mental, that were of immediate concern to his physicians and court alchemists; these men emerged to become just as important in the 1470s as they had been in the previous two decades. For Commines Edward's debauched lifestyle was a medical issue that was intensified after the recapture of his throne and the death of Warwick (who may have exercised a fatherly restraint on him) and he believed that this was the immediate cause of his death. 'He fell upon his pleasures and indulged himself in them after a more violent nature than before. From this time he feared nobody but living a luxurious life, he grew very fat, and his excess inclining him to diseases, and in the very flower of his age he died suddenly (as it was reported) of an apoplexy.'

Edward shared his brother Clarence's addiction to alcohol. Paston, giving an account of Edward's itinerary in East Anglia in 1474, which included an Easter stay in Norwich and then Walsingham, warned 'Will Coyney to provide them with enough for the town shall be drunk as dry as York was when the king was there'. The Croyland chronicler noted that men of every rank and condition marvelled that a man so addicted to conviviality, vanity and drunkenness could have such a capacious memory.[66] He was just as compulsive in his eating. In the regulations of the royal household from the *Black Book* of 1472 there is an illustration showing Edward dining in state. On the king's right there is a bishop quoting Socrates: 'It is necessary to eat to live rather than you live to eat' – advice that Edward ignored.[67] This illustration, showing the king at supper with a fish on a plate and his knife prominently displayed on the table, bears a close resemblance to illustrations in Ripley's *Cantilena* showing the king and queen dining on the flesh of a peacock, and may imply the important role of alchemists like Ripley in trying to influence the king's diet.[68] This same image of the knife appears on Ripley's tomb. There was a morbid quality to Edward's over-eating, a sense of misplaced and negative energy, perhaps relating to his inability to apply himself to the more mundane and mature responsibilities of kingship, his fixation on his own youth and his despair as it fell away from him. The unenviable task of continuous regulation of Edward's eating habits fell to his physicians.[69] According to one household ordinance, each holder of this office

> standith much in the presence of the kinges meles, by the councelyng or awnswering to the kinges grace which dyet is best acording, and to the nature and operacion of all the metes. And camynly he shuld talke with the steward, chambrelayn, assewar, and the master acooke to deuyse by counsayle what metes or drinkes is best according with the kinges dyet; and when he woll at mete and souper in the kinges chambre or hall or in his own chambre deuysyng the kinges medecens.[70]

Mancini, who was a good friend of the prince's physician John Argentine, was in a good position to know about the anxiety such indulgences caused:

> In food and drink he was most immoderate: it was his habit, so I have learned, to take an emetic for the delight of gorging his stomach once more, for this reason and for the ease which was especially dear to him after his recovery of the crown, he had grown fat in the loins whereas previously he had been not only tall but rather lean and active.[71]

Edward's main compulsion, however, was women. When William Paston wrote to his nephew Sir John in 1474 about inducements for their handsome and amorous monarch to prolong his stay in Norfolk, he suggested they commend the beauty and agreeable behaviour of the women of the region.[72] According to Mancini, Edward had three mistresses. Two of them, one witty and one pious, were of reasonably high rank but preferred to remain anonymous, while the third, the king's favourite, was Elizabeth (Jane) Shore, a merry woman of more humble rank. Her husband, a London citizen, left her when she became the royal mistress. According to More, Edward was genuinely fond of Jane, who would mitigate and appease his mind when men were out of favour. Edward never lost the ability to charm and there was something of the dandy about him. According to Commines, his thoughts were wholly employed on ladies, hunting and clothes. In the summer's hunting his custom was to have tents set up for the ladies in which he treated them in a splendid and magnificent manner. But there was a more disturbing side to his womanizing. The court had always had a reputation for being a source of immorality (Henry VI once advised a group of scholars from his foundation of Eton to stay away from the nearby court at Windsor), but during Edward's second reign it took on an increasingly decadent Roman aura. According to More, the queen hated Hastings because she thought he was secretly familiar with the king in wanton company. Mancini provided the details. According to him, Edward was:

> licentious in the extreme: moreover it was said that he had been most insolent to numerous women after he had seduced them, for, as soon as he grew weary of dalliance, he gave up the ladies much against their will to the other courtiers. He pursued with no discrimination the married and unmarried, the noble and lowly – He overcame all by money and promises, and having conquered them he dismissed them – Among the many promoters and companions of his vices were two sons of the queen, Thomas Marquis of Dorset, and Sir Thomas Grey and the queen's brother Sir Edward Woodville and Edward's closest friend William Lord Hastings – one that shared every peril with the king, but was also the accomplice and partner of his privy pleasures.[73]

This of course amounted to a misuse and abuse of his charm, good looks and power. Seduced by the myths accruing around him and the numerous references to his own beauty, he had become Narcissus, in love with his own image, and all the women (and perhaps the men) of his court and his kingdom were his for the taking. By the end of his reign, when he had become fat, his vain obsession with his appearance and his clothes (he paid his Italian tailor a shilling a day) led him to present himself before his court at Christmas 1482 as a puffed-up figure in voluminous fur-lined robes, a grotesque parody of the 'tall and lean' youth who had taken the throne.[74] The sumptuary legislation that he enacted in the last year of his reign stipulating that none but the royal family should wear cloth of gold or purple silk is an indication of the increasing vanity and foppishness of his court.

To some extent Edward would have found an endorsement and encouragement of his hedonistic lifestyle and his collecting of art and illuminated deluxe manuscripts in the alchemical text he had owned since his youth, Bacon's version of the *Secreta secretorum*. The perfect regimen for a prince to achieve humoral balance is to live in comfort and wealth, feared by his enemies, living in pleasure, listening to music, beholding and being delighted with beautiful things, reading pleasant books, hearing joyous songs with beloved friends, wearing fine clothes and conferring with wise men of things past and to come. With these things, the author adds, 'men are made fat'. The opposite picture is presented in the form of a dry and feeble man, eating and drinking little, labouring often without reason, sleeping on hard beds, vexed in mind with bad thoughts, often dreading sorrow.[75] This amounts to an endorsement of Edward's personality (his motto 'comfort and joy' may have been intended as an affirmation of Bacon's humoral philosophy) and a criticism of such opposites as the neurotic Louis XI and Richard duke of Gloucester. It was a medical theory, expounded by Bacon and in such works as *De retardatione senectute*, that recommended the healing properties of laughter and mirth.

The use of emetics for regular vomiting was widely used in Galenic medicine as a prophylactic and in Edward's version of the *Secreta secretorum* vomiting two or three times a month, especially in summer, is recommended to wash the stomach and purge it of all humours, moistures and corrupt matter of the body. However, Mancini, who knew this, was aware that Edward's use of emetics taken in the manner of Trimalchio in Petronius's *Satyricon* to enhance or prolong the sensual pleasure of eating, was wrong and dangerous. Edward took such advice well beyond the point of maintaining humoral balance and being 'sleek and contented o'nights'. Practitioners of Baconian alchemical medicine at Edward's court, such as Roger Marshall (who owned the works of Pliny and Plato) and John Cokkes (the transcriber of Edward's copy of *Secreta secretorum* and Bacon's *Opus tertium* and *De retardatione senectute*) would have integrated their interest in alchemical medicine and knowledge of stoic literature to regulate and moderate the king's diet and lifestyle to ensure humoral balance. The new household ordinances of 1474 stipulated that the royal physicians ought to be responsible for advising the king and his family on their diet. The doctor of physic stood by the king, advising which diet was best and giving instructions to the steward chamberlain to devise the food best for the king.[76] There were many regimens available to provide such advice, including Kymer's *Regimen sanitatis*, originally written for Humphrey duke of Gloucester, and the different versions of the *Secreta secretorum*, and Edward would have had his own. In such works the virtues of a good diet that balanced the humours and controlled the emotions were extolled. Of special relevance to Edward would be discussions of the way choler, the predominant humour of youth, could dry out naturally after forty years of healthy living, and that this could lead to melancholy (the passion for things past and the sorrow for things to come, as fellow-sufferer William Worcester defined it), a condition that afflicted Edward after 1475. This trend could only be reversed with a carefully regulated diet and the frequent application of oils.[77] Anxiety about Edward's promiscuity can be explained by standard medical knowledge known to everyone: immoderate use of the work of Venus led to dehabilitation of the kidneys and genitalia. Frequent emission of semen caused loss of vital fluids and energies, impeding digestion, causing dryness and corruption of the humours; this impoverished the spirit, checked the natural heat suppressing bodily functions and gave rise to diseases. This effeminizing of the sperm produced fatness and neglectfulness and shortened life expectancy.[78] Mancini, who was in communication with the princes' physician John Argentine, attributed Edward's premature death to his promiscuity.

Conventional medicine going back to Galen and Hippocrates was more concerned with lifestyle than with medicinal cures, and these ideas were shared by alchemists following the teaching of Roger Bacon. During his second reign Edward showed little inclination to practise the moderation, pursuit of wisdom and stoic detachment recommended in many of the works of antiquity that he was collecting. George Ripley tried to advise Edward on moderating his diet and lifestyle. In his letter in 1471 he wished for a long life for the king and advised him to eat and drink moderately to quench his natural heat and to exercise after eating. Above all he should pursue philosophy and cultivate the virtue of prudence, taking heed of the way kings such as Adam, Samson and David were undone because they lost wisdom. He directly appealed to Edward, employing the imagery of a besieged castle, and referred to the king's wish to attain the secret of secrets 'according to thy desire'.[79] Ripley's interest in the heroic, mythic aspects of the growth of the self would have compelled him to advise Edward to take careful heed of his dreams. However, his master was like Chanticleer, Chaucer's hypochondriac cock who, instead of heeding the warnings of a disturbing dream about a fox, chose to listen to his wife Pertelote, who saw it as the result of bad digestion and advised laxatives to purge the offending humours.[80] Edward put more pressure on Ripley and his other physicians to procure the only things that satisfied him, purgative medicines. In the dedicatory epistle to Edward that precedes the *Compound of Alchemy*, Ripley suggested different potions to slow down the ageing process, such as hypericum with milk and even spermaticelli with red wine.[81] In Edward's copy of Bacon's version of the *Secreta secretorum* there are instructions on the preparation of food ensuring proper irradiation from the stars, careful choice of substance and good and equal proportions to prolong life.[82] The medicine that probably satisfied both his avarice and his hypochondria was gold. In Chaucer's translation of Boethius's *Consolations of Philosophy*, which was printed by Caxton and owned by Edward's physician Roger Marshall, it is maintained that the best way to health is to avoid material medicine and to behold nurse philosophy. This was the most important aspect of Baconian medicine, to use the stoic philosophy of the ancients to learn patience in sorrow and adversity, to lead a moderate lifestyle which would bring peace of mind and detachment. Edward had built up a collection of the appropriate literature but was unable to practise this way of life. Instead, like Chanticleer, he had recourse to emetics as his hypochondria and addiction to medicines grew. The bills from the royal apothecary John Clark for supplying drugs and oils to the court rose from £87 in 1464 to the considerable sum of £283 in May 1475;[83] some of this expenditure must have contributed to the sovereign's overworked digestion. Edward's physician, probably Clark's personal friend Roger Marshall, was instructed in the household ordinances to spend time in his own chamber devising the king's medicines. Edward's dependence on doctors was beginning to be a cause for concern. Another of his physicians, James Fryse, a knight of St George's Windsor, was accused of exerting a sinister influence on the king.[84] Edward also developed a morbid fear of being poisoned. At Christmas 1472, when entertaining Gruuthuyse and Lord Hastings, he had stag's horn, a powerful antidote, placed in the drinks. At the beginning of 1474 he would not go within forty feet of the French ambassadors for fear of poisoning.[85] In all of this hypochondria, compulsive eating, drinking and womanizing there seems to have been an element of self-absorption perhaps related to his infatuation with his own lost youth. As the reign went on Edward seems to have become more out of touch with the sound and beneficial aspects of alchemy – its ability to sustain one through hardship by tapping into sources of self-belief, and to encourage self-discipline – and more preoccupied by the chimeras that had discredited this art and which his physicians would have warned him about, especially the search for the elixir of lost youth. The sun that had once been the source of light and warmth for his kingdom was now the beguiling and illusionary glow of his lost boyhood.

Edward's hypochondria inevitably increased during the plague of 1472. He made a pilgrimage to Canterbury at this time and in May, before the danger was past, he swallowed ten pounds' worth of medicine 'contra pestem'. Edward had a favourite recipe against the plague to be taken before the appearance of the dreaded 'purple', a 'medesyn that the Kyngis grace usythe every day for the raynyng seknys that now raynthe'. The recipe was reported to have saved seventy-one people in a single year from the pestilence and probably dates from 1472. The king or his physician is instructed to strain handfuls of various herbs including rue and feverfew and an alchemical origin to the recipe is suggested by the addition of 'a quantity of dragonys, the crop or the root', which refers to the medicinal red gum known as dragon's blood, extracted from the dragon tree (*Dracaena draco*) of the

Canary Islands.[86] The plague of 1479 was the worst of the century and must have contributed to the deepening gloom around Edward. The epidemic forced the closure of the courts at Westminster during the summer. According to a London chronicler there was a huge mortality in the city and in many parts of the realm. Sir John Paston recognized that the crowded city was a source of infection but took the risk of returning there in 1479 for a business trip, and he paid the penalty with his life.[87] Edward's fear of the plague was so great that he avoided London and lived in dread at Eltham and Sheen. After his infant son, George (Clarence's namesake) died of the disease in March, his physicians sought a papal dispensation so that Edward could eat meat and food prepared with milk during Lent and on Sundays. The miracle prophylactic drug for those wealthy enough to afford it was theriac, made from the flesh of vipers after the venom had been extracted. In the *Treatise of Remedies Against the Plague* written by 'the noble physician' John Burdus, it is recommended that treacle (or theriac) be taken, along with milk and almonds, as a hot drink, with a little ale.[88] Henry IV had a silver box for theriac. The Pastons consumed large quantities of it,[89] and so did Edward. It took twelve years to mature and consignments of theriac were regularly examined in all major ports. In 1471 the royal physician Roger Marshall was summoned by the mayor of London to declare seventeen barrels of treacle worthless. Marshall too was engaged in making recipes of such drugs for the king. In a Peterhouse manuscript there is, in his hand, a recipe for the preservation of Edward IV.[90] Theriac was closely associated with the activities of alchemists. In the third gate of his *Compound of Alchemy*, George Ripley is concerned with providing the king with instructions on its manufacture. Its potency was in part derived from the fact that it was derived from the flesh of the viper, a creature that produced a deadly venom, and seems have been combined with distilled alcohol:

> Distill it therefore till it be clene
> And thinne like water as it should be,
> This water is like to the venymous Tire,
> Wherewith the mighty triacle is wrought,
> For it is poyson most strong of Ire,
> Aa stronger poyson cannot be thought,
> At Pothecaries often therefore it is sought,
> But no man by it shalbe intoxicate,
> From the time it is into medicine elixerate,
> For then as is the Triacle true,
> It is of poyson most expulsive,
> And in his working doth marveiles shew,
> Preserving many from death to life.[91]

Ripley's vision, the source of much of the imagery in the *Ripley Scrolls*, is dominated by the venomous toad whose carcase, rotting in the gentle fire, creates the medicine of the venom that kills and saves, 'glory be to the granter of such secrets'.

The plague, however, like leprosy, was associated with the malaise of the body politic and its head the king. Outbreaks in 1433 and 1438 had been linked (as we have seen) by the author of Yorkist genealogical histories and prophecies with the usurping house of Lancaster,[92] but the increasing frequency of epidemics in the later years of Edward's reign was inevitably connected to the king's waning powers, in the same way as the plagues of 1368–9 were linked to the senility of Edward III and those of the 1590s with the old age of Elizabeth I. Stephano Trento, the papal envoy, praised his friend George Neville for taking every precaution against the plague. Neville was desirous of removing his friend from the source of infection but Stephano could not resist pointing out that there was another kind of disease, a moral illness, afflicting all those around him, which he linked to the corruption at Edward's court. Plague was linked to planetary constellations that brought a wide variety of disorders, natural and political. Henry Sutton, in his tract on the comet of 1472, saw such phenomena as harbingers of plague and catastrophe.[93] Plague was believed to be connected with leprosy and was seen as a punishment for sins, especially those of the court. The new household ordinances of 1474 stipulated that the royal physician, besides advising the king and his family on diet, was urged to 'espie if any of the court be infected with leprosy or pestilence'.[94] Some chroniclers even associated the arrival of plague with the king's French expedition in 1475. According to Hall, Edward picked up a tertian ague on his trip to France in 1475, and this was a torment to him as long as he lived.

By 1476 there is evidence of an increasingly pessimistic and fatalistic attitude towards the sense of sickness surrounding the king. Ripley was now turning his attention to trying to rejuvenate his sick friend George Neville, whose health and spirit had been broken by his imprisonment. Concern had been expressed by his friend and fellow student of the literature of antiquity, John Shirwood, bishop of Durham, who visited Neville in exile in Calais in 1475 on his return from the papal Curia.[95] By 1476 Neville was being treated in England by the Cambridge physician Walter Lemster for the stone and was prescribed various medicines of barley water and herbs.[96] The oppressive sense of mortality and the search for lost youth that pervades Ripley's *Marrow of Alchemy*, written in 1476, may also be due to the increasingly heavy burden Ripley felt when catering for the king's insecurities. Neville, the recipient of this work, is addressed 'O pastor meek' and urged:

> Yourself preserve and eke know how
> Old age to hide and youth outshine.[97]

Ripley, who repeatedly writes of the body's alchemy, by which he means its humoral balance,[98] promises to teach Neville how to make mixtures pure and by multiplying procure gold:

> By it are things increased soe,
> That health thereby you may renew.

He urges Neville that:

> If you unbroken long would keep
> In perfect health, your vessel still:
> Then for your cannon look you seek.

Ripley made bold claims for the miraculous medicine which 'hath power to turn all bodies into pure gold and to heal all infirmities more than all the potions of Hippocrates and Galen, for this is the true Gold – the highest of all medicines both to heal men's bodies and also to transmute the bodies of metal into most pure gold'. But there was now a persistent reminder of mortality in his work: 'to everyone of us applies this terrible sentence, saying all time is given to you to rende again'.[99] By the middle of the decade there was a growing sense that this heroic king was indeed mortal and there was some anxiety about the future, which was expressed in the various prognostications about Edward's life and health. Marshall (who had written a horoscope for Henry VI at the time of the Eleanor Cobham controversy, which was later copied by Caerleon),[100] wrote a horoscope in his own hand for Edward IV.[101] John Argentine, the princes' physician, also wrote a horoscope for the king.[102]

Picquigny was the defining moment for these alchemists. The pension Edward secured both ensured the end of any heroic quests and also gave him the money and leisure to indulge in his vices of avarice, lust, greed and vanity, and to set himself on a self-destructive path. There is no doubt about the accelerated deterioration of Edward's physical and mental health after this treaty, and it was around this time that the alchemists, increasingly disillusioned with the king, abandoned any hope of redeeming him. The pension at Picquigny would have confirmed that the king's interest in alchemy was no longer related to the triumph of the submersion of the ego in pursuit of the heroic quest, but to his search for gold. Ripley in his prologue to the *Compound of Alchemy* promised 'our secrets to thee I will reveal' and in his letter to Edward IV he promised to reveal to him secrets that would enable him to 'turne all mettals to Sunne and Moone' and to 'make the great Elixir and Aurum potabile.' Picquigny showed that Edward now only understood this in a literal sense, and in *The Bosom Book*, copied from a manuscript in his own hand, he promised 'this groundes dede George Rypley wrote them for you: not struck as phansy sayns, but thynges in proof full time.' The Croyland chronicler intimated that the king's avarice had submerged his heroic idealistic qualities when he observed that Edward used his pension to equip merchant ships and to enter into exchanges with Greek and Italian merchants 'just like a man who earns his living by trade'.[103] On 18 June 1474 Edward granted a licence for four years to the royal servants David Beaupe and John Marchaunt 'that they may practise the faculty and science of philosophy and the turning of mercury into gold and silver'. Ripley, despite his possible implication in the Lincolnshire rebellion of 1470, was still in Edward's service in 1471 when he warned him against becoming avaricious, proud and complacent. The retraction that he wrote in 1471 of all his writings previous to the *Compound of Alchemy* between 1450 and 1471 may have been an attempt to distance himself from the events of Edward's first reign and to assert his hope for a new beginning.[104] However, by 1476 (a key year for court alchemists in the same way that 1456 and 1468 had been) Ripley and his king had drifted irrevocably apart. In the *Marrow of Alchemy* Ripley laments the destruction of friends and family in the wars of 1469–71 and expresses his regret at the disintegration of his relationship with Edward: 'the present king by whose gifts in time past I was refreshed, which now are lamentably dead with many other'. The recipient of this work was Ripley's friend and fellow alchemist George Neville, who, despite a royal pardon, had been imprisoned in Calais in 1472 for entering into correspondence with the earl of Oxford, who had attempted an invasion of England at St Michael's Mount in 1473; although he had been released from prison in 1474,[105] the man who had played such a crucial role in the making and breaking of kings was himself broken in spirit and being treated for various ailments by Ripley. Accustomed to contemplating the emergence of the king from the chaos of civil war in alchemical terms, Ripley now concentrated on the purely personal aspects of alchemy, in its use for treating Neville's various ailments and for catering for his friend's spiritual welfare. He therefore expressed his disillusionment with the court: 'What can now help my heaviness, what can now suage my secret weeping and sighing day and night though I resent them when I should more entangle myself with worldly vanities and hurtful observations or with pleasures so vain and transitory, vanities of vanities all is vanity.' In a manuscript transcribed in 1476 and containing miscellaneous alchemical works, including Ripley's, there is a tract of consolation by a poor canon, George Ripley, which may allude to his fall from royal favour.[106]

By 1476 the two men had entered into a correspondence that expresses their sense of weariness with the court, with politics and with the king. In the letters Ripley wrote to his friend there is a new ascetic tone, a sense of religious vocation that is close to the atmosphere at the close of Malory's *Morte d'Arthur*. Ripley, discussing their interest in alchemy, uses such phrases as 'the illumination of the mind', the 'poor servant of Christ' and expresses a wish to visit the places where Christ lived and died and his plans to find an elixir for pilgrims. In the *Marrow of Alchemy* Ripley, in dedicating his work to archbishop Neville, asks for his support that: 'hereafter I shall no-more busy myself with worldly matters: and seeing that is best to establish the heart with grace, that I may set myself again within the cloister from the world, according to my desire'. Neville was too ill to assist him, but Ripley, using the dispensation he had received from Pope Sixtus IV, retired to the Carmelite priory of St Botulph's, Boston, in the Fens.[107]

Thomas Norton had been a member of Edward's household since 1466, and according to his great-grandson he had accompanied the king on his Burgundian exile. However, he too was becoming disillusioned with Edward and this is reflected in the *Ordinal of Alchemy* which he began writing in 1477. According to Samuel Norton in the *Key of Alchimie*, the reason why he did not reveal the secret of alchemy to the king could be found in a passage in his great-grandfather's *Ordinal of Alchemy* (presumably added by Norton after Edward's death):

> Truly King Edward was nigh thereto
> If sinne had not kept him therefro
> But surelie sinne jointlie with grace
> will not be together in one place
> – grace of consolation
> is deferred while sinne hath domination.[108]

This science, Thomas Norton added, can only honour the king who loves God above all things, and despite the great hopes placed on Edward he laments, 'in a mourning sort', that the stone would not be revealed to him because of his frailties.[109] Norton's rift with Edward was confirmed in April 1476 when, as collector of customs,[110] Norton brought a bill of complaint against the mayor of Bristol, William Spenser, for smuggling cloth, offering him a bribe, and defrauding the king of £700 from the estate of the duke of Clarence and the earl of Warwick.[111] On 12 March 1477 Norton accused Spenser of high treason and Spenser, with the support of the sheriff of Bristol, denounced Norton for keeping riotous company (Norton had been overzealous in the performance of his duties). Norton appeared before the king in London, who 'estranged his look from him' and Norton left court. On Sunday 20 March the case against Spenser was dismissed and the king commended the mayor for his wisdom.[112] From Norton's perspective it must have seemed as if the king was turning a blind eye to corruption. It also appears that in the previous year Norton was moving closer to George Neville. According to Ashmole, the manuscript of Norton's *Ordinal of Alchemy* which he used for his edition contained the arms of George Neville (subsequently cut out and replaced with another miniature). This implies that before Neville's death Norton was seeking the archbishop's patronage or friendship.[113] An eloquent testimony to Edward's loss of interest in the mythological and alchemical ideals that he maintained when he reconquered his kingdom was provided in the concern expressed by members of the Burgundian Order of the Golden Fleece about Edward's inability to sustain his levels of energy and commitment to higher ideals. The statutes of the order, like those of the Garter, called for a revision of the life and deeds of their members. In May 1473 the Order of the

Golden Fleece reviewed Edward IV's own conduct and character. Amidst general praise for his knightly courage and prowess and his qualities as a good friend, two specific criticisms were made: first, that he lacked foresight: it was believed that if he had gauged the political situation more accurately he would never have been forced into exile; and secondly, and more personally, that he could be unduly passive: if those close to him did not praise his plans and undertakings he did not have the confidence to execute them.[114] Further concern was expressed in October 1478 by a Burgundian embassy. Maximilian and Mary sent Seigneur d'Irlain to make anxious enquiry why Edward no longer wore the collar of the Golden Fleece, and Ostriche Herald accompanied them to inform the king that there would be a meeting of the chapter of the Order of the Golden Fleece in April of the following year.[115]

In the period encompassed by Edward's reign there was a powerfully imaginative dimension to the political life of the king, his court and many of his people. The alchemical quest, the national myths and the prophecies, liberated in Edward and his followers creative energies which enabled them to evoke a sense of national pride and well-being. This imaginative component to political life was, however, volatile and unpredictable, with negative and destructive potential that could be expressed in a preoccupation with witchcraft and sinister, self-fulfilling prophecies once public confidence in Edward began to erode away. Writing in 1478, the author of the *Arrivall*, not a credulous man but a scholar who seems to have been aware that Edward had squandered his blessings, saw signs of doom going back to 1473. He noted that in this year of George Neville's arrest there were many tokens of impending disaster: rivers overran their banks in Croydon, and in Hungerford rivers ran foul and troubled, signifying the approach of battle; voices were heard crying in the air between Leicester and Banbury 'Bowes, bowes'; and a headless man was heard crying. Attention was turning to the skies for an explanation of what was going wrong. Henry Sutton, Master of St Nicholas' Hospital in Salisbury, who was later involved in the Perkin Warbeck conspiracy, wrote in a tract on comets about the comet of 1472, which coincided with an outbreak of plague, and noted that comets were harbingers of disaster and sickness to the land.[116] This was the comet that Angelo Cato de Supino of Benevento used to predict the death of the duke of Burgundy after he left the duke's service for that of Louis XI.[117] This preoccupation with comets and eclipses was linked to a growing fear of witchcraft, the conviction, in the face of political crisis, that there was a swallowing of the male energy of the sun by the dark cthonic, feminine, phlegmatic power of the moon. Witchcraft accusations, as we have seen, occurred towards the end of Edward's first reign but this was nothing compared to what would happen in the last six years of his second reign. On 12 April 1477 Clarence, delusional since his wife's childbirth-related death the preceding December, arrested his dead wife's attendant Ankarette Twynho, without a warrant, on a charge of witchcraft, accusing her of causing her mistress's death by a venomous drink of ale laced with poison. She was executed without a trial at Warwick in Clarence's presence. Her execution was soon followed by that of one John Thuresby, charged with poisoning the couple's infant son, who had died in January. Edward responded to this affront to his authority by ordering the arrest for witchcraft of Dr John Stacy, an Oxford astronomer. Stacy's name appears in the sixteenth-century list of prominent British alchemists.[118] His fate illustrates how alchemists, who were inevitably involved in making all sorts of prognostications, could not easily avoid the political risks incumbent in serving the great. Stacy was a servant of Clarence. Under torture he confessed that another member of Clarence's household, Thomas Burdett, enraged by the king's killing of his favourite white buck while hunting in his park in 1474, had wished the king dead. In the following year, according to this confession, he had enlisted the services of Dr Stacy and another astronomer, Thomas Blake, a chaplain of Merton College. By art, magic and necromancy these two established that the king would die in a short time and asserted this to a number of people on 20 May 1475 in an attempt to 'shorten the king's life by sadness' (presumably by exacerbating his hypochondria). Blake was pardoned but Stacy and Burdett were drawn to Tyburn on 19 May 1477 and hanged. Clarence responded the following day by getting one Dr Goddard (possibly the physician who had supplied a recipe for *aqua vitae* to the physician John Green and to William Worcester) to testify that Stacy and Burdett in their confessions had protested their innocence; according to the act of attainder against him, Clarence also got his retainers to spread the word that Burdett had been wrongfully put to death and that the king poisoned his subjects by necromancy.[119]

The application of alchemy in the black arts and in the pursuit of power was a convenient label to apply to political enemies, as Humphrey duke of Gloucester had found out in 1441, and there is little doubt that there were political motives behind the trial in 1441 of Gilles de Rais, the marshall of France and former companion in arms of Joan of Arc, for practising alchemy and the black arts. After being charged in an ecclesiastical court with using alchemical magic to invoke demons and making a pact with the devil, to whom he sacrificed children, he was tried in a secular court for the murder of over a hundred children. He was burnt by the inquisition. The charges may have been exaggerated by his political enemies but there were dark forces involved in this case. Today we would brand de Rais a vicious sexual pervert, but the most sensational aspect of the trial at the time was the involvement of alchemists (de Rais in his retirement employed an Italian alchemist in the 1430s to attempt transmutation to pay his debts) and the suspicion that children were being sacrificed for the pursuit of gold.[120] Deeper descent into the occult certainly occurred in Edward's court. Clarence was arrested and in February 1478 was convicted of treason and accusing Edward of sorcery; he was then accused of sorcery himself.[121] According to John Rous in his *Historia*, written ten years later, Edward had also been told by a soothsayer that one by the name of G would disinherit his children and take the crown.[122] This prophecy has been dismissed as a Tudor myth perpetrated by Shakespeare. But versions of prophecies where one king replaces another through the use of letters were very common in the late Middle Ages. One fourteenth-century prophecy begins 'H will submit to the father. After R, H will rule and after H, E will become king, and after E attends wonderful things.' This was applied to Edward IV and a version of it appears in the *Yorkist Prophecies*, the collection of prophecies foretelling the coming of Edward and known to Richard duke of Gloucester.[123] It was a very easy matter to tamper with such prophecies by altering a letter, and versions of the prophecy of G were certainly circulating immediately after Clarence's death in the Tower on 18 February.

This unprecedented infiltration of black magic into the affairs of state is a reflection of how far things had deteriorated since 1471. The preoccupation with witchcraft at Edward's court and the growing fear of women it implied needs to be seen in the context of a darkening of the general mood in Europe as women found themselves tried both by the Inquisition and in secular courts for witchcraft. A sensational trial at Arras in 1459–60 led to the arrest of thirty-four people and the burning of twelve as witches who served the devil. Secular judges in the Valois condemned large numbers of witches in 1447, and in the Dauphine 110 women and 57 men were executed between 1428 and 1447 in a series of persecutions that produced revelations of witches' covens and revels. In a trial in Dijon in 1470–1 the term witches' sabbat was first used. In a number of bulls Pope Eugenius IV (1431–47) ordered the Inquisition to proceed against magicians and diviners whose crimes he defined in terms of witchcraft, of making pacts with the devil. In December 1484 Pope Innocent VIII (1484–92) published his bull *Summus desiderandis*, effectively establishing that the Inquisition against witches had full papal approval. This paved the way for the appearance in 1485 or 1486 of the *Malleus maleficarum* (*The Hammer of Witches*), written by two German inquisitors Heinrich Institoris and Jakob Sprenger. This influential work organized and systematized the whole system of witch beliefs in the mind of the Inquisition and society, defining witchcraft as the most abominable of heresies.[124] Although nothing as extreme occurred in England, the increasing hostility towards powerful women at Edward's court reflected the changing mood and was a direct response to the growing frustration with the way Edward, caught between his queen and his three regular mistresses (and who knows how many others) was becoming increasingly passive. In Edward's copy of Bacon's *Secreta secretorum* there is a warning that there has been a steady progression in the misleading of people through the magic arts of hydromancy, aeromancy and pyromancy as magicians and parents teach their children and the evil of bewitchment grows until the coming of Anti-Christ and in particular 'from these talismans and charms and figures and magical doings comes errors of old women, witches.[125] Clarence in charging Ankarette Twynho with witchcraft was reviving rumours of the queen's descent from the famous water-witch Melusine. Elizabeth was in turn probably responsible for Clarence's death. Thomas More certainly pointed the finger at her. Apart from the vague charges against Clarence that he was practising the occult, no one seems to have known why Edward, after so much forbearance, finally sanctioned his brother's death. The imprisonment of Bishop Stillington in the Tower shortly after[126] would suggest that Clarence had secured from Stillington (the only witness apart from the king) the story of Edward's contract to marry Eleanor Butler before he had married Elizabeth, which in strict terms of canon law meant that the princes were illegitimate and Clarence was Edward's immediate heir. Clarence and Richard probably regarded themselves as Edward's heirs during the Burgundian exile, especially before the birth of Edward, prince of Wales. One prophecy describes them in October 1470 as 'Edward's heirs driven out of England contrary to God's will'.[127] Elizabeth, in defence of her son's inheritance, probably urged Clarence's immediate dispatch to prevent this story spreading. But Gloucester knew this story in 1483, and probably in 1478, and he, like Clarence, brought accusations of witchcraft against the queen, accusing her, in the act confirming his title in 1484, of complicity with her mother Jacquetta in bewitching the king in order to marry him. According to Vergil, Gloucester accused the witch Elizabeth of afflicting his body with her veneficia and suggested that Mistress Jane (Elizabeth) Shore was her associate: 'That sorceress and that other witch of her council, Shore's wife, of their affinity have by their sorcery, and witchcraft wasted my body.'

By 1477 Edward's carnal past had returned to haunt him and there was at this time a general perception that Edward had become disempowered by women. By this stage Edward may have come to believe, along with those pressing charges against his mother-in-law in 1469, that his profane marriage on the morning after Walpurgisnacht had aroused in him a self-destructive and demonic sensuality. The eclipse of 1482, the devouring of the sun by the feminine moon, would have been seen as an eloquent representation of the way Edward's masculine, martial energies had been swallowed. But fears about the loss of the king's powers went even deeper. Edward, through his long associations with alchemy, going back to 1456, and through the transformations he had effected, must have been regarded as something of an alchemist. Norton, in the *Ordinal of Alchemy*, specifically linked the state of mind of the king, his patron, with the performance of his experiments:

> – merke,
> Whethir his mynde accorde with the werke
> Which shall be harde to pay for all,
> Ells all your labour destroye be shall.[128]

But Edward had lost the ability to transform himself and those around him into a purposeful myth, and the science of alchemy itself was becoming the focus of these fears of a power that was turning malign. Stacy was also an alchemist, and Clarence responded to his execution by encouraging rumours that 'the king our sovereign lord wrought him by nygromancy and used craft to poison his subjects such as he pleased'. Clarence also charged Edward with having designs on his life through witchcraft and the imagery he used powerfully conveys the way, in some minds at least, the sun had degenerated into a more occult consuming force: 'the king intended to consume him [Clarence] in likewise as a candle consumeth in burning'.[129]

The killing of Clarence irreparably damaged Edward in the eyes of his subjects. He had, according to the author of the *Crowland Chronicle*, become a tyrant who 'exercised his office so haughtily thereafter that he seemed to be feared by all his subjects while he himself feared no man'.[130] The court had become increasingly like that of Rome in the time of Nero when no one felt safe. Caxton reflected on the paranoia and suspicion rife in Edward's court in these years by translating and printing Alan Chartier's *Curiale* in 1484 and dedicating it to an earl (probably Rivers). In this work a courtier employs an old topos (found in Walter Mapp) that nevertheless had increasing relevance at the Yorkist court and warns his younger brother to stay away from such an assemblage of mutual deceivers who buy and sell one another in the hall of the great prince which is 'couenly infecte and eschaufed of the breeth of the peple'[131] where no one is safe in his situation, where most serve their own honour rather than the common weal, where traitors bred in the arts of entrapment watch every word so they can turn informer and obtain favour from the great.[132] Edward may have been jealous of his younger brother. Clarence was like him in many ways, handsome, popular, charming, a very fine speaker, but he too was increasingly wasted through self-indulgence. He was moreover the favourite of the dowager duchess of York. The killing of Clarence may have been the result of Edward's narcissistic resentment. The manner of his death, drowning in a butt of malmsey wine, has the hallmarks of a cruel and puerile joke, not unlike Edward's earlier behaviour to George Neville. This rather than *realpolitik* would explain why he came to regret his actions. The killing of a brother was no light matter for Edward. In 1474 he snubbed an envoy of Louis XI because it was rumoured he had poisoned his brother the duke of Guienne, who was in alliance with the dukes of Brittany and Burgundy against his brother Louis XI and who died on 25 May 1474. The Croyland chronicler asserted that in his opinion the king 'privately repented very often' of what had been done. According to the author of the *Chronicles of the White Rose*, whenever anyone kneeled before the king to ask pardon for an offence, he would exclaim: 'O unfortunate brother, that no man would ask thy pardon.'[133] Edward had not become a monster, but he was by now a spent force slipping further into depression.

The role of the youngest brother in all this is difficult to fathom. He did not have Clarence's looks or charm and was therefore never a threat to Edward's vanity. According to Mancini Richard was shocked to hear of his brother's death and kept his grief hidden. Nevertheless he was to some extent implicated, and if there was a dark, demonic force at work from the time of Clarence's murder it was Richard duke of Gloucester, not Edward. Gloucester must have been aware of the pre-contract and would have seen it as the sins of his brothers coming to light, the approach of divine retribution. Richard had been waiting in the wings since late 1475, viewing with silent contempt what he regarded as the Babylonian excesses of Edward and his Woodville in-laws, and waiting for a sign that he was the chosen redeemer. The prophecy of G. could just as easily have been applied to Gloucester, and the execution of Clarence, which Richard may have urged, made him Edward's heir and brought him closer to the throne. The family of York was imploding and Gloucester, who styled himself as a descendant of Brutus in his copy of Geoffrey of Monmouth, would, in the light of these events, have consulted the genealogies that he and Edward had used in the 1471 campaigns, such as the adapted Yorkist chronicle and the *Genealogy of Edward King of Britain*.[134] He would have contemplated the evolution of God's divine plan from Adam to Richard, rather than to Edward. He would have noted how it all began with fraternal strife between Cain and Abel and his ancestor Seth. The prophecy of the coming of the British king chosen by God could also have been applied by Richard to himself, and especially relevant at the time of the Clarence affair was the prophecy of the eagle, found in his copy of Geoffrey of Monmouth, where it was predicted that 'a tusked boar will make his den, and throughout the bushes and briars of fraternal strife one who is unlooked for will reign'.

Richard's messianic conviction that he was the virtuous chosen king of an exiled people punished for their sins, which I have previously traced to the psalms in the king's *Book of Hours* which he used between 1483 and 1485, goes back much earlier and to another source, the prophecies which Richard had grown up with and which were in his volume of Geoffrey of Monmouth. One such prophecy concerned the vision of Edward the Confessor of the rejoined tree of the British line which dominates the *Illustrated Life of Edward IV* and which also occurs in the 1471 version of the *Genealogy of Edward King of Britain*.[135] The sense in these rolls and prophecies, copied and disseminated between 1471 and 1478, of the British race as a chosen people, like the Jews, undergoing punishment and exile and awaiting a redeemer would have appealed to Gloucester's sense of self-righteousness. In 1478 his charter for Middleham College depicted its founder in a similar way as the chosen one elevated by God: 'what am I lord and what is my family that thou hast brought me this far – thou hast raised me to this I give and return thanks'. The sins of Edward and his court, so similar to those of the fallen British of Cadwallader's time and of the Lancastrians, were a further indication that it was the isolated and puritanical Richard who was the chosen one. He therefore would have seen particular appropriateness in the prophecy of Merlin to Vortigern that after a period of oppression the Britons would prevail under the leadership of the Boar of Cornwall (Arthur).

As Gloucester began to establish his power-base in the north and to advance into Scotland, taking Berwick, he must have had a sense of the prophecies unfolding, especially when he consulted the Thomas Becket prophecy: 'When Becket asked our Lady whether a Boar shall come from Britain she said yes and the Boar shall tumble France and not rest till its tusks are grown and he shall be stirred up by Berwick.' In a commonplace book originating from the honour of Richmond, the centre of Gloucester's power-base, from where he made his bid for the throne,[136] there is a prophetic vision of the defeat of the Scots and the French by a British hero. He also owned the prophecy of the eagle concerning the return and victories of a British hero, and in this manuscript Richard signed his own motto on the opening folio.[137] It was from this power-base in June 1483 that the city of York, in response to a letter from Gloucester, sent 8,000 boar badges wrought upon fustian for Richard's coronation.

Contrary to the popular view of historians, Richard was not taken by surprise by Edward's death. The king's physical decline in the preceding years was well known. In the Percy Roll, perhaps finally completed after Bosworth and incorporating Richard III, Edward's bloated and ill-looking face is depicted in a line-drawing.[138] Hastings and Gloucester may have involved themselves in the abortive attempt to provide military assistance to Boulogne from the Calais garrison in 1477 against Edward's wishes because the king was too ill to take control of foreign policy. Louis was certainly corresponding with Hastings rather than with Edward at this time, and in April he enquired whether Edward was suffering from a serious illness. The report of Edward's infirmity had reached Louis by means of certain Scots at his court. Hastings responded that the king was in good health and intended to celebrate the feast of the Garter at Windsor, as he usually did.[139] However, although Edward did attend the Garter feast, it was not the one originally to be held at Windsor on 23 April 1477. Instead it took place over 23–24 April at St John's Priory, where the king was in residence, presumably because he could not travel. A separate feast was then held at Windsor on 10 May but the king was unable to attend and sent a proxy.[140] The promptness with which Hastings and Gloucester worked together in unison at the time of Edward's death to forestall a Woodville takeover may reflect their knowledge of the precarious state of the king's health. It can therefore be argued that Richard did not panic and improvise because he felt threatened when his brother was no longer there to protect him from the power of the Woodvilles. The reality of the situation was closer to the dramatic recreation of Shakespeare. The playwright shows Richard duke of Gloucester plotting his way to the throne, compressing thirteen years into a much shorter interval of time, but this was not such a distortion as the explanation provided by modern historians, myself included, for Richard's motivations. By explaining Richard's behaviour in the four months following the death of his brother and protector as an insecure, uncharacteristic and instinctive reaction to his vulnerable position in the north, dependent on the goodwill of the Woodvilles, we have clouded the previous thirteen years of Gloucester's life with mystery, turning the Gloucester of this period into a bland, uncharismatic loyal subject and brother. Why do people assume Gloucester was so different from Clarence, who spent ten years plotting for the throne? He was just cleverer. The picture I painted of a devout, fanatical man believing he was chosen by God to rule need not now be confined to 1483–5; it can be put back at least to 1475 and to convictions that were deeply rooted not just in the daily reading of the psalms but in the prophecies and genealogies that first inspired Richard as an eight-year-old child when he still saw Edward as the father, head and saviour of his house. Edward's death on 9 April came as no surprise; it was something Richard had been waiting for, and it was the start of the fulfilment of another prophecy, widely circulated and popular at the time, found in Metham's treatise on palmistry. This is one of the prognostications based on Christmas Day, attributed to the prophet Esdras, which foretell the events of the year according to the day of the week on which Christmas Day falls. In 1483 Christmas Day fell on a Thursday and according to the prognostication 'that yere schulde kyngy and lordys dey'.[141] In this year two kings did die, Edward IV and his son Edward V; and many lords also died, including Anthony Woodville, Thomas Grey, Richard Vaughan, William Lord Hastings and Henry Stafford, duke of Buckingham. Richard, although he may not have intended it, had begun to create another myth when, like Macbeth, he attempted to bring these prophecies about. This was to become the antithesis of the myths that Edward had built around himself, the myth of the demonic tyrant. This was not a Tudor invention but something that horrified onlookers could see happening. Louis XI may have had a destructive, indeed demonic influence on Edward, but he took no pleasure in his death and clearly regarded Gloucester as inhabiting another dimension of villainy. When Richard III, on his accession, attempted to correspond with Louis XI, the French king refused to accept letters 'from one so cruel' and returned them. This was the myth that would endure: Richard was unable to convince as the heroic British redeemer.

Edward, on the other hand, with his good looks, charm and confidence in his own good fortune, had been able to inspire his court and the nation with these myths of the British redeemer. Richard was a loner, lacking his brother's advantages, and for him the myths, especially those from the Old Testament, merely reinforced his sense of being different. He could therefore only inspire in others fear and incomprehension. The alchemists would have nothing to do with him because with his catalogue of crimes – regicide, fratricide, infanticide, incest and possibly the poisoning of his wife – he evoked all the primeval taboos in the depths of the unconscious into which the alchemists, especially one like Ripley, penetrated. Richard was Saturn devouring his children, the crow, the venomous scorpion, and from an alchemical perspective the events of 1483 represented a terrifying manifestation of the *nigredo*. As Shakespeare expressed it Richard was 'like to a chaos'. Scorpio was regarded as the sign least favourable to the alchemical work. It was a murderous, watery sign of Autumn associated with inverted energies, with putrefaction and corruption. It is likely that Richard's piety, like that of his mother, would have led him to regard Edward's close interest in alchemy as an indication of his moral degeneration. A collection of alchemical treatises in a fifteenth-century manuscript is followed by a genealogy of historical notes of English kings culminating in Edward IV.[142] The same scribe subsequently added an account of Richard III, referring to him as a diabolic king with an insatiable appetite for power who seized Edward prince of Wales and Richard duke of York under fraudulent circumstances. He goes on to claim that at the instigation and counsel of the Duke of Buckingham, Lord Rivers and Thomas Vaughan were beheaded without due process of law and Hastings was beheaded because he was not prepared to accept the coronation. The nephews too, regarded as impediments to kingship, were murdered on the counsel of Buckingham. A similar account of Richard's reign of terror occurs in a poem about the kings of England in another late fifteenth-century manuscript which describes Richard being made king 'at the occasion of an unhappy deed by the murdering of young Edward our king'.[143] Alchemical language was even used in a Latin elegy on Edward's death, possibly composed by Carmeliano as an epitaph for his unfinished tomb. Mourning the passing of one who was Arthur to his enemies, in habit like Solomon, the ornament of the world, the rose, the sun of triumph, the poet refers to the hiding of the sun, and laments that England is now oppressed by dark cares.[144]

But Richard's sinister image was more widely recognized. As a printer and publisher, Caxton was closely in touch with public opinion, and this, together with the instigation of the most Arthurian of Edward's courtiers, Anthony Woodville (who may have supplied the manuscript), encouraged Caxton to print Malory's *Morte d'Arthur*. In working on his edition between 1483 and 1485 Caxton saw parallels between the bleak conclusion to this epic and what was happening in England. In his dedication of his translation and edition of Lull's *Order of Chivalry* to Richard III in 1484, Caxton lamented the passing of the Camelot era of Edward's court, that there were no heroes in England to compare with the knights of Arthur's day. Knights now, he claimed, went to bathhouses and played at dice instead of reading the volumes of Lancelot and Seynt Grail.[145] By choosing to follow his publication of Higden's *Polychronicon* in 1482 with Malory's *Morte d'Arthur* between 1483 and 1485, he was reflecting what must have been a popular perception, that England was being ruled by Mordred, Arthur's bastard son, who had usurped his father's kingdom and who, against the wishes of the archbishop of Canterbury, 'how may ye wed youre owne fadirs wyff',[146] intended to enter into an incestuous marriage with Arthur's queen. Guinevere, to avoid this fate, escaped to the Tower, which she fortified, while Elizabeth Woodville stayed in the sanctuary of Westminster Abbey with her children. Richard had similarly usurped his nephew's kingdom and it was popularly believed that he was contemplating in 1485 an incestuous union with his niece Elizabeth of York. An indication of the way Richard's reign was seen in terms of the usurpation of Mordred appears in Thomas More's account of Edward's deathbed when he warns the courtiers of the serpents in the commonwealth. Edward had been depicted at the time of his conquests sitting triumphantly on top of fortune's wheel but this description of his deathbed recalls Arthur's dream of sitting on a wheel over a pit of serpents.

NOTES

1. M.G.A. Vale, 'An Anglo-Burgundian Nobleman and Art Patron', in Barron and Saul (eds), *England in the Low Countries*, p. 128; Rymer, *Foedera*, vol. xi, p. 765.
2. *Archeologia*, xxvi (1835), 147; BL MS Bib. Cotton Jul. Caes VI.
3. Rees, *Son of Prophecy*.
4. G. Williams, *Renewal and Reformation in Wales*.
5. BL MS Cotton Vesp. E VII, fo. 89b; Bodley MS 623, fos 76–76b.
6. See Ben Jonson, *The Alchemist*.
7. BL MS Add. 48031, fo. 187. In one manuscript, BL MS Lansdowne 762, fo. 3, this letter is ascribed to Henry V; Scofield, *Edward IV*, vol. ii, p. 107.
8. Scofield, *Edward IV*, vol. i, pp. 73–4, 159.
9. Vergil, *Anglia Historia*, 110, 172.
10. Mancini, *The Usurpation of Richard III*, ed. C.A.J. Armstrong (1969), pp. 64–7.
11. *Crowland Chronicle; Second continuation (1459–86)*, pp. 150–3.
12. Mancini, *Usurpation of Richard III*, pp.64–7.
13. Ross, *Edward IV*, pp. 214–18; Lander, *Hundred Years War*, pp. 231–4; A.J. Pollard, *Late Medieval England 1399–1500* (Edinburgh, 2000), pp. 301–2.
14. *Cal. Milanese Papers*, vol. v, pp. 193–4; *Great Chronicle of London*, p. 221; Scofield, *Edward IV*, ll, 105.
15. Commines, *The Memoirs of Philippe de Commines*, ed. S. Kinser, transl. J. Gazeaun (South Carolina, 1973).
16. Commines, *Memoirs*, p. 105.
17. Commines, *Memoirs*, pp. 54–70; C. Richmond, '1485 and All that'; *Cal. State Papers* in MS existing in archives of Milan, vol. i, pp. 217, 218, 221.
18. *Cal. State Papers Milan*, vol. i, p. 218.
19. *Crowland Chronicle*, p. 138.
20. D. Dunlop, 'The Redress and Reparacions on attemptales: Alexander Legh's instructions from Edward IV, March–April 1475', *Historical Research*, 63 (1990), 340–53.
21. *Cal. State Papers Milan*, vol. i, p. 163; M.K. Jones, '1477 – The Expedition that Never Was: Chivalric Expectation in Late Yorkist England', *The Ricardian*, xii, 153 (June 2001), p. 277 n.10, citing PRO E 405/55r 1.
22. College of Arms MS 21716.
23. BL MS Harl. 7353; A. Sutton and L. Visser-Fuchs, 'The Royal Burials of the House of York at Windsor', *The Ricardian* xi, 143 (December 1998).
24. Robbins, *Hist. Poems*, pp. 218–21.
25. BL MS Harl. 48, fos 78–91.
26. Bodley MS Hatton 56.
27. BL MS Lyell 33, fos 11–12.
28. Ashmole Roll 26.
29. St Petersburg, Saltykov-Shchedrin State Public Library MS Lat. F IV 76. See Sutton and Visser-Fuchs, *Richard III's Books*, p. 157.
30. Ashmole Roll 26.
31. BL MS Royal 15 E IV, fo. 14; printed in Dupont, *Anciennes Croniques d'Engleterre* (Paris, 1858–63), p. xlvi.
32. A. Sutton and L. Visser-Fuchs, 'Richard III and the Knave of Cards'. These authors have correctly established the conventional stereotyped patterns in this miniature, but their claim that the template for this figure is the knave of cards is conjecture and the possibility that it is Gloucester cannot be ruled out.
33. BL MS Royal E II, fo. 338.
34. Bodley MS Hatton 56.
35. Ibid, fos 45a–46b.
36. This manuscript was written after 1460. The date 1460 appears next to the prophecy of St Gildas. It was therefore not written in 1450–3 as claimed in the Bodley summary catalogue. Thus it can be considered with BL MS Cotton Vesp. E VII and Bodley MS 623 and College of Arms MS 20/9 as belonging to the period of Edward's accession.
37. Bodley MS Hatton 56, fo. 40v.
38. C. Weightman, *Margaret of York Duchess of Burgundy 1446–1503* (Gloucester, 1989), p. 120.
39. E. Liot de Northbecourt, 'La Complaint d' Arras', *Bulletin des antiquaires de la marinie*, vol. 2 (1857–61); see Jones, '1477, the Expedition that Never Was' for a translation.
40. *Crowland Chronicle, Continuations*, p. 143.
41. Commines, *Memoirs*, pp. 7–8.
42. *Chronicles of the White Rose*, p. 246.

43. *Lettres de Louis XI roi de France*, ed. J. Naesen and E. Charavay, 12 vols (Paris, 1883–1901), vol. 6, p. 138.
44. Jones, '1477, the Expedition that Never Was', 278; Henry Huntingdon Library MS HA 13879, fo. 3.
45. *Paston Letters*, vol. v, p. 288.
46. Ibid, pp. 287–8.
47. The details of this process survive among the papers of Louis's secretary, Jean Bourre, Paris, Bibliotheque nationale, MS Fr 204494, fos 97–8. For a transcript see Jones '1477, the Expedition that Never Was', 285–7.
48. C.D. Grummit, 'The Defence of Calais and the Development of Gunpowder Weapons in England in the late fifteenth century'.
49. Scofield, *Edward IV*, vol. ii, pp. 478–9.
50. Jones, '1477, the Expedition that Never Was'.
51. Plancher, *Histoire de Bourgogne*, vol. 4, pp. 400–1.
52. BL MS Harl. 3569.
53. M. Biddle, 'The Painting of the Round Table', in *King Arthur's Round Table*, ed. M. Biddle (Woodbridge, 2000), pp. 469–70; S. Laschitzer (ed.), 'Der Theurdank', *Jahrbuch der Kunthistorishe Sammlungen des Allerhochsten Kaiserhauses*, 8 (1888); Gerhild S. Williams, 'The Arthurian Model in Emperor Maximilian's Autobiographical Writings Weisskunig and Theuerdank', *Sixteenth-Century Journal*, 11.4 (1980), 3–22 at pp. 14–15; Gerhard Benecke, *Maximilian I (1459–1519) An Analytical Biography* (London, 1982).
54. Biddle, 'The Painting of the Round Table', 464, 471.
55. BL MS Add. 15549.
56. Mancini, *Usurpation of Richard III*, p. 57.
57. R. Firth Green, *Poets and Prince-Pleasers: Literature and the English Court in the Late Middle Ages* (Toronto, 1980).
58. A. Sutton and L. Visser-Fuchs, 'The Royal Burials of the House of York at Windsor', *The Ricardian*, xi, 143 (1998), 366–407.
59. John Rylands University Library MS Eng 113, fos 3r–v; Sutton and Visser-Fuchs, 'Laments for the soul of Edward IV', 516–18.
60. BL MS Harl. 3952, fo. 105v; Sutton and Visser-Fuchs, 'Laments for Edward IV', 518.
61. Bodley MS Rawl. C 86, fo. 74; Sutton and Visser-Fuchs, 'Laments for Edward IV', 516–18.
62. Shakespeare, *Othello*, Act III, Sc. III, l. 214.
63. Commines, *Memoirs*, vol. ii, pp. 304, 344.
64. *Crowland Chronicle*, p. 149.
65. Ibid, pp. 149–51.
66. Ibid, p. 153.
67. Ross, *Wars of the Roses*, p. 72.
68. Trinity College Cambridge, MS 0.2.16, fos 28v, 33. This is a fifteenth-century manuscript.
69. C. Rawcliffe, 'Consultants, Careerists and Conspirators: Royal Doctors in the time of Richard III', *The Ricardian*, 106 (1988).
70. Myers, *Household of Edward IV*, pp. 123–4; Carole Rawcliffe, 'More than a Bedside Manner: the Political Status of the Late Medieval Court Physician', in *St George's Chapel, Windsor*.
71. Mancini, *Usurpation of Richard III*, p. 67.
72. *Paston Letters*, ed. Fenn, p. 161.
73. Mancini, *Usurpation of Richard III*, p. 67.
74. *Crowland Chronicle*, p. 149.
75. *Secreta secretorum*, p. 60.
76. Myers, *Household of Edward IV*, pp. 123–4.
77. John Somer was the author of a treatise on the virtues of olive oil.
78. See Kymer's *Regimen sanitatis*.
79. Ashmole, *Theatrum Chemicum Britannicum*, p. 43.
80. Chaucer, *The Nun's Priest's Tale* in *Works*, ll. 2837–9; Getz, *Medicine in the English Middle Ages*, p. 88.
81. Ibid, p. 114.
82. *Secreta secretorum*, ch. 7. The kinds of medicine prescribed at the end of Edward's reign can be found in *Stonor Letters*, ed. Kingsford (London Society, 3rd ser. xxx, 1919), vol. ii, pp. 107–8.
83. Rawcliffe, *Medicine and Society*, p. 54.
84. Rawcliffe, 'Consultants, Careerists and Conspirators'.
85. *Cal. State Papers Milan*, vol. i, p. 171.
86. Huntingdon MS 144, fos 152r–v, printed in R.J. Furnival, *Notes and Queries* 9 (1878), p. 343; Issue Roll Easter II Edward IV.
87. R. Virgoe, *Private Life in the Fifteenth Century: Illustrated Letters of the Paston Family* (London, 1989), p. 269.

88. BL MS Egerton 2572, fo. 68v.
89. Rawcliffe, *Medicine and Society*, p. 153.
90. Peterhouse College, Cambridge, MS 95, fo. 108v.
91. Ashmole, *Theatrum Chemicum Britannicum*, pp. 139–48; *Compound of Alchemy*, ed. Linden, pp. 38–9.
92. BL MS Cotton Vesp. E VII; Bodley MS 623.
93. BL MS Harl. 220, fos 74v–75.
94. R.T. Beck, *The Cutting Edge: Early History of the Surgeons of London* (London, 1974).
95. Bodley MS Ashmole 344, fo 34r. Shirwood gave Neville a mathematical game to amuse him during his convalescence.
96. Bodley MS Ashmole 1432, fos 3–4.
97. For preface see Ashmole, *Theatrum Chemicum Britannicum*, pp. 389ff.
98. BL MS Sloane 3580 B, fo. 148v.
99. BL MS Sloane 3667, a sixteenth-century copy, fos 94–104; *Marrow of Alchemy* (*Medulla Philosophorum*); BL MS Sloane 3580 B, fo. 138.
100. Cambridge University Library, MS Ee 3.61.
101. BL MS Harl. 267, fo. 235r.
102. Peterhouse College, Cambridge, MS 95, fo. 108v; Gloucester Cathedral MS 21, fo. 9v; J.D. North, *Horoscopes and History*, p. 141.
103. *Crowland Chronicle*, p. 139.
104. *CPR Edward IV and Henry VI 1467–77*, p. 588; Bodley MS Ashmole 1459, fo. 27b. Ashmole saw Ripley's retraction in John Dee's copy of the *Compound of Alchemy* dated 1471.
105. *Arrivall*, p. 46.
106. Thorndike, *History of Magic*, citing Univ. Bologna MS 142, fo. 60.
107. Ashmole notes to *Theatrum Chemicum Britannicum*, pp. 455–6.
108. This passage is not in the version of the *Ordinal* as we have it, but presumably was in a revised version, done after Edward's death for Henry VII and in Samuel Norton's possession. Norton seems to have revised his work for each patron and this explains why a number of other quotations from Samuel Norton occur in the surviving text but in different chapters. Bodley MS Ashmole 1421, fo. 171v.
109. Bodley MS Ashmole 1421, fo. 171v.
110. *CPR Edward IV 1467–77*, p. 629; *CPR 1475–85*, pp. 22, 71.
111. Reidy, intro. to Norton, *Ordinal of Alchemy*, pp. xlvi–lii. For an account of the affair see *The Great Red Book of Bristol*, ed. E.W.W. Veale, text pt iii (Bristol Record Society Publications), pp. xviii, 39, 57–93.
112. *Adams' Chronicle of Bristol*, ed. F.F. Fox (Bristol, 1810), p. 73; Latimer, 'Some curious incidents in British History', *Transactions of the Bristol and Gloucester Archaeological Society*, xxii (1890), 275–83.
113. BL MS Add. 10302; Ashmole, *Theatrum Chemicum Britannicum*, p. 455.
114. M.K. Jones, '1477, the Expedition that Never Was', 284; Sutton and Visser-Fuchs, 'Chivalry and the Yorkist Kings', 112.
115. Reiffenberg, *Histoire de la Toison d'Or*, pp. 98, 102; Scofield, *Edward IV*, p. 239.
116. BL MS Harl. 22, fos 74r–75r; C.H. Talbot and E.A. Hammond, *The Medical Practitioner in Medieval England, a Biographical Register* (London, 1965), p. 112; *Memorials of Henry VII*, ed. J. Gairdner (Rolls Series, 1858), 19.0.
117. Thorndike, *History of Magic*, p. 436.
118. BL MS Sloane 2218.
119. H.A. Kelly, 'English Kings and the Fear of Sorcery', *Medieval Studies*, 39 (1977), 230ff; Kittredge, *Witchcraft*, p. 84.
120. J. Burton-Russell, *Witchcraft in the Middle Ages* (Cornell, 1972), pp. 262–3.
121. *Rot. Parl.*, vol. vi, p. 232.
122. Rous, *Historia Regem Angliae*, p. 215. According to Rous, Humphrey duke of Gloucester had been murdered for the same reason.
123. Bodley MS Hatton 56, fo. 35r.
124. The *Malleus malifecarum*, transl. Montague Summers (London, 1928); R. Kieckhefer, *Magic in the Middle Ages* (Cambridge, 1990), pp. 196–8; J. Burton-Russell, *Witchcraft in the Middle Ages*.
125. *Secreta secretorum*, ch. 3, 6.
126. *Stonor Letters and Papers*, vol. ii, p. 42.
127. Bradfer Lawrence MS.
128. Norton, *Ordinal of Alchemy*, p. 84.
129. *Rot. Parl.*, vol. vi, p. 194.
130. *Crowland Chronicle*, p. 148.
131. *The Curiale made by Mayster Alain Charetier, transl. William Caxton 1484*, ed. R. Deacon (EETS, 54), p. 10.

132. Ibid, pp. 10–12.
133. *Chronicles of the White Rose*, p. 252.
134. Bodley MSS Lyell 33 and Ashmole Roll 26.
135. BL MS Harl. 7353; Bodley MS Ashmole 26; Sutton and Visser-Fuchs, *Richard III's Books*, p. 353.
136. For the Becket prophecy see Bodley MS Hatton 86 fos 45a–45b. The manuscript contains an inquest for the honour of Richmond; John Rylands Library MS 228.
137. St Petersburg, Saltykov-Shchedrin State Public Library, MS Lat. F iv 76; Sutton and Visser-Fuchs, *Richard III's Books*, p. 288.
138. Bodley Roll 5.
139. M.K. Jones, '1477, the Expedition that Never Was', 278. From a major new source Lord Hastings' Calais Letter Book. Henry Huntingdon Library, San Marino, California, MS HA 13879, fo. 4r.
140. Jones, '1477, the Expedition that Never Was', 290 n.15, from Diethard Schneider, *Der englische Hosenbandorden. Beitrage zur Entstehung und Entwicklung des 'The most noble order of the Garter (1348–1702) mit einem Ausblick bis 1983*, 2 vols in 4 (Bonn, 1988), vol 1, pt 1, pl. 356; pt 2, p.162.
141. These prognostications later became the husbandman's diary; *John Mepham's Treatise on Days of the Moon* (EETS, 1916), ed. Craig; All Souls College, Oxford, MS 81.
142. Johannes Fabricius, *Alchemy, The Medieval Alchemists and their Royal Art* (London, 1976), 106–7. The scorpion represented the opposite of the *uroboros* because it was believed it killed itself when biting its own tail. Bodley MS Ashmole 1448, fos 288v–9; Bodley MS Rawl. C 86, fo. 74; Sutton and Visser-Fuchs, 'Laments for the Soul of Edward IV', *The Ricardian*, xi, 145 (June 1999).
143. BL MS Lansdowne 762, fo. 11.
144. Bodley MS Rawl. C 86, fo. 74. Printed in Sutton and Visser-Fuchs, 'Laments for the Death of Edward IV', 516–18.
145. Caxton, *Book of the Order of Chivalry*; A.F. Sutton and L. Visser-Fuchs, 'Richard III's Books: Chivalric Ideals and Reality', *The Ricardian*, ix, 116 (1992), 120–206. Sutton and Visser-Fuchs, 'Richard III's Books: XI Raymund Lull's Order of Chivalry translated by William Caxton', *The Ricardian*, 114 (1991), 110–30.
146. *Works of Malory*, vol. 1, p. 228.

CHAPTER 11

Conclusion: The Legacy of Edward IV

Celsa petens astri, iam liquit culmina castrii.
He reached for the sky but now has left his castle high.

Anon, *Lament for Edward IV*

Banquo: 'It was said
It should not stand in thy posterity,
But that myself should be the root and father
of many kings. If there come truth from them, –
As upon thee, Macbeth, their speeches shine, –
Why, by the verities on thee made good,
May they not be my oracles as well,
And set me up in hope.'

William Shakespeare, *Macbeth*

The story of Edward IV, on a personal level, is a tragedy about the disintegration of a personality and the destruction of everything, including his family, that he had worked for. But Edward's legacy was considerable. He was the first English king to harness the combined influences of alchemical medicine, myths and prophecies to weld together a nation. He provided, through these forces, for the establishment of a dynastic system that has continued to this day. The myths, history and philosophy of antiquity that he fostered at his court contributed to the formation of a secular state that would dictate the future course of western civilization.

Edward's death in April 1483 provided the same sort of opportunities for the alchemists, physicians and astronomers at his court that the death of his father Richard duke of York had provided in January 1461. It freed them from their allegiance to a king who was a spent force, and allowed them to plan for the alchemical birth of a new dynasty, in which the links between alchemical chemistry and genealogy, which had been explored in 1460 and 1471, took on an exciting new dimension with the possibilities raised by an alchemical marriage between the Houses of York and Lancaster. As soon as it became clear that Gloucester intended to usurp the throne, alchemists and physicians entered into correspondence with the exiled Henry Tudor earl of Richmond, then in Brittany, in an attempt to bring about Gloucester's downfall. John Morton bishop of Ely's interest in alchemy is suggested by his employment of the alchemist Mr T. Ward as his confessor. Ward, an Oxford and Cambridge scholar,[1] was the author of a treatise on the sublimation of mercury which appears in a collection of alchemical treatises.[2] Morton was imprisoned by Gloucester on Friday 13 April when Hastings was

June

executed, but he was soon put into the protective custody of Henry Stafford duke of Buckingham. A scientific community in opposition to Gloucester was forming around Morton. Physicians, by the nature of their trade, using volvelles to follow the paths of the sun and moon and to read off zodiac signs and to define and advise favourable days for blood-letting, were inevitably drawn into making political prognostications. The 1482 eclipse must have represented for them at the very least the increasing feminizing of Edward's masculine energies, and they would have subsequently seen it as the harbinger of the eclipse of the sun king and the rise of the sinister Gloucester. The encroaching darkness was further manifested with the famous eclipse of the sun of 16 March 1484, the day of the death of Richard's queen, Anne Neville. The Welsh physician and astronomer Lewis Caerleon MD, a Cambridge graduate and author of a table of eclipses of the sun and moon,[3] who had written about the eclipse of 1482 as a harbinger of a change of dynasty,[4] served as physician to both Margaret Beaufort, who according to Vergil 'conferred her adversity on the physician',[5] and Elizabeth Woodville. Caerleon used his position as a man of science to visit Elizabeth in her sanctuary in Westminster Abbey in the summer of 1483 to suggest an alliance with Margaret against Gloucester.[6] Notes in a contemporary hand to Caerleon's astrological tables record that he produced other tables and canons while incarcerated in the Tower by Richard III.[7]

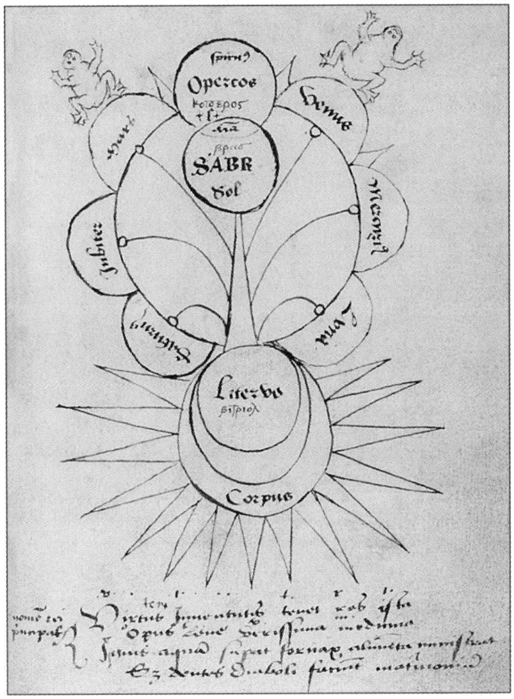

The most extreme manifestation of the conjunction of the sun and moon in an eclipse. This image occurs in the Ripley Scrolls, The Illustrated Life of Edward IV *and in* The Prophetic History of Edward King of Britain. *(British Library Egerton 845, fo. 17)*

Another physician who may have been involved in this attempt to end Richard III's rule was John Argentine, who lectured in Cambridge on astrology and the natural, sciences and medicine in 1470 and cast horoscopes for Edward IV and his son Edward V. Argentine became physician to Henry VII's son Prince Arthur.[8] Lewis Caerleon, Margaret Beaufort and Elizabeth Woodville were implicated in the conspiracy behind the uprisings throughout southern England in late September 1483, aimed at the restoration of Edward V. To this inner council of Duke Henry who 'falsly and traiterously, as false Traitours and Rebells intended, conspired imagined and compassed' the death of Richard III can be added Thomas Nandike. Nandike, who read for the degree of Bachelor of medicine at Cambridge in 1476–7, belongs to the circle of influential Cambridge physicians and astrologers with alchemical interests. Described in a list of individuals attainted by Parliament for their part in the rebellion of autumn 1483 as chaplain, physician and 'nigromansier' to Henry duke of Buckingham, Nandike also practised alchemy of a dubious kind with political objectives in mind. The inventory of his effects taken in 1491 after years of relative poverty and obscurity in Cambridge, with its combination of shabby but once grand Calabrian furs and Tartary silk gowns and such weapons as a pair of crossbows with winches and a brass handgun, imply grandiose and secretive activities. Most suggestive are his books of physic and astronomy, two brass astrolabes and other unspecified instruments and some of the basic equipment required for the alchemical distillation and transmutation of metals. This includes 37lb of wrought lead, 28lb of unwrought lead, books of astronomy and glasses and boxes sold to Master Abbot head of the Glomery, a teachers' college in Cambridge, and a 'melting ladyll of yron', two chalkstones, a handsaw, a 'fier rake', hatchets, shovels, charcoal, pewter and brass pans and basins which were sold to William Buckenham, Fellow of Gonville Hall and executor of John Argentine. Nandike's possession of so much lead is especially interesting. Lead, of the planet Saturn, was conceived to be the *prima materia*, the heavy dull leprous opposite of gold, a hopeless fusion of elements mirroring the heavy formless *prima materia* before the creation of the world. The alchemist's task was to purify and extract the stone from its matrix, bringing light from the darkness, administering to the lead and curing it into gold. Nandike as a physician and alchemist would have applied his warming irons, fires and vessels to this task, by following recipes like George Ripley's for oxidizing the lead, heating and distilling it to create a tincture of colour that could lead to its transmutation. England after Edward IV's death had been plunged into the hellish chaos of the *prima materia* and Nandike probably conceived his involvement in Buckingham's rebellion, which earned him a pardon from Henry VII in 1485, as an alchemical quest to purge the realm of the Saturnian darkness of Richard III's rule.[9] At least one attempt was made to rescue the prince, but when the rebels were joined by Buckingham, his physician Nandike and his prisoner Morton (who according to the chroniclers persuaded Buckingham to join the rebellion) the objective changed to putting Henry Tudor on the throne. Presumably Buckingham brought the news that the princes were dead.

Although Richmond's claim was weak, the Yorkists were attracted by his promise to marry Elizabeth of York. The architects of this plan were Morton and Caerleon, physician to the heads of both houses, Margaret Beaufort and Elizabeth Woodville. The rebellion finally broke out on 10 October, but by 2 November it had been suppressed by Gloucester; Richmond, who had landed at Plymouth too late to be of any assistance, turned back to France. Morton escaped to Flanders, but Nandike and Caerleon were imprisoned in the Tower. Caerleon continued to plan for the union of the two houses. According to Vergil, Margaret Beaufort consulted him regularly as her advocate after the slaughter of Edward's children, and began to hope in her son's fortune and the profit of the commonweal by joining the blood of Henry VI and King Edward. She therefore consulted him about the marriage of Elizabeth of York and her son. The queen in her turn followed his advice because he was a learned physician and he did astronomical calculations in the Tower. On Christmas Day 1483, at Rennes Cathedral, Henry Tudor took an oath to marry Elizabeth of York. This was more than a dynastic

This illustration of an alchemical marriage shows the alchemist (possibly Ripley) presiding over a reconciliation of the fighting dragons. Behind him, bursting through the clouds, is the sun in splendour. This image, which occurs on the Ripley Scroll, *would have increasing significance in 1483 when alchemists were planning to revive the fortunes of Edward IV's decimated family by uniting the houses of York and Lancaster. (British Library Egerton 845, fo. 17v)*

arrangement. Leading intellectuals, who shared an interest in medicine and alchemy, including Ward, Morton, Nandike, Caerleon, Argentine and no doubt others, possibly Norton and Ripley, had all been involved; such a marriage presented exciting possibilities for a permanent resolution of all the conflicts that had bedevilled the English body politic for the previous thirty years.

George Ripley once more proved to be a central figure, as he had been in 1461 and 1471, for his writings, full as they are of sexual imagery of a marriage between a white queen and a red king, of the union of such opposites as the sun and moon, silver and gold, through the agency of mercury, took on new political significance. In a mid-fifteenth century alchemical treatise it was proclaimed that gold and silver were the most highly evolved of the metals (like the heads of the two rival dynastic houses of the period who both employed genealogies to demonstrate their evolution). The royal marriage of December 1483 brought these two opposites together. In the fourth of his twelve gates of alchemy with which he divides up the *Compound of Alchemy*, Ripley dealt with this conjunction of opposites and discusses a secret union whereby 'natures repugnant joyneth to perfect unyte'.[10] This could easily be applied to the marital union of the two houses that had been at war for so long. In the fifth gate the stone flourishes in the form of ruby-red grapes (depicted in the *Ripley Scrolls*) and the elements are joined without strife, the red king rejoicing 'in the whiteness and beauty of his wyfe'.[11] In the *Marrow of Alchemy* he wrote of the mystery of the two sulphurs, the red and the white, which together create the highest of all medicines to transmute bodies of metal to pure gold. What would have most captured the imagination of the physicians who supported this marriage alliance would have been passages such as that in the *Bosom Book* where Ripley writes 'This is the pleasant and dainty Garden of the Philosophers, which beareth the sweet smelling Roses white and red, abbreviated out of all the work of the Philosophers', and the motif of the golden rose of alchemy, a red and white rose, which occurs in some sixteenth-century versions of the *Ripley Scrolls* and which symbolizes the allegorical marriage of the red man (gold) and the white woman (mercury).[12] This was a theme common to all the alchemical writers of the period. Barker wrote of a dyeing of the stone white and red; Norton wrote of a marriage between a white queen and a red king, and the creation of the rose of alchemy. John Sawtry (or Santry), a Benedictine monk of Thorney abbey in the Fens (an abbey with a well-stocked library, where Reginald Pecock was confined after his trial in 1458), was described as an alchemist prominent around 1477 in the sixteenth-century *Lookeing Glasse for Illiterate Alchymists*. He took part in diplomatic missions as a papal nuncio in 1474, and was the sort of person to be consulted on the marriage between the white house of York and the red house of Lancaster. In his alchemical treatise, where his name occurs in acrostic in Latin verse in the preface, he suggested that such a marriage had been proposed by Merlin himself, the original alchemist, and the prophet and architect of Arthur's reign, and by implication the symbolic inspiration for this dynastic union which would produce Prince Arthur: 'Merlin says if the white woman be married to the red man they are combined together and they that were two shall be made as one.'[13] Sawtry's proclamation 'Behold here is the stone', perhaps made in the 1480s, could be interpreted as signifying the united kingdom.

These images were popularized in the scrolls attributed to Ripley. Apart from the first version, which was produced around the time of Edward IV's accession, the earliest surviving images occur not on the scrolls themselves but in two late fifteenth-century alchemical manuscripts.[14] Images very similar to those on the scrolls occur in these two manuscripts, including a couple in a vessel with the inscription 'the red man here to his white wife is married with the spirit of life'. Verses accompanying the *Ripley Scrolls* appear in the sixteenth century, and these are related to the verses written by another alchemist Richard Carpenter (d. 1503). An Oxford graduate, he was a canon of Westbury-on-Trym, and as a West Countryman he may have known his fellow alchemist Norton. One of Carpenter's verses refers to an alchemical marriage that will produce the stone.[15] Sixteenth-century copies of the scroll proliferated the explicit images of a sexual union between a white queen and a red king and the birth of a child, the *homunculus*. Some even prominently display the red and white rose of alchemy, and at the foot of the *Ripley Scrolls* Ripley himself is shown holding his scroll and declaring 'Behold here is the stone', which could signify the kingdom. On some he is even facing a king.

The white rose was one of the badges of the house of York and had been adopted as Elizabeth of York's personal badge; the red rose, which came to be regarded as one of the badges of the house of Lancaster, was probably first used by Henry Tudor, who claimed it had been the badge of his ancestor Edmund Crouchback, when he took his oath of marriage, and this badge was adopted by his mother Margaret Beaufort.[16] After the series of cynical marriages arranged by Warwick in the period between 1469 and 1470 this betrothal must have captured the imagination of the scientific and political community. The Tudor red and white rose, which represented the union of the two houses and which Richmond was supposed to have invented, was in fact a creation of the alchemists.

Richmond's defeat of Gloucester at Bosworth on 22 August 1485 was quickly followed by his marriage to Elizabeth of York on 18 January 1486, and these alchemical images of the conjunction featured in his accession. In April 1486, during his progress to the north of England, Richmond sent ahead instructions on how he was to be received in York. At Micklegate Bar a mechanical device was to show a red rose conveyed to a white rose to create before the citizens of York the Tudor badge, the red and white rose, 'the principal of all the flowers'.[17] The dragon and the rose were prominently displayed in King's College Chapel and on Henry VII's tomb in Westminster Abbey. It is an indication of the enthusiasm that the alchemists had for this marriage that the two most important alchemists of Edward IV's reign, Norton and Ripley, both endorsed the royal marriage. Norton, shortly after Henry VII's accession, rededicated his *Ordinal of Alchemy* to the new king. The earliest surviving manuscript is a presentation copy, probably very similar to the copy presented to Henry VII and mentioned in Ashmole's *Theatricum Chemicum*.[18] Norton made some derogatory remarks about Edward IV that he probably added after his death:[19]

> This science shal draw towarde the kynge
> And many mo gracis ye may be tolde.
> – Grace on that king shalle descende.[20]

Writing of the stone to be revealed to the kings of the land, he added, according to his great-grandson Samuel Norton: 'By the fortune and by the grace of a woman fair of face'.[21] Norton may have originally intended such sentiments to apply to Elizabeth Woodville (and his great-grandson applied them to Elizabeth I)[22] but the sentence as it stands would either have been written in 1477 or added after Edward's death. In the context of the rededication of the work to Henry VII, who had his portrait painted wearing the collar of the Order of the Golden Fleece,[23] these sentiments would have been applied to Henry's bride Elizabeth of York, who like her mother was a descendant of Melusine, the agent of alchemical transformation. But Elizabeth of York was also an active participant in the alchemical marriage, the white sulphur to be combined with the red. Ripley, who lived long enough to witness all these events, probably designed the images that appeared on his tomb in Bridlington priory. Around the tomb, which to judge by the earliest surviving drawings was an elaborate two-tiered structure indicating his importance at the time of his death, occur images of the conjunction of the sun and moon, an allusion to the royal marriage, and, most interestingly, two dragons with their tails intertwined. The dragon was Henry Tudor's personal symbol, with which he defeated Richard III. Throughout Ripley's creative life he had used fighting dragons to symbolize the war between the elements, in a political as well as alchemical sense.[24] Now they were at peace, and beneath them Ripley placed the date of his death, MCCCCXC, with the ninety written in the form of the alchemical cross, the symbol for Mercurius, the agent of transformation,[25] perhaps an allusion to his own part in this successful marriage and the emergence of the nation out of civil war.

A similarly idealistic attitude towards politics and alchemy may have existed for a time at the neighbouring court of James IV, Scotland's cultivated king. Like Edward IV and Henry VII, James came to the throne during a rebellion and he used his position as king to finance and indulge in his empirical, scientific interests, which included the practice of medicine and alchemy. He undertook medical experiments, procured a collection of alchemical texts in 1508, and was engaged in a lifelong search for the quintessence as a cure for disease. His chief associate, the French or Italian alchemist John Damian (best known for his unsuccessful attempt to fly from the walls of Stirling Castle), seems to have occupied a similar position in James's court to that of Ripley in Edward's. Damian, like Ripley, was able to practise alchemy within the security of a religious order. James procured for him a position as abbot of Tunglow so he could proceed with his experiments in his laboratories in Stirling and Lambuskenneth. Like Ripley, he travelled abroad, securing the king's leave for the period 1508–13. James supplied Damian with chemicals, gold, silver, whisky and wine for distillation and they succeeded in several distillations, creating what they thought was *aqua vitae* (pure alcohol). James cherished the ideal of a crusade, which depended on peace between France, England and Scotland. He made a definite peace with England in 1502, and in 1504 he married Henry VII's daughter Margaret. Although all the king's dreams ended in tragedy on Flodden Field in 1513, his marriage alliance, established possibly with the encouragement of alchemists at both courts, was in the long term as influential as the marriage between Henry VII and Elizabeth of York, preparing for the eventual union of the two crowns of Scotland and England. Together with the assimilation of Wales into English political life under Edward IV, these two marriages show that alchemical medicine lay behind the political establishment of the United Kingdom.[26]

Throughout Edward's reign the alchemical quest had been integrated into the fulfilment of prophetic destiny and the living-out of myths, and this was to have an impact on the Tudor successors. Henry Tudor incorporated these myths in his conquest of the throne. He had come under the guardianship of William Herbert, Edward's lieutenant, soon after the surrender of Pembroke Castle to Herbert's forces in September 1461, and for the next decade he spent his life in Herbert's household, absorbing the Arthurian myths and British history with which Herbert so closely identified. As he was Welsh on his father's side, it was natural that he took over Edward's mantle as the son of prophecy, the redeeming British king. He therefore assumed the red dragon of Cadwallader as his badge and saw himself as the returning Arthur.[27] Like Edward before him, he owned and read (both before and after he came to the throne) key prophecies concerning the victory of the redeeming British king. A deluxe volume was specially made for King Henry containing the prophecies of Merlin and Bridlington, the prophecy of the eagle, and a prophecy of a great *rex futurus* of British history who will save England from a *rex inutilis* and reunite the island and restore its ancient name.[28] Another manuscript originating during Henry's reign contains the *Secreta secretorum* and the prophecies of Bridlington and the *Holy Oil of St Thomas*.[29]

This image of a red dragon in the sky, formed by a constellation of stars prophesying the coming of Arthur, occurs in a deluxe collection of prophecies, including those of Merlin, presented to Henry VII. (British Library Arundel 66, fo. 33v)

An indication of the way these myths and prophecies that had been popularized by Edward IV's kingship occupied such a central place in political life, creating a fusion of religion, myth and politics, can be seen in the activities of the entrepreneur William Caxton. He transferred his allegiance from Edward IV to Henry Tudor, and in preparing Malory's *Morte d'Arthur* for print between 1483 and 1485 he used the work as a prophecy. Anticipating that there would be a final showdown between Richard/Mordred and Henry/Arthur, he prepared for it by publishing the dream Arthur has before crossing the Channel to fight the Emperor Lucius. Arthur dreamed of a fight to the death in the sky between a dragon and a bear. The victorious dragon, according to the philosophers interpreting the dream, is Arthur, and the defeated slain bear betokens some tyrant who tormented the people, like Lucius. Caxton changed the wording of bear to boar, to make the dream a direct prophecy of the outcome of the fight between Henry Tudor and Richard III.[30] On 31 July, the final day of the printing of the *Morte d'Arthur*, Henry Tudor, like Edward before him in 1471, set sail for Britain bolstered by myths. As he moved along the Welsh coast he was greeted by the same bardic poets who had hailed Edward as the son of prophecy. Dafyd Llwyd, who was supposed to deliver prophecies to him as he moved inland and stayed overnight at Mathafan, castigated Richard III as the servile boar and proclaimed Henry the leader of the stock of Llewelyn. When the two met at Bosworth Field, it was a meeting they both desired; each was armed with the sets of prophecies he believed in: Richard had the prophecies of the victorious boar, and Henry the prophecies of the victorious dragon. It was to be a trial by battle in which God would decide the outcome, and fittingly it ended when Richard impulsively charged the standard of Tudor bearing the red dragon. After his victory Henry VII was presented with the keys of the city of Worcester and identified as Jason returning with the Golden Fleece and King Arthur, the one who fulfilled the prophecies. Henry VII's belief in the supernatural forces at work at Bosworth was shown when he employed William Parron, an astrologer from Italy, between 1498 and 1503. Parron used planetary conjugations in 1484 to signify approval of this momentous battle.[31]

When, shortly after the royal marriage, it became apparent that the queen was pregnant, preparations were made to complete this alchemical work. Lewis Caerleon (d. 1494), knighted for his service as king's physician and for his role in intriguing against Richard III, was the physician to the baby's mother and in 1488 he was made knight of the king by Henry VII.[32] Alchemy and Arthurian myth converged when careful preparations were made to ensure that the child was born at Winchester, the site of Camelot. The child was a boy, and it must have seemed that this was the *homunculus* that completed the alchemical quest. Ripley's words in the *Compound of Alchemy* about the lying together of the white queen and the red king and the conception of the child, heralded by the appearance of the rainbow, must have seemed like the fulfilment of a prophecy of Merlin.[33] The birth of the prince was the result of a fusion of the Welsh blood of Edward IV through the female line and of the Welsh blood of Henry VII through the male line, and the child was naturally christened Arthur. John Argentine was appointed as the child's physician. The court astrologer compiled a horoscope and commentary on the appearance in the sky of the star Arcturus (where according to Lydgate King Arthur had ascended to live in heaven as the sun of Britain) as signifying the second coming of Arthur, the birth of the royal child at Camelot. At the celebrations of the marriage of Prince Arthur to Princess Katherine of Aragon in 1499 the pageant master devised a golden chariot for Arthur to ride triumphantly around the zodiac through the sphere of the sun while another pageant car was drawn by primitive creatures representing the original ancient Britons. The Round Table at Winchester was subsequently decorated, perhaps after the prince's birth, or more probably in 1516, with images of King Arthur and the names of his knights. The placing of Henry VII as Arthur at the top of the table, under Edward III's sun badge in the roof beams, recalled the images of Edward IV on the top of fortune's wheel, and perhaps was a conscious homage to the true founder of this new Arthurian dynasty, Edward IV. In the centre of the table was the Tudor rose – the rose of alchemy, the philosopher's stone, the nation's soul. The altarpiece, commissioned between 1503 and 1509 from the king's Flemish painter Maynard, commemorated the alchemical perfection of the great work. Henry and Elizabeth kneel at a *prie-dieu* with canopies above their heads showing the Tudor rose. St Michael is between them and above their heads over the royal palaces of Shene and Richmond, St George fights a vast flying dragon, representing the discord of the Wars of the Roses.[34]

The soul of this nation, so graphically illustrated by the Round Table at Winchester, was forged around a largely mythical figure. However, there is some factual basis to Arthur in the form of a Celtic warlord who fought to preserve the Romano-Celtic way of life in the face of the invading Saxons. It was this historical relationship that existed between the original British and the Romans that underlay the mythic depictions of the Roman origins of the British in the genealogical histories of the reign of Edward IV, and in Hardynge's *Chronicle*, which perpetuated the myth of a close working partnership between Rome and Britain rather than a relationship between conqueror and conquered.[35] One of the lasting legacies of the reign of Edward IV was the rediscovery of the Romano-British heritage through the translation, copying and dissemination of works of Roman literature and the incorporation of Roman political and ethical philosophy in the education and public life of Edward's courtiers. The creation of a secular state along Roman lines, in which religion was subservient to the pragmatic interests of the state, was initiated by Edward IV's government. Such a rational construct was intended to override the competing interests of the baronial families and indeed to forestall threats to the common weal posed by religious extremism. This state had been forged through the use of powerful myths of ancient Rome and Britain, which encouraged Edward's subjects to begin to see themselves as an island people separate from the Germanic European traditions of the house of Lancaster, and possessing their own separate Church like their Celtic ancestors. The same process was occurring in other European nations. Maximilian I, the Holy Roman Emperor, believed the blood of all great dynasties of the ancient world flowed through the veins of the Hapsburgs, and claimed for this House descent through the Romans, Franks, Trojans and the Old Testament patriarchs. Besides patronizing alchemists he is shown in a sixteenth-century print visiting a laboratory. Maximilian employed genealogists and historians such as Jacob Mennel to trace his line back to Hector and Aeneas.[36] In Castile the historian Rodriguez de Almela presented a chronicle of Spain to Ferdinand and Isabella in 1491, reminding Isabella of her descent from Alaric, the first king of the Goths, who took Rome by force and established a thousand years of continuity among the kings of Spain. Almela argued for the historic destiny of the kings of Castile to restore the Hispano-Tingitanian province possessed by the Goths.[37] The imperialistic dimension to alchemy which we have observed in England may well have applied to the Hapsburgs. An entire floor of Philip II's palace, the Escoriale, was devoted to alchemical instruments.

The state that began to take shape under Edward IV, and which came to fruition under the Tudors, fostered a profound sea-change in mentality. The seeds of the Reformation lay in this concept of obedience to the state. Through the assimilation of Roman, stoic literature, God was beginning to be perceived as a more remote deity, rational but detached. Caxton, in his prologue to his 1480 translation of the *Metamorphoses* of Ovid (which according to the prologue to the *Legenda Aurea* he printed in 1484, but which only survives in a single manuscript),[38] commended the wisdom of antiquity transmitted through Ovid, and attempted to reconcile Ovid's religious views with his own: 'he argue not in signe pluralitee of goddes, how wel that he afermeth may by nowe see that in alle of his books ryght fynly he speaketh of the unyte of God and of his sapience not comparible. And also of his prudence, which he coleth governes of the universalite.'[39] The wisdom of antiquity in this text, and in other translations of Roman works read by the governing class of Edward IV's court (Seneca too wrote of a single providence) was integrated with Christianity to create a different image of God, one that had more in common with the remote, stoic intellect of Athena than the passionate interventionist Christian God of the Old Testament, or the suffering redeemer of the New Testament. Such a rational outlook involved a change in emphasis from focusing on the next world to concentrating on this one. Henry VI embodied the late fourteenth-century and early fifteenth-century enthusiasm for the contemplative life, a rejection of the world, society, the body and nature, and yet the new works emerging from Caxton's press, the translations of Worcester and Caxton himself of the works of Cato, Seneca and Cicero, and the scientific works of the alchemists all advocated the wisdom of nature, the need to adapt to the various ages of the body, the different humours and to heed the calls of race, language and myth. Intellectuals in this period were in different ways rejecting the contempt for the world represented by contemplative, monastic traditions. Henry VIII, like his grandfather whom he resembled in many ways, also deployed myths, though in a more purposeful and ruthless way; and it is possible to see the state he created and the destruction of the religious houses as the culmination of trends first established in the reign of Edward IV. The reason why such profound changes of outlook have escaped notice while so much emphasis has been placed on Lollardy and the subsequent Reformation is that these changes were so pervasive and subtle (Erasmus's derogatory remarks about the deleterious effects of identifying too closely with figures like Hector are isolated exceptions) and therefore they did not arouse too much controversy at the time.

However, it would be surprising if such a period of social, political and intellectual upheaval, which witnessed the advance of Islam; wars between England and France and among the aristocracy in both countries; various crises of monarchy in the leading states of Europe; the advance of education and social mobility; and such technological innovations as printing, did not inspire some reaction. This was a period of change as profound as those in the first decades of the twentieth century. Modernist art forms after the First World War explored the distorted perspectives brought about by a scientific, social revolution that destroyed centuries of certainties about the origin of man, the nature of time and space and the concept of self. From the late fourteenth century, in a similar way, the images of faith and continuity: the crucified Christ, the Madonna and child and the Trinity were fractured and twisted in such alchemical imagery as the mother copulating with her child the king and the crucified serpent, symbol of knowledge rather than faith. These obscure and disturbing allegorical distortions of iconography similarly expressed the disintegration of the old certainties of faith.

The alchemists bequeathed a far-reaching intellectual legacy at the court of Edward IV. They were perpetuating the methods of the twelfth- and thirteenth-century empirical scientific observers of the natural world: Adelard of Bath, Daniel of Morley, Alfred of Shareshill, Robert Grosseteste and Roger Bacon. Grosseteste in particular used his senses to understand the underlying coherence and structure of things. He attempted to explain the behaviour of light in causing rainbows; the different elevations of the pole star at various points of the horizon demonstrated to him the spherical shape of the earth; the origin of sound he explained as the reverberations caused by dislodging particles from inertia (which took him to the fringes of modern views of matter); the regular flooding of the Nile was explained by the influence of the moon; the economy of nature was seen in organisms' adaptation to the needs of the environment; and his interest in time and its organization in calendars was based on the study of natural seasons and the behaviour of planets.[40] Grosseteste was working in an English tradition of scientific enquiry that displayed a fascination with nature. The alchemists of Edward's court were similarly curious in a scientific way about the natural world around them; the difference was that now scientific empirical curiosity had a much wider currency and was no longer the preserve of cultivated circles of Herefordshire monks and Oxford scholars. Norton was engaged in an empirical investigation of the body and the natural world: he examined the colours of urine; how haystacks were formed; how odours were produced; he observed the changing of metals and the formation of compounds and alloys; the production of perfumes; and the natural processes of putrefaction. Worcester's interest in alchemy was part of his interest in all aspects of the natural world around him. He owned John Free's notes on Pliny's *Natural World*[41] and took notes on observations of natural history, geography, architecture and astronomy. If the monastic and ascetic traditions in the Christian Church, and indeed the pastoral teachings of the secular Church disseminated in such works as the *Prick of Conscience*, emphasized the transitoriness of life and nature and taught people to have contempt for the natural, corporeal world, Norton, Ripley and their fellow alchemists were intent on preserving life as long as possible:

> For above all erthlye thynge
> I mooste desire and love connynge:
> And for the rede stone is preseruatife,
> Moste precious thynge to length my life.[42]

They went against centuries of Christian tradition by accepting and celebrating nature and the flesh. The spirit and the divine were not something to be separated from matter; their redemption lay in matter. In Ripley's words:

> – that the spirite may corporall bee,
> And become fixt with it, and consubstantiall;
> – Then when they thus together depured be,
> They will sublime up whiter than the snowe.[43]

Ripley in particular, by stressing that the preservation of corporeal health was of a piece with the alchemical purification of the soul, was moving away from the conservative Galenic medicine of the universities, which accepted the divorce of body and spirit that was an integral part of the monastic traditions that dominated medieval hospitals, and which prepared patients to follow the suffering Christ for the inevitable and desirable departure of the spirit from the corrupt body.[44] Ripley thought that spirit and body were interchangeable, that 'there is resident in physical bodies a certain incorruptible and occult essence comprising true medicine'.[45] In his holistic approach to medicine, his belief in the inter-relationships of the health of the body and soul and the curative properties of nature, he anticipated Paracelsus: 'It is established that virtue both superior and inferior inheres in all things produced by nature.'[46] Ripley was also interested in the processes of accelerated change in the laboratory, the evaporation of water, the melting of metals, dyeing, tincturing and glazing.[47] Norton, too, was fascinated by the processes of natural change: changes that occurred in a dunghill in summer; in the making of wine and perfumes; how colours are formed; the way fluids clean and feed the body; and the way such fluids were affected by the operations of the planets.[48] In their heated alembics alchemists duplicated the womb, watching the gestation of life, and they went further, reproducing the primordial chaos from which all matter emerged.[49] In Barker's words 'right as this world is made so is our stone'.[50] The phenomenon of transubstantiation was no longer a mystery witnessed by clergy; it was given a scientific, empirical dimension and could be observed by laymen such as Norton.[51] The writings of Edward's alchemists deployed the language of imperialism, expressing the need to dominate nature, to accelerate change from one substance to another, to find the source of gold, of worldly domination. Men like Norton were the forerunners of modern chemistry, but in another way they heralded a new scientific approach. This can be seen in the prologue to Caxton's English edition of *Le Somme le Roi*, the *Mirror of the World*, an encyclopaedia originally written by Goisain of Metz in 1246, which Caxton translated in 1481 for Hugh Bryce, an alderman of London, who presented it to William Lord Hastings.[52] Caxton wrote:

> And emonge alle other this present books whiche is called the ymaage and myrrour of the world, ought to be visyted, redde, knowen, by cause it treateth of the world and of the wondreful dyuision thereof, in whiche book a man resonable, may see and understande more clerer by the visytyng and seeyng of it and the figures therin, the situacion and moeuyng of the firmament, and how the unyuersal erthe hangeth in the myddle of the same.[53]

He adds that he who understands the substance of this book will know:

> the creation of this world, the gretnes of the firmament, lytilnes of therthe in regard of heuen, how the vii sciences were founden and what they bee by whiche he may the betterr avaylle in knowleche alle the dayes of his lyf.[54]

A similar approach can also be seen in this sentence of Tiptoft's: 'Ye wold be glad to speke with sad and connyng persones, and demaunde they mof the merueyllous causes of thynges, of the moeyng of the planetes and the discyplyne of maners.'[55]

Such a scientific outlook, encouraged by the increasingly remote and rational conception of the deity, was to lead to this island nation becoming such a dominant force in the world of science and in terms of imperial expansion it would exceed the Romans. In the long term the humiliation at the hands of the French was an irrelevancy. More important was the establishment of the sense of a British identity as an island separate from Europe that would become increasingly scientific, secular and expansionist in outlook. The seeds of British concentration on the western seas were beginning to be seen in Edward's reign: expeditions were mounted to find Brazil[56] and to explore the coast of Africa. Humanist writers around Charles V of Castile similarly used the myths and history of ancient Rome to develop a sense of imperial destiny of a divinely ordained and superior people now defined by their own language and hostile to the Moors and Jews within the Iberian peninsula. These myths took the Spanish beyond the Pillars of Hercules to establish a western empire.[57] But it could be argued that they were less well prepared than the British would be to establish an empire along Roman lines, and the foundations for the British achievement had been laid in the educational traditions established in the reign of Edward IV. There was also an imperialistic attitude to learning itself in Edward's reign, especially among alchemists. Ripley and Neville in particular desired to integrate all the intellectual traditions of the past, especially Roman and Christian, to create an unbroken succession of knowledge from Egypt, Greece, Rome and Islam, handed down from adept to adept. In Ripley's words: 'Though all philosophers speak plurally all is but one. This you may well trowe.'[58]

This scientific attitude was even applied to the very myths that had helped to forge the new British, expansionist and empirical outlook. The ascetic and mystical traditions of the Church had as little time for the mysteries of the unconscious as for the mysteries of the physical body. This was summed up by the author of the *Cloud of Unknowing* who rejected all thoughts and associations in an attempt to reach God. But alchemists, especially Ripley, were engaged in an exploration of all aspects of nature including the soul, what we would call the unconscious. It is significant that the Middle English words for mind and metal, 'mynde and myny', were so similar.[59] In the mid-fifteenth-century alchemical treatise on *The withdrawing of the accidents of old Age*, attributed to Bacon, there is a reference to the entrails and bowels of thought. The alchemists had an intuition that the soul was a part of nature, that it was the collective source of these myths. Christian tradition taught redemption through the light of faith and scripture; alchemy taught redemption through the light of nature which functions in the human mind while producing the images of the alchemists and the myths of the poets. Worcester, in his translation of Cicero's *Old Age*, wrote of the preternatural origins of knowledge, the unrestrained activity of souls in sleep as evidence of a collective memory. Caxton, in his prologue to the *Metamorphoses* of Ovid, a key source for the myths of the ancient world and alchemy, argued for an intellectual freedom that allowed men to read and gather what they could from the writings of the ancients,[60] the philosophers whose features are sketched in a manuscript of the *Dicts and Sayings of the Philosophers*.[61] Above all these writers Caxton praises Ovid, 'because of the subtlety of the fables wherein is contained great wisdom to those who wish to know and understand'.[62] Caxton understood that these were more than the artistic creation of a single man, that they were the productions of a collective and more powerful source: 'And it ought not to be sustained that Ovid in his person only in his period by himself hath forged all these fables for as much as declaring there have been many of the Greeks and other poets his ancestors and made of them.'[63] He was also aware that these myths held the key to understanding the past imperial and scientific achievements of antiquity, and possible future progress in the imperialistic and scientific development of the realm:

> No man lightly damne these things that before he hath not known, or knowing that he may hereafter know for who so can discover or take away the veil or shadow from the fables he shall see clearly sometime poetry and sometime right high philosophy under the science of Ethics; under other Economics; under other Politics; under other he shall find geste of History composed.

It is hard not to escape the conclusion that men in Caxton's intellectual milieu, perhaps sharpened by the perceptions of the alchemists, were fully aware of what Edward was achieving through the exploration of the myths of the past and how, despite his personal failings, these myths held the key to Britain's future destiny: 'By subtlety of enquiry that one by one showing how they [the myths] depend on each other from the creation of the world to this time – Under the veil of sweet eloquence they comprise the science and advertising of a great part of things coming or at least the possibility of things to come.'[64]

And yet little remains in the popular culture of the sixteenth century of the man who inspired these myths. To Shakespeare and Heywood he was a shallow buffoon and a charming womanizer. Even his role as patron of Ripley (the popularizer of pseudo-Lullian writings), his imprisonment of the alchemist Dalton, and his abandonment of the crusade in favour of an abortive invasion of France, had been distorted into a myth about a King Edward (usually Edward III) who had imprisoned Raymond Lull himself and invaded France. But the sixteenth-century alchemists themselves were interested in the patron of George Ripley and Thomas Norton. Thomas Charnock and Samuel Norton, in their alchemical treatises dedicated to Elizabeth I, described Edward's reign as a great era for the flourishing of the royal art of alchemy.[65]

John Dee, a Welsh alchemist who identified with Merlin and named his eldest son Arthur, wrote to Mary I asking for her help to preserve ancient manuscripts and monuments from the destruction caused by the dissolution of the monastic libraries. He set about preserving Ripley's heritage collecting, copying and annotating the writings of Edward's alchemists in his library at Mortlake. In October 1573 Dee wrote to William Cecil, Elizabeth's chief minister, requesting a recommendation to the keeper of Wigmore Castle (Edward earl of March's childhood home and base for his campaign at Mortimer's Cross) to examine the archives there: 'It is my fancy', he said, 'to go there at my leisure for chronicle or pedigree to find out about heroic deeds and past heroes'.[66]

The first major vision Edmund Kelly brought him through the spirit medium Madini, a nine-year-old girl who would later direct Dee to the court of the alchemist Rudolph II, was of Edward IV. On her earliest appearance in Kelly's scrying glass in 1583 Madini produced a pocket book, opened it and pointed at a picture of a man with a coronet in his hand and a crown on his head. The child asked Dee if he thought the man was pretty.

'What is his name?' Dee asked.

Madini replied: 'My mother saith his name is Edward. Look you, he hath a crown upon his head', and added, 'and this was a jolly man when he was king of England.'

Dee asked her: 'How long since is it that he was king of England?' By way of answer Madini turned the pages back from Richard duke of York to Edward's ancestor, Roger Mortimer earl of March and Lord of Wigmore (in whom the lines of the kings of England and the ancient kings of Britain met in an alchemical compound).[67] Dee and Samuel Norton identified the important place occupied by their own sovereign in a line of queens bearing the name Elizabeth that included Edward's wife, Elizabeth Woodville, and daughter, Elizabeth of York. All were sources of inspiration for the alchemical regeneration of the kingdom. But the role of Edward IV's great-granddaughter, Elizabeth I, as patron of alchemy, imperial endeavours and Arthurian myths is another story.

NOTES

1. He was admitted to study for a BA at Oxford in 1459 after studying for three years in Cambridge. Ward rented a *scola geometrie* in Schools Street, Oxford. Emden, *BRUO*, vol. iii, p. 198.
2. BL MS Sloane 692, fo. 102v.
3. Cambridge University Library MS Ee 3.61, fos 62–108v; J.D. North, *Horoscopes and History*, Warburg Institute Survey Texts 13 (London, 1986); H. Carey, 'Astrology at the English Court', in *Astrology, Science and Society*, ed. A. Curry (Woodbridge, 1987).
4. BL MS Royal G 2.g.1, fos 1–8v.
5. Polydore Vergil, pp. 195–6.
6. Ibid.
7. BL MS Royal g 11, fos 1r and 6r; Rawcliffe, 'More than a Bedside Manner', 88.
8. For Argentine's books see D.E. Rhodes, *John Argentine, Provost of Kings* (Amsterdam, 1962), pp. 16–24; H.M. Carey, *Courting Disaster: Astrology at the English Court and University in the Later Middle Ages* (London, 1992), pp. 157–9.
9. Nandike's inventory preserved among the probate inventories in the Public Record Office PRO, PROB 2/48 is described by C. Rawcliffe in 'More than a Bedside Manner' in *St George's Chapel, Windsor*, p. 90. I am grateful to Carole Rawcliffe for allowing me to use her study and edition of this inventory entitled 'The Inventory of a Fifteenth-Century Necromancer', publication forthcoming. *Rotuli Parliamentorum* vi, p. 245; see George Ripley's *Bosom Book* for recipes on distillation of lead. For the *prima materia* and alchemy see J. Elkins, *What Painting Is* (New York, 2000), ch. 9.
10. Trinity College Cambridge MS R. 14. 52, fo. 67; Ashmole, *Theatrum Chemicum Britannicum*, p. 144.
11. Ibid, p. 148.
12. *The Bosome-Book of St George Ripley* (London, 1683). Jung, *Psychology and Alchemy*, p. 80; *Ripley Scroll*, BL MS 5025. Scroll no. 4.
13. Bodley MS Ashmole 1459.
14. BL MS Egerton 845 has the date 1493 and was copied from BL MS Harl. 2407.
15. Ashmole, *Theatrum Chemicum Britannicum*, pp. 275–7; Trinity College, Cambridge, MS R.14.45, fos 4–5 and 5v 6.
16. Ashdown-Hill, 'The Red Rose of Lancaster', *The Ricardian*, ix, 133 (1996), 406–20.
17. A. Raine (ed.), *York Civic Records*, vol. I (Yorkshire Archaeological Society 98, 1939), p. 156; Pollard, *Wars of the Roses*, pp. 6–7.
18. BL MS Add. 10302.
19. See above.
20. Norton, *Ordinal of Alchemy*, ll. 1424–8.
21. Samuel Norton, *Key of Alchemy*; Bodley MS Ashmole 1421, fo. 171.
22. Bodley MS Ashmole 1421, fo. 171.
23. *Kings and Queens AD 635–1953* (London, 1953), p. 14; Boulton, *Knights of the Crown*, p. 395.
24. BL MS Vitellius Ex, fo. 235v. The cross on the top of his tomb is similar to the cross on George Neville's coat of arms; BL MS Harl. 3346, fo. 4v.
25. Bodley MS Ashmole 971. This contains Ashmole's *Theatrum Chemicum Britannicum*, a collection of the works of Ripley, Norton and Charnock with Ashmole's notes. This drawing is a copy of BL MS Vitellius Ex but also shows the base of the tomb which has been torn off in the Vitellius manuscript. For the symbol

of mercury in the form of the Latin abbreviation for ten see fifteenth-century alchemical symbols in Trinity College, Cambridge, MS R.14.45, fo. 121.
26. *Accounts of Lord High Treasurer of Scotland* (Edinburgh, 1877), vol. 11, p. 362; J.D. Comrie, *History of Scottish Medicine*, 2 vols (London, 1932), vol. 1, pp. 150–7.
27. O.D. Harris, 'Tudor Heraldry at Bosworth', *The Ricardian*, v, 67 (1979), 123–33.
28. BL MS Arundel 66.
29. Society of Antiquaries MS 101.
30. D. Starkey, 'King Henry and King Arthur', *Arthurian Literature*, xvi, ed. J.P. Curley and F. Riddy (1998), pp. 171–96. Taylor, *The Political Prophecy in England* (1967).
31. Sydney Angelo, *Spectacle Pageantry and Early Tudor Policy* (Oxford, 3rd ed. 1997). Geneva, *Astrology in the Seventeenth Century*, p. 134.
32. P. Kibre, 'Lewis of Caerleon, Doctor of Medicine, Astronomer and Mathematician', *Isis*, xliii (1952).
33. Ashmole, *Theatrum Chemicum Britannicum*, pp. 148–51.
34. Kipling, *Triumph of Honour*, p. 83. Riches, *St George*, p. 115.
35. Hardynge, *Chronicle*, pp. 97–8.
36. F. Heer, *The Holy Roman Empire* (London, 1967), p. 141.
37. Ramon Menendez Didal, 'The Significance of the Reign of Isabella the Catholic According to her Contemporaries', in R. Highfield, *Spain in the Fifteenth Century, 1369–1516* (London, 1972).
38. Kathleen L. Scott, *The Caxton Master and his Patrons* (Cambridge Bibliographical Society Monograph 8 (1976), pp. 45–6, 69; A.I. Doyle, 'English Books in and Out of Court', in *English Court Culture in the Later Middle Ages*, ed. V.J. Scattergood and J.W. Sherbourne (London, 1983), p. 179; Magdalen College, Cambridge, Old Library MS F 4 34. A facsimile edition entitled *Caxton's Metamorphoses in English* was published in 2 volumes by George Brazille (New York, 1968).
39. Magdalen College, Cambridge, Old Library MS F 4 34 (facsimile), fo. 14.
40. R.W. Southern, *Robert Grosseteste. The Growth of an English Mind in Medieval Europe* (Oxford, 1986), pp. 82–107, 141–69.
41. Balliol College MS 124.
42. Norton, *Ordinal of Alchemy*, ll. 2595–8.
43. Ashmole, *Theatrum Chemicum Britannicum*, p. 174; *Compound of Alchymy* (1591), ed. Linden, p. 68.
44. Rawcliffe, *Medicine for the Soul*, pp. 104ff.
45. George Ripley, *Ripley's duodecum Axiomata Philosophia* in C. Zetzner (ed.), *Theatrum Chemicum*, 4 vols (Strasbourg, 1613–61), vol. ii (1659), pp. 121–2.
46. Ibid, pp. 121–3; Noel L. Brann, 'George Ripley and the Abbot Trithemius, An Inquiry into Contrasting Medical Attitudes', *Ambix* (26 November 1979), 212–20.
47. *Compound of Alchemy* in Ashmole, *Theatrum Chemicum Britannicum*, p. 179.
48. Norton, *Ordinal of Alchemy*, p. 56.
49. Ashmole, *Theatrum Chemicum Britannicum*, pp. 163ff.
50. BL MS Stowe 1970, fos 26–32.
51. Norton, *Ordinal of Alchemy*, p. 78.
52. Sutton and Visser-Fuchs, *Richard III's Books*.
53. *Caxton Prologues*, p. 52.
54. Ibid, pp. 50–60.
55. Tiptoft, *Declamacion of Noblesse*, pp. 239–40 (Mitchell appendix).
56. Worcester, *Itinerarium*, p. 366.
57. J.H. Elliot, 'Spain and its Empire in the sixteenth and seventeenth centuries', in Elliot, *Spain and its World 1400–1700* (Yale, 1989), pp. 8–26.
58. Ashmole, *Theatrum Chemicum Britannicum*, p. 112 (letter to Edward IV).
59. Trinity College Cambridge MS R. 15. 52 fo. 61. See Norton, *Ordinal of Alchemy*, p. 47, where the two words occur together.
60. Magdalen College, Cambridge, Old Library Ms F4 34 (facsimile), fo. 13.
61. Bodley MS 943.
62. Ibid, fo. 14.
63. Ibid, fo. 13.
64. Ibid, fo. 13v.
65. BL MS Lansdowne 703; Bodley MS Ashmole 1421.
66. BL MS Lansdowne 103 art 23.
67. Diaries of John Dee, ed. E. Fenton (Charlbury, 1998), p. 87.

APPENDIX I

Alchemical Texts and Images of the Fifteenth Century

A series of papers delivered at the *International Congress on Art and Alchemy* at the University of Aarhus, 7–9 December 2001, has demonstrated how the allegories and emblems of alchemical transmutation have provided a fertile source of inspiration for painters from Hieronymous Bosch in the sixteenth century to Vivien Torrence and Leonora Carrington in the twentieth century; for engravers like Michael Maier, photographers and sculptors like Joseph Boyce and Rebecca Horn and writers as diverse as Nathaniel Hawthorne and Michael Ondaatje. The allegories and symbols these artists use are vaguely perceived to be medieval in origin and while Fabricius reproduced a collection of alchemical motifs in 1976 under the title: *Alchemy: The Medieval Alchemists and their Royal Art*, none of the illustrations he chose were in fact medieval: for much of the literature and visual symbolism of the late middle ages only survives in late sixteenth century and seventeenth century printed editions, engravings and manuscripts. John Dee the alchemist and scholar commissioned copies of the *Ripley Scrolls* in Lubeck, Germany, in 1588 and Elias Ashmole, the English antiquary and student of the occult, copied and printed Ripley's writings. The loss of a great deal of medieval alchemical learning can partly be explained by the secrecy of this art. Ripley in the prologue to his *Compound of Alchemy* wrote, 'Our secrets to thee I will disclose,/Keepe thou them secreate'. Few manuscripts were copied in the fifteenth century and when the printing press arrived in England in 1477 alchemical texts were not considered for publication. Ripley's *Compound of Alchemy* was not printed until 1591. Undoubtedly many original fifteenth-century manuscripts in England perished with the dissolution of the monasteries and the destruction of John Dee's library. Approaching medieval alchemy from seventeenth-century sources has its dangers, as the case of Nicholas Flamel, a pious and wealthy fourteenth-century Parisian bookseller on whom French publishers in 1624 foisted a fraudulent work of alchemy, *His Exposition of the Hieroglyphicall Figures*, demonstrates.[1] It is therefore important to stress that alchemical manuscripts do survive from the period of the lifetimes of alchemists such as George Ripley and Thomas Norton. My study of Arthurian myths and alchemy, based largely on this evidence, has I hope uncovered the original seam of much of the alchemical language, written and visual, that has inspired so many artists and placed it within the very precise political context of the reigns of Henry VI and Edward IV. Below, in chronological order, are the most important fifteenth-century sources.

1445 The Pseudo Lullian *Testamentum* Corpus Christi College, Cambridge MS 112, Corpus Christi Oxford MS 244

c. 1460 *The Ripley Scroll* Bodley Roll 1 showing the pursuit of the philosopher's stone

1460–1 Yorkist genealogies with alchemical motifs and symbols: *The Illustrated Life of Edward IV* BL Harl. 7353; College of Arms MS 20/20 Genealogy with alchemical imagery of the evolution of Edward IV from the prima materia; *The Genealogy of the Red Dragon* (BL Add 18268 A) a Yorkist genealogy by a different author applying alchemical cognomens to the lines of Mortimer and Lancaster; *The Coronation Roll* (Philadelphia Free Library MS 201), a genealogy showing family tree of Edward IV with alchemical symbols representing the evolution of the philosopher's stone

1450–70 George Ripley's *Cantilena*, a Latin composition possibly belonging to the twenty-year period of experimentation referred to in the *Compound of Alchemy*. Fifteenth century manuscripts include BL Sloane 3747 *c.* 1475 and Trinity College, Cambridge 0.8.24

1461–4 BL Vesp E VII A Genealogical Roll chronicled and prophecies containing alchemical cognomens for Edward IV and Henry VI

1465 Bodley MS 623 A Genealogical Roll and prophecies with alchemical cognomens for Edward IV and Henry VI

1470 Ripley's *Bosom Book* with the *Vision of George Ripley* appears in BL MS Sloane 3667, a sixteenth-century manuscript, and was copied from a manuscript in Ripley's own hand. In the *Bosom Book* there is also a genealogy of the evolution of the great work with Ripley's name and the date, 1470. The vision occurs in another sixteenth-century manuscript, Bodley Ashmole 1480 pt 1 fo. 36

1471 *Genealogy of Edward IV King of Britain* (Bodley MS Ashmole Roll 26) showing the evolution of Edward IV from *prima materia* and containing alchemical cognomens.

Ripley's *Compound of Alchemy*. Dorothy Singer's identification of seven fifteenth-century manuscripts outside the British Library should be treated with caution.[2] The most important manuscript of *The Compound of Alchemy* is BL Sloane 2598 dated 1471 and subscribed with an alchemical sigil that may be derived from Ripley's name or that of the scribe (fo. 71v). The printed edition of 1591 is similar to this manuscript.[3] This manuscript contains the preface, a prologue written for the king, Ripley's account of his travels in Italy and description of himself as a canon of Bridlington and his retraction of previous writings and experiments. It does not include the letter to Edward IV printed by Ashmole in the *Theatrum Chemicum Britannicum*. This letter does however occur in Sloane 3747 written around 1475 and was therefore probably written separately. The letter also appears in the sixteenth-century manuscript BL Sloane 3667 fo. 157v–160 and may, like *The Bosom Book* in this manuscript, have been copied by Samuel Norton from a manuscript in Ripley's own hand. Other manuscripts that can safely be placed in the late fifteenth century include Corpus Christi College Oxford 172 and Trinity College Cambridge 0.5.31, a prose version with an attribution to Ripley

1475 Some of the Miscellaneous writings of Ripley, probably from the period 1450–76, survive in a fifteenth-century manuscript (Bodley Ashmole 759) written *c.* 1475–1500. This manuscript, a combination of paper and vellum, contains on vellum Ripley's 'As a Philosopher in the Boke of Meteors doth Write' fos 103a to 105b (this appears as a part of the dedication to Edward IV); *The Mystery of Alchymists* fo. 106v–113b beginning 'When Sol is in Aries and Phoebes shyneth'; a note on the philosopher's stone ff 35b, 68b and 77a; an experiment beginning 'First calcine and after putrefy', fo 78a–b. and the *Pupilla Alchemiae*, attributed to Ripley fo 35a–b[4]

1476 Ripley's *Marrow of Alchemy*, originally written in Latin, appears in a sixteenth-century manuscript (BL Sloane 3667 fos 94–104) in an English translation

1477 Thomas Norton's Ordinal *of Alchemy*. There are thirty-one surviving manuscripts, most from the sixteenth century. Elias Ashmole in *Theatrum Chemicum Britannicum* did not print the Ordinal until 1652. There is one fifteenth-century manuscript BL Add MS 10302, which on the basis of the costumes in six accompanying illustrations can be dated between 1480 and 1490[5]

Late fifteenth century

BL Harl 2407 and Egerton 845. Collections of alchemical tests with alchemical images similar to the Ripley scrolls.

BL Harl 2476. A collection of alchemical texts includes the works of John Dastin with diagrams of the golden chain of being.

BL Add 10764. Alchemical diagrams showing the evolution of metals.

NOTES

1. N. Wilkins, *Nicolas Flamel: Des Livres et de l'Or* (Paris, 1993); L. Dixon, *Nicolas Flamel, His Exposition of the Hieroglyphicall Figures*.
2. D.W. Singer, *Catalogue of Latin and Vernacular Alchemical Manuscripts* in 3 vols (Brussels, 1954).
3. S.J. Linden, ed., *George Ripley's Compound of Alchymy* (1591) (Aldershot, 2001).
4. G. Keiser, *Manual of Scientific Writings in Middle English*, 638.
5. J. Reidy, ed. *Ordinal of Alchemy*, p. xi.

APPENDIX II

Glossary of Alchemical Terms

Albedo or whitening
This represents the baptism and purification of the stone and the renewal of the material in alchemical experiments through cleansing and purification. It became associated with the emergence of the white rose of York.

Alembic
A glass or copper vessel used for distillation, wbich was often applied to the head of the still. Distillation was an important part of the alchemical process and the alembic was more than a piece of equipment: it was a symbolic vessel.

Alpha et Omega
Christ declared himself to be *alpha* and *omega*, the first and last, in the *Book of Revelation*. The stone of transmutation was a symbol of the redemptive power of Christ, *Alpha* and *Omega*, and this was applied in alchemy to the *prima materia*, which could be mercury, the *uroboros* and the dragon. The *alpha et omega* was used to convey the working of God's providence in Yorkist genealogies.

Antimony
A metal derived from stibnite (its sulphide) and of significance to alchemists as *lupus* (wolf) because of its use in devouring impurities and purifying gold. Antimony was associated with the house of Lancaster.

Ashmole, Elias
A royalist during the civil war, he founded the Ashmolean Museum and was a student of astrology and hermeticism. Ashmole transcribed late medieval English alchemical manuscripts now in the Ashmole collection in the Bodleian Library and published the leading English alchemists in 1654 in *Theatrum Chemicum Britannicum*.

Astrology
Expertise in astrology was essential in the practice of alchemy and medicine and the understanding of human affairs and politics. The seven planets: the Sun, Moon, Mercury, Venus, Mars, Jupiter, and Saturn governed the growth and maturation of metals within the earth and the behaviour of the four humours within the individual.

Bath
The warming bath used constant, modest heat and was equated with the baptism and purification that followed the *nigredo*. It was associated with the immersion of the king and queen and is depicted in the *Ripley Scrolls*.

Beasts
Beasts were employed in alchemy and had significance in genealogy and heraldry. Creatures of light, the eagle, lion and ram, were associated with Edward IV. Creatures of darkness the raven, toad and wolf, were associated with the house of Lancaster.

Caduceus
The staff of Mercury around which is entwined two serpents symbolizing the marriage of opposites, mercury and sulphur. The caduceus represents the equilibrium of opposites and a symbol of death and resurrection.

Colours
Alchemical distillation and the heating of metals produced colours, the most important of which were white and red. These were to have important political significance with the union of the houses of York and Lancaster in 1485.

Conjunction
The marriage of opposites sulphur and mercury. The conjunction was often depicted sexually, and therefore had political potential in arranging royal marriages.

Distillation
The most important of alchemical processes, including the heating of cinnabar, to extract mercury in vapour form. Distillation of alcohol from wine produced *aqua vitae* and *aqua ardens* which were used for medicinal purposes. Distillation was also a mystical process in which gross material elements, earth and water, became rarefied and pure to approach the climax, the spiritual quintessence.

Dragon
The winged dragon represented volatile mercury and the wingless dragon was fixed mercury. The dragon was also associated with the self-devouring serpent the *uroboros* and chthonic underworld powers. Jung saw the slaying of the dragon as a myth of death and resurrection: the dragon was an archetype of the powers of the unconscious, which the conscious ego had to assimilate if they were to be harnessed. The dragon became an important symbol for Edward IV of the ancestral source of inspirational myths and energies.

Elixir
Often a symbol for the stone and tincture, the medicine of medicines that healed defects and corruption in metals and raised them to perfection. The fourteenth-century English alchemist, John Dastin, expounded the theory of elixirs.

Fountain
Prominent on the *Ripley Scrolls*, the fountain represented the vessel in which mercury was transformed. As mercury was an unpredictable trickster, his fountain was, like the tree of life, ambivalent with the potential for poisoning as well as being a source of health and rejuvenation.

Four Elements
Earth, air, fire and water were believed to be derived from prime matter. Alchemy was concerned with the transmutation of one element into another.

Gold (Sol)
The goal of alchemy is to produce the tincture, elixir or stone, which will accomplish transmutation of base metals into gold. Gold was used as a ferment to aid transmutation and was regarded as a medicine that, through magical sympathy, could improve health and prolong life. It was associated with Edward IV and the Yorkist sun.

Hermaphrodite
A symbol of the mystical marriage of sulphur and mercury. In psychological terms it represented the undifferentiated unconscious which has the potential for masculine and feminine development. The final production of the stone, the crowned hermaphrodite, is an emblem of the culmination of the individuation process, the self-transcending ego. It was used by Ripley and applied to attempts to bring Henry VI to maturity.

Humours
The four humours: choler, blood, bile and phlegm, were each derived from the four elements of fire, air, earth and water and identified with the planetary influence of Mars, Venus, Saturn and the Moon. They were the foundation of alchemical medicine and the understanding of personality and indeed politics. Henry VI was believed to be formed under the influence of phlegm and Edward IV choler and blood.

Jung, Carl
The Swiss psychiatrist who started studying alchemy in 1920. For Jung alchemy was the key to individuation: the growth of the personality from its psychic roots in the unconscious. Though lacking in historical context, his insights have important and underestimated potential for studying the way alchemy was used in this way by high-ranking people during the golden era of alchemy from 1400 to 1600.

King and Queen
They are prominent in alchemical allegories as symbols of sulphur and mercury, sun and moon, gold and silver. The king or *Sol* radiating splendour was a key symbol for Edward IV.

Lead
The sickest of metals, dull, poisonous and composed of compacted waste, it was thought of as degraded leprous gold but also as the humble filth that only the wise notice because it contains the stone. Ruled by Saturn, lead was associated with the melancholy that preceded the work of alchemy and mirrored the heaviness of the *prima materia* and the leaden formless waters before the Creation. The alchemist's task was to purify lead, to extract the stone from its matrix and cure it into gold or nourish it until it matured into gold.

Mercury
The most complex and elusive of alchemical symbols, embracing every aspect of the work from the initial dragon to the stone. The only metal to maintain liquid state at room temperature and responding to minute temperature changes by vaporizing, mercury was extracted from its ore by distillation. Regarded as the water of life and death in which metals decomposed and were resurrected, it was the *Alpha* and *Omega*.

Nigredo
A death necessary for the future progress of the work and represented by Ripley in the form of a crow, a toad and the slaying of the dragon. Metals such as gold and silver were dead,

inert and had to be revived by means of the spirit if they were to make the silver and gold of the philosophers. This was achieved by reducing the metal to its prime matter (the *nigredo*). In 1471 this was to prove a powerful political allegory for Edward IV's exile and revival.

Prima materia
The unformed chaos that preceded the differentiation of matter into the four elements. Diagrammatic representations of the *prima materia* that preceded the intervention of God in the creation of the world and the evolution of Edward IV's line occur in Yorkist genealogies.

Quintessence
A fifth element, incorruptible and pure, from which the four elements were derived. The quintessence was identified with the philosopher's gold, Christ and the arrival of Edward IV. Alchemists attempted by distillation to extract this essence from natural substances. The quintessence also represented the state of perfect balance between the four humours achieved by Christ which resulted in perfect health and well-being. Such a state was claimed by Edward for his realm in 1461.

Tincture
The dyeing or colouring of metals through controlled heating that lends new colour to the substance of a metal. Also known as the rubedo this rainbow-like show of colour heralded the culmination of the work.

Transmutation
The transforming of base metals into gold according to the theory that metals grew in the protection of the womb of the earth as combinations of sulphur and mercury. The alchemist could speed up the process of metallic incubation.

Tree
In alchemy there was a close association of the tree of life and the tree of knowledge of the *Book of Genesis*. The tree was used to demonstrate the evolution of metals and therefore lent itself to adaptation with alchemical symbols and cognomens to demonstrate the evolution of the Yorkist dynasty.[1]

NOTE

1. For further information on alchemical terms see M. Haeffner, *The Dictionary of Alchemy* (London, 1991).

APPENDIX III

Genealogy of Edward IV from a Yorkist Perspective

A simplification of such Yorkist genealogies as Philadelphia Free MS E201, Ashmole Roll 27 and Lyell 35 which presented Edward IV's credentials as a focus for national unity as the redeemer of Britain's past.

Japheth son of Noah

Aeneas of Troy

Celtic Britain

Brutus
grandson of Aeneas
arrives in Albion
c. 1170 BC and calls
it Britain. Founds
New Troy

Romano-Celtic Britain

Cassivedaunus, the first
British king to pay
tribute to Julius Caesar 54 BC

Lud builder of London

Cymbeline brought up
by Augustus

Helen, discoverer of
the true cross, and wife of
Constantine

Constantine the Great,
King of Britain
and emperor of Rome

Departure of the Romans

Vortigern, usurper of the
prophecies of Merlin

Aurelius Ambrose son of Constans
erects Stonehenge on advice of Merlin

Uther Pendragon son of Constantine

Arthur son of Uther

Mordred the usurper
illegitimate son of Arthur

Cadwallader the last
king of Britain dies
in Rome AD 689

**The end of Celtic Britain.
The arrival of the Saxons**

Egbert unifies Anglia
and changes the name
of Britain to England

The Kings of Wales

Cadwaladr ap Cadwallon
king of Gwynedd d. 634

Rhodri Mawr Hywel the Good
c. 900–950

Gruffud ap Llywelyn
king of Wales 1039–63

Gruffudd ap Cyman
king of Gwynedd 1098–1137

Geoffrey of Monmouth's
vision of uniting Britain
under the crown of London

By 1200 the title prince of Wales is being used

Arrival of the Danes

Ethelred

Alfred the Great

Edward the Confessor

Harold 1066

The Norman Kings

William the Conqueror

Henry III

Llewelyn ap Iorwerth (Llewelyn the Great)
prince of Gwynedd 1200–40

Gwladys Ddu daughter of
Llewelyn ap Iorwerth
m. Ralph Mortimer

Llewelyn (the Last) prince of Gwynedd and
Wales 1256–82

The end of the Welsh princes and the rise of the Mortimers

Ralph Mortimer d. 1246
and Gwladys Ddu

Roger Mortimer
of Wigmore

Roger Mortimer
earl of March

Roger Mortimer
earl of March d. 1360

Edmund Mortimer
earl of March m.
Philippa daughter of Lionel
duke of Clarence

Roger Mortimer
earl of March d. 1398

Anne Mortimer m.
Richard earl of Cambridge (ex. 1415)

Richard duke of York
m. Cicely Neville

Edward IV

Edward I

Edward II

Edward III

Richard II
deposed 1399

Lionel duke of
Clarence d. 1369

John of Gaunt
duke of Lancaster

Edmund duke of York

Philippa m. Edmund Mortimer

Henry Bolingbroke

Richard earl of Cambridge
m. Anne Mortimer

The Usurper Kings of the House of Lancaster

Henry IV

Henry V

Henry VI

The Return of the Kings of Britain

The culmination of The Illustrated Life of Edward IV *is the divinely inspired accession of the Mortimer heir seated on the wheel of fortune. The wheel's rotation has been stopped by Reason dressed as a judge. (British Library MS Harl. 7353)*

Bibliography

Primary Sources

Manuscripts

Paris

Bibliothèque Nationale MS na Fr 11673. *Le fait des Romains* (owned Edward IV)

London

PRO SC1/43/182 Summons to Gilbert Kymer to treat Henry VI

Sir John Sloane 1 Edward IV's copy of Josephus's *Jewish Wars*

Society of Antiquaries 101 *Secreta secretorum* and prophecies of Bridlington from the reign of Henry VI

British Library

Add. 10, 099. Poems in praise of Edward IV

Add. 10764. Alchemical manuscript with diagrams of the four elements

Add. 15549. Alchemical manuscript with instructions of Merlin to his son

Add. 37801. Fortescue's *Governance of England*, an alternative version presented to Edward IV

Add. 10302. Fifteenth-century illustrated copy of Thomas Norton's *Ordinal of Alchemy*

Add. 11388. Ripley's *Cantilena* (illustrated)

Add. 11814. English translation of Claudian's *Letter to Stilicho*

Add. 15549. Poem on Edward IV's death

Add. 18268A. *The Genealogy of the Red Dragon*

Add. 34360. Epitaph of Humphrey duke of Gloucester

Add. 46846. Correspondence of Thomas Beckington

Add. 47680. Edward III's copy of *Secreta secretorum* with images of the sun and moon

Add. 48031A. Richard duke of York's articles explaining his assumption of the protectorate

Add. 48976. *The Rous Roll*

Add. 5544. William Worcester's *Itinerarium*

Add. 48031. Fortescue's articles addressed to the earl of Warwick

Arundel 66. Volume of prophecies made for Henry VII

Bib. Cotton Jul. Caes VI. Bluemantle Pursuivant's account of the visit of Louis of Gruuthuse to England

Bibl. Reg B 11. *Tale of Melusine*, compiled 1382–94 by Jean D'Arras

BL Vitellius E X. Drawing of Ripley's tomb

Cotton Domitian A IX. Reference to the birth of Edward IV

Cotton Julius MS FVIII. William Worcester's notebook containing extracts from Roger Bacon's *Book of Wisdom*

Cottonian Vespasian E VII. William Worcester's notebook containing extracts from Roman history and philosophy

Egerton 1076. Seventeenth-century copy of a genealogy of Edward IV

Egerton 2572. The Book of the Barber Surgeons Guild

Egerton 845. Alchemical manuscript of 1493 with images similar to *Ripley Scrolls*

Egerton 2572. John Burdus's *Treatise of Remedies against the Plague*

Harl. 543. Manifesto of Yorkist earls

Harl. 103. John Tiptoft's volume of the proverbs of Seneca and medical tracts
Harl. 1736. English version of 1446 of the surgical treatise of John Bradmore
Harl. 49. Richard duke of Gloucester's *Prose Tristan*
Harl. 220. Henry Sutton's Tract on Comets
Harl. 2407. Alchemical manuscript *c.* 1480 with images similar to the *Ripley Scrolls*
Harl. 2476. Alchemical works of John Dastin containing a diagram of the golden chain of being
Harl. 2637. *Dialogue de Oratoribus* of Tacitus 1462
Harl. 267. Caerleon's horoscope for Edward IV
Harl. 3346. The sayings of the ancient philosophers owned by George Neville
Harl. 372. Richard Roos, *La Belle Dam Sans Merci*
Harl. 3952. 'Laments for Edward IV'
Harl. 48. Funeral procession of Richard duke of York
Harl. 661. Hardynge's *Chronicle* with maps of Scotland to assist Edward IV
Harley 4780. Wardrobe records 1480
Harley 642. Edward IV's *Black Book*
Harley Roll T. 12. The Scroll *Considerans*, a genealogical roll to Henry VI
Roll 5025. *Ripley Scroll* executed Lubeck 1583
Royal 18 E VI. Edward IV's copy of Jean Mansel's *Fleur des histoires*
Royal 12 A xxix. Carmeliano's *Ver (Spring)* dedicated to Edward IV
Royal 12 Ex V. Edward earl of March's copy of Bacon's version of the *Secreta secretorum*
Royal 13 C 1. Worcester's collection of extracts on the Carthaginian war
Royal 14 E ii. Edward IV's copy of *Chemin De Vaillance*, and *the Epistle of Othea* by Christine de Pisan
Royal 14 E III. Elizabeth Woodville's copy of the vulgate cycle of Arthurian romances
Royal 14 E IV. *Waurin's anchiennes et nouuelles croniques angleterre*
Royal 14 E V. Edward IV's copy of Premierfait's French translation of Boccaccio's *De Casibus illustrium*
Royal 15 D VI. Edward IV's copy of Livy's *History*
Royal 15 E IV. Edward IV's copy of Valerius Maximus's *Dicta et facta memorabilia*
Royal 15 E II. Edward IV's copy of Lull's *Book of the Order of Chivalry*
Royal 15 E. VI. Romances and *Chevalier au Cyne* owned by Margaret Beauchamp and John Talbot
Royal 16 E IV. Edward IV's copy of Waurin's *Chronicle of Britain*
Royal 17 D XV. Edward IV's copy of Xenophon's *Cyropoedia*
Royal 17 E II, Poem on Edward IV's recovery of the throne
Royal 17 E IV. Edward IV's copy of *Receuil des Histoires de Troye*
Royal 17 F II. Edward IV's copy of *La Grande Histoire Cesar*
Royal 18 B xxii, William Worcester's *Boke of Noblesse*, presented to Edward IV
Royal 18 D ii. Lydgate's *Troy Book and Siege of Thebes*, owned by William Lord Herbert and Edward IV
Royal 18 E III. IV. Valerius Maximus' *Memorable Deeds and Sayings*
Royal 18 E VI. *La Fleur des Hystoires*
Royal 19 E V. Edward IV's copy of *Le faits des Romains*
Royal D xv. Poem on Edward IV's recovery of the throne
Royal G 2.g.1. Caerleon's table of eclipses of the sun and moon
Royal II G XL. Edward IV's copy of Xenophon's *Cyropedia*
Sloane 1118. Recipes of John Kirkby
Sloane 692. Thomas Ward's alchemical treatise
Sloane 1118. Kirkby's collection of alchemical works of Rupescissa, Geber and Arnold of Villanova
Sloane 118. Text on distillation with references to John Kirkby
Sloane 2218. *The Myrour of Illiterate Alchemysts*
Sloane 2320. Medical treatises associated with John Kirkby
Sloane 2464. Lydgate's translation of the *Secreta secretorum*
Sloane 2523B. Sixteenth century copy of the *Ripley Scroll*, bearing Ripley's name
Sloane 2598. Ripley's dedicatory letter to Edward IV
Sloane 2958. Ripley's *Compound of Alchemy* with the date 1472
Sloane 338. Fifteenth century treatise on distillation
Sloane 3479. Fortescue's *De Laudibus legum Anglie*
Sloane 3580B. A copy made in 1580 of Ripley's *Marrow of Alchemy*
Sloane 3747. Fifteenth-century copies of Ripley's *Compound of Alchemy* and *Cantilena*

Sloane 4. William Worcester's medical notebook
Sloane 56. John Ardene's treatise on surgery
Sloane 59. Tract on the distillation of wine owned by John Somerset
Sloane 965. Mid-fifteenth-century treatise on the four humours and Guy De Chauliac's Treatise on Surgery
Sloane 2580B. Letter of George Ripley to George Neville
Sloane 2948. John Kirkby's treatise on herbal medicine and a treatise on clysters
Sloane 419. John Kirkby's translation of pseudo-Lullian alchemical works
Stow 433. Payment to Edward IV's illegitimate son, Arthur
Stowe 1070. Alchemical treatise of Robert Barker (Friar Bungay) with dedication to Edward, Prince of Wales, aged fourteen

Lambeth Palace Library
Lambeth Palace MS 265. Anthony Woodville's translation of *The Dicts and Sayings of the Philosophers* presented to Edward IV
Lambeth Palace 1176. Genealogy from Brutus to Edward IV
Lambeth Palace MS 506. William Worcester Collection of Documents on the war in Normandy

Royal College of Arms
College of Arms 20/25. *Genealogy of Edward IV King of Britain*, written 1470
College of Arms 20/20. *Genealogy of Edward IV King of Britain*, written 1464
College of Arms 20/6. Genealogy compiled by author of the *Prophetic History of Britain*, compiled 1461
College of Arms 21716. Edward IV's muster roll 1475
College of Arms 3/2. Genealogy compiled by author of the *Prophetic History of Britain*
College of Arms 9/9. Genealogy compiled by author of the *Prophetic History of Britain*

Cambridge University
Cambridge University Library
CUL Ee 3.61. Robert Marshall's horoscope for Edward IV
CUL K.K1.5. Middle English translation of Christine de Pisan's *Livre Du Corps De Policie*
CUL MS Dd xiv2. Extracts from the *Brut* and prophecies of Merlin

College Libraries
Corpus Christi 112. *Testamentum* (Pseudo-Lull)
Emmanuel 1.2 10. William Worcester's copy of *The Dicts and Sayings of the Philosophers* with his marginal notes
Gonville and Caius 181/214. Roger Marshall's copy of the book of alchemy of Albertus Magnus
Gonville and Caius 249. Geoffrey of Monmouth's *Historia regum Britanniae*, Higden's *Polichronicon* and the chronicle of John Herryson 1377–1469
Peterhouse 190. Copy of the *Brut* owned by the author of the *Arrivall*
Peterhouse 95. Recipe of Roger Marshall for the preservation of Edward IV's health
Trinity O.5.31. Fifteenth-century prose copy of the *Compound of Alchemy*
Trinity R 3.21. Poem in praise of Edward IV and prophecies composed between the deaths of Henry VI and Edward IV
Trinity R.14.45. Alchemical manuscript containing verses of Richard Carpenter and table of fifteenth-century alchemical signs
Trinity R.15.52. A mid-fifteenth-century copy of *De retardatione senectutis*
Trinity 0.2.16. Fifteenth-century manuscript of Ripley's *Cantilena*
Trinity 0.8.24. Fifteenth-century illustrated copy of Ripley's *Cantilena*
Trinity 516. John Benet's *Chronicle* and prophecies of the coming of Edward IV
Trinity G3. A Latin genealogical roll issued around May 1471
Trinity R 14.52. John Vale and John Multon's book containing Bacon's alchemical writings and Fortescue's *Governance of England*
Trinity 0.8.31. Roger Marshall's medical collection received from John Somerset
Trinity R.3.21. Fifteenth-century poem in praise of Edward IV
Trinity R.3.29. Prophecies of the coming of Edward IV

Oxford University
Bodleian Library
Ashmole 1432. Medical recipes
Ashmole 1453. Medical recipes of John Welles
Ashmole 1475. Medical works containing the name of John Cokkes
Ashmole 1505. Robert Broke's copy of a treatise on distillation
Ashmole 440. Collection of Ripley's letters and writings with a recipe for the elixir attributed to Merlin
Ashmole 1152. Alchemical manuscript containing the legend of King Edward imprisoning Lull
Ashmole 1394. Ripley's *Cantilena*
Ashmole 1408. Recipes of Robert Barker (Friar Bungay)
Ashmole 1421. Samuel Norton's notes on the *Compound of Alchemy* written by his great-grandfather, Thomas Norton
Ashmole 1421. A Latin translation of the Arabic revelations of Morienus to Kalide, an important influence on Ripley
Ashmole 1426. 1500. Alchemical recipes of George Ripley
Ashmole 1432. Medical recipes for the treatment of George Neville
Ashmole 1445. sixteenth-century translation of the *Cantilena*
Ashmole 1448. Alchemical collection from the 1460s beginning with the motto 'Know thyself'
Ashmole 1459. Alchemical collection containing a copy of *Ripley's Wheel* and alchemical treatise of John Santry
Ashmole 1479. *c.* 1520 Ripley's *Marrow of Alchemy*
Ashmole 1480. Ripley's *Marrow of Alchemy*
Ashmole 1485. *c.* 1520 Recipes of Robert Barker (Friar Bungay)
Ashmole 1490. Alchemical treatise of Robert Barker (Friar Bungay) with dedication to Edward, Prince of Wales, aged fourteen
Ashmole 344. Correspondence of George Neville
Ashmole 396. Fifteenth-century version of Bacon's *Secreta secretorum*
Ashmole 440. Letter of Ripley describing himself as a parish priest
Ashmole 446. Ripley's recipe for the elixir citing Merlin as a source
Ashmole 750. Fifteenth-century. Medical recipes of Robert Barker (Friar Bungay)
Ashmole 750. Fifteenth-century manuscript which contains an order for barley (commonly used in medicines) for my master pere (father) Barker (fo. 195b)
Ashmole 759. Fifteenth-century copy of Ripley's *Compound of Alchemy*
Ashmole 971. Ashmole's *Theatrum Chemicum Britannicum*, with Ashmole's notes and a copy of the drawing of Ripley's tomb in BL Vitellius Bodley MS Ashmole roll 40
Ashmole Roll 26. *The Genealogy of Edward King of Britain* c. *1471*
Ashmole Roll 40. Sixteenth-century copy of *The Ripley Scroll*
Ashmole Roll 53. *Ripley Scroll*, executed in 1530
Ashmole Roll 54. Sixteenth-century copy of *The Ripley Scroll*
Auct F1. 13. John Tiptoft, earl of Worcester's copy of Lucretius' *De Rerum Naturae*
Bodley 362. Medical and alchemical manuscript commissioned by Gilbert Kymer from Herman Zurke
Bodley 456. Rolle's *Emendation Vitae*
Bodley 649. Sermon of 1419 preceding Henry V's invasion of France
Bodley 943. Copy of *The Dicts and Sayings of the Philosophers* with images of the philosophers of Greece and Rome
Bodley BB Art Selden 4. Richard Fleming's *Lucubratiunculae*
Bodley Digby 196. Genealogy of Edward of Lancaster
Bodley Laud Lat 70. John Morton's copy of Seneca's letters
Bodley Laud Misc 558. Medical and alchemical manuscript commissioned by Gilbert Kymer from Herman Zurke
Bodley Laud poet 121. *The Vision of George Ripley*
Bodley Marshall 135. Genealogy written for Henry Percy earl of Northumberland (1416–55)
Bodley 179. Fastolf's copy of Aldobrandinus of Siena's regimen of health
Bodley 264. Richard Woodville's copy of a fourteenth-century Alexander
Bodley 361. Copied 1453–9; Medical and alchemical manuscript commissioned by Gilbert Kymer from Herman Zurke

Bodley 362. Copied 1448–55; Medical and alchemical manuscript commissioned by Gilbert Kymer from Herman Zurke
Bodley 623. *Prophetic History of Britain*
Bodley Arch Selden B 10. Hardynge's *Chronicle* presented to Edward IV with additional material on the 'matter of Britain' not in Ellis' edition
Bodley e Mus 153. Alchemical works of Bacon transcribed by John Cokkes including Cokkes's transcription of Bacon's *Opus Ter*
Bodley e Mus 155. Alchemical works of Bacon transcribed by John Cokkes
Bodley e Mus 35. Lancastrian genealogical roll
Bodley Hatton 56. Book of prophecies written in 1461 on the coming of Edward IV
Bodley Laud Misc 570. Fastolf's illustrated manuscript of Christine de Pisan's *Epitre d'Othea*
Bodley Lib Rawl B 490. *The English Conquest of Ireland* (an English translation of the *Expurgnatio Hibernia* of Giraldus Cambresis made by an Anglo-Hibernian in the early fifteenth century
Bodley Roll 1. *The Ripley Scroll c.* 1460
Bodley Roll 5. Genealogical Roll of Edward IV commissioned by Henry Percy earl of Northumberland
Digby 181. Collection of prophecies dating from Edward IV's reign
Digby 82. Collection of prophecies dating from Edward IV's reign
Jesus College 114. Genealogical chronicle of Thomas of Haseldene, 1468
Lansdowne 762. Fifteenth-century poem in praise of London and Edward IV's hunting letter to Louis XI
Lansdowne 456. Genealogical Roll for Edward IV *c.* 1461
Lansdowne 204. Hardynge's *Chronicle* presented to Edward IV
Lansdowne 103. John Dee's letter to Lord Cecil
Lansdowne 285. John Paston's *Grete Boke*
Lansdowne 456. Genealogical roll for Edward IV *c.* 1461
Lansdowne 703. Charnock's alchemical treatise
Lansdowne 262. Yorkist prophecies and a poem in praise of London
Lat. Misc b 2. Genealogy of Edward IV
Laud Misc 558. Hermann Zurke's copy of alchemical treatises commissioned by Gilbert Kymer
Lyell 33. Genealogy of Edward IV *c.* 1467
Lyell 35. Genealogical Roll of Edward IV
Lyell 36. Fifteenth-century version of Bacon's *Secreta secretorum*
Merton College, 268. Copied 1458–9; Medical and alchemical manuscript commissioned by Gilbert Kymer from Herman Zurke
New College Oxford 162. William Worcester's copy of the medical writings of Arnold of Villanova
Rawl A 338. *Le Quadrilogue Invectif*
Rawl C 274. Fifteenth-century version of Bacon's *Secreta secretorum*
Rawl C 86. Carmeliano's lament for the passing of Edward IV
Rawl C 86. Fifteenth-century alchemical collection with a genealogy of the Kings of England
Reg. 17 D xv. Poem on Edward IV's recovery of the throne
Yelverton 35. Fortescue's *Governance of England* revised for Edward IV

College Libraries
All Souls 81. *John Mepham's Treatise on Days of the Moon*
All Souls Gg1. Alchemical manuscript owned by Robert Marshall
Balliol 124. William Worcester's manuscript containing John Free's notes on Pliny's *Natural World*
Corpus Christi 244. *Il Testamentum Alchemico* attributed to Raymond Lull
Corpus Christi 172. Fifteenth-century copy of *The Compound of Alchemy*
Magdalen 65. Flyleaf referring to William Worcester's copy of Albertus Magnus's *De Virtute Lapidum preciosorum*
Magdalen 198. William Worcester's copy of Boccaccio with his notes
Magdalen Fastolf Paper 43. Inventory referring to Fastolf's copy of Vegetius's *De Re Militari*
Magdalen Old Library F4 34 (facsimile). Caxton's translation of the *Metamorphoses* of Ovid
Magdalen Oxon Norfolk and Suffolk, 75. William Worcester's roll setting out Fastolf's offices
St John's 172. John Aldeward's manuscript containing tracts on the philosopher's stone and phlebotomy
St John's 23. Genealogical Roll to Henry VI The Scroll *Considerans*

Manchester
John Rylands University Library MS Eng 113. Poem on the death of Edward IV

Norfolk
Norfolk County Record Office MS Bradfer Lawrence Xa/15. Prophecies of Merlin adapted in 1470

Philadelphia
Philadelphia Free Library MS E 201. The Coronation Roll of Edward

York
Borthwick Institute Historical Research Register Neville vol. i

Printed Sources

Accounts of Lord Hugh Treasurer of Scotland (Edinburgh, 1877.
Adams' Chronicle of Bristol ed. F.F. Fox (Bristol, 1810).
Aelred of Rievaulx, *'Vita Sancti Edwardi Regis', Patrologiae*, ed. J.P. Migne, 195 (1885).
An English Chronicle of the Reigns of Richard II, Henry IV, Henry V and Henry VI (London, 1856), ed. J.S Davies.
Anglicus, Bartholomaeus, *On the Properties of Things*: John Trevisa's Translation of of Bartholomaeus Anglicus' *De Proprietatibus Rerum*, eds M.C. Seymour and others (3 vols, Oxford, 1975–88).
Annales or General Chronicle of England (London, 1615).
Ashmole, E. *Theatrum Chemicum Britannicum* (London, 1652).
Augustine, St, *The City of God*, ed. D. Knowles (Harmondsworth, 1972).
Aurora Consurgens, transl. R.F.C. Hull and A.S.B. Glover (London, 1966).
Bacon, Roger, ed. J.S. Brewer, *Opus Tertium*, in *Fr Rogeri Baconi opera quaedam hactenus inedita*, I (London, 1859).
Bale, J. *Index Britanniae scriptorum* (Woodbridge, 1990).
Bede the Venerable, *A History of the English Church and People*, transl. L. Shirley-Price (Penguin, 1955).
Benet, G.L. and M.A. Harris, Camden Miscellany, 24, *Camden Society*, 4 ser, 9 (1972).
Biblia Pauperum ed. Schreiber, 8 (Munich, 1961).
Bokenham, Osbern, *A Legend of Holy Women*, transl. Sheila Delany (Notre Dame, Indiana, 1992).
Book of the Order of Chivalry translated by William Caxton, ed. A.T.P. Byles, EETS OS 168 (1926).
Bridget, St, *The Liber Celestis of St Bridget of Sweden*, vol. 1 text EETS, OS, 291 (London, 1987).
Brut, ed. Brie (EETS, London, 1908).
Calendar Close Rolls, Henry VI preserved in the Public Record Office ed. W.H.B. Bird (London, HMSO, 1933–47).
Calendar of Fine Rolls XX (Edward IV, 1461–7, 1949) XXI Edward IV–Richard III, 1471–85 (1961).
Calendar of Fine Rolls, 1461–71 LHMSO (1949).
Calendar of Patent Rolls, Edward IV 1–11 1461–7, 1467–77; Edward IV–Richard III, 1471–85 (1961).
Calendar of State Papers and Manuscripts existing in the Archives and Collections of Milan, I (1385–1618) ed. A.B. Hinds (1913).
Calendar of State Papers Venetian, 1202–1509, ed. R. Brown (London, 1864).
Calendar of the Close Rolls, 6 vols HMSO (London, 1933–9).
Calendar of the Patent Rolls for Henry VI 6 vols (Norwich, HMSO, 1901–10).
Capgrave, John, *Chronicle of England*, ed. F.C. Hingeston Rolls Series I (London, 1855).
Capgrave, John, *Liber de Illustribus Henricis*, Rolls ser (London, 1858).
Caxton, William, *Godfrey de Boleyn*, ed. M.N. Colvin (EETS, London, 1893).
Caxton, William, *Mirror of the World*, ed. O.H. Prior, EETS, ES, 110 (1913, repr. 1966).
Cessolis, James de, *The Game of Chess*, Translated and printed by William Caxton *c.* 1483, introd. N.F. Blake (facsimile edn, London, 1976).
Chastellain, *Oeuvres*, IV, ed. K. Lettenhave (Brussels, 1884).
Chaucer, Geoffrey, *The Canon Yeoman's Tale*, ed. M. Hussey (Cambridge, 1965).
Chaucer, Geoffrey, *The Canterbury Tales*, ed. L.D. Benson, The Riverside Chaucer 3rd edn (Oxford, 1988).
A Chronicle in the Reigns of Richard II, Henry IV and Henry VI, ed. J.S. Davies (Camden Society, 1865), *Register Abbatiae Johannis Whethamsted* (Rolls Series, 2 vols, 1872–3), 386.
Chronicle of the Rebellion in Lincolnshire 1470, ed. J.G. Nichols (Camden Society, 1847).
Chronicle of the Wars of the Roses, ed. E. Hallam (London, 1988).

Chronicles of the White Rose of York, ed. J.A. Giles (London, 1845).
Cicero, *Of Old Age and Friendship*, W. Caxton, 1481, The English Experience Facsimile, no. 861 (Amsterdam, 1977).
Collection of Ordinances and Regulations for the Government of the royal Household (Soc Antiquaries, London, 1770).
Commentaries of Pius II, Bks 97–99, transl. F.A Cragg-Smith, Studies in History 35, Northampton Massauchusetts, 1951.
Commines, P. *The Memoirs of Philippe de Commynes*, ed. S. Kinser, transl. J. Gazeaun (South Carolina, 1973).
Complete Works of St Thomas More, ed. R.S. Sylvester vol. ii, *The History of Richard III* (Yale, 1963).
Cordyale by Anthony Woodville, ed. J.A. Mulders (Nijmegen, 1962).
Coventry Leet Book ed. M.D. Harris (EETS, 1907–13).
Croyland Chronicle Continuation 1459–86, ed. N. Pronay and John Cox (London, 1986).
Curiale made by Mayster Alain Charetier, transl. William Caxton 1484, ed. R. Deacon (EETS, 54).
Dante, Alighieri, *Hell*, transl. S. Ellis (London, 1994).
Diary of John Dee, ed. J.D. Halliwell (Camden Society, 1842).
Dupont, *Anchiennes Croniques d'Engleterre*, Paris, 1858–63.
Earliest English Translation of Vegetius' De Re Militari, Middle English Texts, 21 (Heidelberg, 1988).
Ellis, H., *Original Letters*, 2nd series (London, 1827).
English Conquest of Ireland (an English translation of the *Expurgnatio Hibernia* of Giraldus Cambresis made by an Anglo-Hibernian in the early fifteenth century) in Bodley MS Lib Rawl B 490 ed. J. Furnivall (EETS, OS vol. cvii, 1896).
Erasmus of Rotterdam, *The Correspondence of Erasmus, Letters* 1523–4, transl. R.A.B. Mynors and A. Dalzell (*The Collected Works of Erasmus*, Toronto x 1992).
Excerpta Historica, ed. S. Bentley (London, 1833).
Fabyan, R., *New Chronicles of England and of France*, ed. H. Ellis (1811).
Fifteenth Century Translations of Alain Chartier's Traite de L'Esperance and le Quadrilogue Invectif, ed. M.S. Blayney (EETS, 1974).
Galen on the Usefulness of the Parts of the Body, ed. M.T. May (2 vols, Cornell, 1968).
Gascoigne, Thomas, *Loci e Libro Veritatum*, ed. J.H. Thorold-Rogers (Oxford, 1881), 228.
Geoffrey of Monmouth, *The History of the Kings of Britain*, transl. L Thorpe (Harmondsworth, 1966).
George Ashby's Poems, ed. M. Bateson, EETS, Ex Ser, lxxvi (1899).
Gerald of Wales, *The Journey through Wales and the Description of Wales*, transl. C. Thorpe (Harmondsworth, 1978).
Giles of Rome, *De Regimine Principum Librii III* (Rome, 1567) repr. Facsimile, Frankfurt, 1968.
Giles of Rome, *De Regimine Principum*, ed. P. Molenaer (New York, 1899).
Governance of Princes (Secreta secretorum) Lydgate and Benedict Burgh see Steele EETS Ext Ser 66.
Governance of Princes (Secreta secretorum) transl. James Yonge, 1422 (EETS Ext Ser 74) ed. R. Steele.
Gower, John, *The Complete Works*, ed. G.C. Macaulay (4 vols, Oxford, 1899–1902).
Great Chronicle of London, ed. A.H. Thomas and I.D. Thornley (1938, repr. Gloucester, 1983).
Great Red Book of Bristol, ed. E.W.W. Veale, Text pt iii (Bristol Record Society Publications) xvi.
Gregory's Chronicle in *Historical Collections of a Citizen of London*, ed. J. Gairdner (Camden Society, 1876).
Guido delle Colonne, *Guido de Columnis, Historia Destructionis Troiae*, ed. N.E. Griffin (Cambridge, Mass., 1936).
Habington, Thomas and William, *The Historie of Edward IV* (London, 1640).
Hall, Edward, *Hall's Chronicle Containing the History of England During the Reign of Henry IV and the Succeeding Monarchs* (London, 1809).
Hall, Edward, *Union of the two Illustre Families of Lancaster and York*, ed. H. Ellis (1809).
Hardynge, John, *Chronicle*, ed. H. Ellis (London, 1812).
Henry VI A Reprint of Blacman's Memoir, ed. M.R. James (Cambridge, 1919).
Heywood, Thomas, *The First and Second part of King Edward IV's Histories* (London, 1842).
Historical Poems of the Fourteenth and Fifteenth Centuries, ed. Russel Hope Robbins (New York, 1959).
Historie of the Arrival of Edward IV, ed. J. Bruce in *3 Chronicles of the Reign of Edward IV*, intro. K. Dockray (Sutton, 1988).
Hoccleve, Thomas, *Hoccleve's Works: The Regiment of Princes and Fourteen Minor Poems*, ed. F.J. Furnivall, EETS, ES, LXI (London 1892, repr. 1970).

Household Book of Edward IV, the Black Book and the Ordinance of 1478, ed. A.R. Myers (Manchester, 1959).
Il Testamentum Alchemico Attributo A Raimundo Lullo, Edizione del testo Latino e Catelano del Manuscritto Oxford, Corpus Christi College 244, ed. M. Pereira and Barbara Spaggiari (Firenze, 1999).
Inventaire de la Bibliotheque du Roi Charles VI, fait au Louvre en 1423, ed. L.C. Douet d'Arcq (Paris, 1923).
John Benet's Chronicle for the years 1400–62, ed. G.L. and M.A. Harris, Camden Miscellany, XXIV 4th ser (London, 1972.
John Metham's Treatise on Days of the Moon, in The Works of John Metham, EETS (London, 1916) ed. H. Craig.
Jonson, Ben, *The Alchemist*, ed. F.H. Mares (London, 1967).
Laschitzer, S. (ed), *'Der Theurdank', Jahrbuch der Kunsthistorishe Sammlungen des Allerhochsten Kaiserhauses* 8 (1888).
Le Fevre, Raoul, *The History of Jason*, transl. William Caxton, ed. J. Munro, EETS, ES, 111 (London, 1913).
Letters and Papers Illustrative of the Wars of the English in France during the Reign of Henry VI, ed. J. Stevenson 2 vols (RS London, 1864).
Letters of Margaret of Anjou and Bishop Beckington, ed. Cecil Munro (New York, Camden Society, OS 86, 1969).
Lettres de Louis XI roi de France, ed. J. Naesen and E. Charavay, 12 vols (Paris, 1883–1901), vol. 6.
Literae Cantuariensis: the Letter Books of the Monarchs of Christchurch Canterbury, 3 vols, Rolls Series (London, 1839).
Lull, Ramon, *The Book of the Ordre of Chyvalry*, transl. and printed by William Caxton, ed. A.T.P. Byles, EETS, OS 168 (London, 1926, repr. 1971).
Lydgate's Troy Book, ed. H. Bergen (EETS, Extra Ser xcvii–cvi, London, 1906–12).
Magdalen College, Cambridge Old Library MS F 4 34. A Facsimile edition entitled *Caxton's Metamorphoses in English* in 2 vols, published by George Brazille (New York, 1968).
Maleus maleficarum, transl. Montague Summers (London, 1928).
Mancini, Dominic, *The Usurpation of Richard III*, ed. and transl. by C.A.J. Armstrong (2nd edn, Oxford, 1969).
Maximus, Valerius, *Facta et dicta memorabilia*, ed. C. Kempf (Leipzig, 1888).
Memorials of Henry VII, ed. J. Gairdner, Rolls Series (1858).
Middle English Translation of Christine de Pisan's Livre Du Corps De Policie, ed. from MS CUL K.K1.5 Diane Bornstein (Heidelberg, 1977).
Miracles of King Henry VI, ed. R. Knox and S. Leslie (London, 1923).
More, Sir Thomas, *The Usurpation of Richard III*, ed. R.S. Sylvester (*Complete Works*).
Myroure of Oure Ladye, EETS, Ex Ser 19 (London, 1873).
Norton, Thomas, *Ordinal of Alchemy*, ed. J. Reidy, EETS 272 (London, 1975).
Paston Letters 1422–1509, ed. J. Gairdner, 6 vols (1904).
Paston Letters and Papers of the Fifteenth Century, ed. N. Davis, 2 vols (Oxford, 1976).
Paston's *Grete Boke, A Descriptive Catalogue with an introduction of British Library MS Lansdowne 285*, ed. G.A. Lester (Cambridge, 1984).
Peter Idley's *Instructions to His Son*, ed. Charlotte d'Evelyn (London, 1935).
Political Poems and Songs relating to English History, ed. T. Wright, Rolls Series, 2 vols (London, 1859–61).
Political Religious and Love Poems, ed. F.J. Furnivall, EETS, OS 15 (London, 1866).
Polychronicon Randulphi Higden (from the Creation to 1352 together with English translations of John Trevisa and of an unknown writer of the fifteenth century), 9 vols, Rolls Series (London, 1865–86).
Prologues and Epilogues of William Caxton, EETS, OS 176 (1928).
Proposito Johannis Russel, printed by William Caxton circa A.D. 1476, introd. H. Guppy (Manchester and London, 1909).
Raine, A. ed. *York Civic Records*, vol. I, Y.A.S, 98, 1939.
Recuyell of the Hystoryes of Troye (London, 1894).
Revelations of St Bridget, The Liber Celestis of St Bridget of Sweden, ed. R. Ellis (EETS, 1987).
Ripley, George, *Georgii Riplaei – opera omnia chemica*, ed. L. Combachius (Casselis, 1649).
Ripley, George, *Ripley's duodecum Axiomata Philosophia Theatrum Chemicum, praecipuos selectorum auctorum tractatus de chemiae et lapidis philosophici antiquitate continens*, ed. L. Zetzner (Argent, 1622).
Ripley, George, *The Compound of Alchemy*, in *Theatrum Chemicum Britannicum*, ed. E. Ashmole (London, 1652.

Robbins, R.H., ed. *Historical Poems of the XIVth and XVth Centuries* (New York, 1959).
Rotuli Parliamentorum, ed. J. Strachey, 6 vols (London, 1767–77).
Rous, John *Historia Regum Angliae* (Oxonii, 1716).
Rous, John, *Johannis Rossi, Antiquari Warwicensis Historia Regum Angliae*, ed. T. Herne (Oxford, 1745).
Rous Roll, The, ed. C. Ross (Gloucester, 1980).
Rymer, T., *Foedera, Conventiones, Litterae et cuiusque Acta Publica*, 20 vols (The Hague, 1704–35).
Scrope, Stephen, *The Dicts and Sayings of the Philosophers*, ed. C.F. Buhler, EETS, OS ccxi (1941).
Scrope, Stephen, *The Epistle of Othea*, ed. C.F. Buhler (EETS, 274, London, 1970).
Secreta secretorum, ed. M.A. Manzalaoui, EETS, 276 (1977).
Secreta secretorum cum glossis et Notulis Fratris Rogeri, ed. R. Steele (Oxford, 1920).
Short English Chronicle, ed. Gairdner.
Siege of Rhodes, transl. John Kaye 1482, facsimile repr. (New York, 1975), the English Experience no. 236.
Sir John Fortescue, Works, ed. T. Fortescue Lord Clermont (London, 1869).
Stephani, *Baluze miscelleneorum liber primus (-septimus) Autem opera ac studio Johannis Mansi* (Lucca, 1761–4).
Stevenson J., *Letters and Papers Illustrative of the Wars of the English in France During the Reign of Henry VI*, Rolls Series, 2 vols in 3 parts (London, 1861–4).
Stonor Letters, ed. Kingsford, London Soc 3rd ser xxx (1919).
Stow, John, *Annales* or *A General Chronicle of England* (London, 1631).
Sutton, A. and Visser-Fuchs, L. *Richard III's Books* (Stroud, 1997).
Tanner, Thomas, *Bibliotheca Britannico-Hibernica* (London, 1748, repr. 1963).
Testament of Alchemy, L. Stavenhagen (New Hampshire, 1974).
Testamenta Vetusta illustrations from wills, ed. N.H. Nicolas (London, 1826).
Theatrum Chemicum, 4 vols (Strasbourg, 1613–61, ii, 1659).
Thornley, A.H and I.D., eds, *The Great Chronicle of London* (1937).
Three Books of Polydore Vergil's English History, ed. H. Ellis (London, 1844).
Three Fifteenth Century Chronicles, ed. James Gairdner (Camden Society, London, 1880).
Tiptoft, John, earl of Worcester, *Declamation of Noblesse* in R.J. Mitchell, *John Tiptoft, 1427–1470* (London, 1938), appendix, 215–41.
Travels of Leo of Rozmital, ed. and transl. M. Letts, Hakluyt Soc. 2nd ser (Cambridge, 1957).
Trismoson, Salomon, *Splendor Solis*, ed. J.K. Jordon (1920).
Vergil, Polydore, *Three Books of Polydore Vergil's English History*, ed. H. Ellis (Camden Society, 1844).
Vespasiano de Bistichi, *Vite dii uomini illustri del secolo XV*, ed. L Frati I (1892).
Warkworth, John, *A Chronicle of the First Thirteen Years of the Reign of King Edward the Fourth*, ed. J.O. Halliwell (Camden Society, 1839).
Waurin, Jean de, *Receuil des Croniques et Anchiennes Istories de la Grant Bretaigne, a present nomme Engleterre*, ed. W. and E. Hardy, vol. 5, 14447–71 (Rolls Series, 1981).
Wilkins, David, *Concilia Magnae Britanniae et Hiberniae AD 466–1718*, 4 vols (1737).
Worcester, William, *The Boke of Noblesse*, ed. J.G. Nichols Roxburghe Club (London, 1860).
Worcester, William, *Itineraries*, ed. J.H. Hardy (Oxford, 1969).
Works of Sir John Fortescue in 2 vols, ed. T. Fortescue, Lord Clermont (London, 1869).
Works of Sir Thomas Malory, 3rd edn, ed. E. Vinaver and revised by P.J.C. Field, 3 vols (Oxford, 1990).
Works of Sir Thomas Malory, ed. E. Vinaver (Oxford, 1947).
Wright, ed. *Political Poems and Songs*, Rolls Series 2 vols (London, 1859–6).
Year Books Edward IV; 1461–70 De termino Michaelis anno primo Edwardi quarti (London, 1556).

Secondary Sources

Unpublished

Allan, A., 'Political Propaganda employed by the House of York in England in the mid-fifteenth century, *c.* 1450–71', PhD thesis, Swansea, 1981.
Blanchard, Laura, 'Free Library of Philadelphia Lewis E 201, the Edward IV Roll', libwww.library.phila.gov-/medieval/Lewis E201.
Keir, G., 'The Ecclesiastical Career of George Neville 1432–1476', Oxford Univ. B.Litt, 1970.
Kekewich, M., 'A Yorkist Propaganda Roll: British Library Harleian Manuscript 7353' unpublished paper.

McKendrick, Scott, 'Classical Mythology and Ancient History in works of Art at the courts of France, Burgundy and England, 1364–1500', unpublished Ph.D. thesis, Courtauld Institute, London, 1988.

Selected Printed Secondary Sources

Ackroyd, P., *London, the Biography* (London, 2000).

Allan,. A., 'Royal Propaganda and the Proclamations of Edward IV', *BIHR*, 59.

——, 'Yorkist Propaganda: Pedigree, prophecy and "the British History" in the Reign of Edward IV', in C. Ross, ed. *Pedigree, Patronage and Power in Later Medieval England* (Gloucester, 1979).

Allen, P.S., 'Bishop Shirwood of Durham and his Library', *EHR*, XXV (1910), 445–56.

Anglo, S., 'British History and early Tudor Propaganda', *BJRL*, 44, 1961.

Anstis, J., *The Register of the Most Noble Order of the Garter*, 2 vols (London, 1724).

Armstrong, C.A.J., 'Some Verses by Jean Mielot on Edward IV and Richard earl of Warwick', *Medium Aevum*, 8 (1939).

——, 'The Inaugural Ceremonies of the Yorkist Kings and the Title to the Throne', *TRHS*, 4 Ser xxx (1948).

Ashdown-Hill, J., 'The Red Rose of Lancaster', *Ricardian*, x, 133 (1966).

Backhouse, J., 'Founders of the Royal Library: Edward IV and Henry VIII as Collectors of Illuminated Manuscripts', in *England in the Fifteenth Century, Proceedings of the 1984 Harlaxton Symposium*, ed. D. Williams (Woodbridge, 1987).

Baillie, M., in *Exodus to Arthur: Catastrophic Encounters with Comets* (London, 1999).

Barber, R.W., *The Tournament in England 1100–1400* (Woodbridge, 1986).

Barber, Richard, 'Malory's *Le Morte d'Arthur* and Court Culture under Edward IV', *Arthurian Literature* xii ed. J.P. Carley and F. Riddy (Cambridge, 1993).

Baring-Gould, Sabine, *Myths of the Middle Ages* (1996); ed. (EETS, London, 1895).

Barron W.R.J., ed. *The Arthur of the English. The Arthurian Legend in Medieval English Life and Literature* (Cardiff, 2001).

Baskerworth, G., 'A London Chronicle of 1460', *E.H.R.*, xxviii (1913).

Baudot, J., *Melusine* (Paris, 1908).

Baugh, A.L., 'Documenting Sir Thomas Malory', *Speculum*, xlvii.

Beck, R.T., *The Cutting Edge: Early History of the Surgeons of London* (London, 1974).

Benecke, Gerhard, *Maximilian I (1459–1519) An Analytical Biography* (London, 1982).

Bennet, H.S., *The Pastons and their England*, 2nd edn (Cambridge, 1932).

Benson, L.D., 'The Date of the Alliterative Morte Arthure', in *Medieval Studies Presented to William Herlands Hornstein*, ed. J.B. Bessinger and R.K. Raymo (New York, 1969).

Biddle, M., *King Arthur's Round Table: An Archaeological Investigation* (Woodbridge, 2000).

——, 'The Painting of the Round Table', in *King Arthur's Round Table*, ed. M. Biddle (Woodbridge, 2000).

Blake, N.F., *William Caxton and English Literary Culture* (London, 1991).

Bloch, M., *The Royal Touch: Sacred Monarchy and Scrofula in England and France*, transl. J.E. Anderson (London, 1973).

Blunt C.E. and Whithorn, C.A., 'The Coinages of Edward IV and Henry VI (Restored)', *The British Numismatic Journal* 3rd Ser, vol. v (1945–8).

Boardman, J., Griffin, J. and Murray, O., *The Roman World, the Oxford History of the Classical World* (Oxford, 1988).

Bone, G., 'Extant Manuscripts Printed by W. de Worde with notes on the owner Roger Thorney', The *Library*, 4th Ser 12 (1931).

Bornstein, Diane, *Mirrors of Courtesy* (Hamden, Conn., 1975).

Boulton, D.J.D., *The Knights of the Crown* (Woodbridge, 1897).

Brann, Noel L., 'George Ripley and the Abbot Trithemius, An Inquiry into Contrasting Medical Attitudes', *Ambix* (26 Nov 1979).

Brehm, E., 'Roger Bacon's Place in the History of Alchemy', *Ambix*, ix, 23 Mar 1976.

Brill, R., 'The English Preparations before the Treaty of Arras: A new Interpretation of Sir John Fastolf's report, September, 1435', *Studies in Medieval and Renaissance History*, vii, 1970.

Buhler, T.F., 'Sir John Fastolf's Manuscripts of the Epitre d'Othea and Stephen Scrope's translation of the text', *Scriptorium*, iii (1949).

Burton Russel, J., *Witchcraft in the Middle Ages* (Cornell, 1972).

Campbell, Joseph, *Creative Mythology: The Masks of God* (Arkana, 1991).
Campbell, P.C.G., *L'Epitre d'Othea; Etude sur les sources de Christine de Pisan* (Paris, 1924).
Carey, Hilary, *Courting Disaster: Astrology at the English Court and University in the Later Middle Ages* (London, 1992).
Carey, Hilary, 'Astrology at the English Court', in *Astrology, Science and Society*, ed. A. Curry (Woodbridge, 1987).
Carpenter, Christine, *The Wars of the Roses* (Cambridge, 1997).
——, 'Sir Thomas Malory and Fifteenth Century Local Politics', *Bulletin of the Institute of Historical Research*, 53 (1980).
Christianson, C.P., *A Directory of London Stationers and Book Artisans 1300–1500* (New York, 1900).
——, *Memorials of the Book Trade in Medieval London* (Cambridge, 1987), 12.
Christine de Pisan, *Livre du Corps de Policie*, ed. R.I. Lucas (Droz, 1967).
Cobbam, A.B., *The Medieval English Universities* (Aldershot, 1988).
Comrie, J.D., *History of Scottish Medicine* (London, 1932) vol. 1 and 2.
Coote, L., *Prophecy and Public Affairs in Later Medieval England* (New York, 2000).
Cosgrave, Art, *Late Medieval Ireland 1370–154* (Dublin, 1981).
Crawford, R.H.P., *The King's Evil* (Oxford, 1911).
Cripps-Day, E., *The History of the Tournament in England and France* (London, 1918).
Davies, R.R., *The First English Empire* (Oxford, 2000).
——, 'The People of Britain and Ireland 1100–1400: IV Language and Historical Mythology', *TRHS*, 6 Ser vii, 5.
Davis, N., Review of *Proverbs, Sentences and Proverbial Phrases from English Writings Mainly before 1500* by B.J. Whiting, *Medium Aevum*, xli (1972).
Delaney, Sheila, *Impolitic Bodies: Saints and Society in Fifteenth-century England* (Oxford, 1998).
——, 'Bokenham's Claudian as Yorkist Propaganda', *Journal of Medieval Studies*, vol. 22, no. 1 (1996).
Dixon, L.S., *Nicholas Flamel His Exposition of the Hieroglyphicall Figures*.
——, *Alchemical Imagery in Bosch's Garden of Delights* (Ann Arbor, Michigan, 1981).
Dobbs, Betty Jo Teeter, *The Foundations of Newton's Alchemy* or *The Hunting of the Greene Lyon* (Cambridge, 1983).
Dockray, Keith, 'Edward IV: Playboy or Politician?', *The Ricardian*, x, no. 131, December 1995, 306–24.
——, *Edward IV: A Source Book* (Stroud, 1999).
Doob, P.B.R., *Nebuchadnezzar's Children: Conventions of Madness in Middle English Literature* (Yale, 1974).
Doyle, A.I., 'English Books In and Out of Court', in *English Court Culture in the Later Middle Ages*, ed. V.J. Scattergood and J.W. Sherbourne (London, 1983).
Duff, E.G., *Fifteenth Century English Books* (Oxford, 1977).
Duncan, E.H., 'The Literature of Alchemy and Chaucer's *Canon Yeoman's Tale*: Framework, theme and characters', *Speculum*, 43 (1968).
Dunlop, D., 'The Redress and Reparacions on attemptales: Alexander Legh's instructions from Edward IV, March–April 1475', *Historical Research*, 63 (1990), 340–53.
Dunn, Diana, 'Margaret of Anjou, Chivalry and the Order of the Garter', in *St George's Chapel Windsor*, ed. Richmond and Scarfe.
Eldredge, L.M., *The Index of Manuscripts containing Middle English prose in the Ashmole Collection Handlist IX* (Cambridge, 1992).
Elkins, James, *What Painting Is* (New York, 2000).
Elliot, J.H., 'Spain and its Empire in the sixteenth and seventeenth centuries', in Elliot, *Spain and its World 1400–1700* (Yale, 1989).
Emden, R.B., *Biographical Register of the University of Oxford to 1500*, 3 vols (Oxford, 1957–9).
Emden, R.B., *Biographical Register of the University of Cambridge to 1500* (Cambridge, 1963).
Fabricianus, Johannus, *Alchemy: The Medieval Alchemists and their Royal Art* (Copenhagen, 1976).
Field, P., 'The Malory Life Records', in *A Companion to Malory*, ed. E. Archibald and A.S.G. Edwards (Cambridge, 1996).
Field, P.J.C., 'Sir Thomas Malory', MP *I.H.R. Bull.* xlvii.
——, *The Life and Times of Sir Thomas Malory* (Cambridge, 1993).
Firth Green, R., *Poets and Prince Pleasers: Literature and the English Court in the Late Middle Ages* (Toronto, 1980).
Fleming, P.W., 'The Hautes and their Circle', in *Culture and the English Gentry in the Fifteenth Century*.

Flugel, E., 'Eine mittelengische Claudian-Ubersetzung (1445)', *Anglia*, XXVIII (1905).
Foster, Richard, *Patterns of Thought: the Hidden Meaning of the Great Pavement of Westminster* (Woodbridge, 1991).
Foster, Richard and Tudor Craig, Pamela, *The Secret Life of Paintings* (Woodbridge, 1986).
Fox Davies, A.C., *The Art of Heraldry* (London, 1904).
French, Peter, *John Dee: the World of an Elizabethan Magus* (London, 1972).
Furnivall, F.J., 'Edward IV's Plague Medicine', *Notes and Queries* 9 (1870).
Geddes, Jane, 'The Search for John Tresilian Master Smith to Edward IV', *History Today*, May 2002.
Geneva, Anne, *Astrology and the Seventeenth Century Mind* (Manchester, 1995).
Geoghegan, D., 'A licence of Henry VI to Practice Alchemy', *Ambix*, 6, 1957–8.
Getz, Faye, *Medicine in the English Middle Ages* (Princeton, 1998).
Goldstire, Herman H., *New and Full Moons 1001 BC to AD 1651*, American Philosophical Society (Philadelphia, 1973).
Goodman, A. and Morgan, D., 'The Yorkist Claim to the Throne of Castile', *Journal of Medieval History*, ii (1985).
Goodman, J.R., *Chivalry and Exploration 1298–1631* (Bury St Edmunds, 1998).
Gransden, A., *Historical Writing in England*, 2 (London, 1982).
Grant, A., *Henry VII* (London, 1985).
Green, J.R., *A Short History of the English People* (London, 1874).
Griffin, M.E., 'Cadwallader, Arthur and Brutus in the Wigmore Manuscript', *Speculum*, 16 (1941).
Griffith, R.R., 'The Authorship Question Reconsidered. A Case for Thomas Malory of Papworth St Agnes, Cambridgeshire', in *Aspects of Malory*, ed. Toshiyuki Takamiya and D. Brewer (Cambridge, 1981).
——, 'The Political Bias of Malory's *Morte d'Arthur*', *Viator*, 5 (1974), 365–86.
Griffiths, R. A., 'The sense of Dynasty in the Reign of Henry VI', in *Patronage, Pedigree and Power in Later Medieval England*, ed. C. Ross (Gloucester, 1979).
——, *The Reign of Henry VI* (London, 1981).
——, 'Richard duke of York and the Royal Household in Wales, 1449–50', *Welsh History Review*, 8 (1976).
Grillot de Givry, *Witchcraft, Magic and Alchemy*, transl. J.C. Locke (New York, 1931).
Gross, A., *The Dissolution of Lancastrian Kingship* (Stamford, 1996).
Grummit, C.D., 'The Defence of Calais and the Development of Gunpowder weapons in England in the late Fifteenth century'.
Haines, R.M., '"Our Master Mariner, Our Sovereign Lord": a Contemporary Preacher's View of Henry V', *Medieval Studies*, xxxviii (1976), 85–96.
Halleaux, Robert, *Les textes alchimiques* (Turnhout, 1979).
Halliwell J.D., *Archeologia* (1842).
Hampton, W.E., 'Witchcraft and the Sons of York', *The Ricardian*, v, 68 (1980).
Harris, Gerald, Introduction to *The Scroll Considerans* (Magdalen MS 248) *Giving the Descent from Adam to Henry VI* (Oxford, 1999).
Harris, G.L., ed. *Henry V: The Practice of Kingship* (Oxford, 1985).
Harvey, M., *England, Rome and the Papacy 1417–64* (Manchester, 1993).
Heer, F., *The Holy Roman Empire* (London, 1967).
Hervey, F., *Holbein's Ambassadors* (London, 1900).
Hexter, J.H., 'The Education of the Aristocracy in the Renaissssance', *Journal of Modern History*, xxii (1950).
Hodges, G., 'The Civil War of 1459 to 1461 in the Welsh Marches. 2: The Campaign and Battle of Mortimer's Cross', *Ricardian*, vi, 85 (1984).
Hoffman, E.J., *Alain Chartier, His Work and Reputation* (New York, 1942).
Hughes, Jonathan, *Pastors and Visionaries: Religion and Secular Life in Late Medieval Yorkshire* (Woodbridge, 1988).
——, 'Stephen Scrope and the Circle of Sir John Fastolf: Intellectual and Moral Outlooks', in *Medieval Knighthood IV Papers from 5th Strawberry Hill Conference, 1991*, ed. C. Harper Bill and R. Harvey (Woodbridge, 1993).
——, 'The Administration of Confession in the Diocese of York in the Fourteenth Century', in *Studies in Clergy and Ministry in England*, ed. D. Smith, Borthwick Studies in History, York (1991).
——, *The Religious Life of Richard III: Piety and Prayer in the North of England* (Stroud, 1997).

Ives, E.W. 'The Common Lawyers' in *Profession, Vocation and Culture in Later Medieval England Essays dedicated to A.R. Myers*, ed. C.H. Clough.
James, M.R., *The Abbey of St Edmund at Bury*, Cambridge Antiquarian Society (Cambridge, 1894).
——, *A Descriptive Catalogue of the Manuscripts in the Library of Lambeth Palace* (Cambridge, 1932).
James, Mervyn, 'English Politics and the Concept of Honour 1485–1642', *Past and Present*, Supplement 3 (1978).
Jamison, C., *The History of the Royal Hospital of St Katherine* (Cambridge, 1952).
Joly, Joseph, *Histoire de la Bourgogne*, vol. 4 (Toulouse, 1874).
Jones, M.K., '1477, The Expedition that Never Was: Chivalric Expectation in Late Yorkist England', *The Ricardian*, xii, no. 153.
——, 'Edward IV, the earl of Warwick and the Yorkist Claim to the Throne', *Institute of Historical Research Bulletin*, vol. 70, 173 (1997).
——, Review *Ricardian*, xi (September 1997).
Jones, P.M., *Medieval Medical Miniatures* (London, 1984).
Jonson, P.A., *Richard duke of York 1411–1460* (Oxford, 1988).
Jung, Carl, *Alchemical Studies*, in the *Collected Works*, vol. 13 (Princeton, 1970).
——, *Mysterium Coniunctionis*, transl. R.F.C. Hull (Princeton, 1963).
——, *Psychology and Alchemy* (London, 1953)
Jung, Emma and Von Franz, Marie-Louise, *The Grail Legend* transl. A. Dykes (Princeton, 2nd edn 1970).
Keen, M., *Chivalry* (New Haven, 1984).
Keiser, George, *A Manual of Writings in Middle English 1050–1500, vol. 10 Science and information*. Gen. Ed. Albert E. Hartung (New Haven, 1998).
——, 'The Conclusion of the Canon Yeoman's Tale: Readings and (Mis)readings', *Chaucer Review*, vol. 35, no. 1 (2000).
Kekewich, Margaret, 'Edward IV, William Caxton and Literary Patronage in Yorkist England', *MLR*, 66 (1973).
Kelly, H.A., 'English Kings and the Fear of Sorcery', *Medieval Studies*, 39 (1977).
Kibre, P., 'Lewis of Caerleon, doctor of Medicine, Astronomer and Mathematician', *Isis*, xliii (1952).
Kieckhefer, R., *Magic in the Middle Ages* (Cambridge, 1990).
Kings and Queens AD 635–1953. Catalogue of an Exhibition held in the Royal Academy (London, 1953).
Kingsford, C.L., 'The First Version of Hardynge's Chronicle', *English Historical Review*, xxvii (1912)
——, *English Historical Literature in the Fifteenth Century* (Oxford, 1913).
Kinsman, R., 'A Lament for King Edward IV', *Huntingdon Library Quarterly*, 29 (1966).
Kipling, G., *The Triumph of Honour* (Leiden, 1977).
Lander, J.R., *Government and Community, England 1450–1509* (London, 1980).
Lang, S.J., 'John Bradmore and His Book Philomena', *Social History of Medicine* V, 1992.
Latimer, 'Some curious incidents in British History', *Trans Bristol and Gloucester Arch Soc* xxii (1899).
Linden, S.J., 'The Ripley Scrolls and the Compound of Alchemy', in *Glasgow Emblem Studies vol. 3, Emblems and Alchemy*, ed. A. Adams and S.J. Linden (1988).
Liot de Northbecourt, E., 'La Complaint d'Arras', *Bulletin des antiquaires de la marinie*, vol. 2 (1857–61).
Loomis, R.S., *The Grail from Celtic Myth to Christian Symbol* (Bury St Edmunds, 1993).
Louis, 'A Yorkist genealogical chronicle in Middle English verse', *Anglia* (1991).
McCallum, R.I., *Antimony in Medical History* (Edinburgh, 1990).
——, 'The Ripley Scroll of the Royal College of Physicians of Edinburgh', *Vesalius* II, 1, 39–49 (1996).
McCarthy, T., 'Malory and his Sources', in *A Companion to Malory*, eds E. Archibald and A.S.G. Edwards (Woodbridge, 1996).
MacCracken, H.N., 'Vegetius in English', in *Anniversary Papers by Colleagues and Pupils of George Ryman Kittredge*, eds E.S. Sheldon and F.N. Robinson (Boston, 1913).
McFarlane, K.B., 'William Worcester: a Preliminary Survey', in K.B. McFarlane, *England in the Fifteenth Century* (London, 1981).
——, *The Nobility of Late Medieval England* (Oxford, 1973).
MacGibbon, D., *Elizabeth Woodville* (London, 1938).
McKendrick, S., 'Edward IV An English Royal Collector of Netherlandish Tapestries', *Burlington Magazine*, cxxix (1987), 521–4.
McKendrick, Scott, '*La grande Histoire Cesar* and the manuscripts of Edward IV', *English Manuscript Studies* ii (1990).

——, 'Louis of Gruuthuse and the Library of Edward IV', in *Lodewijk van Gruuthuse mecenam en European Diplomat ca 1427–1492*, ed. M.P.J. Martens (Bruges, 1992).
——, 'The *Romuleon* and the Manuscripts of Edward IV', in *England in the Fifteenth Century: Proceedings of the 1992 Harlaxton Symposium*, ed. N. Rogers (Stamford, 1994).
McNiven, P., 'The Problem of Henry IV's Health, 1405–13', *English Historical Review*, 396 (1985).
Martin, A.T., 'The Identity of the author of the *Morte Darthur*', *Archaeologia*, xlvi.
Mathews, C.G., *The Royal Apothecaries* (London, 1967).
Mathews, W., *The Ill Framed Knight* (Berkeley and Los Angeles, 1966).
Meale, Carole, 'Readers and Patrons in 15th Century England: Sir Thomas Malory and Arthurian Romance,' *Arthurian Literature*, iv (1983).
——, 'Readers and Patrons in Fifteenth Century England: Sir Thomas Malory and Arthurian Romance', *Arthurian Literature*, 4 (1985), 93–126.
Mendelsohn, J. Andrew, 'Alchemy Norton, *Ordinal of Alchemy*, 45 and Politics in England 1649–65', *Past and Present*, 135 (1992).
Mitchell, R.J., 'A Renaissance Library: the collection of John Tiptoft, Earl of Worcester', *The Library*, xviii (1937–8).
——, *John Tiptoft, 1427–1470* (London, 1938).
Mooney, L., 'A Middle English Treatise on Seven Liberal Arts', *Speculum*, 68 (1993).
——, *Index of Middle English Prose Handlist XI The Library of Trinity College* (Cambridge, 1995).
Murdoch, J.E., *Albumen of Science and Antiquity in the Middle Ages* (New York, 1984).
North, John, 'Horoscopes and History', *Warburg Institute*, Survey Texts 13 (London, 1986).
——, *The Ambassadors' Secret: Holbein and the World of the Renaissance* (London, 2002).
Obrist, Barbara, 'Les debuts de l'imagerie alchemique xiv–xv siècles', Paris, *La Sycamore*, 1982, Review.
Ogrinc, W.H.C., 'Western Society and Alchemy from 1200–1500', *Journal of Medieval History*, 6 (1980).
Oman, C., *The coinage in England* (Oxford, 1931).
Orme, N., *From Childhood to Chivalry* (London, 1984).
——, 'The Education of Edward V', *Bulletin Historical Research*, LVII, no. 136 (1984).
Parvus Cato Magnus Cato, transl. Benedict Burgh, ed. from William Caxton's first edition, F. Kuriyawa (Tokyo, 1974).
Pereira, Michela, '*Quintessenza alchemica*', *Kos*, 7 (1984).
——, *The Alchemical Corpus attributed to Raymund Lull*, Warburg Institute Surveys and Texts, xviii.
Piershall, *Scriptorium*, xxiii (1969).
Pollard, A.J., ed. *The Wars of the Roses* (London, 1995).
——, *Late Medieval England 1399–1500* (Edinburgh, 2000).
Porter, Roy, ed. *Cambridge Illustrated History of Medicine* (Cambridge, 1996).
Pouchelle, M.C., *The Body and Surgery in the Middle Ages*, transl. R. Morris (Oxford, 1990).
Pritchert, J.L.G., *La metaphore pathalogique et therapeutique à la fin du moyen age* (Tubigen, 1994).
Pugh, T.B., *Henry V and the Southampton Plot of 1415* (Southampton, 1988).
Ramon Menendez Didal, 'The Significance of the Reign of Isabella the Catholic According to her Contemporaries', in R. Highfield, *Spain in the Fifteenth century, 1369–1516* (London, 1972).
Rawcliffe, Carole, 'Consultants, Careerists and Conspirators: Royal Doctors in the time of Richard III', *Ricardian*, 106 (1988).
——, 'More than a Bedside Manner: The Political Status of the Late Medieval Court Physician', in *St George's Chapel, Windsor, in the Late Middle Ages*, eds C. Richmond and E. Scarfe (Windsor, 2001).
——, 'Royal Doctors at the time of Richard III', *Ricardian*, 106 (1989).
——, 'The Inventory of a Fifteenth-Century Necromancer', publication forthcoming.
——, *Medicine and Society in Later Medieval England* (Stroud, 1997).
——, *Medicine for the Soul. The life, Death and Resurrection of an English Medieval Hospital* (Stroud, 1999).
——, 'Written in the Book of Life: Building the Libraries of Medieval English Hospitals and Almshouses', publication forthcoming.
Ray, C., *Melusine* (Ligage, 1898).
Reddaway, T.E., 'The King's Mint and Exchange in London', *E.H.R.*, cccxii (1967).
Rees, David, *The Son of Prophecy: Henry Tudor's Road to Bosworth* (Ruthin, 1985).
Reidy, J., 'Thomas Norton and the Ordinal of Alchemy', *Ambix*, December 1957, vol. vi.
Rhodes, D.E., *John Argentine, provost of Kings* (Amsterdam, 1962).
Riches, Samantha, *St George: Hero Martyr and Myth* (Stroud, 2000).

Richmond, Colin and Kekewich, M., 'The Search for Stability 1461–83', in *The Politics of Fifteenth Century England*, 43–67.
Richmond, C., '1485 and all that, or what was going on at the battle of Bosworth', in P.W. Hammond, ed. *Richard III: Loyalty, Lordship and Law* (London, 1986).
Riddy, Felicity, 'John Hardynge's Chronicle and the Wars of the Roses', *Arthurian Literature*, 12 (1993).
——, 'John Hardynge's Chronicle and the Wars of the Roses', *Arthurian Literature*, xii (1935) eds J. Carley and F. Riddy.
——, *Sir Thomas Malory* (Leiden, 1987).
Roberts, Gareth, *The Mirror of Alchemy. Alchemical Ideas, and Images in Manuscripts and Books* (London, 1994).
Roskell, J.S., *The Commons and their Speakers in English Parliaments 1376–1523* (Manchester, 1965).
Ross, C.D., 'Rumour, Propaganda and Popular Opinion during the Wars of the Roses', in R.A. Griffiths ed., *Patronage, the Crown and the Provinces* (Gloucester, 1981).
Ross, Charles, *Edward IV* (London, 1974).
Rowe, B.J.H., 'King Henry VI's claim to France in picture and poem', *The Library*, 4 Ser, 13 (1932–3).
Schneider, Diethard, *Der englische Hosenbandorden. Beitrage zur Entstehung und Entwicklung des 'The most noble order of the Garter'* (1348–1702) mit einem Ausblick bis 1983, 2 vols in 4 (Bonn, 1988), vol. 1 part 1.
Scofield, C.L., *The Life and Reign of Edward IV*, 2 vols (London, 1923).
Scott, Kathleen L., *The Caxton Master and his Patrons* (Cambridge Bibliographical Soc Monograph 8, 1976).
Scott, Kathleen, *Later Gothic Manuscripts 1390–1490*, vol. 6.
Scrope, Stephen, *The Epistle of Othea*, ed. C.F. Buhler, EETS (London, 1970).
Seaton, E., *Sir Richard Roos, Lancastrian Poet* (London, 1961).
Shakespeare, William, *Othello, Macbeth, Henry IV Parts I and II and Henry V* (New Arden Shakespeare).
Sherwood Taylor, F. *Ambix*, ii nos 3–4 (December 1946).
Sherwood Taylor, T., *The Alchemists* (London, 1952).
Singer, D.W.,'The Alchemical *Testamentum* Attributed to Raymund Lull', *Arecheion*, 9 (1928–9).
Smith, J.J., Cambridge Antiquarian Society, Quarton Series, 1846.
Southern, R.W., *Robert Grosseteste. The Growth of an English Mind in Medieval Europe* (Oxford, 1986).
St John Hope, W.H., *The Architectual History of Windsor Castle* (London, 1913).
Stannier, R.S., *A History of Magdalen College Grammar School* (Oxford, 1958).
Starkey, David, 'King Henry and King Arthur', *Arthurian Literature*, xvi, eds J.P. Curley and F. Riddy (1998).
Stone, R.T., 'A Brief History of the King's Evil', *Ricardian* (1989).
Storey, R.L., *The End of the House of Lancaster* (new edn, Gloucester, 1986).
Strouff, C., *Essai sur Melusine, Roman du XIVième siècle par Jean d'Arras* (Paris, 1930).
Stubbs, W., *The Constitutional History of England*, vol. 3 (Oxford, 1878).
Summers, Montague, *The History of Witchcraft* (London, 1926).
Sutton, A. and Visser Fuchs, L., 'Chevalerie – in som partie is worthi for to be comended, and in some part to ben amendid: Chivalry and Yorkist Kings' in *St George's Chapel, Windsor, in The Late Middle Ages*, eds C. Richmond and E. Scarfe (Windsor, 2001).
——, 'Richard III's Books: V Aegidius Romanus De Regimine Principum', *Ricardian*.
——, 'Richard III's Books Observed', *Ricardian*, x, 120 (1993).
——, 'Richard III's Books: Ancestry and True Nobility', *The Ricardian*, ix, 119 (1992).
——, 'Laments for the Soul of Edward IV', *The Ricardian*, xi, no. 145 (June 1999).
——, 'Richard III's Books: Chivalric Ideals and Reality', *The Ricardian*, ix, 116 (1992).
——, 'Richard III's Books IV, Vegetius' *De Re Militari*', *The Ricardian*, 7 (1987), 541–2.
——, '"A Most Benevolent Queen" Queen Elizabeth Woodville's Reputation, her Piety and her Books', *The Ricardian*, x, no. 129 (1995).
——, 'Richard III's Books: X 'The Prose Tristran', *Ricardian*, ix, no. 112 (1991).
——, 'The Royal Burials of the House of York at Windsor', *Ricardian*, xi, 143 (1998).
——, 'Richard III's Books XI: Raymund Lull's Order of Chivalry translated by William Caxton', *Ricardian*, 114 (1991).
——, 'Richard III's Books: Ancestry and True Nobility', *Ricardian*, ix, 119 (1992).
——, with P.W. Hammond, *The Reburial of Richard duke of York, 21–30 July 1476* (London, 1996).

Sutton, Anne, 'Sir Thomas Cook and his troubles: an investigation', *Guildhall Studies in London History*, 3 (1978).
——, 'Malory in Newgate', *The Library*, 7 Ser vol. 1, no. 3 (September 2000).
Szulakowska, U., 'The Tree of Aristotle: Images of the Philosopher's Stone and their Transference in Alchemy from the xvth to the xxth century', *Ambix* 33 (1986).
——, 'The Pseudo-Lullian Origins of George Ripley's Maps and Routes as developed by Michael Maier', *Cosmos*, 9 (Edinburgh, 1993)
Talbot, C.H. and Hammond, E.A., *The Medical Practitioners in Medieval England: A Biographical Register* (London, Wellcome Institute, 1965).
Tanner, N.P., *The Church in Late Medieval Norwich, 1370–1532* (Toronto, 1984).
Taylor, R., *The Political Prophecy in England* (1967).
Telle, Joachim, *Sol und Luna: Literar- und alchemiegeschichtliche Studien zu einem altdeutschen Bildgedicht* (Hurtgenwald, 1980).
The Oxford Dictionary of Saints, ed. D.H. Farmer (Oxford, 1978).
The Politics of Fifteenth Century England: John Vale's Book, eds M. Kekewich, C. Richmond, A.F. Sutton, L. Visser-Fuchs and J.L. Watts (Stroud, 1995).
Thomas, Keith, *Religion and the Decline of Magic* (London, 1984).
Thompson, C.J., *The Lure and Romance of Alchemy* (New York, 1996).
Thorndike, L., 'Some Medieval Texts', *Ambix*, vii (1959).
Thorndike, Lynn, *A History of Magic and Experimental Science* (New York, 1941).
Tyerman, C., *England and the Crusades 1095–1588* (Chicago, 1988).
Vale, Juliet, 'Arthur in English Society', in *The Arthur of the English*, ed. Barron.
Vale, M.G.A., 'An Anglo Burgundian Nobleman and Art Patron', in C. Barron and N. Saul, eds, *England and the Low Countries in the Later Middle Ages* (Stroud, 1995).
——, *War and Chivalry* (London, 1981).
Vaughan, R., *Charles the Bold* (London, 1973).
Virgoe, R., *Private Life in the Fifteenth Century: Illustrated Letters of the Paston Family* (London, 1989).
Visser Fuchs, Livia, 'Where did Elizabeth of York Find Consolation?', *The Ricardian*, ix, no. 122 (1993).
——, 'Nicholas Harpsfield, Clerk of the Signet, Author and Murderer', *The Ricardian*, x, no. 125 (1994).
——, 'Choosing a Book', in C. Barron and N. Saul, *England and the Low Countries in the Later Middle Ages* (Stroud, 1995).
——, '*Sanguinis haustor* Drinker of Blood. A Burgundian view of England, 1471', *The Ricardian*, vii, 92 (1986).
Voigts, L., 'Scientific and Medical Books' in *Book Production and Publishing in Britain 1375–1475*, eds Jeremy Griffiths and Derek Pearsall (Cambridge, 1989).
Voigts, Linda, 'A Doctor and his Books: the manuscripts of Roger Marshall d. 1477', in *New Science out of Old Books*, eds R. Beadle and A.J. Piper (Aldershot, 1995). £80-L13
von Franz, Maria Louise, 'The Process of Individuation' in *Man and his Symbols*, ed. C.G. Jung (London, 1964).
Wagner A.R., 'The Swan Badge and the Swan Knight', *Archaeologia*, cxvii (1956).
Waley, D., *Later Medieval Europe* (New York, 1985).
Walker, Simon, 'Political Saints in Later Medieval England', in *The McFarlane Legacy*, eds R.H. Britnell and A.J. Pollard (Stroud, 1995).
Warren, Nancy Bradley, *Spiritual Economies: Female Monasticism in Later Medieval England* (Philadelphia, 2001).
Watts, J. '*De consulatu stilichonis*, texts and politics in the reign of Henry VI', *Journal of Medieval History*, 16 (1990).
Watts, John, *Henry VI and the Politics of Kingship* (Cambridge, 1996).
Weightman, C., *Margaret of York: Duchess of Burgundy 1446–1503* (Gloucester, 1989).
Weiss R., *Humanism in England During the Fifteenth Century* (3rd edn, Oxford, 1967).
Whitteridge, G., 'The Identity of Sir Thomas Malory, Knight-prisoner', *Review of English Studies*, ns xxiv.
Wilkins, C.H., 'A fifteenth century Lawsuit', *Law Quarterly Review* XI (1934).
Wilkins, Nigel, *Nicholas Flamel 'des Livres et de d'Or'* (Paris, 1993).
Williams, Gerhild S., 'The Arthurian Model in Emperor Maximilian's Autobiographical Writings Weisskunig and Theuerdank', *Sixteenth-Century Journal* 11.4 (1980).
Williams, Glanmor, *Renewal and Reformation in Wales, c. 1415–1642* (Oxford, 1993).

Witten II, Laurence C. and Richard Pachella, *Alchemy and the Occult: a Catalogue of Books and Manuscripts from the Collection of Paul Mary Mellor*, 4 vols (New Haven, 1968–77).
Wolffe, B.P., 'Yorkist and Early Tudor government 1461–1509', *Historical Association Pamphlet*, 1966.
——, *The Crown Lands 1461–1536* (London, 1971).
Wright, H.G., *Boccaccio in England from Chaucer to Tennyson* (London, 1957).
Yates, Frances, *The Occult Philosophy in the Elizabethan Age* (London, 1979).
Zaehner, R.C. *Mysticism Sacred and Profane: an enquiry into some varieties of praeternatural experience* (London, 1961).

Index